Model-Driven Software Development

Sami Beydeda · Matthias Book · Volker Gruhn (Eds.)

Model-Driven Software Development

With 195 Figures and 5 Tables

 Springer

Editors
Sami Beydeda
Federal Finance Office
(Bundesamt für Finanzen)
Friedhofstr. 1
53225 Bonn, Germany
sami.beydeda@bff.bund.de

Matthias Book
Volker Gruhn
Chair of Applied Telematics/e-Business
Department of Computer Science
University of Leipzig
Klostergasse 3
04109 Leipzig, Germany
book@ebus.informatik.uni-leipzig.de
gruhn@ebus.informatik.uni-leipzig.de

ACM Computing Classification (1998): D.2.2, D.2.11

ISBN-13 978-3-642-06502-6   ISBN-13 978-3-540-28554-0

Springer is a part of Springer Science+Business Media
springeronline.com

© Springer-Verlag Berlin Heidelberg 2010
Printed in Germany

Cover design: KünkelLopka, Heidelberg

Printed on acid-free paper   45/3142/YL - 5 4 3 2 1 0

Preface

One of the basic principles of software engineering is abstraction, which mainly refers to separation of the essential from the non-essential. In terms of software development, the essential usually refers to the functionality to be implemented and the non-essential to aspects such as the technical platform on which the software will eventually be deployed. However, non-essential aspects are not unimportant. They also have to be considered when designing and developing a software system, but they do not have to be considered at the very first stage when more fundamental issues have to be considered.

Abstractions are provided by models. A model is mainly a representation of the essential aspects of the underlying subject and thus contains less complexity. Less complexity obviously allows the prediction of system characteristics, analyzing specific properties, and also communicating with the various roles involved in the development process more easily. However, implementing a model means expressing it at a very low level of abstraction, i.e. at a level at which it is understood by a computer.

Modeling and model transformation to the required abstraction level constitute the core of model-driven development. In model-driven development, essential aspects of software are expressed in the form of models, and transformations of these models are considered the core of software development. Models can particularly be transformed into a technical implementation, i.e. a software system. Such an approach can avoid restricting oneself to a specific technology in the early stages of the development process and can ensure a consistent architecture throughout the lifecycle of a software system.

The aim of this book is to give an overview of the current achievements in model-driven development. In the introductory chapter *Models, Modeling, and Model-Driven Architecture (MDA)*, Brown, Conallen and Tropeano first explain the terminology used in the following chapters of the book and introduce basic principles and methods in model-driven development. Achievements in model-driven development are then considered from a conceptual point of view in Part I of the book that comprises the following chapters:

- *A Systematic Look at Model Transformations.* Metzger focuses on model transformations and presents a classification scheme to consider the differences between the modeled system, the model itself and the formalism used.
- *Tool-support for Model-Driven Development of Security-Critical Systems with UML.* Jürjens and Shabalin show the use of UML in model-driven development. In particular, they give a formal semantics for a subset of UML which can be used to analyze the interaction of a system with its environment and UML specifications.
- *Caste-Centric Modeling of Multi-Agent Systems: The CAMLE Modeling Language and Automated Tools.* Zhu and Shan introduce the CAMLE approach to model-driven development of multi-agent systems by combining graphical modeling with formal specification.
- *Using Graph Transformation for Practical Model Driven Software Engineering.* In this chapter, Grunske et al. consider model transformations using graph transformation theory, in particular to specify and apply model transformations.
- *A Generalized Notion of Platforms for Model Driven Development.* Atkinson and Kühne consider two of the basic terms in model-driven development, platform and platform model. They show the origin of these terms and propose an alternative definition for them.

Part II then considers technical achievements and technical infrastructures of model-driven development in the following chapters:

- *A Tool Infrastructure for Model-Driven Development Using Aspectual Patterns.* Hammouda introduces a concern-based approach to model-driven development and presents a tool, called MADE, which particularly supports model generation, checking and tracing.
- *Automatically Discovering Transitive Relationships in Class Diagrams.* Egyed considers the problem of abstracting class diagrams of certain complexity with tool support. The approach proposed uses a large number of abstraction rules and is used for model understanding, consistency checking and reverse engineering.
- *Generic and Domain-Specific Model Refactoring using a Model Transformation Engine.* Zhang, Lin and Gray propose an approach for refactoring at the model level with the use of behavior-preserving transformations. Their chapter also covers a model transformation engine for refactoring various types of models.
- *A Testing Framework for Model Transformations.* Lin, Zhang and Gray discuss validation and verification of model transformation at the model level rather than late in the development process at the source code level. The framework presented is integrated in the transformation engine presented in the previous chapter and provides means for typical testing activities.
- *Parallax – An Aspect-Enabled Framework for Plug-in-Based MDA Refinements Towards Middleware.* Silaghi and Strohmeier present the Parallax framework, an open and extensible tool which particularly supports configuring application designs with regard to specific middleware concerns and adapting to different middleware infrastructures.

- *Evolution and Maintenance of MDA Applications.* Seifert and Beneken investigate the life cycle of applications developed according to the model-driven development approach. They particularly focus on long-term aspects and consider the maintenance of such applications and the progress in model-driven development.

The chapters in Part III finally summarize experience gained in actual projects employing model-driven development:

- *Intents and Upgrades in Component-Based High-Assurance Systems.* Elmqvist and Nadjm-Tehrani describe their experience using model-driven development in the area of high-assurance components, particularly components used as part of embedded systems.
- *On Modeling Techniques for Supporting Model Driven Development of Protocol Processing Applications.* Alanen et al. use model-driven development in the area of protocol processing applications. They give an overview of a respective method and summarize their experience.
- *An Integrated Model-driven Development Environment for Composing and Validating Distributed Real-time and Embedded Systems.* Trombetti et al. employ model-driven development in the area of distributed real-time and embedded applications. They present an integration of tool suites for model-driven development and model checking in this area.
- *A Model-Driven Technique for Development of Embedded Systems Based on the DEVS formalism.* Wainer, Glinsky and MacSween propose a model-driven approach to the development of embedded systems with real-time constraints based on the formal technique of DEVS, and summarize their experience using this approach.
- *Model Driven Service Engineering.* Bræk and Melby consider problems associated with expressing platform-independent models and their behaviors, and also discuss how to handle implementation and platform-dependent properties. They suggest possible solutions to those problems based on their experience.
- *Practical Insights into Model-Driven Architecture: Lessons from the Design and Use of an MDA Toolkit.* Brown, Conallen and Tropeano finally summarize their experience in the design and use of a model-driven architecture toolkit at IBM.

Work on this book officially began in April 2004 with an email to the `seworld` mailing list, which was followed by individual invitations sent to the leading experts of the field. Researchers and practitioners have been invited to summarize their research results and experience in model-driven development in the form of book chapters. Fortunately, we received a large number of very high-quality contributions, which shows that model-driven development will not be a short-lived hype in software engineering. We are very grateful for the contributions and would like to thank all authors for their effort.

Leipzig and Bonn,   *Sami Beydeda*
May 2005   *Matthias Book*
                                                                                    Volker Gruhn

Acknowledgments

Inviting the leading researchers guaranteed a high quality of the individual chapters and thus of the book. However, we decided to conduct a peer review to further improve the chapters. The review was conducted with the support of a committee whose members reviewed the individual contributions and gave valuable remarks to revise and improve them. We would like to thank all committee members for their support; without them, the book would not have its quality.

Committee Members

- Marcus Alanen, Johan Lilius, Ivan Porres, Dragos Truscan
  Software Construction and Embedded Systems Laboratories, Turku Centre for Computer Science, Lemminkäisenkatu 14, FIN-20520 Turku, Finland
  {marcus.alanen, johan.lilius, iporres, dragos.truscan}@abo.fi

- Alan W. Brown
  IBM Software Group, 4205 S. Miami Blvd, Durham, NC 27703, USA
  awbrown@us.ibm.com

- Rainer Burkhardt
  JgenCy Project GmbH, Heidegarten 14, 98693 Martinroda, Germany
  Rainer@Burkhardt.com

- Alexander Egyed
  Teknowledge Corporation, 4640 Admiralty Way, Suite 1010, Marina Del Rey, CA 90292, USA
  aegyed@ieee.org

- Jonas Elmqvist, Simin Nadjm-Tehrani
  Department of Computer and Information Science, Linköping University, S-581 83 Linköping, Sweden
  {jonel, simin}@ida.liu.se

- Leif Geiger, Albert Zuendorf
  Department of Computer Science and Electrical Engineering, University of Kassel, Wilhelmshoeher Allee 73, 34121 Kassel, Germany
  {leif.geiger, albert.zuendorf}@uni-kassel.de

- Aniruddha Gokhale
  Department of Electrical Engineering and Computer Science, Vanderbilt University, Box 1829, Station B, Nashville, TN 37235, USA
  gokhale@dre.vanderbilt.edu

- Jeff Gray
  Department of Computer and Information Sciences, University of Alabama at
  Birmingham, 126 Campbell Hall, 1300 University Boulevard, Birmingham, AL
  35294-1170, USA
  gray@cis.uab.edu

- Lars Grunske
  School of Information Technology and Electrical Engineering, University of
  Queensland, Brisbane, QLD 4072, Australia
  grunske@itee.uq.edu.au

- Imed Hammouda
  Institute of Software Systems, Tampere University of Technology, P.O. Box 553,
  FIN-33101 Tampere, Finland
  imed.hammouda@tut.fi

- Jan Jürjens, Pasha Shabalin
  Dept. of Informatics, Software & Systems Engineering, TU München, Boltzmannstr. 3, 85748 München/Garching, Germany
  {juerjens, shabalin}@in.tum.de

- Alpay Karagöz
  Bilgi Grubu Ltd., Gumus Blk. No:3, ODTU Teknokent, 06531 Ankara, Turkey
  alpay.karagoz@bg.com.tr

- Hubert B. Keller
  Forschungszentrum Karlsruhe, Institut für Angewandte Informatik, Postfach 3640,
  76021 Karlsruhe, Germany
  keller@iai.fzk.de

- Philippe Kruchten
  Dept. of Electrical & Computer Engineering, University of British Columbia,
  2356 Main Mall, Room 441, Vancouver, BC V6T1Z4, Canada
  pbk@ece.ubc.ca

- Thomas Kühne
  Darmstadt University of Technology, Hochschulstr. 10, 64289 Darmstadt, Germany
  kuehne@informatik.tu-darmstadt.de

- Michael Kunz
  Stab Architektur IDG, Pohligstr. 3, D-50969 Köln, Germany
  michael_kunz@idg.de

- Andreas Metzger
  Software Systems Engineering, University of Duisburg-Essen, Schützenbahn 70,
  45117 Essen, Germany
  metzger@sse.uni-essen.de

- Raul Silaghi, Alfred Strohmeier
  Software Engineering Laboratory, Swiss Federal Institute of Technology, CH-
  1015 Lausanne EPFL, Switzerland
  {raul.silaghi, alfred.strohmeier}@epfl.ch

- Niels Van Eetvelde, Pieter Van Gorp
  University of Antwerp, Middelheimlaan 1, 2020 Antwerpen, Belgium
  {niels.vaneetvelde, pieter.vangorp}@ua.ac.be

- Dániel Varró
  Department of Measurement and Information Systems, Budapest University of
  Technology and Economics, H-1117, Budapest, Magyar tudósok krt. 2, Hungary
  varro@mit.bme.hu

- Gabriel A. Wainer, Samuel Ajila, Yvan Labiche
  Dept. of Systems and Computer Engineering, Carleton University, 4456 Mackenzie Bldg., 1125 Colonel By Drive, Ottawa, ON K1S 5B6, Canada
  gwainer@sce.carleton.ca

- Yun Yang
  Faculty of Information and Communication Technologies (ICT), Swinburne University of Technology, PO Box 218, Hawthorn, Melbourne, Victoria 3122, Australia
  yyang@it.swin.edu.au

- Hong Zhu
  Department of Computing, Oxford Brookes University, Oxford OX33 1HX, UK
  hzhu@brookes.ac.uk

Last but not least, we would also like to thank Gerald Mücke, Matthias Pätzold and
Falk Schütze for polishing the final manuscript of the book.

Contents

Introduction: Models, Modeling, and Model-Driven Architecture (MDA)

Alan W. Brown, Jim Conallen, and Dave Tropeano

IBM Software Group,
4205 S. Miami Blvd, Durham, NC 27703, USA
{awbrown, jconallen, davetropeano}@us.ibm.com

Summary. Models, modeling, and Model-Driven Architecture (MDA) are the basis for a set of development approaches known as model-driven development (MDD). Models are used to reason about a problem domain and design a solution in the solution domain. Relationships between these models provide a web of dependencies that record the process by which a solution is created, and help to understand the implications of changes at any point in that process.

In addition to creating these models, we can define rules for automating many of the steps needed to convert one model representation to another, for tracing between model elements, and for analyzing important characteristics of the models. This style of MDD is called Model-Driven Architecture (MDA). The MDA approach is being widely discussed in the software industry today as a way of increasing the quality, efficiency, and predictability of large-scale software development. In this paper we explore the role of modeling and the MDA style of MDD, and provide a useful context for understanding current product and research efforts in area of MDA.

1 Introduction

It is tempting to believe that software development is easy. You gain an understanding of the problem that needs to be addressed by talking with people familiar with that domain, and then design a solution to meet those needs and deploy it in the customer's environment. Unfortunately, several issues can get in the way to make the task of software development a lot more challenging:

- We rarely, if ever, get a full understanding of the problem space. Domain experts help, but they, too, have a limited understanding of the areas they work in, view things from different perspectives, or disagree on approaches, processes, and priorities. So in practice, we spend a lot of time analyzing these different inputs and obtaining a common, evolving view of the customer's domain.
- There are many constraints on the solutions to consider: for example, balancing the time and effort required to implement a system, integrating with existing applications and technologies already in place, and coordinating multiple teams producing different components of the deployed system.

- Many kinds of changes must be addressed at all stages of development: errors will be discovered, designs will be updated, requirements will be refined, priorities will be changed, implementations will be refactored, and so on. The dynamic nature of the development process results in a lot of time spent on understanding the impact of a change, defining a plan to address the change, and ensuring that any actions are carried out appropriately.
- A large software development task is an engineering project involving teams of people with different skills interacting over an extended period of time to implement a solution that can never truly be said to be "finished." As a result, all the techniques of managing engineering projects must be taken into account: scheduling, resource management, risk mitigation, ROI analysis, documentation, support, and so on.

Software engineers turn to many techniques to address these challenges. One of the most fundamental is the use of models and modeling. Models provide abstractions of a physical system that allow engineers to reason about that system by ignoring extraneous details while focusing on the relevant ones. All forms of engineering rely on models as essential to understanding complex real-world systems. Models are used in many ways: predicting system qualities, reasoning about specific properties when aspects of the system are changed, and communicating key system characteristics to its various stakeholders. The models may be developed as a precursor to implementing the physical system, or they may be derived from an existing system or a system in development as an aid to understanding its behavior [386].

There are many aspects of a system that may be of interest. Depending on what is considered relevant at any point in time, various modeling concepts and notations may be used that highlight one or more particular perspectives, or views, of that system. Furthermore, in some instances models can be augmented with hints, or rules, that assist in transforming them. For example, it is often necessary to convert between different views of the system at an equivalent level of abstraction (e.g., between a structural view and a behavioral view), and model transformations facilitate this. In other cases, a transformation converts models offering a particular perspective between levels of abstraction, usually from a more abstract to less abstract view by adding more detail supplied by the transformation rules.

These ideas of models, modeling, and model transformation are the basis for a set of software development approaches that are known as model-driven development (MDD). Models are used to reason about the problem domain and the solution domain. Relationships between these models provide a web of dependencies that record the process by which a solution was created, and help us to understand the implications of changes at any point in that process.

In fact, we can be quite prescriptive in the use of models in a software development process. If we define the kinds of models that must be produced, and apply some rigor to the precise semantics of these models, we can define rules for:

- Automating many steps needed to convert one model representation to another.
- Tracing between model elements.
- Analyzing important characteristics of the models.

This style of MDD, called Model-Driven Architecture (MDA), is championed by the Object Management Group (OMG). It is based on a set of emerging standards for how to define a set of models, notations, and transformation rules. The MDA approach provides an open, vendor-neutral basis for system interoperability via OMG's established modeling standards: Unified Modeling Language (UML), Meta-Object Facility (MOF), and Common Warehouse Metamodel (CWM). Platform-independent descriptions of enterprise solutions can be built using these modeling standards and can be transformed into a major open or proprietary platform, including CORBA, J2EE, .NET, XMI/XML, and Web-based platforms [324].

MDA styles of development are being widely discussed in the software industry today as a way of increasing the quality, efficiency, and predictability of large-scale software development [135, 115, 114]. However, few documented experiences with the use of MDA styles of development are available. In this paper we explore the role of modeling and the MDA style of the MDD development, and provide a useful context for understanding current product and research efforts in area of MDA. Our work is based on a number of experiences, including creation and use of an MDA toolkit developed to extend an existing modeling workbench to support MDA styles of development for particular customer situations in which families of related software applications were being created within a single domain. We believed MDA offered the best means to capture commonalty in the problem domain, express transformation rules that convert the problem understanding into a candidate solution, and repeatably to generate major parts of that solution to the customers' environment of choice [51].

2 Modeling Approaches

In the software engineering world, modeling has had a rich tradition from the earliest days of programming. The most recent innovations have focused on notations and tools that allow users to express system perspectives of value to software architects and developers, and to express these perspectives in ways that can be readily mapped into the programming language code compiled for a particular operating system platform. The current state of this practice employs the Unified Modeling Language (UML) as the primary modeling notation [138]. The UML allows development teams to capture a variety of important characteristics of a system in corresponding models. Transformations among these models is primarily manual, although tools can be used to manage traceability and dependency relationships among model elements according to best practice guidance on maintaining synchronized models as part of a large-scale development effort [9].

One useful way to characterize current practice is to look at the different ways in which the models are synchronized with the source code they help describe. This is illustrated in Fig. 1,[1] which shows the spectrum of modeling approaches in use by software practitioners today. Each category identifies a particular use of models

---

[1] This is based on a diagram originally created by John Daniels.

in assisting software practitioners to create running applications (code) for a specific runtime platform, and the relationship between the models and the code.[2]

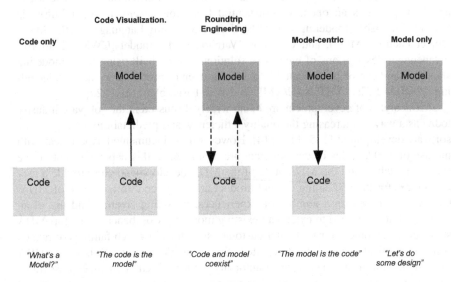

Fig. 1. The modeling spectrum

Today, a majority of software developers still take a *code-only* approach (see the left end of the modeling spectrum, Fig. 1), and do not use separately defined models at all. They rely almost entirely on the code they write, and they express their model of the system they are building directly in a third-generation programming language (3GL) such as Java, C++, or C# within an integrated development environment (IDE) such as IBM WebSphere Studio, Eclipse, and Microsoft VisualStudio.[3] Any "modeling" they do is in the form of programming abstractions embedded in the code (e.g., packages, modules, interfaces, etc.), which are managed through mechanisms such as program libraries and object hierarchies. Any separate modeling of architectural designs is informal and intuitive, and lives on whiteboards, in PowerPoint sides, or in the developers' heads. While this may be adequate for individuals and very small teams, this approach makes it difficult to understand key characteristics of the system among the details of the implementation of the business logic. Furthermore, it becomes much more difficult to manage the evolution of these solutions as their scale and complexity increases, as the system evolves over time, or when the original

---

[2] Many other important life-cycle artifacts also benefit from a model-driven approach (e.g., requirements lists, test cases, and build scripts). For simplicity we concentrate on the primary development artifact – the code.

[3] For this discussion we shall ignore the fact that the code is itself a realization of a programming model that abstracts the developer from the underlying machine code for manipulating individual bits in memory, registers, etc.

members of the design team are not directly accessible to the team maintaining the system.

Developers can frequently gain additional insights when provided with *code visualizations* in some appropriate modeling notation. As developers create or analyze an application they often want to visualize the code through some graphical notation that aids their understanding of the code's structure or behavior. It may also be possible to manipulate the graphical notation as an alternative to editing the text-based code, so that the visual rendering becomes a direct representation of the code. Such rendering is sometimes called a code model, or an implementation model, although many feel it more appropriate to call these artifacts "diagrams" and reserve the use of "model" for higher levels of abstraction. In tools that allow such diagrams (e.g., IBM WebSphere Studio and Borland Together/J), the code view and the model view can be displayed simultaneously; as the developer manipulates either view the other is immediately synchronized with it. In this approach, the diagrams are tightly coupled representations of the code and provide an alternative way to view and possibly edit at the code level.

Further advantage of the models can be taken through *roundtrip engineering (RTE)* between an abstract model of the system describing the system architecture or design, and the code. The developer typically elaborates the system design to some level of detail, then creates a first-pass implementation from that code by applying model-to-code transformations, usually manually. For instance, one team working on the high-level design provides design models to the team working on the implementation (perhaps simply by printing out model diagrams, or providing the implementation team some files containing the models). The implementation team converts this abstract, high-level design into a detailed set of design models and the programming language implementation. Iterations of these representations will occur as errors and their corrections are made in either the design or the code. Consequently, without considerable discipline, the abstract models and the implementation models usually – and quickly – end up out of step.

Tools can automate the initial transformation, and can help to keep the design and implementation models in step as they evolve. Typically the tools generate code stubs from the design models that the user has to further refine.[4] As changes are made to the code they must at some point be reconciled with the original model (hence the term "roundtrip engineering," or RTE). Tools adopting this approach, such as IBM Rational Rose, can offer multiple transformation services supporting RTE between models and different implementation languages.

In a *model-centric* approach, models of the system are established in sufficient detail that the full implementation of the system can be generated from the models themselves. To achieve this, the models may include, for example, representations of the persistent and non-persistent data, business logic, and presentation elements. Any integration to legacy data and services may require that the interfaces to those elements are also modeled. The code generation process may then apply a series of pat-

---

[4] In some cases much more than code stubs can be generated depending on the fidelity of the models.

terns to transform the models to code, frequently allowing the developer some choice in the patterns that are applied (e.g., among various deployment topologies). To further assist in the code generation, this approach frequently makes use of standard or proprietary application frameworks and runtime services that ease the code generation task by constraining the styles of applications that can be generated. Hence, tools using this approach typically specialize in the generation of particular styles of applications (e.g., IBM Rational Rose Technical Developer for real-time embedded systems, and IBM Rational Rapid Developer for enterprise IT systems). However, in all cases the models are the primary artifact created and manipulated by developers.

A *model-only* approach is at the far-right end of the modeling spectrum. In this approach developers use models purely as thought aids in understanding the business or solution domain, or for analyzing the architecture of a proposed solution. Models are frequently used as the basis for discussion, communication, and analysis among teams within a single organization, or across multi-organizational projects. These models frequently appear in proposals for new work, or adorn the walls of offices and cubicles in software labs everywhere as a way of understanding some complex domain of interest, and establishing a shared vocabulary and set of concepts among disparate teams. In practice the implementation of a system, whether from scratch or updating an existing solution, may be practically disconnected from the models. An interesting example of this approach can be seen in the growing number of organizations which outsource implementation and maintenance of their systems while maintaining control of the overall enterprise architecture.

3 MDA Principles

There are four principles that underlie the OMG's MDA approach:

(1) Models expressed in a well-defined notation are a cornerstone to system understanding for enterprise-scale solutions.
(2) Building systems can be organized around a set of models by imposing a series of transformations between models, organized into an architectural framework of layers and transformations.
(3) A formal underpinning for describing models in a set of metamodels facilitates meaningful integration and transformation among models, and is the basis for automation through tools.
(4) Acceptance and broad adoption of this model-based approach requires industry standards to provide openness to consumers, and foster competition among vendors.

To support this approach the OMG has defined a specific set of layers and transformations that provide a conceptual framework and a vocabulary for MDA. Notably, OMG identifies four layers: Computation Independent Model (CIM), Platform Independent Model (PIM), Platform Specific Model (PSM) described by a Platform Model (PM), and an Implementation Specific Model (ISM). This is illustrated in Fig. 2.

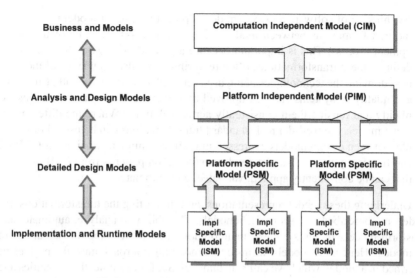

Fig. 2. The layers and transformations of MDA

A key aspect of the MDA approach is to recognize that transformations can be applied to abstract descriptions of some aspect of a system to add more detail to that description, refine that description to be more concrete, or to convert between representations. Three ideas are important here:

- Distinguishing different kinds of models allows us to think of software and system development as a series of refinements between different model representations. These models and their refinements are a critical part of the development methodology for situations that include refinements between models representing different aspects of the system, adding further details to a model, or converting between different kinds of models.
- One way to consider the models is to classify them in terms of how explicitly they represent aspects of the platforms being targeted. In all software and system development there are important constraints implied by the choice of languages, hardware, network topology, communications protocols and infrastructure, and so on. Each of these can be considered elements of the solution "platform." An MDA approach helps us to focus on what is essential to the solution being designed separate from the details of that "platform."
- The notion of what is a "platform" is rather complex, and highly context dependent. For example, in some situations the platform may be the operating system and associated utilities; in some situations it may a technology infrastructure represented by a well-defined programming model such as J2EE or .NET; in other situations it is a particular instance of a hardware topology. Whatever we consider the "platform," it is important to think more in terms of models at different levels of abstraction used for different purposes, rather than be too distracted by defining what a "platform" means.

- By thinking of software and system development as a set of model refinements, the transformations between models become first-class elements of the development process. This is important because a great deal of work takes places in defining these transformations, often requiring specialist knowledge of the business domain, the technologies being used for implementation, or both. Efficiency and quality of systems can be improved by capturing these transformations explicitly and reusing them consistently across solutions. Where the different abstract models are well-defined, standard transformations can be used. For example, between design models expressed in UML and implementations in J2EE we can frequently use well-understood transformation patterns from UML to J2EE that can be consistently applied, validated, and automated.

Underlying these model representations, and supporting the transformations, the models are described in a set of metamodels. The ability to analyze, automate, and transform models requires a clear, unambiguous way to describe the semantics of the models. Hence, the models intrinsic to a modeling approach must themselves be described in a model, which we call a metamodel. So, for example, the semantics and notation of the UML are described in metamodels. Tool vendors turn to the standard metamodels of UML when they want to implement the UML in a standard way. For example, the UML metamodel describes in precise detail the meaning of a class, the meaning of an attribute, and the meaning of the relationships between these two concepts.

The OMG recognized the importance of metamodels and formal semantics for modeling as essential for their practical use. As a result, OMG defined a set of metamodeling levels, and defined a standard language for expressing metamodels, the Meta-Object Facility (MOF). A metamodel uses MOF to formally define the abstract syntax of a set of modeling constructs.

The models and the transformations between them will be specified using open standards. As an industry consortium, the OMG has championed a number of important industry standards for specifying systems and their interconnections. Through standards such as CORBA, IIOP, UML, and CWM the software industry is enjoying a level of system interoperability that was previously impossible, Furthermore, tool interoperation is also facilitated as a result of tool interchange standards such as MOF and XMI.

3.1 A Simple Example

In Fig. 3 we show a simplified example of a Platform Independent Model (PIM) and its transformation into three different Platform Specific Models (PSMs).

In Fig. 3 we show a simple PIM representing a customer and an account. At this level of abstraction the model describes important characteristics of the domain in terms of classes and their attributes, but without making any platform specific choices about which technologies will be used to represent them. Specific mappings, or transformations, will be defined to create the PSMs. Three are illustrated, together with the standards that are used to express the mappings. For example, one approach

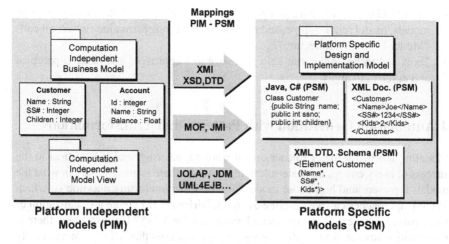

Fig. 3. A simplified example of PIM-to-PSM mappings

is to take the PSM expressed in the UML and export it in XMI format using standard definitions expressed as XML Schema Definitions (XSDs) or Document Type Definitions (DTDs). This can then be used as input to a code generation tool that produces interface definitions in Java for each of the classes defined in the UML. Usually a set of rules is built into the code generation tool to perform the transformation. However, often the code generation tool allows those rules to be specifically defined as templates in a scripting language.[5]

3.2 Summary

Following a long history of the use of models to represent key ideas in both problem and solution domains, MDA provides a conceptual framework for using models and applying transformations between models as part of a controlled, efficient software development process. The following ideas were highlighted:

- Models help people understand and communicate complex ideas.
- Many different kinds of elements can be modeled depending on the context. These offer different views of the world that must be reconciled.
- We see commonality at all levels of these models – in both the problems being analyzed and in the proposed solutions.
- Applying the ideas of different kinds of models and transforming them between representations provides a well-defined style of development, enabling the identification and reuse of common approaches.

---

[5] More detailed examples of this will be described later. However, you may wish to take a look at commercial examples of MDA in action such as IBM Rational's Rose Technical Developer or Rapid Developer products (www.ibm.com/rational), or at open source MDA tools applying this approach (e.g., AndroMDA (www.andromda.org) or Jamda (jamda.sourceforge.net)).

- The OMG has provided a conceptual framework and a set of standards to express models, model relationships, and model-to-model transformations in what it calls "Model-Driven Architecture".
- Tools and technologies can help to realize this approach, and make it practical and efficient to apply.

4 Automating Generation with Patterns and Transformations

Modeling has had a major impact on software engineering, and it is critical to the success of every enterprise-scale solution. However, there is great variety in what the models represent and how those models are used. An interesting question is: which of these approaches can we describe as "model-driven?" If I create a visualization of some part of a system, does that mean I am practicing MDA? Unfortunately, there is no definitive answer. Rather, there is a growing consensus that MDA is more closely associated with model-driven approaches in which code is (semi-)automatically generated from more abstract models, and which employs standard specification languages for describing those models and the transformations between them.

In fact, models are the stepping stones on the path between a description of the business need and the deployable runtime components. As the system under development evolves, the models themselves become more complete, accurate, and consistent with each other. The focus of effort also shifts from the models at the higher level of abstraction toward those at lower levels. Ultimately these models are used to directly create the deployable components.

4.1 How Models Evolve

There are two main activities that happen with models: refinement and transformation. Model refinement is the gradual change of a model to better match the desired system. The model is refined as more information is known and understood about the system. A model may also be refined for purely internal reasons (i.e., refactoring). As the various models evolve, dependent models will also need to change in response. By the end of each iteration of the development cycle, however, all the models should be consistent with each other.

Models are refined either manually or through some form of automation or assisted automation. Automation can be in the form of rules for model refinement implemented as executable patterns or assets. When a pattern is applied to a model it modifies or rearranges the model elements to resemble the pattern. The application of a pattern adds new elements or properties to the model. When a pattern is applied it may involve some user assistance – for example, prompting the developer for an existing model element to bind a pattern parameter with, or other decisions that need to be resolved for the pattern to be executed.

Model transformations, on the other hand, involve two or more models. The most typical example is a high-level abstraction model (a "Platform Independent Model" – PIM) being transformed into a low-level abstracted and technology-dependent one (a "Platform Specific Model" – PSM). For example, a UML PIM could represent a logical data model and consist of a number of entity classes, each with a number of persistent attributes. This model could be transformed through automation into a UML data model that captures the same underlying entities, but now from the viewpoint of database tables. The data model could in turn be used to directly generate SQL scripts that define the database, and could be directly executed on a specific database management system (DBMS).

Model transformations are not necessarily unidirectional. It is possible for some model transformations to be bidirectional. For example, a platform-specific UML model of several Entity JavaBean (EJB) classes could be "synchronized" with the source code implementing these EJBs. New elements (i.e., methods, attributes, associations) defined in the model would generate appropriate elements in the source, and any new elements created in the source (or removed) would generate appropriate elements (or be removed) in the model.

4.2 Understanding Model Transformation

Defining and applying model transformations are critical techniques within any MDA style of development. Model transformations involve using a model as one of the inputs in the automation process. Possible outputs can include another model, or varying levels of executable code. In practice there are three common model transformations: refactoring transformations, model-to-model transformations, and model-to-code transformations.

(1) *Refactoring transformations* reorganize a model based on some well-defined criteria. In this case the output is a revision of the original model, called the refactored model. An example could be as simple as renaming all the instances where a UML entity name is used, or something more complex like replacing a class with a set of classes and relationships in both the metamodel and in all diagrams displaying those model elements. This is illustrated in Fig. 4 which shows a simple refactoring transformation that extracts a class's interface.

(2) *Model-to-model transformations* convert information from one model or models to another model or set of models, typically where the flow of information is across abstraction boundaries. An example would be the conversion of one type of model into another, such as the transformation of a set of entity classes into a matched set of database schema, Plain Old Java Objects (POJOs), and XML-formatted mapping descriptor files. This conversion is illustrated in Fig. 5a through Fig. 5d. Figure 5a shows the high-level entity model as a PIM. Figure 5b shows the resulting logical data model and is considered in this context to be a PSM. Figure 5c shows the matching Java objects, and Fig. 5d shows components that represent the persistence descriptor files.

(3) *Model-to-code transformations* are familiar to anyone who has used the code generation capability of a UML modeling tool. These transformations convert a model element into a code fragment. This is not limited to object-oriented languages such as Java and C++. Nor is it limited to programming languages:

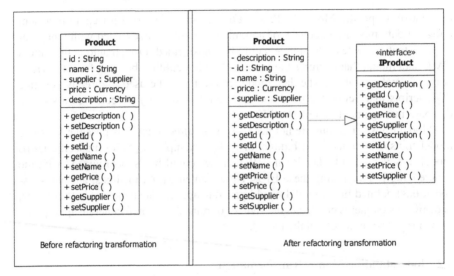

Before refactoring transformation   After refactoring transformation

Fig. 4. An example of a refactoring transformation

configuration, deployment, data definitions, message schemas, and others kinds of files can also be generated from models expressed in notations such as the UML. Model-to-code transformations can be developed for nearly any form of programming language or declarative specification. An example would be to generate Data Definition Language (DDL) code from a logical data model expressed as a UML class diagram. This is illustrated in Fig. 6, which shows the DDL generated with the example database PSM shown in Fig. 5b.

4.3 Applying Model Transformations

Having described different kinds of model transformations, we also note that in practice there are several ways in which model transformations can be applied. In MDA approaches there are four categories of techniques for applying model transformations:

- *Manual.* The developer examines the input model and manually creates or edits the elements in the transformed model. The developer interprets the information in the model and makes modifications accordingly.
- *Prepared Profile.* A profile is an extension of the UML semantics in which a model type is derived. Applying a profile defines rules by which a model is transformed.
- *Patterns.* A pattern is a particular arrangement of model elements. Patterns can be applied to a model and result in the creation of new model elements in the transformed model.

(a) PIM

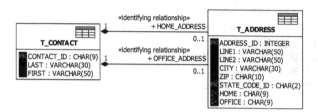

(b) Database PSM

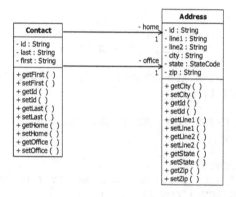

(c) Java Objects PSM

(d) Persistence Descriptor Files PSM

Fig. 5. Examples of model-to-model transformations

```
CREATE TABLE T_CONTACT (
CONTACT_ID CHAR ( 9 ) NOT NULL,
LAST VARCHAR ( 30 ) NOT NULL,
FIRST VARCHAR ( 50 ) NOT NULL
);

CREATE TABLE T_ADDRESS (
ADDRESS_ID INTEGER NOT NULL,
LINE1 VARCHAR ( 50 ) NOT NULL,
LINE2 VARCHAR ( 50 ) NOT NULL,
CITY VARCHAR ( 30 ) NOT NULL,
ZIP CHAR ( 10 ) NOT NULL,
STATE_CODE_ID CHAR ( 2 ) NOT NULL,
HOME CHAR ( 9 ) NOT NULL,
OFFICE CHAR ( 9 ) NOT NULL
);

ALTER TABLE T_CONTACT ADD CONSTRAINT T_C_Constraint1
  PRIMARY KEY ( CONTACT_ID );

ALTER TABLE T_ADDRESS
ADD CONSTRAINT T_A_Constraint1
PRIMARY KEY ( OFFICE, HOME, ADDRESS_ID );

ALTER TABLE T_ADDRESS ADD CONSTRAINT T_A_Constraint6
  UNIQUE ( OFFICE );

ALTER TABLE T_ADDRESS ADD CONSTRAINT T_A_Constraint4
  UNIQUE ( HOME );

ALTER TABLE T_ADDRESS
ADD CONSTRAINT T_A_Constraint5 FOREIGN KEY ( OFFICE )
REFERENCES T_CONTACT ( CONTACT_ID )
ON DELETE CASCADE
ON UPDATE NO ACTION;

ALTER TABLE T_ADDRESS
ADD CONSTRAINT T_A_Constraint3 FOREIGN KEY ( HOME )
REFERENCES T_CONTACT ( CONTACT_ID )
ON DELETE NO ACTION
ON UPDATE NO ACTION;
```

Fig. 6. An example of a model-to-code transformation

- *Automatic.* Automatic transformations apply a set of changes to one or mode models based on predefined transformation rules. These rules may be implicit to the tools being used, or may have been explicitly defined based on domain specific knowledge. This type of transformation requires that the input model be sufficiently complete both syntactically and semantically, and may require models to be marked with information specific to the transformations being applied.

The use of profiles and patterns usually involves developer input at the time of transformation, or requires the input model to be "marked". A marked model contains extra information not necessarily relevant to the model's viewpoint or level of abstraction. This information is only relevant to the tools or processes that transform the model. For example, a UML analysis model containing entities with string types may be marked variable or fixed length, or it may be marked to specify its maximum length. From an analysis viewpoint just the identification of the string data type is usually sufficient. However, when transforming a string-typed attribute into, say, a database column type, the additional information is required to complete the definition.

5 Summary

MDA is a work in progress. The very definition of what "MDA" means is evolving. In the narrowest of contexts, it is about different abstract models of a system, and well-defined model transformations among them. In the more general sense, it is about having models at varying levels of abstraction as the basis for software architecture that ultimately drive into various implementation technologies. So at this time, there is very broad interpretation of MDA to the point that many organizations and solutions claim "support" for, or "conformance" to, MDA. In this paper we emphasize MDA as an emerging set of standards and technologies focused on a particular style of software development – one that highlights the advantages of modeling at various levels of abstraction, and, most importantly, on the integration and flow of information through these models. This approach to software development allows developers to contribute to the project through the types of models that best match the type of information and decisions that they make. This approach also allows senior project members to maximize their effectiveness through their definition and implementations of model-to-model transformations. Additionally, system analysts, testing, and quality assurance staff can leverage models for analysis of the system and its performance before it is complete.

6 Acknowledgements

The work reported in this paper has been carried out by a number of people, and it is our pleasure to acknowledge their contribution. The ideas discussed here reflect the thinking of a broad team at IBM including Grady Booch, Gary Cernosek, Jim

Conallen, Pete Eeles, Sridhar Iyengar, Simon Johnston, Grant Larsen, Martin Nally, Jim Rumbaugh, and Bran Selic. We also thank Mike Perrow for his helpful reviews of the paper.

Part I

Conceptual Foundations of Model-Driven Development

A Systematic Look at Model Transformations

Andreas Metzger

Software Systems Engineering, University of Duisburg-Essen,
Schützenbahn 70, 45117 Essen, Germany
metzger@sse.uni-essen.de

Summary. Model transformations are at the heart of model-driven software development (MDSD). As a typical example, models of a higher level of abstraction are transformed into models that are closer to the target platform. However, there are also other forms of such transformations: for example, a model at a certain level of abstraction can be evolved by applying specific designs or modeling patterns.

We believe that a systematic classification of the kinds of transformations that are performed during an MDSD activity is of great assistance in understanding such transformations and in comprehending the sources of possible errors and difficulties. This chapter provides a systematic look at model transformations and presents a detailed classification scheme that we have found suitable. To support the soundness of this scheme, we provide examples for its application (i.e., for classifying typical transformations) and we demonstrate how such a classification can assist in understanding some of the problems that can occur within MDSD.

1 Foundation

Before the various kinds of model transformations can be discussed, the central term "model" has to be clarified. In general, "a *model* is a set of statements about some *system under study*" ([384], p. 27).

To enable the model users to concentrate on the significant system aspects, thus allowing them to handle complexity, any useful model will exhibit some form of *abstraction* from the system under study. One form of abstraction is the selection of relevant from irrelevant or random properties, which is known as *reduction* (cf. [281], p. 6). Other important forms of abstraction are generalization and classification. *Generalization* is a means by which differences among similar elements are ignored to form an entity in which the similarities can be emphasized ([346], p. 155). *Classification* is the process of identifying types, which are also known as concepts (cf. [327], p. 12-2 and [346], p. 156). Classification is the basic form of abstraction found in object-oriented or object-based modeling, where object types are the main elements of conceptual models and classes their respective realization in design models (cf. [327], p. 12-3).

In traditional scientific disciplines models are usually *descriptive*, which means that a model can be considered a "correct" description of the system under study if all its statements are true for the system (see [384], p. 27).

In the case of software systems, a model can also be considered as the *specification* of a system or rather a whole set of systems that should be built. In the context of such a *prescriptive* (cf. [281], p. 8) form of model application, which can be found in other engineering disciplines also, a specific system is considered as being "correct" relative to its specification "if no statement in the model is false for the system under study" ([384], p. 27). During software development, the models are refined (i.e., the level of abstraction is reduced), whereby a subset of the initial set of systems is selected. If successful, this process leads to the final software product, which realizes the desired system in the end.

As is shown in Fig. 1, each model is based on a *formalism* (or language), which precisely defines the model's syntax (or notation) and its semantics (or meaning). The syntax of a formalism is made up of the concrete and the abstract syntax. The concrete syntax specifies the readable representation of the abstract notational elements. The semantics consists of the dynamic and the static semantics. The static semantics, which should be more correctly called well-formedness rules (cf. [195], p. 16), is implied by the dynamic semantics and represents restrictions on the set of valid models that can be expressed using the underlying formalism.

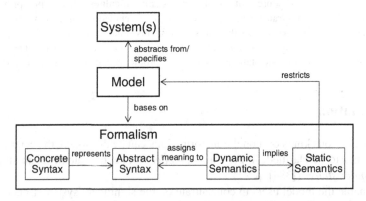

Fig. 1. System, model, and formalism (adapted from [55])

With these definitions of system, model, and formalism, we can more formally describe transformations that can occur during software development. Using a modified form of a formalization that was introduced by Caplat and Sourrouille in [55], we assume that M is the model of a system S (or a specification for a set of systems) and F is the formalism in which the model is described. Any transformation t can then be formulated as

$$t : M_1(S_1)|_{F_1} \rightarrow M_2(S_2)|_{F_2} \tag{1}$$

where M_1 is the *source* model and M_2 is the *target* model of the transformation.

2 Classification of Model Transformations

Note that the transformation t that has been introduced in (1) implies neither that the source model will be modified nor that the target model will be created without modifying the source model. This characteristic should be considered as being orthogonal to the transformation that is described by t. Typically, one would consider the transformation of the latter kind as a *query* because it is free of side-effects (cf. [12]).

A transformation can be *monolithic* (or atomic) or can be composed of many separate steps, which implies a step-wise transformation (cf. [200]).

Caplat and Sourrouille [56] further distinguish model transformations as being *endogen* if the formalism of source and target model is the same ($F_1 = F_2$) or being *exogen* otherwise ($F_1 \neq F_2$).

A further distinction between different kinds of transformations can be exercised upon the purpose of the transformation. There exist transformations that are performed to evolve the model and are therefore called *horizontal* transformations. If a transformation is employed for implementing the model, i.e., for transforming the source model into a model that is closer to the run-time platform, we speak of such a transformation as being *vertical* (cf. pp. 335–339 in [79]). In the first case, the formalism of the source and target model is the same (endogen transformation), where as in the latter case the target model's formalism contains elements that describe concepts that are closer to the final implementation platform (see p. 119 of this book for an in-depth discussion of the term "platform"). Such a vertical transformation is commonly known as *code generation*, when the target model is the actual implementation code (see [12]).

It should be noted that although vertical transformations are exogen transformations, not all exogen transformations have to be vertical transformations. As an example, static analysis tools operate in the reverse direction. These tools usually have implementation code as an input and compute a more abstract model as an output. An example is the computation of the cyclomatic complexity for individual code components (see [229], pp. 348–350).

Another characterization can be performed based on the degree to which model transformations can be automated. As each model transformation represents a query and modification of models, such models have to be machine readable and modifiable for automating such activities. Only formal aspects of a model fulfill this requirement and are thus available for a manipulation through software tools (cf. [327]). Consequently, if the source and target models' syntaxes are fully formalized, a *fully automatic* transformation is conceivable. Otherwise, manual steps are required allowing for *partially automated* or *manual* transformations only.

If a model transformation is exercised by a software tool, this transformation will always be performed in a repeatable and deterministic way. Also, if the transformation specification has been systematically tested (see p. 219 of this book) or formally verified (cf. [439]), the chance for introducing errors into the target model is considerably reduced compared to the manual execution of such an activity.

Finally, model transformations can be classified by the technique that is used for describing (resp. executing) the transformations. Two basic approaches for such a description exist: an operational and a declarative approach.

In a *declarative* approach, transformations are described through rules, which are specified by pre- and post-conditions. The pre-condition describes the state of the model before the transformation is executed. The post-condition specifies the state after a successful transformation. As most of the models or specifications can be expressed as graphs, many of the declarative approaches that are used today are graph transformations (e.g., see p. 91 of this book).

With declarative approaches, a specification of the transformation can be achieved, which is often called a *mapping* (see [256]). Nevertheless, we will not distinguish between "transformation" and "mapping" in the remainder of this chapter but will use the terms interchangeably for readability reasons.

In contrast to declarative approaches, in *operational* (or imperative) approaches, the activities which must be performed to transform the source to the target model are described explicitly by a sequence of actions (see p. 480 in [458]).

Czarnecki and Helsen present further approaches for classifying transformations [80]. Among other aspects, they discuss the notions of model-to-model and model-to-code translations and examine the differences of transformation approaches based on the representation (syntax) of the transformation rules or the form of typing that the "rule language" offers. Favre [120] distinguishes between transformation functions (i.e., transformation specifications) and transformation instances (i.e., the application of a transformation specification to a specific source model).

Although all of the above types of transformations may provide a suitable classification when examining certain properties of model-driven software development (MDSD), we see the need for yet another classification scheme that allows one to reflect on some of the potential pitfalls of MDSD. This scheme is introduced in the following section and is followed by examples for its application in Sect. 3.

2.1 Fine-Grained Classification Scheme

In this section, a fine-grained classification scheme is introduced that considers the possible variations of the systems, the potential changes of models, and the variations in the respective formalisms. To begin with, Fig. 2 shows an overview of the identified types of transformations.

As the reader can observe, we have chosen a very simple scheme for naming the different types of transformations by following the graphical layout of the figure, which should be easy to remember. With this classification scheme, each kind of transformation can be described by a type from the left-hand side of the figure together with a type from the right-hand side of the figure.

Not all of the above transformations are "true" model transformations, as some of them do not require any modification of models ($M_1 = M_2$). However, we will show that such mappings exist in reality and that these can be helpful when evaluating model transformations.

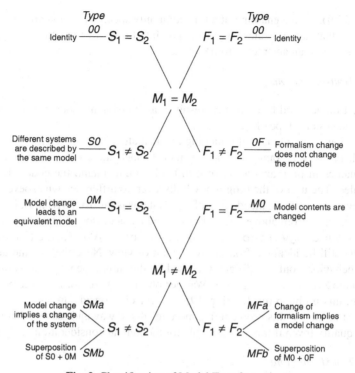

Fig. 2. Classification of Model Transformations

2.2 System and Model Transformations

We start the detailed discussion of our classification scheme by presenting the types of transformations that are introduced on the left-hand side of Fig. 2.

Type S0 Transformations

At the beginning of this chapter, the nature of a model (or a specification) as being an abstraction of a set of systems has been introduced. It is this very nature of a specification that allows several systems to be represented by the same model, thus leading to a "transformation" that can be classified as S0. Whenever two systems differ only in properties either that have been eliminated in the model or that are not reflected in the abstract model elements, we can observe a "transformation" of type S0 between these two systems.

An illustrative example for the abstraction of such a property is provided by Petri nets. In general, a Petri net is a directed bipartite graph with two distinct types of nodes: places and transitions. To describe the dynamics of a Petri net, tokens that can reside within places are introduced. A transition is enabled if and only if there is at least one token in each input place of the transition. When a transition is enabled, it *can* fire, upon which a token is removed from each of the input places and a token is generated in each of the output places (for a more detailed introduction see, e.g., [359]). As the enabling of a transition only specifies its *potential* for firing, each system that demonstrates any of the possible firings of transitions is a correct realization of such an abstract Petri net model.

Type 0M Transformations

There exist model modifications that result in an equivalent model with respect to the modeled system (type 0M).

An obvious example is that renaming an attribute i to countingVariable will result in the very same software system. In fact, there exist tools to obscure variable names in programs to make it difficult to understand the code when it is de-compiled. The user of the program will discover no difference whatsoever.

However, determining the identity of two systems is far from trivial. If, instead of using the variable from above, we were to introduce accessor and mutator methods (i.e., getCountingVariable() and setCountingVariable()), the systems might still be identical from a given point of view. Nevertheless, the detailed run-time behavior would be different, caused by the timing penalty that is imposed by the method calls. As Kleppe and Warmer observe, there does not seem to be a solution to this problem (cf. [256], p. 19). Yet, for our considerations we believe it is sufficient to look at this problem in a more idealistic way and assume that we can identify equality (even if this was possible for theoretical considerations only).

Type SM Transformations

A transformation of type SM comes in two facets. On the one hand, there is the obvious case that a model change implies the change of the specified system (type SMa). For example, if a UML object model is extended by a new class, the thus extended system will most certainly differ from the original system.

On the other hand, the observed changes of the model as well as the system might be attributed to the superposition of two other types of transformations (type SMb). This is possible if a model change does not imply a change of the system (type 0M), yet the system possesses properties that are not described in the model (type S0).

2.3 Model and Formalism Transformations

Now that the different types of transformations considering the variations of model and system have been discussed, the kinds of transformations that can be found on the right-hand side of Fig. 2 are presented.

Type 0F Transformations

A transformation of type 0F can lead to a change of presentation of the model only, i.e., the concrete syntax of formalism F_1 will differ from that of formalism F_2. A change of the abstract syntax or even the semantics of the formalism would force a more drastic change (see type MF below).

As an example of such a transformation, we introduce the Specification and Design Language SDL (see [330]). SDL models can be described in graphical form (SDL-GR) as well as in a textual representation (SDL-PR). In Fig. 3 both forms are presented. The model describes a state transition from Z1 to Z2 after the reception of a signal (or message) S1.

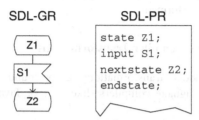

Fig. 3. Different representations of an identical model

Type M0 Transformations

Transformations of type M0 could be considered as "true" model transformations because the model information is changed while preserving the model's formalism.

The above example of adding a UML class to an object model falls into this category as well as the change of an existing model element (e.g., renaming an attribute of a UML class). Type M0 transformations are the typical horizontal transformations that we have introduced in Sect. 2.

Type MF Transformations

This last type of transformation (type MF) exhibits two facets, as is the case for type SM. First, a change of formalism can imply a change of the model (type MFa). This situation always occurs when the abstract syntax or the semantics of the formalism changes.

To illustrate, if one changes the formalism from UML object diagrams (where objects have dependent control flows per default) to the modeling language SDL (where objects are realized as independent processes), this must have wide-reaching consequences for the model (and if more than one object is modeled, for the modeled system as well).

Additionally, a superposition (type MFb) is possible, i.e. although a (syntactical) change of the formalism has no consequences (type 0F), a "true" model transformation (type M0) is performed.

3 Using the Classification Scheme

After the different types of transformations have been introduced and have been illustrated with simple examples, this section presents other more complex examples for the application of the classification scheme. These include the analysis of transformation steps that are performed by a high-level language compiler as well as the classification of activities that are performed within a transformational software development process. Additionally, common transformations that can be found in state-of-the-art MDSD approaches (like OMG's Model-Driven Architecture [294]) are evaluated. An example is provided for applying the scheme when a horizontal model transformation is performed.

3.1 High-level Language Compiler Transformations

A traditional field of "model" transformations can be found when considering the concepts of high-level language compilers (like C++ or Java compilers, e.g., see [10]).

Source "model" M_s for these compilers is the source code in a high-level programming language that should be transformed into the target "model" M_t, i.e., the machine or byte code of the target platform or virtual machine. As a first step, an abstract syntax tree M_s^a is created by parsing the source code (concrete syntax). This tree, which typically can be found as an internal data structure of the compiler, is then transformed into an abstract syntax tree M_t^a that reflects the target model. From this abstract syntax tree, the final "model" in the concrete syntax of the machine or byte code is attained through an unparsing activity. To summarize, the following transformations are performed:

$$M_s \xrightarrow{\text{OF}} M_s^a \xrightarrow{\text{M0}} M_t^a \xrightarrow{\text{OF}} M_t \qquad (2)$$

Transforming the source model to its abstract representation is a pure formalism transformation that does not affect the actual model. The same holds for the unparsing activity. Therefore, both are of type OF. The transformation of the abstract syntax tree, however, requires a model change because the concepts of the source and target language might differ, e.g., there will be no such concept like a for-loop in the machine or assembler language. Therefore, this usually must be mapped to a conditional branch construct (like bne or beq).

It should be noted that in many compiler implementations, the transformation is abbreviated by directly transforming the source to the target model, i.e., by employing a transformation of type MFa.

3.2 Transformational Software Development

The essence of transformational software development is that "from a formal specification of a problem to be solved, programs correctly solving that problem are constructed by stepwise application of formal, semantics-preserving transformation rules" ([345], p. V). It is this very focus on semantics-preserving transformations that allows one to guarantee the correctness of the program by construction.

Typical examples of the application of the transformational approach are the derivation of operational specifications (or code) from a declarative model of the problem as depicted by Partsch in [345], p. 189. The transformation rules that are presented by the author are special forms of inference rules, the systematic application of which will lead to an operational specification. Because of the semantics-preserving nature of the inference rules, all transformations within such a transformational software process can be classified as being of type M0.

To allow for the smooth transition from the formal specification to the actual program, wide-spectrum languages are employed. These languages, in addition to specification constructs (i.e., more abstract concepts), contain concepts that are known from programming languages (cf. [345], p. 51). This means that a wide-spectrum language is a formalism with a single and consistent set of conceptual elements ([32], p. 15). Based on our classification scheme, this implies that transformations between "models" that are expressed in such a language are of type 0M.

3.3 MDSD Transformations

As an important and current example the application of our classification scheme, we discuss the typical kind of transformation that occurs within most of today's model-driven software development approaches, of which the OMG's Model-Driven Architecture MDA (cf. [294]) is the most prominent example. However, also generative approaches that use the Specification and Design Language SDL (see above) are commonly found here.

In all these cases *vertical* transformations are applied to generate models in a less abstract formalism (target model) from models that are described in a more abstract formalism (source model). Less abstract here means that the target model is closer to the run-time platform than the source model was. In the context of the MDA these transformations occur between the *Platform Independent Model* (*PIM*) and the *Platform Specific Model* (*PSM*) as well as between the PSM and the actual implementation code. Currently, many of the MDA tools skip the generation of the intermediate PSM model altogether and directly generate implementation code. Well-known examples of such tools are iLogix's Rhapsody, gentleware's Poseidon, or ARTiSAN's Real-Time Studio. For the modeling language SDL, implementation code is typically also directly generated from models, e.g., when using Telelogic's Tau SDL Suite.

It is this very transformation of source models to implementation code that we want to evaluate in more detail. However, the results could also apply to any vertical transformation of more abstract source to less abstract target models (cf. [256]).

Understanding what occurs during code generation becomes important especially when the running system is being tested. The assumption that the properties of the source model and the properties of the implementation code are identical can lead to the incorrect identification of errors in the source model, or, worse, can obscure errors.

As both the source model and the implementation code are models (both more or less abstract from concrete systems), the creation of the implementation code from the source model (the PIM in the case of MDA) is a kind of model transformation.

As the formalism of the more abstract model and the formalism of the implementation code usually differ in many aspects, such a transformation inevitably implies a major change of the model. One example of a transformation from a PIM to implementation code could be the generation of Java classes from UML classes. Using our classification scheme, such a transformation of the source model to code can be considered a transformation of type MFa, i.e., a "true" formalism and model change.

Ideally, the systems that are realized by the implementation code should be a subset of the set of systems that is described by the specification (semantics-preserving refinement, see Sect. 3.2). Only this relationship would allow for the verification of the considered properties of the specification (the source model) by employing the implementation code for testing. Within the MDA, a model transformation is even defined to be "the process of converting one model to another model of the *same* system" ([294], p. 2-7). We therefore would have to require a transformation of type 0M. As Kleppe and Warmer observe in [256], such a transformation is only realistic in an ideal situation.

The reason is that in a practical context, the required transformation of 0M is complicated by the transformation of type MFa which was identified above. This implies, in many cases, that the transformation of type 0M cannot even be realized. This can be attributed to the fact that the formalisms of source and target models not only differ considering their syntax but almost always differ in their semantics, i.e., in the basic paradigm of the conceptual elements (cf. [210], pp. 7–8) . Preserving the semantics of the models during an MFa-type transformation therefore almost always will be impossible (cf. [256]).

This fact presents a notable difference to the types of transformations that have been illustrated in the previous sub-sections. Traditional compilers work with input "models" that are at a low enough level such that "purely local optimizations are sufficient" ([27], p. 41). A similar observation holds for transformational program development, when a wide-spectrum language, which presents a formalism with a single and consistent set of conceptual elements ([32], p. 15), is used.

Looking at MFa transformations in more detail, three different kinds of mappings of source model elements to counterparts in the target model can be identified:

(1) *Non-ambiguous mapping*: One or more model elements of the source model can be mapped to one ore more elements in the target model without losing their meaning (example: an attribute of a UML class can be mapped to a variable in Java). If this mapping can be applied for all model elements, we would arrive at the ideal case of having a transformation of type 0M.

(2) *Selection*: One or more elements of the source model can be mapped to elements of the target model only after additional decisions have been made. Consequently, such a mapping is ambiguous, which implies that a selection among several alternative mappings must be performed.

(3) *Approximation*: For one or more source model elements, there exist no (semantically equivalent) counterparts in the formalism of the target model. Therefore, the elements of the source model have to be approximated as best as possible by using elements of the target model.

The last two cases are obviously the ones that prohibit the desired transformation of type 0M. If there is no direct or no non-ambiguous mapping from elements in the source model to elements in the target model, the resulting systems can hardly be identical.

To give the reader an in-depth understanding of the critical situations that can occur when a selection or approximation has to be exercised, we will present two examples in the SDL. This language is comparable in many ways to the current version of the UML (i.e., UML 2.0). Therefore, similar observations would apply.

Selection

A situation that requires a *selection* of a mapping alternative occurs when the parallel processes that are described in SDL have to be realized within a monolithic operating system process, which is typically implemented in the programming language C (this is Telelogic Tau's approach). To perform such a realization, an execution order of the processes has to be defined to be able to execute them sequentially.

This sequentialization, however, can obscure errors because critical situations, in which the errors would be visible, will never occur. To illustrate such a situation, we introduce a small SDL example (see Fig. 4), in which the model architecture as well as the behavioral description of the individual processes is shown.

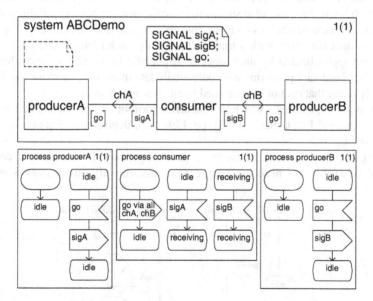

Fig. 4. SDL model of a producer/consumer pair

There are three communicating processes: producerA, producerB, and consumer. Signals from producerB can only be received after producerA has initially sent a signal sigA to the consumer process (the transition from idle to receiving is taken). To start communication, the consuming process sends a go signal to both producing processes.

Depending on the order of execution (i.e., whether producerA or producerB is activated first), the consumer process might be able to receive signal sigB or will lose the signal. These two possible scenarios of execution are shown in Fig. 5 as a Message Sequence Chart (MSC; cf. [330], pp. 356–359), which is similar to UML's sequence diagrams in the form in which it is used here.

If the processes were scheduled according to scenario b) only, the error in the specification would be obscured, as the potential loss of signals could never be observed. This implies that even if the tests had been passed for a very specific test case, the test might have failed when a different code generator was used (although there had been no change of the source model whatsoever).

To increase the confidence of such tests, the selection of the properties should always be considered. One could, as an example, generate code alternatives that use a different form of selection and additionally test these alternatives. However, one should keep in mind that the number of possible combinations that must be evaluated might soon reach a limit above which the effort for testing is no longer feasible.

Approximation

Signals that are exchanged between SDL processes are stored in signal queues (cf. [109], pp. 62–63). As a model abstraction, these queues can hold an infinite number of signals. Because of obvious memory constraints, such queues can only be implemented as data structures with a finite (although dynamic) length, i.e., the infinite queues are approximated by finite queues. Especially in reactive systems that are executed on hardware platforms with only small data memories, memory overflows can easily occur that cannot be attributed to an error in the specification.

The following example, which is a modified form of an SDL model that is presented in Queins' Ph.D. thesis ([353], pp. 179–180), depicts this situation in more detail (see Fig. 6).

Using the timer perT, the sensor process periodically measures a certain physical value that is sent to the logger process. Initially this process is in the

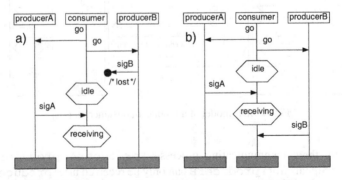

Fig. 5. Different execution scenarios for SDL model of Fig. 4

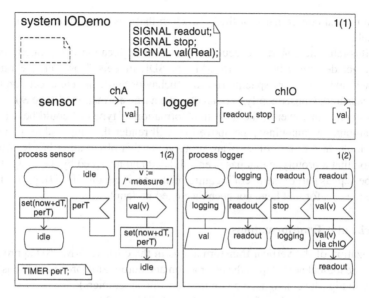

Fig. 6. SDL model of a data logger

logging state and does not consume the val signals (the rhomboid symbol denotes that the signals are kept, i.e. "saved", in the input queue). As soon as the
logger process receives the readout signal from the environment (i.e., when
the user wants to receive a readout of the logged sensor data), all val signals in the
input queue are consumed and a respective signal is sent to the environment until the
stop signal is received.

Assuming that the period dT of the sensor process is Δt and the maximal
queue size of our implementation is s (this upper limit can be imposed by either a
static data structure or the actual memory available to the running system), a memory
overflow will occur if the readout signal is not received within $s\Delta t$ after system
start.

If the arrival of the readout signal can be guaranteed, the observed fault will
not be critical. However, in a reactive system the arrival of external signals can typically not be guaranteed (the user cannot be forced to read out the data before the
memory overflow occurs). As a consequence, the source model would have to be
changed, although the specification was correct. Unfortunately, this implies that the
chosen abstraction might not have been suitable or that the ideal of MDSD might not
be accomplished as easily as thought.

Additional Properties

In addition to the properties that differ between the systems that are described by the
source and the target model, the target system (in our case the running application)
can exhibit *additional* properties that have not been described in any of the models.

This is a natural consequence of the abstraction that has been employed to achieve the models.

To illustrate, the concrete execution time of an application is a property that is typically not described by standard UML or SDL models. However, the running system will exhibit a very specific run-time behavior and concrete execution times can be measured. Consequently, we can observe a transformation of type S0.

This implies that even if the ideal transformation of type 0M could be achieved by non-ambiguous mappings, the above fact will render this impossible on a more detailed look. In the field of software prototyping this observation has lead to the suggestion that a prototype that has been validated and accepted by the users should always be kept as part of the overall requirements specification (cf. [54], p. 40). However, the reasons for that have not been discussed in detail.

3.4 Horizontal Transformations

The realization of the vertical transformations in the context of MDSD approaches has been the logical next step in the abstraction and automation process that has been started with high-level language compilers (or even assemblers).

Interestingly, examples of the automation of horizontal (i.e., evolutionary) transformations can rarely be found. This might be attributed to the fact that source code – even the one of a high-level programming language – is not semantically rich enough to allow for such an automated evolution. Only with the introduction of modeling languages and domain specific modeling (e.g., through meta-models) does this seem to become possible. Czarnecki and Eisenecker even postulate that the more abstract development information a source model contains, the more automated the support for model evolution can become ([79], p. 338).

One such transformation is the automatic instrumentation of a model for debugging or testing purposes. In the SDL example, a special output statement could be added to each transition to monitor the execution of the system. This extension of the model consequently is a transformation of type M0 (the source and the target models are SDL models).

Because the instrumentation will produce additional output, the systems that are finally derived from such an instrumented model will be different from the systems that are derived from the initial source model. This means that this instrumentation activity has to be classified as being of type SMa. This poses the problem that the system that is being tested (the one *with* the instrumentation) differs from the system that finally will be deployed, and thus the results of the tests might become questionable.

Another example of such a vertical transformation is "model refactoring", which is introduced in detail by Gray et al. on p. 199 of this book.

4 Conclusion

In this chapter, we have shed light on the essential activity that is performed in any model-driven software development: model transformation. After the most basic terms and current classification schemes were introduced, a more fine-grained scheme has been presented that considers the differences between the modeled system, the model itself, and its formalism.

With this classification scheme, different examples of transformations have been evaluated. These were transformations performed by high-level language compilers as well as transformations within a transformational software development process. Further, important forms of transformations have been discussed for state-of-the-art MDSD approaches (like MDA), which included vertical transformations (code generation) and horizontal transformations (where the instrumentation of a model has been chosen as an example).

With this classification, problems that are eminent in all model-driven software development approaches have been uncovered and the reasons for their existence have been explained. In detail, we have illustrated why test results that have been attained by testing systems that have been automatically derived from specifications have to be evaluated critically. We believe that understanding what happens during each type of model transformation is an important prerequisite for properly applying MDSD approaches and for correctly using the associated tools. Therefore, we hope that the concepts and views that have been depicted in this chapter will help "model-driven software developers" in solving their challenging yet enthralling tasks.

5 Acknowledgments

I want to thank the anonymous referees for their critical and productive comments that have led to the improvement of this contribution. I further would like to thank Stefan Queins, who first brought the difference between a prototype (the target system) and the specification (the source model) to my attention. I also have to acknowledge Christian Floyd's 1984 paper "A Systematic Look at Prototyping", which inspired the title to this chapter. Finally, I am grateful to my aunt Anna-Lee Adams for fine-tuning the English.

Tool Support for Model-Driven Development of Security-Critical Systems with UML

Jan Jürjens* and Pasha Shabalin

Software & Systems Engineering, TU Munich, Germany
Boltzmannstr. 3, 85748 München/Garching, Germany
{juerjens, shabalin}@in.tum.de

Summary. The high-quality development of critical systems is difficult. We propose to use the Unified Modeling Language (UML), the de facto industry standard specification language, as a notation together with a formally based tool support for model-based critical systems development.

We introduce UML Machines, which is a formal notation designed to reflect properties of the UML execution semantics relevant to criticality requirements. We use it to define a foundation that puts models for the different diagrams into context and gives a precise meaning to mechanisms such as message passing between objects or components specified in different diagrams, while offering the possibility to analyze criticality requirements.

We present tool support for this approach developed at the TU München, which facilitates transfer of the methodology to industrial contexts.

1 Introduction

High-quality development of critical systems (be they real-time, security-critical, or dependable systems) is difficult. Many such systems are developed, deployed, and used that do not satisfy their criticality requirements, sometimes with spectacular failures. However, critical systems on whose correct functioning human life and substantial commercial assets depend need to be developed especially carefully.

Unfortunately, in critical systems development, correctness is often in conflict with cost. Where thorough methods of system design pose high costs through personnel training and use, they are all too often avoided. The Unified Modeling Language (UML) [318] offers an unprecedented opportunity for high-quality critical systems development that is feasible in an industrial context:

- As the de facto standard in industrial modeling, a large number of developers are trained in UML.

---

* http://www4.in.tum.de/~juerjens. This work was partially funded by the German Federal Ministry of Education, Science, Research and Technology (BMBF) in the framework of the Verisoft project under grant 01 IS C38. The responsibility for this article lies with the author(s).

- Compared to previous notations with a user community of comparable size, UML is relatively precisely defined.

Nevertheless, the UML semantics is given only in prose form [318], leaving room for ambiguities. However, to provide advanced tool support (for example, automated checking of behavioral properties of a UML specification) to assist application of our approach in industry, we need a mathematically precise semantics for UML.

There has been a substantial amount of work towards providing a formal semantics for UML diagrams (including [48, 133, 358, 237]; specifically, [43] gives a statechart semantics using Abstract State Machines which was a starting point for the current work). However, most work only provides models for single UML diagrams in isolation. When trying to give a precise mathematical meaning to whole UML specifications, one needs to be able to combine the formal models for the different kinds of diagrams. In this chapter, we provide a formal framework to support this using of UML Machines.

Our approach is based on *Abstract State Machines* (ASMs) [44] where states are represented by algebras. We use ASMs to present our semantics because this notation, essentially a more formal pseudo-code, seems to be relatively accessible. At the same time the notation is mathematically precise. For a given proof tool (for example, the model-checker Spin, Prolog, or the automatic theorem prover Setheo), we translate the semantics into the relevant input notation (such as Promela, Horn formulas, or the TPTP notation, resp.). We feel that this approach of using an intermediate representation in ASMs may be more flexible and universally usable than directly using a notation closer to a given input notation.

For our purpose, we use an extension of ASMs with UML-type communication mechanisms called UML Machines, inspired by the *Algebraic State Machines* from [52]. Also, we define the concept of UML Machine System (UMS) that allows one to build up specifications in a modular way (corresponding to the use of UML subsystems). We use this to define a semantics for a simplified fragment of UML supporting the combined use of different kinds of UML diagrams including actions, activities, and message passing between different diagrams, and which allows one to easily include different adversary and failure models to analyze specifications for criticality requirements.

Furthermore, we present work by the UMLsec group at TU München aimed at the development of automated tools for analyzing UML models for criticality requirements, to facilitate technology transfer to industry.

The work presented here builds on previous work including [238] but extends to diagram types not treated in [238] (such as sequence diagrams) and to the development of tool support for automated verification. Part of the material has been presented in [241].

Outline

After giving some background in Sect. 1.1, we recall the necessary definitions and introduce the notion of UML Machine used for our semantics in Sect. 2. We show how several UML Machines can be composed into a UML Machine System (UMS).

In Sect. 3, we sketch how we use our framework for a simplified formal semantics of UML combining different diagram types in the example of UML sequence diagrams. In Sect. 4, we explain how UML, together with an XML-based analysis of UML models, can be used as a basis for a formally based method for critical systems development. In Sect. 5, we present some information on tools for advanced XML-based processing of UML models. We describe a framework that incorporates automated tools for the analysis of UML models against critical requirements. We end with pointers to related work and a conclusion.

1.1 Overview and Background

Traditionally, there exist different methods for ensuring reliability of critical systems:

Break-And-Fix This approach accepts that deployed systems may fail; whenever a problem is noticed and identified, the error is fixed. The Break-And-Fix approach is probably the most obvious one, but it has a lot of drawbacks. It is inherently disruptive – fixing the system often implies distributing patches, which disturbs users, annoys customers, and destroys their confidence. What is worse, the method is unsafe and insecure – we can never be sure that the new problem will not disturb critical functionality, or that it will not be spotted at first by a malicious person, who will try to compromise the system further.

Traditional formal methods, on the other hand, offer very good quality of the developed critical systems. There has been a lot of successful research in this direction (for an overview see [240]). However, formal methods are rarely applied in practice because of the high costs arising from the necessary training for the developers of the system, and from the construction of the formal specification of the system.

The UML [431], the de facto industry standard in object-oriented modeling, together with XML-based processing of UML models, offers an unprecedented opportunity for high-quality critical systems development that is feasible in an industrial context:

- A large number of developers are trained in UML, as the de facto standard in industrial modeling, making less training necessary. Also, UML specifications of systems under development may already be available for analysis, which again saves time and cost.
- Compared to previous notations with a user community of comparable size, UML is relatively precisely defined, opening up the possibility for advanced tool support to assist the development of safety-critical systems.
- After several years of evolution, an XML/XMI-based standard for UML model representation has evolved, enabling interchange and automated processing of the UML models.

2 UML Machines and UML Machine Systems

UML Machines are based on the *Abstract State Machines* notion. We recall central concepts here; for a formal definition see [44]. They are inspired by the *Algebraic State Machines* from [52].

In this section we will use the following technical definitions. A *multi-set* (or *bag*) is a set which may contain multiple copies of an element, with notation $\{\!\{\ \}\!\}$ instead of the usual brackets. For example, $\{\!\{1,1,1,1,1,1,1,1,1,1\}\!\}$ is the multi-set consisting of ten copies of the element 1. For two multi-sets M and N, $M \uplus N$ denotes their union and $M \setminus N$ the subtraction of N from M. For a multi-set M and a set X, we write $M\backslash X$ for the multi-set of those elements in M, preserving their cardinalities, that are also elements of X. Intuitively, in $M\backslash X$, all elements except those in X are filtered out. We write $M \subseteq N$ for two multi-sets M, N if $M\backslash N = M$. We write $\lfloor M \rfloor$ for the set of elements in the multi-set M and $\sharp M$ for the number of elements in M.

Abstract State Machines

A *state* A is a non-empty set X containing distinct elements *true*, *false*, and *undef* together with a set $\mathbf{Voc}(A)$ of function names with interpretations in the base set X. An *Abstract State Machine* (ASM) consists of an *initial state* and an *update rule*, where the variable assignment of the initial state sends each variable to the value *undef*. An ASM is executed by iteratively firing the update rule. Thereby, its current state is *updated*; that is, the interpretations of its functions are redefined in terms of the previous interpretations. The syntax and informal semantics of update rules are given inductively as follows (the formal semantics can be found in [44]):

skip : causes no change.
$f(\bar{s})$:=t : updates f at the tuple $\bar{s}$ to map to the element t.
if g **then** R **else** S : If g holds, the rule R is executed, otherwise S.
do − **in** − **parallel** $R_1, \ldots, R_k$ **enddo** : R_i execute simultaneously, if for any two update rules $f(\bar{s}) := t$ and $f(\bar{s}) := t'$, we have $t = t'$; otherwise the execution stops.
seq R S **endseq** : R and S are executed sequentially.
loop v **through list** X $R(v)$: iteratively execute $R(x)$ for all $x \in X$.
case v **of** x_1 : **do** R_1 $\ldots$ x_n : **do** R_n **else** S : execute by case distinction.

Extending ASMs to UML Machines

We define UML Machines as an extension of ASMs with a UML-like communication mechanism that uses buffers. We will use UML Machines to specify components of a system that interact by exchanging messages from a set **Events** which are dispatched from (resp. received) in multi-set buffers (*output queues*, resp. *input queues*). Note that this way, incoming signals can be processed in an arbitrary order, which is what is specified by the UML definition.

Definition 1. *A* UML Machine $(A, \mathsf{inQu}_A, \mathsf{outQu}_A)$ *is given by an ASM A and two multi-set names* $\mathsf{inQu}_A, \mathsf{outQu}_A \in \mathbf{Voc}(A)$ *such that the rules in A change* inQu_A *only by removing and* outQu_A *only by adding elements.*

The set names inQu_A, outQu_A model the input buffer and the output buffer of the UML Machine A. We assume that at the initial state of the UML Machine, they always have the value $\emptyset$.

The behavior of a UML Machine $(A, \mathsf{inQu}_A, \mathsf{outQu}_A)$ is captured in the following definition, where a multi-set of input (resp. output) values represents the input (resp. output) during a time interval of a given finite length. Possible non-determinism in the UML Machine rules leads to *sets* of output sequences.

Let $\mathsf{toinQu}_A(X) \stackrel{\mathrm{def}}{=} \mathsf{inQu}_A := \mathsf{inQu}_A \uplus X$. Given a UML Machine $(A, \mathsf{inQu}_A, \mathsf{outQu}_A)$, and a sequence $\mathbf{I}$ of multi-sets, consider the UML Machine $\mathbf{Behav}(A(\mathbf{I}))$ with the vocabulary $\mathbf{Voc}(\mathbf{Behav}(A(\mathbf{I}))) \stackrel{\mathrm{def}}{=} \mathbf{Voc}(A) \cup \{\mathsf{outlist}(A)\}$, and the rule $\mathbf{Behav}(A(\mathbf{I}))$ given in Fig. 1. For any given run $r \in \mathbf{Run}(\mathbf{Behav}(A(\mathbf{I})))$ of the UML Machine $\mathbf{Behav}(A(\mathbf{I}))$, after completion of r, $\mathsf{outlist}(A)$ contains a sequence of multi-sets of values $\mathsf{outlist}(A)^r$.

Definition 2. *The input/output behavior of a UML Machine* $(A, \mathsf{inQu}_A, \mathsf{outQu}_A)$ *is a function* $[\![A]\!]()$ *from finite sequences of multi-sets of values to sets of sequences of multi-sets of values defined by* $[\![A]\!](\mathbf{I}) \stackrel{\mathrm{def}}{=} \{\mathsf{outlist}(A)^r : r \in \mathbf{Run}(\mathbf{Behav}(A(\mathbf{I})))$.

Intuitively, given a sequence $\mathbf{I}$ of multi-sets of input values, the rule $\mathbf{Behav}(A(\mathbf{I}))$ computes the set of possible sequences of multi-sets of output values by iteratively adding each multi-set in $\mathbf{I}$ to inQu_A, calling A, and recording the multi-set of output values from outQu_A in $\mathsf{outlist}(A)$.

We would like to build up UML specifications in a modular way, by combining a set of UML Machines together with communication links and connecting them to form a new formal specification. To achieve this, we define the notion of a *UML Machine System* (UMS). Our approach allows a rather flexible treatment of the communication since the UMS *main loop* (Fig. 2) can be modified as necessary. For example, our explicit way of modeling the communication links and the messages exchanged over them allows modeling exterior influence on the communication within a system (such as attacks on insecure connections, or quality-of-service aspects of networks).

Rule $\mathbf{Behav}(A(\mathbf{I}))$
    loop I **through list I**
        $\mathsf{toinQu}_A(I)$
        $\mathbf{Exec}(A)$
        $\mathsf{outlist}(A) := \mathsf{outlist}(A).\mathsf{outQu}_A$
        $\mathsf{outQu}_A := \emptyset$

Fig. 1. Behavior of a UML Machine

Definition 3. *A UML Machine System (UMS)* $\mathcal{A} = (\text{Name}_{\mathcal{A}}, \text{Comp}_{\mathcal{A}}, \text{Sched}_{\mathcal{A}}, \text{Links}_{\mathcal{A}}, \text{Msgs}_{\mathcal{A}})$ *is given by*

- *a name* $\text{Name}_{\mathcal{A}} \in \textbf{UMNames}$,
- *a finite set* $\text{Comp}_{\mathcal{A}}$ *of UML Machines called* components,
- *a UML Machine* $\text{Sched}_{\mathcal{A}}$, *the* scheduler *that may call the components as subroutines,*
- *a set* $\text{Links}_{\mathcal{A}}$ *of two-element sets* $l \subseteq \text{Comp}_{\mathcal{A}}$, *the communication links between them, and*
- *a set of messages* $\text{Msgs}_{\mathcal{A}} \subseteq \textbf{MsgNm}$ *that the UML Machine System is ready to receive.*

Rule $\langle \mathcal{A} \rangle$
seq
    forall S **with** $S \in \text{Comp}_{\mathcal{A}}$ **do**
        $\text{inQu}_{\langle S \rangle} := \text{inQu}_{\langle S \rangle} \uplus$
            $\{\!\!\{ \textbf{tail}(e) : e \in (\text{inQu}_{\langle \mathcal{A} \rangle} \setminus \text{Msgs}_{\mathcal{A}}) \uplus$
            $\uplus_{l \in links_S} \text{linkQu}_{\langle \mathcal{A} \rangle}(l) \wedge \textbf{head}(e) = S \}\!\!\}$
    $\text{inQu}_{\langle \mathcal{A} \rangle} := \emptyset$
    $\langle \text{Sched}_{\mathcal{A}} \rangle$
    forall l **with** $l \in \text{Links}_{\mathcal{A}}$ **do**
        $\text{linkQu}_{\langle \mathcal{A} \rangle}(l) := \{\!\!\{ e \in \text{outQu}_{\langle S \rangle} :$
            $S \in \text{Comp}_{\mathcal{A}} \wedge l = \{\textbf{head}(e), A_i\} \}\!\!\}$
    $\text{outQu}_{\langle \mathcal{A} \rangle} := \text{outQu}_{\langle \mathcal{A} \rangle} \uplus \uplus_{S \in \text{Comp}_{\mathcal{A}}} \{\!\!\{ \textbf{tail}(e) :$
        $e \in \text{outQu}_S \wedge \textbf{head}(e) = \langle \mathcal{A} \rangle \}\!\!\}$
    forall S **with** $S \in \text{Comp}_{\mathcal{A}}$ **do**
        $\text{outQu}_{\langle S \rangle} := \emptyset$
endseq

Fig. 2. Main loop of a UML Machine System

The set $\textbf{MsgNm}$ consists of finite sequences of names $n_1.n_2.\ldots.n_k$ where $n_1, \ldots, n_{k-2}$ are names of UMSs, n_{k-1} is a name of a UML Machine, and n_k is the local name of the message. We define the set $\textbf{Events}$ of events to consist of terms of the form $msg(exp_1, \ldots, exp_n)$ where $msg \in \textbf{MsgNm}$ is an n-ary message name and $exp_1, \ldots, exp_n \in \textbf{Exp}$ are expressions, the *parameters* or *arguments*, of the event (for a given set of expressions $\textbf{Exp}$).

We recursively define the behavior of any UMS A as a UML Machine $\langle A \rangle$. For any UML Machine A, we define $\langle A \rangle \overset{\text{def}}{=} A$. Given a UMS $\mathcal{A}$, the UML Machine $\langle \mathcal{A} \rangle$ models the joint execution of the components of $\mathcal{A}$ and their communication by exchanging messages over the links. The execution rule for $\langle \mathcal{A} \rangle$ is given in Fig. 2 (where $links_S \overset{\text{def}}{=} \{\{A, B\} \in \text{Links}_{\mathcal{A}} : A = S\}$ is the set of links connected to S).

3 Formal Semantics for a Fragment of UML

We sketch our approach to defining a formal semantics for UML models on the example of sequence diagrams. Further UML diagrams are formalized similarly [238] (where also more details about this approach can be found).

In UML, messages can be synchronous (meaning that the sender of the message passes the thread of control to the receiver and receives it back together with the return message) or asynchronous (meaning that the thread of control is split in two, one each for the sender and the receiver). Accordingly, we partition the set of message names **MsgNm** into sets of operations **Op**, signals **Sig**, and return messages **Ret**. Because of the space restrictions, we only give here a formalization of the asynchronous communication.

In our model, every object or subsystem O has associated multi-sets inQu_O and outQu_O (*event queues*). We model sending a message $msg = op(exp_1, \ldots, exp_n) \in$ **Events** from an object S to an object R as follows:

(1) The object S places the message $R.msg$ into its multi-set outQu_S.
(2) The dispatching component distributes the messages from out-queues to the intended in-queues (while removing the message head); in particular, $R.msg$ is removed from outQu_S and msg added to inQu_R.
(3) The object R removes msg from its in-queue and processes its content.

This way of modeling communication allows for a very flexible treatment; for example, we can modify the UMS main loop (Fig. 2) to take account of knowledge of the underlying communication layer (such as security or performance issues).

Objects may execute *actions*. We write **Action** for the set of actions which are expressions of the following forms:

Send action: $\text{send}(sig(a_1, \ldots, a_n))$ for an n-ary signal $sig \in$ **Sig** and argument $a_i \in$ **Exp**.
Void action: nil.

For any action a, we define the expression **ActionRule**(a) (where $\mathcal{A}$ is the UML machine in which **ActionRule**(a) is executed).

$$\textbf{ActionRule}(\text{send}(e)) \equiv \left(\text{outQu}_{\mathcal{A}} := \text{outQu}_{\mathcal{A}} \uplus \{\!|\, e \,|\!\} \right)$$
$$\textbf{ActionRule}(nil) \equiv \textbf{skip}$$

The set of *Boolean expressions* **BoolExp** is the set of first-order logical formulas with equality statements between elements of **Exp** as atomic formulas.

3.1 Sequence Diagrams

To demonstrate how behavioral diagrams can be included in our framework for defining a formal semantics for UML, we exemplarily consider a (again simplified and restricted) fragment of sequence diagrams.

For readability, the prefix obj on the messages sent to an object obj which is contained in a sequence diagram may be omitted in that diagram (since it is implicit).

Abstract Syntax of Sequence Diagrams

A sequence diagram $D = (\mathsf{Obj}(D), \mathsf{Links}(D))$ is given by:

- a set $\mathsf{Obj}(D)$ of pairs (O, C) where O is an object of class C whose interaction with other objects is described in D and
- a sequence $\mathsf{Links}(D)$ consisting of elements of the form $l = (\mathsf{source}(l), \mathsf{guard}(l), \mathsf{msg}(l), \mathsf{target}(l))$ where
  - $\mathsf{source}(l) \in \mathsf{Obj}(D)$ is the source object of the link,
  - $\mathsf{guard}(l) \in \mathbf{BoolExp}$ is a Boolean expression (the guard of the link),
  - $\mathsf{msg}(l) \in \mathbf{Events}$ is the message of the link, and
  - $\mathsf{target}(l) \in \mathsf{Obj}(D)$ is the target object of the link.

Behavioral Semantics

We fix a sequence diagram $\mathcal{S}$ modeling the objects in $\mathsf{Obj}(\mathcal{S}) \stackrel{\mathrm{def}}{=} \bigcup_{D \in \mathcal{S}} \mathsf{Obj}(D)$ and an object $O \in \mathsf{Obj}(\mathcal{S})$. Further we assume that the set $\mathbf{Var}$ contains elements $arg_{O,l,n}$ for each $O \in \mathsf{Obj}(\mathcal{S})$ and numbers l and n, representing the nth argument of the operation that is supposed to be the lth operation received by O according to the set of sequence diagrams $\mathcal{S}$, and define $args_{O,l} = [arg_{O,l,1}, \ldots, arg_{O,l,k}]$ (where the operation is assumed to have k arguments). Then we give the behavior of O as defined in $\mathcal{S}$ as a UML Machine $(\llbracket \mathcal{S}.O \rrbracket^{SD}, \{\mathsf{inQu}_{\llbracket \mathcal{S}.O \rrbracket^{SD}}\}, \{\mathsf{outQu}_{\llbracket \mathcal{S}.O \rrbracket^{SD}}, \mathsf{finished}_{\llbracket \mathcal{S}.O \rrbracket^{SD}}\})$. The rule of the UML Machine $\llbracket D.O \rrbracket^{SD}$ is given in Fig. 3.

Rule $\mathbf{Exec}(D.O)$
if cncts $= [\,]$ then finished$_{D.O} := true$
else
    if source(head(cncts)) $= O \wedge$ guard(head(cncts))
        then
                $\mathbf{ActionRuleSD}$(msg(head(cncts)));
                if target(head(cncts)) $\neq O$ then
                    cncts $:=$ tail(cncts);
    if target(head(cncts)) $= O$ then
        choose e with $e \in$ inQu$_O \wedge$
        msgnm(msg(head(cncts))) $=$ msgnm(e) do
           inQu$_O :=$ inQu$_O \setminus \{\!\{ e \}\!\}$;
           $args_{D,\mathsf{lnum}} :=$ $\mathbf{Args}(e)$;
           lnum $:=$ lnum $+ 1$;
           if msgnm(e) $\in \mathbf{Op}$ then
                sender($\mathbf{msgnm}(e)$) $:=$
                    sndr(e).sender($\mathbf{msgnm}(e)$);
        cncts $:=$ tail(cncts)

Fig. 3. UML Machine for sequence diagram

Given a sequence l of links and an object O, define $l\!\downarrow_O$ to be the subsequence l of those elements l with source(l) $= O$ or target(l) $= O$.

3.2 Reasoning about Model Properties

The UML Machines framework allows formal inspection of the UML model for certain properties. In case of a security-critical system, these can be for example "data security" (indicating that a certain data item should not leak out of a system component). The desirable security properties can be introduced in the model using UML extension mechanisms and further the whole model can be checked for consistency; that is; whether the required properties are met by the design.

To investigate security properties of a system, it is extended with a subsystem modeling behavior of a potential adversary. The notion of UMS allows its natural modeling. We can create specific types of adversaries that attack different parts of the system in a specified way. For example, an attacker of type *insider* may be able to intercept the communication links in a company-wide local area network. We model the behavior of the adversary by defining a class of UML Machines that can access the communication links of the system in a specified way. To evaluate the security of the system with respect to the given type of adversary, we consider the joint execution of the system with any UML Machine in this class.

Security evaluation of specifications is done with respect to a given type A of adversary. For this, in particular, one has to specify a set $\mathcal{K}_A^p \subseteq \mathbf{Exp}$ of previous knowledge of the adversary type A. Also, $\mathcal{K}_A^a \subseteq \mathbf{Exp}$ contains knowledge that may arise from accessing components (see below). We define $\mathcal{K}_A^0 = \mathcal{K}_A^a \cup \mathcal{K}_A^p$ to be the initial knowledge of any adversary of type A.

Given a UMS $\mathcal{A}$ we define the set $int_\mathcal{A}$ of (recursively) contained components:

- for a UML Machine A, $int_A := \{A\}$ and
- for a UMS $\mathcal{A}$, $int_\mathcal{A} := \bigcup_{\mathcal{B} \in \mathsf{Comp}_\mathcal{A}} int_\mathcal{B}$.

Similarly, for a UMS $\mathcal{A}$ we define the set $lks_\mathcal{A}$ of (recursively) contained links:

- for a UML Machine A, $lks_A := \emptyset$ and
- for a UMS $\mathcal{A}$, $lks_\mathcal{A} := \mathsf{Links}_\mathcal{A} \cup \bigcup_{\mathcal{B} \in \mathsf{Comp}_\mathcal{A}} lks_\mathcal{B}$.

To capture the capabilities of a possible attacker, we assume that, given a UMS $\mathcal{A}$, we have a function $\mathsf{threats}_A^\mathcal{A}(x)$ that takes a component or link $x \in int_\mathcal{A} \cup lks_\mathcal{A}$ and a type of adversary A and returns a set of strings $\mathsf{threats}_A^\mathcal{A}(x) \subseteq \{\mathsf{delete, read, insert, access}\}$ under the following conditions:

- for $x \in int_\mathcal{A}$, we have $\mathsf{threats}_A^\mathcal{A}(x) \subseteq \{\mathsf{access}\}$,
- for $x \in lks_\mathcal{A}$, we have $\mathsf{threats}_A^\mathcal{A}(x) \subseteq \{\mathsf{delete, read, insert}\}$, and
- for $l \in lks_\mathcal{A}$ with $i \in l$ and $\mathsf{threats}_A^\mathcal{A}(i) = \{\mathsf{access}\}$, the equation $\mathsf{threats}_A^\mathcal{A}(l) = \{\mathsf{delete, read, insert}\}$ holds.

The idea is that $\mathsf{threats}_A^\mathcal{A}(x)$ specifies the *threat scenario* against a component or link x in the UMS $\mathcal{A}$ that is associated with an adversary type A. On the one hand, the threat scenario determines which data the adversary can obtain by *accessing* components; on the other hand, it determines which actions the adversary is permitted by the threat scenario to apply to the concerned links. Thus each function $\mathsf{threats}()$ gives rise to the set of accessed data $\mathcal{K}_A^a$ mentioned above and a set of permitted actions $perm_A$:

- $\mathcal{K}_A^a$ consists of all expressions appearing in the specification for any $i \in int_A$ with access $\in$ threats$_A^{\mathcal{A}}(i)$.
- $perm_A$ consists of
  - all actions delete$_l \equiv$ linkQu$_A(l) := \emptyset$ for any $l \in lks_A$ with delete $\in$ threats$_A^{\mathcal{A}}(l)$ (deletes all elements from linkQu$_A(l)$),
  - all actions read$_l(m) \equiv m :=$ linkQu$_A(l)$ for any $l \in lks_A$ with read $\in$ threats$_A^{\mathcal{A}}(l)$ and any variable name m (copies the content of linkQu$_A(l)$ to the variable m), and
  - all actions insert$_l(e) \equiv$ linkQu$_A(l) :=$ linkQu$_A(l) \uplus \{\!\!\{ e \}\!\!\}$ for any $l \in lks_A$ with insert $\in$ threats$_A^{\mathcal{A}}(l)$ and any $e \in \mathcal{K}_A^0$ (adds an element e to linkQu$_A(l)$).

Intuitively, $perm_A$ consists of those actions that an adversary of type A is capable of doing with respect to the multi-set linkQu$_A(l)$ for any link l.

3.3 Using External Verification Tools

One of the goals of this work is to provide tool support for security analysis of models in *UMLsec*, the UML-based language for secure-critical system development which was introduced in [239]. Verification of complex dynamic properties of UMLsec models requires application of an external verification tool, for example model checker, theorem prover, or Prolog interpreter. Following the semantics presented above, the relevant model fragment is translated into the language of the target verification tool. Exemplarily, verification of the « secrecy » property using the model checker implies translation of three UMLsec diagram types, extracting from them the following information.

Class Diagrams

These are used to define classes in the model and associations between them. A class contains a set of *attributes* (local variables) with optional *initial values* and a set of *operations*. An attribute can be marked by a *stereotype*. Each operation can have zero or more parameters. An association has two *association ends*, each connected to a class. An association in our semantics intuitively means "knows about". Operations defined by a class can be invoked by sending a message to it by any object in the system (including itself).

Statechart Diagrams

These define dynamic behavior and changes in the internal state of the UML classes in response to incoming messages. This behavior is inherited by all objects instantiated from the class. Following the UMLsec formal semantics, each statechart diagram is translated into a *run-to-completion* loop ensuring that a message can only be dequeued and dispatched after the previous message has been fully completed. In the case when the new message does not make any transition selection, it is dropped and the next message from the input queue is consumed. The execution blocks on an attempt to read from an empty input queue until a new message arrives.

Deployment Diagrams

These describe the physical layout of the system. *Objects* in a deployment diagram represent instances of classes; there can be more than one instance of the same class. Each object is contained in a *component instance*, and each component instance is contained in a *node instance*. A *link* represents a physical connection between two node instances. Physical properties of the link are defined by attaching one of the UMLsec stereotypes «LAN », «Internet », or «Encrypted ».

Objects in a Deployment diagram are connected by associations which represent logical dependencies between them. During model translation, logical connections between classes, defined by associations in the class diagram, are mapped to associations and further to links in the deployment diagram. Later adversary capabilities for every logical association in the class diagram are calculated from these mappings.

4 UML and XML-Based Analysis for Critical Systems Development

We will now explain how UML, together with an XML-based analysis of UML models, can be used as a basis for a formally based method for critical systems development. We will first analyze our requirements on the proposed method, and demonstrate how the UML-based solution meets them. To keep the presentation concise and intelligible, we will restrict ourselves to security-critical systems. However, our approach is generic, and can be applied to other criticality requirements like safety, quality-of-service, etc.

An inherent problem of any model-based verification method, including our approach, is the possibility of an attack exploiting inconsistencies between the model and the modeled system. On one hand these are human errors in the modeling process. On the other hand the adversary can attack some system features which are normally not included in the abstraction. Exemplarily, this can include cryptanalysis of the underlying algorithms, and statistical analysis of the system physical characteristics including time, energy consumption, or electromagnetic radiation monitoring.

The UML-based formal methodology for the development of security-critical systems should meet the following requirements:

- Given a system model described with UML, it should *automatically* evaluate it for security-related vulnerabilities in design.
- The methodology should be available to developers *that are not necessarily security experts*, and still allow them to ensure the necessary security properties of the system under design.
- Security properties are often imprecisely defined or misunderstood. Formulating security properties of a system can often be a challenge by itself. Therefore we should enable the user to define easily and unambiguously both *security features* and *security requirements* of the system. The latter step is often considered as

granted, but for many security properties it can be very difficult and normally requires the developer to have special qualifications in cryptography.

- Costs of correcting flaws in a software system grow dramatically in the process of development; therefore we would like to consider security from *early design phases*.
- Consider security on *different levels of abstraction*, and *in system context*. Security of a complex distributed computer system can be violated on different levels. Even worse, security properties are generally not preserved by the composition [240] and therefore blindly combining even proven security mechanisms may result in a faulty system. The method should detect these kinds of errors.
- Make use of the powerful pattern concept and *encapsulate established rules of prudent security engineering*.
- For certain security-critical software products, such as firewalls, the acceptance procedure is comparable to the development itself in laboriousness. Thus we want to make *certification cost-effective*.

Now we will look closer at some of the requirements listed. It is obvious that today any software development methodology which aims for broad acceptance needs to provide the end user with software tools supporting it. We are facing two challenges in this regard.

First, we need a uniform and standardized way of acquiring and processing UML models. Until recently there were no standards on storing UML models, and different UML editing tools were producing files in proprietary format. The development and spreading of XML as a universal data representation language motivated the development of the XML Metadata Interchange (XMI) [313] language for storing UML models in a file.

For developing critical systems using UML and XML-based analysis, one needs a precise semantics of the used notation. The UML is relatively precisely defined, but its semantics is given partially in prose, leaving room for ambiguities [431]. We have refined the semantics by giving mathematically precise meaning to UML constructs, as shown in the previous chapter.

5 Tools for Advanced XML-Based Processing of UML Models

Using the UML notation has two important aspects:

- *Standardized notation* helps to capture, store, and exchange knowledge about the system under design.
- *Semantics*, although semi-formal, assures that different developers understood the common meaning of UML diagrams.

Initially, different UML tools implemented proprietary UML storage formats which made exchange and reuse of the models impossible. Having chosen a UML tool, the developer was tied to using it through the whole project. Applying emerging technologies the UML modeling on an industrial level was virtually impossible. To suggest any custom UML processing, one would have to develop a complete UML editor and persuade the auditorium to use it.

Development of the XML as a universal data storage format changed this situation dramatically. In the year 2000 The Object Management Group (OMG) [322] issued the first specification for the XML Metadata Interchange (XMI) language [313] which – among other applications – became a standard for serializing UML models in a file.

The XMI language is compliant with MOF (Meta-Object Facility [312]), which is a framework for specifying meta-information (also called metamodels). Initially it was developed to define CORBA-based services for managing meta-information. Currently its applications include definition of modeling languages such as UML and CWM (Common Warehouse Model). The framework operates on a four-level data abstraction model, shown in Fig. 4.

M3	Meta-Metamodel	MetaClass, MetaAssociation - MOF Model
M2	Metamodel	Class, Attribute, Dependency - UML (as a language), CWM
M1	Model	Person, City, Book - UML Model
M0	Data	Bob Marley, Bonn - Running program

Fig. 4. MOF framework

We consider the abstraction levels from bottom up. The lowest level M0 deals with the data instances, for example *Mr. Smith, 35 years old, lives in New York*. The level M1 describes data models; in software development this corresponds to the UML model of the application. An example for this layer is a *Person* with attributes *Name, Age, Address*. The next abstraction level M2 is the modeling language itself. There exist different modeling languages for different application domains, and the last abstraction level M3 is the common environment for defining these modeling languages, standardized by the MOF. It operates with three elements:

MOF Object defines object types for the target model. It includes a *name*; a set of *attributes*, both predefined and custom; a set of *operations*; a set of *association references*; a set of *supertypes* it inherits, and some other information. The MOF object is a *container* for its component features; that is, any *attributes, operations*, and *association references*. It may also contain MOF definitions of *data types* and *exceptions*.

MOF Association defines a link between two MOF objects. The MOF links are always binary and directed. A link is a *container* for two *association ends*, each representing one object the link is connected to.

MOF Package groups related MOF elements for reuse and modularization. It is defined by a *name*; a list of *imports* which defines a set of other MOF packages whose components may be reused by components defined within the package; a list of *supertypes* which defines a set of other MOF packages whose components form a part of the package; and a set of contained elements including other objects, associations, and packages.

The MOF also defines the following secondary elements:

Data Types can be used to define *constructed* and *reference* data types.
Constants define compile-time constant expressions.
Exceptions can be raised by object operations.
Constraints can be attached to other MOF elements. Constraint semantics and verification are not part of the MOF specification, and therefore they can be defined with any language.

The MOF is related to two other standards:

XML Metadata Interchange (XMI) is a mapping from MOF to XML. It can be used to automatically produce an XML interchange format for any language described with MOF. For example, to produce a standardized UML interchange format, we need to define the UML language using MOF, and use the XMI mapping rules to derive DTDs and XML Schemas for UML serialization. MOF itself is defined using MOF itself, and therefore XMI can be applied not only for metamodel instances, but for metamodels themselves (as they are also instances of a metamodel, which is MOF).

Java Metadata Interface (JMI) standard   defines   MOF-to-Java   mapping (similar to the MOF-to-XML mapping provided by XMI). It is used to derive Java interfaces tailored for accessing instances of a particular metamodel. As MOF itself is MOF compliant, it can be used to access metamodels too. The standard also defines a set of *reflective* interfaces that can be used similar to the metamodel-specific API without prior knowledge of the metamodel.

After the standards were introduced, major producers of UML editors eventually picked it up, and currently support model interchange in the XMI format. Together with the wide support for the XML in industry, including a broad range of libraries, editors, and accompanying technologies, this enables development of the lightweight UML processing tools, tailored to carry one particular task.

The whole story is applicable to the formalized critical system development with UML. To facilitate acceptance of the formalized UML-based software development, automated processing of UML models was greatly required. Prototype tools supporting this functionality have been developed at the TU München; some results of these projects are presented below. Especially we hope that the publicly available Web-based interface will provide a simple and accessible entry into the methodology.

5.1 XML-Based Data Binding with MDR

Technically the central question was how to work with UML/XMI files. There exist three possible approaches:

- XML parsing and transformation languages coupled with the XML standard (XPath, XSLT).
- Any high-level language with appropriate libraries (Java, C++, Perl).
- Data binding.

The first two methods, although more flexible, require more development effort. However, for UML processing we are concerned about the data contained in documents rather than about the document itself and its structure. For this purpose, data binding offers a much simpler approach to working with XML data.

There exist several libraries supporting data binding for XML. It was important to use one with an appropriate data abstraction level. For example, the widely used Castor library [57] would leave the developer with a very abstract representation of the UML model, on the level of MOF constructs. However, there exist data-binding libraries which provide a representation of a UML XMI file on the abstraction level of a UML model. This allows the developer to operate directly with UML concepts (such as classes, statecharts, stereotypes, etc.). We use the MDR (MetaData Repository) library which is part of the Netbeans project [299], also used by the freely available UML modeling tool Poseidon 1.6 Community Edition [146]. Another such library is the Novosoft NSUML project [302].

The MDR library implements an MOF repository with support for XMI and JMI standards. Figure 5 illustrates how the repository is used for working with UML models.

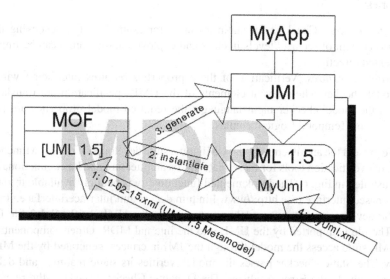

Fig. 5. Using the MDR library

The XMI description of the modeling language is used to customize the MDR for working with a particular model type, UML in this case (step 1). The XMI description of UML 1.5 is published by the Object Management Group (OMG) [322]. A storage customized for the given model type is created (step 2). Additionally, based on the XMI specification of the modeling language, the MDR library creates the JMI (Java Metadata Interface) implementation for accessing the model (step 3). This allows the application to manipulate the model directly on the conceptual level of UML. The UML model is loaded into the repository (step 4). Now it can be accessed through the supplied JMIs from a Java application. The model can be read, modified, and later saved as an XMI file again.

Because of the additional abstraction level implemented by the MDR library, using it in the UML suite should facilitate upgrading to upcoming UML versions, and promises the highest available standard compatibility.

5.2 XML-Based UML Tools Suite

To facilitate the application of our approach in industry, automated tools for the analysis of UML models using the suggested semantics are required. We describe a framework that incorporates several such verifiers currently beeing developed at the TU München.

Functionality

We can group all the UML model features, which can be verified, into two major categories:

- *Static features.* Checkers for static features (for example, a type checking like enforcement of security levels in class and deployment diagrams) can be implemented directly.
- *Dynamic features.* Verification of these properties requires interfacing with a model checker. The relevant elements of the UML specification are translated into the model-checker input language; the required model properties are presented by Temporal Logic formulas.

We present the architecture of the UML tools suite developed at the TU München, providing verification tools for these features. Its architecture and basic functionality are illustrated in Fig. 6. The implemented functionality is publicly available through a Web-based interface (see http://www4.in.tum.de/ csduml/interface/interface.html).

The developer creates a model and stores it in the UML 1.5/XMI 1.2 file format. The file is imported by the UML into the internal MDR. Other components of the UML suite access the model through the JMI interfaces, generated by the MDR library. The Static Checker parses the model, verifies its static features, and delivers the results to the Error Analyzer. The Dynamic Checker translates the relevant fragments of the UML model into the input language of the relevant analysis engine (currently, the Promela language for the Spin model checker and the TPTP format for the automated theorem prover Setheo). The analysis engine is spawned by the UML suite as an external process; its results (and a counterexample in case a problem was found) are delivered back to the Error Analyzer. The Error Analyzer uses

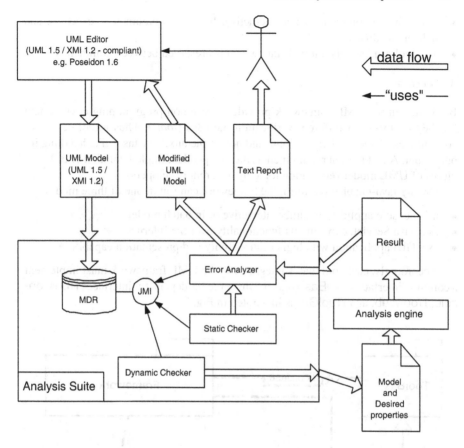

Fig. 6. UML tools suite

the information received from both Static Checker and Dynamic Checker to produce a Text Report for the developer describing the problems found, and a Modified UML Model, where the errors found are visualized and/or corrected.

The idea behind the tools suite is to provide a common programming framework for the developers of different verification modules (*tools*). Thus a tool developer should concentrate on the verification logic and not on the handling of input/output. Different tools, implementing verification logic modules (*Static Checkers* or *Dynamic Checkers* in Fig. 6), can be independently developed and integrated. Currently there exist *Static Checkers* for most static UMLsec properties, and *Dynamic Checkers* for some dynamic properties.

The tool implementation follows the following simple concepts:

- The tool is given a default UML model to operate on. It may load further models if necessary.
- The tool exposes a set of commands which it can execute.

- Every single command is not interactive. It receives parameters, executes, and delivers feedback.
- The tool can have its internal state which is preserved between commands.

Architecture

By its design the UML framework provides a common programming environment for the developers of different verification modules (*tools*). Thus a tool developer concentrates on the verification logic and not on the auxiliary tasks like handling input/output. An additional requirement is the independent implementation of different pieces of UML model verification logic by different developers.

On any Java-enabled platform, the framework can run in one of three modes:

- as a console application, either interactive or in batch mode;
- as a Java Servlet, exposing its functionality over the Internet;
- as a GUI application with higher interactivity and presentation capabilities.

Accordingly, each tool that is integrated in the UML framework must implement a common interface IToolBase plus the three media-dependent interfaces IToolConsole, IToolWeb, and IToolGui as illustrated in Fig. 7.

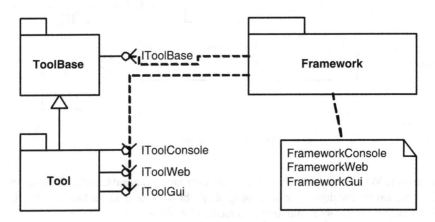

Fig. 7. Tool interfaces

However, the requirement to implement all three media-dependent interfaces for a tool would mean a serious overhead for the tool developer. To assist the developer in this regard, the framework provides default implementations for the IToolWeb and IToolGui interfaces, as illustrated in Fig. 8. These default wrappers render the plain text output, generated by the tool through the IToolConsole interface, into the HTML page or scrolling text window respectively. Thus each tool plugged into the framework must implement at least the IToolBase and IToolConsole interfaces. If the tool developers want to exploit all capabilities of the Web or GUI media, they have to implement the IToolWeb and/or IToolGui interfaces, which provide more

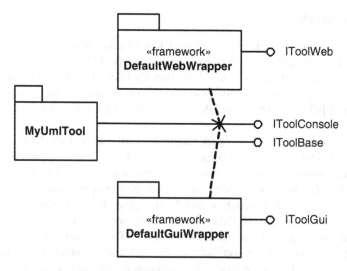

Fig. 8. Default interface wrappers

control over the tool input and output. In the GUI mode the developer is then requested to provide an instance of the **JPane**-derived class which hosts the complete UI of the tool and has the ability to customize the menu and toolbar of the framework. In the Web mode the developer can fully control the rendered HTML document.

The UML framework uses the **IToolBase** interface to retrieve general information about the tool, and one of the three tool media-specific interfaces to call commands provided by the tool and receive the output. The output is further rendered by the framework on the current media.

Each tool exposes a set of commands which can be executed through the functions **GetConsoleCommands**, **GetWebCommands**, and **GetGuiCommands** of the corresponding interface. Thus the tool can provide different functionality on different media, adapting to its specifics.

The tool can execute several commands sequentially, preserving its internal state and the changes to the UMLsec model between command calls. The set of available commands for each tool may vary depending on the execution history and current state. This allows use of the UML framework for complex and interactive operations on the UML model.

To achieve the media-independent operation of the tools their parameter input, as well as their output, is handled by the framework and not by the tools themselves. Each single command during its execution defines the set of required input parameters, and receives them from the framework. On behalf of the tool, the UML framework collects the parameters from the user using the current input/output media (console, Web, or GUI). Currently supported parameter types are **Integer, Double, String,** and **File.** Further types can be easily integrated into the framework as necessary.

6 Related Work

There has been a considerable amount of work toward a formal semantics for various parts of UML. A complete overview has to be omitted, but [133] discusses some fundamental issues concerning a formal foundation for UML. [358] gives an approach using algebraic specification; [48] uses a framework based on stream-processing functions; and [43] uses ASMs for UML statecharts which was a starting point for the current work.

There are several existing tools for automatic verification of the UML models. The HUGO Project [374] checks behavior described by a UML collaboration diagram against a transitional system comprising several communicating objects. The vUML Tool [276] analyzes the behavior of a set of interacting objects, defined in a similar way. A related approach to ours is also given by the CASE tool AUTO-FOCUS [212] which uses a UML-like notation. However, neither tool can be directly extended for our purpose. First, our approach allows formalization and verification of different UML diagrams in combination. Second, our implementation explicitly models data types, which is necessary for handling, for example, encryption primitives.

Work on model-based development of systems with other non-functional requirements besides security includes pp. 289, 305, 329, and 363 in this book on embedded systems. Other work on tool support for model-based development can be found for example on pp. 91 and 139 of this book.

7 Conclusion

The development and spreading of the UML within the last few years, especially its standardization and introduction of supporting technologies, is changing its role in software development from a notational aid to a powerful framework with support for the automation of many development tasks.

We presented work for formal critical systems development using the UML. We provided a formal semantics for a fragment of the UML using UML Machines, which puts diagrams into context. The semantics is particularly useful to analyze the interaction between a system and its environment and to analyze UML specifications in a modular way. In particular, we explained how to use the semantics to analyze UML specifications for criticality requirements, by including an adversary model.

We have demonstrated a framework for automated processing of UML models, which facilitates technology transfer to industry. This framework has been used to connect various analysis engines (the model checker Spin, the automated theorem provers Setheo and SPASS, and a Prolog verification engine) to support the automated analysis of criticality requirements (in particular, behavioral properties).

The proposed method of XML-based analysis of UML models has been successfully tried out on several industrial projects.

We believe that the suggested approach to critical system development using UML and XML-based processing of UML models will find widespread acceptance in the modern software development industry for the following reasons:

- It is based on UML, which is the de facto standard in software development, and which facilitates acceptance in industrial software development teams.
- The application of the methodology requires no special training in security (in the case of UMLsec) or the other criticality domains.
- The suggested formal semantics for a simplified fragment of the UML lays a foundation for advanced XML-based tool support for the methodology, making automatic verification of the criticality features possible.

The tools presented in this chapter have been successfully used in industrial projects with partners including German Telecom, BMW, Allianz insurance, and others.

We plan to continue work on the project. Some important aspects for the future development are listed below:

- When targeting external verification tools, complexity of the produced model is an issue for our method. Several approaches can help to address this problem. Highly non-deterministic adversary behavior, which is mostly responsible for the complexity issue, can be significantly restricted by using simple rules for cutting out uninteresting scenarios. Separate verification of different scenarios can be possible. Additional, possibly automatic model abstraction while preserving desired requirements is an interesting approach in this regard.
- Improving feedback to the user is an important step toward broad application of the methodology in industry. Currently we support rudimentary annotation of UML models with labels indicating potential problems. The feedback can be significantly extended, for example an error trace produced by a model checker could be translated into a UMLsec sequence diagram, which would illustrate for the developer the sequence of actions which led to the problem. The upcoming UML 2.0 standard is particularly interesting in this regard as it supports diagram interchange.

Caste-centric Modelling of Multi-agent Systems: The CAMLE Modelling Language and Automated Tools

Hong Zhu[1] and Lijun Shan[2]

[1] Department of Computing, Oxford Brookes University,
   Wheatley campus, Oxford OX33 1HX, UK
   hzhu@brookes.ac.uk
[2] Department of Computer Science, National University of Defence Technology,
   Changsha, 410073, China
   lijunshancn@yahoo.com

Summary. Agent technology is widely perceived to be a viable solution for large-scale industrial and commercial applications in dynamic environments such as the Internet. However, the lack of rigour and language support in the analysis, specification, design and implementation of multi-agent systems has hampered the wide adoption of agent technology. This chapter proposes a model-driven approach to the development of multi-agent systems. It combines graphic modelling with formal specification through automated tools. The chapter reports an agent-oriented modelling language CAMLE and the automated tools in its modelling environment. Two aspects of particular importance in the model-driven development methodology are addressed in this chapter. The first is the definition and implementation of consistency constraints on graphic models. The second is the automated transformation of graphic models into formal specifications.

1 Introduction

Agent technology has long been predicted to be the next mainstream computing paradigm; see, for example, [230, 371, 340]. It is widely perceived to be a viable solution for large-scale industrial and commercial applications in dynamic environments such as the Internet [234]. One of the key factors that contributed to the progress in software engineering over the past two decades is the development of language concepts and facilities that directly support increasingly powerful and natural high-level abstractions with which complex systems are modelled, analysed and developed. From a software engineering point of view, one of the most appealing features of agent technology is its natural way to modularize a complex system in terms of multiple, interacting and autonomous components that have particular objectives to achieve [233]. Such modularity achievable by multi-agent systems (MASs) is much more powerful and natural than any kind of modularity that can be achieved by existing language facilities such as type, module and class.

However, the research on agent-based systems has been mainly an AI endeavour so far. The majority of extant agent applications are developed in an ad hoc fashion without proper analysis and specification of requirements, and without systematic verification and validation of the properties of the implemented systems. We believe that there are two major factors that hamper the wide adoption of agent technology in software development. First, being autonomous, proactive and adaptive, agent-based systems can be very complicated. They may demonstrate emergent behaviours which sometimes are neither designed by the developers nor expected by the users. The new features of agent-based systems demand new methods for the specification of agent behaviours and for the verification and validation of their properties to enable software engineers to develop reliable and trustworthy agent-based systems. It has been recognized that the lack of rigour is one of the major factors hampering the wide-scale adoption of agent technology [47]. Second, extant MAS are mostly developed without a proper language facility that directly supports the effective and efficient utilization of the modularity and abstraction underlying the concept of agents. Due to the lack of language support, the advantages and merits of agent technology are inevitably overwhelmed by the inefficiency of the implementations in incompatible languages, and the high cost and poor productivity due to the unnecessary complexity in design, coding, debugging, and testing at a lower level of abstraction etc.

In this chapter, we propose a model-driven approach to the development of agent-based systems. It combines graphic modelling of MAS with implementation-independent formal specifications in order to provide the rigour in the analysis, specification and design of MAS. The central concept of the approach is caste, which is a language facility introduced as a natural evolution of the notion of data type in procedural programming and class in object-oriented paradigm. It is the classifier of agents. It serves as the template of agents and the organizational unit of MASs. This language facility is intended to bridge the gap between the abstract concepts of agent and their concrete representations in computer software so that MAS applications can be developed effectively and efficiently. In this chapter, we present an informal introduction to the modelling language CAMLE, which stands for Caste-centric Agent-oriented Modelling Language and Environment [389]. We also report an automated modelling environment that supports the users to construct MAS models at the requirements analysis and specification stage in CAMLE graphical notation with multiple views and at different abstraction levels. We will focus on two aspects of particular importance in the tool support to model-driven software development. They are the consistency problem of graphic models and the automation problem of model-based development. Diagrammatic models in CAMLE serve as a representation of users' requirements and are used as the bases for further design and implementation of MAS. It is therefore of vital importance to ensure the model's consistency [390]. A set of consistency constraints is defined on CAMLE models and an automatic consistency checker is designed and implemented to help the detection of inconsistency according to the constraints. As in many existing modern modelling languages that employ the so-called multiple view principle, the information that specifies one caste of agents is scattered over various diagrams. It is therefore desirable to specify each caste of agents in one 'module' that contains all necessary information for its further design and implementation without unnecessary knowledge of other parts of the system. This is achievable through an automated tool that transforms graphic models into formal specifications in SLABS (a Specification Language for Agent-Based Systems) [468, 470], which describes an MAS with a set of specifications of the castes that the system contains.

The remainder of the chapter is organised as follows. Section 2 presents the meta-model of MAS, which is independent of the implementation platforms and applicable to all types of agent theories and techniques. Section 3 is an informal introduction to the modelling language CAMLE. Section 4 defines the consistency constraints on models in CAMLE. Section 5 describes the algorithms and rules that transform graphic models in CAMLE to formal specifications in SLABS. Section 6 describes the architecture and main functions of the automated modelling environment and reports the case studies with the modelling language and environment. Section 7 concludes the chapter with a discussion of further research.

2 Meta-model of Multi-agent Systems

Because the concepts of agents and MAS are controversial, it is worth saying a few words to clarify what we mean by agent and MAS and how such systems work. Generally speaking, a consistent definition of the basic concepts, structures and mechanisms underlying a specific type of system forms a conceptual model (sometimes also called meta-model) of these systems. A conceptual model of MAS, therefore, must answer a set of fundamental questions about agents and MAS. For example, what is the structure of an agent? How do agents perform their activities? What constitute an MAS? How do agents in an MAS communicate with each other? How are agents in an MAS organized? And so on.

Our conceptual model can be characterized by a set of pseudo-equations. Each pseudo-equation answers such a question and thus defines a key feature of MAS. A formal definition of the model can be found in [468, 470].

Pseudo-equation (1) states that agents are defined as real-time active computational entities that encapsulate data, operations and behaviours, and are situated in their designated environments:

$$Agent = \langle Data, Operations, Behaviour \rangle_{Environment} \qquad (1)$$

Here, data represent an agent's state. Operations are the actions that the agent can take. Behaviour is described by a set of rules that determine how the agent behaves, including when and how to take actions and change state in the context of its designated environment. By encapsulation, we mean that an agent's state can only be changed by the agent itself, and the agent can decide 'when to go' and 'whether to say no' according to an explicitly specified set of behaviour rules. Figure 1 illustrates the control structure of the agent's behaviour.

There are two fundamental differences between objects and agents in our conceptual model. First, objects do not contain any explicitly programmed behaviour

```
Begin
    Initialise state;
    Loop
            Perceive the visible actions and states of the agents in the
                environment;
            Take actions and change state according to the situation in the
                environment and the agent's internal state;
    end of loop;
end
```

Fig. 1. The control structure of an agent's behaviour

rule. Second, objects are open to all computation entities to call their public methods without any distinction of them. However, as argued in [468], objects can be considered as agents in a degenerate form. In particular, object is a special case of agent in the sense that it has a fixed rule of behaviour, i.e. 'executes the corresponding method when receives a message'. Consequently, in our conceptual model, an MAS consists of agents and nothing but agents, as stated in pseudo-equation (2):

$$MAS = \{Agent_n\}, \ n \in Integer \tag{2}$$

Notice that an agent's state variables and actions are divided into two kinds: visible ones and invisible (or internal) ones. An agent taking a visible action can be understood as generating an event that can be perceived by other agents in the system, while an agent taking an internal action means it generates an event that can only be perceived by its components, which are also agents. Similarly, the value of a visible state variable can be obtained by other agents, while the value of an internal state can only be obtained by its components. Notice that our use of the term 'visibility' is different from the traditional concept of scope.

The concept of visibility of an agent's actions and state variables forms the basic communication mechanism in our conceptual model. Agents communicate with each other by taking visible actions and changing visible state variables, and by observing other agents' visible actions and visible states, as shown in pseudo-equation (3):

$$Communication(A \rightarrow B) = A.Action\&B.Observation \tag{3}$$

However, an agent's visible action is not necessarily observed by all agents in the system. It is only observed by those interested in its behaviour and considering it as a part of their environments. In other words, the environment of an agent in an MAS at time t is a subset of the agents in the system. As illustrated in pseudo-equation (4), from a given agent's point of view, only those in its environment are visible. In particular, from agent A's point of view, agent B is visible means that agent A can perceive the visible actions taken by agent B and obtain the value of agent B's visible part of state:

$$Environment_t(Agent, MAS) \subseteq MAS - \{Agent\} \tag{4}$$

To enable our model to deal with open and dynamic environments, we introduced the concept of 'designated environment', i.e. the environment of an agent is specified when the agent is designed, but the specification allows the environment to vary within a certain range. Therefore, the set of agents in the environment of an agent depends on time, hence, the subscription t in pseudo-equation (4). The language facility that enables us to achieve the variation of environment is the concept of caste.

In our conceptual model, the classifier of agents is called caste. Agents are classified into various castes in a similar way as to that data are classified into types, and objects are classified into classes. However, different from the notion of class in object orientation, caste allows dynamic classification. That is, an agent can change its caste membership (called casteship in the sequel) at run-time. It also allows multiple classifications, i.e. an agent can belong to more than one caste at the same time. As all classifiers, inheritance relations can also be specified between castes. As a consequence of multiple classifications, a caste can inherit more than one caste. Caste is the basic organizational unit in the design and implementation of MAS. As a modularity language facility, a caste serves as a template that describes the structure and behaviour properties of agents. Pseudo-equation (5) states that a caste at time t is a set of agents that have the same structural and behavioural characteristics:

$$Caste_t = \{agents | structure \ \& \ behaviour \ properties\} \qquad (5)$$

The weakness of the static object–class relationship in current mainstream object-oriented programming has been widely recognized. Proposals have been advanced, for example, to allow objects' dynamic reclassification [92]. In [471], we suggested that an agent's ability to dynamically change its roles is represented by dynamic casteship. In our model, dynamic casteship is an integral part of agents' behaviour capability. Agents can have behaviour rules that allow them to change their castes at run-time autonomously. To change its casteship, an agent takes an action to join a caste or retreat from a caste at run-time. Therefore, which agents are in a caste depends on time even if agents can be persistent, hence the subscript of t in pseudo-equation (5). We believe that this feature allows users to model the real world by MAS naturally and to maximize the flexibility and power of agent technology.

Moreover, dynamic caste membership enables us to describe agents' designated environments in a flexible and effective way. The environment description of an agent (or a caste) defines what kinds of agents are visible. With the concept of caste, we can describe an environment, for example, as the set of agents in a number of particular castes. An environment so described is neither closed, nor fixed – nor totally open. Since agents can change their casteships dynamically, an agent's environment may change dynamically as well. For example, an agent's environment changes when it joins a caste and hence the agents in the caste's environment become visible. The environment also changes when other agents join the caste in the agent's environment.

It is worth noting that the conceptual model defined above is independent of any implementation platform and applicable to all types of agent theories and techniques.

3 The CAMLE Modelling Language

In this section, we give an informal introduction to the modelling language CAMLE and illustrate its uses by a simple example.

3.1 The Overall Structure of Models

CAMLE employs the multi-view principle to model complicated systems. There are three types of models in CAMLE: caste models, collaboration models and behaviour models. Each model may consist of one or more diagrams. A caste model specifies the castes of agents in the system and the relationships between them, such as the inheritance and whole–part relations. A collaboration model specifies how the agents interact with each other. A behaviour model specifies how an agent decides its actions and state changes.

A caste is called a compound caste if its agents are composed from a number of other agents; otherwise, it is called atomic. An MAS can, therefore, be considered as a compound agent. For example, as shown in Fig. 2(a), the system is directly composed of castes A and B. Each of them can be further decomposed into smaller components N_1 and N_2, and M_1 and M_2, respectively. To each compound caste, such as the system, A and B in Fig. 2, a collaboration model and a behaviour model are associated. Atomic castes only have no collaboration models because they have no components, thus no internal collaboration.

The overall structure of a system's collaboration models and behaviour models can be viewed as a hierarchy, which is isomorphic to the whole–part relations between castes described in the caste model; see e.g. Fig. 2(b).

The following subsections describe each model and discuss their uses in agent-oriented software development.

3.2 Caste Model

We view an information system as an organization that consists of a collection of agents that stand in certain relationships to one another by being a member of certain groups and playing certain roles, i.e. in certain castes. They interact with each other by observing their environments and taking visible actions as responses. The behaviour of an individual agent in a system is determined by the 'roles' it is playing. An individual agent can change its role in the system. However, the set of roles and the assignments of responsibilities and tasks to roles are usually quite stable [326]. Such an organizational structure of information systems is captured in our caste model.

Figure 3 shows the notation and an example of caste diagrams. A caste diagram identifies the castes in a system and indicates the relationships between them. In CAMLE, there are three types of relationships on castes represented in caste models. They are inheritance, aggregation and migration relations.

The inheritance relationship between castes defines sub-groups of the agents that have special responsibilities and hence additional capabilities and behaviours. For

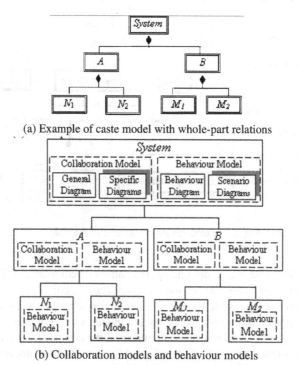

(a) Example of caste model with whole-part relations

(b) Collaboration models and behaviour models

Fig. 2. Overall structure of CAMLE models

example, in Fig. 3, the members of a university are classified into three castes: students, faculties and secretaries. Students are further classified into three sub-castes: undergraduates, postgraduates and PhD students.

Migration relations specify how agents change their casteships. There are two kinds of migration relationships: migrate and participate. A migrate relation from caste A to B means that an agent of caste A can retreat from caste A and join caste B. A participate relation from caste A to B means that an agent of caste A can join caste B while retaining its casteship of A. For example, in Fig. 3, an undergraduate student may become a postgraduate after graduation. A postgraduate student may become a PhD student after graduation or become a faculty member. Each student becomes a member of the alumni of the university after leaving the university. A faculty member can become a part-time PhD student while remaining employed as a faculty member. From this model, we can infer that an individual can be a student and a faculty member at the same time if he/she is a PhD student.

An aggregate relation specifies a whole–part relationship between agents. An agent may contain a number of components that are also agents. The former is called compound agent of the latter. In such a case, there exists a whole–part relationship between the compound and the component agents, which is represented through an aggregate relation between castes. We identify three types of whole–part relationships between agents according to the ways a component agent is bound to the com-

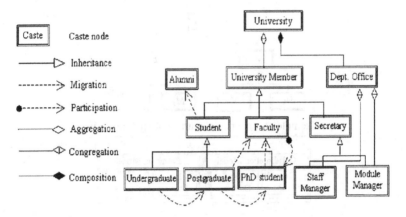

Fig. 3. Caste diagram: notations and example

pound agent and the ways a compound agent controls its components. The strongest binding between a compound agent and its components is composition in which the compound agent is responsible for the creation and destruction of its components. If the compound agent no longer exists, the components will not exist. The weakest binding is aggregation, in which the compound and the component are independent, so that the component agent will not be affected for both its existence and casteships when the compound agent is destroyed. The third whole–part relation is called congregation. It means that if the compound agent is destroyed, the component agents will still exist, but they will lose the casteship of the component caste. For example, as shown in Fig. 3, a university consists of a number of individuals as its members. If the university is destroyed, the individuals should still exist. However, they will lose the membership as the university member. Therefore, the whole–part relationship between University and University Member is a congregation relation. This relationship is different from the relationship between a university and its departments. Departments are components of a university. If a university is destroyed, its departments will no longer exist. The whole–part relationship between University and Department is therefore a composition relation. The composition and aggregation relation is similar to the composition and aggregation in UML, respectively. However, congregation is a novel concept in modelling languages. It was introduced by CAMLE. There is no similar counterpart in object-oriented modelling languages, such as UML. It has not been recognized in the research on object-oriented modelling of whole–part relations; cf. [28]. We believe that it is important for agent-oriented modelling because of agents' basic features, namely dynamic casteship.

3.3 Collaboration Model

While caste model defines the static architecture of MAS, collaboration model defines a dynamic aspect of the MAS organization by capturing the collaboration dependencies and relationships between the agents.

Agents in an MAS collaborate with each other through communication, which is essential to fulfil the system's functionality. Such interactions between agents are captured and represented in a collaboration model. In CAMLE, a collaboration model is associated to each compound caste and describes the interactions between the component agents of the compound caste through a set of collaboration diagrams. Figure 4 gives the notations of collaboration diagrams.

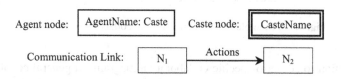

Fig. 4. Notation of collaboration diagram

There are two types of nodes in a collaboration diagram. An agent node represents a specific agent. A caste node represents any agent in a caste. An arrow from node A to node B represents that the visible behaviour of agent A is observed by agent B. Therefore, agent A influences agent B. When agent B is particularly interested in certain activities of agent A, the activities can also be annotated to the arrow from A to B.

Although this model looks similar to the collaboration diagrams in UML, there are significant differences in the semantics. In the OO paradigm, what is annotated on the arrow from A to B is a method of B. It represents a method call from object A to object B, and consequently, object B must execute the method. In contrast, in CAMLE the action annotated on an arrow from A to B is a visible action of A. Moreover, agent B does not necessarily respond to agent A's action. The distinction indicates the shift of modelling focus from controls represented by the method calls in the OO paradigm to collaborations represented by signalling and observation of visible actions. It fits well with the autonomous nature of agents.

3.3.1 Scenarios of Collaboration

One of the complications in the development of collaboration models is to deal with agents' various behaviours in different scenarios. They may take different actions, pass around different sequences of messages and even communicate with different agents. Therefore, it is better to describe different scenarios separately. The collaboration model supports the separation of scenarios by including a set of collaboration diagrams. Each diagram represents one scenario. In such a scenario-specific collaboration diagram, actions annotated on arrows can be numbered by their temporal sequence. Figure 5 gives an example of a scenario-specific collaboration diagram. It describes the collaborations of an undergraduate student with his/her personal tutor, the faculty members who give lectures and the PhD students who are practical class tutors.

Fig. 5. An example of a scenario-specific collaboration diagram

In addition to scenario-specific collaboration diagrams, a general collaboration diagram is also associated to each compound caste to give an overall picture of the communications between all the component agents by describing all visible actions that the component agents may take and all possible observers of the actions. Fig. 6 describes the communications within a department between various agents.

3.3.2 Refinement of Collaboration Models

The modelling language supports modelling complex systems at various levels of abstraction. Models of coarse granularity at a high level of abstraction can be refined into more detailed fine granularity models. At the top level, a system can be viewed as an agent that interacts with users and/or other systems in its external environment. This system can be decomposed into a number of subsystems interacting with each other. A subsystem can also be viewed as an agent and further decomposed. As analysis deepens, a hierarchical structure of the system emerges. In this way, the compound agent has its functionality decomposed through the decomposition of its structure. Such a refinement can be carried on until the problem is specified adequately in detail. Thus, a collaboration model at system level that specifies the boundaries of the application can be eventually refined into a hierarchy of collaboration models at various abstraction levels. Of course, the hierarchical structure of collaboration diagrams can also be used for bottom-up design and composition of existing components to form a system.

Figure 7 gives an example of a general collaboration diagram that refines the caste Dept Office. In this diagram, the agents in the castes of Student and Faculty as well as a specific agent called Dept Head in the caste of Faculty form the environment of the caste Dept Office. Therefore, they are visible to the component agents of the caste.

3.4 Behaviour Model

While caste and collaboration models describe MAS at the macro-level from the perspective of an external observer, the behaviour model adopts the internal or first-person view of each agent. It describes an agent's dynamic behaviour in terms of how

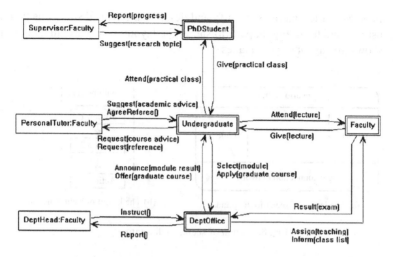

Fig. 6. An example of a general collaboration diagram

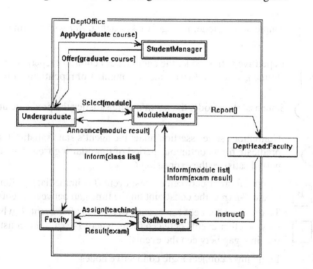

Fig. 7. An example of a general collaboration diagram that refines a caste

it acts in certain scenarios of the environment at the micro-level. A behaviour model consists of two kinds of diagrams: scenario diagrams and behaviour diagrams.

3.4.1 Scenario Diagrams

We believe that each agent's perception of its environment should be explicitly specified when modelling its behaviour. From an agent's point of view, the situation of its environment is characterized by what is observable by the agent. In other words, a scenario is defined by the sequences of visible actions taken by the agent in its environment. Scenario diagrams identify and describe the typical situations that the agent must respond to. In Fig. 8, part (a) shows the layout of scenario diagrams and part (b) shows the layout of swim lanes.

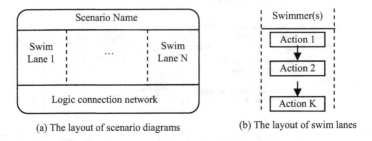

(a) The layout of scenario diagrams   (b) The layout of swim lanes

Fig. 8. Format of scenario diagram

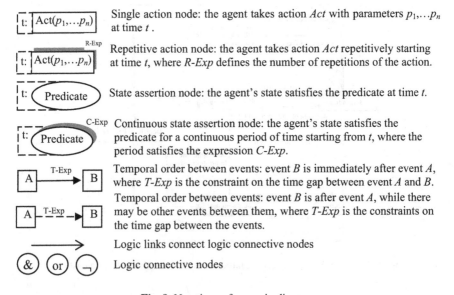

Fig. 9. Notations of scenario diagram

The swimmer(s) of a swim lane can be in one of the following forms: (a) $\forall x \in C$, where C is a caste and x is a bounded variable; this means all agents of caste C take the same sequence of actions specified in the swim lane. (b) $\exists x \in C$, where C is a caste and x is a bounded variable; this means there is at least one agent in caste C that takes the sequence of actions specified in the swim lane. (c) $\alpha \in C$, where α is an agent in caste C; this means that agent α takes the sequence of actions specified in the swim lane.

Figure 9 depicts the notations to specify visible events by nodes and temporal ordering by arrows in scenario diagrams, as well as logic connective nodes and links for the combination of situations.

For example, Fig. 10 describes a scenario where Greenspan announces that the interest rate will decrease by 0.25 points and all stock market analysts recommend buying Microsoft shares.

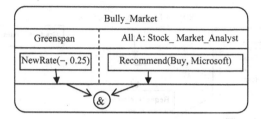

Fig. 10. Example of scenario diagram

3.4.2 Behaviour Diagrams

A behaviour diagram is associated to a caste to define a set of behaviour rules for the agents of the caste. The notation of behaviour diagrams includes the notation of scenario diagrams plus those in Fig. 11.

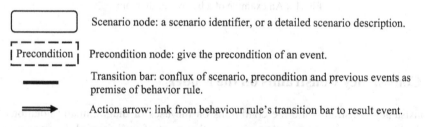

Fig. 11. Notation for behaviour diagrams

A behaviour diagram contains event nodes linked together by the temporal ordering arrows as in scenario diagrams to specify the agent's previous behaviour pattern. A transition bar with a conflux of scenario, precondition and previous pattern and followed by an event node indicates that when the agent's behaviour matches the previous pattern and the system is in the scenario and the precondition is true, the event specified by the event node under the transition bar will be taken by the agent. In a behaviour diagram, a reference to a scenario indicated by a scenario node can be replaced by a scenario diagram if it improves the readability.

For example, the behaviour diagram in Fig. 12 defines the behaviour of an undergraduate student. It states that if the student is in the final year and the average grade is 'A', he/she may request a reference from the personal tutor for the application to a graduate course. If the personal tutor agrees to be a referee, the student may apply for a graduate course. If the department office offers a position in a graduate course, the student will join the Graduates caste and retreat from the Undergraduates caste.

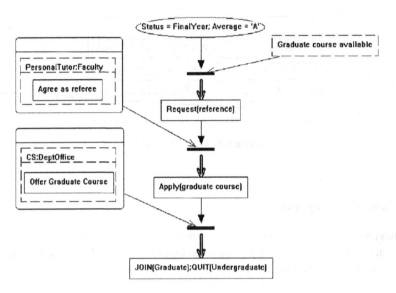

Fig. 12. An example of a behaviour diagram

4 Consistency Constraints on the Models

Consistency constraints are the conditions on the uses of diagrammatic notations, variables and names, types and symbols so that a set of well-formed diagrams can be regarded as a meaningful model. These conditions are usually related to the semantics of the diagrams. However, in order to enable the automated checking of a model effectively and efficiently, consistency constraints often have to be simplified and represented as syntactic rules.

A typical example of such a consistency constraint is that the same identifier that occurs at different places must refer to the same entity and an entity should be referred to by the same identifier even if it occurs at different places in the model. This rule cannot be mechanically checked directly. Instead of checking the consistency against this rule directly, we check a set of syntactical rules that represents the consistency in some more concrete forms. For example, we can use one model as the declaration of all entities and check all other occurrences of identifiers against the declaration. An alternative approach is to check if the entities referred to by the same identifier have the same features. Such rules are necessary conditions of the consistency rather than sufficient ones. However, well-defined consistency conditions can significantly improve the quality of models just like type compatibility checking in programming languages can detect programming errors.

In this section we define the consistency constraints for the CAMLE language. These constraints are classified into two types. Intra-model consistency constraints are those conditions that only involve the diagrams of the same type. Inter-model constraints involve more than one type of diagrams.

4.1 Intra-model Consistency

4.1.1 Constraints on Caste Models

As discussed in Sect. 3.2, a caste diagram defines the castes in the system and three kinds of relationships between them: inheritance, aggregation and migration. A well-formed caste diagram must satisfy the following conditions.

Constraint (1a) *A caste diagram defines a naming space. In this naming space each node defines a caste with a unique name.*

Constraint (1b) *Each link defines a binary relation on castes by linking two nodes in the diagram.*

Constraint (1c) *An inheritance relation and a migration relation must be associated to two different caste nodes.*

Constraint (1d) *Inheritance relations must not form any loops in a caste diagram.*

Aggregation and migration relations are allowed to form loops. It is not required for an aggregation relation to be associated to different caste nodes.

4.1.2 Constraints on Collaboration Models

A collaboration model may contain a number of collaboration diagrams including a general collaboration diagram (GCD) and a set of scenario-specific collaboration diagrams (SCDs). A GCD serves as a declaration of what castes and their instance agents are involved in the collaborations, while SCDs define the details of the collaboration protocols in various scenarios. Each SCD specifies a linear sequence of actions taken by the agents in a specific scenario of collaboration. To be well formed a collaboration diagram must satisfy the following conditions.

Constraint (2a) *A caste or agent node in a collaboration diagram must have a unique name.*

Constraint (2b) *The number assigned to an action must be unique, if any.*

Let G be a GCD, S be the set of SCD and $D \in S$ be any given SCD. Let $ANode(X)$, $CNode(X)$ and $Node(X)$ denote the set of agent nodes, the set of caste nodes and the set of all nodes in the collaboration diagram X, respectively. Let $CName(x)$ denote the caste name of a node x. The nodes and arrows in G and those in S must satisfy the following consistency conditions.

Constraint (2c) *Every agent node in the GCD G must appear in at least one SCD. Formally,*

$$\forall n \in ANode(G).\exists D \in S.(n \in ANode(D)) \qquad (6)$$

Constraint (2d) *A caste node in the GCD must appear at least once in an SCD as either a caste node or an agent node representing a specific agent of the caste. Formally,*

$$\forall n \in CNode(G).\exists D \in S.$$
$$(n \in CNode(D) \vee \exists n' \in ANode(D).(CName(n') = CName(n))) \qquad (7)$$

Constraint (2e) *Every caste node in an SCD must also appear in the GCD. Formally,*

$$\forall D \in S.\forall n \in CNode(D).(n \in CNode(G)) \qquad (8)$$

Constraint (2f) *For every agent node in any SCD, there must be either a node of the same agent or the caste of the agent in the GCD. Formally,*

$$\forall D \in S.\forall n \in ANode(D).$$
$$(n \in ANode(G) \vee \exists n' \in CNode(G).(CName(n') = CName(n))) \qquad (9)$$

Assume that $a = Act(p_1, p_2, \ldots, p_n)$ is an action associated to an arrow from node b to c. We call $\langle a, b, c \rangle$ an interaction from b to c with action a and define $Action(\langle a, b, c \rangle) = a$, $Begin(\langle a, b, c \rangle) = b$ and $End(\langle a, b, c \rangle) = c$. Let $Interaction(X)$ be the set of all interactions in a collaboration diagram X.

Constraint (2g) *Every interaction in the GCD must appear in at least one SCD, where a caste node in GCD can be replaced by an agent node of the same caste in the SCD. Formally,*

$$\forall \alpha Interaction(G).\exists D \in S.\exists \beta \in Interaction(D).$$
$$(CName(Begin(\alpha)) = CName(Begin(\beta))$$
$$\wedge CName(End(\alpha)) = CName(End(\beta))$$
$$\wedge Action(\alpha) = Action(\beta)$$
$$\wedge Begin(\alpha) \in ANode(G) \Rightarrow Begin(\beta) \in ANode(D)$$
$$\wedge End(\alpha) \in ANode(G) \Rightarrow End(\beta) \in ANode(D)) \qquad (10)$$

Constraint (2h) *Every interaction in any SCD must also be defined in the GCD. Formally,*

$$\forall D \in \boldsymbol{S}.\forall \alpha \in Interaction(D).\exists \beta \in Interaction(G).$$
$$(CName(Begin(\alpha)) = CName(Begin(\beta)))$$
$$\wedge CName(End(\alpha)) = CName(End(\beta))$$
$$\wedge Action(\alpha) = Action(\beta)$$
$$\wedge Begin(\alpha) \in CNode(G) \Rightarrow Begin(\beta) \in CNode(D)$$
$$\wedge End(\alpha) \in CNode(G) \Rightarrow End(\beta) \in CNode(D)) \tag{11}$$

As discussed in Sect. 3.3.2, CAMLE supports the decomposition of an agent into a number of component agents in the same way as the analysis of the whole system. The collaboration among the component agents can also be defined by a set of collaboration diagrams. Thus, the consistency between diagrams at different levels in the hierarchy of collaboration models of a system must be ensured. Let X be a collaboration diagram for a caste. We use $Env(X)$ to denote the environment of X, i.e. the set of agent and caste nodes on the border of X.

Constraint (2i) *The environment of an SCD must be identical to the environment of the GCD. Formally,*

$$\forall D \in \boldsymbol{S}.(Env(D) = Env(G)) \tag{12}$$

For the sake of simplicity, we assume that a collaboration model M satisfies the consistency constraints within one model discussed above. Therefore, we can overload the notation $Env(X)$ defined on diagrams to be the environment of the model, i.e. for a model M and any diagram D in M, define $Env(M) = Env(D)$, provided that M satisfies condition (2i).

Let C be a compound caste in a collaboration model M, and M_C be the collaboration model for C. That is, M_C specifies the collaborations between C's components. The environment of C defined in M should be consistent with the environment description in M_C. The following two constraints are imposed on the models at different levels.

Constraint (2j) *The set of agents and castes in C's environment described in M must be equal to the set of agents and castes in M_C's environment description. Formally,*

$$\forall n.(n \in Env(M_C) \Leftrightarrow$$
$$\exists \alpha \in Interaction(G).(n = Begin(\alpha) \wedge C = End(\alpha))) \tag{13}$$

where G is the GCD in M.

Constraint (2k) *The interactions that C participates in as an observer described in M must be realized as interactions between environment elements and C's components in M_C. Formally,*

$$\forall \alpha \in Interaction(G). \exists \beta \in Interaction(G_C).$$
$$(End(\alpha) = C \Rightarrow Begin(\alpha) = Begin(\beta)$$
$$\wedge Action(\alpha) = Action(\beta)$$
$$\wedge Begin(\beta) \in Env(G_C)$$
$$\wedge End(\beta) \in Component(G_C)) \tag{14}$$

where G_C is the GCD in M_C and $Component(G_C)$ is the set of C's components depicted in G_C.

4.1.3 Constraints on Behaviour Models

A behaviour model associated to a caste may contain two kinds of diagrams: scenario diagrams (SDs) and behaviour diagrams (BDs). The following well-formedness conditions are imposed on BDs and SDs.

Constraint (3a) *The temporal order between events must be linear, i.e. the in-degree and out-degree of an event node must be less than or equal to 1.*
Constraint (3b) *The logic connective nodes 'AND' and 'OR' are binary operators, and 'NOT' is the unitary operator.*
Constraint (3c) *A transition bar has at most three nodes directly connected to it: at most one scenario (may be a logical combination of several scenario nodes), at most one precondition node and at most one event node.*

Each scenario reference node in a BD refers to a scenario defined in an SD. Therefore, a consistency condition on the relationship between a BD and the SDs in one behaviour model is defined as follows.
Constraint (3d) *The set of scenarios referred to in a BD by using scenario reference nodes is a subset of the scenarios defined by SDs. Formally, let C be a caste, D_C be the behaviour diagram of caste C, and S_C be the set of scenario diagrams of C. Fromally,*

$$\forall n \in ScenarioNode(D_C). \exists S \in S_C.(Name(n) = Name(S)) \tag{15}$$

4.2 Inter-model Consistency

This subsection discusses the consistency between different types of models, namely the inter-model constraints. In the sequel, models are assumed to be consistent with regard to the intra-model constraints defined above.

4.2.1 Consistency Between Collaboration Models and Caste Models

Let CD be the set of collaboration diagrams in a collaboration model, and C the caste model for the system in question.

Constraint (4a) *The set of castes in the collaboration model must be a subset of the castes in the caste model. Formally,*

$$\forall D \in CD. \forall n \in Node(D). \exists n' \in Node(C).(CName(n) = Name(n')) \quad (16)$$

It is possible that a caste in the caste model does not appear in any collaboration diagram. For example, a caste can be an abstract caste, which has no direct instance agent and any instance of the caste is always an instance of its sub-caste. The behaviours of the agents of the abstract caste can be defined by its sub-castes. Consequently, the abstract caste may not occur in any collaboration diagram.

Let CM be the collection of collaboration models of the system. Let x be a caste in the system, and M_x be the collaboration model for x. For models M_A and M_B in CM, we say that M_B is an immediate refinement of model M_A and write $M_B \lhd M_A$, if B is the component caste of caste A. Let $Aggr(C)$ be the set of aggregation relations in the caste model C.

Constraint (4b) *The hierarchical structure of the collaboration models must be consistent with the whole–part relations between castes defined in a caste diagram. Formally,*

$$\forall M_A, M_B \in CM.(M_B \lhd M_A \Rightarrow \exists R \in Aggr(C).(R(B, A))) \quad (17)$$

4.2.2 Consistency Between Behaviour Models and Caste Models

Due to the existence of inheritance relations, some castes may have no explicit behaviour definition. Therefore, we have the following consistency conditions on the relationship between a caste model and the set of behaviour models.

Let BM be the set of behaviour models of a system, and C the caste model. The caste with a behaviour model X defining its behaviour is denoted by $Caste(X)$.

Constraint (4c) *Each behaviour model B in BM defines the behaviour of a caste and the caste must be in the caste model. Formally,*

$$\forall B \in BM. \exists n \in Node(C).(Caste(B) = n) \quad (18)$$

In a behaviour model, say, of caste B, the description of scenarios may refer to the agents in the environment of B. Let $Agents(B)$ be the set of agents referred to in a behaviour model B, and $CasteOf(x)$ the caste of such an agent.

Constraint (4d) *Every agent in a scenario in a behaviour model must have its caste defined in the caste model. Formally,*

$$\forall B \in BM.\exists a \in Agents(B).\exists n \in Node(C).(CasteOf(a) = Name(n)) \quad (19)$$

In a caste model, an agent's change of casteship is described through a migration relation between the castes. In a behaviour model, an agent's change of casteship is defined through actions $JOIN(caste)$, $MOVETO(caste)$ and $QUIT$. Such information in the behaviour model must be consistent with the caste model.

Constraint (4e) *Let BC be the behaviour model for caste C.*

* BC contains an action $JOIN(C')$, where C' is a caste name, if and only if there is a participate migration relation from C to C' in the caste model.
* If BC contains an action $MOVETO(C')$, where C' is a caste name, there must be a migrate relation from C to C' in the caste model.
* If BC contains an action $QUIT$, there must be a migrate relation from C to some caste in the caste model.
* If there is a migrate from C to some caste (say C') in the caste model, there must be either a $MOVETO(C')$ or $QUIT$ action in the behaviour model of C.

By 'an action in a behaviour model', we mean a result action of a behaviour rule, depicted as an action node immediately after a transition bar in a BD.

4.2.3 Consistency Between Collaboration Models and Behaviour Models

Both collaboration models and behaviour models define the behaviour of agents. However, collaboration models define the behaviours of agents from an inter-agent interaction point of view, while behaviour models are from the view of agents' internal activities. Due to the overlap in the information provided by these two types of models, consistency between them is of particular importance.

Let $Components(C)$ be the set of C's component castes.

Let $VisibleActions(C)$ be the set of visible actions of caste C defined in the collaboration model. Let B_X be the behaviour model for caste X, $Rules(B)$ be the set of rules in the behaviour model B, and $Action(r)$ be the result action of the rule r.

Constraint (4f) *Every visible action of caste C defined in the collaboration models must occur in the behaviour model of C or at least one of C's components as a result action. Formally,*

$$\forall a \in VisibleActions(C).$$
$$((\exists r \in Rules(B_C).(a = Action(r))$$
$$\lor(\exists M \in Components(C).\exists r \in Rules(B_M)).(a = Action(r))) \quad (20)$$

Let G be a caste or agent that has a communication link to caste C in the collaboration model. We call G a collaborator of caste C and write $Collaborators(C)$ to denote the set of C's collaborators. Let $Scenarios(B)$ be the set of scenarios used in a behaviour model B, and $Ref(Sc)$ denote the set of castes or agents that a scenario Sc refers to.

Constraint (4g) *For each scenario used in the definition of caste C's behaviour, the agents and/or castes that the scenario refers to must occur in the collaboration model as C's collaborators. Formally,*

$$\forall Sc \in Scenarios(BC).\forall G \in Ref(Sc).(G \in Collaborators(C)) \qquad (21)$$

Notice that an actor in a scenario may be specified with a qualifier, e.g. '$\forall A : CasteX$', and '$\exists Y : CasteX$'. In such cases, the caste $CasteX$ must be a collaborator of caste C. If the actor of a scenario refers to a specific agent, i.e. in the form of '$AgentM : CasteX$', the agent $AgentM$ of caste $CasteX$ must be a collaborator.

Constraint (4h) *The agents and castes referred to in a scenario must be elements in the environment of the caste described by the collaboration model. Formally, let C be the caste described by a behaviour model B. Formally,*

$$\forall Sc \in Scenarios(B).\forall G \in Ref(Sc).(G \in Env(C)) \qquad (22)$$

where $Env(X)$ is the set of castes and agents in X's environment description.

The collaboration between an agent A of caste C and other agents may be realized through the collaboration of A's component agents. Therefore, we do not require all collaborators of caste C to be referred to in the definition of caste C's behaviour.

Let $p_1, p_2, \ldots, p_n$ be the sequence of actions of a caste C (or an agent of caste C) described in a scenario Sc. Each p_i, $i = 1, 2, \ldots, n$, is called a referred action of caste C in scenario Sc. We write $ReferredActions(C, Sc)$ to denote the set of all such actions.

Constraint (4i) *Every referred action in a scenario used in a behaviour diagram must be a visible action of the caste described by the scenario. Formally,*

$$\forall Sc \in Scenarios(BC).\forall a \in ReferredActions(C, Sc).$$
$$(a \in VisibleActions(C)) \qquad (23)$$

It is not required that all visible actions of a collaborator should be referred to in the definition of a caste's behaviour, because the collaboration may be realized through component agents.

4.3 Discussion

Consistency conditions can play at least two important roles in model-driven development. First, consistency conditions serve as check points for quality assurance in the modelling process. Violation of consistency conditions indicates the existence of contradictions in the model. Therefore, automatic consistency checks can help engineers to detect errors at the modelling stage, hence prevent errors from being propagated to later stages. Inconsistency may also be caused by conflict in requirements. Consistency checks on requirement models help to identify and thereafter to resolve and manage such conflict. Second, in model-driven development of software systems, it is desirable to transform automatically one model to another model (maybe partial model), and to generate code (or code framework) from models. Design and implementation of such tools must ensure that the transformation rules preserve the models' meanings. Therefore, consistency between the original and the resultant must be guaranteed. Consistency conditions provide a means to specify formally the correctness of the transformation rules.

The consistency constraints defined above have been used for both of the above purposes in the implementation of the CAMLE environment [234]. The consistency constraints defined in this chapter are computable and have been directly implemented in the environment as consistency check tools. Diagnostic information as the result of the check is recorded to help users to locate and correct errors. The partial diagram generator in the environment generates partial models (incomplete diagrams) from existing diagrams to help model construction. The rules to generate partial models are based on the consistency constraints so that the generated partial diagrams are consistent with existing ones. Preliminary case studies show that both consistency check and partial model generation are very helpful to improve the quality of models and software engineers' productivity. Besides model construction and consistency check, another main function of the CAMLE environment is to transform graphic models automatically into the formal specifications in SLABS. Consistency check also simplifies the implementation of the automatic transformation because less error processing is required.

Well-defined visual notations for modelling software systems' structures and behaviours have the advantages of readability and preciseness due to their semi-formal nature. A common feature of such visual notations is that multiple views are utilized to model a system's different aspects and/or at different levels of abstraction. Since different views emphasize different aspects of a system or different levels of abstraction, consistency between the views has become a serious problem in the development of models. It is a crucial quality attribute of software models. It is widely recognised as very desirable to check automatically the consistency of software models [463, 265]. However, due to the semi-formal nature of modelling languages, the definition of effective and computable consistency constraints is a difficult and non-trivial problem [297]. Most existing modelling languages, e.g. UML, have no explicitly defined consistency constraints.

The past few years has seen a rapid increase in the research on defining consistency conditions and implementing consistency check tools for modelling languages, especially for UML [342, 19, 341, 21]. Among the related works on consistency check, Xlinkit is a flexible tool for checking the consistency of distributed heterogeneous documents [298]. It comprises a language for expressing constraints between such documents, a document management mechanism and an engine that checks the documents against the constraints. In comparison with Xlinkit, our approach is language specific. The direct implementation of consistency constraints as a part of the modelling environment is highly efficient and effective in detecting errors. In addition, the explicitly defined constraints form a base for automatic transformations between models. Formal methods, such as model checking, have also been used for checking the consistency between multiple views of software specifications, e.g. in [220, 374]. It requires translating models into a formal notation as the input to a model checker, while assuming that syntactic errors have been removed before the translation. Therefore, to check consistency before translation is still necessary.

5 Automatic Generation of Formal Specifications

As shown in the previous sections, graphic models in the CAMLE notation are suitable for the representation of users' requirements. To develop MAS further in a modular way in which castes are used as the templates of agents and the basic organizational units of software systems, it is desirable to specify MAS with modularity. That is, all information required to design and implement a caste should be specified in one module, but nothing more. However, in the CAMLE language, the information about a caste is scattered over various diagrams. This section presents the rules and algorithms that transform models in CAMLE to formal specifications in SLABS, which provide modular specifications of MAS.

5.1 The Specification Language SLABS

SLABS is a model-based specification language with the conceptual model described in Sect. 2 as its meta-model [468, 470].

A formal specification in SLABS consists of a set of descriptions of castes. Figure 13 shows the structure of the description of a caste in SLABS. The clause '$C \Leftarrow C_1, C_2, \ldots, C_n$' specifies that caste C inherits the structure, behaviour and environment descriptions of existing castes $C_1, C_2, \ldots, C_n$. The environment description explicitly specifies a subset of the agents in the system that may affect the agent's behaviour. The state space of an agent is described by a set of variables with keyword VAR. The set of actions is described by a set of identifiers with keyword ACTION.

A behaviour rule has the following structure:

$BehaviourRule ::=$
$\quad [\langle RuleName \rangle] Pattern[Prob] \rightarrow Event, [\textbf{if } Scenario][\textbf{where } PreCond];$

A pattern describes the behaviour of an agent by a sequence of observable state changes and actions. In addition to the pattern of individual agents' behaviour, SLABS also provides the facility of scenario to describe the global situation of the whole system. Informally, a scenario is a set of typical combinations of the behaviours of related agents in the system. The syntax of scenarios is given below:

$Scenario ::= AgentName : Pattern \mid AtomicPredicate$
$\quad \mid \exists_{[ArithmeticExp]} AgentVar \in CasteName : Pattern$

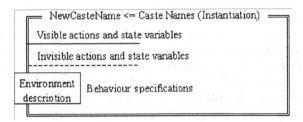

Fig. 13. Caste descriptions in SLABS

$\quad | \ \forall AgentVar \in CasteName : Pattern$
$\quad | \ Scenario \& Scenario | Scenario \vee Scenario | \ Scenario$
$Pattern ::= [\{ Event[\ \| \ Constraint]/, \}]$
$Event ::= [TimeStamp :][Action][!StateAssertion]$
$Action ::= AtomicPattern[^\wedge ArithmeticExp]$
$AtomicPattern ::= \$ \ |\sim| \ ActionVariable$
$\quad | \ ActionIdentifier[(\{ArithmeticExp\})]$
$TimeStamp ::= ArithmeticExp$

An informal definition of the semantics of various forms of scenarios and patterns is given in Table 1. The following are some examples of scenarios:

$$\exists p \in Parties : t2004 : [Nominate(Bush)] \ \| \ t2004 = (March/2004) \quad (24)$$

This describes the situation that at least one agent in the caste called Parties took the action $Nominate(Bush)$ at the time of March 2004.

$$(\mu x \in Voter : [vote(Bush)] > \mu x \in Voter : [vote(Kerry)]) \quad (25)$$

This describes the situation that there are more agents in the caste Voter who took the action of $vote(Bush)$ than those in the caste who took the action of $vote(Kerry)$.

An important feature of the formal specification language SLABS is that it provides a modular specification of MAS in which each caste is specified by one caste description. Each caste description contains all necessary information about one caste but nothing more. The analysis, design and implementation of a caste can be based on the caste description without referring to other units. The modular specifications in SLABS are composable and reusable [467]. Therefore, it is more suitable to be used for further development of MAS than graphic models where the specification of a caste is spread over a number of diagrams due to the multiple view principle.

5.2 The Overall Transformation Algorithm

The following algorithm translates each caste in a CAMLE model into a caste description in SLABS. Various parts of caste description are generated according to the information spread in various models. In the sequel, we assume that graphic models

Table 1. Semantics of scenario descriptions

Pattern/Scenario	Meaning
$\$$	The wild card; it matches with all actions
$\sim$	The silence event
Action variable	matches an action
$P^{\wedge}k$	A sequence of k events that match pattern P
$Action(a_1, \ldots, a_k)$	An action takes place with parameters that match $(a_1, \ldots, a_k)$
$!Predicate$	The state of the agent satisfies the $Predicate$
$[p_1, \ldots, p_n]$	The previous sequence of events matches the patterns $p_1, \ldots, p_n$
$A : P$	Agent A's behaviour matches pattern P
$\forall X \in C : P$	The behaviours of all agents in caste C match pattern P
$\exists_{[m]} X \in C : P$	There are at least m agents in caste C whose behaviour matches pattern P. The default value of m is 1
$\mu X \in C : P$	The number of agents in caste C whose behaviour matches P
$S_1 \wedge S_2$	Both scenario S_1 and scenario S_2 are true
$S_1 \vee S_2$	Either scenario S_1 or scenario S_2 or both are true
$\sim S$	Scenario S is not true

are consistent with regards to the consistency constraints defined in Sect. 4.

ALGORITHM 1. {Overall}

```
INPUT: ⟨CM, CLM, BM⟩, /* CM is a caste model,
                       /* CLM is a collaboration model, and
                       /* BM is a behaviour model
OUTPUT: {C_i}_{i∈I}, /* C_i is a caste description, i ∈ I.
BEGIN
      FOR each node N in caste model CM DO
      BEGIN /* Generate a caste description with caste name N
      /* Step 1: Generate inheritance clause
      IF there is an inheritance arrow from node N to node A in CM,
      THEN A ∈ Ancestors(N);
       /* Step 2: Generate environment description
      IF there is an arrow from node X to node N in a CD in CLM
      THEN
          CASE X OF
          X is an agent node with label 'A : CasteName':
              'A : CasteName' ∈ Environment(N)
          X is a caste node with label 'CasteName':
              'All : CasteName' ∈ Environment(N)
          END_CASE;
      /* Step 3: Generate visible actions and variables
      FOR each collaboration model CD in CLM that contains N
      DO IF there is an arrow from N to X with 'Action' annotated
                on the arrow
          THEN 'Action' ∈ VisibleAction(N);
```

```
END_FOR;
/* Step 4: Generate invisible actions and variables
FOR each collaboration diagram of caste N
DO IF there is an arrow from caste N to a component node X
          with 'Action' annotated on the arrow
     THEN 'Action' ∈ InvisibleAction(N);
END_FOR;
/* Step 5: Generate behaviour rules
GenerateBehaviourRule(BM_N),
     /* BM_N is the behaviour model of caste N.
  END_FOR
END_ALGORITHM
```

The generation of castes' behaviour rules is more complex compared with other parts of caste's structure. It is discussed in the next subsection.

5.3 Generation of Behaviour Descriptions

Generation of a caste's behaviour description from a behaviour diagram consists of two main steps. The first is to recognize the rules in a network of interconnected nodes in the diagram. The second is to generate a behaviour rule in SLABS syntax from each rule recognized in the first step. The algorithm is as follows:

```
ALGORITHM 2. {Generate Behaviour Rules};
    INPUT: BM_N /* a behaviour model for caste N
    OUTPUT: R = {r_i}_{i∈I},
                 /* a set of behaviour rules in SLABS syntax for caste N
    VARIABLE: P = {p_i}_{i∈I}, /* a set of rules recognized from BM_N
    BEGIN
        P := RecogniseRules(BM_N);
        FOR each p_i in P DO r_i := TranslateRule(p_i) END_FOR
END_ALGORITHM
```

5.3.1 Recognition of Behaviour Rules

In a behaviour diagram, several behaviour rules may be depicted independently or interconnected. The recognition of behaviour rules is achieved through an analysis of the diagram's structure. It converts a diagram into a set of graphically unconnected rules. Figure 14 shows the structure of rules.

When a behaviour diagram contains several interconnected behaviour rules such as in Fig. 15, the number of transition bars in the diagram determines the number of rules contained in the diagram. For example, three rules can be recognized from the behaviour diagram given in Fig. 12. The recognition algorithm uses the transition bars in the diagram as boundaries between various rules. For instance, in Fig. 15 the sequence of event nodes between the first and the second transition bar are the first rule's result events. They are also the second rule's pre-events. Generally, the event nodes on the path from transition bar T_1 to transition bar T_2 are result events of the rule corresponding to T_1. They are also the pattern of the rule corresponding to T_2.

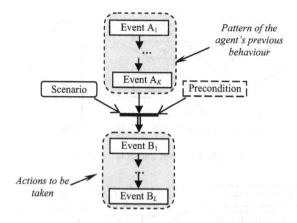

Fig. 14. Structure of behaviour rule in behaviour diagrams

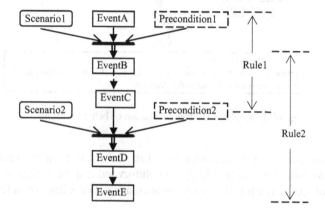

Fig. 15. Recognition of rules in behaviour diagrams

5.3.2 Translation of Rules into SLABS Format

As shown in Fig. 16, a behaviour rule defines the cause and effect of an agent's behaviour through five parts: (a) a scenario that describes the situation in the environment, (b) a pattern that describes the agent's own previous behaviour, (c) a precondition on the agent's internal state, (d) a sequence of resulting events that specifies
the actions to be taken, and (e) a transition bar that links these parts together. The
first three parts, which are connected to the transition bar through logical and temporal links, constitute the premise of a rule to define 'when to go'. The transition
bar is connected to one or a sequence of event nodes, which indicates 'what to do'.
Figure 16 gives the rule for transforming a behaviour rule in diagrammatic notation
to SLABS syntax. Figure 17 shows a typical behaviour rule, which governs UN-SC
member's behaviour in a voting process, and its equivalent form in SLABS syntax.

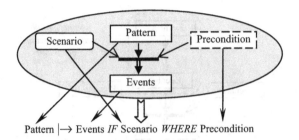

Pattern $\mapsto$ Events *IF* Scenario *WHERE* Precondition

Fig. 16. Top-level transformation rule

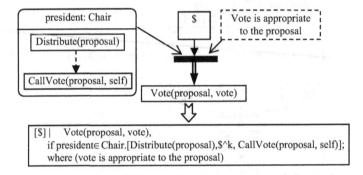

[$] | Vote(proposal, vote),
   if president∈ Chair.[Distribute(proposal),$^k, CallVote(proposal, self)];
   where (vote is appropriate to the proposal)

Fig. 17. Example of the transformation of behaviour rules

The translation of the precondition of a behaviour rule from the precondition node in the behaviour diagram is fairly straightforward and the details are omitted for the sake of space. The translation of scenarios and patterns deserves a few words.

5.3.3 Transformation Rules for Behaviour Patterns

In a behaviour diagram, a pattern as a list of events in a behaviour rule is depicted as a set of action nodes or state nodes connected by temporal links. Therefore, the formal specification of a pattern can be derived as a combination of the specifications of the events. Figure 18 illustrates some of the transformation rules for various kinds of nodes and links.

5.3.4 Transformation Rules for Scenarios

A scenario description node consists of three parts: the scenario name, a set of swimming lanes and a logical connective network comprising logical connective nodes and links which connect the set of swimming lanes. Figure 19 shows the transformation rule for swimming lanes, where Qu is a qualifier $\forall$ or $\exists$.

Figure 20 shows the formal specification generated by the CAMLE tools from the behaviour diagram given in Fig. 12.

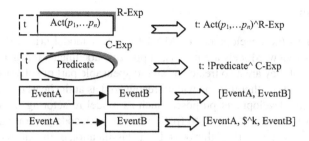

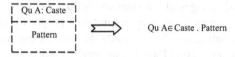

Fig. 18. Transformation rules for nodes and links

Qu A: Caste

Pattern ⟹ Qu A∈ Caste . Pattern

Fig. 19. Transformation rule for pattern nodes

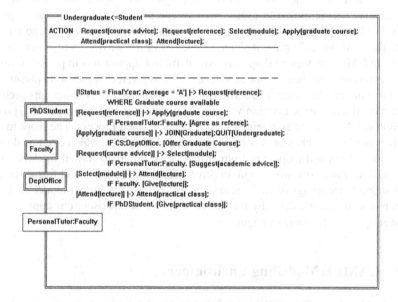

Fig. 20. An example of an automatically generated formal specification

5.4 Discussion

Our approach to the development of MAS follows a model-driven development (MDD) point of view. Models are not just supportive documents for facilitating implementation, but they are also treated as an indispensable part of software artefacts. Model transformation, therefore, is widely recognized as at the heart of MDD. It can serve for various development purposes, such as model refactoring (p. 199 of this book), PIM-to-PIM and PIM-to-PSM (p. 91 of this book), code generation (p. 237 of this book), etc.; see e.g. p. 19 of this book for a classification of the kinds of transformations that can be performed during MDD activities. Different to the above works, our purpose of transformation from CAMLE models to SLABS formal specification is for combining the advantages of informal and formal methods.

In the software engineering literature, a number of proposals have been advanced to combine graphic notation and formal methods, such as the employment of dual languages and method integration [86]. In our previous work, an automated tool was developed to translate structured models of software requirements definitions into Z [235]. A flexible framework to define mappings from graphic models to formal specifications was proposed in [338]. A prototype program to convert an adapted form of UML class diagrams into specifications in the B language was reported in [399]. The work in [267] presented some schemes of the derivation of B specifications from UML behavioural diagrams. An alternative approach is to project formal specifications back to diagrammatic models. For example, techniques were presented in [86] to transform the integrated formalism to UML diagrams. Another approach is to combine diagrammatic notation with formal notation in one language: [213] discussed how UML can be augmented with Z in the Unified Process. The work most closely related to this chapter is perhaps that reported in [338], which employed two languages and defined mappings from front-end notations to formal models. The customizable framework works with different front-end notations and formal models. It supports mappings of analysis results obtained on the formal model back to the front-end notation chosen by the practitioners. In comparison, our approach is language specific, but more efficient.

6 The CAMLE Modelling Environment

Modelling environments containing automated tools can play a significant role in MDD as discussed on p. 139 of this book and demonstrated on pp. 289, 35, 199, 329 and 237 of this book for the tools that support various MDD activities. This section gives a brief description of our automated modelling environment.

6.1 The Overall Architecture

A software environment to support the process of system analysis and modelling in CAMLE has been designed and implemented. The main functionalities of the environment are:

(1) *Model construction.* This consists of a set of graphical editors to support the construction of models and tools for version control and configuration management.
(2) *Model consistency check.* This checks if a model satisfies the consistency constraints defined in Sect. 4.
(3) *Automated generation of formal specifications.* This provides the function of transforming graphic models into the corresponding formal specifications in SLABS.

Figure 21 shows the architecture of the environment.

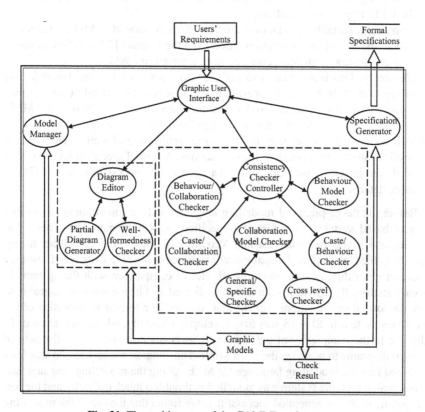

Fig. 21. The architecture of the CAMLE environment

In addition to the consistency checker and formal specification generator that have been discussed in detail in Sect. 4 and 5, respectively, the diagram editor supports the manual editing of models through a graphic user interface. The well-formedness checker ensures that the user-entered models are well formed. The diagram generator can generate partial models (incomplete diagrams) from existing diagrams to help users in model construction. The rules to generate partial models are based on the consistency constraints so that the generated partial diagrams are consistent with existing ones according to the consistency conditions.

6.2 Case Studies

A number of systems have been modelled in CAMLE and their formal specifications in SLABS generated as the case studies of the modelling language and its modelling environment. The following are these systems:

(1) *United Nations' Security Council.* The organizational structure and the work procedure to pass resolutions were modelled and a formal specification of the system in SLABS was generated. Details of the case study as well as modelling in other agent-oriented modelling notations can be found on AUML's website at the URL: http://www.auml.org/.

(2) *Amalthaea.* Amalthaea is an evolutionary MAS developed at MIT's Media Lab to help the users to retrieve information from the Internet [295]. A formal specification of the system was generated from a model in CAMLE.

(3) *University.* This is a partial model of the university organization. The objective of the case study was not to provide a complete model; instead, it aims at providing illustrative examples to demonstrate the style of modelling in CAMLE. Examples given in this chapter were taken from this case study.

(4) *Web services.* The case study modelled the architecture of web services and an application of web services on online auctions. A formal specification in SLABS of the architecture and application was generated successfully. See [472] for more details.

Before the development of modelling language and the environment, a number of agent-based systems were formally specified in SLABS manually. These systems include Maes' personal assistant Maxims [283, 468], the speech-act theory [396, 397, 468], a simplified communication protocol [467], a distributed resource allocation algorithm, an ant colony [468], etc. In comparison with the systems in the case studies, these systems are less complicated and hence more manageable to write the formal specifications without tool support. The formal specification of the Amalthaea system in SLABS was first developed manually, which met much difficulty due to the complexity of the system. It was only completed with the help of informal diagrams to organize the ideas [469]. This diagrammatic notation was later developed into the modelling language CAMLE. Using the modelling language and the automated tool, the system was modelled without too much difficulty and the formal specification was generated successfully. We found that the use of the modelling language was very helpful. It is much more efficient to develop formal specifications through modelling with the help of automated tools than manual approaches; especially, the automated consistency checking facility helped to remove syntax errors in the models. In the case studies, we found that the CAMLE language was highly expressive to model information systems' organisational structures, dynamic information processing procedures, individual decision making processes, and so on. The models in CAMLE were easy to understand because they naturally represent real-world systems.

7 Conclusion

In this chapter, we proposed a model-driven approach to the development of MAS. It combines graphical models with formal specifications through the employment of automated tools. It is based on a common meta-model of MAS, which is independent of implementation platforms and applicable to all types of agent theories and techniques. A modelling language CAMLE was introduced and an automated modelling environment was reported. We addressed two important issues in model-driven software development of MAS. The first was the consistency problem of the models with multiple view representations. We formally defined consistency constraints as a set of computable rules and implemented them as automated consistency checkers. The second was the automation problem in model-based development. An automated specification generator was designed and implemented to transform graphic models into formal specifications. While graphic models containing a number of diagrams in various views and at different levels of abstraction are more suitable to the representation and understanding of users' requirements involving various stakeholders, modular formal specifications are more suitable to be used by software engineers as the bases for further design and implementation of the specified system. The automated specification generator bridges the gap between them. Case studies show that the approach is effective and efficient for the development of MASs, especially at the requirements analysis and specification and system design stages.

We are further investigating language facilities that directly support efficient implementations of MASs and the techniques that enable graphic models and formal specifications to be automatically transformed into executable code.

8 Acknowledgements

The work reported in this chapter is partly supported by China High-Technology Programme (863) under the Grant 2002AA116070. The authors are grateful to colleagues at FIPA's Modelling Technical Committee for the invaluable discussions on various issues related to modelling multi-agent systems via emails and at meetings. The authors would also like to thank colleagues at the Department of Computing of Oxford Brookes University, especially Prof. David Duce, Mr David Lightfoot and other members of the Applied Formal Method Research Group and the Computer, Agent and People Research Group.

Using Graph Transformation for Practical Model-Driven Software Engineering

Lars Grunske[1], Leif Geiger[2], Albert Zündorf[2], Niels Van Eetvelde[3],
Pieter Van Gorp[3], and Dániel Varró[4]

[1] School of Information Technology and Electrical Engineering, University of Queensland,
Brisbane, QLD 4072, Australia
grunske@itee.uq.edu.au
[2] Department of Computer Science and Electrical Engineering, University of Kassel,
Wilhelmshöher Allee 73, 34121 Kassel, Germany
leif.geiger|albert.zuendorf@uni-kassel.de
[3] University of Antwerp, Middelheimlaan 1, 2020 Antwerpen, Belgium
niels.vaneetvelde|pieter.vangorp@ua.ac.be
[4] Department of Measurement and Information Systems, Budapest University of
Technology and Economics, H-1117, Budapest, Magyar tudósok krt. 2, Hungary
varro@mit.bme.hu

Summary. Model transformations are one of the core technologies needed to apply OMG's model-driven engineering concept for the construction of real-world systems. Several formalisms are currently proposed for the specification of these model transformations. A suitable formalism is based on graph transformation systems and graph transformation rules. The chapter provides an overview about the needed concepts to apply graph transformations in the context of model driven engineering and we show the technical feasibility based on several tools and applications.

1 Introduction

Model-driven engineering (MDE) is a software engineering approach that promotes the usage of models and transformations as primary artifacts. The Object Management Group (OMG) [306] proposed the Model-Driven Architecture (MDA) as a set of standards for integrating MDE tools. These standards focus on the usage of Platform Independent Models (PIMs), which help to develop software on a higher level of abstraction by hiding platform specific details. Thus they solve some of the problems that are caused by the ever-increasing complexity of software systems. For further reduction of complexity PIMs can be modeled with several viewpoints (e.g., structure models, behaviour models, quality assurance models, test cases), in order to focus on particular concerns within the system separately.

For the construction and evolution of these viewpoint models, it is necessary to ensure consistency between the different models. To enable this consistency, model transformations are used to update all other viewpoint models in case one model has been changed. Furthermore, model transformations can help to construct a new viewpoint model based on the existing models. All these model transformations are PIM-to-PIM transformations or model-to-model transformations, which can also be called horizontal transformations, because they are used to transform models on the same level of abstraction. To execute the PIM on the target platform, a Platform Specific Model (PSM) must be generated. This generation also needs appropriate model transformations that enrich the PIM with platform specific details. These model transformations are vertical transformations, respectively called as PIM-to-PSM transformations.

To conclude this, model transformation is the heart and soul of model driven software engineering [388]. To standardize these model transformations the OMG recently announced a request for proposals (RFP MOF 2.0 Query/Views/Transformation) [165], which includes requirements for the transformational language. This transformation language and the underlying formalism should provide the following characteristics:

(1) The formalism should support the specification of horizontal and vertical model transformations.
(2) The formalism should enable the automatic application of the model transformation rules.
(3) The transformation rules should be easy to understand.
(4) The transformation rules should be adaptable and reusable.

Based on these requirements, we propose to use graph transformations to specify and apply model transformations in MDE. The reasons for this are: (a) graphs are a natural representation for models, since most modeling languages are formalized by a visual abstract syntax definition, (b) graph transformations provide a formal theory and some established formalisms for the automatic application, (c) we believe that graph transformation rules can be easily and intuitively specified (unfortunately there are currently no empirical studies to prove this) and (d) the complexity of the graph transformation rules and the application formalisms can be hidden for the end user.

This chapter is structured as follows. Section 2 summarizes the theoretical background of graphs and graph transformations. Furthermore, alternative approaches are discussed. In Sect. 3 and 4 the state-of-the-art graph transformation tools are described to illustrate their applicability for horizontal and vertical model transformation. In Sect. 5 it is shown how the correctness of the applied graph transformations can be verified. Finally, conclusions are drawn and directions for future work are discussed.

2 A Basic Introduction to the Graph Transformation Concepts

In this section, we introduce the basics of graph-based structures. Furthermore, we describe the fundamental graph transformation theory and give an overview of useful graph transformation variants that can be used to specify model transformations.

2.1 Directed Typed Graphs and Graph Morphisms

We choose directed typed graphs as the basic structure for graph-based model transformations, because they are well suited for specifying different types of models [29]. These graphs contain nodes and edges, which are instances of node and edge types. The instance relation between the nodes and edges and their types is similar to the relation between objects and classes in object-oriented software engineering. Due to this, a node or edge type can contain a set of application specific attributes and operations. To model the graph-based structure each edge is associated to a source and a target node. Formally, a typed graph can be defined as follows:

Definition 1 (Directed Typed Graphs). Let L_V be a set of node types and L_E be a set of edge types; then a directed typed graph G from the possible set of graphs $\mathcal{G}$ over L_V and L_E is characterized by the tuple $\langle V, E, source, target, type \rangle$, with two finite sets V and E of nodes (or vertices) and edges, a function $type : V \rightarrow L_V \cup E \rightarrow L_E$ which assigns a type to each edge and node and two functions $source : E \rightarrow V$ and $target : E \rightarrow V$ that assign to each edge a source and a target node.

Another preliminary for the definition of graph transformation systems is graph morphisms. These graph morphisms are structure and type-preserving mappings between two graphs, which can be defined as follows:

Definition 2 (Graph Morphism). Let $G = \langle V, E, source, target, type \rangle$ and $G' = \langle V', E', source', target', type' \rangle$ be two graphs; then a graph morphism $m : G \rightarrow G'$ consists of a pair of mappings $\langle m_V, m_E \rangle$, with $m_V : V \rightarrow V'$ and $m_E : E \rightarrow E'$, which satisfy the following conditions:

- $\forall e \in E : type'(m_E(e)) = type(e)$
- $\forall v \in V : type'(m_V(v)) = type(v)$

If both mappings $m_V : V \rightarrow V'$ and $m_E : E \rightarrow E'$ are injective (surjective, bijective) then the mapping $m : G \rightarrow G'$ is injective (surjective, bijective).

2.2 Graph Variants

In addition to the introduced directed typed graphs, several other variants have been proposed in the graph transformation community. One basic variant uses undirected edges. These undirected edges can be modeled in a directed graph with two contrary edges for each undirected edge. Another variant are hypergraphs [181], where each edge is associated to a sequence of source and target node. Due to this, these edges are also called hyperedges. For the construction of hierarchical models, hierarchical graphs are important. These hierarchical graphs model the hierarchical structure ether by (hyper)edge [91] or node [352] refinement.

2.3 Graph Transformation and Graph Transformation Systems

Basic Principles

Graph transformation systems make use of graph rewriting techniques to manipulate graphs. A graph transformation system is defined with a set of graph production rules, where a production rule consists of a left-hand side (LHS) graph and a right-hand side (RHS) graph. Such rules are the graph equivalent of term rewriting rules, i.e., intuitively, if the LHS graph is matched in the source graph, it is replaced by the RHS graph. Formally, a graph transformation rule can be defined as follows:

Definition 3 (Graph Transformation Rule). A graph transformation rule $p = \langle G_{LHS}, G_{RHS} \rangle$ consists of two directed typed graphs G_{LHS} und G_{RHS} which are called the left-hand side and right-hand side of p. Furthermore the graph G_I is an interface graph, satisfying $G_I \subseteq G_{LHS}$ and $G_I \subseteq G_{RHS}$.

For the application of a graph transformation rule to an application graph G_{APP} the following simplified algorithm can be used, which contains the following steps:

(1) Identify the LHS G_{LHS} within the application graph G_{APP}. For this, it is necessary to find a total graph morphism $m : G_{LHS} \to G_{APP}$ that matches the LHS G_{LHS} in the application graph G_{APP}.
(2) Delete all corresponding graph elements, w.r.t m, in the application graph G_{APP} that are part of the LHS G_{LHS} and are not part of the interface graph G_I.
(3) Create a graph element in the application graph G_{APP} for each graph element that is part of the RHS G_{RHS} and is not part of the interface graph G_I. Connect or glue these added graph elements to the rest of the application graph G_{APP}.

For a formal description of the rule application formalisms, we refer to [74, 108], where the formal foundations of the single pushout (SPO) and double pushout (DPO) approach are reviewed. Currently these approaches have the most impact in the graph transformation community.

Application Conditions

In graph transformation systems with a large number of graph transformation rules it is often necessary to restrict the application of single rules. Therefore, in [182] the concept of positive and negative application conditions (PACs and NACs) are introduced. These application conditions are formally graphs that define a required context (i.e., the presence of some nodes or edges) or a forbidden context (i.e., the absence of some nodes or edges). The fulfillment of these application conditions must be checked before the rule is applied. Therefore, the presented algorithm must be extended with an additional step between the first and the second step that checks the application conditions. With the introduction of application conditions graph transformation rules become conditional productions, which enhances the expressiveness of the graph transformation system (especially if NACs are used) [182].

Specification of a Graph Transformation Rule

In traditional approaches for specification of graph transformation rules, the RHS and the LHS of a rule are drawn separately. Throughout this chapter, the notation of story diagrams [475] is used, which combines both sides. Story diagrams use UML collaboration diagrams to model graph transformation, cf. [126, 476]. Consequently, nodes become objects and edges become links between objects. Objects and links in such collaboration diagrams marked with the ≪*destroy*≫ stereotype appear only on the LHS of the corresponding graph transformation, i.e., they are deleted. The stereotype ≪*create*≫ marks elements only used on the RHS, i.e., such elements are created. Objects and links that have no stereotypes appear on both sides of the graph transformation rule (see Fig. 1).

Story diagrams use programmed graph transformation rules. Due to this, a control structure can be specified that manages the order of the execution of transformation rules. Such a control structure is modeled using UML activity diagrams. The transformation rules are then embedded into the activities.

Story diagrams use typed graphs. Graph schemata are modeled using UML class diagrams (see Fig. 2 below). In graph transformations, the type is specified after the object name separated by a colon. By omitting the type, bound objects are marked. Bound objects are objects that are already known to the system either from previous matchings or because they are passed as parameters to the transformation rule (as done for the object *afterElem* in Fig. 1). Thus, a bound object does not compute a new match but it reuses its old match.

More elaborate elements of graph transformations, like negative application conditions, multi-objects, non-injective matching, are also supported by the story diagram language. Some of these features will be discussed in Sect. 3.

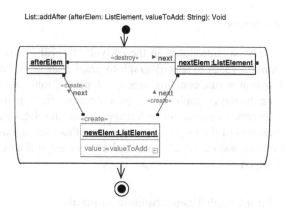

Fig. 1. Graph transformation "Fujaba-style"

The rule shown in Fig. 1 models the behavior of the *addAfter* method of a class emphList. This method simply adds a new String value (passed as parameter *value-*

ToAdd) into a list after a given element (passed as *afterElem*). This method consists only of one activity; that means only one transformation rule. The pattern matching starts with the bound *afterElem* node. From this node, an edged labeled *next* to a node of type *ListElement* is searched. If such an edge is found, the targeting node is called *nextElem*. Having found such a node, the pattern matching is completed and the changes can be executed. First the *next* edge between *afterElem* and *nextElem* is deleted. After that a new node *newElem* is created and its *value* attribute is set to the passed *valueToAdd* parameter. Then two new *next* edges connecting this node with the other two nodes are created. After that, the rule is completed and the method is left.

2.4 Graph Transformation Variants

In this section we briefly introduce two alternative approaches that are suitable to specify model transformations as presented in the following sections. These approaches are pair grammars [352] and triple graph grammars [382].

Pair Graph Grammars

Pair grammars and pair grammar rules were introduced by Pratt [352] in the early 1970s to specify graph-to-string translations. A pair grammar rule rewrites two models: a source graph and a target string. Thus it contains a pair of production rules (a graph and a string production rule), which modify simultaneously the two participating models. Based on this, pair grammars are well suited to specify transformations between graphs and strings. If the string production rule is substituted by a graph production rule, pair grammars can be used for graph-to-graph translations.

Triple Graph Grammars

Triple graph grammars, as introduced in the early 1990s [382], are an extension of pair graph grammars [352] to specify graph-to-graph translations and evolution. Each triple graph grammar rule contains three graph productions: one operates on a source graph, one on the target graph and one on a correspondence graph. This correspondence graph describes a graph-to-graph mapping, which relates elements of the source graph to elements of the target graph. Based on this mapping an incremental change propagation is possible, which updates the target graph if an element in the source graph is changed.

2.5 Alternatives for a Graph Transformation Approach

Gerber et al. provide a good overview of mainstream transformation approaches [147]:

- One alternative for graph transformation, developed by the OMG, would be the Common Warehouse Metamodel (CWM) specification [344], which provides concepts for *black-box* and *white-box* transformation specifications. Still, fine-grained graph transformations can complement these CWM concepts. CWM white-box specifications leave the actual production of target model elements from source model elements unspecified in a string of source code that can be implemented in any programming language. CWM black-box transformations are even more abstract.

- XSLT [460] has become a popular alternative for describing model transformations. Peltier et al. [347] propose to consider metamodels as models: they use MOF [312] as the metamodel of such models and use XMI [170] to serialize their instances. An XSLT specification is also an XML document, describing a transformation using both declarative and imperative constructs. Gerber et al. found that the verbosity of the XML syntax leaded to specifications that were difficult to read and to maintain.

- Text-based tools like perl and awk are also useful but only for simple transformations, because they cannot cope with the abstract syntax of models.

- Their own tool, GenGen, describes transformation rules as instances of a CWM-inspired metamodel. The rules are implemented by transforming them to Java code which can then manipulate models in MOF repositories. It is a rather procedural transformation language, and therefore, although powerful, lacks the capabilities like unification from declarative languages.

- The Mercury programming language [402], in contrast, is a purely declarative, strongly typed logic language and offers these pattern matching features. This leads to rules that are more compact and easier to understand. However, the main problem experienced with this approach is that it is necessary, and hard, to capture the semantics of the source and target models using the language type system.

- Finally, F-Logic [254] is a complete formal model for deductive object-oriented languages. It offers a flexible and compact syntax for defining rules that can be interpreted at both the model and instance levels, and does not suffer from the restrictions of the Mercury language.

The authors describe their attempt to map an EDOC Business Process [172] model to the Breeze Workflow [93] model, using both the declarative and procedural approaches. From their experiment the authors derive a set of both functional and usability requirements, needed to model mapping rules. They conclude that a declarative approach is preferred, due to the simpler semantic model required to understand the transformation rules, but acknowledge that for certain types of transformations a procedural specification may remain necessary.

Küster et al. performed an initial comparison between a graph transformation approach and a relational approach to model transformation [264]. Using the translation of statecharts to CSP as a benchmark for comparing the Consistency Workbench [112] to the QVT-Merge proposal [165], the authors concluded that both approaches were similar regarding the matching of patterns in a host model. Therefore, the new relational approach can build upon the insights of efficient model matching as discussed by Dorr [87], Vizhanyo et al. [448] and Varró et. al. [440].

From a consistency maintenance viewpoint, the relational approach is currently more generic than graph transformation since the former provides a framework to automatically keep the related source and target models synchronized. Graph transformation theory needs to be extended with the notions of consistency contracts and traceability links to support such incremental updates. Consistency contracts can be described declaratively in OCL while the graph transformation approach described in Sect. 3.2 can be used to establish and maintain the contracts [432]. Initial ideas on graph transformation with incremental updates are discussed by Varró [441].

On the other hand, from a model analysis viewpoint, graph transformation has clear advantages. In such cases, the transformation should describe either a complex computation (e.g., flattening hierarchical statecharts' concurrent regions into flat statecharts) or powerful abstractions need to be performed to avoid state space explosion (thus the descriptive power of source and target languages is very different). Declarative (relational) approaches have not yet proved their practical feasibility in these areas.

3 Graph Transformations for Vertical Model Transformation

Vertical transformations are transformations towards PSMs and towards a specific model implementation. Generally, vertical transformations may use the same techniques as horizontal transformations just for a different purpose. Only some aspects, e.g., code generation, require additional concepts.

3.1 The Fujaba Approach

Our approach uses the Fujaba project and tool set developed at the University of Paderborn [475]. Fujaba is a graph-based tool which uses the Unified Modeling Language UML for design and realization of software projects. Fujaba uses UML class diagrams for the specification of graph schemata. As mentioned earlier, it uses a combination of activity diagrams and collaboration diagrams, so-called story diagrams for the specification of operational behavior. The semantics of story diagrams is based on programmed graph rewriting rules [476]. The story diagrams offer many powerful constructs of graph transformation like multi-objects, non-injective matching, NACs, etc., to create a powerful language which is usable for modeling even complex problems in an elegant way. The operational behavior modeled with such story diagrams can then be tested using the graph based object browser DOBS (Dynamic Object Browsing System, see Fig. 3 below) which is part of the Fujaba Tool Suite, cf. [143].

In contrast to other graph-based tools (cf. [418, 177]), Fujaba does not rely on proprietary runtime environments. Instead, Fujaba generates standard Java source code that is easily integrated with other Java program parts and that runs in a common Java runtime environment. The Fujaba code generation for graph rewrite rules uses a sophisticated query optimizer that translates the LHS of a rule into nested search loops, cf. [474, 476]. In general this results in efficient rule execution. Altogether, this enables the use of graph-based concepts in all kinds of Java applications. Support for other target languages is planned, too.

Metamodel

To illustrate our approach, a small case study on a statechart environment is used. This case study was first introduced in [144]. The Fujaba approach is used to describe how model transformation to the PSM and operational semantics of the PSM can be done.

The statechart case study is used to show Fujabas abilities to model a visual language. Since the Fujaba approach uses typed graphs, one needs a graph schema to model graph transformations. Such graph schemata are modeled using UML class diagrams in Fujaba. Note that the usage of MOF would be applicable here, too. Figure 2 shows such a graph schema/metamodel/class diagram for the statechart environment.

From such a class diagram, Fujaba generates Java classes for the different kinds of objects, their attributes and their relationships. From the developer's point of view, Fujaba's implementation of relationships turns Java object structures into graphs with bi-directional edges. Provided with a class diagram, our dynamic object browser DOBS may already be used as a simple editor for models/object diagrams/graphs, see Fig. 3. DOBS shows the abstract syntax of our model.

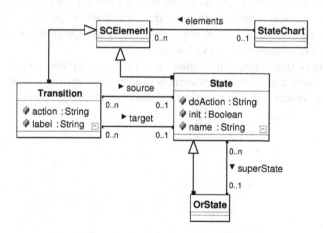

Fig. 2. Class diagram for statechart metamodel

100   Lars Grunske et al.

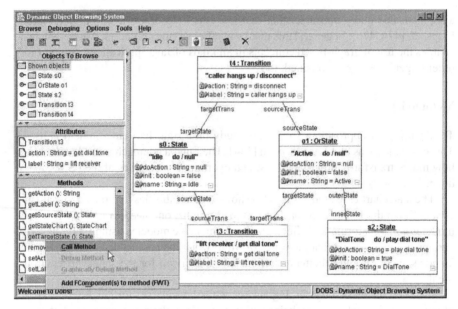

Fig. 3. Abstract syntax in DOBS

Model Transformations to PSM

Based on the metamodel, model transformations are discussed in the sense of Model-Driven-Architecture (MDA). As an example of a simple model transformation the flattening of complex statecharts to plain state machines is specified. This flattening is discussed first, since this allows us to simplify the specification of operation semantics and of consistency checks later on.

Flattening of statecharts with or-states deals with the replacement of transitions targeting or-states, and with the replacement of transitions leaving or-states and with the removal of or-states that have no more transitions attached.

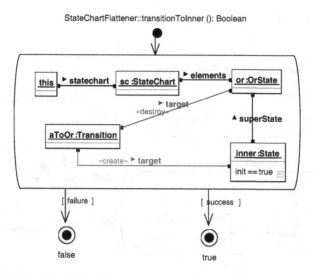

Fig. 4. Replacing transitions targeting or-states

Figure 4 specifies the replacement of transitions targeting or-states. Such transitions are simply re-targeted to the initial state of the statechart embedded within the or-state. Note that Fig. 4 employs a new (functional) class *StateChartFlattener* that has a *statechart* reference to *StateChart* objects. The graph transformation in Fig. 4 matches a statechart object *sc* containing an or-state *or* that is targeted by a transition *aToOr*. In addition, the graph transformation identifies a sub-state object *inner*, where the *init* attribute has value *true*, i.e., the initial sub-state. As indicated by the ≪*destroy*≫ and ≪*create*≫ markers, the graph transformation of Fig. 4 removes the *target* link connecting transition *aToOR* and or-state *or* and adds a new target link leading to sub-state *inner*. If this rule is applied as often as possible, all transitions leading to or-states are redirected to the corresponding initial states.

In Fig. 2 class OrState inherits from class State. This means that when we need a node of type State, a node of type OrState does the job as well (substitutability). For our graph rewrite rule this means that node inner may match either a plain state or an or-state. Thus, our graph transformation works for nested or-states as well.

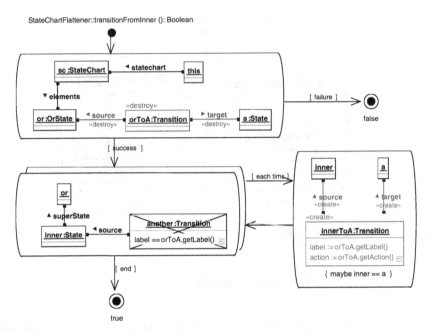

Fig. 5. Replacing transitions leaving or-states

The graph transformation of Fig. 5 replaces transitions leaving or-states. This is done in three steps. The first graph rewrite rule identifies a transition *orToA* with a source link to an or-state *or* and destroys it. If this rule has been applied success-fully, the second graph rewrite rule identifies inner states of *or* that do not already have a leaving transition with the same label. Story diagrams use crossed out elements to specify negative application conditions. The second graph rewrite rule has two stacked shapes. Such a rule is called a *for-each activity*. For-each activities are iteratively applied as long as new matches are found. Due to the *each time* transition in Fig. 5, each time when the second graph rewrite rule identifies an inner state without an appropriate leaving transition, the third graph rewrite rule is executed. The negative node *another* prevents the creation of a new transition if the *inner* state already has such a transition. This implements the priority rules of UML statecharts. The third graph rewrite rule creates a new transition leaving the corresponding *inner* state, targeting the same state *a* as the old transition. In addition, the transition label and the transition action are transferred.

In general story diagrams employ isomorphic rule matching only. However, the *maybe inner==a* clause of the third graph rewrite rule allows nodes *inner* and *a* to be matched on the same host graph object. This handles self-transitions.

The graph rewrite rule of Fig. 6 employs two negative nodes ensuring that the considered or-state has no outgoing and no incoming transition. For simplicity, a third negative application condition ensures that the considered or-state is not em-bedded in another or-state. This means that we handle nested or-states outside in. If all conditions hold, the or-state is destroyed and all its sub-states are added to the statechart *sc*. In addition, the init flag of the or-state is transferred to its initial sub-state. Thus, if the or-state was a usual state, its initial sub-state becomes a usual state, too. If the or-state was the initial state of the whole statechart, its initial sub-state becomes the new initial state of the statechart.

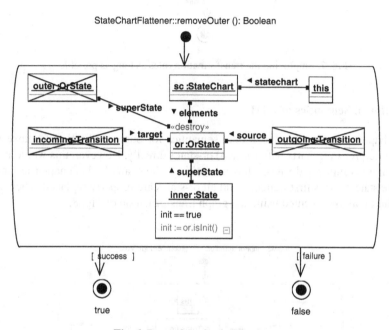

Fig. 6. Removing obsolete or-states

In story diagrams, the graph grammar-like application of a set of rules as long as possible needs to be programmed explicitly. This may be done as shown in the (pseudo) graph transformation of Fig. 7, which employs a Boolean constraint calling our three model transformations. If one of the above transformations is applied (and returns true), we follow the *success* transition, and the Boolean constraint is evaluated, again. If no transformation succeeds, the transformation terminates. Thus, the application of transformation *flattenStateChart* removes all (even nested) or-states and results in a simple state machine.

Note that the Boolean *or* operators connecting our three basic model transformations use left precedence and short-circuit evaluation. This means that transitionFromInner has higher priority than transitionToInner which again has higher priority than removeOuter. Thus, the proposed way of applying a set of graph transformation implies precedences on the transformation rules. Relying on these precedences, the negative nodes of Fig. 6 could have been omitted.

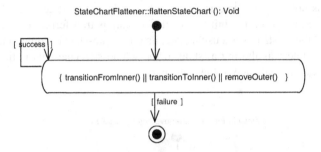

Fig. 7. Employing the transformation rules as long as possible

Operational Semantics of PSM

This chapter provides the operational semantics for our statecharts. Of course we could interpret statecharts with (nested) or-states directly. However, this would need some more complicated rules. Thus, to facilitate the example this chapter assumes that the state chart is first flattened and all or-states are properly replaced. Then, the statechart may be executed using the graph transformation of Fig. 8.

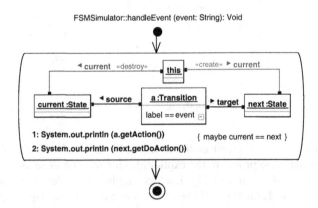

Fig. 8. Firing transitions

For handling events, we employ an object of type *FSMSimulator*. This simulator object has a *current* edge marking the currently active state. If method *handleEvent* is called, it tries to identify an outgoing transition *a* with the label provided in parameter *event*. The *maybe current==next* clause allows us to handle self transitions. If such a transition exists, the *current* edge is redirected to the target state of the transition. In addition, the transition action and the do-action of the target state are executed. For simplicity reasons, this is simulated using *System.out.println*. Alternatively, the actions might employ Java syntax and a Java interpreter like the bean shell [301] could have been used to actually execute the actions.

3.2 Comparison with other Related Approaches

Since vertical transformations and horizontal transformations are just transformations for different purposes, the comparison given in the following chapter holds here, too. However, there are some specific techniques in current CASE tools related to vertical transformations.

Usually, platform specific information is added to a PIM with the help of stereotypes. For example, a platform independent server class might be stereotyped to use CORBA as its underlying communication mechanism. Such a stereotype parameterizes the code generator of the underlying CASE tool to generate platform specific stub classes and communication means. Similarly, a stereotype might specify different priority options within a statechart. Again, this parameterizes the code generator of the underlying CASE tool. In some CASE tools, stereotypes may be exploited in template-based code generators. This means the user may provide a meaning for new stereotypes by editing specific code generation templates. Alltogether, we do not consider such stereotype mechanisms as actual model transformations. For example, they seem inappropriate for statechart flattening or other more complex transformation tasks.

The only notable mechanism for model transformation provided by CASE tools so far is the design pattern expansion mechanism provided, for example, by Rational ROSE XDE [215] and Artisan. This is a kind of macro mechanism allowing us to instantiate and adapt multiple design elements with a single pattern expansion command. In addition, methods generated by such a pattern expansion may already have an implementation that is adapted to the specific pattern occurrence during pattern expansion. Actually, this is a helpful mechanism for vertical model transformations. However, in graph grammar terms this is a specific node replacement system. Compared to a full graph rewriting system, such node replacement systems provide very limited modeling means. While both kinds of graph grammars in principle generate the same classes of graphs, our experiences have shown that comfortable modeling of complex transformations requires complex object patterns in the LHS, various kinds of application conditions and control structures for the combination of simple rules to complex transformation algorithms.

While the design pattern expansion mechanism provided by some CASE tools is not rich enough from the point of view of graph grammars, the design pattern expansion mechanism in these tools has the advantage that the rules are written in an extended UML notation, i.e., at the level of concrete syntax. Story diagrams are a general modeling language. Therefore, story diagram rules work on the metamodel level, i.e., at the level of abstract syntax. For end users, dealing with the internal metamodel of some tool is a major obstacle. To facilitate the writing of story diagram rules for such end users we plan to allow concrete syntax in story diagram rules, too.

The example transformations, shown in this chapter, utilize many of the more sophisticated features of story diagrams, e.g., programmed graph rewriting, method invocations, for-each activities, multi-objects, maybe clauses, negative application conditions, path expressions, etc. Similar language elements are provided by Progres graph transformations [177] only. In our experience, such sophisticated modeling constructs are mandatory for the specification of complex functionality as required for CASE tools.

The MoTMoT approach [129, 376] also uses story diagrams to specify model transformations. But unlike Fujaba, MoTMoT does not offer an editor to create story diagrams, but provides a UML 1.4 profile which uses annotated UML class diagrams and annotated UML activity diagrams to model story diagrams. This way, story diagrams can be drawn with every UML 1.4 compliant editor, like Together, MagicDraw or Poseidon.

The MOLA language [242] developed at the University of Latvia uses very similar concepts as used in story diagrams. MOLA also uses typed graphs and programmed graph transformations. But until now, MOLA has remained only a language specification and an editor. Interpreter or compiler support is still missing.

The GReAT tool [243] uses similar transformation rules. To structure more rules, GReAT makes use of data flow diagrams rather that control flow diagrams used in Fujaba.

The VIATRA tool [78] uses a combination of graph transformation rules (to describe structural modifications) and abstract state machines [44] (used as control structures to arrange elementary rules into complex transformations) and it is integrated into the Eclipse environment.

ATOM3 [81] is a multi-paradigm visual modeling framework also using graph transformation for defining the semantics of individual modeling languages and transformations. In addition to discrete modeling languages (like Petri nets, statecharts, etc.) the tool also aims at integrating domains of continuous models (as widely used control theory).

4 Graph Transformations for Horizontal Model Transformation

The vertical model transformations from the previous section are used to implement a refinement (or its inverse abstraction) relationship. The input and output models conform to metamodels that represent system properties at different levels of abstraction. In contrast, horizontal model transformations are used to implement mappings between models at the same level of abstraction.

In some cases, the output model is an in-place updated version of the input model. Using refactorings as an example, it will be illustrated that one implements such transformations by rephrasing a system in the same language: a transformation is defined on only one metamodel that serves as input and output.

In other cases, the output models are constructed from the input models by translating their information to other modeling languages. In this section, it will be shown that such horizontal translations are defined on a different metamodel for input and output. The generative programming community also recognizes the distinction between horizontal and vertical transformations that are defined either within the same metamodel or across different metamodels [79]. For a brief classification, we refer to the introduction of Visser's survey of rewriting strategies in program transformation systems [446].

4.1 The Fujaba Approach

Refactoring as an Example of Horizontal Rephrasing

Refactorings are transformations that change the structure of a program while maintaining its external behavior [131]. Other examples of horizontal rephrasings are normalization and optimizations. In an MDE context one implements such program transformations following the same approach: the program is parsed to a model which is then transformed horizontally while preserving certain properties.

When implementing refactorings, one first has to decide what properties characterize external program behavior. From this, one has to agree upon a metamodel on which the transformations and properties can be formalized without navigating through irrelevant details. In order to express the transformations, one finally needs a language that assists reasoning about the correctness of a refactoring implementation, again while hiding unimportant details. In [290], it is shown that graph rewriting is a promising formalism for this.

A typical example of a graph rewriting rule implementing a refactoring is given in Fig. 9. It represents the Pull Up Method refactoring expressed as a Fujaba SDM specification. The metamodel used to express the refactoring, is Fujaba's internal metamodel. The diagram shows how *method*, which is implemented in *container*, is moved to *superclass*. By expressing the refactoring on Fujaba's internal metamodel,

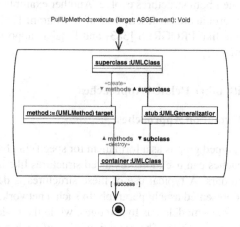

Fig. 9. Pull Up Method refactoring expressed using Fujaba's Story-Driven Modeling (SDM) language

the code generated from this graph rewriting can be called from a Fujaba plugin for refactoring UML class diagrams [433].

Refactorings are not the only applications of horizontal rephrasing with the target of improving an existing infrastructure. Similar approaches exist for the restructuring of software architectures: for example, Fahmy and Holt [119] use graphs to represent software architectures and conditional graph rewriting rules to improve quality attributes of a software architecture.

Horizontal Translation

To be able to focus on different aspects of a program, software engineers usually employ different views of the software. A typical example, which was introduced in [382], considers syntax trees and flow diagrams. Both diagrams contain the same information, but allow one to extract a certain type of information more easily. For example, a syntax tree representation of a method is excellent for specifying low-level code transformations, while flow diagrams help the programmer to get a better understanding of parts of the code, and the calculation of certain properties like cyclomatic complexity. Since the same program is represented in different modeling languages, horizontal translations are required for maintaining the consistency between the models. Pair grammars and triple graph grammars offer a declarative solution to implement this.

For the example, a triple graph grammar rule is given in Fig. 10. It relates the addition of an assignment construction to an abstract syntax tree to that of a control flow diagram. This rule is triggered whenever the syntax tree is adapted and updates the control flow graph. Apart from this forward rule, two other rules are part of the triple rule. The backward rule specifies how the addition of the assignment in the flow graph must update the syntax graph. The last rule analyzes and updates the correspondence graph when both structures evolve. Another example relates a program structure graph to an architectural description of a program [76]. Different graph rewriting environments like PROGRES [383] and Fujaba support the specification of triple graph grammars.

4.2 Comparison with other Related Approaches

Hypergraph Transformation Approaches

Next to using simple, typed graphs as a formalism for specifying horizontal transformations, other approaches can use more advanced structures like hypergraphs [181] and hypergraph grammars. A typical use of these structures is described in [207], where a network is represented as a hypergraph. In such a network, the basic entities like servers and clients are modeled as hyperedges, while the nodes represent communication between these entities. The reconfiguration of such a network architecture is then described as a set of hyperedge replacement rules. The main advantages of using hypergraphs are the improved flexibility in modeling, and the possibility of creating hierarchical graphs. Hierarchical graph transformation [91] can then be used to specify high-level translations or rephrasings as described in [179].

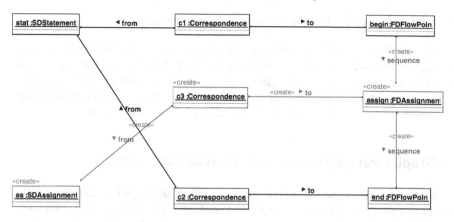

Fig. 10. Forward triple graph rule

Metamodel Design

Fujaba's metamodel is similar to the UML metamodel. In [155], it is shown which key shortcomings of the UML metamodel need to be resolved for expressing source-consistent refactorings. By extending the UML 1.4 metamodel with constructs for modeling method bodies in a language-neutral way, one can reuse (parts of) refactoring implementations (and related bad code smell specifications) for different OO languages.

Based on a list of criteria for UML refactoring (like simplicity, backward compatibility with previous UML versions, the ability to integrate with code smell detectors and maintain the consistency with the source code), the action semantics package of UML 1.5 was found inadequate as a basis for expressing UML refactorings. Therefore, the authors proposed a refactoring-oriented set of extensions to the UML 1.4 metamodel. Research on the FAMIX metamodel [83] indicated that the notion of access, call and updatebehavior had to be augmented with the notions of type-casting and nested scopes containing local variables.

In 2001, researchers from the reengineering community [96] agreed on the Dagstuhl Middle Metamodel [270] for representing software at a medium level of abstraction and on Datrix [209] for a low-level representation. It appears to be unfeasible to design a metamodel that satisfies the needs of both low-level refactoring tools and high-level visualization tools. Therefore, it may be more promising to investigate how the consistency between models in different modeling languages can be maintained. Source code refactorings could be implemented on full-fledged abstract syntax graphs while visualization tools could be implemented using minimalistic metamodels for class diagrams, statecharts, sequence diagrams, etc. Changes resulting from refactoring applications on the concrete models could be propagated to the visualization models by triggering model translations.

Consistency Through Distributed Graph Transformation

Bottoni et al. use distributed graph rewriting to decompose a refactoring on a redundant metamodel into several smaller units [139]. This technique is useful in a UML context where structural program information is redundantly stored in both the core package and the class diagram package of the metamodel. By coordinating the distributed rules, one can maintain the consistency between all diagrams.

5 Graph Grammars for Model Analysis and Verification

Although graph grammars provide a visual yet formal language for capturing a wide range of model transformations with automated code generation and tool support, automation and formality do not alone guarantee correctness as the specifications of model transformations can also be erroneous. This problem can be severe since, if some bugs are detected during model-driven development in a PSM or in the target program, the designers have to be reassured that the automated model transformations do not introduce new flaws into the system model. As a consequence, one has to prove precisely (and automatically, if possible) that a model transformation is correct [439].

5.1 Correctness Criteria for Transformations

The most elementary requirements of a model transformation are syntactic. The minimal requirement is to assure *syntactic correctness*, i.e., to guarantee that the generated model is a syntactically well–formed instance of the target language. An additional requirement (called *syntactic completeness*) is to completely cover the source language by transformation rules, i.e., to prove that there exists a corresponding element in the target model for each construct in the source language (and we did not forget about any situations when specifying the transformation rules).

However, in order to assure a higher quality of model transformations, at least the following *semantic requirements* should be verified for a model transformation. First one must guarantee that a transformation is *terminating* and *confluent* (thus it yields a unique result). As model transformations may also define a projection from the source language to the target language, semantic equivalence between models cannot always be proved. Instead we aim to prove the *property preservation* of a transformation for certain (transformation specific) correctness properties. For instance, in a statechart-to-code transformation, one may prescribe the natural criterion for correctness that each state configuration that is reachable from the initial configuration in a statechart model should be reachable in the target code as well.

5.2 CheckVML: A Tool for Model Checking Graph Grammars

The main idea of the CheckVML approach [437, 438, 377, 362] is to exploit off-the-shelf model checker tools like SPIN [211] for the verification of graph grammars.

More specifically, it translates a graph transformation system parameterized with a type graph and an initial graph (via an abstract transition system representation) into its Promela equivalent to carry out the formal analysis in SPIN. Furthermore, graph properties that capture the requirements for the system visually are also translated into equivalent temporal logic formulae.

Graph and Rule Model.

CheckVML uses directed, typed and attributed graphs as model representation. Inheritance between node types is also supported.

Concerning the rule application strategy, it prescribes that a matching in the host graph should be an injective occurrence of the LHS (and NAC) graphs. Furthermore, all dangling edges are implicitly removed when deleting a node. Arbitrary creation and deletion of edges are allowed while there is an a priori upper bound for the number of nodes (of a certain type) potentially created during a verification run, which is passed as a parameter to the translator.

The Model Checking Problem

The *model checking problem* is to automatically decide whether a certain correctness property holds in a given system by systematically traversing all enabled transitions in all states (thus all possible execution paths) of the system. The correctness properties are frequently formalized as LTL formulas.

Traditional model checkers are based on so-called *(state-)transition systems (TSs)*, where the structure of a state consists of a subset of a finite universe of propositions. This determines the storage structures used (usually Binary Decision Diagrams or a variant thereof), the logic used to express properties (propositional logic extended with temporal operators, usually LTL or CTL) and the model checking algorithms (automata-based or tableau-based).

From Graph Grammars to Transition Systems: An Overview

In graph grammars, a state is constituted by a graph, while a transition means the application of a rule for a certain matching of the LHS in such a graph. Traversing all enabled transitions then means applying all rules on all possible matchings. During this process, it is important to realize whether a certain state has been investigated before; therefore the model checker has to store all the graphs that it has encountered.

Since graph transformation is a meta-level specification paradigm (i.e., it defines how each instance of a type graph should behave), while the transition system formalism of Promela is a model-level specification language (i.e., a Promela model describes how a specific model should behave), the main challenge in this approach is *rule instantiation*, i.e., to generate one Promela transition for all the potential application of a graph transformation rule *in a preprocessing phase* at compile time.

State Variables and Initialization

A model element (object, link or attribute) is considered to be dynamic if there is at least one rule that potentially modifies (creates, destroys, updates) the element. The encoding of dynamic model elements into state variables is driven by the metamodel (type graph). A one-dimensional Boolean state variable array (a unary relation symbol) is defined for each dynamic node type; and a two-dimensional Boolean state variable array (a binary relation symbol) for each edge type.

In traditional model checker tools, the dimension of each array and all the enumeration types must be restricted to be finite at compile time. For the corresponding graph grammar, this restriction implies that there exists an a priori upper bound for the number of nodes in the model for each node type given explicitly by the user of CheckVML. In this respect, we suppose that when a new node is to be created it is only activated from the bounded "pool" of currently passive objects (deletion means passivation, naturally), and the same applies to the interpretation of links.

Note that the restriction for the existence of a priori upper bounds is a direct consequence of using SPIN, which prescribes that the domains of all state variables have to be a priori finite. Fortunately, one can insert special assert statements in the Promela code which check if these limits were exceeded during verification, and then the user can increase the corresponding upper bound before the next compilation and verification run. Alternatively, one can switch to another model checker (like dSPIN [221]) that supports object creation without restrictions, which needs further investigations.

In general terms, the initial configuration of the application model is projected into the initial state of the TS. In this respect, exactly those locations of state variable arrays evaluate to true in the initial state for which the related model elements exist in the initial configuration.

Translation of Rules.

Potential applications of the graph transformation rules that specify the dynamic behavior of the style are encoded into transitions (guarded commands) of the corresponding TS.

Since the encoding only introduces state variables for dynamic model elements, we also have to eliminate conditions that refer to the static parts of the model. For that reason, the generation process of transitions is driven by a graph pattern matching engine, which collects all the matching instances of the static parts of the preconditions of a rule. If the guard of a certain guarded command can never be satisfied due to the failure of pattern matching in the static structure then this transition is not generated at all in the target TS.

Although this compile-time preprocessing can be time-consuming, since all the potential matches of a rule have to be encountered, we only have to traverse a relatively small part of the state space for this step as graph transformation rules define local modifications to the system state; thus it is typically negligible when compared with the time required for traversing the entire state space during model checking.

Properties To Be Verified.

The requirements for system under design are most typically captured by *safety* and *reachability* properties. A safety property defines a desired property that should always hold on every execution path or (equivalently) an undesired situation which should never hold on any execution path. A reachability property describes, on the contrary, a desired situation which should be reached along at least one execution path. From a verification point of view, safety and reachability properties are dual: the refutation of a safety property is a counter-example which satisfies the reachability property obtained as the negation of the safety property. On the other hand, if a safety property holds (or a reachability property is refuted) the model checker has to traverse the entire state space.

A safety or reachability property can be interpreted as a special graph pattern (called *property graph* in the sequel) which immediately terminates the verification process if it is matched successfully. It is shown in [361] that the properties expressible in this way are equivalent to the $\exists\neg\exists$ fragment of ($\forall$-free) first-order logic with binary predicates.

The CheckVML Tool: Pros and Contras

The potential benefits of the CheckVML tool are the following:

(1) The tool considers typed and attributed graphs, which fits well with the meta-modeling philosophy of UML and other modeling languages.
(2) The size of the state vector depends only on the dynamic model elements (i.e., elements that can be altered by at least one graph transformation rule) while immutable static parts of a model are not stored in the state vector. This is a typical case for data flow-like systems (e.g., data flow networks, Petri nets, etc.).
(3) CheckVML can be easily adapted to various back-end model checker tools (like SAL [37], Murϕ [1]) due to the usage of XML input and output formats.

The essential disadvantage of the approach is that dynamic model elements (that are not restricted by static constraints) easily blow up both the verification model and state space; moreover, symmetries in graphs can be handled only for limited cases.

Verification Experiments

Concerning the practical usefulness of the approach, two questions might immediately arise: (i) what is the size of the models that can be verified, and (ii) how does one obtain meaningful initial models?

To answer the first question, detailed experiments have been carried out in [362] where two main roads of model checking graph transformations (namely, GROOVE [360] vs. CheckVML) were compared on various case studies having essentially different characteristics concerning the dynamic and symmetric nature of the problem.

For instance, SPIN (CheckVML) managed to verify the graph transformation version of dining philosophers problem with ten philosophers – which is a relatively good problem size concerning (i) the use of explicit state model checkers and (ii) the automatic generation of the Promela code without further manual optimizations. On the other hand, verification failed much sooner in the case of inherently dynamic and symmetric problems (like the mutual exclusion example of [205]).

These experiments also revealed that (i) the space consumption of these tools were comparable, (ii) SPIN (CheckVML) had a clear advantage concerning the time required for verification of problems of the same size, but (iii) GROOVE were able to handle problems with a larger dimension due to its sophisticated algorithms for graph isomorphism checks.

Now, to answer the second question based upon these experiments, it seems unrealistic that correctness properties could be verified on a large initial graph (of a complex system model). But the practical use of model checkers is most frequently to automatically find conceptual flaws in the specification (i.e., refutation instead of verification), for which one can use much smaller initial models. Furthermore, the execution traces retrieved during the verification of reachability properties can immediately be used as (automatically derived) *test cases* for a more complex system. The exploitation of these issues is a direction of future research.

5.3 Reachability Analysis of Flattened Statecharts

Based upon the operational semantics rule of statecharts (see Fig. 8), a reachability analysis is carried out to decide whether all states of a flattened statechart are reachable or not. For this purpose, we first translate a sample flattened statechart model (consisting of states s1, s2 and s3 and transitions t1: s1->s2, t2: s2->s3 and t3: s1->s3) and the rule into a corresponding TS.

Since there is a single dynamic element in the class diagram (namely, the current edge type), the TS encoding of our model contains only a single state variable array. All other static elements are eliminated by CheckVML in the pre-processing phase since they will never change during the verification (model execution).

```
/* upper bound for the domain of variables */
#define MAXFSM 1
#define MAXSTATE 3
/* instances (individuals) */
#define a1 0 #define s1 0 #define s2 1 #define s3 2

/* state variable: one- or two-dimensional arrays */
/* for dynamic node, edges, and attributes */
 bool current[MAXFSM][MAXSTATE];

/* Initialization of state variables */ init{
/* All locations in the state variable array */
/* are set properly */
 current[a1][s1] = true; current[a1][s2] = false;
 current[a1][s3] = false;
}
```

All potential matches of the graph transformation rule of the statechart semantics are collected also at compile time and translated into the following guarded commands (which are, essentially, a pair of guards and elementary update operations). Below we present the TS equivalent of one potential matching, namely, for transition t1.

```
/* transition: Boolean guard -> update1; update2; */

:: atomic {
 fsm[a1] && current[a1][s1] && state[s1] && source[t1][s1] &&
 transition[t1] && target[t1][s2] && state[s2] ->
   current[a1][s1] = false; current[a1][s2] = true;
}
```

Static parts of the model and dead guarded commands with a guard always evaluated to false because some static parts of the model are removed this time as well. As a result, we end up with the following very compact representation of our statechart model.

```
/*  non-deterministic selection between transitions; */
/*  executed as an atomic step; */
do :: atomic{ current[a1][s1] ->
   current[a1][s1] = false; current[a1][s2] = true; }
:: atomic{ current[a1][s2] ->
   current[a1][s2] = false; current[a1][s3] = true; }
:: atomic{ current[a1][s1] ->
   current[a1][s1] = false; current[a1][s3] = true; }
od
```

The required reachability property stating that each state of the statecharts should be reachable can be expressed by the graph pattern of Fig. 11. The parametric property graph in the upper part (expressing that a state S never becomes current, which is an undesired situation) is first instantiated to enumerate all potential matchings in the instance graph. Then the corresponding LTL formula for the safety property can be easily derived, which simply collects all these matchings into a disjunctive formula with global (G) temporal quantifiers (which prescribes that the formula should hold for all states on all execution paths).

When running the model checker, a counter-example for the property of Fig. 11 shows an execution of the flattened statechart where it is proved that all states of the statechart become reachable.

5.4 Comparison with other Related Approaches

The theoretical basics of verifying graph transformation systems by model checking have been studied thoroughly by Heckel et al. in [205, 204] (and subsequent papers). The authors propose that graphs can be interpreted as states and rule applications as transitions in a TS. This idea is adopted more or less in all existing model checking approaches of graph grammars.

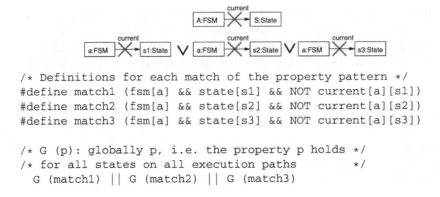

```
/* Definitions for each match of the property pattern */
#define match1 (fsm[a] && state[s1] && NOT current[a][s1])
#define match2 (fsm[a] && state[s2] && NOT current[a][s2])
#define match3 (fsm[a] && state[s3] && NOT current[a][s3])

/* G (p): globally p, i.e. the property p holds */
/* for all states on all execution paths          */
  G (match1) || G (match2) || G (match3)
```

Fig. 11. The reachability property of states

The main current alternative for CheckVML is provided by the GROOVE framework [360], which uses the core concepts of graphs and graph transformations all the way through during model checking (instead of translating them into existing model checking tools). This means that states are explicitly represented and stored as graphs, and transitions as applications of graph transformation rules; moreover, properties to be checked should be specified in a graph-based logic, and graph specific, model checking algorithms should be applied. A more detailed comparison between GROOVE and CheckVML can be found in [362].

A theoretical framework by Baldan and König [26] aims at analyzing a special class of hypergraph rewriting systems by a static analysis technique based on foldings and unfoldings of a special class of Petri nets. This framework is able to verify infinite state systems by calculating a representative finite complete prefix. Unfortunately, no supporting tools have been reported in the literature.

Dotti et al. use object-based graph grammars [88] for modeling OO systems and define a translation into SPIN to carry out model checking. The main difference (in contrast to CheckVML) is that the authors allow a restricted structure for graph transformation rules that is tailored to model message calls in OO systems. Therefore, CheckVML is more general from a pure graph transformation perspective (i.e., any kind of rules are allowed). However, the framework of [88] relies on higher-level SPIN/Promela constructs (processes and channels), which might result in better run-time performance.

6 Conclusions and Future Work

In this chapter we used graph transformation to specify and apply model transformations in the context of model-driven software engineering. For this reason, we presented the theoretical background of graphs and graph transformations. Thereafter, we demonstrated the practical feasibility of graph transformations for horizontal (PIM-to-PIM) and vertical (PIM-to-PSM) model transformations and the verification of these model transformations. For each domain typical case studies were introduced and the existing tool support was described. Based on these examples, we believe that graph rewriting systems are well suited to the context of model transformations. Especially, pair grammars and triple graph grammars can become the dominant formalism for automated PIM-to-PIM and PIM-to-PSM transformations.

Throughout the examples, we used the syntax of Fujaba's graph rewriting language which is very close to standard UML activity diagrams and object diagrams. In order to realize the MDA vision of platform independence, a recent investigation demonstrated how this syntax could be completely aligned with UML stereotypes and MOF [376]. The result of this work makes it possible to specify model transformations in one UML tool and deploy them on the repository of another UML tool.

To continue this movement toward standardization and cross-fertilization among formalisms and tools, one may investigate how OCL can be integrated with the standardized graph transformation language to support textual constraint specifications embedded in graph rewriting rules. This may result in a concrete proposal for supporting queries, views and transformations on models based on the synergies between graph transformation and UML/MOF.

A Generalized Notion of Platforms for Model-Driven Development

Colin Atkinson[1] and Thomas Kühne[2]

[1] University of Mannheim, L15, 16, 68161 Mannheim, Germany
`colin.atkinson@ieee.org`
[2] Darmstadt University of Technology, Hochschulstr. 10, 64289 Darmstadt, Germany
`kuehne@informatik.tu-darmstadt.de`

Summary. The notions of "platform" and "platform model" have a fundamental role to play in the MDA vision of software engineering, since they form the basis for distinguishing between Platform Independent Models (PIMs) and Platform Specific Models (PSMs) and for defining the input that allows transformation tools to map PIMs into PSMs. However, the de facto notions of platform and platform model that prevail in the MDA community today are overly narrow and only vaguely defined. In the MDA literature, the basic capability that an artifact is required to have to be characterized as a platform is the ability to support the execution of a software application. Beyond that, there is no consensus on what features a platform should possess or what form platform models should take. One school of thought holds that a platform model is essentially a Domain Specific Language (DSL) and that MDA technology is essentially about the definition and use of DSLs, but this fails to capture some important properties that are usually associated with the notion of platform. In this chapter we explain why this is the case and discuss what information a generalized platform notion should encapsulate and what form a model of such a platform should take. We present a notion of "platform" based on four minimalistic, orthogonal elements: Language, predefined types, predefined instances and patterns, and explain how this notion can be applied to contemporary software platforms such as Java, J2EE and .NET.

1 Introduction

Model-driven development (MDD) is based on the principle of separating the description of an application's abstract properties and logic from a description of its platform specific implementation, and of automating the transformation of the former into the latter using advanced model transformation tools (MTTs). The most mature formulation of this vision at present is the OMG's "Model-Driven Architecture" (MDA) which refers to a high-level description of an application as a Platform Independent Model (PIM) and a more concrete implementation-oriented description as a Platform Specific Model (PSM). Figure 1, taken from the OMG's MDA Guide [317], provides a "suggestive" picture of the MDA vision by illustrating how PIMs are automatically transformed into PSMs with the help of additional input describing the properties and services offered by the target "platform". While this is undoubtedly a very powerful and elegant metaphor for software development, there are some significant issues which need to be sorted before this vision becomes a reality in mainstream software engineering. Chief among them is the question of what precisely a platform is and what a platform model looks like. Of the three fundamental ingredients of MDA referred to in Fig. 1, "model", "transformation" and "platform", "platform" is currently the vaguest and least well defined. This may be because most of the research on MDA to date has focused on the "transformation" challenge (p. 19, p. 91 of this book) [387]. There are few explicit definitions of the notion of "platform" or platform model in the MDA literature and those that do exist are rather vague and high level. However, without a precise and concrete definition of what a platform is and what a platform model looks like it is impossible to formulate a precise notion of PIMs, PSMs and the additional "input" depicted in Fig. 1.

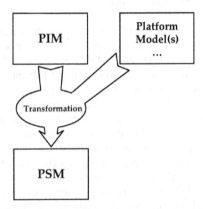

Fig. 1. Core principle of MDA

The most explicit definition of the concept of a platform in the MDA context is probably to be found in the MDA Guide [317], which states:

> *"A platform is a set of subsystems and technologies that provide a coherent set of functionality through interfaces and specified usage patterns, which any application supported by that platform can use without concern for the details of how the functionality provided by the platform is implemented."*

Although this is a very high-level definition which leaves a lot of scope for interpretation, it does make it clear that a platform is intended to be viewed as a vehicle for the *execution* of a software application. This is reinforced by the "flagship" text that accompanies the MDA logo on the OMG's website:[3]

> *"Platform-independent applications built using MDA and associated standards can be realized on a range of open and proprietary platforms, including CORBA, J2EE, .NET and Web Services or other Web-based platforms."*

---
[3] http://www.omg.org/mda/

This is no accident of course, because the word "platform" is generally used in the IT industry to refer to machines or systems that are built to support the execution of software applications in their end-user environment. In addition to the platforms already mentioned, examples include hardware such as the Intel Pentium or Power PC processors, operating systems such as Linux or Windows, and virtual machines such as the Java Virtual Machine and the .NET Common Language Runtime. If one views a platform as an execution infrastructure, it seems self-evident that a "platform model" is a "model of an execution infrastructure". However, this is as concrete a definition as one can extract from the OMG's MDA literature, which is clearly unsatisfactorily vague to drive the transformation from PIMs to PSMs. The most concrete definition of "platform model" available today comes from the school of thought that characterizes MDA in terms of transformation between Domain Specific Languages (DSLs) [70, 69, 162]. According to this school of thought, the essential difference between the input and output models in the MDA transformation illustrated in Fig. 1 is that they are written in different languages (or languages dialects). In other words, the information that has to be input into the MTT to effect the transformation is a description of the languages that the models are written in. Therefore, although it is not stated explicitly, language definitions essentially play the role of platform models in the DSL view of MDA. Thus, if one takes a DSL interpretation of Fig. 1, the PIM is written in one DSL, the PIM in another DSL, and the platform model(s) input to the MTT is a description of one or both of these DSLs. In this chapter we challenge both of these implicit assumptions that underpin the generally accepted notions of "platform" and "platform model", namely the "platform = execution infrastructure" assumption and the "platform model = language definition" assumption. In the next section we start by discussing the traditional view of a platform as an execution vehicle and identify the various elements from which a platform is typically constructed. Section 3 follows with a description of the traditional ways in which these platform elements are described. In Sect. 4 we then present a more general notion of "platform" which is sufficient to provide a sound foundation for MDA. Finally, in Sec. 5 we discuss the ramifications of this model for the MDA transformation approach depicted in Fig. 1 and the model transformation tools which are expected to enact them.

2 What Is a Platform?

In the context of MDD, as mentioned above, a platform is regarded as "a set of subsystems and technologies" that provide the capabilities needed to support the execution of a software application. Because of their complexity, modern execution platforms are generally visualized and organized as a hierarchy of layers.

Figure 2 gives a schematic view of the layers that one typically finds in an execution platform. A software application may have access to all the layers in this hierarchy or some of the layers may completely hide layers below them. For instance, an operating system may make some aspects of the underlying hardware completely transparent (as in the "DirectX" video driver scheme), or a virtual machine may

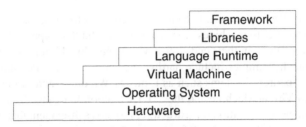

Fig. 2. Typical Platform Layers

completely abstract away the choice of an operating system (as accomplished in Smalltalk [154]). The notion of a platform that is relevant for a particular application depends on the set of layers that it makes use of. For instance, if a virtual machine is not able to completely hide the idiosyncrasies of an operating system's file system or scheduling policy, and these features are utilized by an application, then these aspects of an operation system need to be part of the application's perception of its execution platform. In the following we consider each of these elements in turn.

2.1 Hardware

Computer hardware is the most basic kind of platform on which a computer application can run, and forms the base of the hierarchy of layers. A hardware platform makes a set of basic capabilities available to applications in terms of a set of machine language instructions, memory and various assisting components, such as a floating point arithmetic unit etc. Thanks to compiler technology, these rarely if ever have to be considered in application development. However, sometimes the performance criteria of a platform may only be met if certain special-purpose hardware (such as a digital signal processor) is used. In such cases, these hardware capabilities have to be included in the platform model.

2.2 Operating System

The second layer in the hierarchy of platform elements is usually regarded as being the operating system. This provides a whole host of additional capabilities such as file systems, processes, threads, etc. Operating systems are rarely regarded as covering or hiding the underlying hardware because they do not reproduce the execution capabilities offered by the hardware, but rather augment it with many additional services. It is quite common for software applications to depend on the specific capabilities offered by an operating system just as much as on the underlying hardware. For example, one often speaks informally of the "Wintel" platform. Thus an operating system also needs to be part of an application's perception of its platform.

2.3 Virtual Machine

Not all platforms have a virtual machine layer, but if present, this layer is typically regarded as being on top of the operating system layer. The role of a virtual machine is to make the actual choice of operating system and hardware transparent. By doing so it obviates the need to compile all parts of the application down to the layer of the operating system and hardware. A virtual machine may completely hide the underlying layers from the layers above, or it may let some of the underlying layer's functionality or properties shine through.

2.4 Language Support

Any layer above the virtual machine layer, or in its absence the operating system layer, assumes a certain language which library, framework and application are expressed in. While most of the support for executing the language is provided by the virtual machine or hardware, the compiler adds important functionality in the form of a language runtime system that is a part of the execution platform. Also, high-level language constructs made available to layers above are expressed as templates of low-level byte code or machine code. In addition, predefined values available to programmers may be supported by an underlying virtual machine but are part of, and are typically generated by, the corresponding language support. The classic "runtime" system that compilers bundle with their application hence also needs to be counted as "language support".

2.5 Libraries

Object-oriented programming languages like Java, C++ or Smalltalk typically come with a rich set of libraries providing additional, predefined functionality. Some of these libraries are regarded as standard, and must be present in any platform that aims to support the language, while others are "optional" and provide solutions only for specific domains or purposes. Libraries are the basic mechanism by which middleware technologies that form the foundation of distributed platforms are realized. All of the main capabilities associated with middleware technologies, ranging from "remote message interchange" and "transaction support" to "components and services", are made available to developers in the form of so called "Application Programming Interfaces" (APIs) as libraries. Thus, the libraries upon which an application depends form an essential part of its perception of its platform.

2.6 Framework

In contrast to libraries, which can be regarded as passive building blocks for the assembly of software, frameworks contain active control code. They pre-structure applications built using them according to some standard control scheme and provide standard solutions for a family of applications. A middleware solution featuring services like "transaction control" or cleverly managed persistence which embodies certain standard usage styles, is much more akin to a framework than a library. The special utility of a framework in providing an execution infrastructure over and above a library is not only the generic control code but also the design of how to use parts of the framework (or a library) in a generic way across a family of applications. Technically, one could subsume frameworks under "Libraries" as well, since they also represent standard, predefined code. However, if we want to characterize the purpose and nature of the predefined code, it makes sense to distinguish between library and framework layers.

3 Describing Platforms

Having discussed the various elements that comprise a modern execution platform, in this section we now discuss what information needs to be captured to fully characterize a platform from the perspective of an application.

3.1 Hardware

A hardware platform is characterized by the set of instructions, memory model and further functionality that it supports. In general, some form of assembler language plus a description of available hardware components is sufficient to formally capture the properties of a particular type of hardware platform.

3.2 Operating System

An operating system is characterized by the set of services or so-called "system calls" that it makes available to applications. Although these services are ultimately realized in terms of routines implemented in the underlying hardware platform, application programmers, or users interacting directly with the operating system, invariably invoke them using a high-level linguistic representation. Therefore, the definition of the system calls supported by an operating system usually involves the use of a language to describe the signatures of the calls that can be invoked. For instance, in the case of the Unix operating system this interface (and implementation) language is "C". Furthermore, an operating system generally offers standard instances which applications can use. Unix , for example, offers instances such as */dev/null, /dev/zero*, or a system timer.

3.3 Virtual Machine

The description of a virtual machine is usually more complex than that of an operating system because it involves the definition of some of the programming language features as well as the predefined system calls that the language environment provides. In other words, it needs to cover both hardware and operating system layers plus an additional language support layer (see below).

3.4 Language Support

The description of a (programming) language is generally captured in terms of four main elements:

(1) abstract syntax
(2) concrete syntax
(3) static semantics (or well-formedness rules)
(4) dynamic semantics (or behavior semantics)

Usually the static semantics (3) is checked prior to execution (e.g., by a compiler), so it is not normally necessary to include it in the description of the runtime infrastructure, i.e., the platform model. Likewise, the concrete syntax (2) typically plays no role at runtime, as it will have been compiled to byte code, or machine code prior to execution. In some cases, one might rely on runtime interpretation or compilation of (program-generated) source code, in which case (2) and (3) become relevant again for a complete platform description.

3.5 Library and Framework

Apart from "native classes", which are really part of the underling language cast in terms of library elements, the library and framework aspects of a platform are invariably expressed using the features of the language support by the language support and virtual machine layers.

4 Platforms and Platform Models for MDA

Having discussed how platforms are typically structured and described in traditional IT technology, we are now in a position to explain how we believe these approaches should be generalized to support the notions of "platform" and "platform model" in MDD. In doing this we have four goals in mind. We want to provide a notion of platform and platform model that

- is consistent with OMG MDA terminology
- accommodates the approaches described in the previous two sections
- is complete
- is composed of orthogonal concepts, avoiding redundancy and overlap

To achieve these goals we need to move away from two of the fundamental assumptions which implicitly underpin the notions of platform and platform models in the MDA literature today, namely the assumptions that

(1) platform = execution infrastructure
(2) platform model = language definition

Although platforms are most commonly thought of as execution infrastructure in the IT industry, this is not always the case. In general, a platform can be viewed as any system capable of supporting the fulfillment of some goal with respect to a software application. Executability is certainly one important goal, but it is not the only one. Next to execution, useful goals to support are checking, presentation and even the creation of models, i.e., model development. Thus, the concept of a platform in its full generality also embraces what is typically viewed as the development environment as well the execution environment. In this sense, a system which supports the model-based representation of an application as part of development is just as much a platform as systems that support its execution, testing, validation (see p. 329 of this book) or benchmarking for example. Generalizing the concept of "platform" to encompass both *deployment* and *development* environment brings several benefits as explained below. Ideally, a model of a platform should provide a complete and accurate description of that platform, so that any application that is consistent with the platform model is guaranteed to be processable by that platform. Although language definition is an important element of such a platform definition, as discussed in the previous section it is not by itself enough. There are aspects of a platform that are not captured using the classic language description techniques, such as the functionality provided as system calls and libraries. Thus, the concept of a platform model needs to be extended to include other elements.

4.1 Generalized MDD Platform Model

Analyzing the various platform elements and description techniques discussed in Sects. 2 and 3 we can identify four basic facets through which information about the capabilities and rules of an object-oriented platform is conveyed.

Language The first facet is a language facet which describes the basic concepts with which applications designed to use the platform can be constructed. This, of course, corresponds to the language support element of the platform description techniques discussed in Sect. 3.

Predefined types The second facet consists of a set of predefined types (e.g., classes) which augment the core language capabilities with additional services. This corresponds roughly to the library element in traditional platforms, but includes predefined types coming from the language support layer (e.g., class "Object" in Java).

Predefined instances The third facet consist of a set of predefined instances (e.g., objects), which are ready to be used out of the box. This facet contains the pre-instantiated objects that are found in some libraries such as Java's standard I/O streams "in, out, err" or Smalltalk's "true" and "false" instances, but also pre-existing system timers etc. Furthermore, if predefined operations are thought of as belonging to a single unified system (in the sense of systems calls) this is the facet which contains the system as a pre-instantiated object ready to receive system calls.

Patterns This fourth facet consists of the additional concepts and rules that are needed to use the capabilities found in the previous facets in a meaningful fashion. We use the terms "patterns", but in general any "usage rules", such as those that characterize a framework, are found in this facet. Typically, software may be used in many contexts and ways and displays different properties accordingly. In order to achieve exactly the functionality and properties intended for a particular standard platform, one must associate the corresponding usage patterns with the platform. A complete platform description therefore needs to specify not only the available parts but also the intended ways in which to use these parts. This knowledge can be expressed in a variety of ways, including as patterns in the style of design patterns [140].

In Fig. 3 we represent all the facets including their role by representing patterns as a circle covering the three other facets. The language facet sits above "Types" and "Instances", since it is the defining layer for both. Layer "Language" corresponds to language *definition*, whereas "Types" and "Instances" correspond to language *usage*. We refer to this view of a platform as the General Platform Model (GPM). We only show two logical metalevels (types and instances) in this picture since most mainstream languages do not offer more than two levels of language use. In general, Fig. 3 may feature further facets below "Language", such as "Metatypes" etc.

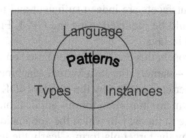

Fig. 3. General Platform Model

An important point about the GPM illustrated in Fig. 3 is that it is not intended to correspond to a cumulative collection of platform model elements as discussed in Sect. 2, but rather is intended to provide a way of characterizing *each* element. Each element may place a different emphasis on the different platform facets, but can nevertheless be expressed using the same overall notion of platform. For example, an operating system, which offers most of its capabilities in the form of system calls, will have a platform model that is predominantly centered on the instance facet. On the other hand, a virtual machine, which offers a large proportion of its capabilities in the form of a language, will naturally have a platform model that is predominantly centered on the language facet. It is our contention that any kind of platform can be modeled through the appropriate combination of these facets, and, in fact, is typically incomplete if one more of the facets is ignored. In Fig. 4 we illustrate this by showing how each of the traditional platform notions discussed in Sect. 2 can be represented in terms of the GPM.

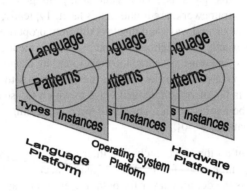

Fig. 4. Full platform description

4.2 Stack Example

To illustrate that these four facets are indeed sufficient and minimal let us consider how a small example would be modeled using the GPM. Figure 5 shows a highly simple stack class written in Java.

According to our approach, this Stack is written based on a model of the platform that is going to execute it – namely, the Java Virtual Machine and its predefined execution environment – after compilation by the standard JDK compiler. To ascertain what aspects of the platform are important for this application we simply have to ask whether a potential change to the way in which the application is represented would render it non-executable by the target platform. Clearly the features of the core Java language are important (language facet), because if we were to use any non-Java features the program would no longer compile. In the extreme case we could write the code in another language like C++, but then the application would be targeted to a different platform and would not be executable on the Java platform. Another important feature of the stack class is its use of the utility class "Vector" from the predefined Java library (types facet). This is clearly another dependency on the Java platform, since if this class were not available, or were given a different semantics to that expected, the application would not run or would not run as expected. This dependency has nothing to do with the basic language (language facet), however. It would be perfectly possible to define another platform based on the same Java core language but with a different library of predefined classes. Another dependency of the stack class on the Java runtime environment is its use of the standard output stream "out" to output messages (instances facet). Although the stream is accessed via the library class System, in effect, "out" references a predefined stream object. As with the predefined classes such as Vector, the absence of the standard output

```
import java.util.Vector;

public class Stack {
    protected int max, elems;
    protected Vector entries;

    public Stack (int maxValue) {
        max = 10;  elems = 0;
        entries = new Object[max];
    }

    public void push (Object o) throws Exception {
        if (elems < max) {
            entries.addElement(o);
            elems++;
        } else {
            System.out.print ("Stack is full")
            throw new Exception("FullStackException");
        }
    }

    public Object pop () throws Exception {
        if (elems >= 0) {
            return entries.lastElement();
        } else {
            System.out.print ("Stack is empty")
            throw new Exception("EmptyStackException");
        }
    }
}
```

Fig. 5. Java Stack example

stream, or a change to its semantics, would change the Stack's ability to execute on the platform, or would change its intended effect.

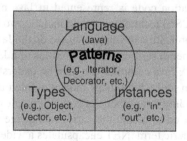

Fig. 6. GPM representation of the Java platform

Figure 6 illustrates how the various elements of the standard Java platform can be represented according to the GPM approach. For simplicity we have refrained from extending the example to feature a full application of a "Handle Body" pattern, such as the Bridge pattern [140], and therefore left out the patterns facet. As illustrated by this example, a platform changes if any one of the facet elements in the GPM changes. Thus, a change to the types or to the instances results in a different platform even if the core language remains the same. In fact, this is precisely how Java, as a general technology foundation, has been adapted by Sun to support the many middleware and enterprise technologies that it is now known for. The core Java language remains untouched whenever possible, but the set of predefined set of types and instances is extended or changed. Figure 7 shows how the J2EE platform is defined by adding additional predefined types and instance features to those available in the basic J2SE platform, leaving Java as the base language in the language facet. In addition, the platform contains a well-defined set of new patterns which describe how these types and instances should be used.

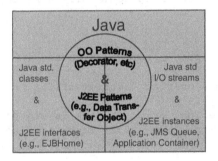

Fig. 7. J2EE platform

An advantage of explicitly separating the distinct aspects of a platform in a GPM is that the relationship between high-level and intermediate-level representations of applications is clarified. Java technology, for example, actually defines two platforms: the high-level language platform in which application code is represented in the Java high-level language (like the Stack class in Fig. 5), and the byte code platform in which application code is represented in Java byte code. Thus, a full model of standard Java (J2SE) technology would include two GPMs, one describing the capabilities used by application developers based on the Java high-level programming language and the other describing the capabilities of a Java Virtual Machine in terms of Java byte code. A Java compiler can then be understood as a very specialized model transformation tool which maps models written according to one GPM into models written according to another. As a more complex example we consider how the GPM might be used to model the various language and capabilities in the ".NET" platform. The generic term .NET encapsulates a wide range of development technologies ranging from enterprise servers to web services. However, the core of the technology is the so-called .NET framework which provides a variety of different execution platforms. The basic architecture of this family of platforms is described in an ECMA standard, known as the Common Language Infrastructure (CLI) [63]. One of the key goals of this standard is to make it possible for code written in different languages to interoperate. To achieve this, the CLI defines a language-spanning type system, known as the Common Type System (CTS) and a core set of features (the Common Language Specification (CLS)) that all compliant languages must support. Code written in a language that is compliant with the CLS is referred to as managed code and is guaranteed to be able to execute all .NET features and to interoperate with all other managed code, regardless of the managed language used to write it. Figure 8 illustrates how the GPM can be used to represent the family of platforms encapsulated by the .NET framework.

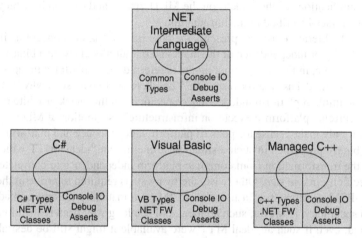

Fig. 8. .NET platform family

The GPM at the top of Fig. 8 represents the low-level execution platform defined by the CLI in terms of the CTS and the intermediate language. This is implemented as the Common Language Runtime. The lower three GPMs in Fig. 8 represent some of the different managed language environments currently implemented. The only aspect that differs in these GPMs is the base language in the language facet and the availability of extra language specific types, such as Visual Basic specific types in the second GPM, C++ specific types in the third GPM, etc. Several of the GPMs in addition contain specific features in their instance facet. For example, the C++ GPM contains the system instances as an abstraction of the underlying runtime system responsible for realizing system calls, the J# GPM contains the usual standard I/O instance objects such as "in" and "out", etc. Furthermore, each of the platforms in the platform family defines a set of patterns (usage guidelines) for the use of the common and specialized features.

Most of the ".NET" features are wrapped up in the predefined type library captured in the type facet of the GPM. In the case of .NET, the framework library contains a vast collection of classes which provide a wide range of capabilities ranging from basic network and middleware services through to features for database access, dynamic web page generation, GUI development and web service creation.

5 Model Transformation Tools

In the previous section we introduced the concept of the GPM, and explained how it can be used to model all of the different kinds of execution platforms encountered in MDD. We also introduced the notion that all environments which perform some useful function with respect to a software application should be regarded as platforms and characterized using GPMs, not just execution platforms. In this section we discuss the ramifications of these ideas on the MDD vision, and explain how they help resolve the issues identified in the introduction.

The MDA literature usually presents the core transformation concept as if platform specificity or independence of the input and output models were a binary property. For example, in Fig. 1, the input model is referred to as "platform independent" and the output model as "platform specific", but there are two reasons why it is inappropriate to think of platform independence/specificity in this black or white manner given the current "platform = execution infrastructure" assumption of MDA.

First, it only makes sense to speak of platform independence and platform specificity as binary properties in such a situation if one has an "ideal" MTT which can perform the transformation from complete platform independence to complete platform specificity in *one* step. Otherwise, the many steps required to arrive at the bottommost PSM, starting from a high-level PIM, automatically introduce shades of platform specificity. However, such an ideal tool is a long way from realization.

Second, even if such an ideal MTT were available it might still be desirable to produce the models at intermediate levels of abstraction which highlight a particular aspect of the architecture or reveal a certain aspect of the application (p. 139, p. 363 of this book) [22]. Thus, for the foreseeable future, the MDA transformation step illustrated in Fig. 1 is likely to be applied in the context of a chain of transformation steps, each creating a model of the application which is closer to the final execution platform than the previous model. Only the first and last application models in such a chain would then be characterizable as either (fully) platform independent or (fully) platform specific, and the intermediate models would have a certain degree of platform independence/specificity which lies somewhere between. This view is in fact explicitly acknowledged in the MDA Guide which states that:

> *"Platform independence is a quality, which a model may exhibit. This is the quality that the model is independent of the features of a platform of any particular type. Like most qualities, platform independence is a matter of degree."*

Given this situation, therefore, Fig. 9 represents the currently prevailing view of how MDA transformation technology will be used in practical software engineering scenarios.

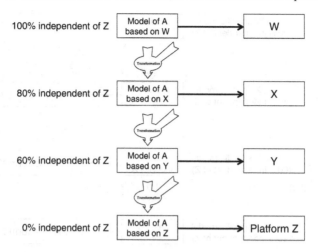

Fig. 9. Existing view of the MDA transformation chain

Several aspects of Fig. 9 are worthy of note. First, although all of the application models in the chain are "based on" (i.e., represented in terms of) something, only the bottom model is based on an actual executable platform. According to the "platform = execution infrastructure" assumption, X, Y and Z upon which the other models are based are not platforms, since the associated models are not yet executable. The question is: if they are not platforms, what are they? The DSL school of MDA would answer that these are DSLs. However, as explained in the previous sections, DSLs described using the traditional language definition techniques are not in general sufficient to describe all the characteristics/facets which such models might need. In particular, they do not capture type libraries, instances and patterns.

Figure 10 shows the alternative view of the model transformation chain based on the proposals put forward in this chapter. The main point to note is that W, X and Y on the right-hand side of the picture are now also viewed as platforms, not just Z. They may not be platforms supporting execution but in our approach they would nevertheless be considered platforms and would ideally be represented as GPMs. This in turn means that all of the application models can be viewed in one sense as PSM because they are all based on (and thus 100% specific to) the platform they are written in terms of. It is still of course possible to assign each model a measure of independence or specificity with respect to another particular platform, such as the ultimate target platform model for the which the application is being developed. But by requiring every model to be "based on" exactly one platform model, the original terminology and intention of the fundamental MDA transformation step once again becomes meaningful. Every model is specific to one platform and (relatively) independent of all the others. The final question which needs to be addressed is how the proposed model shapes the additional input that drives the transformation. Because the MDA literature uses the phrases "independence" and "specificity" in relation to the *output* model of the basic transformation step, there is an implication that MTTs

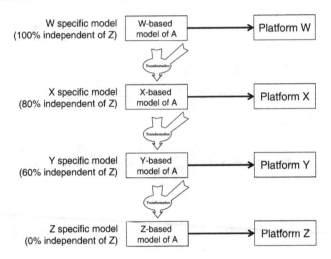

Fig. 10. Proposed view of the MDA transformation chain

will be specific to the *input* model platform but parameterized with respect to the *output* model platform. Such an MTT might, for example, be tied to the UML platform as the base for its input models but parameterized with respect to the platform model of its output. This situation is illustrated in Fig. 11, which enhances Fig. 10 with information about the input models driving the transformation step.

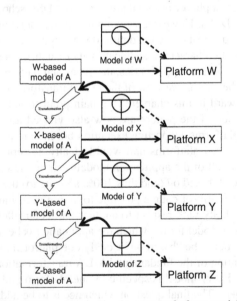

Fig. 11. Parameterization by ouptut platform models

In Fig. 10, it is the model of the platform upon which the output model is based that serves as the additional input to the transformation. This represents only one point on a spectrum of possible tool parameterization, however. Other tools which provide a different balance are also feasible. At one extreme, there are MTTs which are specific to both the input and the output platforms, and cannot handle models which are targeted to other platforms. Today's compilers are examples of this kind of MTT. At the other extreme, one can envisage MTTs which are fully parameterized with respect to both the input and output platform models as illustrated in Fig. 12.

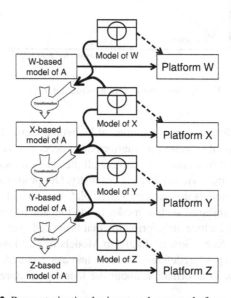

Fig. 12. Parameterization by input and output platform models

For the foreseeable future it is likely that we will see MTTs which occupy the full spectrum of genericity between these two extremes, as illustrated in Fig. 13. Initially one can expect to see MTTs that are similar to compilers and are hardwired to transform between two specific platform models, but gradually more generic tools will be developed which will be parameterized with respect to increasingly more aspects of the target *and* source platforms.

6 Summary

In this chapter we have identified two significant problems with the notion of platform and platform model in the current vision of MDA technology and have suggested a possible approach for solving them. The first problem is that the concept of platform promoted in the MDA literature is strongly associated with the notion of execution infrastructure, and thus implicitly rules out the consideration of other kinds of environments as platforms. The second problem is that the prevailing vision

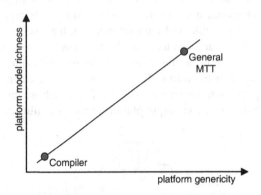

Fig. 13. Spectrum of transformation tools

of MDA as a vehicle for supporting families of Domain Specific Languages (DSLs) leads to a de facto way of representing platforms (or descriptions that play the roles of platforms) that is not rich enough to capture all the characteristics of platforms as they have traditionally been viewed in the IT industry. Our proposed solution is to expand the set of environments that are considered platforms to include those that offer development time capabilities, such as model validation, and to generalize the notion of a platform model to include all information that is needed to capture the necessary features of platforms. Such General Platform Models (GPMs) include information about the predefined types, predefined instances and usage patterns that characterize a platform *in addition to* information about the language features supported, as is currently the case.

7 Acknowledgements

The authors would like to thank Clemens Szyperski for clarifying discussions on the ".NET" platform family.

Part II

Technical Infrastructure of Model-Driven Development

Part III

Technical aspects of Medical Data
Development

A Tool Infrastructure for Model-Driven Development Using Aspectual Patterns

Imed Hammouda

Institute of Software Systems, Tampere University of Technology,
P.O.BOX 553, FIN-33101 Tampere, Finland
imed.hammouda@tut.fi

Summary. A software system can be viewed as a combination of separate concerns covering various artifact types and cross-cutting the primary structure within each artifact type. This chapter presents a concern-based approach to model-driven development. An aspectual pattern concept is used to represent concerns at different model levels. We back our approach with a concrete tool implementation called MADE (Modeling and Architecting Development Environment). The tool has been used in a number of development scenarios providing support for variability management, framework specialization, maintenance, and system comprehension. The tool introduces a task-based model-driven development environment and provides facilities for model generation, checking, and tracing.

1 Introduction

In software engineering, a model of a system is a description or specification of that system and its environment for some certain purpose [317]. A single system can be represented using multiple models at various abstraction levels ranging from requirement models to source code. Different models can be expressed using different forms. Requirements documents can be written in natural language, design models can be expressed using visual modeling languages such as the Unified Modeling Language (UML), and implementation is usually coded using high-level languages such as Java. Even though these models take different forms, they all represent properties of the same software system, realized in machine instructions. A clear benefit of this diversity is that each form may serve the need of different stakeholders in the software development cycle. Business managers, for example, are mostly comfortable with informal textual information and simple visual diagrams. System designers, however, prefer to analyze systems using more detailed design diagrams whereas programmers express their software solutions in terms of code.

Model-driven development (MDD) [288] is a practice where models not only are used as documentation but also become the backbone of the development process. In MDD, models of the same system are usually derived from each other; a new model can be generated from an existing one. A model and its derivations are usually connected using various kinds of relationships. These relationships can be formal or informal, complex or simple [180]. One way of building and expressing the inter-model relationships is the use of mapping functions. Mapping functions represent expert knowledge to transform between one model and another [288]. As the model is transformed, the new model may be expressed in another form. For example, a UML design model can be mapped into Java code. Automation has been recognized as a key factor when deriving models from others [386]. The idea is that most application code, for example, should be automatically generated from design models.

Separation of concerns (SoC [85]), which is a principle to modularize a system into manageable parts, can be used to structure a model into smaller sub-models that are easier to handle. Each sub-model represents a specific concern (i.e., matter of interest) in the system. For example, it is important to separate platform-specific concerns from application-specific concerns. However, because software systems are typically specified in terms of models at multiple abstraction levels, individual concerns must be addressed at all levels. Thus, the same concern can be represented at different levels using different notations and languages.

Generally, the key issues in MDD, such as the ability to generate new models from existing ones or to express the relationships between a model and its derivations, are judged according to tool support. In fact, the need for MDD tool support has been widely acknowledged by software developers, as the success of MDD is strongly dependent on tools. Nowadays, a variety of tools with various capabilities of applying MDD principles is available on the market. Another key factor for the usage of an MDD tool is the support for different software development activities. Ideally, the same tool should fulfill the need of different stakeholders in the development process, as every stakeholder might use the tool in a different development scenario such as model generation, maintenance, or customization.

This work proposes an approach and a tool for MDD by structuring models into separate concerns at different abstraction levels. The various features and capabilities of the tool allow developers to interact with the environment in different usage scenarios. The remainder of the chapter is organized as follows. Section 2 discusses the main characteristics of MDD tools. In Sect. 3, a pattern-oriented infrastructure for MDD tools is described. Using this infrastructure, Sect. 4 presents a concrete implementation of an MDD tool. Section 5 illustrates experiences in applying the proposed methodology and the implemented tool. Related methodologies and tools are briefly discussed in Sect. 6. Finally, Sect. 7 concludes the chapter.

2 Characteristics of MDD Tools

The main purpose of MDD tools is to facilitate the development of software by raising the abstraction level at which software solutions are defined. As the rise in the level of abstraction from assembly languages to high-level programming languages has improved productivity and increased the quality of software, it is believed that the same improvements could be achieved by moving the focus of software development from programs to models of programs. In order to achieve the goals set for MDD, these tools should meet the following functional and quality requirements.

The requirements have been abstracted from research on MDA (Model-Driven Architecture) [317] tools such as [35, 369]:

(1) Mapping and tracing of models: new models can be derived from existing ones; for example, generating code from visual models or customizing models themselves. Using MDD tools, developers should also be able to trace elements in one model to the elements they are derived from in other models. Consequently, an MDD tool should be able to relate different models expressed in heterogeneous notations and languages. In addition, developers should also be able to modify the derived models by, for example, updating design models or adding code fragments to the generated code.
(2) Support for different software engineering activities such as specifying requirements, constructing design models, and code generation as well as other development-process activities such as comprehension and maintenance.
(3) Ability to separate and represent different subject matter in models so that relevant matters are considered and non-essential aspects are deferred to later development phases. An MDD tool should also be able to represent the various relationships between these matters of interest.
(4) Model mappings and transformations should be performed in a controlled manner. The tool user should be given clear instructions on how to perform the transformations and which model parts are being transformed.

Based on requirements 1–2, we can see that one of the technical foundations of MDD tools is the support for heterogeneous artifacts expressed in different languages and notations. This is essential for managing models at different abstraction levels. A second implication of these two requirements is the support for various development scenarios corresponding to different phases of software development. Requirements 3–4 suggest that every model abstraction level may define its own matter of interest. For example, some platform-specific information is not required for models at higher abstraction levels. Therefore, a desired quality of MDD tools is the ability to express separate concerns of a software system. In the following, these three characteristics are discussed in more detail.

2.1 Support for Multiple Artifact Types

Software development involves different phases ranging from requirements specification to final deployment and maintenance of applications. Each phase is associated with specific software artifacts that are usually expressed using different languages (notations). For example, requirements artifacts can be represented using text documents, design models may be expressed in UML diagrams, and implementation can be written in Java. MDD tools aim at transforming these different artifacts from each other. For this reason, these tools should support heterogeneous artifact types (requirements document, design models, implementation) and different languages used to express these artifacts (UML, Java, XML).

The approach to support multiple artifact types is illustrated in Fig. 1. An MDD tool, which is represented by a cubical shape, handles different software artifacts.

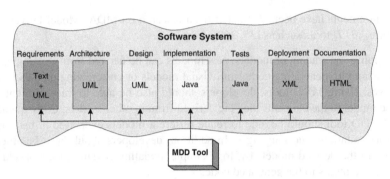

Fig. 1. MDD tool support for multiple artifact types

The idea is that such a tool should support various software development processes handling different modeling artifacts given with different notations. Usually, there is a many-to-many relationship between software artifact types and the notations used. A single software artifact can be expressed using different notations. For example, requirement specification documents can be described using both informal textual files and UML use case diagrams. The same language can be used to express different software artifacts. For example, implementation and test code can both be written in Java.

2.2 Support for Various Development Activities

The success of an MDD tool strongly depends on the diversity of the usage scenarios it suggests and on the extent the tool supports the needs of different stakeholders. This is important, especially for developers who play multiple roles in the development process. Generally, using one integrated development environment instead of independent tools minimizes the overhead of learning and switching between tools and enhances the inter-tool communication. MDD tools supporting heterogeneous development activities should incorporate a number of core functionalities including the ability to represent models, to derive new models from existing ones, and to define different kinds of relationships between models.

Generating application code from (visual) models residing at higher abstraction levels has been regarded as the primary expectation of MDD tools. Nevertheless, these tools might help developers deal with the complexity of other development tasks. For example, models may be used for verification and simulation purposes and for increasing the level of automation of testing activities by automatically deriving test cases [35]. Furthermore, MDD tools can be used to facilitate maintenance of existing models. For example, the tool might generate maintenance tasks based on earlier maintenance decisions. Another example scenario is to use the tool to facilitate learning complex system models, for instance through model abstraction (p. 179 of this book) or model customization [188].

2.3 Support for Decomposing Systems into Separate Concerns

The development of a software system can be divided into sub-problems according to the different concerns the application needs to incorporate. Applications are then modeled as hierarchical combinations of concerns. Each concern tackles a specific matter of interest in the application, such as a specific application functionality or quality. It has been shown that separation of concerns improves the alignment between requirements, design, and code of applications and leads to better reuse and evolution of systems [62].

Decomposing systems into separate concerns is particularly beneficial when developing applications of multi-tier architecture such as J2EE systems. The architecture of a J2EE system can be decomposed into three layers: presentation, business logic, and data. Each of these layers represents a separate concern in the system. Different concerns may serve the needs of different stakeholders in the development team. For example, graphic designers are usually interested in user interface matters reflected by the presentation tier only. Even in the case of single-layered systems, separation of concerns proves to be a useful practice. Software development becomes easier if the essential aspects of software such as business logic are separated from other concerns which involve technology-related matters such as security.

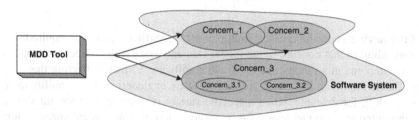

Fig. 2. MDD tool support for separation of concerns

Figure 2 shows an arbitrary software system decomposed into a number of concerns. MDD tools should provide a two-way support for such decomposition. First, the tool should be able to represent the individual concerns as separate entities. Second, using the tool, it should be possible to model the various inter-concern relationships. There are two kinds of relationships: overlapping and containment. Figure 2 shows an overlapping relationship between Concern_1 and Concern_2, meaning that those model elements represented by the overlapping region treat both concerns. As an example of a containment relationship, Concern_3 is modeled as the composition of Concern_3.1 and Concern_3.2.

2.4 A Two-Dimensional Development Approach

Figure 3 illustrates a two-dimensional approach for model-driven software development. The figure can be seen as a union of Fig. 1 and Fig. 2: an MDD tool should represent the different development phases (and the artifact types); an artifact type is structured into separate concerns. Following this approach, an MDD tool can be used to support various development activities as shown in the right part of Fig. 3. The development approach brings a number of benefits including better traceability, comprehensibility, and maintainability, which are essential qualities in model-driven software development.

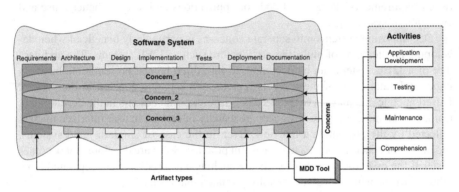

Fig. 3. A two-dimensional development approach

First, having a concern crosscut multiple software artifacts links the requirements corresponding to that concern to the model elements satisfying the requirements, to the code implementing them, and to all other software artifacts reflecting that concern. This is important in various areas of software engineering. In variability management [82], for example, when a specific variant is selected, that variant should be represented at all model levels. Second, separation of concerns enhances system comprehensibility because a concern localizes the focus of software developers to one specific matter of interest at a time. Furthermore, understanding a certain design model fragment can be enhanced by backward tracing that fragment to the requirement it satisfies. Finally, with a combination of good traceability and good comprehensibility, system maintainability becomes simpler and more obvious. For example, when a requirement is changed, the affected design solution or code is easily tracked so the propagation of change is better controlled.

In a typical situation, however, a concern might not cover all levels of abstraction, as shown in Fig. 3. Some concerns, for example, are first expressed at the requirements level but deferred to later stages in the development process. For instance, user authentication is usually not discussed at the architecture or design levels since at these levels developers prefer to focus on business logic instead. Some other concerns might not be represented in the deployment or documentation levels. An example of such concerns is comprehensibility. Other concerns such as maintainability concerns are not discussed at the requirements level but are often anticipated during the architecture or design phase.

3 Concepts for MDD Tool Infrastructure

We propose the use of a generic role-based pattern concept called aspectual pattern to represent the concern-based decomposition and composition of software systems as discussed in the previous section. First, we review the principle of separation of concerns in software development. Then we discuss the main characteristics of aspectual patterns.

3.1 Separation of Concerns

In software engineering, separation of concerns refers to the ability to identify those parts of software artifacts that are relevant to a particular concept, goal, task, or purpose. Aspect-oriented software development (AOSD) [124] is a paradigm that addresses crosscutting concerns by providing means for their systematic identification, separation, representation, and composition [357]. According to Kiczales [250], two crosscutting structures imply that neither can fit neatly into the other. Aspect-oriented programming (AOP) is a recent programming paradigm incorporating the ideas of AOSD. AOP organizes the crosscutting concerns into separate modules called aspects.

Aspects are merged with base programs or models of programs. The process of merging is called weaving. There are two ways in which aspects are weaved: static or dynamic. Static weaving modifies a structural base model by inserting new model elements. Dynamic weaving consists of adding at runtime new behavior to applications.

Traditionally, aspects have been used to encapsulate the different concerns cutting across several classes or other units of decomposition within the same level of abstraction, for instance implementation classes. Recent research work (e.g. p. 237 of this book, [419]), however, extends the ideas of aspect orientation to support the representation of concerns within and across software artifacts. Similarly, this work argues that the crosscutting nature of concerns could be extended to cover the different features of software cutting across various levels of abstraction. A single concern would then have a specific representation at different model levels expressed using different artifact types. In the next section, we describe a concrete pattern concept for implementing such concern-based composition and decomposition of systems.

3.2 Aspectual Patterns

A solution for modeling the two-dimensional development approach shown in Fig. 3 is to use the so-called aspectual patterns [191]. An aspectual pattern[1] can be viewed as a configuration that captures an aspect cutting across various software artifacts. It is an organized collection of software elements capturing a concern that is relevant for some stakeholder of a software system.

---

[1] Aspectual patterns have little to do with, say, design patterns: an aspectual pattern is a low-level mechanism that can be used to represent a design pattern or some other concern. Generally, aspectual patterns are system specific.

Aspectual patterns are described in terms of roles and the relationships between them. A role has a type, which determines the kind of software elements that can be bound to the role. A pattern can be associated with multiple sets of role types (e.g., UML, Java, etc.). Each set groups together related role types. For example, there is a set of role types for representing UML class diagram elements. In order for an aspectual pattern to crosscut multiple software artifact types, it should support heterogeneous sets of role types. For simplicity, the term pattern will be used in the remainder of the discussion to refer to aspectual patterns.

Pattern roles are attached with a number of properties. Each role may have a set of constraints. Constraints are structural conditions that must be satisfied by the concrete element bound to a role. A constraint of a UML association role P, for example, may require that the UML association bound to P must appear between the UML classes bound to certain other UML class roles Q and R.

A cardinality value is defined for each role. The cardinality of a role gives the lower and upper limits for the number of the elements bound to the role in the pattern. For example, if a role of type UML operation has cardinality value 0..1, the operation is optional, because the lower limit is 0.

Roles may depend on other roles. For example, there is a dependency from role P to role Q since the binding of P depends on the binding of Q. In this case, a UML class should be bound to role Q before that class is used when binding a UML association to role P.

A default element can be defined for a role. If a role with a default element specification is to be bound during the pattern instantiation process, the binding can be carried out by first generating the default element according to the specification, and then binding the role to this element. The specification of a default element may refer to the (elements bound to the) other roles, implying dependencies between the roles. Often, it is sufficient to calculate the value of the element name before the element gets generated.

In this work, aspects are represented using a role structure that can be instantiated and weaved into base models. The weaving corresponds to the binding of the roles: each role stores the information of a joint point. The constraints that are associated with a given role can be used to determine the context where the aspect may appear, and the constraints can be used to check whether the aspect, implemented by the pattern, is correctly weaved. There are a number of advantages in representing aspects as role-based patterns:

- Flexible weaving process: In contrast to traditional weaving, the weaving of aspectual patterns is considered as an interactive, incremental process where the join points are located under the guidance of a pattern tool, rather than in a fully automated fashion. The weaving process is performed as simple tasks in the context of the developer, rather than as a large black-box operation. By task we mean a simple action that adds an element or enforces a property on the base model. In the context of aspectual patterns, a task stands for binding an unbound element or enforcing a role constraint.

- Addressing several key challenges in aspect orientation: First, aspect overlapping can be represented and implemented in a straightforward way using role-based pattern composition techniques where a model element can play different roles in different patterns. Second, aspectual patterns offer a symmetric model where there is no explicit distinction between "base-level" elements and "aspect" elements. Yet, using binding information it is still possible to highlight the effect of aspects in base models. Another desired property of aspectual patterns is the ability to support various phases of the development process as roles can be bound to software and non-software elements covering various kinds of system artifacts. Finally, aspectual patterns can be reused in multiple contexts. Roles are attached with parameterized properties whose values are calculated and adapted to the context where the patterns are applied.

3.3 Pattern Role Diagrams

In order to improve the comprehensiveness of pattern structures, Fig. 4 introduces a notation for visual pattern specification. The figure depicts a role diagram of an aspectual pattern for managing system security. For simplicity, we discuss the pattern structure specified using a single set of role types, i.e., UML element types. In the next section, the representation is extended to multiple sets. Security is recognized as a critical concern, for example, when developing business applications. The aspectual pattern illustrated in the figure shows how security should be modeled in the system under development.

A ConcreteSecurityManager class provides a checkPermission operation which checks the security policy of a custom permission ConcretePermission. The nodes, marked in white, depict the pattern roles. The ConcreteSecurityManager role, for example, stands for any concrete element (in this case a UML class) that implements a custom security policy. The type of the role is specified above the role name. The edges in the upper part of the figure denote the dependencies between the roles. There are two kinds of dependencies: 1) the dependency from role checkPermission to role SecurityManager, which is marked with a diamond-headed line, represents the containment relationship between the elements that may play these two roles; and 2) the dependency from role ConcreteSecurityManager to role SecurityManager, which is marked with a light-arrow-headed broken line, stands for a logical relationship. In this case, any element that plays role ConcreteSecurityManager should implement the concrete element that plays role SecurityManager. The cardinality value ("1" for exactly one, "?" for optional, "*" for zero or more, "+" for at least one) of a role comes together with the role name. For instance, the cardinality value of ConcreteSecurityManager is "+" meaning that there should be at least one element bound to this role. If not otherwise indicated, the cardinality of the role is 1.

In order to show how the pattern can be applied, the bottom part of the figure gives a possible concrete binding (weaving). The concrete element FilePermission, represented by a dark-gray node, plays role ConcetePermission. This is marked by the double-arrowed line between FilePermission and ConcetePermission. There are two elements that play role ConcreteSecurityManager. This is a direct implication

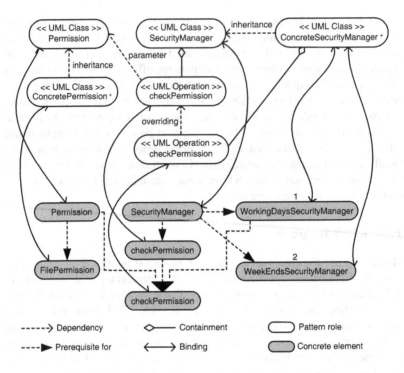

Fig. 4. Role diagram of an aspectual pattern for security

of the "+" cardinality symbol associated with this role. In case several concrete elements play the same pattern role, the order of the binding is indicated by an integer index. Moreover, the dark-headed arrows in this part of the figure denote the order of how the bindings should be performed. For instance, the binding of SecurityManager to its concrete element is a prerequisite for the binding between ConcreteSecurity-Manager and WorkingDaysSecurityManager.

3.4 Using Aspectual Patterns for Multiple Artifact Types

As described earlier, an aspectual pattern captures an aspect cutting across various software artifacts. This situation can be described using a heterogeneous aspectual pattern supporting multiple sets of role types (i.e., UML, Java, etc.). Considering the pattern discussed in Fig. 4, a heterogeneous aspectual pattern for security, for example, can be used to illustrate how security is represented in a software system implementation and documentation in addition to its design model.

Figure 5 shows the security pattern covering three different artifact types. The artifact types are represented by roughly circular shapes. For brevity Fig. 5, which can be regarded as an extension to Fig. 4, does not show role bindings. In addition to the design model, the pattern has roles for implementation and documentation. At the implementation level, there is a role named ConcreteSecurityManager. This

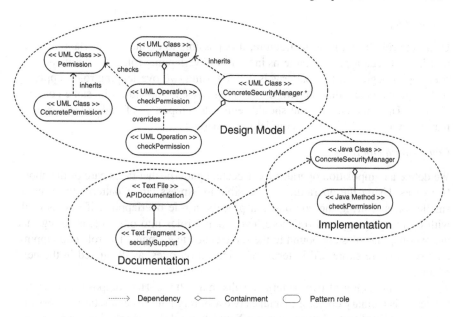

Fig. 5. Role diagram of a heterogeneous aspectual pattern for security

role is of type Java class and is used to represent a class implementing a specific security policy. Furthermore, there is a role at the documentation level for registering the used Java implementation in the system API documentation. This role is named securitySupport and should be bound to a text fragment providing the API documentation fragment. The text fragment should be stored in the API documentation file that should be bound to the APIDocumentation role.

3.5 Composition of Aspectual Patterns

In Sect. 2.3, two kinds of relationships between concerns have been identified: containment and overlapping. Assuming that aspectual patterns are used to specify system concerns, one needs to define proper techniques for representing such kinds of relationships. Let us first discuss containment and overlapping in the context of aspectual patterns.

Containment

This relationship is the simpler of the two. In the context of aspectual patterns, this relationship basically means that it should be possible to group together a number of patterns in order to express a larger concern. Realizing such a concern means applying all the constituent patterns defining that concern.

Overlapping

Using the role-based pattern structure, it is possible to define the overlapping relationship between aspectual patterns in terms of overlapping roles. Assuming that the overlapping region of two patterns is defined using two overlapping roles, applying both patterns means that the two overlapping roles are bound to the same concrete element. The concrete element should reflect the properties of both roles assuming that the two roles do not have conflicting properties.

Composition Operator

We define a composition operator for aspectual patterns that takes care of the above two cases. Using the operator, it is possible to express larger patterns in terms of smaller ones. During the composition process, a role overlapping, if any, is dealt with by merging any two (or more) overlapping roles into one role, meaning that the overlapping roles are bound to the same concrete element. The role overlapping relationships are expressed in terms of composition rules, as illustrated in the next example.

The composition of two patterns results in a pattern. The composition operator we define is a binary operator that takes two arbitrary patterns and returns a possibly larger one. Given two arbitrary patterns X and Y, if roleX and roleY are overlapping roles in patterns X and Y respectively, then the composition of X and Y can be expressed as follows:

$$Z = +(X, Y, \{(roleX, roleY)\})$$

Z is said to be the composite pattern of X and Y. The composition formula specifies the two patterns to be composed followed by a set of tuples defining the overlapping roles. In the composite pattern Z, the role representing the overlapping of roleX and roleY, say roleZ, is said to be the unified role of roleX and roleY.

Given the above definition, we can define the following composition properties:

- Two roles roleX and roleY can overlap only if they are of the same role type.
- Two roles roleX and roleY can overlap only if the parent roles of roleX and roleY (the roles where roleX and roleY are contained), if any, are overlapping too.
- If roleX and roleY are two overlapping roles, then the cardinality of the unified role roleZ is reduced to the more restricted cardinality of the two roles.
- If roleZ is the unified role of roleX and roleY, then roleZ has at most the total number of dependencies (both outgoing and incoming) of roleX and roleY. If roleX has n dependencies and roleY has m dependencies, then roleZ has at most n+m dependencies and at least max(n, m) dependencies. This is because some of the dependencies (dependencies having the same target role) of roleX and roleY can be the same.
- Similarly, roleZ is associated with the constraints of roleX and roleY. If roleX has n constraints and roleY has m constraints, then roleZ has at most n+m constraints and at least max(n, m) constraints. The constraints having the same type and value are treated as the same.

- Patterns X and Y are said to be disjoint if they have no overlapping roles. X and Y are said to be fully composed if there is a one-to-one mapping between all roles of X and Y.

Example

Figure 6 illustrates a situation where the security policy in a software system is log based. When designing a software system, security and logging are usually identified as two separate concerns. A common situation, however, is to compose these two concerns in one important concern, called log-based security. This new concern can be considered, for example, in order to check if the software system comes under attack by unauthorized sources at runtime.

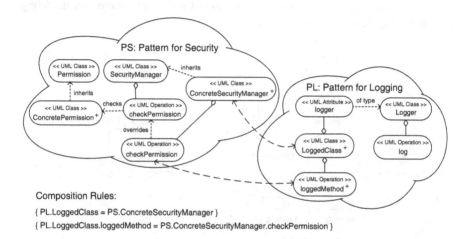

Fig. 6. Composing security and logging

Figure 6 shows two composed patterns. The pattern for security has the structure explained in Fig. 4. The pattern for logging defines roles for specifying the concrete logger to use and the logged operations to be logged. Role Logger should be bound to a UML class representing the used logger class. Role LoggedClass should be bound to the class to be logged, while loggedMethod represents the individual logged methods of that class.

In the above situation, the log-based security concern can be implemented by applying the two patterns PS (for security) and PL (for logging). During the binding process, roles ConcreteSecurityManager of PS and LoggedClass of PL should be bound to the same concrete element. The purpose is to log the security manager operations being called. The two class roles are said to be overlapping. Furthermore, roles loggedMethod and checkPermission should also be bound to the same concrete operation. The implication of this overlapping relationship is that the method implementing the security policy is recorded in the system logs. An overlapping relationship between two roles is graphically represented using a dashed double-headed arrow linking these two roles and is textually expressed in terms of composition rules. The composition rules in Fig. 6 are defined in terms of two role pairs. Each pair represents two overlapping roles.

3.6 Identifying and Documenting Aspectual Patterns

In order to be able to identify and structure system concerns (and thus the aspectual patterns), a high-level modularization technique based on concern architecture views is used. Concern architecture views are introduced in [247]. Typically, each concern in a concern architecture view tackles a specific area of interest in the software system. Concerns can, in turn, be composed of smaller units of interest. Each of these small units is treated as an aspectual pattern. In this way, concern architecture views are used to define and structure a system of aspectual patterns for modeling the software system.

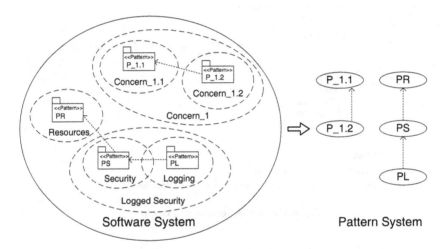

Fig. 7. Identifying aspectual patterns

The left part of Fig. 7 depicts the concern architecture view of an arbitrary software system. The log-based security concern, discussed in the previous section, is used as one of the example concerns. In addition, the figure shows three other concerns. There is a concern named Resources. This concern stands for adding to the system new resource types such as printer jobs or database connections. There are two other arbitrary concerns, Concern_1.1 and Concern_1.2. The aspectual patterns modeling these concerns are represented using rectangular shapes. In addition to illustrating concerns and patterns, the figure shows, using dashed arrows, possible dependencies between individual patterns. For example, there is a dependency from the pattern for logging (PL) to the pattern for security (PS) since the model elements for security need to be identified before they are logged. Another dependency links pattern PS to the pattern handling resources. The reason is that system developers want to define a security policy for every added resource type. As explained earlier, the log-based security concern is defined using two overlapping patterns. However, it is possible that a concern is formed using two disjoint smaller concerns. In this case, this concern is modeled using two disjoint aspectual patterns. This is the example of Concern_1.

The right part of Fig. 7 shows the list of patterns identified using the concern architecture view. Assuming a pattern-based MDD tool, it is essential to be able to model both the individual patterns and the various relationships between them. The next section presents a concrete implementation of a pattern-based tool that can be used to specify and apply heterogeneous aspectual patterns.

3.7 Aspectual Patterns as Transformations

As discussed earlier, transformation is an essential property for MDD. The main goal of model transformation is to document the relationships between models and to provide rules for deriving a model from another. Models at both ends of the transformation can be either within the same level of abstraction or at different levels. Furthermore, transformation can be applied instantly or incrementally. Instant transformation means that the transformation is carried out in a single batch operation whereas incremental transformation implies that the transformation is performed through a number of transformation steps.

Aspectual patterns can be thought of as a mechanism for incremental transformation, where a transformation step involves generating the possible default elements for unbound roles based on their specifications. The order of the transformation steps is implied by role dependencies. Thus, the relationships between model elements are in fact embedded in the role specification. Because aspectual patterns are heterogeneous, the transformation can be performed from and to any level of abstraction. The idea has been applied to achieve an open MDA environment [393].

4 Implementation – MADE

This section discusses the main components and features of the MADE (Modeling and Architecting Development Environment) tool and shows how heterogeneous aspectual patterns are represented and composed in MADE. However, the way patterns are applied is discussed in Sect. 5.

4.1 MADE Toolset

In order to demonstrate the heterogeneous aspectual pattern concept, a prototype tool known as MADE [193] has been developed. The MADE platform itself is the result of integrating three different tools: JavaFrames [183], xUMLi [348], and Rational Rose [368]. JavaFrames is a pattern-oriented development environment built on top of Eclipse [98]. Rational Rose is used as the UML editor. The third component, xUMLi, is a tool-independent platform for processing UML models and is used for integrating JavaFrames and Rational Rose. In addition to acting as a Java IDE, Eclipse offers a number of facilities useful for software development including a variety of integrated editors (such as for Java and text) and other project management tools. The MADE toolset can be downloaded from http://practise.cs.tut.fi/fred.

Originally, JavaFrames was developed as a pattern-driven specialization environment for Java-based frameworks. For this reason, the pattern role types have initially been Java specific. In order to support the heterogeneous pattern concept, however, support for new role types has been added. For modeling purposes, a set of UML-specific role types has been developed. A third set of role types has been designed for supporting general text file operations. In addition, there are a number of other role types representing informal tasks, reminders, and user input values.

When constructing new role types, the only thing one assumes is that the tools used to process the relevant system artifacts offer an API which allows the MADE tool to access the elements of those artifacts and to catch certain events (e.g., when an artifact has been modified). It is also possible to construct new kinds of constraints and associate them to proper role types. The same constraint kind can be applied to different role types, for instance a naming constraint which requires that the name of an artifact element should conform to a given regular expression.

Figure 8 shows an overall view of MADE. Rational Rose represents the upper part of the environment. As an example of an integrated editor, implementation code is displayed in a Java editor (middle view). The left view represents the part of the environment where patterns are specified and applied. In the next two subsections, pattern specification is discussed in more detail. Patterns are represented by circular graphical icons. In the MADE environment, patterns are instantiated as extensions of other patterns. For example, the Access pattern under the FileSystemAccess node is an instantiation of the Security pattern specified under the Catalogue node. In the MADE terminology, pattern Access extends pattern Security.

When a pattern is selected, MADE transforms the pattern into a task list. This is done by generating a task for each unbound role that can be bound in the current situation, taking into account the dependencies and cardinalities of roles. The task view displays the tasks implied by the pattern. This view is divided into two panes: task titles are shown in the upper pane and detailed task descriptions are presented in the lower one. In the example figure, a task for providing a logger field is displayed. There are two kinds of tasks: mandatory and optional. Mandatory tasks are marked using a red circular dot attached to the task title whereas optional tasks are marked with a white circular dot. The task presented in the figure is mandatory.

Tasks can be performed in two different ways. The developer might bind the pattern role to an existing model element. In this case, a binding between a pattern role and an existing model element is established but the model does not change. In most cases, however, executing a task means generating a new model element. In this case, a binding between a pattern role and the generated element is established and the element is added to the proper editor depending on the type of the element. If the model element is a UML class, for example, the element is shown in the UML editor. The middle view depicts the bindings that have been performed. Models can be freely edited through their dedicated tools: if an artifact is modified, the worst that

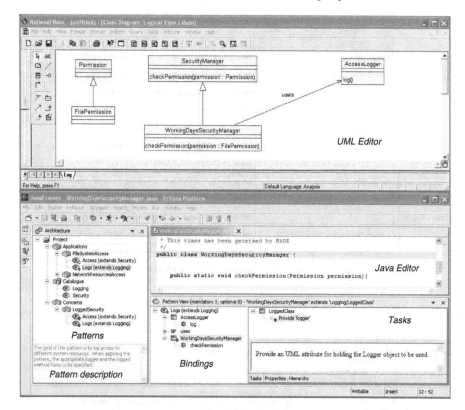

Fig. 8. MADE

can happen is that some bindings in an existing pattern become invalid or certain constraints defined by the pattern are violated. In this case, the pattern tool warns the developer about the inconsistencies and proposes corrective actions. It is then up to the developer to either correct the situation or ignore the warning.

4.2 Presenting Heterogeneous Aspectual Patterns in MADE

Considering the aspectual pattern for security discussed earlier, the actual pattern specification in MADE adds a number of properties to the role information shown in Fig. 5. These properties are mainly used by the tool for guiding the user through the development process. Figure 9 illustrates some of these role properties. For brevity, the figure does not show all the roles and properties. The roles have been grouped into three categories; each category represents a particular artifact type.

At the design model level, the definition of role ConcreteSecurityManager includes a defaultElementName, which is used as a default name when generating the UML class to be bound to the role. The value of this property is expressed as a template referring to the name of the concrete element bound to role SecurityManager,

Heterogeneous Aspectual Pattern: Security		
	Roles	**Properties**
Design Model	**SecurityManager:** UML Class (1)	**description:** Abstract class encapsulating security managers.
	ConcreteSecurityManager : UML Class *(+)*	**defaultElementName:** My<#:/SecurityManager.i.shortName>
		description : Concrete security manager implementation.
		taskTitle : Provide a UML class for concrete security manager.
	inheritance : Constraint	**value:** <#:/SecurityManager.i.shortName>
	checkPermission : UML Operation *(1)*	**description:** UML operation encapsulating a concrete security policy.
	parameter : Constraint	**value:** <#:/Permission.i.shortName>
	Permission : UML Class *(1)*	**description:** A UML class encapsulating the kinds of permissions.
Implementation	**JavaConcreteSecurityManager:** Java Class (1)	**description** : Java implementation for a concrete security manager.
		defaultElementName : <#:/ConcreteSecurityManager.i.shortName>
	checkPermission : Java Method (1)	**description**: Java implementation of a concrete security policy.
Documentation	**APIDocumentationbstract** : Text File (1)	**description** : A text file for documenting system API.
	securitySupport : Text Fragment *(1)*	**description**: Recording API for security support.

Fig. 9. Properties of the pattern for security

Fig. 10. MADE aspectual pattern

which in this example represents a base class of all security managers. The property taskTitle is used by the tool for generating a title for the corresponding task. The inheritance constraint is used to enforce the generalization/specialization relationship between concrete elements bound to role ConcreteSecurityManager and the concrete element bound to role SecurityManager. In this case, the specification says that any UML class bound to role ConcreteSecurityManager should inherit from the UML class bound to role SecurityManager. The cardinality of roles is given in parentheses after the role names. At the implementation level, role JavaConcreteSecurityManager refers to role ConcreteSecurityManager for generating the default name of concrete elements. In this case, the specification suggests sharing the same name.

Figure 10 shows a view of the MADE pattern editor specifying the pattern for security. The left pane shows the hierarchical structure of the pattern roles and constraints. In this case, role checkPermission is selected. The right pane is composed of two parts. The upper view displays the list of roles which the selected role depends on. The lower portrays exposes the checkPermission role properties discussed in Fig. 9.

4.3 Composing Aspectual Patterns

Section 3 discussed two kinds of relationships that may exist between different aspectual patterns: containment and overlapping. A composition operator was then defined in order to represent these relationships. Figure 11 shows how patterns are organized and applied in the MADE tool environment. In particular, the figure shows how individual patterns can be composed to treat larger concerns. Patterns are organized using architecture nodes. There are three types of architecture nodes: catalogue, concern, and application. Individual patterns are created under the Catalogue root node. At this stage, each aspectual pattern is regarded as a separate entity treating a specific concern in a software system and completely unrelated to other patterns. In the example case, there are two patterns named Logging and Security. The two patterns respectively implement the concerns discussed in Sect. 3.

The concerns of a software system are represented using concern nodes and are hierarchically represented under the Concerns root node as shown in Fig. 11. The figure depicts a single concern named LoggedSecurity. As discussed in Sect. 3, this concern is the composition of two component concerns: logging and security. If a concern is implemented by multiple aspectual patterns, that concern may define rules on how the patterns are composed. Composition rules are specified as a property of concern nodes and are currently specified in a text area as shown in Fig. 11. Each composition rule is formulated using a pair of pattern roles. The first rule, for example, says that role LoggedClass in the pattern for logging overlaps with role ConcreteSecurityManager in the pattern for security.

Currently, pattern composition in MADE requires manual enumeration of the composition rules, which might become a challenging task as the number of rules grows high. This problem can be partially resolved by keeping MADE patterns small in size and loosely coupled. Another solution we are investigating is the possibility to build the composition rules on the fly and compose the patterns when applied to base models.

Application development is carried out by considering those concerns relevant to the application needs. Using MADE, the developer selects which concern he or she wants to realize. The environment then takes care of which patterns to instantiate. The Application root node in Fig. 11 shows a concrete realization of the LoggedSecurity concern. The concrete application is named FileSystemAccess and stands for developing a security policy for file system access. Access and Logs represent respectively the instantiation of patterns Security and Logging. When a pattern is selected, the environment displays the tasks corresponding to that pattern. When tasks are executed, the composition rules are taken into account. If a developer binds a role that has an overlapping counterpart, the overlapping role is automatically bound to the same concrete element.

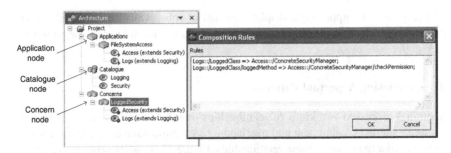

Fig. 11. Composing aspectual pattern in MADE

4.4 Main Features of MADE

MADE comes with a number of qualities desirable for MDD. The main characteristics of the tool are:

(1) Stepwise development environment: MADE transforms a pattern specification into a task list guiding developers step by step through model development.

(2) Automatic detection and repair of broken model conventions: If a model is manually edited, the environment provides immediate validation of the model against the pattern specifications. In the case of a constraint violation, a repair task is created to inform the user about the violation. In most cases, the tool provides the option to automatically repair the violation, for example, restoring a generalization/specialization relationship between two classes.

(3) Adapting to developer's context: MADE is able to record the history of developers' tasks and use the recorded information when documenting next tasks. The tool, for example, uses the names of concrete elements in the textual descriptions of related tasks.

(4) Support for separation of concerns in models: Using MADE, individual concerns in a software system are represented as a set of aspectual patterns.

(5) Support for traceability and visualization: Aspectual patterns are used to represent a concern crosscutting various abstraction levels. When a pattern is applied, MADE records role binding information which can be used later to link together different representations of a concern at different abstraction levels or simply to highlight the effect of a concern in a base model.

(6) Openness to new design conventions: MADE is not bound to a fixed set of patterns. As new concerns are identified, new patterns can be easily introduced to the existing architecture. In addition, as the application domain evolves, existing pattern specification can be updated and outdated patterns can be removed. It is also possible to change the specification of patterns if the roles are not yet bound.

Category	Purpose	Creator	User
Feature variation pattern	Manage feature variability across different software artifacts	Product line architect	Product developer
Maintenance pattern	Document anticipated maintenance tasks at different model levels	Designer	Maintainer
Framework specialization pattern	Document the specialization interface of application frameworks at different model levels	Framework architect	Application developer
Comprehension pattern	Learn complex system models through model customization at different levels of abstraction	System architect/ designer	Developer/ Maintainer

Fig. 12. Example categories of aspectual patterns

5 Supporting Different Activities

The MADE tool has been applied to support MDD in a number of ways. In the subsequent sections, four applications of heterogeneous aspectual patterns are presented. Figure 12 depicts four pattern categories relevant to each application: feature variation patterns, maintenance patterns, framework specialization patterns, and comprehension patterns. In addition to the purpose of the pattern, the figure shows the different stakeholders that are involved in creating the patterns and those involved in applying them. In the first category, for example, feature variation patterns have been used to manage feature variability in software systems. In this case, heterogeneous aspectual patterns are used to represent the different variation points and to make sure that when a specific feature variant is selected, that decision is propagated to all models of the application. These kinds of patterns are usually created by product-line developers specifying the different variation points in the system architecture. Product developers then apply these patterns to design and implement new products.

In the remainder of the discussion, each subsection discusses a pattern category, together with an example application. In addition to validating the approach, the aim of the examples is to discuss the details of MADE from different perspectives. In the first two applications, the focus will be on the specification and the deployment of aspectual patterns. The first example shows how the specification of a pattern can be transformed into a task list and how the tasks are carried out in the MADE tool. The second example discusses the issue of viewing and browsing the model fragments that are relevant to a particular concern. In the third and fourth applications, the focus will be on the role of concern architecture views in the identification of aspectual patterns, as discussed in Sect. 3.6. The third case study illustrates the use of concern architecture views to specify the extension points in an example framework specialization interface. The last application shows the use of concern architecture views to describe the customization principles of an example complex model.

5.1 Feature Variability Management

In software product lines, variability means variation in the definition and implementation of a specific feature or additional features [82]. Variability can occur at different levels in the design: product-line level, product level, component level, subcomponent level, and code level [412]. Assuming that variation is represented at different model levels, it is essential to reflect the choice of a particular variant in all levels. Typically, every variation point is represented using a separate aspectual pattern. A single variation point may crosscut various model levels. To represent this crosscutting nature, feature variation patterns [190], which have roles covering different artifact types, can be used.

Example

In EJB component architecture [226], for example, the persistence of a BMP (Bean-Managed Persistence) entity bean can be realized by the use of different database products. In order to achieve maximum portability, bean providers choose to support multiple database implementations. Database variation in a BMP entity bean is considered as a variation point in the bean implementation. In order to manage this variation point, bean developers use a solution called Data Access Object (DAO) defining a common interface for all possible data source implementations. When a BMP bean is deployed, only one database implementation is used.

There are two common solutions to select a data source implementation. The first is to hardcode the name of the implementation class in a specific registration method in the bean. When the data source changes, the implementation of that method changes so that it would return the proper implementation class. Another solution is to store the name of the implementation class in the deployment descriptor of the bean, as an environment variable. The bean decides at runtime which data source to use by looking up the value of this environment variable. In both techniques, either the Java code or the deployment descriptor should change according to the data source selected. However, even if the developer decides to hardcode the implementation class in the bean code, storing the information of the used data source in the deployment descriptor might serve other purposes such as application documentation.

Let us assume that the database variation is given as a feature model and that one needs to reflect the database choice in the design model of the bean as well. Both the feature model and the design model are expressed in terms of UML class diagrams. In addition to filling the variation point in the design model, the class corresponding to the selected data source should be represented in the registration method and the deployment description of the bean.

The MADE solution for the above situation is to use a feature variation pattern for managing the database variation. In this context, the concern that the pattern encapsulates is the database implementation feature. The pattern covers four abstraction levels: feature model, design model, implementation, and deployment information. The pattern has roles for representing UML model element (feature model and design model), Java element (bean implementation), and XML entities (deployment descriptor).

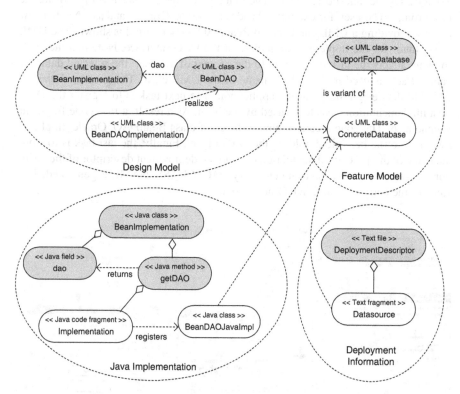

Fig. 13. Pattern role diagram for database product variation

Figure 13 shows a pattern role diagram for database product variation. The diagram uses the notation introduced in Fig. 5. The shaded roles represent pre-bound roles that define the context of applying the pattern. The pre-bound role DeploymentDescriptor, for example, is bound to the XML file that represents the deployment descriptor of the bean. At the level of the feature model, role ConcreteDatabase represents the database product variation point. When the pattern is applied, the role should be bound to a concrete UML class reflecting the selected data source. Several roles in other abstraction levels depend on this role. At the design model level, role BeanDAOImplementation reflects the data source selection in the design model of the bean. At the Java implementation level, role Implementation represents a Java code fragment that registers the proper database implementation class. Finally, at the deployment information level, role Datasource represents an XML tag that stores the name of the selected database implementation into an environment variable.

Figure 14 shows a scenario for applying the pattern shown in Fig. 13. MADE presents a role binding as a task, shown as a textual prompt. The execution of the task results in binding the role to a concrete element. The first task is to select the data source to be used. The developer is shown the list of available data sources: MySQL, Oracle, and PostgreSQL. The outcome of the task is shown following the task prompt. The user, for example, decides to use the Oracle database. Next, a new task for providing a UML class named BeanDAO_Oracle_Impl is shown. The UML class stands for the implementation class of the DAO interface. Note that the environment adapts the task description to the context of the user: the selected database name Oracle is used in the default name of the UML class. The generated class is added to the design model of the application. The next task is to register the DAO Java implementation class to be used by the bean. As a result, a Java code fragment is generated. The code creates a new instance of class BeanDAO_Oracle_Impl and assigns it to the bean field holding the DAO object. Finally, the last task is to store the name of the DAO implementation class in the deployment descriptor of the bean. For this purpose, a new environment entry DAO_CLASS_NAME is generated. The value of the entry is BeanDAO_Oracle_Impl.

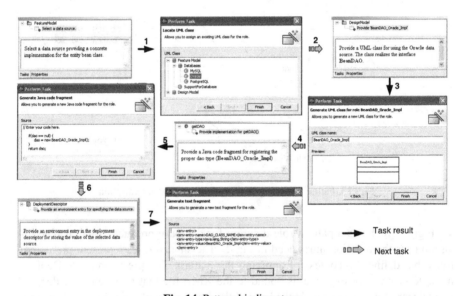

Fig. 14. Pattern binding steps

Figure 15 depicts an overall view of MADE after the tasks described above have been carried out. In the upper left part, the feature model is displayed in the UML editor. Using the same editor, the design model of the bean is presented in the upper right view. A proper database implementation class named BeanDAO_Oracle_Impl is used. The Java editor in the middle shows the generated Java implementation of the database registration method whereas the right-hand side shows the environment variable stored in the deployment descriptor file of the bean. The Bindings view groups together all the role bindings at all abstraction levels. Using the tool, it is possible to trace back the concrete elements bound to the pattern roles. However, it is also useful to know to which roles an artifact element is bound. This feature will be implemented in future versions of the tool.

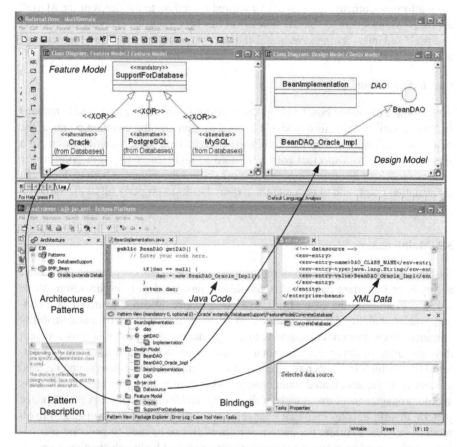

Fig. 15. Managing database product variation in MADE

Experiences

The aim of this section was to illustrate the details of MADE by studying the use of a simple feature variation pattern. An important question is "Can the approach scale up?" To address the question of scalability, we are currently studying the practical applicability of the approach in an industrial product line [190]. The example case study is to use the MADE approach to identify, express, and manage variability in a Nokia GUI platform. The early results have been positive. It was possible to conveniently present a number of variation points in the platform with a set of heterogeneous patterns covering four abstraction levels: the feature model representing services provided by the platform, the design model of the product, the Java implementation of the application, and the product service registry files.

The biggest challenge in the case study has been identifying the variation points in the GUI platform and expressing them using feature models. The reason is that the platform documentation was not structured according to the needs of the MADE approach. Consequently, considerable effort has been spent on studying the product line itself and interviewing several stakeholders participating in the development and use of the platform.

Concluding Remarks

This example discussed how heterogeneous aspectual patterns can be used to manage feature variability. A feature model is defined to represent the variation points at the requirements level. Application developers need to bind these variation points to a specific variant. An aspectual pattern is used to represent a variation point in the various models of a software system. The purpose of the pattern is both to document the variation points and to generate the required tasks to properly fill in the variation points at different model levels.

5.2 Maintenance

System maintainability is considered as a development-process concern. Maintainability is an important concern that should be considered early in the design phase [413], especially in the case of adaptive maintenance. When considered as a concern, maintainability can be expressed in terms of a related set of maintainability concerns. Each concern corresponds to a large maintenance task that may crosscut different units of decomposition such as classes or modules. A maintenance pattern [189], which is a concrete usage of the aspectual pattern concept, can be used to document the anticipated maintenance tasks. Furthermore, maintenance actions should propagate to all the models of the system under maintenance. A maintenance pattern, therefore, takes care that changes due to maintenance are propagated to all model levels. In addition, the pattern specification can be used to generate maintenance tasks based on maintenance actions carried out at higher abstraction levels. It is important, for instance, that the implementation code of a software system adapts to any maintenance changes occurring in the design model.

Example

Measuring human–computer interaction is very important for improving interactive systems and their user interfaces. In order to conduct this kind of measurement, proper measuring tools have to be implemented. When designing such tools, it is impractical to fix all aspects of the measurement process as new measurements and measuring strategies are discovered after the tool is in use. It is important therefore to anticipate at the design phase those extension points.

As an example, consider some measuring software for making user tests of a web search engine user interface. Using the measuring tool, it is possible to both log and analyze the results of these tests. The measuring tool first writes user interactions with the search engine into log files, then parses the stored log files, and builds an object structure based on the logged information. In a second phase, a specific component is used to make measurements based on the observed data. There are a variety of possible measurements such as average time needed to complete a task, average number of selections made in one task, or total number of selections made during the test. Many others can be discovered as information is being logged. Furthermore, a measurer component can be defined by combining any of these measurements. Therefore, it is possible to design and use new measurer components as the system runs.

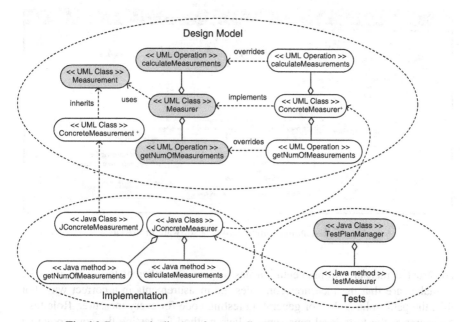

Fig. 16. Pattern role diagram for extending some measurement software

Considering the example, one can define a maintenance pattern for extending measurements and for building new measures. Figure 16 shows a structure for such a pattern. For brevity, some roles have been omitted. The pattern has roles in three model levels. At the design model level, for example, role ConcreteMeasurer stands for a new measurer component and should be bound to a UML class in the design model of the measuring software. The role has two child roles: getNumOfMeasurements represents the operation returning the number of used methods and role calculateMeasurements stands for the operation that performs the actual measurements.

As a new measurer is added to the design model, a corresponding Java implementation class should be defined at the implementation level. This is marked by the dependency from role JConcreteMeasurer at the implementation level to role ConcreteMeasurer at the design model level. Further, let us suppose that every newly

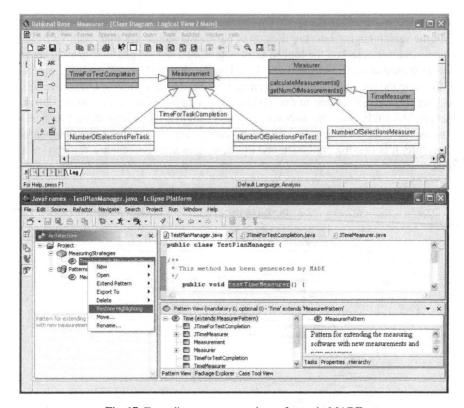

Fig. 17. Extending some measuring software in MADE

constructed measurer implementation has to pass a number of test cases in order to make sure that the measurer combines the measurements in a correct way. For this, the pattern has roles for generating testing code for every measurer. Role test-Measurer at the tests level represents a Java method for testing the corresponding measure. Similarly to Fig. 13, pre-bound roles are shaded.

Figure 17 shows a possible deployment of the maintenance pattern in MADE. The pattern has been used to provide a new measurement strategy (TimeForTest-Completion) and a new measurer component (TimeMeasurer). Using MADE, it is possible to view the effect of applying the pattern to different model levels. The UML model elements rendered in darker color show the effect of highlighting the maintenance pattern at the design model level. At the Implementation level, the Java source files associated with the pattern are shown in the Java editor. In addition, a method for testing the new measurer is highlighted in the existing TestPlanManager Java class reflecting the effect of the maintenance pattern at the tests level. Pattern highlighting is regarded as a tool for tracing a single concern across multiple software artifacts.

Experiences

As another example of adaptive maintenance, we have applied the approach to the MADE system [189]. The motivation was to show that if the approach works for general anticipated maintenance tasks, it should work for maintaining MADE itself. The pattern engine, which is an integral part of the MADE system, has been designed to support new artifact types and notations. Thus, the case study was to use the tool to construct new role types.

An experiment for creating two new role types has been carried out in [201]. As a result, a total of 11 Java classes (400 lines of code) have been created. Out of these, 315 lines of code have been generated automatically while 85 lines of code have been manually created or edited. Thus, the MADE approach achieved a ratio of 79% of automatic code generation. The other 21% was not automatically generated since it stands for knowledge that is not captured by the pattern specification. In this case, for example, it was not possible to anticipate how to resolve an artifact element bound to a role of the newly constructed type since this depends greatly on the tool where that artifact element is managed.

Concluding Remarks

In this example application, heterogeneous aspectual patterns have been used to document and generate the maintenance tasks required for maintaining a software system. In this case, an example of adaptive maintenance is considered. However, other forms of maintenance can also be supported [189]. Here, maintenance is considered as an activity that is mainly dealt with at the design and implementation phases. In contrast, variability management is addressed in the requirements and architecture levels. Maintenance patterns have roles covering multiple sets of role types in order to reflect the maintenance actions at all possible model levels. For brevity, the discussion does not show how the pattern is applied in MADE. Typically, individual maintenance tasks are similar to the ones described in Fig. 14.

5.3 Framework Specialization

An object-oriented framework is a reusable design expressed as a set of classes implementing the basic architecture for a family of software systems [121]. Framework specialization is the process of adapting a framework to meet the requirements of a specific application. Framework specialization is usually regarded as a complex task. The reason is twofold. First, following the specialization instructions often lack tool support and can be tedious. Second, there is a lack of assisting application developers to carry out the specializations at the level of visual modeling languages, such as UML. As a solution, special-purpose aspectual patterns, called framework specialization patterns [193], can be used to structure and document the specialization interface of frameworks into different specialization concerns. A specialization concern crosscuts different software artifacts of the framework specialization. Patterns are used in order to make the specialization process easier by grouping the specialization tasks into meaningful parts (concerns) and propagating the specialization

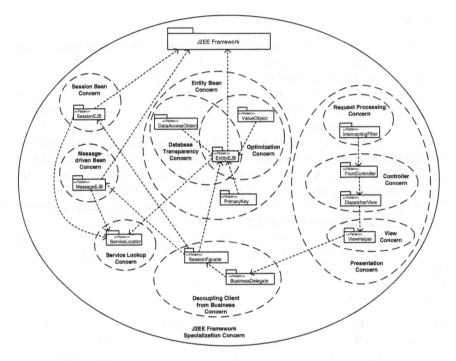

Fig. 18. Specialization concern architecture view for J2EE

decisions to all generated application models including design and implementation, and documentation.

Example

J2EE is a component-based and platform-independent architecture for building enterprise applications. J2EE applications are constructed by following the architectural rules imposed by the J2EE framework. On top of these architectural rules, several design conventions have been proposed to bring better reuse, maintainability, and portability to these applications [192]. Figure 18 depicts a concern architecture view structuring the specialization interface of the J2EE platform into a number of concerns reflecting these architectural rules and design conventions.

There are three concerns for the creation of the three bean types: session, message-driven, and entity beans. Each of the first two concerns is represented using a single aspectual pattern whereas the third is composed of several smaller concerns and thus implemented using more than one pattern. Patterns SessionEJB and MessageEJB are used to generate a session bean and a message-driven bean respectively. In order to generate an entity bean, four patterns should be applied. Pattern EntityEJB models the core components of an entity bean. Pattern ValueObject is used to optimize the communication between business components and clients. Pattern DataAccessObject is applied to make the enterprise components transparent to the data source used. This solution has already been discussed in Sect. 5.1. This pattern is applied for generating entity beans with BMP only. The fourth pattern PrimaryKey is responsible for generating primary key classes for the corresponding entity beans. In order to locate other business components, patterns SessionEJB, MessageEJB, and EntityEJB get the service of a pattern named ServiceLocator whose role is to abstract the complexity of the lookup process.

In order to decouple client access from the core business layer of the application, two patterns are used: pattern SessionFacade is used to reduce the complexity of the interaction between clients and business objects by grouping together the access to multiple beans. In addition, pattern BusinessDelegate is used to achieve loose coupling between clients at the presentation tier and the business services implemented by the enterprise beans.

The presentation layer is defined using three concerns. There is a concern for pre-processing requests. This concern is represented by a pattern named InterceptingFilter. The aim of this pattern is to process requests and responses before being passed to clients. The second concern is for defining a control strategy of how to process requests and view navigation. It is represented by two patterns. Pattern FrontController centralizes the decision how to retrieve and process the requests and pattern DispatcherView separates the logic on deciding which view comes next from the view components themselves. Finally, the third concern deals with the view component of the presentation layer and is modeled using one pattern named ViewHelper. This pattern processes business data for getting presentation content.

Figure 19 shows the patterns and the concerns, which have been identified in Fig. 18, specified in the MADE tool. First, patterns are defined under the Catalogue node, then they are grouped into separate concerns under the Concerns node. In addition, the figure depicts a concrete application implemented according to the architecture proposed by the pattern system. The application is a web-based to-do list where a list of users and their associated tasks can be accessed, manipulated, and stored in a relational database. The Entity_Bean concern is considered to implement an entity bean for representing users. This is depicted in the figure by the node User_Entity_Bean. The Session_Bean concern is used to implement a session bean modeling user tasks. This is illustrated by the Task_Session_Bean. Since the application does not need asynchronous communications, no message-driven bean is developed. This is why the concern Message-driven_Bean is not considered in the application.

Experiences

Using MADE, it was possible to automatically generate up to 60% of the total lines of code for the to-do list application discussed above [192]. Manually, it could take up to 20 hours to construct the code from scratch. Using MADE, the same task took a couple of hours. Approximately, one-third of the development time was spent with using the environment for automatic code generation. The rest was to manually provide custom business code and user interface implementation. The overall design was made according to the widely used J2EE design patterns.

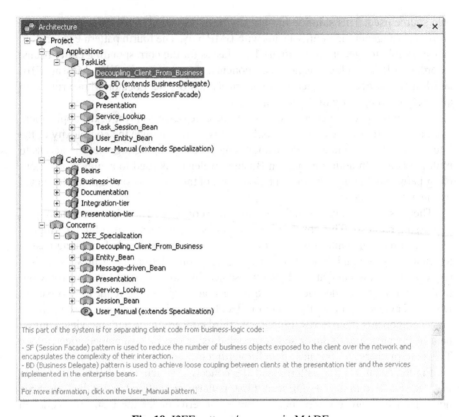

Fig. 19. J2EE patterns/concerns in MADE

Therefore, the MADE tool could be used to improve the quality of the application and reduce the development effort. Nevertheless, identifying the proper concerns and patterns requires effort and domain expertise. Besides, modeling the patterns in MADE, in terms of roles and their properties, can be a laborious task. For instance, it took a couple of hours to model the EntityEJB pattern and several deployment checks to validate the pattern against its specification.

Concluding Remarks

This section shows how concern architecture views can be used to identify and document the relationships between framework specialization patterns specified as aspectual patterns. Framework specialization is another example of variability management. In this case, however, the decision on the variation points is not bound to a specific feature model. Instead, the specialization decisions are open. For brevity, the structural specification of the patterns is not discussed and the actual deployment of the pattern system has been omitted.

Framework specialization patterns are heterogeneous aspectual patterns. Using MADE, it is possible to generate the design model, the implementation, and the deployment descriptors of the enterprise application. If servlets are used for implementing the presentation layer, the standard Filter approach can be used when applying the InterceptingFilter pattern, which means that the pattern has roles for representing XML files. Furthermore, the patterns at the presentation layer may have roles for supporting different client implementations such as HTML, JSP, or WML.

5.4 Comprehension

Customization is an essential activity for comprehending complex model structures since it is easier to study a system one part at a time [343]. Model customization can be used to adapt a model to specific purposes by identifying only those parts of the model that correspond to these purposes. Assuming that software systems are represented using different forms of models, customization decisions should cover all these model levels. For example, the same customization principles should be used to customize a design model and the source code of a software system. In this way, the implementation of the system remains aligned with the design model. Comprehension patterns [188], which are aspectual patterns reflecting system comprehensibility issues, are used to group related model parts of complex systems into separate comprehensibility concerns. Using comprehension patterns, it is possible to show those parts of the system that are relevant for a specific purpose and to make sure that models remain aligned following the customization actions.

Example

JPEG (Joint Photographic Experts Group) [417] is one of the well-known file formats for compressed images. The structural model behind this standard is an example of a complex system since it comprises a large number of components, defines complex inter-component dependencies, and is subject to extension. An efficient way of learning this complex system is to customize its model according to the specific needs of the learner, focusing on those parts relevant to the actual context and leaving out the irrelevant parts.

Figure 20 presents the different relationships between the various JPEG-related file formats. The file formats are shown using cubical shapes. There are, however, four main file formats: JPEG, JFIF, EXIF, and DCF. These formats are discussed in more detail in [188]. The dashed arrows describe the dependencies between these formats. The DCF format, for example, is an extension of the EXIF format. Consequently, for learning the DCF format, it is required to learn the EXIF format as well. However, it is not necessary to learn the DCF extensions in order to learn EXIF.

Figure 21 shows a concern architecture view for structuring the comprehensibility of the JPEG-related file formats. There are four concerns; each concern corresponds to learning the corresponding file format and is modeled using a number of comprehension patterns. The DCF format concern, for example, represents the structural components and rules that correspond to DCF file formats. It is composed of the EXIF format concern and three DCF-specific comprehension patterns. These three patterns represent the model elements that are specific to the DCF extensions

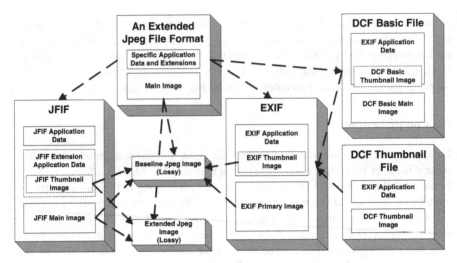

Fig. 20. The JPEG file formats

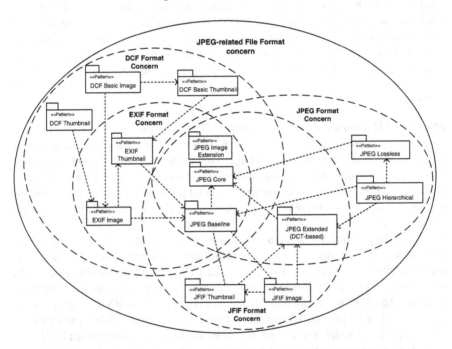

Fig. 21. Comprehensibility concern architecture view for JPEG-related file formats

only. The EXIF format concern, in turn, is modeled using two EXIF-specific patterns and three JPEG-related patterns. The latter three patterns represent the core model elements required for defining any of the file formats.

Given the above concern architecture view, it is clear that in order to comprehend the DCF part of the JPEG-related file formats, there is no need to study the model elements relevant to JPEG or JFIF formats only. Using MADE, only those patterns corresponding to the DCF format concern have to be applied. The environment provides learning tasks corresponding to the model elements reflecting the structure of DCF.

Figure 22 depicts the MADE specification of the architecture identified in Fig. 21. Individual patterns and concerns are specified in the Catalogue and Concerns nodes respectively. Furthermore, the figure shows three example customization scenarios for learning different formats of the JPEG standard: EXIF, JFIF, and basic JPEG formats. As an example, the environment displays the patterns that should be applied for learning the EXIF format. The complete case study is discussed in more detail in [188].

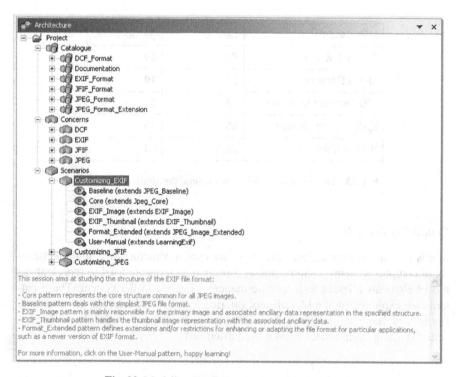

Fig. 22. Modeling JPEG patterns/concerns in MADE

Experiences

Comprehension patterns are used to represent a structured collection of model elements. Using MADE, developers are able to view only the artifact elements resulting from the application of patterns. The whole original model can be obtained by applying all the patterns. A number of experiments have been conducted to determine the customization capabilities of the MADE tool in the context of the case study. Figure 23 shows a comparison between the original model of the JPEG library structure and several customized models. The customized models represent different concerns in the library. Depending on the selected concern, the customization resulted in a reduced number of model elements. For example, this number is reduced by 50% when the user focuses on the JFIF-related features.

In the case of the JPEG library, it was relatively easy to identify the comprehension patterns based on the concern architecture views. However, in case the architecture does not clearly separate different concerns, it might become harder to identify the patterns. Comprehension patterns, on the other hand, are more useful when the crosscutting concerns are not directly reflected by the architecture.

UML Model	Classes	Associations
Original Model	70	50
JPEG Baseline	27	19
EXIF without thumbnail	49	37
EXIF with thumbnail	55	43
Whole JFIF	32	24

Fig. 23. The original model versus several customized models

Concluding Remarks

In this section, concern architecture views are used to structure the comprehensibility of complex systems. Heterogeneous aspectual patterns are used to represent the model elements relevant to a specific matter of interest in the system. These patterns are exploited by the MADE tool offering a task-based learning environment. For brevity, however, the detailed specification of the patterns is not shown and the actual learning environment has not been discussed.

6 Related Work

In this section, we discuss work related to the notion of aspectual patterns and the principle of separation of concerns. We then compare our methodology for MDD to other approaches and tools.

6.1 Aspectual Patterns

The term aspectual pattern used in this paper is inspired by the work on aspectual components [274]. The constructs in both approaches are represented in terms of a graph of nodes. In the case of [274], a graph node, called a participant, is a class in the participant graph that should be bound to classes in other participant graphs or to a concrete class graph. In the context of MADE, the graph nodes represent the pattern roles. Roles may overlap with other roles and need to be bound to concrete elements. The key difference between the two approaches is that aspectual components operate at the programming level whereas aspectual patterns apply to different artifact types expressed in different notations.

Glandrup and Aksit [149] independently use the term aspectual pattern in a slightly different context. In their work, an aspectual pattern is a language-independent extension for a pattern. The extension is used to describe the crosscutting behavior of a pattern. Similar to the MADE approach, a role-model is used to represent how patterns are superimposed in the implementation and role constraints are used for tracing and verification of patterns in the implementation. MADE can be used to implement the concepts proposed in [149].

6.2 Separation of Concerns

The issue of separation of concerns has already been discussed in the context of MDD. According to Kulkarni and Leddy [263], separation of concerns should be dealt with at both the model and code levels. The authors propose a development architecture that uses parameterized package abstractions to specify and compose concerns at the model level. At the code level, these concerns are managed using aspect-oriented programming. The MADE approach extends the ideas of [263] by supporting separation of concerns at all model levels including documentation, test code, and deployment information if possible. Instead of using different techniques to represent concerns at different levels, the methodology presented in this work uses a solution applicable to all levels. This leads to better traceability between models.

The idea of representing concerns within and across different artifacts has been addressed in the work on multi-dimensional separation of concerns [419]. The authors present a model for encapsulating concerns using so-called hyperslices. These are entities independent of any artifact formalism. Aspectual patterns, presented in this work, can be considered as a concrete realization of the hyperslice concept. Other concepts such as subjects [62], contracts [208], aspects [124], and viewpoints [304] also correspond to aspectual patterns. Subjects are class hierarchies representing a particular viewpoint of a domain model. Contracts operate on object-oriented artifacts and are used to represent objects and their interactions separating them from other interactions involving the same objects. Aspects, on the other hand, have been mostly used to represent concerns at the programming level. Viewpoints, in turn, are used to represent developers' views at the requirements level. Different viewpoints can be described using different notations. Compared to these concepts, aspectual patterns are not bound to a specific artifact type and can be used to represent any type of structural configuration including text document for example.

6.3 MDD

MDA (Model-Driven Architecture) is a recent initiative by OMG for supporting MDD principles. MDA defines three views of a system: a Computation Independent Model (CIM), which is a representation of a system from a business viewpoint, a Platform Independent Model (PIM), which is a representation of a system ignoring platform (technology) specific details, and Platform Specific Model (PSM), which is a model of a system that covers both platform independent information and details about a specific platform. OMG claims that this hierarchy offers better control for software development and brings up desired qualities such as portability, interoperability, and reusability. In response to the needs of MDA, the QVT-Partners have released a revised proposal for the OMG's QVT RFP [165]. QVT stands for Queries/Views/Transformations and represents a standardized transformation language to allow UML models to be transformed into usable software. The MADE approach solves some of the issues mentioned in the RFP. The aspectual pattern concept can be used as a technical infrastructure for managing the various transformations between models [393].

Batory et al. treat models as a series of layered refinements [31]. Individual features (reflecting different concerns) are composed together in a stepwise refinement fashion to form complex models. Models can be programs or other non-code representations. In order to support their concepts, the authors have developed a number of tools for feature composition, called the AHEAD toolset. The toolset provides similar functions to those of the MADE tool. MADE, however, solves two problems not otherwise addressed in [31]: tracing concerns in the generated models and checking the validity of models against the architectural rules.

6.4 Tools

As MDA is considered as the most popular approach for MDD, MDD tools are generally referred to in the software community as MDA tools. A number of these tools along with a detailed comparative evaluation are presented in [35]. Some of these tools were not originally built for MDA but were later tuned to support its principles. Similarly, the MADE pattern concept and pattern engine wereinitially implemented for specializing Java-based frameworks. Most tools (if not all) do not implement all the features of MDD (or MDA). Instead, each tool considers a restricted set of features. MADE takes the same line: the tool supports separation of concerns across models at different abstraction levels.

The Concern Manipulation Environment (CME) [64] shares similar ideas and goals as those of MADE. The idea of CME is to offer end users an open suite of tools for use in creating, manipulating, and evolving aspect-oriented software, across the full software lifecycle. The environment helps in interoperating and integrating different AOSD tools and paradigms and comes with an initial set of components. For instance, the Concern Manager (ConMan) tool models software in terms of arbitrary concerns and their interrelationships. A strong similarity between MADE and

ConMan is the support for a wide variety of concern structures and software decompositions – artifact types.

The most closely matching MDD tool related to the MADE approach is Rational XDE [400]. Similarly to our approach, XDE includes a pattern engine that can be used for model transformation. However, patterns are applied differently in MADE than they are in XDE. In MADE, it is possible to apply a pattern in small increments whereas an XDE pattern is only applied in full. The reason is that MADE treats each role binding as a separate task. After an XDE pattern is applied, the integrity of the pattern against the model is not automatically supervise; one has to revalidate the pattern bindings each time the model changes. Also, XDE does not detect all violations (e.g., a deleted generalization relationship between two classes) when the model is manually edited. In MADE, the conformance to the architecture expressed by patterns is supervised all the time and it is possible to detect all constraint violations in the model against pattern specifications. When a violation is detected, a new task is immediately generated informing the developer about the violation and suggesting an automatic repair. Another significant difference is that aspectual patterns can have roles representing non-software entities like text files and user input values or even roles representing informal entities like reminders. Furthermore, in XDE, there is no support for explicit modeling of concerns.

7 Conclusions

In this work, we have presented a tool infrastructure for model-driven development. The methodology consists of a two-dimensional development approach that is based on separating the different concerns in a software system and representing these concerns at different abstraction levels. In order to implement the proposed tool concept, we have used a structural entity called heterogeneous aspectual pattern. As tool support, we have built a pattern-driven modeling environment known as MADE. In MADE, a pattern is used to represent a concern cutting across multiple levels of abstraction.

We have applied the MADE tool in a number of development scenarios. Depending on the nature of the problem, aspectual patterns provided support for managing feature variability, documenting maintenance tasks, annotating framework specialization, and facilitating system comprehension. We have tested the MADE tool against small illustrative examples and larger industrial-level case studies.

So far, experience indicates that the proposed task-based development environment realizes many of the principles of model-driven development, namely automatic model derivation, controlled artifact generation, and traceability between models. We think that MADE can be further applied to support other software engineering activities such as architecture validation and software testing. Another direction for future work is to generalize the aspectual pattern concept to represent other dimensions in software development. For example, a pattern can be used to encapsulate different views of a given concern. Similarly, one concern may be represented at the same level of abstraction using different formalisms. Furthermore, one concern may crosscut multiple software systems.

8 Acknowledgements

This work is supported financially by the Academy of Finland (project 51528) and by the National Technology Agency of Finland (projects 40183/03 and 40226/04). The author would also like to thank Nokia Foundation for a grant toward his postgraduate studies and Kai Koskimies, Tommi Mikkonen, Tarja Systä, and the anonymous reviewers for their comments.

Automatically Discovering Transitive Relationships in Class Diagrams

Alexander Egyed

Teknowledge Corporation,
4640 Admiralty Way, Suite 1010, Marina Del Rey, CA 90292, USA
aegyed@ieee.org

Summary. Large-scale class diagrams are overwhelming to designers of software systems. They expose the designer to a level of detail that is often inappropriate for basic understanding and they complicate evolutionary changes in that the broader impact of changes is obscured by details. This chapter presents an approach for the automated abstraction of class diagrams that allows designers to "zoom out" of class diagrams to investigate and reason about their bigger picture. The approach is based on a large number of abstraction rules that individually are not very powerful but, when used together, abstract complex class diagrams quickly. The technique was validated on over a dozen models where it was shown to be well suited for model understanding, consistency checking, and reverse engineering.

1 Introduction

Refinement is often considered the natural course of software development where a problem is evolved into a solution. Yet, the more a class diagram is refined, the more there is a need to step back to investigate the bigger picture. We define abstraction to be the reverse of refinement. Abstraction is a transformation process (p. 19 of this book) that transforms lower-level class diagrams into higher-level ones, containing fewer elements. Class abstraction has a number of vital uses. It allows designers to (1) focus a class diagram on a particular problem or goal, omitting details that are not needed in that context; and it allows designers to (2) zoom out of a class diagram to investigate its entirety through a selected set of key elements.

In essence, abstraction is the simplification of models by removing details that are deemed unimportant by the designer. This naturally improves the understanding of class diagrams; supports reverse engineering by transforming low-level models into higher-level ones; and supports consistency checking by comparing existing higher-level models or architectures [106] with abstracted ones. The technique may also help the designer in restructuring class diagrams (p. 199 of this book).

This chapter presents a technique for abstracting class diagrams [42] where designers decide which classes to keep (i.e., called *important classes*) and which ones to temporarily remove (called *helper classes*). Since it is not semantically correct to simply remove helper classes, the technique reinterprets the helper classes in terms of their effect on the important classes. A designer may guide the abstraction to emphasize different goals or concerns (p. 139 of this book).

Our technique computes how the important classes would interact with one another if their interaction were not obscured by the helper classes. The technique first identifies the paths of helper classes that span between any two important classes. These paths are then abstracted and replaced by single relationships that approximate the meanings of the paths. The technique is supported through small yet numerous abstraction rules that define how simple class/relationship paths are replaced by single relationships. The application of abstraction rules is guided by the paths of helper classes that span between any two important classes. These paths are abstracted individually by applying the abstraction rules in the order in which classes are traversed while one important class interacts with another (through these helper classes). This problem is similar to the graph transformation discussed on p. 91 of this book but avoids the pattern matching problem by dealing with strings of classes only.

We evaluated the technique on over a dozen real-world case studies ranging from in-house developed models to third-party models. Most notably, we used the technique in connection with the Inter-Library Loan System [6], a part of a Satellite Ground System [16], C2SADEL to UML integration [106], Video-On-Demand System, SDS Statechart Simulator [107], and other projects. The sizes of the models ranged from several dozen to several hundred classes. The validation showed that the technique produces correct abstractions 96% of the time. This chapter presents the technique, originally introduced in [103], and then discusses two key extensions:

- The number of paths between important classes rises exponentially with the number of helper classes involved. We present an optimization that identifies in linear time the actual classes and relationships used that reach between any two helper classes, thus minimizing the path exploration problem.
- Complete paths are no longer computed before abstraction (i.e., due to the exponential problem) but are stepwise abstracted while the paths are explored. This avoids unnecessary path exploration because a partially non-abstractable path is also not abstractable in its entirety.

Also, a new tool was built as an add-in to IBM Rational Rose™. Rose is used to draw class structures and, using Rose's selection mechanism, a designer selects important classes for abstraction. The abstraction results are visualized in Rose also.

2 Illustrative Example

For illustrative purposes, this chapter uses a simple UML class diagram [42] of a Hotel Management System (HMS) that provides support for reservations, check-in/check-out procedures, and associated financial transactions (see Fig. 1). The figure defines that a *Person* may have an *Account* and that a single account may belong to multiple persons; it also defines that an account may have *Transaction*s and transactions may be either *Expense*s or *Payment*s. Furthermore, it defines that a *Guest* is a *Person* who provides services for reservation and check-in/out procedures. Both *Room* and *Reservation* are part of *Hotel* to indicate that instances of *Room* and *Reservation* are unambiguously associated with particular instances of *Hotel*. *Guest* is also related to *Room* and *Reservation* but less tightly via calling dependencies. These two calling dependencies describe that an instance of *Guest* may stay at a *Room* of a *Hotel* or may have several *Reservation*s for any given *Hotel*.

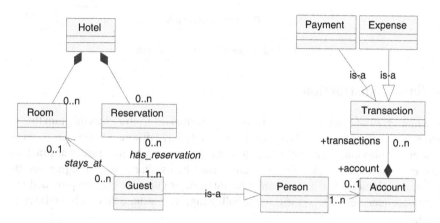

Fig. 1. Illustrative class diagram of a Hotel Management System (HMS)

While this class diagram is simple enough for human comprehension, we have worked with class diagrams that include thousands of classes and many more relationships. It is impossible for humans to comprehend such class structures and designers resort to abstraction as a means of coping with this complexity. Abstraction allows a designer to depict class structures from a particular point of view, concern, requirement, or other form of interest.

Figure 2 depicts a couple abstractions of Fig. 1 that emphasize different sets of important classes. For example, Fig. 2 (a) depicts the important classes *Guest*, *Payment*, and *Expense* but it also depicts relationships among these three classes that are not to be found in Fig. 1. These relationships are the abstract interpretation of the hidden classes. Fig. 2(b) and (c) depict yet other abstractions that "slice" across the classes in Fig. 1.

Clearly, there are a range of benefits associated with working with abstractions. Each abstraction depicts a "slice" of the class diagram and is easier to understand. Also, in this case, each abstraction relates to some form of requirement or system goal and designers may intuitively benefit from seeing the HMS in terms of these individual goals.

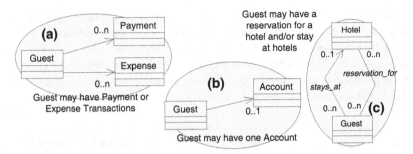

Fig. 2. Abstractions of the HMS system

3 Simple Abstraction

The main goal of class abstraction is to hide information from a class diagram that is perceived as not important. Since designers likely have different notions as to what classes are important (i.e., reflecting different goals or problem), a class abstraction technique needs to be guidable. Guidance may be as simple as a designer selecting model elements that are of particular interest; or guidance may be provided via trace dependencies [104], [156]. In the following, we presume that such guidance is available.

Abstraction replaces all unimportant helper classes in the class diagram such that the resulting diagram depicts only the important classes and their computed relationships. The main challenge of abstraction is to compute relationships out of the helper classes. That is, if we simply hide the class *Reservation* and its relationships in Fig. 1 then the class diagram loses the knowledge that a *Guest* may have a *reservation for* a *Hotel*.

This section presents generic abstraction rules (patterns) that are based on the UML notation for class diagrams [42]. Currently supported are class diagrams with four types of relationships: generalization (inheritance), association (calling direction), aggregation (part-of), and dependency. The presented abstraction rules are generic and applicable to a wide range of software projects. Designers are not required to extend or modify this rule set unless they wish to fine-tune it (e.g., domain specific rules).

3.1 Semantic Rules

The class abstraction technique interprets the transitive meaning of classes and their relationships. For example, the information that a *Person* may have an *Account* (association relationship in Fig. 1) implies a property of the class *Person* (class properties are methods, attributes, or relationships). Furthermore, the information that *Guest* is-a *Person* (inheritance) implies that *Guest* inherits all properties from *Person*. It follows that *Guest* inherits the association to *Account* from *Person* implying that a *Guest* may have zero or one *Account*s. This knowledge of the transitive relationship between *Guest* and *Account* (via *Person*) implies that the class *Person* (and its two relationships to *Guest* and *Account*) could be "collapsed" into a composite, more abstract relationship linking *Guest* and *Account* directly. That composite relationship should be of type "association" with the cardinality "0..1". This example shows a case where knowledge about the semantic properties of classes and relationships makes it possible to eliminate a class and derive a slightly more abstract class diagram. The example above can be seen as a class abstraction pattern of the following form (cardinalities are discussed later):

{1} GeneralizationRight - Class - AssociationRight -> AssociationRight

We use relationship names post-fixed with either "Left" or "Right" to indicate directionality. "GeneralizationRight - Class - AssociationRight" implies a generalization relationship terminating in the given class and an association relationship originating from that same class. On the other hand, "GeneralizationRight - Class - AssociationLeft" implies both generalization and association relationships terminating in the same class. Given that the above abstraction rule captures an observation that is universally true (meaning true for all instances), this rule collapses any occurrence of the given pattern (before ->) into an occurrence of the implies pattern (after ->).

The transitive property of inheritance may also be used for other types of relationships. For instance, *Guest* could also inherit other relationships from *Person* (e.g., aggregation, dependency, or reverse association relationships – see rules 2–7 below).

{2} GeneralizationRight - Class - DependencyRight -> DependencyRight
{3} GeneralizationRight - Class - AssociationRight -> AssociationRight
{4} GeneralizationRight - Class - [Agg]Assoc.Right -> [Agg]Assoc.Right
{5} GeneralizationRight - Class - DependencyLeft -> DependencyLeft
{6} GeneralizationRight - Class - AssociationLeft -> AssociationLeft
{7} GeneralizationRight - Class - [Agg]Assoc.Left -> [Agg]Assoc.Left
{8} GeneralizationRight - Class - Association -> Association

UML class relationships are usually uni-directional requiring us to differentiate "Left" from "Right". The only exception is the association relationship which may also be bi-directional. Rule 8 in the above block of patterns states that the bi-directionality of the association is maintained if abstracted together with a generalization.

{9} GeneralizationRight - Class - GeneralizationRight -> GeneralizationRight

The previous assumption about inheritance is true for all relationship types except for generalization relationships. On the one hand, it is valid to state that A inherits from C if A inherits from B and B inherits from C (see rule 9); however, if both A and C inherit from B (A and C share a common parent) then transitively this does not imply a relationship between A and C. It follows that no relationship exists between *Payment* and *Expense* in Fig. 1. Similar restrictions apply if two classes share a common child (multiple inheritance). Rules 10 and 11 express these situations. The symbol "Ø" is used to indicate that no abstraction is possible.

{10} GeneralizationRight - Class - GeneralizationLeft -> Ø

{11} GeneralizationLeft - Class - GeneralizationRight -> Ø

To find more abstraction rules, consider the relationship between *Guest* and *Hotel* in Fig. 1. The class diagram uses the class *Reservation* to define that a *Guest* may have *reservation for* a *Hotel*. If a designer were to derive the transitive relationship from *Guest* to *Hotel* through *Reservation* then the helper class *Reservation* and its relationships need to be replaced. In order to do that, it is again necessary to investigate the transitive meaning of the to-be-replaced model elements. The class diagram shows the class *Hotel* with an aggregation relationship from *Reservation* to *Hotel* implying that *Reservation* is a part of *Hotel*. The class diagram also defines that *Guest* has an association relationship to *Reservation* (instance of *Guest* may call instance of *Reservation*). Given that *Reservation* is a part of *Hotel* implies that the class *Reservation* is conceptually within the class *Hotel*. If, therefore, *Guest* depends on *Reservation* and *Reservation* is part of *Hotel* then *Guest* must also depend on *Hotel*. It follows that *Guest* relates to *Hotel* in the same manner as *Guest* relates to *Reservation*. We thus have found another abstraction rule (rule 12). As before, the same reasoning is applied to other relationships (e.g., rules 13–15):

{12} Association - Class - Association [Agg] -> Association
{13} AssociationRight - Class - Association [Agg] -> AssociationRight
{14} AssociationLeft - Class - AssociationLeft[Agg] -> AssociationLeft
{15} AssociationLeft[Agg] - Class - Assoc.Left[Agg] -> Assoc.Left[Agg]

Note that aggregations are UML associations with the aggregate property [Agg] at one of their ends. The directionality of aggregations also has relevant semantic meaning. For example, if *Hotel* were part of *Reservation* then one could not readily apply the above patterns (e.g., as with the relationship between *Person* and *Transaction* in Fig. 1).

3.2 Living with Ambiguous Class Definitions

The example of determining the relationship between *Person* and *Transaction* (Fig. 1) introduces a new challenge. If one were to derive the transitive relationship between *Person* and *Transaction* then one would need to abstract away the helper class *Account* and its relationships. *Person* currently has an association to *Account* and *Transaction* is part of *Account* ("AssociationRight - Class - [Agg]Association"). By *Person* having an association to *Account* one could argue that *Person* relates to every part of *Account*. Since *Transaction* is a part of *Account* it follows that *Person* must also relate to *Transaction*. Although this argument is true in many situations, it is flawed nonetheless. We make the assumption that by *Person* relating to *Account* it relates to all its parts. It is, however, conceivable that *Person* relates to a subset of *Account* only – a subset other than *Transaction* (i.e., mostly the case where classes provide independent services, e.g., a math library).

Taking a more critical stance toward our abstraction rules, one may find that this is not the first case of uncertainty. Consider again the very first rule 1 "GeneralizationRight - Class - AssociationRight -> AssociationRight". Previously, it was stated that *Guest* has an association relationship to *Account* simply because it inherited one from *Person*. To illustrate this reasoning more precisely, assume that *Person* has a method "foo" that creates an instance of *Account* ("0..1" association between *Person* and *Account*). Based on that assumption, surely, one can infer that *Guest* also has a "0..1" association relationship to *Account* because *Guest* inherits method "foo" from *Person*. Yet the flaw in this reasoning becomes apparent if *Guest* inherits method "foo" but overwrites its body such that it no longer creates an instance of class *Account* nor calls the overwritten method of the parent class. In such a case, *Guest* would not inherit the "0..1" association relationship from *Person* to *Account*. Abstracting the pattern "GeneralizationRight - Class - AssociationRight" is thus "AssociationRight" in some cases but not abstractable (no relationship) in other cases.

Observations such as this one naturally cause a dilemma. We are opposed to using abstraction rules that are not 100% reliable but we encounter imprecise model definitions that take away from our ability to reason precisely. We refer to these uncertainties as "model ambiguities" because imprecise model definitions lead to potentially different, ergo ambiguous, interpretations. A simple solution to this ambiguity problem is to create a semi-automated abstraction process that lets the designer decide in case of uncertainty (e.g., [355]). Given the large and complex nature of models, semi-automated abstraction becomes very costly. Indeed, it has been our observation that not computing time but human intervention constitutes key complexities in activities such as model transformation and consistency checking. A similar unsatisfactory solution to this problem is to make arbitrary decisions about the most likely abstraction case and ignore less likely scenarios (e.g., ignore that the child may overwrite method "foo" of the parent). This solution is unsatisfactory because it makes our approach less reliable, producing potentially erroneous abstraction results without the designer being aware of it.

UML class diagrams, like many other graphical description languages, are somewhat imprecise and ambiguous [227]. Indeed, we find that their relaxed nature often encourages their use since designers are sometimes either unable or unwilling to make precise design decisions. For instance, in UML it cannot be modeled whether class A overwrites methods it inherits from class B. Although a lack of precision on the part of UML, one may argue that it may not always be obvious during design time when to overwrite methods. More recent research has shown that formal annotations can improve the precision of UML (or notations alike) [117], [339], [285] but their use is generally optional and left to the discretion of the designer.

Since the basic notation of UML is ambiguous, we take the stance that automated abstraction needs to handle ambiguities. Our solution to the ambiguity problem is to maintain the ambiguity during abstraction. For instance, if it is unknown whether methods get overwritten during inheritance then we argue that "GeneralizationRight - Class - AssociationRight" is "AssociationRight" in some cases and "Ø" (no relationship) in other cases. This implies that abstract relationships indicated by our approach may or may not factually exist. In cases where more complex abstractions allow multiple abstract interpretations, our approach suggests all of them indicate this uncertainty (ambiguity). Our solution has the advantage that no abstract results are omitted although false positives may happen. Section 6 will show that the likelihood of false positives is very low ($\sim 4\%$). Note that an alternative solution would be to use a subset of abstraction rules that are known to be 100% correct. The problem with this alternative solution is that only very few such rules exist and large-scale abstraction would be rather ineffective as a consequence.

3.3 Other Abstraction Rules

Thus far we have focused on class patterns that use generalization and aggregation relationships. In the following, we briefly discuss some abstraction patterns that use association and dependency relationships (refer to [104] for more details).

An association relationship describes calling operations among classes. For instance, *Person* having an association relationship to *Account* implies that a method of *Person* may call methods of *Account*. If class A calls methods of class B and class B calls methods of class C then, transitively, class A might also call methods of class C ("AssociationRight - Class - AssociationRight -> AssociationRight"). In case a uni-directional association is abstracted together with a bi-directional association, the bi-directionality is replaced. For instance, if class A can only call class B but classes B and C can call one another then, transitively, class A can still only call class C but not the other way around ("AssociationRight - Class - Association -> AssociationRight").

Dependency relationships are used in UML to indicate a required presence of classes. For instance, if class A depends on class B then class B must be present for class A to function. The notion of a dependency is other than calling (association) and is used to single out classes that are used as parameters in method calls (i.e., class A does not call class B but class A has a method that expects an instance of class B as a parameter). It is thus safe to state that "DependencyRight - Class - DependencyRight" must also abstract to a "DependencyRight". Since dependencies can also be inherited (generalization) and a dependency of a part also implies a dependency of the whole (aggregation) the usual assumptions can be made about their abstraction.

3.4 The Complete List

To date, we have validated our approach in the context of UML class diagrams and the relationship types: generalization, association, dependency, and aggregation. Considering directionality, this implies eight uni-directional relationship types such as "GeneralizationRight" or "AggregationLeft" plus three bi-directional relationship types "Association", "[Agg]Association", and "Association[Agg]". Alltogether, those relationships may form 121 different patterns (11*11). Table 1 gives the complete list of abstraction patterns as they are currently defined in our approach.

It is interesting to observe that 29 patterns cannot be abstracted whereas the remaining 92 patterns have abstract counterparts. Given that it should not matter from what direction a pattern is viewed (or abstracted) it follows that mirror images of abstraction patterns must have the same values. For instance, the pattern "GeneralizationRight - Class - GeneralizationRight" (rule 1) is equivalent to the pattern "GeneralizationLeft - Class - GeneralizationLeft" (rule 16).

Table 1. Complete list of abstraction rules for class diagrams

---

1. GeneralizationRight - Class - GeneralizationRight -> GeneralizationRight
2. GeneralizationRight - Class - DependencyRight -> DependencyRight
3. GeneralizationRight - Class - AssociationRight -> AssociationRight
4. GeneralizationRight - Class - [Agg]AssociationRight -> [Agg]AssociationRight
5. GeneralizationRight - Class - GeneralizationLeft -> Ø
6. GeneralizationRight - Class - DependencyLeft -> DependencyLeft
7. GeneralizationRight - Class - AssociationLeft -> AssociationLeft
8. GeneralizationRight - Class - AssociationLeft[Agg] -> AssociationLeft[Agg]
9. GeneralizationRight - Class - Association -> Association
10. GeneralizationRight - Class - [Agg]Association -> [Agg]Association
11. GeneralizationRight - Class - Association[Agg] -> Association[Agg]

---

12. GeneralizationLeft - Class - GeneralizationRight - Class -> Ø
13. GeneralizationLeft - Class - DependencyRight -> Ø
14. GeneralizationLeft - Class - AssociationRight -> Ø
15. GeneralizationLeft - Class - [Agg]AssociationRight -> Ø
16. GeneralizationLeft - Class - GeneralizationLeft -> GeneralizationLeft
17. GeneralizationLeft - Class - DependencyLeft -> DependencyLeft
18. GeneralizationLeft - Class - AssociationLeft -> AssociationLeft
19. GeneralizationLeft - Class - AssociationLeft[Agg] -> AssociationLeft[Agg]
20. GeneralizationLeft - Class - Association -> AssociationLeft
21. GeneralizationLeft - Class - [Agg]Association -> AssociationLeft
22. GeneralizationLeft - Class - Association[Agg] -> AssociationLeft[Agg]

---

23. DependencyRight - Class - GeneralizationRight -> DependencyRight
24. DependencyRight - Class - DependencyRight -> DependencyRight
25. DependencyRight - Class - AssociationRight -> DependencyRight
26. DependencyRight - Class - [Agg]AssociationRight -> DependencyRight
27. DependencyRight - Class - GeneralizationLeft -> DependencyRight
28. DependencyRight - Class - DependencyLeft -> Ø
29. DependencyRight - Class - AssociationLeft -> Ø
30. DependencyRight - Class - AssociationLeft[Agg] -> Ø
31. DependencyRight - Class - Association -> DependencyRight
32. DependencyRight - Class - [Agg]Association -> DependencyRight
33. DependencyRight - Class - Association[Agg] -> DependencyRight

---

34. DependencyLeft - Class - GeneralizationRight -> Ø
35. DependencyLeft - Class - DependencyRight -> Ø
36. DependencyLeft - Class - AssociationRight -> Ø
37. DependencyLeft - Class - [Agg]AssociationRight -> Ø
38. DependencyLeft - Class - GeneralizationLeft -> DependencyLeft
39. DependencyLeft - Class - DependencyLeft -> DependencyLeft
40. DependencyLeft - Class - AssociationLeft -> DependencyLeft
41. DependencyLeft - Class - AssociationLeft[Agg] -> DependencyLeft
42. DependencyLeft - Class - Association -> DependencyLeft
43. DependencyLeft - Class - [Agg]Association -> DependencyLeft
44. DependencyLeft - Class - Association[Agg] -> DependencyLeft

---

45. AssociationRight - Class - GeneralizationRight -> AssociationRight
46. AssociationRight - Class - DependencyRight -> DependencyRight

---

47. AssociationRight - Class - AssociationRight -> AssociationRight
48. AssociationRight - Class - [Agg]AssociationRight -> AssociationRight
49. AssociationRight - Class - GeneralizationLeft -> AssociationRight
50. AssociationRight - Class - DependencyLeft -> Ø
51. AssociationRight - Class - AssociationLeft -> Ø
52. AssociationRight - Class - AssociationLeft[Agg] -> Ø
53. AssociationRight - Class - Association -> AssociationRight
54. AssociationRight - Class - [Agg]Association -> AssociationRight
55. AssociationRight - Class - Association[Agg] -> AssociationRight
56. AssociationLeft - Class - GeneralizationRight -> Ø
57. AssociationLeft - Class - DependencyRight -> Ø
58. AssociationLeft - Class - AssociationRight -> Ø
59. AssociationLeft - Class - [Agg]AssociationRight -> Ø
60. AssociationLeft - Class - GeneralizationLeft -> AssociationLeft
61. AssociationLeft - Class - DependencyLeft -> DependencyLeft
62. AssociationLeft - Class - AssociationLeft -> AssociationLeft
63. AssociationLeft - Class - AssociationLeft[Agg] -> AssociationLeft
64. AssociationLeft - Class - Association -> AssociationLeft
65. AssociationLeft - Class - [Agg]Association -> AssociationLeft
66. AssociationLeft - Class - Association[Agg] -> AssociationLeft
67. [Agg]AssociationRight - Class - GeneralizationRight -> [Agg]AssociationRight
68. [Agg]AssociationRight - Class - DependencyRight -> DependencyRight
69. [Agg]AssociationRight - Class - AssociationRight -> AssociationRight
70. [Agg]AssociationRight - Class - [Agg]AssociationRight -> [Agg]AssociatRight
71. [Agg]AssociationRight - Class - GeneralizationLeft -> [Agg]AssociationRight
72. [Agg]AssociationRight - Class - DependencyLeft -> Ø
73. [Agg]AssociationRight - Class - AssociationLeft -> Ø
74. [Agg]AssociationRight - Class - AssociationLeft[Agg] -> Ø
75. [Agg]AssociationRight - Class - Association -> AssociationRight
76. [Agg]AssociationRight - Class - [Agg]Association -> [Agg]AssociationRight
77. [Agg]AssociationRight - Class - Association[Agg] -> AssociationRight
78. AssociationLeft[Agg] - Class - GeneralizationRight -> Ø
79. AssociationLeft[Agg] - Class - DependencyRight -> Ø
80. AssociationLeft[Agg] - Class - AssociationRight -> Ø
81. AssociationLeft[Agg] - Class - [Agg]AssociationRight -> Ø
82. AssociationLeft[Agg] - Class - GeneralizationLeft -> AssociationLeft[Agg]
83. AssociationLeft[Agg] - Class - DependencyLeft -> DependencyLeft
84. AssociationLeft[Agg] - Class - AssociationLeft -> AssociationLeft
85. AssociationLeft[Agg] - Class - AssociationLeft[Agg] -> AssociationLeft[Agg]
86. AssociationLeft[Agg] - Class - Association -> AssociationLeft
87. AssociationLeft[Agg] - Class - [Agg]Association -> AssociationLeft
88. AssociationLeft[Agg] - Class - Association[Agg] -> AssociationLeft[Agg]
89. [Agg]Association - Class - GeneralizationRight -> [Agg]AssociationRight
90. [Agg]Association - Class - DependencyRight -> DependencyRight
91. [Agg]Association - Class - AssociationRight -> AssociationRight
92. [Agg]Association - Class - [Agg]AssociationRight -> [Agg]AssociationRight
93. [Agg]Association - Class - GeneralizationLeft -> [Agg]Association

94. [Agg]Association - Class - DependencyLeft -> DependencyLeft
95. [Agg]Association - Class - AssociationLeft -> AssociationLeft
96. [Agg]Association - Class - AssociationLeft[Agg] -> AssociationLeft
97. [Agg]Association - Class - Association -> Association
98. [Agg]Association - Class - [Agg]Association -> [Agg]Association
99. [Agg]Association - Class - Association[Agg] -> Association

100. Association[Agg] - Class - GeneralizationRight -> AssociationRight
101. Association[Agg] - Class - DependencyRight -> DependencyRight
102. Association[Agg] - Class - AssociationRight -> AssociationRight
103. Association[Agg] - Class - [Agg]AssociationRight -> AssociationRight
104. Association[Agg] - Class - GeneralizationLeft -> Association[Agg]
105. Association[Agg] - Class - DependencyLeft -> DependencyLeft
106. Association[Agg] - Class - AssociationLeft -> AssociationLeft
107. Association[Agg] - Class - AssociationLeft[Agg] -> AssociationLeft[Agg]
108. Association[Agg] - Class - Association -> Association
109. Association[Agg] - Class - [Agg]Association -> Association
110. Association[Agg] - Class - Association[Agg] -> Association[Agg]

111. Association - Class - GeneralizationRight -> AssociationRight
112. Association - Class - DependencyRight -> DependencyRight
113. Association - Class - AssociationRight -> AssociationRight
114. Association - Class - [Agg]AssociationRight -> AssociationRight
115. Association - Class - GeneralizationLeft -> Association
116. Association - Class - DependencyLeft -> DependencyLeft
117. Association - Class - AssociationLeft -> AssociationLeft
118. Association - Class - AssociationLeft[Agg] -> AssociationLeft
119. Association - Class - Association -> Association
120. Association - Class - [Agg]Association -> Association
121. Association - Class - Association[Agg] -> Association

4 Composite Abstraction

The previous section discussed abstraction in the context of numerous simple rules. These abstraction rules are not very powerful but this section demonstrates how complex class diagrams are abstracted using those rules.

4.1 Path Abstraction

We refer to a sequence of helper classes between two important classes as a path. Abstraction rules are serialized to abstract a path of classes. Fig. 3 (top) depicts a path from *Guest* to *Payment*, taken from Fig. 1. If it is of interest to know the transitive relationship between *Guest* and *Payment* then the abstraction rules in Table 1 have to be applied in sequence to eliminate the helper classes *Person*, *Account*, and *Transaction*.

The abstraction rules are applied in the order in which the classes are visited. That is, if *Guest* calls *Transaction* then this call first passes through *Person*, then

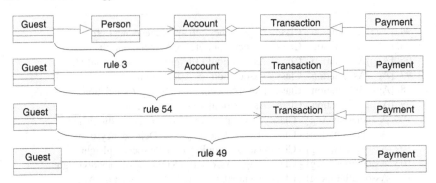

Fig. 3. Abstraction of a path of classes

through *Account*, next through *Transaction*, before, finally, reaching *Payment*. Thus, rule 3 (Table 1) is applied first to replace *Person* (and its relationships to *Guest* and *Account*); rule 54 is applied next to replace *Account*, and rule 49 is applied finally to replace *Transaction*. As a result, we discover a transitive association relationship between *Guest* and *Payment*. Of course, the path could also be explored in reverse from *Payment* to *Guest*.

The abstraction of a path is different from [103] in that no longer are all path combinations explored. This was previously done to ensure that all rules are treated equally during abstraction. For example, the problem in Fig. 3 could have also been resolved by applying the rules in a different order. That is, rule 54 could have been applied first (replacing *Account*), rule 3 next (replacing *Person*), and rule 49 finally (replacing *Transaction*). In this particular case, the outcome of the abstraction would have been identical. While there is no guarantee that all combinations of all rules produce identical abstraction results, we have not encountered a case where it would. Furthermore, given that it is computationally expensive to explore all combinations of rules, the technique now resolves a path in the order it is traversed.

4.2 Paths among Neighboring Important Classes

A path is a sequence of helper classes between two important classes. A path should not contain important classes. Consider, for example, that a designer is interested in the relationships among the important classes *Hotel*, *Guest*, *Payment*, and *Expense*, ignoring helper classes such as *Account*, *Reservation*, or *Person*. If one were to investigate all paths among *Hotel*, *Guest*, *Payment*, and *Expense* then one would find nine (Fig. 4 (top)): one path between *Payment* and *Expense*, one path between *Payment* and *Guest*, one path between *Expense* and *Guest*, two paths between *Hotel* and *Guest*, two paths between *Hotel* and *Payment*, and two paths between *Hotel* and *Expense*.

All nine paths reflect ways for the important classes *Hotel*, *Guest*, *Payment*, and *Expense* to interact with one another. However, it is not desired to know about all possible transitive relationships among all classes of the *Hotel–Guest–Payment–Expense*

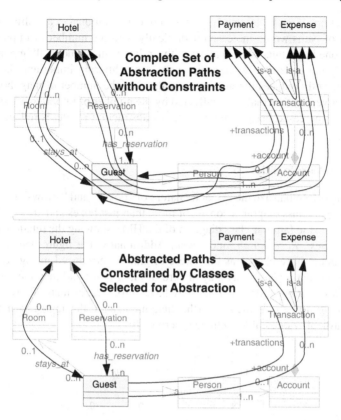

Fig. 4. All transitive relationships (top) and transitive relationships of neighboring classes (bottom)

set. Instead it is desired to know about transitive relationships between neighboring important classes only. Take for instance the path *Hotel–Reservation–Guest–Person–Account–Transaction–Expense* in Fig. 4 (top). Abstracting this path reveals a unidirectional association from *Hotel* to *Expense*. However, this path also eliminates the important class *Guest* because it is part of this path between *Hotel* and *Expense*. This is invalid here since one should not declare *Guest* an important class for abstraction but at the same time eliminate it in some abstraction path. This is invalid because the abstract relationship between *Hotel* & *Expense* would be redundant with other abstract relationships between *Hotel* & *Guest* and *Guest* & *Expense* where the former relationship (*Hotel–Expense*) is an abstraction of the latter two relationships. That is, *Hotel* is not capable of calling *Expense* directly but requires *Guest*. It is thus sufficient to show that *Hotel* calls *Guest* and that *Guest* calls *Expense*. Fig. 4 (bottom) depicts the subset of paths from Figure 4 (top) that do not contain any important classes.

This restriction of paths is also important for computational scalability. That is, the number of paths would increase quadratically with the number of important classes. Yet, if one is not interested in all transitive relationships among all important classes but only the transitive relationships among neighboring important classes, then this significantly reduces the number of paths (i.e., the number of neighboring classes is a relative constant that is not affected by the number of important classes). Usability is also increased because the number of abstraction results is reduced by the same degree.

4.3 Abstracting Cardinalities

The rules in Table 1 emphasize the syntactic nature of "boxes" and "arrows" in class diagrams. However, class diagrams consist of more than just boxes and arrows. Figure 5 (left), depicts the familiar class diagram of the HMS showing the relationships among *Hotel*, *Guest*, *Reservation*, and *Room*. Additionally, the figure depicts the cardinalities among those classes as they were originally introduced in Fig. 1. For example, it shows that a *Guest* may stay at zero or one *Room*s and may have zero, one, or more *Reservation*s. Also, a *Hotel* may have zero, one, or many *Room*s and each *Room* belongs to exactly one *Hotel* (the diamond head of the aggregation relationship has cardinality one unless defined otherwise).

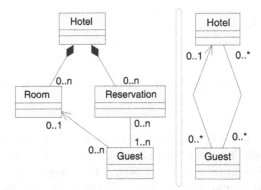

Fig. 5. Abstracting cardinalities

Figure 5 (right) shows that the *Hotel–Room–Reservation–Guest* class structure is abstractable into two relationships between the important classes *Guest* and *Hotel*: a bi-directional association and a uni-directional association (Fig. 5 (right)). These two relationships are based on the two distinct paths that exist between *Guest* and *Hotel*. Since an instance of *Guest* interacts with zero or one instances of *Room* and, in turn, an instance of *Room* is always associated with exactly one instance of *Hotel* (semantic implication of aggregation relationship), a *Guest* may stay at zero or one *Hotels* at any given point in time. This is a transitive property. Since associations and aggregations have two ends, there are always exactly two cardinalities one has to consider. The second cardinality investigates the reverse where an instance of *Hotel* may interact with zero, one, or more instances of *Room* and an instance of *Room* may interact with zero, one, or more instances of *Guest*. This implies that multiple guests may stay at any given *Hotel* room. Other cardinality scenarios follow the same pattern and are described in more detail in [103].

4.4 Path Exploration

Section 4.2 discussed how important classes restrict the exploration of paths in that only paths among neighboring important classes are considered. In spite of this restriction, path exploration is still a computationally expensive activity as there are often many paths between any two neighboring important classes. We address this problem in the form of two optimizations that avoid unnecessary path explorations.

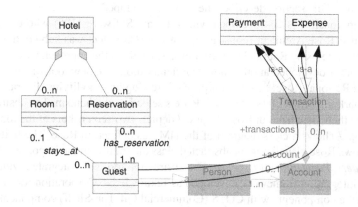

Fig. 6. Helper classes and paths between important classes

The first optimization computes in advance what helper classes (and their relationships) are part of paths between two given important classes. For example, if it is desired to understand the transitive relationships among *Guest*, *Payment*, and *Expense* (Fig. 6) then it is not necessary to explore paths that involve classes such as *Room* or *Hotel*. Yet, the path exploration algorithm in [103] explored paths recursively without knowing, in advance, what paths would succeed in connecting the desired important classes. The technique now computes in linear time what classes span between desired important classes. In the case of the example, the technique computes that only the classes *Person*, *Account*, and *Transaction* bridge the important classes *Guest*, *Payment*, and *Expense*. All other helper classes are ignored during the path exploration.

The second optimization limits the exploration of paths by continuously evaluating the abstractability of paths. That is, there are potentially many paths between any two helper classes but most of them are not abstractable. It is thus not necessary to explore a path in its entirety if a partial exploration and abstraction of that path already determines that it is not abstractable (i.e., if a path is not abstractable partially then it is also not abstractable in its entirety). This optimization avoids the exploration of subsequent path alternatives not yet explored.

The two optimizations discussed in this section minimize the path exploration problem in that only those helper classes are considered that yield useful paths and paths are only abstracted for as long as they are abstractable.

5 Automation and Tool Support

The abstraction technique requires a designer to guide the abstraction by defining important classes in a class diagram. The technique then replaces the remaining helper classes with transitive relationships. The tool support fully automates the replacement of helper classes. This reduces manual effort and makes abstraction results reproducible. This section describes the tool we developed.

Our approach was co-developed with Rational Software [105] who developed a tool called Rose/Architect (construction of Rose/Architect was sub-contracted to Ensemble Systems by Rational Corporation). Since then, the approach was extended and the author developed another non-proprietary tool. The new tool was integrated with IBM Rational Rose™ for the purpose of creating and modifying diagrams. Designers mark important classes through Rose's selection mechanism. The abstraction results are then visualized in Rose. Figure 7 depicts two screenshots of the tool. The top of Fig. 7 shows a class diagram of the HMS as defined in Rose. The bottom of Fig. 7 shows Rose visualizing an abstracted class diagram with the important classes *Hotel*, *Guest*, *Payment*, and *Expense*. The abstraction tool was integrated with Rose using an integration framework developed at Teknowledge Corporation for integrating software components with COTS (Commercial Off-The-Shelf) components.

6 Validation

This section discusses the validity of our approach in terms of its correctness and manual overhead.

6.1 Validity of Abstraction Rules and Algorithm

We evaluated the validity of abstraction results on a representative set of 12 models. Many of the models were built by third parties. Some models were implemented into systems although we did not have access to some of the implemented systems. Some models we reverse engineered from the implemented system. The sizes of the models varied substantially, with up to several hundred classes.

In total, considering the large number of models, experiments, and model elements involved, we found that our technique produces reliable results 96% of the time (only 4% false positives). For about two-thirds of the experiments, our approach

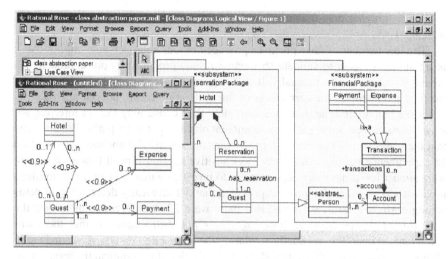

Fig. 7. Class abstraction tool integrated with IBM Rational Rose™

did not produce any false positives. For the remaining one-third, our approach produced less than 10% bad results – with one exception: in one case study, our approach produced 40% incorrect results. This is a very high number, but given the small size of the model (26 classes), higher fluctuations are to be expected. Although our approach produces highly reliable results most of the time, all results have to be investigated to reason about their correctness. Section 6.2 (manual versus automated abstraction) discusses that it is significantly cheaper to manually inspect abstraction results produced by our approach instead of abstracting manually.

Our rules are tailored in a fashion that prevents false negatives. This implies that the lack of an abstraction truly means that no abstraction exists. Because of this, our abstraction technique has 100% sensitivity. Note that sensitivity refers to the proportion of paths that are abstractable that have positive abstraction results. It is computed as (True Positives)/(True Positives+False Negatives). Our abstraction technique also has 99.3% specificity. Specificity refers to the proportion of paths that are not abstractable that have no abstraction results: (True Negatives)/(True Negatives+False Positives). True negatives were computed by subtracting abstracted paths from all investigated paths. For more details about these metrics, refer to [103].

6.2 Manual Abstraction Versus Automation

Despite our approach's preference to err in favor of abstracting too much instead of too little, it produces mostly correct abstraction results. This has the advantages that the designer does not get overwhelmed with too much (wrong) information and consequently incorrect abstraction results can be identified with reasonable effort. We observed during validation that our approach produced a total of 418 abstract relationships among 170 abstract classes (ratio of 2.45 relationships per class). This is not much higher than the ratio among original relationships and original classes, which is 1.83.

The low number of false positives produced by our approach also implies that it is significantly easier to validate abstraction results produced by our approach than having to abstract paths manually. It still requires a human decision maker to make the final judgment on the correctness of the abstraction result, but our approach relieves the human designer from the extremely time consuming task of inferring abstract relationships among all class combinations and potential paths. We observed that there were 21024 potential dependencies among all 170 abstract classes of all 18 experiments; but there were only 258 transitive relationships. It follows that there were almost 100 times more dependencies to investigate than transitive relationships to validate. Even if tool support is provided that automatically determines all paths among abstract classes, we found that there were 2374 different paths among the 170 abstract classes. Most of those paths were not abstractable and thus there was still a tenfold benefit in manually validating the abstraction results versus manually abstracting those paths. This data showed clearly that it is significantly better to investigate the abstracted diagrams without having to do all the abstraction work. The task of validating abstraction results is additionally simplified through trace information (mapping) between abstraction results and their original input. This makes it straightforward for designers to trace back particular abstraction results to investigate their origin and consequently their correctness. As for the actual effort required for validating results, this is entirely dependent on the designer's familiarity with the models. We found that if a designer is very familiar with a model then it was generally straightforward and fast to judge the correctness of abstraction results. For more details about these metrics, consult [103].

7 Related Work

Many techniques have been proposed to aid the understanding of complex class diagrams. There are reading techniques such as inspection [118] that use group effort to cope with complexity. Most of these techniques are manual and involve high effort and staff time. Using multiple views is an effective form of separating concerns [419]. Class diagrams can be subdivided into multiple views [14], [125], [142] where partial and potentially overlapping portions of the diagram are depicted. The sum of all views (diagrams) is the complete class diagram itself. Multiple views make use of the fact that one does not need access to all classes to understand a particular concern. Although multiple views can make classes belonging to individual concerns more understandable, they generally do not project a high-level, simplified abstraction of the overall class diagram.

Lieberherr et al. [275] defined class transformation methods to capture evolution. They argue that class evolution is inevitable and results in new class models that, preferably, should be as consistent as possible with earlier versions. Although one could argue that evolution is a form of refinement, we take a more narrow stance. For us, refinement has to maintain consistency within a given model. Their work thus addresses evolutionary "refinement" and "consistency issues" that are considered outside the scope of this chapter. Nonetheless, one can envision a strong need for our approach to be combined with theirs so that model refinement and abstraction can be complemented with model evolution.

Fahmy and Holt [119] examined structural aspects of models in the form of graph rewriting. In their work, they define rules on how to transform graph patterns. They do not single out class diagrams; however, their work is applicable since class diagrams can be seen as graphs containing vertices (classes) and edges (relationships). They also define transformation rules for "lifting" and "hiding interior/exterior" which could be seen as analogous to our approach. Indeed, graph rewriting could provide a more generic framework for our work and we are considering the integration of some of their ideas; however, currently they do not define class abstraction rules at the level of detail we do, nor do they define an algorithm that can avoid problems of race conditions. Furthermore, their transformation algorithm is computationally very expensive since they can define complex patterns and anti-patterns. Instead, our approach relies on relatively simple patterns that can be abstracted quickly.

The work of Schürr et al. [383] is similar to Fahmy and Holt's. They also propose a graph rewriting approach called PROGRES with similar limitations. However, an interesting feature of PROGRES is the improved performance of pattern matching which they recognized as being a severe problem. They propose a heuristic-based approach that optimizes the use of a limited set of graph rewrite rules to achieve faster performance. The limitation of their approach is that it works best on small sets of rules. We took an alternative approach with a large number of graph rewrite rules (abstraction rules) but only very simple rule patterns (string of relationships). Our pattern matching approach is thus as simple and as efficient as string matching. As such, we see their work as an interesting alternative in dealing with the computationally expensive problem of pattern matching.

Snelting and Tip [398] devised a technique in restructuring class hierarchies by investigating how classes are used by applications. In a form they abstract the essence of classes by creating perspectives of class hierarchies as relevant to individual applications. They then combine those individual perspectives to yield a better class hierarchy. Although their work reinterprets class diagrams (hierarchies) it cannot be used to reason about abstract interdependencies among classes. It is, however, a good example that class hierarchies (or diagrams) are ambiguous and information within them (i.e., methods) can be moved around without destroying behavioral consistency.

Racz and Koskimies [355] created an approach to class abstraction that is probably the closest to ours. They also recognized the powerful but simple nature of abstracting relationships with classes into abstract relationships. However, they only defined a small set of abstraction rules and they did not investigate the issue of path abstraction. As a result, they did not devise an automatable abstraction technique but instead developed a tool for semi-automated use. In Sect. 6, we pointed out the disadvantages of semi-automated abstraction on large-scale class diagrams. Irrespective of the drawbacks of their approach, we see their work as a confirmation of the validity of our abstraction technique because like us they acknowledge the usefulness of abstracting class patterns based on the transitive meaning of relationships.

Our abstraction technique is conceptually related to transformation techniques such as Sequence to Statechart transformation [258], [380], Collaboration to Statechart transformation [248], and Sequence to Class transformation [430]. All these approaches recognized the fact that model transformation in general can be done without the use of intermediate, third-party language. For instance, [258] describes an approach for combining sequence diagrams into statechart diagrams directly without creating the overhead of using an additional languages. These works demonstrate that it is possible to define precise, formal transformations using informal languages (UML diagrams) as input and generating other informal languages as output. Our approach is also well defined and formal and like their approaches we avoided using third-party languages to represent UML although such languages exist.

8 Conclusion

This chapter presented an approach for the automated abstraction of class diagrams. The approach investigated the semantic meaning of paths of classes to infer transitive properties. Although our abstraction rules are primitive in form, they are rich enough in number to abstract large-scale class diagrams. To date we have validated the technique and its rules on numerous third-party applications and models with up to several hundred model elements. We showed that our technique scales and produces correct results most of the time. We demonstrated various forms of ambiguities and showed that there are ways of living with them – even preserving them during transformation.

Our abstraction approach is fully tool supported and integrated with IBM Rational Rose™. We believe our abstraction technique to be well suited for model understanding, reverse engineering, and consistency checking. During model understanding, our technique provides a lightweight, fast, and easy to use method for "zooming out" of a model for inspection (e.g., whenever the model changes). For reverse engineering, our technique helps in creating higher-level interpretations of implementation classes and their relationships. And for consistency checking, our approach makes a lower-level class diagram easier to compare with existing higher-level ones.

9 Acknowledgements

We wish to thank Philippe Kruchten for the initial idea and support. We also wish to thank Barry Boehm, Cristina Gacek, Paul Grünbacher, Nenad Medvidovic, Dave Wile, and the anonymous reviewers for insightful discussions. This work was supported by Rational Corporation and DARPA through contracts F30602-99-1-0524, F30602-00-C-0200, and F30602-00-C-0218.

Generic and Domain-Specific Model Refactoring Using a Model Transformation Engine

Jing Zhang, Yuehua Lin, and Jeff Gray

Department of Computer and Information Sciences,
University of Alabama at Birmingham,
126 Campbell Hall, 1300 University Boulevard, Birmingham, AL 35294-1170, USA
{zhangj,liny,gray}@cis.uab.edu

Summary. Refactoring is an essential approach toward improving the internal structure of a software system while preserving its external behavior. Traditional refactoring techniques have focused on the implementation stage, with source code as the primary artifact of the refactoring process. However, a recent trend is to apply the concepts of refactoring to higher levels of abstraction. Consequently, model refactoring is emerging as a desirable means to improve design models using behavior-preserving transformations.

This chapter describes a practical approach toward implementing model-level refactoring. A model transformation engine has been developed and provides a generalized underlying refactoring tool for manipulating models. A model refactoring browser is integrated within the model transformation engine to enable the automation and customization of various refactoring methods for either generic models or domain-specific models. A result of this work is the capability to perform model refactoring rapidly using user-specified transformation rules.

1 Introduction

Refactoring was first proposed by Opdyke [335] in 1992 as a methodology for restructuring programs. Over the past decade, refactoring has grown into a disciplined technique to improve the maintainability of software systems by changing the internal structure of software without altering its external behavioral properties. With proper tool support, refactoring can be an efficient and effective way to help improve the design of software, make software easier to understand, and to assist in identifying errors [131]. In addition, lightweight development methods, such as eXtreme Programming (XP) [405], have promoted refactoring as a core development practice.

The majority of previous research into refactoring is focused at the code level (i.e., the implementation and maintenance phases during the software life-cycle), and less concerned with the earlier stages of design. It is well known that errors made early in the design process, but discovered late, are much harder to fix than errors made and found earlier in the development process [372]. Thus, a strong need exists for tools that enable designers to discover errors early in development, and to better modularize designs captured in models, not just code [33]. Applying refactoring as early as possible during the software life-cycle can improve the quality of design and reduce the complexity and cost in successive development phases. According to a recent survey on software refactoring [291], several researchers have begun to investigate refactoring at the design level, specifically in terms of UML models. The concept of model refactoring is emerging as a desirable means to improve design models using behavior-preserving transformations.

The main contribution of this chapter is to describe a customizable environment for performing model-level refactoring. In our previous work, a model transformation tool was developed to provide a generalized underlying engine for manipulating models. A new model refactoring browser has been built on top of the transformation engine to enable the automation and customization of various refactoring methods for either generic models or domain-specific models. The work described in this chapter differs from previous model refactoring research because it provides the ability for users to create their own rules that specify the effect of a refactoring. A set of pre-existing refactoring rules can be applied to a generic model, or a user may customize refactoring rules that pertain to a particular domain-specific modeling language.

The chapter is structured as follows. Section 2 gives an overview of the modeling tool and transformation engine. The model refactoring browser is introduced in Sect. 3. In Sects. 4 and 5, examples are presented to illustrate generic and domain-specific model refactorings. The chapter concludes with a section on related and future work.

2 Background: Model Transformation with GME and C-SAW

This section briefly introduces the modeling tool and transformation engine that are used throughout the remainder of the chapter. The overview provides references and links to additional details describing specific features and use of the tools. The particular focus of the chapter is to extend the concepts of this section in order to provide a generic model refactoring tool.

2.1 The Generic Modeling Environment

Model-integrated computing (MIC) [414] has been refined at Vanderbilt University over the past decade to assist with the creation and synthesis of computer-based systems. In MIC, multiple-view models are used to capture the information relevant to the system, represent the dependencies and constraints among different modeling views, and automatically synthesize different kinds of software artifacts. As a variant of the Model-Driven Architecture (MDA) [289, 135], a key application area for MIC is those domains that tightly integrate the computational structure of a system and its physical configuration (i.e., embedded system domains such as avionics and automotive software). In such systems, MIC has been shown to be a powerful tool for providing adaptability in frequently changing environments.

A specific instance of the type of domain-specific modeling supported by MIC is implemented using the Generic Modeling Environment (GME) [128]. The GME is a UML-based meta-modeling environment that can be configured and adapted from meta-level specifications (called the modeling paradigm) that describe the domain. When using the GME, a modeling paradigm is loaded into the tool to define an environment containing all of the modeling elements and valid relationships that can be constructed in a specific domain [269]. Model interpreters supply an ability to generate other software artifacts (e.g., code or simulation scripts) from the models. The GME provides a meta-environment for constructing system and software models using notations that are familiar to the modeler. It was developed before the OMG Meta-Object Facility (MOF) [135] existed, but an MOF-compliant model editor is near completion [111].

2.2 Constraint-Specification Aspect Weaver

The Constraint-Specification Aspect Weaver (C-SAW) is a model transformation engine implemented as a plugin component for GME. C-SAW unites the ideas of aspect-oriented software development (AOSD) [251] with MIC to provide better modularization of model properties that are cross-cutting throughout multiple layers of a model [160]. C-SAW offers the ability to explore numerous modeling scenarios by considering cross-cutting modeling concerns as aspects that can be rapidly inserted and removed from a model. This permits a modeler to make changes more easily to the base model without manually visiting multiple locations in the model. Until C-SAW, these transformations and translations have largely been performed manually in practice. Additional information about C-SAW, including software downloads and video demos, is available at: http://www.cis.uab.edu/gray/Research/C-SAW.

The C-SAW model transformation engine is depicted in Fig. 1. In this figure, a source model serves as input to the model weaver, and the output is a target model that has a cross-cutting concern dispersed across the original base. To perform this process, the transformation specifications describe the binding and parametrization of strategies to specific entities in a model. A transformation specification is composed of an aspect and several strategies. An aspect is the starting point of a transformation process. A strategy is used to specify elements of computation and the application of specific properties to the model entities.

The specification aspects and strategies are based on a special underlying language, called the Embedded Constraint Language (ECL) [161]. ECL is an extension of the Object Constraint Language (OCL) [457], and provides many of the common features of OCL, such as arithmetic operators, logical operators, and numerous operators on collections (e.g., size, forAll, exists, select). ECL also provides special operators to support model aggregates (e.g., models, atoms, attributes), connections (e.g., connpoint, target, refs), and transformations that provide access to modeling concepts that are within the GME (e.g., addModel, setAttribute, removeNode).

ECL is distinct from OCL with respect to side-effects and model manipulation features. OCL is a declarative language and cannot support operations to create, update, or remove the entities within a model, whereas the use of ECL requires the capability to introduce side-effects into the underlying model. This is needed because the strategies often specify transformations that must be performed on the model.

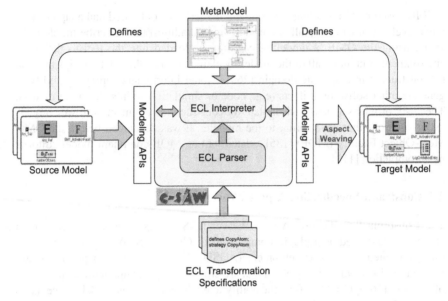

Fig. 1. C-SAW overview

This requires the ability to make modifications to the model as the strategy is applied. ECL supports an imperative transformation procedural style with numerous operations that can alter the state of the model. The application of ECL to model refactoring will be presented later in Sects. 4 and 5.

3 Model Refactoring Browser

C-SAW was originally developed as an aspect weaver at the modeling level. It has evolved into a general model transformation engine. In this chapter, C-SAW is applied specifically to a special case of model transformation, i.e., model refactoring. In particular, ECL is used to specify and implement the model refactoring process. The following definition of model refactoring is adapted from Roberts' refactoring definition [365]:

Definition 1. *A model refactoring is a pair R = (pre; T) where pre is the precondition that the model must satisfy, and T is the model transformation.*

Within this definition, several trivial properties are also implied, such as the name and parameters of the refactoring. In the following sections, detailed explanations will be presented regarding the way C-SAW passes the parameters to strategies and how the strategies are used to specify the precondition and transformation rules.

A model refactoring browser (see Fig. 2) has been implemented as a plugin within GME. This plugin operates with the underlying C-SAW transformation engine. The overall aim of this refactoring browser is to provide an interactive and automated framework for refactoring models. The model refactoring browser provides automation of generic pre-defined refactoring methods within the GME meta-model domain. It also enables the specification of user-defined refactoring strategies, either in the generic model or in any domain-specific model. For pre-defined refactorings, users select a subset of the models to be refactored from the browser menu list, and provide the appropriate parameters to the specified refactoring method. After that, the refactoring process will be carried out automatically. A partial list of the implemented UML class diagram refactorings contains: Add Class, Extract Superclass, Extract Class, Remove Class, Move Class, Rename Class, Collapse Hierarchy, Add Attribute, Remove Attribute, Rename Attribute, Pull Up Attribute, and Push Down Attribute. These generic refactorings are pre-defined within the refactoring browser and can be used for any GME meta-model. During the automated refactoring of a model, the error messages that occur during model transformation will be displayed as soon as a violation is discovered. For user-defined refactorings, users specify their own refactoring strategies using ECL. Such customized refactorings will be stored in the browser for later reuse. Sections 4 and 5 provide more details and examples regarding the implementations of pre-defined and user-defined refactorings.

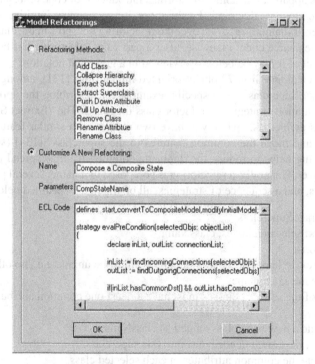

Fig. 2. Model refactoring browser in GME

4 Generic Model Refactorings

During the meta-modeling process, the basic step is to determine the modeling paradigm that contains all of the syntactic, semantic, and other information of the domain to be modeled. Generic modeling, i.e., meta-modeling, is the mapping of specification concepts onto entities, relations, and attributes of a specific domain. The GME meta-modeling paradigm is based on UML. The syntactic definitions are modeled using pure UML class diagrams and the static semantics are specified with OCL. Hence, it is quite natural to regard GME meta-models as class diagrams in order to perform UML class diagram refactorings [411]. In addition, GME meta-models extend the notations of UML to support various generic modeling concepts, which give rise to analysis on GME meta-specific refactorings.

4.1 Class Diagram Refactorings

UML class diagrams are widely adopted to help design and visualize software structure [39]. It is apparent that some refactorings introduced for code representation can also be applied to class diagrams. Furthermore, it may be more intuitive for the system developer or maintainer to discover the refactoring hot spots in the class diagram rather than the source code. Likewise, after a particular refactoring has been carried out, the impact of it may be better overviewed in a graphical notation.

Fowler's catalogue lists 72 object-oriented refactorings [131], among which we select "Extract Superclass" as a specific example for describing the application of ECL transformation strategies to refactor class diagrams. The "Extract Superclass" refactoring is defined as, "when you have two classes with similar features, create a superclass and move the common features to the superclass" [134] (see Fig. 3). This refactoring helps to reduce the duplicate common features spread throughout different classes. Generally, a refactoring is composed of a name, several parameters, preconditions, and a sequence of strategies, all of which are specified below.

Name: Extract Superclass
Parameters: selectedClasses, className
Preconditions:
    (1) The className for the new superclass must be unique, i.e., no other classes have the same name.
    (2) All of the selected classes must have at least one common attribute.
Strategies:
    (1) Create a new superclass named as className.
    (2) Insert the common attributes into this superclass.
    (3) Delete the common attributes in each selected class.
    (4) Make an inheritance relationship from the superclass to the selected classes.

Figure 4 contains the complete ECL specification of the "Extract Superclass" refactoring. Here, the "start" aspect defines the starting point of a transformation

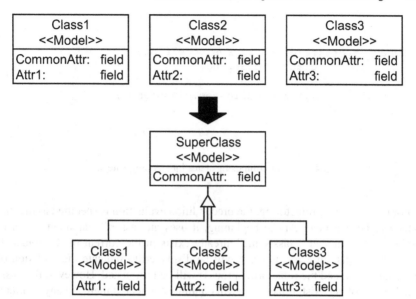

Fig. 3. Extract superclass refactoring

process. It takes parameters that are provided by users (obtained from the refactoring browser) and passes them to strategies that define the necessary transformation semantics to implement the refactoring.

```
1   defines start,evalPrecond,extractSuper;
2
3   strategy evalPrecond(classes   :modelList;
4                        className:String)
5   {
6       assert(currentFolder().select(m|
7           m.name()==className)->size()==0);
8       declare commonAttrs:attributeList;
9       commonAttrs:=findCommonAttributes(classes);
10      if (commonAttrs.size()>0) then
11          extractSuper(classes,commonAttrs,className);
12      endif;
13  }
14
15  strategy extractSuper(classes:modelList;
16          commonAttrs:attributeList; className:String)
17  {
18      declare super:model;
19      super:=createModel("SuperClass", className);
20      super.addAttributes(commonAttrs);
21      classes->removeAttributes(commonAttrs);
22      super.connectedTo("Inheritance", classes);
```

```
23    }
24
25    aspect start(selectedClasses:modelList;
26                 className:String)
27    {
28        evalPrecond(selectedClasses,className);
29    }
```

Fig. 4. ECL for composing states into a composite state

For this particular refactoring, the precondition evaluation is specified as the first strategy to be executed. At the beginning, it uses an "assert" statement to verify whether a class named "className" already exists in the current model folder. If the assertion fails, an error message will be displayed to indicate the violation of the precondition, and the refactoring process will be terminated. However, if "class-Name" does not yet exist, refactoring will continue to check if there are any common attributes within the selected classes. If common attributes are found in the current modeling scope, the second strategy "extractSuper" will begin to execute. As a result of this refactoring, a new superclass will be introduced with extracted common attributes in the selected classes. This ECL code fragment can be applied to any number of classes within a specific scope of a model.

4.2 GME Meta-model Refactorings

This section presents several GME meta-specific refactorings. The GME meta-model extends the concepts of UML entities and relationships to support a set of generic modeling stereotypes, such as model, atom, connection, set, and reference [128]. Fig. 5 illustrates a simple meta-model that represents a system administration domain. This meta-model contains entities acting as the major roles in the domain, such as Administrator, PC, and Server, as well as the Administrate relationship (represented by "Connection") between these entities. In this domain, an Administrator is responsible for a set of PCs and Servers. A Server or PC may be controlled by several Administrators.

The meta-model is rather simple. Nevertheless, it requires every system device managed by an administrator to have an "Administrate" connection. The drawback is that 100 devices would require 100 separate connections. Even if a new visualization was assigned to the connection lines, the vast number of associations would render the diagram unreadable and error prone. This suggests the need for a "multi-connections" refactoring. The following subsections describe two refactoring methods that use different entity concepts from the GME meta-model.

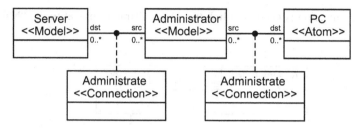

Fig. 5. A system administration meta-model

Replace Connections with Set

The first refactoring utilizes the idea of "set," which is the GME concept recommended for situations in which an object has to be associated with a relatively large number of neighboring objects in a diagram. The members of a set are "owned" by the set through the "SetMembership" connection defined in the GME. The concept of sets is not as indispensable as that of connections because sets can usually be replaced by connections. However, sets should be regarded as an alternate association technique that supplies greater convenience in many situations. The refactored meta-model that is based on a set is shown in Fig. 6, which is semantically equivalent to the meta-model in Fig. 5. However, Fig. 6 provides a more concise and clearer model structure than Fig. 5 and addresses improved scalability of devices. This refactoring process includes removing all of the "Administrator" connections from each device (PC and Server), replacing the "Administrator" model by a set, and connecting each device to the new set through a "SetMembership" association.

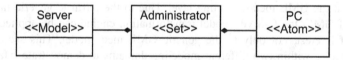

Fig. 6. Refactoring the meta-model using Set

Introduce FCO

Another kind of refactoring can be implemented on this meta-model by introducing a first class object (FCO) [128], which is a generic concept representing a general class for all of the entities and relations in GME. The purpose of using an FCO is to enable objects that are inherently different (such as model, atom, reference, connection) to inherit from a common base class. Figure 7 illustrates the refactored meta-model for the system administration domain by inserting an FCO. In this case, a generic entity that represents anything that a system administrator can govern is specified by the FCO named "Network." All of the devices inherit from this FCO. Consequently, only one connection is needed to link the "Administrator" model to the "Network" FCO.

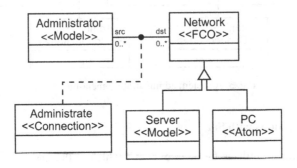

Fig. 7. Refactoring the meta-model using FCO

Because of the rich set of concepts in the GME meta-model, there exist other feasible methods for GME meta-specific refactorings, such as Introduce Reference, Compose Atoms into Model, and Replace General Inheritance with Implementation/Interface Inheritance. These refactorings have been specified using ECL and integrated into the model refactoring browser.

5 Domain-Specific Model Refactorings

The previous section described general refactorings that were applied to UML class diagrams at the GME meta-modeling level. Due to the intrinsic generic modeling features of GME, the C-SAW model transformation engine can be applied to any domain of interest, not only to the generic GME meta-model. This section provides examples within two different modeling domains to demonstrate refactoring of domain-specific models with user-defined customizations.

5.1 Refactoring Quality of Service Models

The Adaptive Quality Modeling Language (AQML) [296] is a domain-specific graphical modeling language developed for modeling Distributed Real-Time Embedded (DRE) systems with quality-of-service (QoS) adaptation configurations. The key objective of AQML is to raise the level of abstraction in specifying QoS policies by providing a control-centric design for the representation and analysis of adaptation of bandwidth for video streaming software.

Within the QoS Adaptation Modeling category, the designer can specify numerous details, such as: the different state configurations of the QoS properties, the legal transitions between the different state configurations, the conditions that enable these transitions, the data variables that receive and update QoS information, and the events that trigger the transitions. These properties are modeled using an extended finite-state machine (FSM) formalism. Figure 8 shows a QoS adaptation model of a video streaming scenario in AQML. The application of QoS adaptation is used to minimize the latency on the video transmission. Cutting frame size is one of the feasible strategies to reduce the transmission rate to compensate for the increased load.

There are six different states that are possible in Fig. 8. After initialization, the camera is tracking over a specific area and transmitting the video. The video is initially transferred at the full frame rate with 100% full frame size (in "Nominal" state). As load increases on the communication resources, each image frame has to be cropped to 90% ("Crop_90pc" state) or even 80% ("Crop_80pc" state) of the original size.

In fact, these three states perform the same task (i.e., adjusting the frame size). In order to improve comprehensibility and modularity, we can apply the model refactoring technique to group related states together into a composite state by specifying ECL model transformation strategies. Because the AQML model is based on state machines, the generic analysis regarding state diagram refactoring is provided below. This refactoring is composed of a name, a couple of parameters, preconditions, and strategies. The selected objects are those states that users are willing to group, as well as their internal transitions. The new state name is for the composite state. These parameters are provided by the user of the refactoring browser. The details of the ECL strategies are specified in Fig. 9.

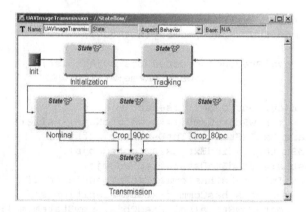

Fig. 8. AQML model before refactoring

Name: Compose states into a composite state
Parameters: selectedObjects, newStateName
Preconditions:
   (1) This newStateName must be legitimate, i.e., no other state has the same name.

(2) Find out all of the external states from which the selected states have the incoming transitions, in the name of "ExtInStateLs." Each found state in this list must have the identical set of transitions ("ExtInTransitionLs") leading to the identical set of selected states ("IntSourceLs").

(3) Find out all of the interior states in the selected set outward connecting to the external states, named "IntDstLs." Each found state in such a list must have the identical set of transitions ("ExtOutTransitionLs") leading to the identical set of external states ("ExtOutStateLs").

Strategies:

(1) Create a new state model, under the name of newStateName.

(2) Move all of the user-selected states along with all of the internal transitions into this new composite state. According to the GME meta-model definition, a connection is just an attachment to FCO (e.g., model, atom); whenever the objects are copied, moved, or removed, those connections will lose one of their ends automatically. Consequently, all of the transitions in "ExtInTransitionLs" as well as "ExtOutTransitionLs" will be removed.

(3) Within this new state, insert an "Init" state and connect it to all of the states in "IntSourceLs."

(4) Within the composite state, insert an "End" state and make a transition from each state in "IntDstLs" to the end.

(5) Go back to the initial outer model, and make a transition from each state in the "ExtInStateLs" to the new composite state that will also be connected to each state in the "ExtOutStateLs."

```
1    defines start,evalPrecond,createNewState,
2            modifyNewState,modifyInitModel;
3
4    strategy evalPrecond(selectedObjs:objectList;
5                         newStateName:String)
6    {
7       assert(currentFolder().select(m|
8              m.newStateName()==newStateName)->size()==0);
9       declare ExtInStateLs,IntDstLs:objectList;
10      ExtInStateLs:=findExtIns(selectedObjs);
11      IntDstLs:= findIntDsts(selectedObjs);
12      if (ExtInStateLs.hasCommonExtInTransitionLs()
13         && IntDstLs.hasCommonExtOutTransitionLs())
14      then createNewState(selectedObjs, newStateName);
15      endif;
16   }
17
18   strategy createNewState(selectedObjs:objectList;
19                           newStateName:String)
20   {
21      declare IntDstLs,IntSourceLs:objectList;
22      declare newState:model;
23      IntSourceLs:=findIntSources(selectedObjs);
```

```
24    IntDstLs:=findIntDsts(selectedObjs);
25    newState:=newModel("State", newStateName);
26    moveObjects(selectedObjects, newState);
27    newState->modifyNewState(selectedObjects,
28                                 IntDstLs,IntSourceLs);
29  }
30
31  strategy modifyNewState(selectedObjects,IntDstLs,
32                          IntSourceLs:objectList)
33  {
34    declare init,end:atom;
35    init:=createAtom("Init");
36    IntSourceLs->connectFrom(init);
37    end:=createAtom("End");
38    IntDstLs->connectTo(end);
39    currentFolder().select(m|m.newStateName()==
40     "initialModel")->modifyInitModel(this,selectedObjs);
41  }
42
43  strategy modifyInitModel(newState:model;
44                          selectedObjs:objectList)
45  {
46    declare ExtInStateLs,ExtOutStateLs:objectList;
47    declare compositeState:model;
48    ExtInStateLs:=findExtIns(selectedObjs);
49    ExtOutStateLs:=findExtOuts(selectedObjs);
50    compositeModel:=copyModel(newState);
51    ExtInStateLs->connectTo(compositeModel);
52    ExtOutStateLs->connectFrom(compositeModel);
53  }
54
55  aspect start(selectedObjects:objectList;
56              newStateName:String)
57  {
58    evalPrecond(selectedObjects, newStateName);
59  }
```

Fig. 9. ECL for composing states into a composite state

Figure 10 shows the refactored AQML model as a result. The upper model delineates the new state diagram with a composite state "AdjustingFrameSize" and the bottom model illustrates the three sub-states contained by this composite state.

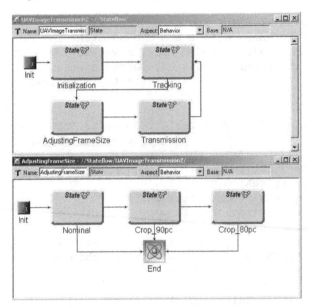

Fig. 10. AQML model after refactoring

5.2 Refactoring Petri nets

Petri nets (PNs) [349] are well known as a basic model for the general theory of concurrency, and as a formal specification technique for distributed and concurrent systems. Petri nets have obtained extensive usage and acceptance due to their easy-to-understand visual notation and a wide range of available tools. A Petri net is primarily characterized by places, transitions, and arcs and is graphically represented by a directed bipartite graph in which places are drawn as circles, transitions are drawn as bars, input and output arcs (from a place to a transition or a transition to a place) are drawn as arrows. The execution of a Petri net is controlled by the position and movement of markers (tokens). It incorporates the notion of a distributed state, called the marking, which is graphically represented by black dots (tokens) in places. The dynamic behavior of a Petri net is governed by transition firing rules. A transition can fire if all of its input places contain at least one token, and if all of its inhibitor places do not contain tokens. If these conditions are satisfied, the transition is said to be enabled, and its firing removes one token from all its input places and generates one token in each of its output places (assuming the weight of each arc is 1).

Figure 11 shows a Petri net model describing a simplified version of the classic Dining Philosophers problem. This problem consists of philosophers sitting at a table who do nothing but think and eat. The philosophers each have a chopstick next to them, both of which they need in order to eat. The initial marking for this model will have all philosophers in the "Thinking" state, and all of the chopsticks available. Because there is only a finite set of chopsticks, it is not possible for all philosophers to eat at the same time. The Petri net shown here models a philosopher who takes both chopsticks simultaneously, thus preventing the situation where some philosophers have one chopstick, but are not able to pick up the second one.

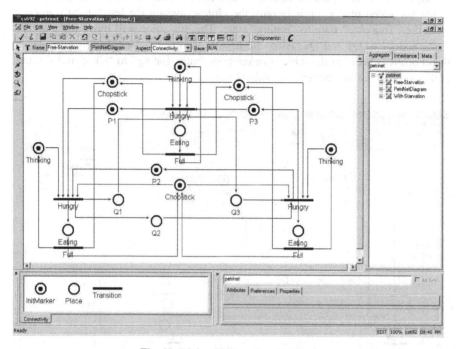

Fig. 11. Dining Philosophers Petri net

This Dining Philosophers Petri net model is deadlock free (i.e., there always exists at least one philosopher whose state is able to transfer from "Thinking" to "Eating"). Nevertheless, partial starvation is still possible because the firing of one transition named "Hungry" prevents the other neighboring transition from firing. If one philosopher rapidly alternates between "Thinking" and "Eating," then the neighboring philosophers may never obtain the "Chopstick" that they need, which will result in starvation. In such a case, the "Chopstick" place models a semaphore to guarantee only one of the two adjacent philosophers can eat at the same time.

One possible solution to avoid starvation is to refactor the Petri net model in order to enforce that every transition must be fired in alternating turns. A generalized semaphore refactoring for this transformation can be specified as follows:

(1) Pick out the semaphores from among the places in the model.
(2) For each semaphore and its two output transitions, insert two new places, one with a marker and the other without a marker. Connect the two new transitions to the existing model to form a cycle (see highlights in Fig. 12).

To verify that the refactored Dining Philosophers Petri net is starvation free after applying this refactoring, we might keep track of the control flow among the transitions one by one. Figure 12 illustrates this Petri net model after refactoring. Due to the six added places, initially only the philosopher on the left can be triggered from the "Thinking" state to "Eating" state. This transition will move the markers in P1 and P2 to Q1 and Q2. After the first philosopher finishes eating and places the chopsticks back on the table (marker goes from "Eating" to "Chopsticks"), the philosopher in the middle will be enabled to eat.

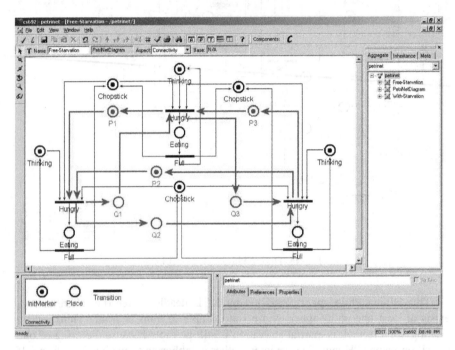

Fig. 12. Dining Philosophers Petri net

Likewise, the philosopher on the right will eventually start to eat in turn. Therefore, all of the philosophers will obtain the opportunity to eat in turn. The corresponding ECL code fragment for implementing this particular refactoring is illustrated in Fig. 13. An iteration over the selected list of the Petri net places checks to see if they meet the precondition of being semaphores, and then inserts two new places with appropriate connections. This strategy is suitable for any number of semaphores involved in the refactoring. For simplicity, it is assumed that each semaphore controls two transitions and it is the user's responsibility to select the semaphores to be transformed.

```
 1   defines freeStarvation, refactorPetriNet;
 2
 3   strategy freeStarvation()
 4   {
 5       declare dstList:modelList;
 6       declare dst1,dst2,p,q:model;
 7       declare static num:Integer;
 8       dstList:=findOutConnections();
 9       assert(dstList.size()==2);
10       dst1:=dstList.get(0);  dst2:= dstList.get(1);
11       p:=createModel("InitMarker","P"+intToStr(num));
12       q:=createModel("Place",  "Q" + intToStr(num));
13       num:=num + 1;
14       addConnection(dst1,p);   addConnection(p,dst2);
15       addConnection(dst2,q);   addConnection(q,dst1);
16   }
17
18   aspect refactorPetriNet(selectedObjs:objectList)
19   {
20       selectedObjs->freeStarvation();
21   }
```

Fig. 13. ECL for starvation free Petri net

6 Related Work

There are several ongoing investigations into the topic of software refactoring. This section briefly acknowledges some of the work that has been done in this area. Mens and Tourwé [291] made a comprehensive literature survey on the existing research of general software refactoring, which is based upon various research perspectives such as refactoring activities, specific techniques to support these activities, types of the software artifacts to be refactored, and refactoring effects.

Opdyke [335] first initiated the concept of refactoring. He identified a set of program refactorings that were applied to an object-oriented framework and presented the theory for automating refactorings in a behavior/semantics preserving way. Fowler et al. [131] provided a catalog of dozens of refactoring techniques for improving code. The focus on these works is at the code level, which is different from our approach to perform the refactoring at a higher level of modeling.

With respect to the research of model refactoring at a higher level of abstraction, Sunyé et al. [411] proposed an initial set of refactorings for UML class diagrams and statecharts. Their research provided a fundamental paradigm for model refactoring to improve the design of object-oriented applications; nevertheless, they do not have any concrete implementation of representative tools. Boger [41] implemented a refactoring browser for a UML case tool to automate the process of system-defined refactoring methods. However, this browser can only provide the automation of pre-existing refactorings; it does not allow a user to specify their own customized refactoring strategies. Porres [351] defines model refactorings as rule-based model transformations, which is similar to our approach. But, his experimental tool does not represent the capability to support refactoring automation and domain-specific model refactorings.

In contrast to the related literature, our model refactoring browser is built on top of an underlying model transformation engine that can enable the automation and customization of refactorings for either generic meta-models or domain-specific models.

Additionally, there exist other related model refactoring approaches, but with different contexts from our approach. Astels [20] presented techniques for detecting bad smells in UML. Correa and Werner [75] primarily contribute several smells and refactorings to OCL specifications. Several researchers are concentrating on a refactoring based on design pattern models [134, 20]. Van Gorp et al. [155] extend the UML meta-model for automating the consistency between the model and the code. Tichelaar et al. [425] developed a specific meta-model to support language-independent refactorings for Smalltalk and Java.

Several of the approaches cited above provide theoretical investigations that do not have concrete implementations of representative tools. Some of the implementation tools provide the automation of pre-existing refactorings, but do not offer the extensibility of user-defined refactorings. Some tools cannot support refactoring automation.

7 Conclusions and Future Work

This chapter described an approach to model refactoring that is based on the existing C-SAW model transformation engine. With ECL, users can express their objectives in a more concise manner than using traditional programming languages. It also permits a modeler to make changes flexible to the base model without manually visiting multiple locations in the model (for instance, imagine such a case when there are 100 semaphores within one Petri net model). The C-SAW model transformation engine and its associated language ECL permit the modeler to make quantifiable statements across the model in a style that supports improved reusability and scalability of models.

An initial prototype model refactoring browser tool serves as a front-end to C-SAW and exists as a plugin within the GME. A set of pre-defined refactorings have been integrated within the browser in order to facilitate automated refactorings. The ECL can be used also to specify new refactoring strategies. This interactive tool permits users to request refactorings to either a GME meta-model, or a domain-specific model (e.g., Petri Nets, or finite-state machines). The current research project is integrated with the GME, whose meta-meta-model is based on its own specification instead of the Meta-Object Facility (MOF). The existence of GME's UML/OCL meta-meta-model predates the adoption of MOF as the OMG's standard meta-meta-model. In addition, although MOF offers some advantages over the GME UML/OCL meta-meta-model, such as package importation and merge, it is also lacking some features that are important for defining domain-specific modeling languages, such as stateful associations, facilities for multi-view modeling, and a standard way to specify the concrete syntax of models [111]. However, there is an ongoing project that incorporates MOF into the GME. It is believed that the same model refactoring technique can be applied to GME-MOF. Furthermore, this research is not limited to GME. We believe that it can be adapted into other modeling tools and plan to generalize a tool-independent version of the model refactoring browser.

With respect to future work, there are several extensions that will be integrated into the model refactoring browser. Behavior/semantics preservation is an important issue with regard to model refactoring. To preserve the semantics of a model, it is necessary to measure the impact of a model transformation in such a way that it can be proved that the behavior/semantics of the model is unchanged. In the GME, a meta-model is specified with UML and OCL constraints. The meta-model can assist in the determination of behavior/semantics preservation [411]. However, a more precise formalism is required for semantic and behavior analysis to ensure the preservation of the model behavior. Because the behavior/semantics of different models may have different specification, and various aspects of the behavior/semantics may depend on various user-specific concerns [291], it is essential to allow the modelers to provide the information of the behavior property that will remain invariant during a model refactoring. We are in the process of developing a model testing suite to assess behavior/semantics preservation by executing user-specified test cases on target and refactored models (p. 219 of this book). In addition, a debugging toolkit is planned for C-SAW. This will be indispensable for detecting errors in the ECL specification during the refactoring execution process.

8 Acknowledgements

This project is supported by the DARPA Information Exploitation Office, under the Program Composition for Embedded Systems (PCES) program.

A Testing Framework for Model Transformations

Yuehua Lin, Jing Zhang, and Jeff Gray

Department of Computer and Information Sciences, University of Alabama at Birmingham,
126 Campbell Hall, 1300 University Boulevard, Birmingham, AL 35294-1170, USA
{liny,zhangj,gray}@cis.uab.edu

Summary. As models and model transformations are elevated to first-class artifacts within the software development process, there is an increasing need to provide support for techniques and methodologies that are currently missing in modeling practice, but provided readily in other stages of the development lifecycle. Within a model transformation infrastructure, it is vital to provide foundational support for validation and verification of model transformations by investigating and constructing a testing framework focused at the modeling level, rather than source code at the implementation level. We present a framework for testing model transformations that is based on the concepts of model difference and mapping. This framework is integrated with an existing model transformation engine to provide facilities for construction of test cases, execution of test cases, comparison of the output model with the expected model, and visualization of test results. A case study in model transformation testing is presented to illustrate the feasibility of the framework.

1 Introduction

To improve the quality of software, it is essential to be able to apply sound software engineering principles across the entire lifecycle during the creation of various software artifacts. Furthermore, as new approaches to software development are advanced (e.g., model-driven software development – MDSD), the investigation and transition of an engineering process into the new approaches is crucial. Model transformations are the heart of model-driven research that assists in the rapid adaptation and evolution of models at various levels of detail (p. 19). As models and model transformations are elevated to first-class artifacts within the software development process, they need to be analyzed, designed, implemented, tested, maintained, and subject to configuration management. For models representing embedded systems that perform critical functions, the importance of correct model transformations is elevated further (p. 289 of this book) [414]. A holistic approach to model transformation can help to assure that the transformation process is reusable and robust [39]. At the implementation level, testing is a popular research area that has obtained widespread attention [473]. Various tools and methodologies have been developed to assist in testing the implementation of a system (e.g., unit testing, mutation testing, and white/black-box testing). In addition to source code, testing has been applied to other software artifacts (e.g., component systems [197] and executable models [95]). However, in current model transformation environments, there are few facilities provided for testing transformation specifications in an executable style. The result is a lack of an effective and practical mechanism for finding errors in transformation specifications. The goal of our research is to describe a disciplined approach to transformation testing, along with the development of the required tools, to assist in ensuring the correctness of model transformations.

In general, model transformation techniques can be categorized as either model-to-model transformation or model-to-code translation [80]. Model-to-model transformation translates between source and target models, which can be instances of the same or different meta-models. In a typical model-to-model transformation framework, transformation rules and application strategies are written in a special language, called the *transformation specification*, which can be either graphical [8] or textual [159]. The source model and the transformation specification are interpreted by the transformation engine to generate the target model. In a model transformation environment, assuming the model transformation engine works correctly and the source models are properly specified, the model transformation specifications are the only artifacts that need to be validated and verified. A transformation specification, like the code in an implementation, is written by humans and susceptible to errors. Additionally, a transformation specification may be reusable across similar domains. Therefore, it is essential to ensure the correctness of the transformation specification before it is applied to a collection of source models.

Model transformation testing as defined in this chapter focuses on *transformation specification testing* within the context of model-to-model transformation where source models and target models belong to the same meta-model. Specification testing involves executing a specification with the intent of finding errors. Such execution-based testing has several advantages that make it an effective method to determine whether a task (e.g., model transformation) has been correctly carried out. These advantages are: 1) the relative ease with which many of the testing activities can be performed; 2) the software artifacts being developed (e.g., model transformation specifications) can be executed in their expected environment; 3) much of the testing process can be automated [197]. Specification testing can only show the presence of errors in a specification and not their absence. However, as a more lightweight approach to specification verification and validation compared to model checking [198, 425, 211] and other formal methods (e.g., theorem proving), testing can be very effective in revealing such errors. This chapter describes our initial work on a testing framework that supports construction of test cases based on test specifications, execution of test cases, and examination of the produced results.

We define execution of a test case to involve the application of a deterministic transformation specification with test data (i.e., input to the test case) and a comparison of the actual results (i.e., the target model) with the expected output (i.e., the expected model), which must satisfy the intent of the transformation. If there are no differences between the actual target and expected models, it can be inferred that the model transformation is correct with respect to the given test specification. If there exist differences between the target and expected models, the transformation specification needs to be reviewed and modified. Within this context, model transformation testing has three core challenges:

(1) **Automatic comparison of models:** During model transformation testing, comparison between two models (i.e., the expected model and the target model) must be performed to determine if there is a mismatch between the models. Manual comparison of models can be tedious, exceedingly time consuming, and susceptible to error. An effective approach is to compare the actual model and the expected model automatically with a high-performance algorithm. Pre-existing graph matching algorithms are often too expensive for such a task [249]. A model transformation testing engine requires an efficient and applicable model comparison algorithm.

(2) **Visualization of model differences:** To assist in comprehending the comparison results, comprehensive visualization techniques are needed to highlight model differences intuitively within modeling environments. For example, graphical shapes, symbols, and colors can be used to indicate whether a model element is missing or redundant. Additionally, we needed to decorate these shapes, symbols and colors onto models even inside models. Finally, a navigation system is needed to support browsing model differences efficiently. Such techniques are essential to understanding the results of a model transformation testing framework.

(3) **Debugging of transformation specifications:** After determining that an error exists in a model transformation, the transformation specification must be investigated in order to ascertain the cause of the error. A debugging tool for model transformations can offer support for isolating the cause of a transformation error. Of course, debuggers at the programming language level cannot be reused at the modeling level due to the semantic differences in abstraction between the artifacts of code and models. A model transformation debugger must understand the model representation, as well as possess the ability to step through individual lines of the transformation specification and display the model data intuitively within the host modeling environment.

This chapter focuses on challenges 1 and 2 from above (i.e., the model difference and visualization problems) and introduces a framework for model transformation testing that is based on model comparison techniques. Theoretically, our approach renders models and meta-models as graphical notations such that the model comparison problem corresponds to graph comparison. The method and tools collaborate with an existing model-to-model transformation engine to provide facilities for construction of test cases, execution of test cases, comparison of the output model with the expected model, and visualization of test results. Currently, we assume test specification and test cases are generated manually by model transformation developers or testers; and the expected models used to compare with the actual results are also specified manually. We also recognize that the expected models in most modeling practices can be built from the base models instead of from scratch so that less manual effort is involved. The automation provided by our testing framework is the execution of the tests for ensuring the correctness of the transformation specification. The chapter is structured as follows: Sect. 2 reviews the background necessary to understand the remainder of the chapter. The importance of model mapping and difference is described in Sect. 3, along with an algorithm for model comparison. The core of the chapter can be found in Sect. 4, which presents the framework for model transformation testing. Section 5 illustrates the feasibility of the framework via a case study of model transformation. Section 6 is a discussion of related work. Finally, Sect. 7 provides concluding remarks and discusses future work.

2 Background

This section briefly introduces the concepts of model-driven software development and the role of model transformation. Specifically, the modeling tool and transformation engine used in this research is described.

The Model-Driven Architecture (MDA) [135] is an initiative by the Object Management Group (OMG) to define Platform Independent Models (PIMs), which can be transformed to intermediate Platform Specific Models (PSMs), leading to synthesis of source code and other artifacts [39]. The current OMG standards for defining PIMs and PSMs include the Meta-Object Facility (MOF) and the UML. To provide a well-established foundation for transforming PIMs into PSMs, the OMG initiated a standardization process by issuing a Request for Proposal (RFP) on Query/Views/-Transformations (QVT) [165]. Driven by practical needs and the OMG's request, a large number of approaches to model transformation have been proposed recently [80]. The primary approaches for model-to-model transformation include graph-based transformation [8], XSLT-based transformation [101], and specialized OCL-based transformation (e.g., the Embedded Constraint Language [160]). Based on these approaches, associated tools have been developed to facilitate rapid adaptation and evolution of models.

Over the past four years, we have developed a model transformation engine, the Constraint-Specification Aspect Weaver (C-SAW), which unites the ideas of aspect-oriented software development (AOSD) [251] with model-integrated computing (MIC) [244] to provide better modularization of model properties that are crosscutting throughout multiple layers of a model [160]. MIC has been refined over the past decade at Vanderbilt University to assist in the creation and synthesis of complex computer-based systems [244]. The Generic Modeling Environment (GME) [269] is a domain-specific modeling tool that realizes the principles of MIC. The GME provides meta-modeling capabilities that can be configured and adapted from meta-level specifications (representing the modeling paradigm) that describe the domain. The GME is generic enough to construct models of different domains and has been proven in practice on several dozen international research projects that were sponsored by industry and federal governments.

C-SAW is a model transformation engine that is integrated into the GME as a plug-in. C-SAW provides the ability to explore numerous modeling scenarios by considering cross-cutting modeling concerns as aspects that can be inserted and removed rapidly from a model. Within the C-SAW infrastructure, the language used to specify model transformation rules and strategies is the Embedded Constraint Language (ECL), which is an extension of OCL [160]. ECL provides many of the common features of OCL, such as arithmetic operators, logical operators, and numerous operators on collections (e.g., size, forAll, exists, select). It also provides special operators to support model aggregates (e.g., models, atoms, attributes), connections (e.g., source, destination), and transformations (e.g., addModel, setAttribute, removeModel) that render access to modeling concepts within the GME.

There are two kinds of ECL specifications: a specification aspect describes the binding and parameterization of strategies to specific entities in a model, and a strategy, which specifies elements of computation and the application of specific properties to the model entities. C-SAW interprets these specifications and transforms the input source model into the output target model. An example ECL specification of a model transformation is provided in Sect. 5.

The C-SAW website is a repository for downloading papers, software, and several video demonstrations that illustrate model transformation with C-SAW in the GME (see: http://www.cis.uab.edu/gray/Research/C-SAW/). In this chapter, we do not emphasize the aspect-oriented features of C-SAW; information on that topic can be found in [159, 160]. For the purpose of this chapter, we consider C-SAW as a general model transformation tool with ECL serving as the transformation specification language.

Although we use C-SAW in the example of Sect. 5, we believe the general process of testing model transformations can be adopted for any combination of modeling tool and transformation engine, provided that there is a mechanism for integration (i.e., a plug-in architecture, such as that provided in GME). Figure 1 shows the integration of GME, C-SAW and the testing engine (the core testing tool described in this chapter). This framework is based on the concepts of model mapping and difference, as well as the techniques of model comparison presented in the next section.

3 Detecting the Differences Between Models

A distinction between actual and expected results is critical in software testing. Model comparison is vital to model transformation testing in order to discover the mapping and differences between the output model and the expected model. From a mathematical viewpoint, GME models can be rendered in a graphical representation, permitting graph-theoretic operations and analysis to be performed. This section explores model difference based on graphical notations and presents an algorithm for model comparison.

3.1 Graph Representation of Models

In GME, meta-models are described in UML class diagrams and OCL constraints, which define the schema and constraint rules for models. GME models can be repre-

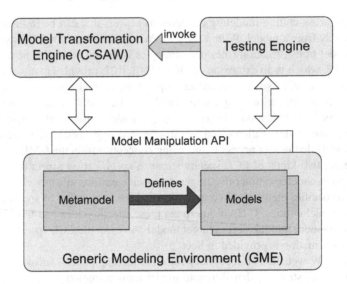

Fig. 1. Integration of GME, C-SAW, and testing engine

sented as typed and attributed multi-graphs that consist of a set of vertices and edges [8]. The following definitions are given to describe a GME model.

Vertex. A vertex is a 3-tuple (name, type, attributes), where name is the identifier of the vertex, type is the corresponding meta-modeling element for the vertex, and attributes is a set of attributes that are predefined by the meta-model.

Edge. An edge is a 4-tuple (name, type, src, dst), where name is the identifier of the edge, type is the corresponding meta-modeling element for the edge, src is the source vertex, and dst is the destination vertex.

Graph. A graph consists of a set of vertices and a set of edges where the source vertex and the destination vertex of each edge belong to the set of vertices. Thus, a graph G is an ordered pair (V, E), $\forall e \in E, Src(e) \in V \wedge Dst(e) \in V$.

Elements and features. In GME, a model can be represented as a graph. We define a model element as a vertex or an edge in a graph. A feature is any attribute of a model element.

In practice, more graphical representations are needed to describe complicated model systems (e.g., GME also supports model hierarchy and multi-views [269]). However, as a first step toward model comparison, the following discussions on model mapping and difference are based on these definitions.

3.2 Model Mapping and Difference

The comparison between two models, M1 and M2, always produces two sets: the mapping set (denoted as MS) and the difference set (denoted as DS). The mapping set contains all pairs of model elements that are mapped to each other between two models. A pair of mappings is denoted as Map $(elem^1, elem^2)$, where $elem^1$ is in

M1 and $elem^2$ is in M2, which may be a pair of vertices or a pair of edges. A vertex v^1 in M1 mapping to a vertex v^2 in M2 implies matching names and types, disregarding whether their features are matching or not. An edge e^1 in M1 mapping to an edge e^2 in M2 implies matching names and types (i.e., source vertices are a mapped pair, and destination vertices are also a mapped pair). When finding the mappings between two models, the name match and type match are considered as a structural mapping to simplify the process of model comparison. This mapping is based on the syntax of a modeling language. In complicated situations, two models can be syntactically different but semantically equivalent, which is also acceptable in the testing context. However, these situations are not considered in this chapter.

The difference set is more complicated than the mapping set. The notations used to represent the differences between two models are operational terms that are considered more intuitive [13]. There are several situations that could cause two models to differ. We define DS = M2 - M1, where M2 is the actual output model, and M1 is the expected model in model transformation testing. The first differing situation occurs when some modeling elements (e.g., vertices or edges in graph representation) are in M1, but not in M2. We denote this kind of difference as New (e^1) where e^1 is in M1, but not in M2. The converse is another situation that could cause a difference (i.e., elements in M2 are missing in M1). We denote this kind of difference as Delete (e^2) where e^2 is in M2, but not in M1. These two situations occur from structural differences between the two models. A third difference can occur when all of the structural elements are the same, but a particular value of an attribute is different. We denote this difference as Change $(e^1, e^2, f, val^1, val^2)$ where e^1 is in M1 and e^2 is in M2, which are a pair of mapping vertices, f is the feature name (e.g., name or an attribute), val^1 is the value of $e^1.f$, and val^2 is the value of $e^2.f$. Thus, the difference set actually includes three sets: DS = N, D, C where N is a set that contains all the New differences, D is a set that contains all the Delete differences, and C is a set that contains all the Change differences.

3.3 Model Comparison

In GME, models can be exported and imported to an XML representation. A possible approach to the model comparison problem is to compare the XML representations of two models. However, with this approach, applications need to be developed to handle the results retrieved from the XML comparison in order to indicate the mapping and difference on models within the modeling environment. A more exact approach is to regard model comparison as graph comparison so that model elements (e.g., vertices and edges) can be compared directly via model navigation APIs provided by the underlying modeling environment.

The graph matching problem can be defined as finding the correspondences between two given graphs. However, the computational complexity of general graph matching algorithms is the major hindrance to applying them to practical applications. For example, the complexity of graph isomorphism is a major open problem and many other problems on graphs are known to be NP-hard [249]. Thus, it is necessary to loosen the constraints on graph matching to find solutions in a faster way. In model transformation testing, one of the goals is to automate model comparison with less labor-intensive integration. It is well known that some parts of model comparison algorithms are greatly simplified by requiring that each element have a universally unique identifier (UUID) which is assigned to a newly created element and will not be changed unless it is removed [13]. To simplify our model comparison algorithm, it is necessary to enforce that every model element has a unique identifier, such that the model comparison algorithm is based on name/id matching. That is, the corresponding elements are determined when they have the same name/id, which will simplify the comparison algorithm. For example, to decide whether there is a vertex (denoted as v^2) in M2 mapped to a vertex (denoted as v^1) in M1, the algorithm first needs to find a vertex with the same name/id as v^1's and then judge whether their type and attributes are equivalent.

Figure 2 presents an algorithm to calculate the mapping and the difference between two models. It takes two models (M1: the expected model and M2: the target model) as input, and produces two sets: the mapping set (MS) and the different set (DS) that consists of three types of differences (N: the set of the New differences, D: the set of the Delete differences, and C: the set of the Change differences). When this algorithm is applied to model comparison within the testing framework, its output can be sent to the visualization component to display test results and to generate test reports.

```
Input: M1, M2
Output: MS, DS {N, D, C}

Begin
1. For each vertex v¹ in M1
        If there is a vertex v² in M2 mapped to v¹
            Mark v¹ and v² mapped
            Add pair (v¹, v²) to MS
            For each attribute f of v¹ and v²,
                If the value of v¹ (val¹) is not equal to
                the value of v² (val²)
                    Add (v¹, v², f, val¹, val²) to C
        Else
            Add v¹ to N
2. For each edge e¹ in M1
        If there is an edge e² in M2 mapped to e¹
            Mark e¹ and e² mapped
            Add pair (e¹, e²) to MS
        Else
            Add e¹ to N
3. For those elements in M2 without mapped mark
        Add them to D
End
```

Fig. 2. A ModelComparison algorithm

4 A Framework for Model Transformation Testing

In the context of C-SAW, a model transformation is performed by interpreting the ECL transformation specification. This section describes a framework (see Fig. 3) for testing model transformation specifications that assists in generating tests, running tests, and documenting tests automatically and efficiently.

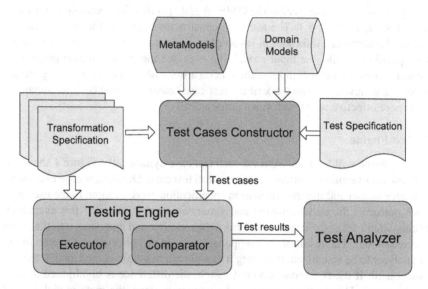

Fig. 3. A framework for model transformation testing

There are three primary components to the testing framework: test case constructor, test engine, and test analyzer. The test case constructor consumes the test specification and then produces test cases for the to-be-tested transformation specification. The generated test cases are passed to the test engine that interacts with C-SAW and the GME to exercise the specified test cases. Within the testing engine, there is an executor and a comparator. The executor is responsible for executing the transformation on the source model and the comparator compares the target model to the expected model and collects the results of comparison. The test analyzer visualizes the results provided by the comparator and provides a capability to navigate among any differences.

4.1 Test Case Constructor

In testing a model transformation, there are different ways to construct test cases. For example, tests can be constructed according to different coverage criteria or test specifications [373]. In our testing framework, we assume tests are planned by the user and defined in a textual test specification. A test specification defines a single test case or a suite of test cases in order to satisfy the testing goal. A simple test case specification defines: a transformation specification to be tested (i.e., an ECL specification file describing a single strategy or a collection of strategies); a source model and an expected model (i.e., a specification of the expected result); as well as the criteria for determining if a test case passed successfully (such as the equivalence between the target and expected models). The test specification can be written by a user or generated from a wizard by selecting all of the necessary information directly from the browser within the GME. A test specification example is shown in the case study of Sect. 5.1. The test case constructor interprets the specification to retrieve the necessary information involved in a test case, such as: the to-be-tested ECL specification file, the input model, the expected model, and the output model. The test case constructor composes the specification with the input model to generate an executable test case. The work of the test case constructor can be done manually, but is more effective when performed automatically.

4.2 Test Engine

The test engine will load and exercise each test case dynamically. Figure 4 shows an overview for executing a model transformation test case. During test case execution, the source model and the transformation specification serve as input to the executor, which performs the transformation and generates a target model. After execution, the comparator takes the target model from the executor and compares it to the given expected model. The result of the comparison should be collected and passed to the test analyzer to be visualized. If the target model matches the expected model, the test is successful. If the two models do not match, the difference is highlighted to help find the errors. During the executor and comparator steps, the meta-model is used to provide the required structure and constraints for test case execution and model comparison (i.e., type information from the meta-model will be used to perform the model comparison).

As mentioned in Sect. 3, there are several situations that could cause the output model and the expected model to differ. If there are differences between the target model and the expected model, this suggests that there is an error in the transformation specification. These differences are passed to an analyzer that can visualize the difference clearly in a representation that is easily comprehended by a human.

4.3 Test Analyzer

When rendered in a graphical notation, models typically have complicated internal data structures; thus, it is difficult to comprehend the differences by visual observation. It is also hard for humans to locate and navigate the differences between two models without automated assistance. To solve the visualization problem, a test analyzer is introduced to indicate the differences directly on the model diagrams and attribute panels within the modeling environment.

The test analyzer provides an intuitive interface for examining the differences between two models. It contains model panels, attribute panels, a difference navigator, and a difference descriptor, as described in the following list.

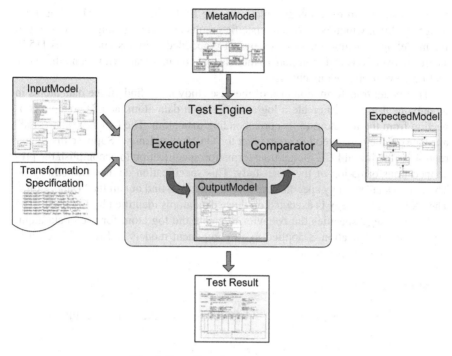

Fig. 4. Overview of a test case execution

(1) **Output model panel and attribute panel:** Displays the target output model and its attributes. Various shapes and colors are used for marking numerous types of difference: a red circle is used to mark the "New" difference, a green square is used to mark the "Delete" difference, and a "Change" difference is highlighted in blue. Generally, structural differences are shown on the diagram and feature differences are shown on the attribute panel. An example is given in Sect. 5.3.

(2) **Expected model panel and attribute panel:** Displays the expected model diagram and attributes. It illustrates the expected results for the tested model transformation.

(3) **Difference navigator:** Hierarchically displays the differences between two models.

(4) **Difference descriptor:** Textually shows the detailed description of the currently selected difference.

5 Case Study: Example Application of Model Transformation Testing

To illustrate the feasibility and utility of the transformation testing framework, this section describes a case study of testing a model transformation. This case study is performed on an experimental platform, the Embedded System Modeling Language (ESML), which is a domain-specific graphical modeling language developed for modeling real-time mission-computing embedded avionics applications [159]. There are over 50 ESML component models that communicate with each other via a real-time event-channel mechanism.

The model transformation task of the case study is: 1) find all the data atoms in a component model, 2) create a log atom for each data atom, and 3) create a connection from the log atom to its corresponding data atom. The type (i.e., the "kind" attribute) of the generated log atom is set to "On Method Entry." Suppose that Fig. 5 represents the initial ECL model transformation specification to accomplish the prescribed transformation of the case study. This specification defines two strategies. The "FindData" strategy specifies the search criteria to find out all the "Data" atoms. The "AddLog" strategy is executed on those data atoms identified by FindData. The AddLog strategy specifies the behavior to create the log atom for each data atom. Before this specification is applied to all component models and reused later, it is necessary to test its correctness.

```
strategy FindData()
{
    atoms() → select(a | a.kindOf() == "Data") → AddLog();
}


strategy AddLog()
{
    declare parentModel : model;
    declare dataAtom, logAtom : atom;
    dataAtom := self;

    parentModel := parent();

    logAtom := parentModel.addAtom("Log","LogOnMethodEntry");
    parentModel.addAtom("Log", "LogOnRead");
    logAtom.setAttribute("Kind", "On Write");
    logAtom.setAttribute("MethodList", "update");
}
```

Fig. 5. An untested transformation specification

5.1 Test Specification Definition

A test specification is used to define the test plan. In this example, there is only one test being performed, with the test specification defined in Fig. 6.

```
Test test1
{
    Specification file: "C: \ ESML \ ModelComparison1
                         \ Strategies \ addLog.spc"
    Start Strategy: FindData
    GME Project: "C: \ ESML \ ModelComparison1
                    \ modelComparison1.mga"
    Input model: "ComponentTypes
                    \ DataGatheringComponentImpl"
    Output model: "ComponentTypes \ Output1"
    Expected model: "ComponentTypes \ Expected1"
    Pass: Output1 == Expected1
}
```

Fig. 6. An Example Test Specification

A test is composed of a name (e.g., "test1") and body. The test body defines the locations and identifiers of the specification file, the start strategy, a GME Project built for testing, the input source and output target models, the expected model, as well as the criteria for asserting a successful pass.

A sample input model and expected model are shown in Fig. 7. The input model contains a data atom named "numOfUsers." According to the transformation task, a log atom should be created for this data atom and a connection should be generated from the log atom to the data atom.

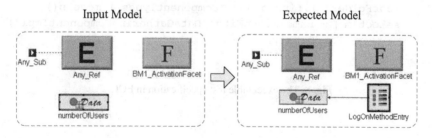

Fig. 7. The input model and the expected model

5.2 Test Case Construction

According to the test specification, the test engine generates a new ECL specification that can be executed by the executor (see Fig. 8). The italicized text is the ECL code to be tested and the other ECL code (i.e., the "test1" aspect) is added by the test case generator in order to construct an executable specification that composes strategies with an aspect. In this case, strategies are the to-be-tested ECL code and the aspect specifies the input model as the source model to be transformed.

```
strategy FindData()
{
    atoms() → select(a | a.kindOf() == "Data") → AddLog();
}


strategy AddLog()
{
    declare parentModel : model;
    declare dataAtom, logAtom : atom;
    dataAtom := self;

    parentModel := parent();

    logAtom := parentModel.addAtom("Log",
          "LogOnMethodEntry");
    parentModel.addAtom("Log", "LogOnRead");
    logAtom.setAttribute("Kind", "On Write");
    logAtom.setAttribute("MethodList", "update");
}

aspect test1()
{
    rootFolder( ).findFolder("ComponentTypes").models().
    select(m | m.name().endWith("DataGatheringComponentImpl"))
          → FindData();
}
```

Fig. 8. The executable test specification in ECL

5.3 Test Results and Difference Indication

After the test case is executed, the output target model and the expected model are sent to the comparator, which performs a comparison using the model comparison algorithm and passes the result to the test analyzer. Figure 9 shows the output model with the difference indication when compared to the expected model. There are three differences indicated on the model diagram:

- Difference 1: missing connection from LogOnMethodEntry to numberOfUsers, which is a "New" difference and marked by a red circle.
- Difference 2: an extra atom "LogOnRead" is inserted, which is a "Delete" difference and marked by a green square.
- Difference 3: the kind attribute of the LogOnMethodEntry has a different value ("On Write") from the expected value ("On Method Entry"), which is a "Change" difference and highlighted in blue.

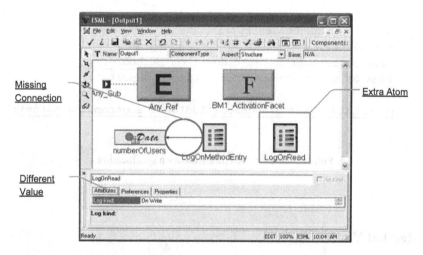

Fig. 9. The output model with difference indication

5.4 Correction of the Model Transformation Specification

According to the test results, it is obvious that there are three corrections that need to be made to the transformation specification. One correction to be added will create the connection between LogOnMethodEntry and numberOfUsers. The second correction is to delete one of the lines in the specification (i.e., the line that adds a LogOnRead: "parentModel.addAtom("Log", "LogOnRead")"). The third correction is to change the value of the Kind attribute from "On Write" to "On Method Entry." The modified transformation specification is shown in Figure 10 with the corrections underlined. We do not imply that Figure 10 is automated - the transformation in this figure represents the correct specification that would be required after observing the test results.

```
strategy FindData()
{
    atoms() → select(a | a.kindOf() == "Data") → AddLog();
}

strategy AddLog()
{
    declare parentModel : model;
    declare dataAtom, logAtom : atom;
    dataAtom := self;

    parentModel := parent();

    logAtom := parentModel.addAtom("Log",
        "LogOnMethodEntry");
    parentModel.addAtom("Log", "LogOnRead");
    logAtom.setAttribute("Kind", "On MethodEntry");
    logAtom.setAttribute("MethodList", "update");

    parentModel.addConnection("AddLog", logAtom, dataAtom);
}
```

Fig. 10. The corrected transformation specification

6 Related Work

There are a variety of techniques for validation and verification of model and model transformation (e.g., model checking [211, 377], simulation [464] and formal proof [436]). Model checking is a widely used technique for validation and verification of model properties (e.g., the Cadena model checking toolsuite [198], the SPIN model checker [211], and the CheckVML tool [377]). However, transformation specification testing is different from model checking in its focus on the correctness of transformations that also requires engineering processes [435]. A mathematically proven-based technique for validating model transformations is proposed in [436]; however, such an approach requires a mathematical description and analysis of models and transformation rules. Compared with these approaches, our contribution to transformation testing is a lightweight approach to finding transformation faults by executing them within the model transformation environment without the need to translate models and transformation specifications to mathematical representations.

Based on an RFP issued by the OMG for a standard test instrumentation interface (TII) for executable models (see "Model-Level Testing and Debugging Interface" [164]), Eakman presents an approach to test executable PIMs where instrumentation code is added during transformation from a PIM to a PSM [95]. This approach requires execution at the source code levels, but our contribution does not involve source code executions.

Toward realizing our vision of execution-based testing of model transformations, we need to solve the problems of model difference detection and visualization. There has been some work on model difference detection and visualization in current modeling research [13, 329]. Algorithms for detecting differences between versions for UML diagrams can be found in [329] where UML models are assumed to be stored as syntax trees in XML files or in a repository system. Several meta-model-independent algorithms regarding difference calculation between models are presented in [13], which are developed primarily based on some existing algorithms on detecting changes in structured data [59] or XML documents [455]. In the above approaches, a set of operations such as "create" and "delete" is used to represent and calculate model differences. However, these research results have not been used to construct testing tools within model transformation environments. In addition, the commonly proposed technique to visualize the model differences is coloring [329]. However, coloring alone is not sufficient in visualizing model differences in complicated modeling systems that support model hierarchy and composition. Our research involves utilizing shapes, symbols, and textual descriptions to advance visualization of model differences and constructing a navigation system for browsing model differences.

7 Conclusions and Future Work

This chapter presents a testing framework for model transformation that provides the facilities for test case construction, execution of test cases, comparison of the output model with the expected model, and visualization of test results. This framework is based on the concepts of model mapping and model difference to provide a technique for model comparison. The main purpose of the framework is to automate testing of model transformation to ensure the correctness of the changes made to a source model; the focus is neither on generation of model-driven test cases for the implementation (programming language) development phase nor on test-driven development of models [203]. This initial framework is integrated within the C-SAW model transformation engine and the GME. Although we target GME models in this chapter, we believe the general idea of transformation testing is also applicable to other modeling tools that can support integration with a plug-in architecture. To utilize the framework in other modeling tools, the test engine would need to adjust to the tool-specific model semantics in order to support model mapping and difference within the host modeling tool.

There are several opportunities to expand the work presented in this chapter. Models are often represented visually as a hierarchical graph with complex internal representations. Several modeling tools (e.g., the GME) capture the hierarchy and containment within models explicitly, whereby the modeler recursively clicks on higher-level models in order to reveal the contents of the containment. The hierarchical nature of models makes it difficult to calculate and observe visually the mapping and difference between two models. Moreover, the multiple views of models also increase the complexity of transformation testing. Other research issues that will be investigated in the near future include: study on effectiveness of this approach to detecting errors in transformation specifications, and evaluation of test adequacy and coverage in the context of model transformation test cases.

We are beginning work to address the debugging issue of challenge 3, as mentioned in Sect. 1. To assist in locating the particular transformation specification error, it is necessary to investigate the concept of a debugger for a model transformation engine. This would allow the stepwise execution of a transformation to enable the viewing of properties of the transformed model as it is being changed. The testing tool suite and the debugging facility together will offer a synergistic benefit for detecting errors in a transformation specification and isolating the specific cause of the error. All of the tools will be designed to integrate seamlessly within the host modeling environment.

8 Acknowledgements

This project is supported by the DARPA Information Exploitation Office, under the Program Composition for Embedded Systems (PCES) program.

Parallax – An Aspect-Enabled Framework for Plug-in-Based MDA Refinements Towards Middleware

Raul Silaghi and Alfred Strohmeier

Software Engineering Laboratory,
Swiss Federal Institute of Technology in Lausanne,
CH-1015 Lausanne EPFL, Switzerland
{raul.silaghi,alfred.strohmeier}@epfl.ch

Summary. MDA has been around for more than three years already. Nevertheless, besides the lack of a standard model transformation language to support the MDA vision, there is even a lack of tool support to implement the platform-specific mappings promoted by the same MDA. For quite some years now, tool vendors have offered the possibility to generate code for different programming languages, but the spectrum of tools is very limited when it comes to generating code for different middleware infrastructures. Parallax, based on aspect-oriented support and through a well-defined system of plug-ins, addresses this issue by providing a framework that enables developers to first (re)configure their designs and enhance them with middleware-specific concerns at different MDA levels of abstraction, and then adapt the implementation of these concerns to different middleware infrastructures and see how they are actually implemented at the code level. Moreover, developers and middleware vendors can contribute and enrich Parallax by implementing and providing the community with new plug-ins for its favorite middleware infrastructures.

1 Introduction

A longstanding goal in software development is to construct applications that are easily modified and extended. The desired result is to achieve modularization such that a change in a design decision is isolated to one location of a program. The proliferation of software in everyday life has increased the conformity and invisibility of software. As the demand for software increases, future requirements will necessitate new strategies for improved modularization in order to support the requisite adaptations.

Adaptability of software is actually partitioned between two stages: modifiability *during development*, and adaptation *during execution*. The first type of adaptation is concerned with design-time, or compile-time, techniques that permit the modification of the structure and function of software in order to address changing stakeholder requirements. To support such evolution, techniques such as aspect-oriented programming and object-oriented frameworks are but a few of the ideas that have shown promise in assisting a developer in the isolation of points of variation and configurability. The second type of adaptation occurs at runtime during the execution of the application. This type of adaptation refers to a system's ability to modify itself and to respond to changing conditions in its external environment. To accommodate such changes, research in meta-programming and reflection have offered some recourse, especially in the area of adaptive middleware.

With the Internet becoming the de facto way by which corporations extend their enterprise business, distributed systems become an increasingly important and integral part of everyday life. To realize distributed systems, *middleware* is needed in order to integrate diverse heterogeneous software components and to allow them to interoperate effectively, addressing at the same time several middleware-specific concerns that crosscut the boundaries of software components, such as distribution, concurrency, transactions, security, etc. In this chapter, we address the first type of adaptation (during development) in the context of middleware-mediated distributed systems from two different perspectives, one focusing on the *(re)configuration* of such systems to incorporate different *middleware-specific concerns* at the *design level*, and the other one focusing on the *adaptation* of the implementation of these concerns to different *middleware infrastructures* at the *code level*.

To abstract away from the ever emergent middleware infrastructures and to avoid drowning in their implementation complexities, models are proposed as a far more accessible and easier means for developers to build, extend, and evaluate applications than working directly at the code level. The Model Driven Architecture (MDA) [324, 309], an Object Management Group (OMG) [322] initiative, promotes the separation of concerns between two modeling dimensions: one focusing on the business functionality (resulting in *Platform Independent Models – PIMs*), and the other one focusing on the implementation of that functionality on a specific middleware platform, such as COM/DCOM/COM+ [292], RMI [406], CCM/CORBA [311, 321], Jini [408, 305], EJB/J2EE [410, 407], .NET [293], Web Services [461], or other message-oriented middleware platforms (resulting in *Platform Specific Models – PSMs*). While model transformations should be used to refine PIMs into PSMs, code generators are supposed to map PSMs to concrete middleware-based implementations, providing thus an elegant approach to adapt PIMs to the peculiarities of the new middleware infrastructures that do not cease to appear.

Before going any further, referring to the "myth of absolute platform independence" and "platform relativism" [136], and in order not to leave any doubts or to risk any misinterpretations, we would like to make clear that, in the context of this work, we consider the *middleware* to be our MDA platform, and not the operating system, or anything else. Moreover, even though MDA is completely independent of any modeling language, the Unified Modeling Language (UML) [318, 116] established itself as the de facto standard. As a consequence, we only focus on the UML support for MDA.

Even though it has been around for more than three years already, MDA still remains a vision in many different aspects. In order to proliferate this vision and make it a reality, and at the same time to facilitate the development of middleware-mediated distributed applications, there is an imperative need for tool support. Unfortunately, so far there is very little in terms of concrete tools that actually support MDA beyond traditional UML modeling and skeleton-class generation. In order to fill this gap, and to make a clear stand in the MDA arena, we designed the Parallax framework that allows developers to look at the system under consideration from different perspectives (or viewpoints) through a well-defined system of plug-ins and based on aspect-oriented support. Besides presenting the Parallax framework, we will mainly focus in this chapter on the (re)configuration and adaptation facilities promoted by Parallax, which enables developers to incorporate middleware-specific concerns in their designs at different MDA levels of abstraction, and to view their enhanced designs through a prism of middleware platforms and see how middleware-specific concerns are actually implemented at the code level. Implementation details are discussed as well, emphasizing the powerful combination of AspectJ aspects with Eclipse plug-ins, which enables aspects to encapsulate concerns that crosscut plug-in boundaries.

The rest of this chapter is structured as follows. Section 2 introduces the architecture of Parallax focusing mainly on its core and on the way it handles several middleware-specific concerns as promoted by the Enterprise Fondue software development method on which it relies, Section 3 presents the framework of Parallax plug-ins that addresses the (re)configuration and adaptation of systems based on AspectJ aspects and Eclipse plug-ins. Section 4 discusses the Parallax tool support and presents typical usage scenarios, Section 5 gives an overview of the currently available tools promoting the MDA vision and emphasizes the points in which Parallax is different, and Sect. 6 draws some conclusions and presents future work directions.

2 Parallax and Enterprise Fondue

In this section, after a concise overview of Enterprise Fondue's terminology, we show how the MDA-oriented UML profiles, defined for addressing middleware-specific concerns in the context of the Enterprise Fondue method, form a solid basis for the Parallax framework in its goal of providing tool support for (re)configuring application designs with middleware-specific concerns, on the one hand, and adapting them to different middleware infrastructures, on the other hand. The architecture and the core of Parallax are presented as well.

The *Enterprise Fondue* software development method [395] brings together four important paradigms in software engineering, namely component-based software engineering (CBSE), separation of concerns (SoC), Model-Driven Architecture (MDA), and aspect-oriented programming (AOP), and shows how they can complement each other at different stages in the development life cycle of middleware-mediated enterprise applications. The method identifies five layers corresponding to different levels of abstraction, each layer addressing specific concerns that pertain to enterprise applications in general. Model transformations are used to refine design models inside the same layer, or between different layers, along specific concern-dimensions.

For consistency reasons, we tend to use the terms middleware-specific *concern-dimensions* in relation with the *refining* activity ("refining along a dimension"), and middleware-specific *concerns* in all other contexts. Nevertheless, both terminologies refer to the same concepts, i.e., distribution, concurrency, transactions, security, and so on.

For the MDA approach to software development to become a reality for distributed enterprise systems, MDA needs to provide support for understanding, describing, and implementing such middleware-specific concerns, also referred to as *pervasive services* in MDA's PIM terminology [309]. However, the current UML does not provide any specific or standard support for modeling pervasive services. What it does offer, is the possibility to "extend" the UML metamodel through, and only through, *profiling*, which defines how specific UML model elements are customized and extended with new semantics as if they were instances of new "virtual" metamodel constructs.

The Enterprise Fondue method defines MDA-oriented UML profiles that address middleware-specific concerns at different levels of abstraction. It also promotes a systematic approach to addressing pervasive services in an MDA-compliant manner, at different levels of abstraction, through incremental refinement steps along middleware-specific concern-dimensions according to the proposed UML profiles. A complete example has already been carried out for the distribution concern. The *UML-D Profiles* proposed in [394] address the distribution concern in an MDA-oriented fashion at three different levels of abstraction: *platform-independent* level, *abstract realization* level, and *concrete realization* level. The CORBA [321] technology was used in [394] to illustrate how the refinement process is applied to a concrete example.

Figure 1 reconsiders the UML-D profiles in the context of this chapter and defines the *RMIDistributionRealizationProfile*, which addresses the realization of the distribution concern when the implementation is supposed to use the RMI technology [406]. It takes advantage of the `AbstractDistributionRealizationProfile` by adapting its abstract concepts to the RMI technology, so that a code generator has enough information to generate the necessary distribution code. Since we kept unchanged the first two MDA-levels of abstraction in the hierarchy presented in [394], we will not explain them once again here. We show nevertheless the entire hierarchy for the sake of completeness and because we need the `DistributionProfile` when configuring designs with distribution elements at a platform-independent level, as we will see in Sect. 3.2.1.

The *«RMINameExposition»* stereotype represents a «NameExposition» using the RMI technology. It extends the «NameExposition» but does not add particular information to it. The idea is to state clearly that a «PublishedServant» instance is registered by *name* using the RMI technology. The same holds for the *«RMIRegistry»* stereotype that extends the «NamingRegistry». In order for an actor of the environment to find the «RMIRegistry», we add the host and port tag definitions. An OCL [456, 457] constraint (④) enforces that these two stereotypes work together and only together. This constraint also enforces that exposition names are all different within the context of a «Publisher».

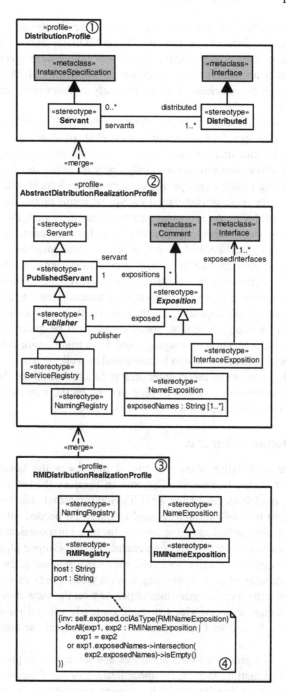

Fig. 1. RMI distribution realization profile

The UML-D profiles are just an example of how the Enterprise Fondue method addresses middleware-specific concerns at different MDA-levels of abstraction. Other such profiles have already been defined for other middleware-specific concerns, such as concurrency and transactions, moving towards defining MDA-oriented UML profiles for middleware services, or more precisely middleware-specific concerns (*UML-MS profiles*).

Based on the solid foundations of the MDA-oriented UML profiles for addressing different middleware-specific concerns at several levels of abstraction in the context of the Enterprise Fondue method, and in order to provide developers with integrated tool support that allows them to incrementally apply these profiles for refining their design models along middleware-specific concern-dimensions at different stages in the development life cycle of distributed enterprise applications, we designed the *Parallax* framework [401]. As it is promoted by its name as well, Parallax[1] enables developers to view the system under development from different perspectives (or viewpoints) through a well-defined system of plug-ins and based on aspect-oriented support. Developers may choose to (re)configure their designs in order to incorporate middleware-specific concerns at different MDA-levels of abstraction, and then to adapt their enhanced designs to different programming languages and different middleware infrastructures depending on the plug-ins that have been loaded. As we will see later, by such an adaptation, specific code will be generated (out of design elements) in a programming language and for a middleware infrastructure, if middleware-specific elements have to be addressed as well.

The remaining sections of this chapter present in more detail the Parallax framework, focusing mainly on its system of plug-ins and on the way they address both the (re)configuration and adaptation of existing systems.

2.1 The Architecture of Parallax

The architecture of Parallax shown in Fig. 2 introduces the basic components building up the Parallax framework. The core of Parallax (`PrlxCore`) is responsible for storing models (loaded from XMI files) into internal object-oriented models (`PrlxModels`) that will further be used to query all needed information. The `PrlxCore` along with the `PrlxMetamodel` are discussed in more details in Sect. 2.2.

Since Parallax was designed and implemented as an Eclipse plug-in, it has to define its own Eclipse perspective. `PrlxPerspective` represents the Parallax perspective of the Parallax plug-in, containing several views (`PrlxViews`) that enable developers to perform specific operations depending on the view they are currently browsing. The complete set of views that are currently offered inside Parallax is presented in Sect. 4 with brief descriptions of their intended use and the provided functionality.

`PrlxUtilities` groups all sorts of classes that serve various purposes, such as support for the highlighting facility, the specialization of the character parser (scanner and rules), some logging facilities using aspects, support for managing icons and

---

[1] [Webster] the *apparent* change in the *position* of an object resulting from the change in the *direction* or *position* from which it is *viewed*

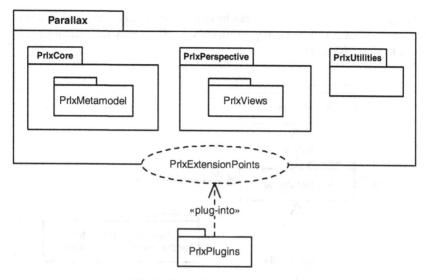

Fig. 2. The architecture of Parallax

color objects, since their total number that can be displayed in the same time is restricted by the underlying operating system, and thus they have to be disposed of when no longer used, and so on.

Parallax plug-ins (PrlxPlugins) represent the most important part of the Parallax framework providing the developer with support for loading application designs exported as XMI files from different UML modeling tools, for configuring the developer's designs to incorporate middleware-specific concerns at different MDA levels of abstraction, and for adapting the enhanced designs to different programming languages and different middleware infrastructures depending on the plug-ins that have been loaded. The main section of this chapter (Sect. 3) is entirely dedicated to the framework of PrlxPlugins that we designed around the Parallax platform, and less on the extension points (PrlxExtensionPoints) defined in order to allow PrlxPlugins to plug new functionality into Parallax. The latter information is rather spread throughout the entire chapter and can be inferred by looking at the description of the PrlxPlugins and their impact on Parallax.

2.2 The Parallax Core (PrlxCore) and the Input Adaptor Plug-ins (PrlxInputAdaptorPlugins)

From the very beginning of this work, Parallax was intended to load application designs exported as XMI files. As a consequence, it became immediately clear that the model information read from such XMI files will have to be stored internally in object-oriented models in order to provide an easy mechanism to query and to deliver such information to other parts of Parallax that require it.

Figure 3 illustrates the model hierarchy of Parallax presented at two different layers of the four-layer metamodeling architecture [318], namely the metamodel (M_2) and the model (M_1) layers.

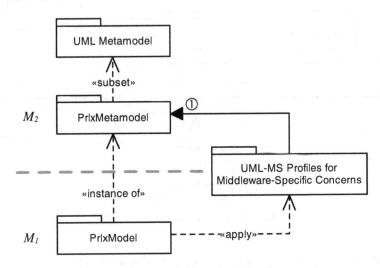

Fig. 3. The model hierarchy of Parallax

Starting from the top, the «subset» dependency shows that the Parallax metamodel (PrlxMetamodel) is just a subset of the full UML metamodel, excluding, for instance, some of the Behavioral Elements packages, such as the Use Cases, the State Machines, or the Activity Graphs packages, which are not needed for the intended purpose of Parallax, i.e., generating code targeted at different programming languages and different middleware infrastructures relying on class diagrams (for the static structure) and on the interactions described in collaboration/sequence diagrams (for the behavior), while also taking into account the UML-MS profiles when applied to a design. Moreover, even for the elements that we considered to include in the PrlxMetamodel, e.g., UML:Class, UML:Operation, etc., we decided to drop certain attributes or features, such as isActive, isSpecification, or isQuery, simply because they are not needed in the code generation process.

Further down, at the M_1 layer, a Parallax model (PrlxModel) incorporates instances from the PrlxMetamodel and applies extensions defined in the UML-MS profiles for the different middleware-specific concerns that we want to address. It is at this layer that a model loaded from an XMI file will be stored in objects that are instances of the PrlxMetamodel classes and that are filled with information found in the XMI input file. This means, for example, that an object instance of the PrlxInterface class (from the PrlxMetamodel level) is responsible for encapsulating a concrete UML:Interface read from the loaded XMI. Note that the (UML 2.0) base class arrow notation (Fig. 3 ①) ends on the Parallax metamodel, instead of the UML metamodel, only because we want to stress that all the base classes that were considered for defining the stereotypes in the UML-MS profiles must be part of the subset included in the `PrlxMetamodel`.

In order to avoid dealing with the peculiarities of the different XMI [308, 313, 320] and UML [318, 116] specifications, we did not want to parse the XMI input files ourselves. Instead, we considered the support provided by third-party products, such as the Eclipse Modeling Framework [99], or the Meta-Data Repository (MDR) [409]. The former one being ECore based [100] and the latter one being MOF based [312], and taking into account the lack of specification behind ECore as opposed to MOF, on the one hand, and our intent to support XMI files exported from the currently used UML modeling tools (most of them MOF-based), on the other hand, we decided to choose MDR as our model repository tool. Implementing the Java Metadata Interface (JMI) specification [231], MDR takes as input a specific MOF-based metamodel (as an XMI file), and generates a complete JMI-based repository (as Java source files) for storing, managing, and querying information from models that are compliant with the considered metamodel. In the concrete case of Parallax, we provided MDR with the `PrlxMetamodel`, and hence MDR generated the complete JMI-based repository for storing, managing, and querying `PrlxModels`, as illustrated graphically in Fig. 4. All the `PrlxViews`, along with the rest of Parallax, rely on these generated interfaces in order to access the information they need from the `PrlxModel` in order to generate their own content.

However, in order to take advantage of the XMI `Reader` and `Writer` implementations provided by MDR, for automatically reading XMI files into `PrlxModels` (deserialization), and saving `PrlxModels` into XMI files (serialization), the XMI file itself and the JMI-based repository must be compliant with the same metamodel. Unfortunately, this is not the case when trying to load application designs exported as XMI files from different UML modeling tools, since such XMI files are compliant with the UML metamodel supported by the modeling tool. As a consequence, in order to have automatic loading and saving facilities between UML-compliant XMI files and `PrlxModels`, *adaptors* have to be implemented between the different JMI-based repositories for UML 1.x or 2.0 models, and the JMI-based repository for `PrlxModels`, as shown in Fig. 4. To be more precise, since none of the currently available UML modeling tools (to our knowledge) support one entire UML specification, and mainly because their XMI export facilities are not fully compliant with the UML Model Interchange, each UML modeling tool introduces new *variation points* in the adaptation process, as we tried to illustrate in Fig. 4. Therefore, the `PrlxInputAdaptorPlugins`, which are responsible for the adaptation step that is necessary when loading XMI files exported from different UML modeling tools into internal `PrlxModels`, have at least two dependency dimensions (*2-DD*); they are at the same time:

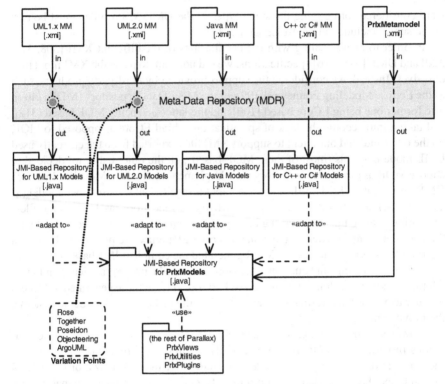

Fig. 4. The Parallax input support (`PrlxInputAdaptorPlugins`)

- *CASE-tool-provider dependent*
  e.g., IBM Rational Rose, Poseidon, Borland Together, Objecteering, ArgoUML, etc.; sometimes, as in the case of Rose, it is the CASE-tool-XMI-exporter (Unisys) that introduces the dependency;
- *UML-specification dependent*
  e.g., UML 1.x, UML 2.0, etc.

For some repositories, the XMI specification (e.g., XMI 1.1, 1.2, 2.0, etc.) might be a third dependency dimension. However, since we use MDR for our model repository, and since MDR transparently handles this dimension, we decided not to include it in the list of dependencies for the time being.

For each CASE-tool-provider, the associated `PrlxInputAdaptorPlugins` are responsible for reading the header of the XMI input file, identifying the corresponding (pretended) UML-specification compliancy, reading the XMI file into the JMI-based repository for the appropriate UML 1.x or 2.0 models, and adapting it to the JMI-based repository for `PrlxModels`. Following this pattern, and relying on the `prlxinputadaptors` extension point that has been defined and published for the `PrlxCore`, the "input" facilities of Parallax can be easily extended to support new XMI file formats exported from different UML modeling tools and compliant with different UML specifications, provided that the appropriate `PrlxInputAdaptorPlugin` has already been implemented. Currently, we are able to load application designs exported as XMI 1.1 (UML 1.3, UML 1.4) and XMI 1.2 (UML 1.4) files from several UML modeling tools, such as IBM Rational Rose, Borland Together, or Poseidon. We plan to include in this list the Objecteering and ArgoUML tools as well.

As a further step down the road, we would like to extend the input facilities of Parallax and allow developers to import Java/C++/C# projects into Parallax. Besides defining the metamodels for Java/C++/C#, special parsers will have to be implemented to extract the information needed from the source code of such projects and to fill the JMI-based repositories for Java/C++/C# models accordingly. Moreover, adaptors will have to be implemented between these repositories and the JMI-based repository for `PrlxModels` as well. Once such projects are loaded into `PrlxModels`, developers will be able to use Parallax just as if the design model had been loaded from an XMI file. We consider that such a reverse engineering facility would be very useful for the huge number of legacy applications that exist out there but do not have any explicit design to start with. Developers might not want to invest in a CASE tool for performing the reverse engineering step, but they would like nevertheless to distribute their applications, or to incorporate other middleware-specific concerns, without too much effort.

3 The Framework of Parallax Plug-ins (`PrlxPlugins`)

After a brief overview of the main concepts and paradigms involved in the Parallax project, and after some details explaining the technical support for the Parallax approach, we present in this section the framework of Parallax plug-ins that addresses the (re)configuration and adaptation of systems, based on AspectJ aspects and Eclipse plug-ins.

Separation of concerns [343] and modularization are fundamental techniques of software engineering. Decomposing software into smaller, more manageable, and comprehensible parts, each of which encapsulates and addresses a particular area of interest, called a *concern*, is a well-proven method for developing applications that are easy to configure, adapt, or extend according to changes in the requirements specification.

The Eclipse Platform [98] is an integrated development environment (IDE) "for anything, and for nothing in particular", as it is stated in one of the technical overviews [325]. The Eclipse Platform is built on a mechanism for discovering, integrating, and running modules, called *plug-ins*, which extend in some way the Java notion of `packages`. Coded in Java, a plug-in is the smallest Eclipse Platform function unit that can be developed and delivered separately. Each plug-in has a *manifest* file, `plugin.xml`, declaring its interconnections to other plug-ins. The interconnection model is simple: a plug-in declares any number of named *extension points*, and any number of *extensions* to one or more extension points in other plug-ins. A plug-in's extension points can be extended by other plug-ins. Except for a small kernel, known as the Eclipse Core Runtime, all of the Eclipse Platform's functionality is located in plug-ins, which makes Eclipse the most extensible platform ever designed. For more details about contributing to Eclipse, its principles, patterns, and plug-ins, refer to [141].

Aspect-oriented programming (AOP) [253] has been proposed as a technique for improving separation of concerns in software. This approach makes it possible to separately specify various kinds of concerns and modularize them into separate units of encapsulation, called *aspects*. One can deal with both the concerns and the modules that encapsulate them at different levels of abstraction, not only at the code level. AspectJ [252, 97] is a general-purpose aspect-oriented extension to Java. It defines one new concept, a join point, and adds a few new constructs, such as pointcut, advice, introduction, and aspect. *Join points* are well-defined points in the program flow; *pointcuts* are a means of referring to collections of join points and context values at those join points; *advices* define code that is executed when pointcuts are reached during execution; *introductions* can be used to affect the static structure of Java programs, namely the members of its classes and the relationships between classes; and *aspects* are AspectJ's modular units of cross-cutting implementation, defined in terms of pointcuts, advices, introductions, and ordinary Java member declarations. Similar extensions exist for other programming languages, such as C++, C, Smalltalk, or Ruby.

When developing applications using AspectJ, a compilation or *weaving* step is always required. Typically, the AspectJ compiler would take all the parts of the application (aspects, sources, classes, and libraries) and produce a complete weaved (and enhanced) system ready for running. This basic assumption breaks with the modularization approach promoted by Eclipse plug-ins. When Eclipse plug-ins are developed, the compiler typically knows all the source code of the plug-in itself and the byte code of the required plug-ins – and no more than that. As a consequence, an aspect would have to be weaved in the classes of a plug-in in order to obtain first the enhanced plug-in, which will be further loaded into Eclipse. Because of this intermediate weaving step, aspects can only define pointcuts that are completely inside a single Eclipse plug-in. To tell the whole truth, they can define more, but the weaving functionality of the AspectJ compiler will find only those targets of the pointcuts that are inside the plug-in in which the aspect is defined, which amounts to a single plug-in, as mentioned before.

In order to overcome this drawback of Eclipse plug-ins with respect to AspectJ support, and to allow developers to define pointcuts beyond the boundaries of plug-ins, the AspectJ-Enabled Eclipse Core Runtime was implemented [278]. Without entering too much into implementation details, we just want to mention that *load-time weaving* is used to weave aspects into classes at the moment when these classes are actually loaded into the virtual machine (in the case of Java). Although load-time weaving was not available for the AspectJ 1.0 language, the byte code weaving implementation of AspectJ 1.1 allows load-time weaving to be realized for the complete AspectJ 1.1 language, i.e., all AspectJ 1.1 constructs lend themselves to load-time weaving functionalities. Because the class-loading mechanism of the Eclipse Core Runtime was not designed to be modified or enhanced through standard Eclipse

```xml
<?xml version="1.0" encoding="UTF-8"?>
<plugin
    id="edu.demo.prlxaspect"
    name="PrlxAspect Plugin"
    version="1.0.0">

    <runtime>
        <library name="prlxaspect.jar"/>
    </runtime>
    <requires>
        <import plugin="org.aspectj.weavingruntime"/>
    </requires>

    <extension
            id="demoaspect"
            name="Demo Aspect"
            point="org.aspectj.weavingruntime.aspects">
        <aspect
                class="edu.demo.PrlxAspect">
        </aspect>
    </extension>

</plugin>
```

Fig. 5. An eclipse plug-in promoting an aspect in its `plugin.xml`

plug-ins, a basic load-time byte code modification *hook* had to be inserted in the class-loader itself. It is through this special hook that the weaving functionality is injected exactly when the byte code of a class is loaded. For defining the weaving functionality, a new extension point for the weaving runtime is provided, called `aspects`, which allows other Eclipse plug-ins to define, in their `plugin.xml` description, the aspects they want to promote for weaving. Such an *aspect-promoting Eclipse plug-in* is illustrated in Fig. 5, which shows how an Eclipse plug-in called `PrlxAspectPlugin` defines an extension for the `aspects` extension point in order to promote the `edu.demo.PrlxAspect` aspect. The AspectJ-Enabled Eclipse Core Runtime is available for download at [279] along with more documentation on its implementation, installation, and some running examples.

Figure 6 depicts in a graphical way the difference between the standard Eclipse Core Runtime support for aspects and its AspectJ-enabled counterpart. We used numbers in order to show the sequencing of operations and to emphasize how in the standard version the aspect is weaved in only one plug-in (①a), which is further plugged into Eclipse (②a), while in the AspectJ-enabled version, the aspect is first plugged into the Eclipse class loader (①b) and then it is weaved in all subsequently loaded classes (②b), and thus all subsequently loaded plug-ins. Note that in order to achieve such a functionality, the aspect `PrlxAspect` had to be encapsulated in a standard Eclipse plug-in `PrlxAspectPlugin`, which extends the `aspects` extension point, just like it was defined in Fig. 5.

Thanks to the enhanced (but compatible) version of the Eclipse Core Runtime, aspects may now be designed using pointcuts that crosscut plug-in boundaries, also referred to as cross-plug-in pointcuts, just like the currently supported cross-objects pointcuts; more importantly, such aspects may be implemented and compiled separately, and may be modularized in *stand-alone* Eclipse plug-ins without the need for weaving them explicitly in their target plug-ins, following therefore the general idea behind plug-ins in the Eclipse world. Cross-cutting concerns that spread across the boundaries of plug-ins may nevertheless be encapsulated in stand-alone plug-ins, which define and promote aspects that address the cross-cutting concern under consideration across several plug-ins and could affect their code accordingly.

Based on the previously introduced concepts and with the technological support of the AspectJ-Enabled Eclipse Core Runtime, we designed and implemented the framework of Parallax plug-ins (PrlxPlugins) illustrated in Fig. 7. Dependencies between plug-ins and their impact on other constituent parts of the Parallax platform are shown in Fig. 7 as well. Since all Parallax plug-ins (PrlxPlugins) are specifically designed to serve some developer needs, they will all have to define entries in one of the views (PrlxViews) building up the Parallax perspective (PrlxPerspective) so that developers can invoke them easily. More details about the intended purpose of the different PrlxViews and their entries will be given in Sect. 4 when describing the Parallax tool support. Nevertheless, there are some PrlxPlugins that go beyond the PrlxViews and impact other graphical user interface elements, such as contextual popup menus, as is the case of PrlxConcernAspectPlugins. These cases will be presented to some extent in the subsections dedicated to the corresponding PrlxPlugin.

Taking into account that the PrlxInputAdaptorPlugins have already been described in Sect. 2.2, the remainder of this section discusses in more detail the other three major parts of the framework of plug-ins, namely the plug-in support for code generation (PrlxCodeGeneratorPlugins), the plug-in support for addressing middleware-specific concerns at the design level (PrlxConcernAspectPlugins and PrlxConcernTechnologyAspectPlugins), and the plug-in support for addressing middleware-specific concerns at the implementation level (PrlxConcern-

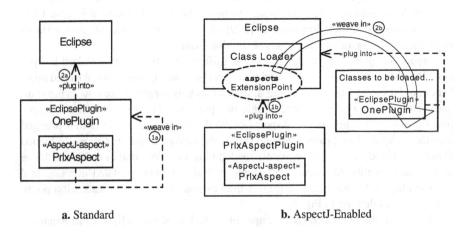

a. Standard   **b.** AspectJ-Enabled

Fig. 6. Eclipse Core Runtime: loading plug-ins and weaving aspects

`PlatformAspectPlugins`). We end with a discussion that shows how Parallax addresses both the (re)configuration and the adaptation of systems through the proposed framework of plug-ins.

3.1 Code Generator Plug-ins (`PrlxCodeGeneratorPlugins`)

Code generator plug-ins are pure standard Eclipse plug-ins, without promoting any aspects for the weaving runtime. By taking the code generation support out of the `PrlxCore`, and by defining and publishing an extension point for it, called `prlxcodegenerators`, developers can start writing their own plug-ins for generating code (`PrlxCodeGeneratorPlugins`) for their favorite programming language, e.g., Java, C++, C#, etc. At the same time, instead of having only one code generator for a programming language, several plug-ins may exist for generating code for the same programming language. Moreover, the aspects defined in `PrlxConcernPlatformAspectPlugins` (as we will see in Sect. 3.2.2) will be weaved in each `PrlxCodeGeneratorPlugin` as their code gets loaded by the AspectJ-Enabled Eclipse Core Runtime, enhancing the code generators with middleware-specific code generation capabilities. It will be the responsibility of the `PrlxConcernPlatformAspectPlugins` to match the programming language they support with the programming language promoted by `PrlxCodeGenerator-Plugins`, and to avoid, for instance, weaving CORBA code generation capabilities for the Java language inside a `PrlxCodeGeneratorPlugin` for the C# language.

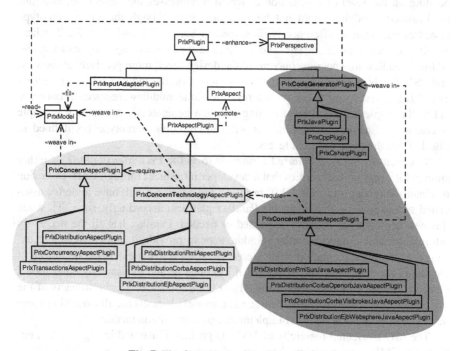

Fig. 7. The framework of Parallax plug-ins

3.2 Parallax Aspect-Plug-ins (`PrlxAspectPlugins`)

Parallax aspect-plug-ins are the special type of plug-ins supported only by the AspectJ-Enabled Eclipse Core Runtime. Besides standard Eclipse plug-in functionalities, they also promote AspectJ aspects (`PrlxAspects`) to the weaving runtime through the `aspects` extension point.

The main purpose of these aspects is to act as "model transformations" inside the Parallax platform. They rely on the UML profiles defined for each middleware-specific concern in the context of the Enterprise Fondue method, and they apply these profiles inside Parallax at different MDA levels of abstraction, just like MTL [137] model transformations did in [394].

UML profiles [318, 116] define a coherent set of extensions for a *specific domain* or *purpose*. Each UML standard extension mechanism specifies how UML model elements can be customized and extended with *new semantics*. For instance, a stereotype creates a "virtual" metaclass with new meta-attributes and *additional semantics*.

As one may notice, the main emphasis in all these definitions is placed on additional semantics, purpose, or meaning that these extensions add to a design model. Because of this new semantics, all the modules of Parallax that have to deal with such new elements sooner or later need to be adapted accordingly. It is the job of `PrlxAspects` to perform such an adaptation that crosscuts different Parallax modules. Moreover, each such aspect defines a different semantics for a stereotype depending on the level of abstraction at which it addresses the stereotype, and thus the cross-cut modules might not be the same, even though the same stereotype is addressed. Such a difference is illustrated in Sect. 3.2.1 and Sect. 3.2.2, where `PrlxConcernAspectPlugins` and `PrlxConcernTechnologyAspectPlugins` address middleware-specific concerns at the design level, more precisely at the PIM and PSM levels of abstraction respectively (acting on the model), while `PrlxConcernPlatformAspectPlugins` address the same middleware-specific concerns but at the implementation level (acting on code generators). A concrete example is considered, namely addressing the «`Distributed`» stereotype (as defined in Fig. 1 ①) at the three different levels.

To conclude, the *rule*, referred further on to as the *PrlxExtensionRule*, is rather simple: for every new semantics that a developer introduces through UML extension mechanisms (encapsulated in UML profiles), the developer will have to define associated `PrlxAspects` that adapt the Parallax platform accordingly, such that when this new semantics is actually addressed or needed, Parallax has all the necessary information and support in order to address or to provide it immediately. For example, at the implementation level, stereotyping typically impacts the definition of the model element itself, the definition of its contents, and its usage by other model elements. In the concrete case of the `DistributionProfile`, the impacts of the «`Distributed`» stereotype on `Interface` model elements are illustrated in more details in Sect. 3.2.2 at the RMI implementation level of abstraction.

The MDA-oriented hierarchy of UML-D profiles illustrated in Fig. 1 relies entirely on UML's extension mechanisms. Moreover, since the structure of the XMI (for exchanging UML models) is based on the UML metamodel, which incorporates extension mechanisms as well, there is no problem in exporting design models that were refined according to the profiles introduced in Fig. 1, i.e., models that contain new stereotypes, tag definitions, or tagged values. When loading such enhanced models into Parallax, new object instances of the `PrlxStereotype` class (from the `PrlxMetamodel`) will be created and filled with the information found in the XMI that defines the stereotype under consideration. Moreover, since each `UML:Core:ModelElement` may be associated with several stereotypes, each class in the `PrlxMetamodel` has its own list of stereotypes, which is also filled when loading an XMI model into Parallax.

Therefore, in the case of the distribution concern and the corresponding UML-D profiles, we are able to load and store in our internal models information about distribution without having plugged into Parallax any distribution-related plug-ins in advance. It is a straight forward support that is provided when models are compliant with the UML metamodel. Saving is not a problem either because we deal with the same stereotypes, we already know what they contain, and there is a standard way of serializing stereotypes into XMI. However, besides loading and saving, there is no more than that. Developers cannot modify any information related to distribution. Everything is treated in a standard way, and there are no special functionalities.

3.2.1 Concern-Oriented and Concern-on-Technology Aspect-Plug-ins (`PrlxConcernAspectPlugins`, `PrlxConcernTechnologyAspectPlugins`)

From the model transformation point of view, we could say that `PrlxConcern-AspectPlugins` and `PrlxConcernTechnologyAspectPlugins` refine Parallax along middleware-specific concern-dimensions, enabling it to store, manage, and query middleware-specific concern-related information at the PIM, respectively PSM, MDA levels of abstraction.

By extending the `prlxprofiles` extension point in the Parallax core (`Prlx-Core`), `PrlxConcernAspectPlugins` and `PrlxConcernTechnologyAspect-Plugins` are responsible for providing Parallax with the corresponding UML profiles that address middleware-specific concerns at the platform-independent and platform-specific levels of abstraction, respectively. It is these very UML-MS profiles, through the new stereotypes they define, that enable the internal `PrlxModel` to store and manage middleware-specific concern-related information. One should notice that the dependency between profiles («merge» in Fig. 1) implies a dependency between plug-ins («require» in Fig. 7), since the stereotypes defined at the PIM level must have been already loaded in order for the PSM-level stereotypes to be able to extend them. An aspect defined in the `PrlxCore` is responsible for collecting all such `prlxprofiles` extensions and for loading the encapsulated profiles immediately after a design model has been successfully loaded.

By extending the `aspects` extension point, `PrlxConcernAspectPlugins` and `PrlxConcernTechnologyAspectPlugins` promote AspectJ aspects, which define explicit high-level interfaces that enable developers to easily query the internal object-oriented `PrlxModel` for the middleware-specific concern-related information.

Moreover, relying on the standard Eclipse plug-in functionalities, these plug-ins also have the responsibility to enhance the Parallax graphical user interface (GUI) so that developers may apply the profiles that have been loaded, i.e., configure stereotypes and tag definitions, through simple GUI interactions.

In the particular case of the distribution concern and considering its associated platform-independent profile (`DistributionProfile`) and RMI platform-specific profile (`RMIDistributionRealizationProfile`) as defined in Fig. 1, while the `PrlxDistributionAspectPlugin` and `PrlxDistributionRmiAspectPlugin` are loaded into Parallax and the encapsulated aspects are weaved in different constituent parts of Parallax, the following actions occur:

- Load the stereotypes promoted by the `DistributionProfile` and `RMIDistributionRealizationProfile` into the `PrlxModel` (if not already there) in order to be able to apply them to model elements.
- Insert new entries in the Concerns and Technologies views of the Parallax perspective (see Fig. 11 ⑤ and ⑦).
- Provide the *"Distribute..."*, *"Create Servant..."*, and *"Servant..."* contextual popup menu options on interfaces, classes, and objects, respectively, in order to allow developers to distribute interfaces (i.e., stereotype them «Distributed») and to create servant objects (i.e., stereotype them «Servant»). In order to further assist the developer in the refinement process, several inference algorithms are running behind the scenes to ensure the consistent application of the `DistributionProfile`, e.g., for each «Distributed» interface that a developer enables through the appropriate contextual popup menu option, a recursive algorithm infers all the other interfaces that must be «Distributed» as well because of their involvement in the newly enabled distributed setting. Similarly, when enabling a «Distributed» interface or a «Servant» object, the corresponding list of all possible «Servant» objects, or «Distributed» interfaces respectively, is presented to the developer as a result of an inference algorithm so that the developer can make a selection immediately, reducing in this way the risk for inconsistencies.
- Provide a configuration tab that would allow developers to configure distribution-specific realization elements on the RMI technology, such as the name of the «Servant» object, and the host and the port of the «RMIRegistry». This PSM-level deployment configuration information will be saved in a special technology-dependent XML-Config-File in order to give the possibility for easy deployment customization, as explained in [394]. It is the RMI-XML-Config-File that the client and the server applications will both read at startup time in order to know how to find each other; the distribution-on-RMI configuration tab is triggered from the Technologies view.
- Define the special semantics for the newly loaded stereotypes in the particular contexts of these aspect-plug-ins and in accordance with the MDA levels of abstraction that they address (i.e., the PIM and PSM levels), as requested by

the `PrlxExtensionRule` introduced in Sect. 3.2; for instance, the example in Fig. 8 shows how the `PrlxDistributionAspect` enhances the `PrlxModel` by defining a new interface (`IDistributionPrlxInterface`) for querying the PIM-level distribution-related information from a `PrlxInterface`. A similar interface is defined for the `PrlxObject` in order to be able to identify the «`Servant`» object. Note the relationship between the classes on which we are defining these extra interfaces and the metaclasses that have been extended in the `DistributionProfile`; without entering into details at this time, similar interfaces are defined by the `PrlxDistributionRmiAspect` for querying the PSM-level RMI distribution-related information from the `PrlxModel`.

- Enable the highlighting of distribution-related information across all currently opened views, e.g., we look in the XMI for the «`Distributed`» and «`Servant`» stereotypes and for all elements that have been stereotyped with one of them, and we highlight all these elements with the color that is associated to the distribution concern.

- Provide special distribution-related icons for «`Distributed`» and «`Servant`» model elements in order to emphasize them even in the absence of distribution highlighting.

```
public aspect PrlxDistributionAspect{
  // on PrlxInterface

  public interface IDistributionPrlxInterface {
    public boolean isDistributed();
  }
  declare parents:
    PrlxInterface extends IDistributionPrlxInterface;

  public boolean PrlxInterface.isDistributed() {
    Iterator it = this.getStereotypes().iterator();
    for ( ; it.hasNext(); ) {
      PrlxStereotype s = (PrlxStereotype) it.next();
      if (s.getName().equals("Distributed")) return true;
    }
    return false;
  }
}
```

IDistributionPrlxInterface

PrlxInterface

(MDR-generated, JMI-compliant interface)

Fig. 8. Code snippet of the `PrlxDistributionAspect`

Several constraints that have been defined on the MDA-oriented hierarchy of UML-D profiles in [394] are enforced inside Parallax as well, such as «`Distributed`» should only be applied to `UML:Interfaces`, «`Servant`» should only be applied to `UML:Objects`, «`Distributed`» interfaces cannot exist without a «`Servant`» object, «`Servant`» objects cannot exist without at least one «`Distributed`» interface, the exposed names within the context of a «`Publisher`» (in this case, an «`RMIRegistry`») must all be different, and so on.

The entire analysis presented in this subsection for the distribution-on-RMI case can be extended to other middleware-specific concerns and other middleware technologies through their own associated `PrlxConcernAspectPlugins` and `PrlxConcernTechnologyAspectPlugins` respectively, e.g., concurrency, transactions, distribution-on-CORBA, transactions-on-EJB, etc. If we look at the inheritance model in the top-right corner of Fig. 8, other `PrlxConcernAspectPlugins` might define their own interfaces (at the same level as `IDistributionPrlxInterface`) in order to query concern-related information, provided that the `UML:Interface` model element has been semantically extended in the profiles for those concerns.

3.2.2 Concern-on-Platform Aspect-Plug-ins (`PrlxConcernPlatformAspectPlugins`)

Concern-on-platform aspect-plugins address middleware-specific concerns at the implementation level. They are weaved in code generator plug-ins, enhancing the code generators with middleware-specific code generation capabilities. More precisely, they address the implementation of those model elements that have been *previously* refined according to a UML profile for a middleware-specific concern, i.e., model elements that have been *previously* refined through a `PrlxConcernAspectPlugin` and `PrlxConcernTechnologyAspectPlugin`. As an immediate consequence, one may infer that, for a particular middleware-specific concern, a dependency must exist between the corresponding `PrlxConcernAspectPlugin`, `PrlxConcernTechnologyAspectPlugin`, and `PrlxConcernPlatformAspectPlugin`, since the former two need to weave in the model certain information that will be further read by the latter one. Another obvious dependency exists between `PrlxCodeGeneratorPlugins` and `PrlxConcernPlatformAspectPlugins`, since the latter ones require the presence of appropriate code generators (with respect to the supported programming language) in order to be able to enhance their behavior. While both such dependencies are illustrated in Fig. 7, one may enforce them by defining appropriate `requires` entries at the `plugin.xml` level of Eclipse plug-ins, as shown in Fig. 5.

Because of the different layers promoted by the Enterprise Fondue method [395], each `PrlxConcernPlatformAspectPlugin` has four dependency dimensions (*4-DD*); it is at the same time:

- *middleware-concern dependent*
  e.g., distribution, concurrency, transactions, security, etc.;
- *technology dependent*
  e.g., RMI, EJB/J2EE, CORBA, .NET, Web Services, Messaging, etc.;
- *platform dependent*
  e.g., WebSphere, WebLogic, JBoss, JOnAS, Axis, JMS, MQSeries, MSMQ;
- *language dependent*
  e.g., Java, C#, C++, C, Smalltalk, etc.

Examples of such plug-ins are: plug-in for distribution, with EJBs, on IBM Web-Sphere, using Java; or, plug-in for transactions, with CORBA, on Borland VisiBroker, using C++.

In the particular case of the distribution concern and its associated UML-D profiles as defined in Fig. 1, while the `PrlxDistributionRmiSunJava-AspectPlugin` is loaded into Parallax and the encapsulated `PrlxDistribution-RmiSunJavaAspect` is weaved in different constituent parts of Parallax (more precisely in the `PrlxJavaPlugin`), the following actions occur:

- Insert an entry in the Platforms view of the Parallax perspective (see Fig. 11 ⑧).
- Define the special semantics for the newly loaded stereotypes in the context of this particular aspect-plug-in and in accordance with the currently addressed MDA level of abstraction (i.e., the implementation level), as requested by the `PrlxExtensionRule` introduced in Sect. 3.2. The example in Fig. 9 shows how the `PrlxDistributionRmiSunJavaAspect` modifies the `PrlxJavaCodeGe-nerator` by prescribing it to add `java.rmi.Remote` in the `extends` clause of all interfaces that have been declared as «Distributed» by a previous refinement, i.e., all interfaces for which the `isDistributed()` method returns `true`. One should notice that we relied on the interface introduced by the `PrlxDistributionAspect`, i.e., the method `isDistributed()`. In a similar way, the signatures of the methods defined in «Distributed» interfaces are enhanced to throw `java.rmi.RemoteException`, and `try/catch` blocks are generated around all remote calls to such methods, covering in this way all the typical impacts that the «Distributed» stereotype has on `Interface` model elements at this RMI implementation level of abstraction, i.e., the impact on the definition of the `Interface` itself, on the definition of its contents, and on its usage by other model elements.

```
public aspect PrlxDistributionRmiSunJavaAspect {

    pointcut allInterfaces(
            PrlxJavaCodeGenerator jgen,
            PrlxInterface prlxi):
        call(String
          PrlxJavaCodeGenerator.getInterfaceCode(PrlxInterface))
        && target(jgen)
        && args(prlxi);

    after(PrlxJavaCodeGenerator jgen,
            PrlxInterface prlxi): allInterfaces(jgen, prlxi) {
        if (prlxi.isDistributed()) {
            jgen.addExtends(prlxi, "java.rmi.Remote");
        }
    }
}
```

Fig. 9. Code snippet of the `PrlxDistributionRmiSunJavaAspect`

Moreover, the semantics for the «Servant» stereotype is addressed by the `PrlxDistributionRmiSunJavaAspect` as well, but we do not enter into more details besides mentioning that it concerns mainly the code that has to be generated for the interactions with the «RMIRegistry».

Since all `PrlxConcernPlatformAspectPlugins` for a given programming language act on the same code generator, it seems that we might have a problem with all the weaved functionality. One obvious question is: if we load the `Prlx-DistributionRmiSunJavaAspectPlugin` and the `PrlxTransactionsCorba-OpenorbJavaAspectPlugin`, and both associated aspects get weaved in the same code generator, how will the code generator know to display only the distribution-related code in a view and the transactional code in another view, depending on what the developer wants to see at a given moment? Or, how will the code generator know to display the code for the `PrlxDistributionCorbaOpenorbJavaAspectPlug-in` and for the `PrlxTransactionsCorbaOpenorbJavaAspectPlugin` inside the same view?

In order to answer these questions, we consider the 4-DD of a plug-in as an identifier (`ID`) that uniquely identifies a plug-in inside the set of all loaded plug-ins. Furthermore, we notice that two plug-ins can be displayed in the same view if and only if they differ only in the *middleware-concern*-dependency dimension. If this is the case, then we say that the two `ID`s are *compatible*.

Based on this identifier and using the AspectJ *Pointcut Method Idiom* as defined in [194], we managed to answer the previously raised questions. The Pointcut Method Idiom is typically used when the execution of certain advice depends on runtime-specific elements that cannot be expressed by the underlying pointcut language. In this case, a `pointcutMethod()` is defined and it will be called in order to determine whether the advice should be executed or not. An important issue is how the computation of the `pointcutMethod()` depends on the execution context of the application. Usually, context information is directly passed by the piece of advice to the `pointcutMethod()`. This implies that either the referring pointcut passes some parameters to the advice or the advice extracts context information using the introspection capabilities of AspectJ, i.e., `thisJoinPoint` or `thisStaticJoinPoint`. Another possibility is that the aspect itself has a state, which is set by the application's execution context. Moreover, just like the case of design patterns [140], several AspectJ idioms can be combined in order to increase the modularity and extensibility of designs with respect to the ever-changing requirements, and thus to increase their reusability. In the case of Parallax, the Pointcut Method Idiom was integrated with other idioms, such as Abstract Pointcut, Template Advice, Chained Advice, all defined in [194].

Figure 10 depicts in a graphical way the proposed solution in which the `ID` is shared by the constituent parts of a plug-in, i.e., the Eclipse part that plugs in the new GUI elements that will trigger the special functionality offered by the plug-in (like the new entry in the Platforms view), and the encapsulated aspect that weaves the new functionality in the code generator. When the developer selects options in the provided views, the `ID` of the currently selected view is known, and thus the code generator will also know what branches to take.

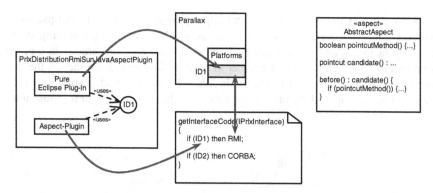

Fig. 10. The Pointcut Method Idiom and ID solution

3.3 Discussion

Even though all aspect-plug-ins (PrlxConcernAspectPlugin, PrlxConcern-
TechnologyAspectPlugin, and PrlxConcernPlatformAspectPlugin) are addressing the same middleware-specific concern, namely distribution, they address
the concern at three different levels of abstraction (platform-independent, platform-
specific, and implementation), and therefore they might impact different Parallax
modules, as was the case in our example (PrlxModel and PrlxJavaCodeGene-
rator). Nevertheless, there is a clear dependency between them as we have seen in
the distribution example. The former ones, which are weaved first, enable the core to
store concern-related information and define interfaces through which this information can be queried afterwards. The latter one, which is weaved in a code generator
plug-in, will read the concern-related information from the core through the enabled
interfaces and it will generate middleware-specific code accordingly.

To conclude, we can group the plug-ins presented in Fig. 7 into two groups: the
first one, which is shaded in light gray, groups plug-ins that offer developers the possibility to *configure* their designs to address middleware-specific concerns at different
MDA levels of abstraction by incorporating concern-related elements into the model
and filling them with relevant information; the second one, which is shaded in dark
gray, groups plug-ins that offer developers the possibility to *adapt* their enhanced designs to different programming languages and different middleware infrastructures,
and to view how middleware-specific concerns are actually implemented at the code
level. Both the configuration and adaptation features are provided through a well-
designed framework of plug-ins, each such plug-in promoting aspects that address
specific concerns that may crosscut plug-in boundaries.

4 The Parallax Tool Support

In this section we provide a brief description of the GUI of Parallax, explaining its
different views and their purposes, and presenting some typical usage scenarios.

260   Raul Silaghi and Alfred Strohmeier

Since Parallax is implemented as an Eclipse plug-in, it follows the Eclipse look-and-feel in terms of perspectives, views, menus, windows, editors, positioning, drag-and-drop facilities, and so on. Figure 11 shows a screenshot of Parallax in a given configuration, i.e., with a certain number of plug-ins installed. Even though the different views shown in Fig. 11 had to be shrunk and moved around in order to best fit the width of the imposed layout, we hope they are illustrative enough for presenting their intended purpose inside Parallax.

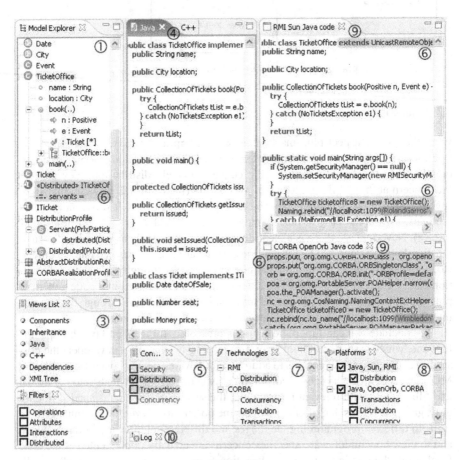

Fig. 11. Parallax

The *Model Explorer* view (①) is responsible for presenting the UML model loaded from an XMI file in a form that is easily accessible to the developer. In this view, we only present a selection of all the model elements that exist in the XMI, such as packages, classes, interfaces, methods, attributes, stereotypes, object instances, and so on. The selection is made from the point of view of their involvement in the code generation process and in the way middleware-specific concerns are addressed at both the model and implementation levels. Moreover, the level of detail for each element is restrained as well. By double-clicking on an element in the Model Explorer, the *property sheet* of that element is displayed containing the exhaustive list of properties that were set for that element.

The *Filters* view ((2)) allows developers to define new filters and to enable/disable them according to their needs at different stages in the development process. Filters are set in order to eliminate certain model elements from the current presentation of the model. As an example, a filter including the `UML:Operation` model element will "logically" remove all currently existing operations from the model. Note that the operation of enabling filters is not necessarily commutative, i.e., enabling filter A before filter B might not result in the same subset of model elements as enabling filter B first. A filter is enabled through its associated check-box.

The *Views list* view ((3)) displays the list of all possible design-specific views that the developer can open. Even though the list can be extended to support new design-specific views, the currently supported ones are: the XMI view, the XMI-Tree view, the Code view, the Inheritance view, the Dependency view, and the Components view. Since most of these views have appropriate names that suggest their intended purpose, we will not explain them in more detail here. However, the meaning of the XMI-Tree view might not be very clear and might require an extra explanation. This view represents a one-to-one mapping of the loaded XMI file onto a `TreeViewer` (a Standard Widget Toolkit component) and allows the developer to browse the *entire* XMI structure in a more friendly way than the text-based version provided in the XMI view. In the XMI-Tree view, for instance, developer's are able to collapse XMI elements at different imbrication levels and focus only on the elements they require. Even though not yet implemented, and therefore not on the screenshot, the Code view will be an Eclipse tabbed view with several tabs corresponding to the different programming languages that are supported through the `PrlxCodeGeneratorPlugins` that have been loaded. These features are currently presented as stand-alone views to the developer (e.g., Java and C++, as shown in (4)).

The *Concerns* view ((5)) presents the list of middleware-specific concerns that Parallax has been enabled to deal with (at the *PIM* level) through the different `PrlxConcernAspectPlugins` that have been loaded. Even though it is difficult to see in Fig. 11, each middleware-specific concern is associated with a different color, which is hardcoded for the moment but will become customizable in the near future. When selecting such a middleware-specific concern in the Concerns view (through its associated check-box), all concern-specific information in all currently opened views is highlighted with the color associated with the selected concern ((6)). When selecting several such concerns, color overlapping may occur in some views, in which case we use a predefined color (`gray`) to highlight the overlapping parts. A message is also displayed to inform the developer that overlapping has occurred.

The *Technologies* view ((7)) groups together the different middleware technologies that Parallax has been enabled to provide configuration for through the different `PrlxConcernTechnologyAspectPlugins` that have been loaded. Each such plug-in provides Parallax with a configuration tab that enables developers to configure a middleware-specific concern with concrete realization details on a specific middleware technology (i.e., at the *PSM* level). For example, if `distribution` is the middleware-specific concern, and `RMI` is the specific middleware technology, then the `PrlxDistributionRmiAspectPlugin` is responsible for providing Parallax with a configuration tab that would allow developers to configure `distribution`-specific realization elements on the `RMI` technology, such as the `host` and `port` of the «`RMIRegistry`» to be used (as defined in Fig. 1 ③). With respect to the Parallax GUI organization, all concern-configuration tabs specific to a technology are enclosed in one technology-configuration window.

The *Platforms* view (⑧) shows the implementation support that has been loaded into Parallax in order to address middleware-specific concerns at the *implementation* level. Each entry in this view corresponds to a `PrlxConcernPlatformAspect-Plugin` that was designed and implemented to address a specific middleware concern, with a specific middleware technology, on a specific middleware platform, and using a specific programming language, e.g., a plug-in for distribution, with CORBA, on Borland VisiBroker, using Java. Each such plug-in may be enabled through its corresponding check-box. Once enabled, a new view is opened and the enhanced generated code is displayed (⑨). We decided to open a new view for each platform plug-in in order for developers to be able to compare and see the changes that middleware, in general, and middleware-specific concerns, in particular, induce at the implementation code level. However, thanks to the `ID` feature that was introduced in Sect. 3.2.2, two enabled plug-ins that have compatible `ID`s, i.e., that differ only in the concern they are addressing, will display the implementation code for the two concerns in the same view.

One should notice that the entries in the Views and Platforms views (③ and ⑧) are *opening* new Parallax views but are displaying information or code in pure text, without any special highlighting besides syntax coloring. It is through the Model Explorer and Concerns views (① and ⑤) that *highlighting* facilities are provided in order to emphasize model-related or concern-related information in all opened views. Moreover, opening new views automatically takes into account all the currently enabled highlighting settings.

While the Concerns and Technologies views show developers to which extent they will be able to *configure* or *reconfigure* their designs by addressing some of the middleware-specific concerns shown in these views, the Platforms view shows developers to which extent they will be able to *adapt* their systems to different middleware infrastructures. The contents of the three views, along with the enabled functionalities, depend on the `PrlxConcernAspectPlugins`, `PrlxConcernTechnolo-gyAspectPlugins`, and `PrlxConcernPlatformAspectPlugins` that have been loaded into Parallax.

A typical usage scenario starts by deciding what plug-ins to load according to what middleware-specific concerns the developer would like to address, and depending on the middleware infrastructures the developer would like to generate code for. After that, the developer can start Eclipse, open the Parallax perspective, load an application design from a previously exported XMI file, and start browsing the model and navigate between the different views provided by Parallax. Provided that the appropriate plug-ins have been loaded and properly installed, the developer can start applying the enclosing UML-MS profiles in order to incrementally refine the centralized design along several middleware-specific concern-dimensions, such as distribution, concurrency, transactions, etc., the available concerns being shown in Fig. 11 ⑤. Contextual popup menu options are enabled, configuration windows are made available, wizards guide and survey the profile application process, providing the developer with messages that point out the missing elements that still have to be set in order to obtain a consistent model with respect to the profile that is being applied. For instance, having in mind the semantics defined by the UML-D profiles for addressing the distribution concern both at the PIM and PSM levels of abstraction (Fig. 1 ① and ③), the developer is able to configure what «Distributed» interfaces are to be made available in a distributed setting, what is the location of the «Publisher» (e.g., the host and port of a «RMIRegistry») to be used, what are the «Servant» objects to be registered with such a «Publisher», and so on. Furthermore, in terms of assistance, when applying the UML-D profiles at the PIM level of abstraction (Fig. 1 ①) for example, a wizard shows the message *"The object obj has been stereotyped as «Servant». Please provide its associated «Distributed» interface"*, and the list of possible interfaces is presented to the developer as a result of an inference algorithm. Once the model has been filled with middleware-specific information, the developer can start selecting the different options in the Platforms view in order to see how the configured concerns are actually implemented at the code level. At this point, the highlighting facilities might be useful in order to see all concern-related information across different views.

Other facilities that are provided but do not appear in the views presented above include: loading and saving a model, searching the model for specific model elements, saving a specific view of generated code, saving all views containing generated code, saving all the code that can be generated from the loaded model based on the plug-ins that have been loaded, etc. Moreover, navigation and highlighting facilities between the different views are also provided, e.g., selecting a model element in the Model Explorer automatically highlights that element in all the views that are currently opened. Messages for the developer are displayed in the *Log* view (⑩).

5 Related Work

Since the MDA approach addresses the development of software at different levels of abstraction, relying on several concepts and techniques to describe and to move between such levels but without imposing any specific modeling language to be used at these levels, the variety of MDA-compliant tools is very broad. It includes model repository tools, domain-specific tools that consider different modeling languages for their specific purposes (either UML or other MOF-based metamodels), tools that promote model transformation languages and provide support for defining and applying model transformations, tools that provide code generation facilities targeting specific platforms, where a platform may be either a programming or scripting language, a middleware platform, a database, an operating system, or anything else that may be seen as a platform in the context of an application, and so on. A non-exhaustive list of the companies committed to support the MDA vision and their products is kept by the OMG at [323].

As clearly stated in the introduction of this paper, we consider the *middleware* to be our MDA platform, and providing support for generating code targeted at different middleware infrastructures is the main goal of Parallax. As a consequence, we will only refer to some of the mature commercial products in this specific MDA-market niche, namely ArcStyler, OptimalJ, and Codagen. Even though it is always difficult to compare tools resulting from academic research with true commercial products, we will point out nevertheless some key concepts that each of these commercial products relies upon and then we will show how Parallax is different.

Mainly focused on increasing the development productivity of Web, EJB/J2EE, and .NET applications, ArcStyler [218] promotes model transformations (model-to-model and model-to-code) as *MDA-Cartridges* based on its MDA-CARtridge ArchiTecture (CARAT). In addition to containing transformation rules, a Cartridge can provide verification rules, which check the input model for correctness with regard to the transformation implemented by the Cartridge. ArcStyler distinguishes between MDA-Cartridges that enable the model-driven development of software applications for standard architectures (Java2, C#, EJB1.1, and EJB1.2), and those supporting the MDA-compliant development of four-tier applications (J2EE, .NET, and ASP.NET). Moreover, the latter category includes MDA-Cartridges for standard J2EE application servers, such as BEA WebLogic, Borland Enterprise Server, IBM WebSphere, and JBoss. ArcStyler also provides an MDA-Cartridge IDE with its Architect edition, giving developers the possibility to define their own MDA-Cartridges or to extend existing ones.

The core of OptimalJ [67] contains models and *patterns*, allowing developers to refine models by sequentially applying a series of customizable patterns. The OptimalJ models are defined at different levels, including the Domain Model, the Application Model, and the Code Model (Java code). Moving between these models is achieved by applying technology and implementation patterns, also referred to as transformation patterns. Another type of patterns, referred to as functional patterns (including domain, application, and code patterns), are more like code templates, providing developers with reusable predefined functionalities that speed up development and reduce errors. A Pattern Editor is provided with the OptimalJ Architecture Edition, allowing developers to define their own patterns or to change the behavior of the existing ones. OptimalJ focuses exclusively on the development of J2EE applications, providing deployment facilities to several J2EE Application Servers, such as IBM WebSphere, BEA WebLogic, Sun ONE (formerly iPlanet), Oracle 9iAS, ObjectWeb JOnAS, and JBoss.

Codagen Architect [66] promotes a model–extend–transform development process, relying on several pre-built transformation templates and UML profiles that are known as *Technology Accelerators*. After modeling the application that needs to be implemented, developers may extend their UML models using transformation markers, which encapsulate design decisions associated with the platform that has been chosen, be it J2EE or .NET. Integration schemas describe how common services provided by the selected infrastructure are reused by business objects from the previously defined models. Transforming business models into source code is achieved using Technology Accelerator templates, which define the model-to-code transformation in terms of XML tokens that control the logic of code generation. A dedicated XML-based environment is provided for editing templates. Codagen Architect provides Technology Accelerator templates for ADO.NET and ASP.NET, on the .NET platform side, and EJB, JSP, and Struts, on the J2EE platform side.

If we were to base our comparison on the number of provided functionalities (wizards, IDEs, editors, code generators, etc.), or on the robustness of the product when it comes to providing support for developing enterprise-level applications, Parallax would not stand a chance of winning against these colossal products that rely on decades of experience in the ever-demanding software industry. However, Parallax manages to distinguish itself as a pioneer in this specific MDA-market niche, proposing a new approach to code generation for different middleware infrastructures by relying on:

- *separation of concerns* for refining designs along one middleware-specific concern-dimension at a time,
- *UML-MS profiles* for addressing middleware-specific concerns at different MDA levels of abstraction,
- *aspect-oriented programming* for encapsulating such middleware-specific concerns into AspectJ aspects that enable the Parallax framework to address them at different MDA levels of abstraction,
- *Eclipse plug-ins* for promoting such aspects in an open source fashion and in this way making unlimited the number of middleware-specific concerns that can be addressed using Parallax (through `PrlxConcernAspectPlugins` and `PrlxConcernTechnologyAspectPlugins`) and the number of middleware infrastructures that may be used as target implementation platforms for the previously addressed concerns (through `PrlxConcernPlatformAspectPlugins`).

6 Conclusions and Future Work

In times of constant and rapid change, with new requirements to satisfy and new technologies to adapt to, tool support is crucial. Built on top of the MDA-oriented UML profiles defined for addressing middleware-specific concerns in the context of the Enterprise Fondue method, the Parallax framework presented in this chapter allows developers to look at the system under consideration from different perspectives (or viewpoints) through a well-defined system of plug-ins and based on aspect-oriented support. In addition to presenting the Parallax framework, we focused on the support provided for (re)configuring application designs with middleware-specific concerns, on the one hand, and adapting them to different middleware infrastructures, on the other hand. Parallax enables developers to incorporate middleware-specific concerns in their designs at different MDA levels of abstraction, and to view their enhanced designs through a prism of middleware platforms and see how middleware-specific concerns are actually implemented at the code level. Implementation details were discussed as well, emphasizing the powerful combination of AspectJ aspects with Eclipse plug-ins, which enables aspects to encapsulate concerns that crosscut plug-in boundaries.

Besides the tremendous support that the Eclipse platform offered and continues to offer in order to design, build, and improve the Parallax framework, Parallax takes a rather specific direction, in both the MDA and Eclipse worlds, targeting middleware-specific cross-cutting concerns, on one hand, and middleware infrastructures (technologies and platforms) on the other hand, while still relying on aspect-oriented support for modularizing concerns that tend to crosscut plug-in boundaries.

Note, however, that both the Enterprise Fondue method and the Parallax tool support are relatively young, and still undergoing refinement and improvement as we move along. Nevertheless, they are both applied to case studies and tests are carried out to determine their limitations and extensibility problems, and to adjust them accordingly. Once the extension points that we have been experimenting with become stable, we intend to follow the Eclipse contribution circle and publish them, so that other developers and middleware vendors may contribute and enrich Parallax by implementing and providing the community with new Parallax plug-ins (PrlxPlugins) addressing middleware-specific concerns for their favorite middleware infrastructures, or simply the code generation for their favorite programming language.

With respect to the Code view, based on the information that can be stored in PrlxModels (according to the current PrlxMetamodel), PrlxCodeGenerator-Plugins should be able to generate application code corresponding to the static structure (from class diagrams) and – to some extent – to the behavior (from interactions in collaboration/sequence diagrams). While we have already implemented support for the Java and C++ programming languages (through a PrlxJavaPlugin and a PrlxCppPlugin), we are currently investing efforts for supporting the C# programming language as soon as possible (through a PrlxCsharpPlugin). Looking forward, UML 2.0 [116] defines new modeling elements that can appear in sequence diagrams for describing enhanced interactions, such as seq, alt, opt, break, loop, etc., defined in Fragments::InteractionOperators. As soon as UML modeling tools provide XMI export facilities for these enhanced interactions, we will extend the PrlxMetamodel in order to incorporate them as well. As a consequence, PrlxCodeGeneratorPlugins will be able to take advantage of these new interaction elements and generate enhanced code in the programming language they promote.

In the current state, aspects are only used to enhance the core of Parallax in order to be able to store and query concern-specific information, and to enhance the code generators with middleware-specific code generation capabilities. As the language imposed by Eclipse plug-ins is Java, all aspects are written in AspectJ, and thus we use a Java aspect-plugin to enhance, for instance, the C++ code generator (which itself is written in Java as well) with CORBA code generation capabilities. However, the final code that is generated no longer supports the separation of concerns. All concerns have their code tangled as it was generated by the enhanced code generator. The developer needs Parallax's highlighting support in order to see clearly what concerns are addressed where. In order to overcome this problem, we are very much interested in the possibility of *generating aspects* as separate units, outside of the code itself, and to encapsulate in these generated aspects the middleware-specific cross-cutting concerns that we are addressing. For example, we would generate the C++ code that addresses the pure functionality of the system to be implemented, and in addition, we would generate separate aspects for each middleware-specific concern that the final system has to incorporate. Moreover, note that such aspects would have to be generated for aspect-oriented extensions of the targeted programming language, i.e., for an aspect-oriented extension to C++ [4] in the case of the previous example. Assistance could be further provided in order to weave the aspects into the pure functional code. With this approach, the developer would get several separate building blocks (code and aspects) that implement the final system in a pure concern-oriented fashion. In a first step, this approach will be tested for generating AspectJ aspects, i.e., aspects for the Java programming language, since we do not have any experience with aspect-oriented extensions to other programming languages.

7 Acknowledgements

We would like to thank Thierry Monney for the insights he provided on the Eclipse platform, and especially on the Eclipse plug-in architecture, and for his major contribution to the implementation of the current version of Parallax. This work has been partially supported by the Swiss National Science Foundation grant 200020–101596/1.

Evolution and Maintenance of MDA Applications

Tilman Seifert and Gerd Beneken

Software & Systems Engineering, Technische Universität München,
85748 München/Garching, Germany
{seifert,beneken}@in.tum.de

Summary. The aim of MDA and its related concepts is to increase the quality and speed of system development by raising the level of abstraction, using modeling techniques, model transformation, and code generation. However, in order to take advantage in a professional development environment, some obstacles need to be overcome.

This chapter considers the complete life cycle of MDA applications which starts with the set-up of a development environment. We put a special emphasis on the long-term perspective of applications developed using the MDA, including maintenance and enhancements of the application itself, as well as of the model transformation languages, templates, and tools.

1 Software Evolution

Long-lived software systems have to be changed and adapted because they are subject to multiple innovation cycles. Several technologies, among them the OMG's Model-Driven Architecture (MDA) [309], claim to improve the evolvability of software systems. We are interested in the evolution of software systems developed using the MDA approach in the long run, when not only the requirements for the system, but also the infrastructure and development tools, change. Therefore we consider the different innovation cycles and the respective maintenance activities.

1.1 Innovation Cycles

Changes to software systems are driven by one out of the following four motivations. Figure 1 shows software as the link between the user requirements and the technical implementation. This simplistic view allows us to deduce four types of maintenance activities: perfective, adaptive, corrective, and preventive maintenance.

The terms "perfective" and "adaptive" are used with slightly different meanings by different authors. We briefly explain our view on different types of maintenance.

Requirements for software systems change over time. Reasons are manifold; consider for example information systems. Business processes change, new increments of the software support a wider scope of business processes, or new laws require a

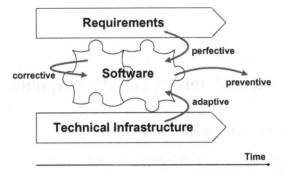

Fig. 1. Innovation cycles and maintenance types

different set of information to be available. Since the implementation of more requirements improves the functionality of a system, this type of maintenance is called *perfective maintenance.*

Technology changes as well. The system has to be adapted to a changed technical environment; therefore the related activities are referred to as *adaptive maintenance.* The term "technology" includes the run-time environment, any third-party components, interfaces to neighboring systems, as well as the tools used in the development process. The last must not be omitted when reasoning about the maintainability of a system, as we will see in this chapter.

Adaptive maintenance exposes two interesting properties. Even though a software system itself might not need an update of its technical infrastructure, often the adaption is inevitable due to external constraints. At the same time, it does not increase the functionality of a system.

Errors are detected and have to be fixed. *Corrective maintenance* includes all related activities. Corrective maintenance is important, but according to Pigoski [350] it accounts for about 20% of all maintenance tasks and is out of the scope of this chapter.

Preventive maintenance are actions taken to avoid difficulties in either one of the above-mentioned maintenance types at some time in the future. These actions are driven by expectations about changes in the future. Preventive maintenance is often not explicitly considered in the literature as well as in practice; however, it is indispensable for a pro-active technology management.

1.2 Dependency Chains

Changes on the level of the technical infrastructure are typically triggered by external events such as upgrades or changes in the run-time environment (e.g., the operating system, the application server, the GUI framework, etc.), or changes in the development tool chain. Due to service level contracts, diminishing support for older versions, or new components that need the newer version, the user of a technology often has little choice but to follow the upgrades.

Therefore it is an important maintenance activity to precisely analyze and keep track of dependency chains of each system. This analysis includes the components of the system itself, all components in the run-time environment, any third-party components like libraries or other systems, as well as compilers and the whole development tool chain.

Run-time Environment

Complex software systems consist of many different components, and are usable only in a specific configuration. A software system usually depends not only on a number of services (as provided by an application server or a database) and tools, but also on specific versions of these software components. This includes middleware, technical services, third-party tools like databases, application servers, and neighboring systems. These components or systems change for the very same reasons. If the interface of a third-party component or a neighboring system is changed, the system in question might also have to be changed. Often enough the decisions about upgrades of any one of these components are largely beyond the control of the project team [462]. In those cases the project team is put into a reactive role and has to respond to the change in the environment.

Third-Party Components

Any software system depends on libraries and other third-party components which might be used by static or dynamic linking, or by dynamic run-time lookup. Changes in those third-party components imply changes in the software system.

Consider for example the popular logging library *log4j* for Java development (see [280]). When changing from version 1.1.3 to version 1.2, the `Category.assert` method has been replaced by `Category.assertLog`. This change was necessary because `assert` is a language reserved word in JDK 1.4. Log4J 1.1.3 does not compile under JDK 1.4, and client code using log4J 1.1.3 has to be adapted in order to work with version 1.2.

This example seems trivial, since the change can be done automatically, using either the refactoring abilities of modern IDEs, or a relatively simple script. As soon as not only the method name but also the parameter types change, the changes quickly become more complicated. But the major concern is that there are many changes that occur without leaving a choice about whether to follow the upgrade or not.

Development Tool Chain

Development tools like IDEs and compilers, modeling tools, and support tools like configuration management, bug tracking, and documentation tools, and even the text processor, are subject to their respective innovation cycles. Upgrades of the tools might allow changes in the system (because a powerful new feature is offered), or even force certain changes to the system (e.g., because an old feature is no longer supported). Section 3 discusses the evolution of the development tool chain in detail.

1.3 Maintainability

There are several definitions for the maintainability of a software system (see Pigoski [350, ch. 16]), but they all remain rather vague. Maintainability is defined to be *the ease with which software can be maintained, enhanced, adapted, or corrected.* It includes the ability to operate the system over a long period of time.

There is a common understanding that maintainability can be "high" or "low", but so far there are no objectively measurable properties of software or its environment that clearly define its (degree of) maintainability. According to Martin and McClure, a system has to be *understandable, modifiable, testable, reliable, efficient, usable, portable* in order to be maintainable [284]. These attributes seem to be sensible; they are more or less compatible with ISO 9126 [219], which postulates that a system is maintainable when it is *analyzable, changeable, testable, and stable.* Throughout this chapter, we will use the properties given by Martin and McClure to analyze the maintainability of a software system. The scope of our analysis will include all four types of maintenance tasks.

However, these attributes only consider the source (i.e., the code and the models, if they are used for generation) of the software system itself. From the perspective of maintenance, the system has to be viewed with its context, i.e., its complete environment, as explained above. Therefore, we will also analyze the evolution of the environment and the dependencies, as discussed in Sect. 1.2.

2 MDA Development Environment

2.1 "Funcar" Application Case Study

Are systems that are built using the MDA approach easier to maintain than systems built using traditional approaches? The OMG claims so: *The MDA provides an open vendor neutral approach to the challenge of business and technology change* [324].

We conducted a case study to learn more about the influences of the current MDA approach on the maintainability of systems. Using the MDA approach we developed a simple application example for the Java J2EE platform. The application is a reservation system with a web interface for a car sharing service called *Funcar*.

2.2 Run-time Environment

We use the Java 1.4.2 Virtual Machine. On top of that the JBoss J2EE application server constitutes the run-time environment. The final version of the reservation system is implemented using the Enterprise JavaBeans (EJB) specification 2.1 [410]. Some code examples are presented below. To analyze a change of the run-time environment in the case study, the EJB 1.1 run-time environment is replaced by the EJB 2.1 environment.

2.3 Development Tool Chain

The tool chain is typical of a Java project, and consists of easily available tools, most of which are open source, except for MagicDraw (Fig. 2). The UML models are developed with MagicDraw and saved in the XMI 1.1 standard file format. Other modeling tools such as Poseidon, Together, or Rational XDE could also be used, because they provide a similar storage format. The MDA tool AndroMDA [18] reads the UML models and generates Java code. The code generation templates are implemented using the scripting language Velocity [442]. We completed the generated code by adding business logic with the Eclipse IDE.

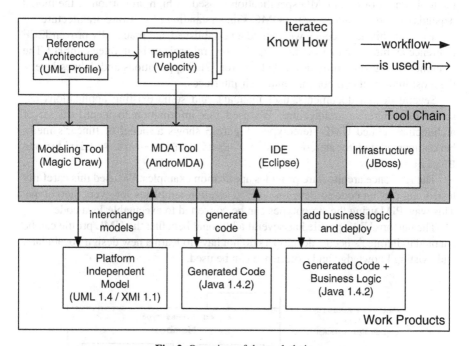

Fig. 2. Overview of the tool chain

2.4 Reference Architectures

Plain UML models do not contain enough information about the meaning of modeling elements. For example, a plain UML class might just be interpreted as a plain programming language class. Several modeling tools provide such a direct mapping between models, which are primarily class diagrams, and code. Therefore plain UML models and the code are at the same level of abstraction. To raise this level, a more expressive *vocabulary* for PIM and PSM models is needed.

The MDA itself does not specify the content of PIM and PSM models. Neither diagram types nor model elements are defined. For some domains the OMG provides specific UML profiles that specify parts of the PIM and PSM [334]. Some further examples of problem-specific languages are presented in this book.

Tool vendors often define their own stereotypes. For example, AndroMDA uses stereotypes such as `Service` and `Entity`, which are quite similar to the withdrawn EJB profile in the Java community process [232]. Other tool vendors use J2EE patterns [15] to identify stereotypes and profiles. For example, the UML J2EE profile contains a stereotype called *Business Facade*, according to the pattern with the same name.

If a proprietary UML profile is applied, the architecture behind it is used, too. Hence, by using the UML profile, the implicit or explicit reference architecture of the tool vendor or of an OMG specification is used. A high proportion of the model depends on a tool vendor's or the OMG's understanding of software architecture.

To avoid this dependency we applied an established and practically proven J2EE reference architecture that has been used in several projects by iteratec GmbH.[1] The reference architecture provides a skeleton for J2EE applications and defines layers, the most important components, and their interfaces.

Several design documents, user manuals, and some existing applications describe the reference architecture. We used this information to identify a set of architecture-related UML stereotypes. Figure 3 shows a model of funcar's member component with the stereotypes: `Core Entity`, `Business Activity`, and `Business Type`.

The reference architecture provides application examples. We used this carefully tested and proven code to develop code generation templates for every stereotype. This way, PIM using the stereotypes can be converted to executable Java code.

The custom UML profile has several additional benefits: the UML profile can be adapted to iteratec's needs, developers do not have to learn a new design vocabulary, and existing knowledge and experience can be used.

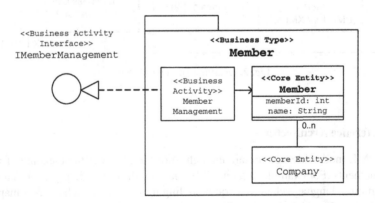

Fig. 3. Member component of the car sharing system in UML

---

[1] Iteratec is a medium-sized software and consulting company located in Munich.

2.5 Business Modeling with UML

As in most MDA approaches, just the static structure of the reservation system is modeled using UML 1.4 class diagrams, which are extended by stereotypes. The diagrams consist of core entities, business activities, business interfaces, and business types (components). Business logic such as computations or checking of correctness rules are hard to express using UML, because either modeling is too complex or applicable modeling elements are missing in tools.

2.6 Model Interchange with XMI

The XMI file format is an OMG standard to exchange UML models between different tools. Listing 1 shows the simplified XMI 1.1 description of the `Core Entity` *Member*. The description of *Member* is similar to a simple UML class; it is qualified by a stereotype `Core Entity`. The stereotype is defined according to the iteratec reference architecture.

Listing 1. XMI description of member

```
<UML:Class xmi.id='MEMBER' >
 <UML:ModelElement.name >Member</UML:ModelElement.name>
 <UML:ModelElement.visibility xmi.value='public' />
 ...
 <UML:ModelElement.stereotype >
       <UML:Stereotype xmi.idref='CORE_ENTITY' />
 </UML:ModelElement.stereotype>
 <UML:Classifier.feature >
   <UML:Attribute xmi.id='IGNORE_1' >
    <UML:ModelElement.name >
    memberId
    </UML:ModelElement.name>
    <UML:ModelElement.visibility xmi.value='private' />
    ...
   </UML:Attribute>
   <UML:Attribute xmi.id='IGNORE_2' >
    <UML:ModelElement.name >
    name
    </UML:ModelElement.name>
    <UML:ModelElement.visibility xmi.value='private' />
    ...
   </UML:Attribute>
 </UML:Classifier.feature>
</UML:Class>
```

Note that XMI 1.x just contains tags for plain UML elements, omitting information on diagrams and graphical positions of model elements. Diagrams are stored in a tool-specific manner, e.g., using specialized XML tags.

MagicDraw stores graphical information, such as the coordinates of a model element in a diagram, using MagicDraw tags in the XMI file (Listing 2). Hence, the diagram interchange works well for plain UML information but problems occur with the graphical presentation of diagrams. In the worst case each diagram has to be redrawn. The UML 2.0 standard solves this problem and provides a notion of diagrams and their graphical elements, with position, size, and rendering order [332].

Listing 2. Coordinates in tool-specific format

```
<mdElement elementClass='ClassView' xmi.id='IGNORE' >
  <elementID xmi.idref='MEMBER' />
  <geometry >10, 110, 308, 76</geometry>
</mdElement>
```

2.7 Code Generation with Velocity

Proven and carefully tested code is required to develop code generation templates. Class names, attribute names, data type names, and other information in the code are replaced by variables and control structures in a scripting language. During code generation the variables are replaced by the corresponding values that are defined in the UML model.

In AndroMDA at least one code generation template is defined for every stereotype in the model. During code generation AndroMDA identifies the required template by the stereotype. Listing 3 shows Velocity code that generates abstract get and set methods, which are mandatory for Entity Beans in the Enterprise JavaBeans 2.1 specification [410].

AndroMDA provides several templates for Enterprise JavaBeans in a cartridge. We modified or exchanged these templates according to the reference architecture.

Listing 3. Velocity template for EntityBean class

```
// ...
public abstract class ${class.name}Bean
     implements javax.ejb.EntityBean
{
  // ...
  #foreach ( $att in $class.attributes )
  #set ($atttypename = "#javaMapping($att)")
  // ...
  public abstract $atttypename
    get${str.upperCaseFirstLetter(${att.name})}();
  // ...
  public abstract void
    set${str.upperCaseFirstLetter(${att.name})}
      (${atttypename} newValue);
  #end
```

```
// ...
public abstract void validate();
// ...
}
```

The template contains a loop (#foreach). For each attribute of the Core Entity, get and set methods are generated. Plain text of the template is directly copied to the Java code file (e.g., public abstract class), whereas the variables are replaced by the information contained in the model (e.g., ${class.name}).

We observed that the generation templates tend to increase their complexity over time, the number of loops and control structures grows significantly. The understandability of the template, which mixes the target language Java with the scripting language Velocity, decreases continuously. Simple code can easily be described using a template language, whereas particular situations have to be handled using the programming language facilities of the template language.

2.8 Business Code in the Target Language Java

The generated code must not be edited. AndroMDA promotes the idea of inheriting a business class from the generated code and adding modifications there. AndroMDA generates a base class such as MemberBean, and also generates an inherited class, such as MemberBeanImpl, that may contain extensions. If the model is modified and the code needs to be updated, just the non-modified base classes are exchanged. Round trip engineering is not supported. The output of the template shown above is depicted in Listing 4.

Listing 4. Generated code for EntityBean class

```
public abstract class MemberBean
      implements javax.ejb.EntityBean
{
  // ...
  public abstract int getMemberId(); // ...
  public abstract void setMemberId(int newValue); // ...
  public abstract java.lang.String getName(); // ...
  public abstract void setName(java.lang.String
     newValue); // ...
  public abstract boolean validate();
  // ...
}
```

For example, the validate() method has to be completed with business code in the inherited class, because the complex business logic is easier to implement in Java. Listing 5 shows a simple data verification rule that requires the memberId to be between 10000 and 20000 for members who work for non-commercial organizations. Note that the listing is simplified. The business rule implementation uses the EJB 1.1 interface. An EJB 2.0 based implementation rather uses container managed relationships instead of calling a `findByPrimaryKey` method to find the member's company. Such dependencies between platform-specific code and business logic are hard to avoid.

Listing 5. Manual extensions in inherited class

```
public abstract class MemberBeanImpl
       extends MemberBean
       implements javax.ejb.EntityBean
{
  //...
  public boolean validate()
  {
    // Filter correct memberIds
    // EJB 1.1 Code; no Container Managed Relationships
    // and no Local Interfaces
    CompanyHome companyHome = ...;
    Company c = companyHome.findByPrimaryKey(
        this.getCompanyId());
    if (c.isNonCommercial() &&
      (memberId >= 10000 && memberId < 20000))
      return true;
    else if (memberId >= 20000 && memberId <= 99999)
      return true;

    return false;
  }
  //...
}
```

Some MDA tools such as OptimalJ use protected areas in the generated code for the handwritten business logic. For example, the `validate()` method is completed directly in the generated code. The handwritten code is protected by special Java comments. If the model is modified and new code generation is necessary, the tools parse the existing files and reuse the business logic in the protected areas.

2.9 Model Transformation

In the case study no model transformation is applied. In principle the model transformation is similar to code generation. The stereotypes in the PIM are interpreted and transformed to other model elements in a PSM. For this purpose tools use model generation templates or transformation patterns. Therefore the argumentation concerning the maintainability of code generation also holds true for model transformation.

Most of the modeling tools available today have a proprietary model transformation approach. The model transformation descriptions are as maintainable as the code generation templates described above. A language as requested in [165] is still in an OMG standardization process.

3 Maintainability of MDA Applications

In order to understand the maintainability of systems developed using the MDA, Table 1 considers the properties introduced in Sect. 1.3 and compares them to the "classical" way of developing the same system, using models only for understanding and specifying (if used at all), but developing the code manually. For our analysis, we consider systems in the context of their development and run-time environment; we refer to the results from our case study in Sect. 2.

Table 1. Maintainability attributes of MDA systems, compared to "classical" software development

Attribute	MDA Systems
Understandability	depends on skill
Modifiability	depends on change request
Testability	depends on tools
Reliability	indifferent
Efficiency	indifferent
Usability	indifferent
Portability	depends on which component to change

A system is **understandable** when it is relatively easy to overview the complete system, to grasp its architecture (i.e., the structure of software elements and their connections and dependencies [30]), and to read and understand the respective documents – be they specification, models, code, or documentation. Using models, model transformation, and code generation instead of prose in the specification and manual code development is not a guarantee for better readability. But using an appropriate and powerful modeling technique, and then choosing the right models, allow zooming in and out of models, giving more abstract views or as much detail as possible. Therefore, models offer chances for better readability. However, there are two drawbacks. First, it depends on the skill of the developer to develop *good* models, and on the skill of the maintainer to deal with existing models. Second, the logic of the system is distributed in the models, in the templates, and in handwritten code. The models represent the business aspects; the templates represent the reference architecture as well as the implementation details for the respective platform; and the handwritten code contains the parts of the business logic that cannot be formulated on the model level. This is a classic constellation for subtle development errors that are hard to find.

The **reliability, efficiency**, and **usability** of a software system depend on many factors. Among them are: thorough analysis of the environment and the requirements, thorough understanding of the implementation platform and its behavior, and a thorough understanding of the system itself. The last is discussed above. The other two are independent of the implementation method. The quality of the platform-specific elements is improved by reusing these elements, which is a major goal of the MDA approach. The advantages and disadvantages of software reuse are examined in the software reuse discussion. Regarding these three quality properties, there is no intrinsic advantage of systems developed using MDA compared to "classic" development.

Testing systems developed on the basis of models is difficult. Every time a model is changed, the code has to be regenerated. Regression tests should be available to test every module automatically. Writing test cases in a conventional programming language (e.g., the target language of the system) seems odd; instead, test cases should be formulated on the same level of abstraction as the model that is to be tested. This is not possible as long as the business logic is not even completely defined on the level of the model. Note that this has dramatic consequences for the development cycle, even before the maintenance phase has started. Especially in projects with short iterations and quick release cycles – which the MDA obviously aims to support – easy regression and unit testing is an essential requirement for the development method.

Debugging MDA systems is also a problem. Currently there is no debugger available that connects the steps being executed to the model at run-time – if there is any logic formulated in the model at all. A developer therefore has to debug generated code which is usually difficult. Another difficulty is that errors can be either in the model, or in the template, or in the handwritten code. Maybe the tool situation will change in the future, but today we have to state that testing and debugging MDA systems is problematic.

The most obvious question for judging the maintainability is how easy it is to **modify** a system. For MDA systems, this cannot be answered in general; it depends on which part of the system needs to be modified. We will use examples to demonstrate both easy and hard modifications for MDA systems in the following sections.

The **portability** of a system is the ease with which it is possible to use the existing system on a new platform without (major) changes. MDA is designed for changing the implementation platform by generating a different PSM. But MDA systems turn out to be highly dependent on the development tool chain, as our examples will show in the following sections.

3.1 Change in the Run-time Environment

Portability is relevant when a system is brought into a new run-time environment or when the deployment platform is changed or upgraded. MDA claims that the run-time platform can easily be replaced. A problem is that the OMG does not clearly define the term "platform". See [309, p. 5]:

"In the MDA, the term platform *is used to refer to technological and engineering details that are irrelevant to the fundamental functionality of a software component."*

A platform can be an operating system, a technology in general (like J2EE or .NET), a specific version of any of these (e.g., JBoss version 4.0), or a target language. In the stepwise refinement from a CIM over a PIM and one or more PSMs to finally generate code, some decisions restrict the set of possible target platforms. E.g., models that use multiple inheritance do not allow Java as the target language but only C++ realizations.

Restricting the focus of the term "platform independence", however, allows us to define which changes of the platform do not affect the business model. In our example, the deployment platform was changed from EJB 1.1 to EJB 2.0. This implied a number of changes. Public attributes in Entity Beans were replaced by abstract access methods (see Listing 4) because the data access mechanism changed with the new EJB version. While this is not a major change in terms of technological options, in "classical" programming, it would still involve major changes in the source code: in some cases, those changes might be done using refactoring tools or small scripts; using MDA it is achieved by simply changing the code generation template.

A second novelty in EJB 2.0 is the concept of "local interfaces" which allows access to Entity Beans more efficiently from within the EJB container. The third major invention of EJB 2.0 is the *container-managed relationship* which extends the concept of managing persistent entities by also managing the relations between these entities.

The principle of the MDA is that only the transformation rules or the code generation templates have to be adapted to reflect a change in the underlying technology. Tool vendors claim that the change from EJB 1.1 to EJB 2.0 can be done amazingly quickly using the MDA approach (see, e.g., [337]). This example of changing from one version of EJB to the next is far more realistic than a change from a CORBA implementation to, say, the .NET framework.

However, it is possible that a technology change has consequences that even influence the PIM. The architecture must be carefully checked to see whether the PIM has to be adjusted or not. In the reference architecture, there are some architecture decisions that are driven by properties of the chosen technology. The fact that accessing Entity Beans used to cause a performance penalty in EJB 1.1 influenced the decision on how business entities are mapped to Entity Beans. The way EJB 2.0 handles relationships between entities offers the chance to remove some code that used to be considered business logic, since relations are now dealt with by the container. Recall our example in Fig. 3; using the new possibilities the relation between members and the companies they work for can now be modeled explicitly and dealt with on the level of the application server instead of in the business logic. In our example, the PIM can remain unchanged, but parts of the implementation of the handwritten business logic, e.g., the `validate()` method of the *Member* entity in Listing 5, have to be adapted manually.

A platform change is always a migration project that involves effort and risks. Without using the MDA, that effort could be moderate or considerable, depending on the system's architecture. But in the light of the MDA's promises, we expected the transition to be smoother. In general, the business aspects are fairly well separated from the mapping to a particular technology which eases the transition. Nevertheless, we found that once again the devil is in the detail.

To sum up our experiences, we observed that the technological change from EJB 1.1 to EJB 2.0 was accomplished with changes in the reference architecture, the generation templates, and the handwritten extension of the generated code. In our case, the MDA approach did not cover the transition completely transparent but required some manual adaptation. Changing the access logic was easy and had no influence on the architecture and the PIM, but changing the relationships involved substantial changes in the architecture. However, it would have been possible to use the new technology without our changes to the architecture and the code, but that would have implied not taking full advantage of the new features.

It is important to bear in mind that after the system is ported to a new platform, a complete and systematic test has to show that the system functions and behaves as expected.

3.2 Evolution of the Reference Architecture

The reference architecture (see Sect. 2.4) is a set of reusable structures and best practices regarding the system architecture. It is likely that the reference architecture will change over time. In this situation there are two options: either the changes are disregarded, or instead only the original reference architecture is used. This strategy avoids changes to the models, all the necessary testing, and so on. However, it implies that from now on, there are two versions of the reference architecture and its generation templates in productive use. A sophisticated configuration management system, accompanied by an appropriate process, is required. In this case study, we analyze only one system. Even here, a versioning problem between the templates and the system is visible. MDA aims at an environment where several similar systems can reuse the same templates in order to build on reliable, proven technical solutions. In such an environment, the versioning issue might well become a real challenge.

The second strategy is to adopt the new architecture, which gives us the chance to take advantage of improved architecture concepts, possibly improved implementations for parts of it, and so on. In this case, the changes are reflected in the UML stereotypes and in the code generation templates. It is the task of the architect to check whether the PIMs have to be adjusted or not.

Note that applying the MDA without using any reference architecture is not possible. Relying on the tool vendor's set of UML stereotypes and transformation or generation rules is nothing more than implicitly using the vendor's reference architecture. In our example we decided to use our own architecture in order to remain independent of yet another innovation cycle.

3.3 Change in the Development Tool Chain

MDA systems depend on a complex tool chain. Section 2.3 demonstrated an example that can be used for MDA development. Now consider changes in that tool chain.

Replacing the modeling tool becomes quite complicated since many modeling tools use their own dialect or extensions of the XMI standard which are not completely compatible with each other; porting models from one modeling tool to another often proves difficult. One of the reasons is that the XMI 1.1 standard does not clearly define how to store diagram information (size and position of the model elements); therefore, if that information cannot be converted, models have to be re-drawn. See Listing 2 for a proprietary, non portable solution.

Exchanging the MDA tool would imply rewriting and retesting all templates for all generation steps because they are specific to AndroMDA and cannot be used by any other tool. Since these templates are intended to be usable in more than one context, the effort can become enormous because more than one system might depend on it.

The MDA does not clearly define the term "platform", and does not clearly state the properties of a PIM or PSM. Therefore, all tools that claim to be "MDA compliant" have to interpret these concepts. Not only that, but also the transformation and generation process works differently in all MDA tools on a technical level. Even worse, every tool can have a different notion of which information exactly is expressed in a PIM, and which information comes in only in the PSM or in further generation steps. The consequence is that a PIM that can be used with one tool might possibly not be used with another tool. Not only the templates, but even the PIMs would have to be re-written if the MDA tool was to be exchanged. The same holds true for the business logic. Consider using *OptimalJ* [337] instead of AndroMDA: OptimalJ uses different mechanisms to generate code and to integrate the handwritten business logic. Hence, exchanging the MDA tool implies massive changes to the system, or even a complete rewrite.

In our example set-up, we use AndroMDA which in turn uses the Velocity scripting language for code generation. Velocity is an open source product with its own release and innovation cycle; changes in the Velocity language are beyond the control of AndroMDA's developers. If the Velocity language should change or be replaced by something else, the templates, which represent the architecture and its technical realization, will need to be rewritten.

The currently available MDA tools are young and actively evolving – and therefore provide a very dynamic development environment. Using commercial tools instead of open source tools, the situation is no different, as MDA and UML are both standards that are continuously being evolved. The MDA specification still leaves a lot of room for interpretation; tool vendors have to define what exactly to include in a PIM and how to translate a PIM via a PSM to compilable and deployable code. The effect is that MDA systems are not really portable from one set of tools to another.

3.4 External Evolution of UML, XMI, or MDA

As discussed in Sect. 1.1, changes to the infrastructure (run-time or development tools) might be beyond the project team's control, but might have a major impact on the project. The same holds true for the modeling method used in the development of the system.

In the same way as other systems depend on the programming language being used, MDA systems depend on the modeling language – which the OMG defines to be UML. The UML standard itself is still evolving [333]. As present, UML 2.0 will soon be defined. It will bring in new elements which will be useful for modeling components of MDA systems, which is not easy with the current version of UML.

Consider as an example the new feature to define *components*. So far, the *package* element was "abused" to declare business components, as Fig. 3 shows. Now the maintainer of the reference architecture has to decide whether to use this feature or not. If it is being used, PIMs will have to be adjusted accordingly. If it is decided to offer both options, some PIMs will use *components*, while other PIMs will use *packages*, so the PIMs will become inconsistent and harder to maintain.

On the one hand, ongoing improvement is an indicator of an innovative environment which will provide modern development methods and tools. On the other hand, it does not provide a stable environment as desired for a long-term development and maintenance project. The evolvement of UML 2.0 and beyond cannot be foreseen today.

This has two consequences. First, we know that tools will be upgraded, and compatibility issues will come in. Second, newer modeling languages will be more expressive, more detailed, more powerful. If we want to use new features, the existing part of the system soon becomes a legacy system. The modeling method introduces another external innovation cycle into the project, in addition to the ones discussed in Sect. 1.1.

It is hard to exclude external innovation cycles from a software system because the line between internal and external components is difficult to draw, e.g., the reference architecture is typically external to the project; however, if a proprietary architecture is used instead of a vendor's architecture, it might be internal to the company.

Note the difference between the MDA approach and the compilation process of higher-level programming languages. After compilation of a higher-level language program, the resulting assembler code or object code will not be modified. But this is exactly what happens using the MDA approach: a PIM is used to generate a PSM and finally code, and the PSM as well as the generated code are fine-tuned for the platform and enhanced by the business logic. Different tools that produce different code are incompatible since the business code that is added after the generation step might not be reused without a change.

This argumentation is in line with what the OMG say about the MDA [331]; they hope to reduce those dependencies in the future:

"Still, developers will have to fine-tune the produced PSMs to some extent, more in early days of MDA but less and less as tools and algorithms advance."

3.5 New Requirements

Consider the following enhancement of business requirements to our example in Fig. 3. The car sharing company extends its business area and becomes international. Invoices need a new attribute for the currency in which each invoice item is billed.

It is easy to add the attribute – no matter whether the system is developed with MDA or handcoded. The hard part of this change request is its complete definition on the business side. How is the invoice item to be coupled with the exchange rate component? Is there an exchange rate component at all? How do you deal with historical exchange rate data? What other components will have to be considered: only the invoice component, or also the customer component to save the currency in which a customer wishes to receive the invoice?

Those questions and their answers have a major impact on the maintenance costs and risks, regardless whether the change is actually implemented by hand either in the code or in a model. Maintenance costs for changed user requirements are largely driven by clearly defining the requirements. This is not an area that the MDA tries to improve, but it is where a large part of the maintenance effort and cost is utilized [350].

In any case, it is necessary to develop new test cases and to regenerate all modified components, which again requires thorough testing.

4 Related Work

Aspects of software maintenance and properties of maintainable systems are discussed in [350, 284] and in the software architecture literature, e.g., in [30], to name just a few sources.

Critical views on the MDA are expressed by Dave Thomas [424], Steve Cook [68], and Martin Fowler [130] who compare the MDA approach to the ideas of CASE tools in the 1980s, "and CASE clearly failed to live up its promises" [68]. Cook promotes Microsoft's MDA alternative. All authors mainly discuss the development of systems using MDA. The maintainability of such systems is not treated.

Parts of this chapter were previously published in [385] and in [36].

5 Conclusion

MDA offers an interesting approach to model-based software development. The core concept of the MDA is to formulate the business logic in a Platform Independent Model (PIM) that uses stereotypes such that elements in the model are explicitly related to the architecture concepts of the system. Platform-specific properties and the mapping from architecture concepts to the technical realization come in via model transformation and code generation steps.

In this chapter, we analyzed this approach with respect to the maintainability of software systems in the long run. Since the MDA promises to make the business aspects independent of the technical platform, we focused our analysis on changes at the technical level. The results are ambivalent. We found changes in the technical run-time infrastructure where it is relatively easy to adapt the software system, whereas other show a major impact on the system at several levels. Pattern-based model transformations and template-based generation of uniform code are easy using current MDA tools. Changes that are structurally fairly simple but have a wide scope on the system are easy to realize.

The most important lesson of our study is that while the MDA at least partly manages to decouple some business aspects from the technical infrastructure, it introduces new dependencies between the software system, the tool chain, the modeling method and language, a reference architecture that has to be used, and a generic implementation of that architecture.

All these elements have their own innovation cycles; so for the maintenance of a software system built using this approach, one has to keep track of all dependencies as well as of all innovation cycles. This is a challenging task, especially since the MDA is an evolving technology. The MDA specification, the UML standard, tools, and languages for model transformation as well as for code generation evolve quickly as more experiences using the MDA become available. A standardization process is ongoing. In the meantime, this leads to strong dependencies on the tool chain because proprietary solutions have to be widely used in all software artifacts, models, and code. There is certainly the danger that software systems implemented today will become legacy in just a few months.

The reason is that currently, the MDA is under-specified. Several gaps in the MDA have to be filled with corporate knowledge, for example, with an in-house reference architecture, or with a tool vendor's standard definitions for stereotypes used for the PIM and PSM. Also, the UML itself is not expressive enough; it is enhanced by appropriate profiles, containing all needed stereotypes. These profiles, again, are subject to evolution.

The high dependency of MDA systems on the tool chain is visible in Fig. 2. Even though there are high-level models that are only concerned with business aspects at the beginning of the tool chain, the other artifacts that are generated on the way to the deployable code like PSMs and generated code, have to be fine-tuned and enhanced. Here lies the fundamental difference between the MDA approach and the compilation process of higher-level programming languages: no one would go and change the assembler code generated by a compiler in order to optimize it for specific hardware. Therefore, the MDA as of today is a supporting process but not a new programming paradigm.

Outlook and Further Research

Our analysis is only a starting point for bringing MDA into a productive environment. Further important research areas include the development and maintenance process. The specific requirements for configuration management and release management must be addressed in order to synchronize the maintenance of templates and tools on the one hand, and the business applications, on the other hand. An environment with such young and actively evolving technologies requires sound technology management. On the technological side, expressive and reliable standards for the transformation of UML models and for the generation of source code are required.

Part III

Case Studies

Case Studies

Intents and Upgrades in Component-Based High-Assurance Systems

Jonas Elmqvist and Simin Nadjm-Tehrani

Department of Computer and Information Science, Linköping University,
S-581 83 Linköping, Sweden
{jonel, simin}@ida.liu.se

Summary. This chapter addresses challenges for model-driven development of embedded systems in industrial practice. These are rooted in the necessity of flexible development of new functionality at low development cost. Where a dependability requirement is added, e.g. support for assurance of safety requirements, then extending functionality by plugging in a new component, or modifying an existing component, without extensive safety-related and fault tolerance tests, is far from today's industrial practice.

The chapter highlights lessons learnt from three applications of model-driven development for high-assurance software components. The components were embedded in vehicular safety restraints, aerospace, and secure radio communication systems respectively. While our experiences in these three fields of application are compared and contrasted, the emphasis will be placed on the specific requirements of safety-critical software in aerospace systems with the following three characteristics: long life, high level of assurance, and forthcoming demands on efficient upgrades of assemblies of components. We discuss the need for relating intent specifications to formally verified design models from which safety-critical code is generated.

1 Introduction

Model-based development of embedded software is promoted as a means to achieve cost-efficient development of code, and platform-independent design. If successful, the model-based approach is a means of realising the "correct by construction" philosophy whereby flaws in a product design are discovered early at the design stage. Once adequate analysis of the design models assures adherence to system requirements, generating executable code is a systematic process that translates models to platform-independent and platform-dependent parts respectively. The idea is very attractive amid the increasing drive for higher efficiency in producing embedded software. Software is undoubtedly the essential ingredient in introducing flexibility in product upgrades and achieving shorter time-to-market for novel products. The questions that are central to the studies in this chapter are: does model-based development of software aid in developing embedded software that has specific extra-functional requirements such as dependability and small footprint, and does it support future upgrades including integration with legacy code?

The chapter summarises experiences from three case studies performed during year 2003 and points out the important aspects that need to be strengthened in today's tools before the vision of model-driven embedded system development can be a reality in high-assurance systems. All three applications were in domains where some element of assurance is present: a future car airbag system being developed at the Swedish subsidiary of the company Autoliv [113], an encryption terminal (Tiger XS) for secure communication on top of any communication equipment at the company Sectra [158], and a sanitised version of an unmanned vehicle with multi-mode control (also human operated) at Saab Aerospace [110]. All three case studies aimed to ascertain the benefit of the current modelling environments to the developers of these systems, including the above criteria: efficient generation of usable code, ease of assuring dependability requirements, and support for system upgrades and integration.

The three application areas also have individual characteristics that are distinctive for the different classes. In the airbag system the main goal is to enable rapid product development amid changing technology. Thus, the company requires a faster and more reliable means of porting a subsystem that was, for example, developed for a 16 bit processor that has 128kb ROM to a 32 bit processor with 256kb ROM. For the company, automatic code generation was studied as a means to increase efficiency in product development. Another main characteristic was the timeliness requirements – having 30 ms between the crash detection and firing of a restraint implies that some algorithms have to be computed predictably (and within 500 μs).

In the Tiger XS communication platform the main requirements are integration with legacy code , platform independence, and security assurance. Tiger XS acts as a component in defence systems. It acts as a bridge that makes any secure application (e.g. encrypted phone calls or encrypted SMS) run on top of any communication hardware (e.g. PDA or phone), and transforms "black" clear text data to "red" encrypted data. Hence, automatically generated code that refers to operating system primitives has to be easily adaptable to new underlying platforms. Moreover, the security-intrinsic applications demand that the generated code should follow a predefined coding style and be suitable for human inspection.

Both of the above applications have small footprint requirements and thus essentially expect the size of the automatically generated code to be comparable to the handwritten code (the airbag system being at the extreme with its byte-optimal handwritten code). In the third category of systems, the aerospace-related case study, footprint is a less dominant requirement. Instead the long lifetime and the safety-critical requirements of the system imply that any upgrades made to the system over its lifetime should be easily traceable to the original intent specifications. Since an aerospace product has to go through well-established assurance procedures and the certification of the new generation of a product is as strict as the certification of the earlier generation, the upgrade verification has a special status. Efficiency in code generation has to be followed by efficiency in the verification process, assuring that component upgrades do not jeopardise system, level safety requirements. This requirement is the one that is least covered by the literature on model-based development and therefore deserves special attention in the current chapter.

2 Intents and Upgrades

From the three case studies one could initially deduce that automatic code generation (to enhance shorter time to development) is an essential property of tools that intend to bridge the gap between user-level requirements and the implemented code. Safety-critical code has, however, the additional characteristic that the original sources of its requirements, often linked to system-level hazard analysis and mitigation of fault/error scenarios by architectural solutions, need to be clearly documented as intents, and traced to any future changes in the design or implemented code. Moreover, all changes to the design are followed by studying their impact on the documentation of the safety case. Also, a modelling tool that supports formal verification makes the extra difference in this context.

Upgrades necessitate replacing one component with another, or modifying one component in some respect. The upgrade process is especially costly for safety-critical systems as much of the analysis and review of the safety arguments has to repeated for every significant change to the system. We believe that tool support in this industrial sector needs not only to encompass fast time-to-market and support for formal analysis, but also to support cost-effective upgrades. In this section we briefly review the potential approaches for developing high-assurance systems that are built from components. These may range over components that are acquired off-the-shelf (no source code) to components that are developed in accordance with model-based development techniques with design specifications and automatically generated code. We briefly cover two broad areas that gained attention in recent years: the component-based approach to development of software-intensive systems, and the approach that can be labelled as "constructing the correct".

2.1 Dependability and Components

The software engineering community [416, 77] is promoting methods for development of systems from components and is, to begin with, trying to define the notion of components by providing a number of examples (e.g. [434]). However, the emphasis in the work up to now has been on the efficiency in the development process as opposed to assurance procedures. Especially, the compositionality of the extra-functional properties has only recently gained attention. The problem with extra-functional properties is that they are typically defined at the system or service level. It is therefore not trivial to pin down the properties that a component should have in order to satisfy the system-level properties when placed in the context of other components. In some sense there is an inherent conflict between separation of concerns (thereby restricting some design analyses to the component level) and overall guarantees for system/service-level properties.

Let us consider a few examples of non-functional properties. A prime concern in most high-assurance embedded systems is adherence to end-to-end timing constraints, and the two specific attributes of dependability [23], namely reliability and safety. Real-time properties are cross-cutting concerns and it is not possible to assure a real-time service by a system assembled from components unless the component model captures the parameters needed for real-time analysis in a well-defined manner [423, 422]. This is an area of work that has recently attracted attention with some progress in sight. But what can be said about component assemblies and assessing the safety of the system from characteristics of the components? The first obstacle that one meets is that assessing system safety and reliability has been predominant in hardware-intensive systems, so many approaches to assessment are hardware-oriented. Extending these methods in a systematic way to software components is only at early stages of research [379].

A widespread myth about software is that the smaller the software unit, the higher its reliability. A study by Jones shows for example that the number of delayed and cancelled projects dramatically increases as the number of function points (a measure of size) increases beyond 5000 [236]. At this level of complexity (roughly corresponding to 500k lines of code in languages like Fortran) 79% of the projects are cancelled or delayed by over 6 months. Thus, the ability to deliver a software-intensive product that satisfies the specification efficiently is obviously a major problem.

A valid question is therefore: can we increase the reliability of a system by breaking it down is to small manageable components? A follow-up question is: if we have demonstrated/estimated the reliability for a component how can we derive the reliability for the whole system based on a composition of the reliability measures for the parts? There are some initial attempts at answering these questions based on historical studies of modular designs. Hatton shows for example that the size–complexity–fault frequency relation is not linear and there are some medium-sized components that exhibit higher reliability compared to both smaller and larger components [199]. With regard to aggregation at system level, Hamlet et al. propose a theory for the compositional calculation of reliability metrics based on component metrics. Nevertheless, they contend that the theory needs to be validated in experimental settings [185].

Safety is the ability of a system to avoid harm to people and the environment. Hence, a car that never starts may seem to be safe by definition (although not quite reliable!). However, a car that does not start can indeed pose a threat to safety if it happens to stall on a railway crossing. In both cases the car fails to meet its reliability requirements. In the latter case it creates a potential threat to safety. Thus, safety is a property that intrinsically emerges from the behaviour of the system under design and the conditions in its environment.

Since there is no way that software on its own harms people or the environment, it is incoherent to allocate attributes such as safety to a piece of software or digital hardware. Software or digital hardware can only be examined in terms of the ways they may contribute towards the appearance of hazards. Hazards are failures that may potentially lead to violation of safety. Hence, traditional analysis of system safety starts by considering the potential unsafe scenarios, characterising the risks for the hazard to take place (both in terms of probability and in terms of severity of consequences), and making a quantified decision on which scenario to consider as one that should never happen – no matter how the constituent components in the system are designed, developed, or operated.

Traditional analysis of system safety rests on techniques that focus specifically on "things that may go wrong". Fault-tree analysis (FTA) and failure modes and effects analysis (FMEA) are old techniques that grew within the era of building systems from hardware (mainly mechanical) components. One can contrast FTA and FMEA by considering one a top-down and the other a bottom-up technique. In other words, in FTA analysis one is interested to know, given a potential failure in the system (a top-level event), what are the combinations of conditions that necessarily cause that event. In FMEA one tries to consider each and every constituent of the system, and trace the effects of errors manifesting in that constituent. An interesting area of work is to extend the traditional safety analysis techniques so that they can indeed be applied to software-based systems too [187, 178].

According to aerospace experts most errors are found in the interface between components, either because the original specification was incomplete (had forgotten to specify some aspect), or because it simply made wrong assumptions. A typical case is that one forgets the dependencies between several components, and when one component is updated/changed, the potential changes in other subsystems are not fully considered, or corresponding changes introduced there. An example is an attribute such as measured wheel velocity. If one reduces the number of pulses per rotation the resolution of the measurement is decreased. This might be favourable in terms of costs in the landing gear system, but the change might affect other consumers of the information. So the supplier of the landing gear system may move on to a cheaper realisation, not considering the changes implied in the flight control system or pilot information system. The way such changes are propagated in the system are by administrative processes: meetings, agreements, reviews. Thus, we are interested in studying whether component-based or model-based development paradigms can support the assurance procedures for a system that is upgraded by changing one or more of its components.

2.2 Constructing the Correct

The traditional formal development process that can be labelled "correct by construction" has a natural extension in the model-based development paradigm. The claim is: if the design can be formally analysed, one can demonstrate that the known causes of failures that may violate safety, as identified by hazard and risk analysis, have been removed. Such a design model can thus be a sound basis from which automatic code generation can produce high-assurance components. A seemingly opposite approach that may be labelled by the slogan "constructing the correct" amounts to applying formal verification techniques directly to source code. Since this approach has gained momentum in recent years, we believe that the proponents of model-based development need to consider the impact of these techniques in future development processes.

The "constructing the correct" school is both old and new. Early versions of the idea can be traced back to the work by Hoare and Floyd on the formal analysis of programs (late 60's). In those years, the ability to reason about the behaviour of a structured program in terms of assertions at entry and exit points, based on deductions after execution of every program statement, was put forward as a fundamental argument for constructing correct programs. One might argue that the early structured languages of 70's were equivalent to the high-level modelling notations (e.g. UML family of languages) of today. Thus, early proponents of "constructing the correct" were indeed acting as today's proponents of the model-based formal verification (and thereby correct by construction idea). However, high level programming languages are no longer at the top of the abstraction hierarchy today. Instead, one could characterise the proponents of this approach by goal to find errors in real executable software in an efficient manner. The claim is that in the end what is running in the system to be delivered is the code. So, high-assurance systems have to find a way to guarantee a predicable behaviour by the control software.

A good overview of the recent trend in program verification can be found in articles by Havelund, Visser, and co-authors [202, 447] where it is clearly emphasised that the purpose of investigating verification techniques for program code is not that design verification is fruitless. Rather, it is recognised that many software engineers, instead of detailing construction decisions in a design, prefer to write the code directly. Also, tools that support design models, e.g. UML, allow the modeller to include code fragments in a UML model. Hence, verifying the code is promoted as an efficient assurance method. This approach is followed for several programming languages, among them Java, C, Ada, and hardware design languages, e.g. [65, 40, 58].

2.3 Dependable Assemblies of Correct Components

Based on the short review above we believe that upgrading dependable systems based on updating and replacing components is an area that model-based development needs to address in the future. The overall methodology can be sketched as follows. Each developed component needs to carry with it information about its effect on overall system behaviour with respect to extra-functional properties. These could be interfaces that capture timing behaviour of the component, or interfaces that tell what behaviour can be expected from a component if the assumptions on its environment are invalidated by external (unintended) faults. The latter can be used in a similar manner to FTA/FMEA that is carried out on assemblies of hardware components. How the interfaces are derived and how they are used in an upgrade process are an interesting field of study, but it seems that there will be potential use for both paradigms, correct by construction using model-based development, and constructing the correct, where the source code of a component is assured to satisfy its contracted interfaces by its team of developers. In either case, the remaining step would be to assure that given certain interfaces the assembly of (upgraded) components satisfies its system-level properties, e.g. safety-related requirements. This requires proof techniques that build up incremental proofs based on earlier analyses and thus achieve the overall assurance in an efficient manner.

None of the tools and environments for model-based development are mature enough to satisfy the above needs. We use the details of three case studies to illustrate this gap and hopefully provide a benchmark for future studies. Two of the case studies concentrate on the needs related to the automatic generation of code. Since there is more maturity on the tool front in those respects, we will report on these in less detail. The third case study, a sanitised example of an unmanned vehicle that was provided by Saab Aerospace, serves to illustrate the need for tracing intents to formally verified component code. This example, although much simpler than any realistic aerospace application, has some elements that illustrate the need for (1) support for intent specifications and tracing the system-level requirements over a long lifetime, including the need for tracing changing requirements all the way down to new design models of upgraded components, and (2) the necessity of support for formal verification to achieve efficient verification of safety-related properties; in particular, incremental verification of such properties upon component upgrades.

3 Intent Specifications

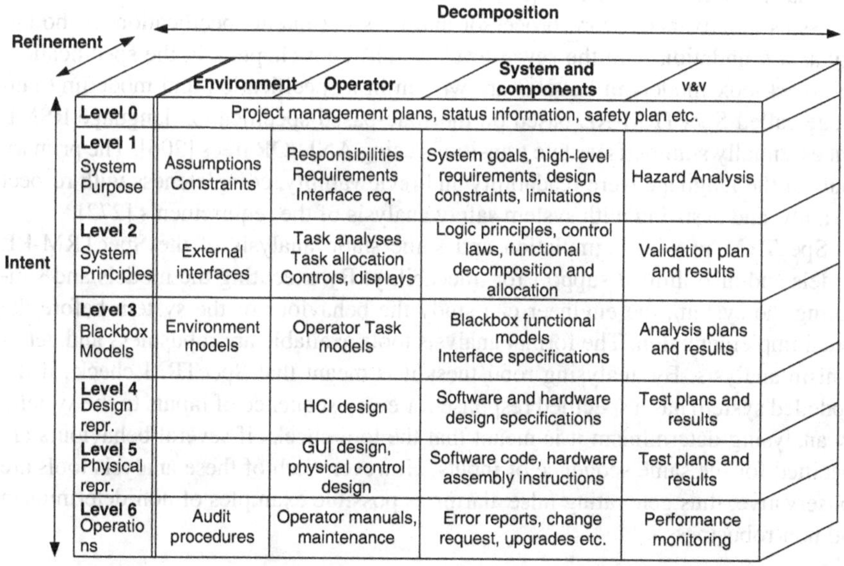

Decomposition
Refinement
Intent
Environment
Operator
System and components
V&V
Level 0
Project management plans, status information, safety plan etc.
Level 1 System Purpose
Assumptions Constraints
Responsibilities Requirements Interface req.
System goals, high-level requirements, design constraints, limitations
Hazard Analysis
Level 2 System Principles
External interfaces
Task analyses Task allocation Controls, displays
Logic principles, control laws, functional decomposition and allocation
Validation plan and results
Level 3 Blackbox Models
Environment models
Operator Task models
Blackbox functional models Interface specifications
Analysis plans and results
Level 4 Design repr.
HCI design
Software and hardware design specifications
Test plans and results
Level 5 Physical repr.
GUI design, physical control design
Software code, hardware assembly instructions
Test plans and results
Level 6 Operatio ns
Audit procedures
Operator manuals, maintenance
Error reports, change request, upgrades etc.
Performance monitoring

Fig. 1. The structure of an intent specification [72]

Intent specifications [271] is a new approach for specifying and designing systems that is based on research in both system engineering and psychology. The primary difference from other approaches is the structure (see Fig. 1). An intent specification is structured in seven levels, each level answering the question "why?", i.e. providing intentions about the level below, as opposed to traditional specification methods where levels are divided into answering what to do from how to do it. Each level is mapped to levels below providing traceability of system goals and high-level requirements down to implementation and vice versa. Each level has its own view of the system and is a different model of the system [157]:

- Level 0 is the project management's view of the system.
- Level 1 is the customer's view, including system goals, high-level requirements, hazards, design constraints, assumptions, and system limitations.
- Level 2 is the system engineer's view of the system and it describes the system design principles.
- Level 3 describes the black-box behaviour of the system and its modules. Formal analysis methods can be used on this level.
- Levels 4–6 provide information on the physical and logical representation of the system down to implementation and maintenance information. These levels were not the focus of this study.

In the unmanned vehicle case study below, the tool used for implementing an intent specification was SpecTRM (Specification Toolkit and Requirements Methodology), a commercial tool from Safeware Engineering [72]. It is a document-oriented tool that focuses on system requirements and specification. The tool works more or less as an advanced word processor and uses the intent specification methodology as a foundation with the seven levels as different chapters in the specification. The black-box models in Level 3 are written in a specification and modelling language called SpecTRM-RL based on the state-based specification language RSML that essentially summarises state transitions using AND/OR trees [206]. The primary goals of the language were readability and reviewability, completeness with respect to safety, and assisting with system safety analysis of the requirements [272].

SpecTRM provides simulation and some static analysis of the SpecTRM-RL models and also limited support for traceability. By executing the models and simulating the system, the engineer can study the behaviour of the system before the actual implementation. The formal analysis tools available are robustness and determinism analysis. By analysing robustness it is meant that SpecTRM checks if the modelled system has a specified response for every sequence of inputs to the system. By analysing determinism it is meant that the tool checks if several behaviours are specified for the same sequence of inputs. However, both of these analysis tools are conservative, thus generating false alarms as possible examples of non-determinism and non-robustness.

4 Support for Upgrades

The development process followed by most companies today, at least in the safety-critical arena, follows what can be considered as a variant of the V method. It essentially assumes a strict control of the integrator company over the developed components (in-house or subcontracted).

Model-driven tools and especially the UML-based support have grown from the world of software development, with the advent of object-oriented design, in the last two decades. The safety requirements of aerospace systems can, however, hardly be traced to a software component alone. Software is typically not harmful to the environment and can only contribute to violation of safety. Achieving safety is typically ensured by a mix of architectural decisions [266] and rigorous process for system development based on functional decomposition. Examples of architectural decisions are incorporation of fault tolerance via redundancy, hardware interlocks as a backup for software failure, watchdogs, monitors, and so on. An interesting question is: how to support the engineers who primarily perform system development in the old worlds of structured design, to encompass the "new" world of software design, and link the two in the systems and safety engineering process? An orthogonal question is, how to support the process of upgrading an existing component when new functional or safety requirements arise?

In current system development processes all the safety analyses, including FTA and FMEA mentioned in Sect. 2.1, and component-level and system level verification have to be redone for every upgrade in the life-cycle of the system. Model-based development needs to address how this process can be "shortened" by making an efficient analysis that assures preservation of safety properties.

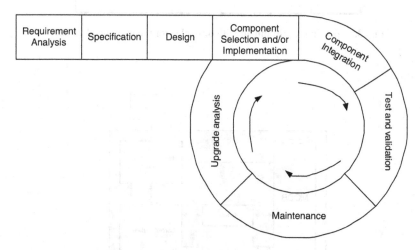

Fig. 2. The Sigma development process model

Elmqvist [110] presents the Sigma development metaphor as a model for system level upgrades based on component updates (see Fig. 2).The model captures the iterative upgrade process of existing components as well as the analysis processes that are essential during a system's life-cycle.

4.1 Example: Unmanned Vehicle

The unmanned vehicle is controlled by the Remote Vehicle Control Unit (RVCU). The vehicle operates inside a closed area (see Fig. 3) consisting of a work area, a parking area, and (stationary) obstacles. The vehicle can be controlled by the operator either hands-on with a joystick or by planning missions. Once it leaves the parking area, the vehicle is not allowed to stop.

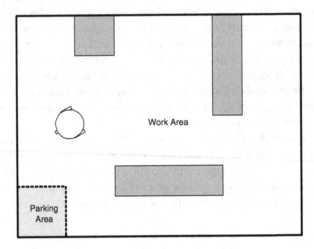

Fig. 3. A possible environment with obstacles for the unmanned vehicle

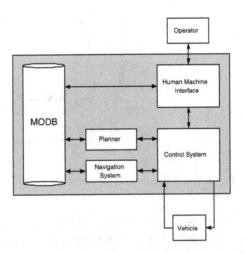

Fig. 4. The RVCU architecture

The role of the RVCU is to make sure that the vehicle is controlled safely inside the area, i.e. avoiding collisions with obstacles and stopping the vehicle navigating outside the closed area.

The Dynamic Window Approach by Fox et al. [132] was used for obstacle avoidance. The algorithm calculates an optimal trajectory by reducing the search space of possible velocities based on the dynamics of the vehicle and the position of the obstacles. The algorithm was slightly modified to fit in the context of the unmanned vehicle example.

The five components of the RVCU are presented in the architectural model in Fig. 4:

- The Human Machine Interface is the interface between the operator and the system.
- The Map and Obstacle Database (MODB) provides a representation of the map and the obstacles.
- The Planner takes care of high-level mission planning during unmanned missions.
- The Navigation System handles the final control of the vehicle by using the Modified Dynamic Window Algorithm.
- The Control System is the coordinating module that besides interacting with both the Planner and Navigation system also communicates with the robot.

The RVCU can be considered a safety-critical real-time system as the collisions with the obstacles or moving outside the designated area can be considered to result in harming people or the environment.

To illustrate lifetime changes we have added a new system requirement, and considered the effects of an upgrade to satisfy that requirement on the existing design. The stationary obstacles in the first design are considered to be moving objects in the new upgraded version.

5 From Specification to Design

The third level of intent specifications described in Sect. 3 is quite close to a design model but does not (yet) have the ambition of supporting model-driven development. Level 3 in SpecTRM provides an input/output interface for each component, and a description of the internal states and externally visible modes of the system. In addition, it gives a human-readable logic for state transition conditions in terms of AND/OR tables. However, to go from intents to implementations, and in particular via designs whose dynamic properties are formally analysable, we need a bridge to a tool that supports both code generation and formal analysis.

In the RVCU case study we chose the Esterel Studio programming environment for further development of the model [420, 38]. The choice was primarily motivated by the support for formal verification in Esterel, using the Prover plug-in model checker that can deal with systems with large state spaces using Stålmarck's method [392]. It also exemplifies a tool that is suitable for this class of applications due to its ability to deal with heterogeneity. Esterel designs have Mealy machines as formal semantics and are as such suitable for hardware/software co-design. A high-level description of an application can be translated after formal analysis to code that is the basis of a software implementation (C code) or hardware implementation (VHDL code).

Another benefit of using this environment in our safety-related case study was that the same environment (the same design model) can in fact be used as a test bed for study of the FTA and FMEA by systematically plugging in failure modes for various inputs or outputs of a component and studying the effects of single or multiple faults in terms of violations of safety at system level [186]. This combines model-based development with formal analysis of safety (in the spirit of FTA/FMEA) using the same design model, and without building fault trees.

6 Results and Lessons Learnt

This section outlines the results of the application of model-driven development to all the three application domains, and in each case summarises the remaining challenges facing the application developer. We begin with the unmanned vehicle example as it was described in more detail here, and then briefly describe the comparison with the other two studies mentioned in Sect. 1.

6.1 Upgraded Unmanned Vehicle

An upgrade of the requirement was done after the initial design and verification of the unmanned vehicle control system. Instead of having static obstacles inside the closed area, the vehicle should be able to avoid moving obstacles.

The study proved SpecTRM (version 1.0.14) to be a rather immature tool and more suitable for the design of control-handling modules such as the Control System than data-intensive modules such as the Navigation System. Further, SpecTRM does not yet provide any automatic traces or any overview of the traces, i.e. the traceability must be created explicitly by the developer as hypertext links. A more sophisticated support for traces would be appropriate in order to make the tool suitable for industrial use.

One could question the use of an intent specification tool when there are already more mature requirements engineering tools (such as CORE [73] and DOORS [421]) available on the market. The reason we thought a tool like SpecTRM was interesting in the context of the case study was that the tool was supposed to support the hierarchy of models described in Fig. 1 that is well-suited for safety-critical systems development. Also, earlier experience with the SpecTRM-RL language had proven to be positive in terms of communication with non-experts and thereby ease of validation of the early requirements. In contrast to the structure of the above Level 3 models, which are quite understandable to engineers from different disciplines, the software-engineering-oriented tools like DOORS that build upon the object-oriented notation have so far been less accessible to other engineers. However, the SpecTRM tool was not able to provide convincing support to the involved engineers to justify its use in the current status.

By manually converting the SpecTRM-RL models to Esterel modules, Esterel Studio could be used to verify the system and its components. Esterel Studio and its built-in model checker were able to prove a majority of the control properties of the RVCU. However, Esterel Studio does not provide any framework for modular or compositional verification. After the upgrade, the original verification process had to be redone. Furthermore, dealing with numerical properties in the 2003 version of the Prover plug-in was insufficient for our purposes.

We conclude that a tool environment that aids the developer, beginning with a specification language such as SpecTRM-RL down to verified code, is needed but is not fully available today. The unmanned vehicle example was indeed tried on a tool chain that combines SpecTRM and Esterel Studio, but with a lack of automatic translation between the tools, any of the tools could be replaced by another alternative. A case study by Leveson and Weiss also addresses the use of SpecTRM and intent specifications in model-based development [272]. However, their focus is on reuse at the software behavioral specification level and they do not address the issue of generating and verifying code.

A positive aspect of the SpecTRM implementation is its use of the Java-based Eclipse [98] environment that allows plug-in translators to be added conveniently. A trial plug-in, SpecTerel, that automatically translates very simple SpecTRM-RL models to very simple Esterel models, was implemented within a few days as a proof of concept.

6.2 Secure Communication Platform

The Tiger XS module is a software platform that provides a middleware function in a larger software system development. Here it was obvious that tools that support the object-oriented design process are the main candidates. Among the UML-based tools for code generation two representatives were studied in terms of the requirements of the case study: Rhapsody from iLogix [216] and Visual State from IAR systems [214]. However, in both cases it was found that both tools provide too much and too little support respectively.

Rhapsody provides too much support in the sense that it has a powerful extended UML language having a comparatively steeper learning curve. However, the primary reason for not being considered as a candidate for tool generation at Sectra was that it targets complete systems and some difficulty was experienced in merging existing (legacy) C-code for other parts of the application and the automatically generated Target XS code.

Visual State, on the other hand, was a lightweight tool with little extra functionality. In particular, it was possible to adjust the coding style to the style required by Sectra by implementing the translation of the action language (the part that defined effects of state transitions in terms of new value assignments to variables) so that it suits the in-house requirements. The main weakness of the tool in this specific case was the support for integration of the generated C code with other legacy code, and, in particular, that it was cumbersome to use user-defined types. Also, the automatically generated code was organised in terms of a number of arrays that were not human readable and satisfactory for security assurance-related inspections.

Although both tools were considered to generate small enough footprint compared to the Sectra handwritten code, they were not adopted for the above reasons. To suit the needs of this case study, in the end, an interpreter-based translation scheme was deemed the most useful. It resulted in an in-house code generator based on a subset of statecharts [158].

6.3 Airbag Software

Rhapsody was also tested as a candidate for the design and code generation of the airbag software. Here, the architecture of the system was clearly divided into two types of modules: those that were control intensive and those that were data intensive. Rhapsody in C was found to be a useful environment for modelling the structure and control-intensive parts of the application as class diagrams and statecharts, respectively. The automatically generated code was tested on a target micro controller (TX 19A). For the data-intensive parts, the code that implements signal processing algorithms to detect when the vehicle i.e. has crashed, another tool that is closer to the data flow abstractions used by the control engineer was deemed useful. The tool Scade [420] was studied for code generation in this part of the application. Another useful feature of Scade was the formal verification support with the Prover plug-in that was tested to a limited extent on the crash algorithm model. Scade is a tool that is based on the language Lustre [184] with a formal semantics, and has a history of usage in European aerospace applications (the code is generated by a DO-178B certified compiler that makes the tool an appropriate candidate for safety-critical applications).

The use of both modelling languages was found to reduce the time for development of code (after excluding the learning time). For a particular airbag function, this gain was quantified as a 60% decrease compared to the estimated time taken for handwritten code. The main drawback for the Rhapsody-generated code was the code size, still a significant factor in choosing such technology in the airbag systems. The low cost constraints of the ROM violate this option, as the size of the generated code was twice as large as the optimised handwritten code. In both cases support for timing analysis of the airbag software was missing, and this needs to be performed separately.

6.4 Final Remarks

Our studies support the claim by providers of tools for model-based development that these tools do indeed reduce the time taken for the development of executable target code from high-level models that are easier to inspect, to communicate, and to use as a documentation of a fairly complex system. The needs of various application areas in terms of requirements on the generated code were illustrated by three examples ranging from very tough code size (memory) restrictions in the airbag system to less demanding requirements on code size in the secure communication support and the unmanned vehicle case. None of the tools, however, have component-based support. This is perhaps not expected from tools like Esterel and Scade that have a state-based or data-flow-oriented style, close to the environment that other engineering disciplines are used to (state machine or function blocks). But the enhancement from object-oriented tools like Rhapsody to component-based modelling is needed if compositional analysis of upgrades is to be supported.

Support for documentation of upgrades in a long lifetime, and in particular when the traceability of the rationale of early design decisions and intents is a prerequisite to maintaining safety arguments, is an obvious shortcoming of the pure "code-generators" in model-based development today. Where intents can be documented and traced (e.g. SpecTRM), the support for code generation, formal verification, and compositional analysis of upgrade effects are still missing. Where design-level models were the starting point (Rhapsody, Visual State, Esterel, Scade), no such support for component upgrade verification or longer-term documentation of intents and safety-related arguments was part of the picture. In two of the applications we observed the dichotomy between data flow abstraction and the state-based control abstraction. UML diagrams syntactically host both styles of modelling, but the semantic gaps still need to be addressed in tools that aim to support development of high-assurance heterogeneous systems. In particular, combining the worlds of structural design (hardware and mechanics) and object-oriented design (software) is a key to model-based development of component-based high-assurance systems.

7 Acknowledgements

This work was supported by the Swedish strategic research foundation project SAVE on component-based safety-critical vehicular systems, and the national aerospace research program NFFP. The lessons learnt were partly based on the work of two Masters students, Andreas Eriksson and Anders Grahn, who did their final year projects under the supervision of the second author. The experimental SpecTerel plug-in translator was developed by Erik Sundvall. The state of practice and the problem definition from the aerospace sector have benefited from numerous discussions with Lars Holmlund, Rikard Johansson, and Jan-Erik Ericsson from Saab AB, whose cooperation is gratefully acknowledged.

On Modeling Techniques for Supporting Model-Driven Development of Protocol Processing Applications

Marcus Alanen, Johan Lilius, Ivan Porres, and Dragos Truscan

Software Construction and Embedded Systems Laboratories,
Turku Centre for Computer Science,
Lemminkäisenkatu 14, FIN-20520 Turku, Finland
{marcus.alanen, johan.lilius, iporres, dragos.truscan}@abo.fi

Summary. The Model-Driven Architecture (MDA) as supported by the Object Management Group (OMG) describes the structural requirements of an engineering discipline where models, instead of source code, comprise the primary artifact. In this chapter we provide an overview of the methods and modeling techniques used to support an MDA methodology for developing protocol processing applications. We demonstrate our approach with examples from an IPv6 router specification targeted to a customized processing architecture.

1 Introduction

The Model-Driven Architecture (MDA) by the Object Management Group (OMG) tackles the elusive problem of system development by promoting the usage of models as the primary artifact to be constructed and maintained. Models are categorized into Platform Independent Models (PIMs) and platform models which can be realized using a variety of middleware and programming languages into Platform Specific Models (PSMs). This is possible only with suitable query and transformation technology for navigating and modifying well-defined models using common modeling languages.

As a consequence, software development can be seen as the process of transforming a model into another until it can be executed outside its development environment. The combined field of model-integrated computing (MIC) and MDA is worth mentioning here. The first joint effort exploring the synergy between MIC and MDA was held in October 2004 [176], and MIC itself has been explored over a decade, for example, at ISIS, Vanderbilt University [223]. The current OMG standards present a static and structural view of models. They define several standard modeling languages and standards related to modeling, such as what a valid model is in a given language using Object Constraint Language (OCL) [169] constraints and how to store a model in a file using XML Metadata Interchange (XMI) [167]. However, they do not discuss how models are created or how models evolve. This may be explained by reviewing the origins of UML: it was developed as a method-independent notation to document software artifacts. UML can be used in combination with practically any software development method and, as a consequence, the OMG standards do not contain any reference or support for software development. We believe that the OMG standards should also consider the dynamic aspects of model development. This ranges from the basics of model evolution using algorithms for model transformation to more sophisticated reasoning about why a model transformation meets new requirements. We may consider that the Software Process Engineering Metamodel (SPEM) [168] standard addresses this issue. However, SPEM tells us how to document a process, while "planning and executing a project using a process described with SPEM is not in the scope [of the standard]". In order to learn more about the requirements of such aspects, we are pursuing a methodology and a case study utilizing such methodology throughout this chapter.

We investigate a possible approach to defining MDA methodology by analyzing the collection of concepts, methods, and tools needed to support such methods. We also try to classify and evaluate the requirements for the tools supporting the approach. MDA was primarily created to be used for the specification of software systems, but some of the ideas can be extended and applied to other domains (e.g. embedded systems). We propose as an example a design methodology applicable to the specification and design of embedded systems, and especially of protocol processing applications. The methodology was used in a larger case study, where an IPv6 router was specified and designed from scratch. To verify the validity of our approach, the specification of the router was targeted (implemented) both on a software platform, using the Java programming language, and on a hardware platform, using the TACO [445, 443] protocol processing architecture. TACO (Tools for Application-specific hardware/software CO-design) is an integrated design framework for fast prototyping, simulation, estimation and synthesis of programmable protocol processors. In this chapter we will focus on the latter approach, because it emphasizes important aspects of model-driven development.

We proceed as follows. Next, we position ourselves with respect to what modeling provides us and needs to provide us in the form of languages and facilities. We describe in Sect. 2 our view on the features that tool support should provide in order to realize a model-driven approach. In Sect. 3 our design methodology is briefly introduced, including our case study for protocol processing applications and we discuss challenges in light of MDA philosophy. We show in Sect. 4 how we used the concepts and tools introduced in Sect. 2 to automate our methodology. We conclude the chapter with final remarks on the benefits of using model-driven approaches for system development.

1.1 Models and Modeling Languages

From our point of view, the two main advantages of using models versus source code to describe our system are that, besides enabling a better abstraction level for analysis of systems' properties, we can store all the relevant information needed in a software project in the model and that all the information in a model is stored in a standardized and uniform way that can be processed and transformed easily.

The idea that we can use the same modeling language to describe the analysis, design, and implementation of a system has always been one of the most repeated features of UML. Actually, UML lacks in certain areas such as describing non-functional requirements and real-time domains, but successive extensions to the standard could alleviate these problems. Indeed, real-time UML is a well-studied topic [89, 90]. However, there is a clear danger in believing in the silver bullet of UML. A more realistic scenario is that we have to be able to experiment with new methodologies and languages, without giving up on what we already possess.

In light of this stepwise incorporation of novel technologies, the need for new metamodels comes forward. There is a strong need to explore new modeling languages and concepts, without trying to incorporate everything into UML. *Metamodeling* is the field of describing, evolving, maintaining, and extending metamodels providing mathematical rigor where possible in the form of (possibly heuristic) verification, and practical statistics of the models in question. A sound practice is to try to map between our various metamodels and the UML, which has become the de facto standard. Transparent mapping of models to other domains provides us with the required integrity and seamless interoperability.

Many developers see UML as a graphical representation of the source code in the system. This view prevents us from including other artifacts such as a spreadsheet or a Mathematica document in our model, even when the contents of those documents can be relevant to our software. We prefer to consider a modeling language as a taxonomy of the most important concepts that can occur in an abstract description of a design.

Another important feature of modeling languages such as UML is that while the models may be represented diagrammatically using icons, they are stored using an object graph similar to the abstract syntax tree of a programming language. In the case of UML, the abstract syntax is defined by the UML metamodel. The metamodel representation is akin to a directed graph. Each node of the graph represents a metamodel element and each arc a relationship between two metamodel elements. Some arcs represent compositions, i.e. whole–part relationships. In the case of UML, if we consider only the composition arcs, the resulting graph is also a tree. The advantage of storing a software project as an object graph is that we can traverse the project, collect, add, and remove information from it in a way that is independent of the target programming language. This task is simplified by languages such as OCL that have specific constructs to navigate models. Using OCL or a similar query language is not restricted to UML, but to the language of metamodels, which in MDA is the Meta-Object Facility [166].

1.2 Model-Driven Software Development Methods

We define a model-driven software development method as a software construction method where all the relevant information in the project is stored in some kind of an abstract model. Model development is then carried out as a sequence of model transformations.

Model-driven engineering is the result of recent developments in computer languages, awareness of the need of software development methodologies, and the constant need to tackle larger and more complex development projects. These forces are not new. Indeed, we could use the same naming pattern to create terms such as punched-card-driven development, to describe the development methods used when compiler time was a luxury, or source-code-driven development, to describe the methods used in Extreme Programming [34] and many open source projects, where source code is the key artifact. However, we believe that MDA opens a window for new development methods and tools that are not available or are too expensive to implement in other approaches such as source code driven development. These tools and methods can take advantage of the fact that the artifacts describing our software are stored in a standardized way and are, to a certain extent, independent of the implementation technology.

The description of an MDA method should contain all the elements that are usually present in any software development method. It should describe which final deliverables and intermediate milestones should be produced, which language should be used to create the previous artifacts, and which tasks we should perform, and in which sequence, so that we can effectively create the required artifacts. However, we consider that there exists two main differences in an MDA method with respect to a traditional development method. First, all artifacts are represented using well-defined modeling languages. Secondly, and as a consequence, we can create tools that process and transform all the artifacts in our projects. Therefore, we will require that all tasks in an MDA method should be performed with the assistance of specialized tools.

2 Tool Support for MDA

CASE tools have a huge role in the MDA initiatives due to the graphic nature of models, the way models are stored, and the fact that many of the benefits of these approaches only arise through automation. Our vision is that a typical MDA project will be carried out using not one but several development tools. There are many different variables in a project such as translation to the target platform, knowledge of the application domain, analysis, estimation (e.g. the TACO framework), and we cannot expect that one single tool will be able to cover the whole development process for all the necessary variables. Thus ease of communication between these tools is of essence.

A true common file format for model interchange would allow a market for new specific tools for model transformation and code generators. Some of these tools could be specialized in application domains such as real-time systems. In many cases the selection of tools such as a model editor would be just a matter of personal preferences as it is now with text editors. This scenario is described in [404] and it requires two components: a standard interchange file format, and tools that comply with it. Unfortunately, in the case of UML, this is still not a reality, as different tools implement the XMI standard differently. Furthermore, by providing multiple ways to serialize the same model parts, the standard has only made it more complex for multiple implementations to co-exist. Also, XMI is designed for the abstract model and does not contain any information about graphical parts. The XMI-DI standard for diagrammatic interchange [175] is not yet so widespread, but we hope that this situation will change in the near future.

We will assume tool support in the form of diagram editors, transformation frameworks, and similar frameworks as an issue of quality of implementation, and concentrate on the facilities that they must provide.

2.1 SMW Tool

To create and manipulate the models, we make use of the freely available Software Modeling Workbench (SMW) [24] toolkit. The tool is built upon the MOF and UML standards from the OMG, allowing editing, storage, and manipulation of metamodels.

SMW is organized in four main layers: the SMW kernel, a generic editor layer, the language-specific editors, and the method-specific scripts. The SMW kernel is in charge of representing models in memory. The kernel ensures that the models are wellformed. It also provides support for XMI, OCL-like idioms for model query and navigation, and user-defined modeling languages. We have used the basic facilities provided by the kernel to create a generic diagram editor. The generic editor provides functionality such as printing or a clipboard that is implemented independently of the actual modeling language used in a given model. The generic editor can be customized into a language-specific editor such as the UML editor, an extension to standard UML, and even other modeling languages, such as the SMW extension to model data flow diagrams (the SA/RT profile [222]) that we use in our design flow.

2.2 Scripts

An MDA script is a small application that processes a software model in order to extract information from it, transform it, or create a derived artifact such as source code. Several transformation languages have already been specified, and others are in the planning stages. Examples of transformation languages are QVT [354], MOLA [242], UMLX [459] and GREAT [61]. In our case, we have decided to use the scripting language provided by the SMW tool.

The actual method engineering support is provided by customized scripts. We have identified three script types that are required to be supported by an MDA process. They operate over model elements as well as over entire models.

(1) *Queries* are applied on a model expressed in one language and return a set of elements of the same model expressed in the same language.
(2) *Model transformations* are applied on a model expressed in a given language and either modify the model in place, or create a model, possibly expressed in a

different language. Model transformations conceive a plethora of new interesting questions and topics, such as transformation taxonomy, correctness-preserving transformations, consistency checking, and/or verification.

(3) *Code generation*, although a form of transformation, is sufficiently different from a model-to-model transformation to merit its own classification. The goal is to produce suitable input to a second-stage compilation or analysis tool. The target language is not a metamodel.

The main difference between queries and transformations is that the queries are free of side-effects, meaning that when applied on a model they do not change the model in any way. A more comprehensive and systematic classification of model transformation is discussed on p. 19 of this book.

2.3 Queries: Metrics, Constraints, and Guidelines

The simplest script is a *query*. A query gathers information from a model but does not update it. OCL is probably the standard and best known language for UML queries. Usually a query gathers information from a model in the form of a collection of elements. In addition, we consider that there are still three other specific uses of queries: defining software metrics, model constraints, and design guidelines.

The main purpose of a query is to extract, from a model, parts of or all model elements corresponding to the query condition. An example of such a query is obtaining a list of all objects that are instances of a given class. In order to perform the query we use the method **getAllParts** that returns all the elements transitively owned by the object. If we invoke this method with the root element of the model we obtain a collection that contains all other elements in the model.

```
1   instances=model.getAllParts().select(lambda c:
2      c.oclIsKindOf(Instance)
3      and c.classifier==someClass).name
```

A query can represent a design guideline when it is used to verify that all elements in the model have been created and are consistent with the development method. In the following example, the lines 1–3 collect all stereotype names (ucStereotypes) present in the use case diagram of the system. Consequently, lines 4–8 create a collection of classes (unRelated) whose stereotype names are not present in the use case diagram.

```
1   ucStereotypes=model.ownedElement.select(lambda uc:
2      uc.oclIsKindOf(UseCase)).stereotype.select(lambda st:
3         st.oclIsKindOf(Stereotype)).name
4   unRelated = model.ownedElement.select(lambda cl:
5      cl.oclIsKindOf(Class) and
6      cl.stereotype.select(lambda st:
7         st.oclIsKindOf(Stereotype) and
8         st.name not in ucStereotypes))
```

Of course, more complexity can be added to the previous verification in order to gather more details on the relation between each class and different use cases. One should note that one class can belong to several use cases or the reverse, i.e. one use case can be contained by one class, even though this situation occurs less frequently.

Finally, a query can be used to ensure that a design can be implemented in a given target platform. In our example, we check that the design is still *implementable* onto the target platform after a refactoring has been performed. In practice, this means that all the class methods should still have at least one implementation solution provided by the target platform.

```
1   implementable = model.getAllParts().forAll(lambda actDiag:
2     actDiag.oclIsKindOf(ActivityGraph) and
3     actDiag.ownedElement.forAll(lambda tran:
4         tran.oclIsKindOf(Transition) and
5         tran.source.oclIsKindOf(ActivityState) and
6         belongsTo(tran.source.name, platformOperations)))
```

The example interrogates all activity diagrams inside a model, and checks that each state is expressed using a platform operation provided in the `platformOperations` list (line 6).

Software Metrics

Software metrics are an application of model queries. We can extract design and implementation metrics from a software model by applying an aggregation operator over a set of queries of a model. Let us take as an example the *total number of classes* in a model. This simple metric may give us a rough estimation of the effort needed to implement the model. Here, we begin by selecting all the classes in the model, and use the **size** operator to count the number of classes.

```
1   NOC=model.getAllParts().select(lambda c:
2     c.oclIsKindOf(Class)).size()
```

Another interesting metric is the *number of operations per class*. The following query creates a collection that contains an integer with the number of operations for each class.

```
1   MpC = model.getAllParts().select(
2     lambda c: c.oclIsKindOf(Class)).collect(
3       lambda c: c.feature.select(lambda f:
4         f.oclIsKindOf(Operation)).size())
```

In this query we first find all classes in the model. Then we use the **collect** operator to calculate the number of operations in each class. Once we have created the final collection we can calculate the average and maximum number of methods per class in the model. We can also use the **stats** Python module to print a histogram of the metric.

```
1   AverageNumberOfMethods = MpC.sum() / MpC.size()
2   MaximumMethodsPerClass = max(MpC)
3   import stats
4   print stats.histogram(MpC)
```

The histogram may reveal that some classes are too large. Probably these classes represent several abstractions and can be refactored into two or more simpler classes. The following query returns the names of the classes in the model that have the most number of operations.

```
1  model.getAllParts().select(lambda c:
2    c.oclIsKindOf(Class) and c.feature.select(lambda f:
3    f.oclIsKindOf(Operation)).size() >= max(MpC) * 0.9).name
```

Target Platform Constraints

Another important type of query is to check if a model fulfills a given constraint of the target platform. These constraints can be dictated by the implementation programming language, the target operating system, or, in our case, by the hardware platform.

For instance, in our design flow one would like to avoid using the multiple implementation inheritance (especially if we are talking about mapping the specification into hardware). For this we have to identify (see the script below) the presence of the classes that use multiple inheritance in our design.

```
1  model.getAllParts().select( lambda c:
2      c.oclIsKindOf(Class) and
3      not c.isAbstract and
4      c.generalization.size()>1
5  ).name
```

In this script we select from all classes in the model (lines 1–2) those representing a concrete class to be implemented (line 3) and have more than one superclass (line 4). Then we collect the names of the selected classes (line 5).

Design Guidelines

Another application for queries is to check whether or not a model follows some design guidelines. Some tools such as Together Control Center from TogetherSoft provide an auditing feature that reveals common design and programming mistakes. ArgoUML [364] provides a similar mechanism with its critics system. Argo critics give advice in real time, while the designer manipulates the model diagrams.

As an example, the following method returns true if a class has an invariant. The invariant may be defined in the given class (line 2) or in any of its superclasses (line 4).

```
1  def hasInvariant(c):
2    if c.constraint.exists(lambda e: e.name=="invariant"):
3      return true
4    else:
5      return c.generalization.exists(lambda g:
6        hasInvariant(g.parent))
```

Given the function **hasInvariant** the next query returns the name of the classes that do not have an invariant defined.

```
1  model.getAllParts().select(lambda c: c.oclIsKindOf(Class)
2    and not hasInvariant(c)).name
```

2.4 Model Transformations

Model transformations can be categorized based on the scope of their effect on a given model. They can be applied to modify internal parts (elements) of a model (update transformation) or to create a new model expressed in the same language or in a different language (mapping transformation). Usually, a model transformation requires a script with a higher complexity than a query. In fact, a transformation is composed of one or many queries that select from the model the required elements satisfying a given condition or being in a certain relation, and then one or many create, edit, or delete operations performed over the target model elements.

A *mapping transformation* translates each element from a source model into zero, one, or more elements of a target model. The source and target models may be described in the same or in different modeling languages. In a mapping transformation, the original model is not altered. Recently, Akehurst and Kent proposed to use relations to define these mappings [11]. Also, the OMG is going to release a new standard for model transformations. We consider that mapping transformations is more suited to describing transformations where a whole model is translated from one language to another.

In contrast, an *update transformation* modifies a model in place: it adds, deletes, and updates elements in one model. The source and target models are the same and the effects of the transformation are visible while performing the transformation. There can be two possible ways in which an update transformation can be performed: to modify an already existing element or to create a new element of the same type followed by the deletion of the initial element. The update transformation is obviously a more efficient approach when only a small subset of the source model will be changed by the transformation. A trivial example is the addition of a new UML class to a package. This involves the creation of a new model element, and modifying the bidirectional association between the class and the package.

Model Refinement and Refactoring

Model refinement and refactoring is a new area of research. We have experience in source code refactorings and refinements, but in modeling it is quite a new concept – probably because a de facto standard for expressing transformations has not yet been developed. Different definitions of a refactoring have been given in the literature. Fowler says that *"The process of changing a software system in such a way that it does not alter the external behavior of the code, yet improves its internal structure"* [131], while Beck considers that a refactoring is *"a change to the system that leaves its behavior unchanged, but enhances some non-functional quality— simplicity, flexibility, understandability, ... "* [34]. A more comprehensive discussion on model refactoring is given on p. 199 of this book.

We consider that model refactoring is a more complex case of model transformation where the update transformation is applied on the entire model. We define a refactoring as a behavior-preserving transformation in a model with the objective

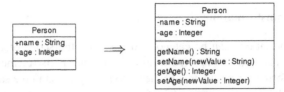

Fig. 1. Attribute encapsulation

of improving the design described in it. In our work, we have used a rule-based approach [351] provided by the SMW tool. It allows us to mix OCL-style queries and preconditions with imperative statements that modify the model. Part of a script for a standard example, encapsulating an attribute of a class, is shown below. The script modifies a public attribute to become private, and adds a suitable getX() method instead. The effects of the refactoring are presented in Fig. 1.

```
1   transformation EncapsulateAttribute:
2     rule AddGetter(a: Attribute):
3       when: a.visibility==VisibilityKind.vk_public and
4             not a.owner.feature.select(lambda f:
5             f.name=="get"+string.capitalize(a.name))
6       do: a.owner.feature.insert(
7           Operation(
8           name="get"+string.capitalize(a.name),
9           visibility=VisibilityKind.vk_public,
10          parameter=[
11          Parameter(name="result",type=a.type,
12          kind=ParameterDirectionKind.pdk_return) ],
13          specification="return "+a.name)
14          )
15      rule Privatize(a: Attribute):
16        when: a.visibility==VisibilityKind.vk_public and
17             not AddGetter.guard([a]) and not AddSetter.guard([a])
18        do: a.visibility=VisibilityKind.vk_private
```

3 A Design Methodology for Protocol Processing Applications

Protocol processing is a sub-domain of digital telecom applications that deals with switching, analysis, buffering, and transformation of units of information used in communication protocols. Among the requirements of protocol processing applications we can enumerate high throughput, physically constrained implementation platforms, and flexibility/upgradeability of functionality. In order to meet all these requirements, these kind of applications are usually implemented on dedicated configurable hardware platforms (e.g. network processors). One of the challenges in designing such applications is how one can choose/configure the implementation platform to better implement the applications, starting from the initial requirements specification of the application.

As mentioned earlier, we see MDA as an integration of languages, models, tools, methods, processes, and frameworks that allow us to specify and analyze systems in a consistent manner, starting from the requirement specification and down to the

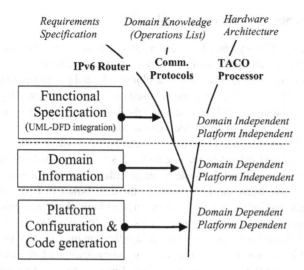

Fig. 2. Design methodology for protocol processing applications

physical implementation. In order to provide a systematic approach to system design, a methodology that guides the designer and provides the necessary tool support has to be defined. Our design methodology (Fig. 2) starts with the functional specification of the application, and when the necessary level of detail is reached, we map the specification onto the target platform. This is exactly what MDA proposes: to use several models (e.g. Platform Independent Model (PIM), Platform Specific Model (PSM), etc.) to describe the system at different layers of realization.

As mentioned in the introduction, MDA was intended for software development. In the case of embedded systems, a more liberal approach has to be adopted, since embedded systems are a combination of hardware and software providing some functionality to the environment. In our case study we specified and implemented an IPv6 router targeted on a protocol processing platform. In this situation, the implementation platform is a programmable processor which, by its nature, not only is a hardware platform but is also configurable.

Therefore, in talking about both hardware and software we are facing a conceptual gap between the two. To alleviate this problem, we used what we call *domain information* to narrow the gap between the functional specification and the platform, and at the same time, to provide basic support for reuse of platform components. Moreover, in our approach we wanted to be able to implement the functional specification of the application on an implementation platform chosen only after the functional specification process was performed. Also the methodology was intended to enable us to configure a target (hardware) platform while starting from the application specification, in contrast to traditional approaches where the application has to be mapped onto a fixed given platform. In the following we briefly present the main phases of the design methodology.

3.1 Functional Specification of the Application

In the area of embedded systems there are mainly two categories of approaches promoting concepts and artifacts that can be viewed as common modeling languages. The first category is based on the use of the object-oriented paradigm, which was the starting point of UML. The second one is based on the data flow paradigm that promoted data flow diagrams (DFDs) as its main modeling language. Both models offer important views, but each of them focuses on certain aspects of the system under consideration. We presented in [429] a combined approach where both paradigms are used to develop embedded software. The method is tool supported, allowing the usage of well-defined models of the system and in order to provide automation, model transformations have been specified between the data-flow and UML views of the system. An argument for the necessity of integrating both views was given in [122].

Below, we briefly go through the main steps of the functional specification phase. We extract the functional requirements of the application into a functional specification performed in a *domain-independent* and *platform-independent* manner. At this point no details about the target domain and platform are being taken into consideration.

The design flow (Fig. 3) is composed of a number of steps that represent different views of the system. At each step, new information is added in the specification, until the necessary level of detail is reached. Briefly, the steps in the figure are:

a. Extract the application requirements.
b. Extract functionality of the system into a Use Case Diagram.
c. Specify the textual description for each use case.
d. Obtain the Initial Object Diagram of the system from the Use Case Diagram.
e. Refactor the Initial Object Diagram based on the use cases' textual description by grouping, splitting, or discarding objects.
f. Transform the Initial Object Diagram into a Data Flow Diagram and build the Data Dictionary of the system.
g. Specify the internal behavior of the DataTransformations using Activity Diagrams.
h. Transform the Data Flow Diagram into a Class Diagram.
i. Transform the Data Flow Diagram into a DFD-like Object Diagram.

Between steps, the designer changes the view of the system several times and, consequently, the modeling paradigm. To provide automation in going from one step to another model transformations have been specified and implemented. We show later (Section 4) in this chapter how we have implemented and used these transformations. A more detailed view of the design flow and how we automated these transformations between different views of the system can be found in [428]. In this chapter we only intend to analyze the methods used in the approach, and based on this analysis, to identify the general requirements of a model-driven development process.

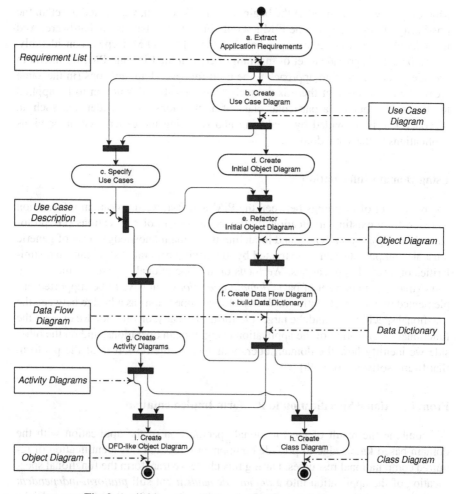

Fig. 3. Available options during the system generation process

3.2 From General Specifications to Specific Implementations

One of our aims is to keep our design methodology applicable to a wider range of embedded systems. Once the functional specification of the application has been performed, different target platforms can be chosen for implementation. The approach is in consensus with the MDA philosophy, where the PIM can be mapped onto a PSM to provide specific implementations of a given specification.

The MDA standard does not mention either a concrete way in which a PIM is transformed into a PSM, or how tool support should be provided for this transformation. Clearly additional information of the target platform is required and for this a Platform (description) Model (PM) is proposed. Still, to be able to perform the PIM-to-PSM transformation, a set of mappings between the PIM and PM is needed.

Moreover, as we mentioned in the beginning of this section, we wanted to retain the possibility of implementing the PIM not only in software, but also in hardware. And in the latter case, the conceptual gap between the PIM and PM deepens considerably.

To be able to provide a set of mappings between the PIM and PM, we intend to provide a general enough approach to be used for several applications (in the same area). We are aware that there is no such "one-size-fits-all" solution to be applied to all systems, but for a particular class of applications we consider that such an approach can be provided by analyzing and (re)using the experience of previous applications in the same domain.

Using Domain Information

To create a set of mappings between the PIM and PM, we use domain information gathered from existing applications in the same domain of applications (i.e. protocol processing). By analyzing and modeling the domain knowledge, a set of generic reusable components can be extracted by identifying general abstractions and similarities of a set of applications. We focus on the operational features of the system and extract a common set of basic *domain operations* that have to be supported/implemented by the target platform. We use domain operations as a bridge between the functional specification and the target platform. Basically, on one side we express the functional specification of the application using domain operations, and on the other side we identify how the domain operations map to the resources of the platform (hardware, software, or both).

From Functional Specification to Platform Implementation

We combine the result of the functional specification of the application with the domain-based knowledge to provide component reuse and fast identification of required computational resources. During this phase we transform the functional specification of the application into a *domain-dependent* but still *platform-independent* specification (phase two of Fig. 2). Seen in the context of an MDA approach, the PIM-to-PSM transformation is presented in Fig. 4.

The diagrams in the final steps of the functional specification (Fig. 3) represent possible outputs of the specification process and can be seen as the PIM of the approach. Although not evident due to typographical reasons, the behavior of the object is specified using UML activity graphs, where the activity states of the graphs are refined until they can be expressed with domain operations. At the same time, for each domain operation we identify how it is supported/implemented by the resource(s) of the target platform (i.e. PM), thus allowing us to identify what platform resources are required to implement the application. The approach can be used to implement the application both on fixed-configuration platforms, as well as on configurable ones. Keeping the application specification independent of the target platform allows designers to take implementation-specific decisions later in the design flow, thus addressing an important issue of the hardware/software co-design domain.

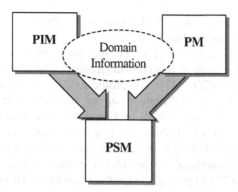

Fig. 4. Using domain information for the PIM-to-PSM transformation

The main benefit of the approach is that it does not restrict us to only one implementation platform. Although specified using domain information, the PIM is still completely independent of the target platform. Consequently, several implementation platforms can be addressed, where the PM can be any kind of implementation platform starting from high-level programming language applications (e.g. C, Java, etc.) to hardware circuits. For instance, to provide an executable model of the functional specification, it is enough to choose the C language as the PM. By specifying how each domain operation is implemented in C, we provide a mapping between the PIM and PM. Of course, identifying how domain operations are implemented by the platform is not always a trivial task. But once the mapping is created, it can be reused for several application specifications (in the same application domain). Another advantage of this approach is that, with the precondition that the behavior of the PIM is expressed with domain operations and that mappings between the domain operations have been built, the transformation of the PIM into the PSM remains the same. This fact enables us to reuse the transformation for trying out several applications implemented on different implementation platforms.

Modeling the Implementation Platform

In one of our case studies (IPv6 router specification), we chose to target the PIM in the previous subsection on the TACO protocol processing platform. TACO is a framework built around the TACO processor, whose resources are implemented and simulated using SystemC [336] (an object-oriented extension of C++ for hardware specification), their physical parameters (like area and power use) are estimated in Matlab, and the processor configurations are synthesized using VHDL. The resources of the processor are organized in a library of components, the *TACO Component Library*, from which the designer can create, at design time, *processor configurations* by selecting those resources needed to implement a given application. The SystemC, Matlab, and VHDL models coexist, enabling one to estimate and simulate processor configurations at system level before going to hardware implementation by selecting resources of the processor. When these configurations are validated with respect to the requirements, VHDL implementations of the processor can be obtained to synthesize the processor in hardware.

In our case, the PM models the TACO Component Library in the form of a UML class diagram. The elements of this class diagram are customized based on a UML profile definition for TACO [427]. The profile models two kinds of information: an architectural description of the processor (i.e. type of resources and their relationships) and library-related information (physical estimations for each resource, as well as SystemC and VHDL corresponding implementations). More additional constraints associated with the profile elements have been specified using OCL-like constructs, to enforce additional architectural properties not enforced by the graphical models. Since the TACO profile is not in the scope of this chapter we avoid going into more detail.

We only mention that the functionality of the processor is implemented by its processing units and their computation is triggered by the processor program code. In Fig. 5 left, we present one of the processing units of the processor, modeled as a «TACOFu» class. Each processing unit, and consequently each class representing it, contains information about what domain operations it implements (e.g. __do_add()) and how each operation is implemented in practice by the platform. In the context of TACO, a domain operation is implemented by a sequence of TACO machine instructions (Fig. 5-right).

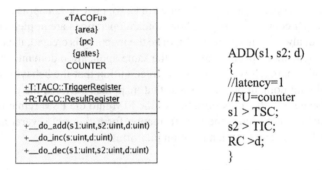

Fig. 5. Domain operations specified in the COUNTER class (left). A domain operation is a sequence of machine instructions (right)

It is worth mentioning that when developing applications for TACO processors, the program code is created and the processor is configured at the same time (by identifying what resources are needed to run that code). Thus, by performing the PIM-to-PSM transformation [426], we obtain simultaneously both the application code and the corresponding hardware configuration.

The resulting diagrams of the process in Fig. 3 model the behavior of the system using UML activity graphs, whose states are further refined into other states expressed with domain operations. On the TACO processor side, each domain operation is implemented (see Fig. 5) by a resource of the processor (i.e. processing unit) and the corresponding processor code to exploit that resource.

We again mention that having domain information "embedded" with both the PIM and PM, the PIM-to-PSM transformation could be fully automated. Basically the transformation selects all processor resources needed to implement the activity states in PIM to obtain the processor configuration, and each state in its turn is transformed into a sequence of processor instructions that will constitute the program code. Due to lack of space, we will not go into detail. We only mention that we applied techniques and concepts similar to those discussed in Sect. 2.2.

This enabled us to check constraints of the platform imposed by the requirements of the application. For instance, often used constraints of embedded systems are the area occupied, the power consumption of the system, or the latency or the throughput of communication channels. In the case of TACO, all resources have this information available in the PM and, as a consequence of the PIM-to-PSM transformation, in the PSM (see `area` and `pc` tagged values in Fig. 5-left). Therefore, using a script that computes the total area and power consumption of the processor, we can ensure that the PSM obtained complies with the initial physical constraints of the application, before going to the hardware synthesis process.

3.3 System Generation

System generation is the translation of a PSM into source code that can be compiled into the "final" system. Here the word final can be seen in relative terms. We can see it as the final system the PSM obtained during the PIM-to-PSM transformation in case it is the end-product of our implementation, or, as an alternative, to generate from the PSM new models or code that can be further transformed or compiled into other models or implementations, respectively. In fact, according to the MDA specification, any PSM can be regarded as a new PIM that can be, in its turn, transformed into a new PSM.

For instance, during our case study, once the PSM (i.e the TACO processor configuration and the corresponding processor code) was obtained, we were able to successively generate automatically several perspectives of the system depending on the design needs (Fig. 6). The approach could be seen as similar to code generation or as transforming the PSM into other models.

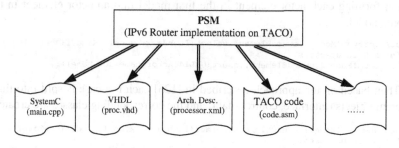

Fig. 6. Possible options for system generation

For instance, from the PSM we can directly generate the SystemC model of the processor (i.e. configuration) to simulate the entire functionality of the system, before going to the hardware design process. This can be done either at the metamodel level, where we map elements of the PSM (TACO processor) into a model of the SystemC language using, say, a SystemC UML profile, or just simply generating the SystemC code files. In parallel, the TACO code (automatically obtained from the configuration) is input to the TACO compiler that performs necessary optimizations and other compiler-specific tasks, and the processor is simulated. In its turn, the SystemC model/code of the processor can be further processed (transformed) into C and/or VHDL code/models, this being one of the current approaches in using SystemC for hardware designs.

In a similar way, and as a consequence of how the TACO Component Library is built, we obtained the VHDL model of the processor that serves as input for hardware synthesis tools to implement the processor in hardware. To connect our design flow with other design tools (e.g. TACO design tool [444]), where the design space exploration is performed, the obtained processor configurations can be exported in XML format. We mention that, due to the way the PSM is created and with the benefit of the scripting facilities presented in the previous section, all these transformations are fully automated.

4 Automating Model Transformations in the Methodology

In the methodology presented in the previous section, a number of models have been used to specify an IPv6 router at different levels of detail during the development process. Also in Sect. 2.2 we defined a set of scripts that operate over well-defined models allowing model creation and manipulation. In this section, we exemplify the way we used scripts to automate the model transformations between the steps of our design methodology.

In the functional specification of the application presented in Sect. 1.2, we apply a number of such transformations. One example is the transformation (step d. of Figure 3) of a UML use case diagram (Fig. 7 - top) into a UML object diagram (Fig. 7 - bottom), remaining within the UML formalism. Basically, the algorithm consists of transforming each actor element in the first model into an actor element in the second model.

```
1    ucActors=umlModel1.ownedElement.select(lambda x: x.oclIsKindOf(Actor))
2    for act in ucActors:
3        p=umlModel2.ownedElement.insert(UML14.Actor(name=act.name))
```

Then based on the approach described in [123] each use case is split into three different objects (interface, control, data) and the corresponding classes are created.

```
4    useCases=umlModel1.ownedElement.select(lambda x: x.oclIsKindOf(UseCase))
5    for el in useCases:
6        classInterface=umlModel2.ownedElement.insert(UML14.Class(name=el.name,
7                              stereotype.append(Stereotype(name="interface"))))
8        classControl=umlModel2.ownedElement.insert(UML14.Class(name=el.name,
9                              stereotype.append(Stereotype(name="control"))))
```

```
10      classData=umlModel2.ownedElement.insert(UML14.Class(name=el.name,
11                          stereotype.append(Stereotype(name="data"))))
```

In this transformation we use an approach where interface objects are the only objects communicating with the external environment, while the communication among interface and data objects is always done through control objects. Thus, we draw by default associations between interface and control objects, and also between control and data objects.

```
12      assoc1=umlModel2.addAssociation(classInterface, classControl)
13      assoc2=umlModel2.addAssociation(classControl, classData)
```

Finally, for each association actor use case in the initial model, an association is drawn between the corresponding actor and the interface object corresponding to the initial use case.

```
14      ucAssocs=ucd.ownedElement.select(lambda x: x.oclIsKindOf(UML14.Association))
15      ucAssocs.select(lambda assoc: ucd.ownedElement.select(lambda el1:
16          (el1.oclIsKindOf(Actor) or el1.oclIsKindOf(UseCase)) and
17          assoc.connection[0] in el1.association and
18          ucd.ownedElement.select(lambda el2:
19              (el2.oclIsKindOf(Actor) or el2.oclIsKindOf(UseCase))  and
20              assoc.connection[1] in el2.association and
21              model.addAssociation(el1,el2,assoc.name))))
```

One should note that, although OCL is specified in the standard to be a declarative language, the Python lambda functions allow us to use OCL-like idioms in an imperative manner. This enabled us to mix queries with model manipulations, making the scripts shorter and more effective.

We mention that the object diagram obtained in Fig. 7 bottom does not represent the exact output of the transformation. As mentioned in step d. of our functional specification design flow, a refactoring process is performed on the object diagram resulting from the transformation. The refactoring is done manually (and based on the designer's experience) and consists of giving a direction to the associations between objects and also deciding which objects are grouped and/or discarded. For instance, in Fig. 7-bottom, data objects {2.d}, {3.d}, {4.d}, {5.d}, and {6.d} represent the same functionality of the system, so they can be grouped into one single object {5.d}, and the others are discarded.

A second example of mapping between two different models, this time also changing the formalism/language, is the transformation that supports the creation of an object diagram in the UML model, starting from a data flow diagram in the DFD model (Fig. 3, step i.). The transformation is applied to a data flow diagram (Fig. 8). The four modeling concepts that are present in a DFD are: data flows (movement of data in the system), data stores (repositories for data that is not moving), processes (transformation of incoming data flows into outgoing data flows), and external entities (sources or destinations outside the specified system boundary). The end-product of the transformation is the diagram in Fig. 9. The diagram proved to be suited for prototyping purposes and functional testing of the specification. Additionally, it is already a good candidate for being mapped onto a hardware-based platform, because its granularity is at a relatively low level of detail. The model transformation starts by gathering model information using a number of basic queries.

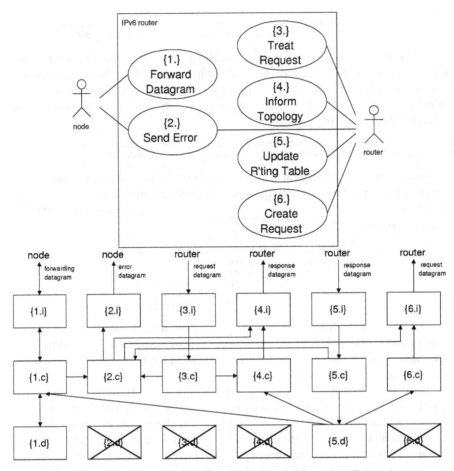

Fig. 7. Transformation of a use case diagram into an object diagram

```
1   dataFlows=dfdModel.ownedElement.select(lambda x:
2       x.oclIsKindOf(DataFlow) and not x.oclIsKindOf(DataStore))
3   externalEntities=topDfd.ownedElement.select(lambda x:
4       x.oclIsKindOf(ExternalEntity))
5   dataStores=topDfd.ownedElement.select(lambda x:
6       x.oclIsKindOf(DataStore))
7   dataTransformations=topDfd.ownedElement.select(lambda x:
8       x.oclIsKindOf(DataTransformation))
```

Next, each DataTransformation and DataStore element in the DFD model is transformed into a class in the UML model.

```
9    dfdModel.ownedElement.select(lambda ts:
10       (ts.oclIsKindOf(DataTransformation) or
11       ts.oclIsKindOf(DataStore)) and
12       classDiag.addClass(name=ts.name))
```

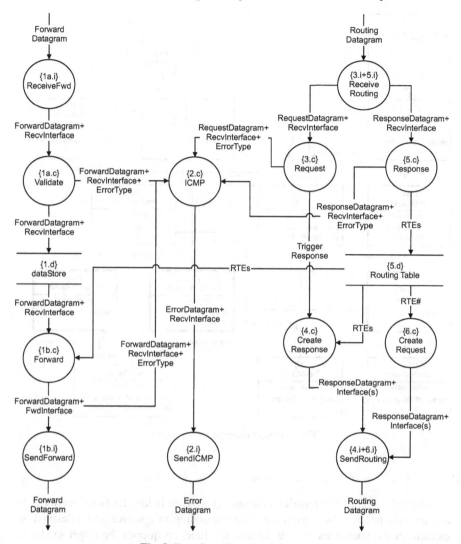

Fig. 8. Data flow diagram of the router

Then we add associations among classes. An association among two classes is obtained from the data flow among the two Data Transformations or Data Stores corresponding to those classes.

```
13    dfdModel.ownedElement.select(lambda f:
14        f.oclIsKindOf(DataFlow) and
15        dfdModel.ownedElement.select(lambda src:
16            src.oclIsKindOf(DataTransformation) and
17            f.connection[0] in src.association and
18            dfdModel.ownedElement.select(lambda dst:
19                dst.oclIsKindOf(DataTransformation) and
20                f.connection[1] in dst.association and
```

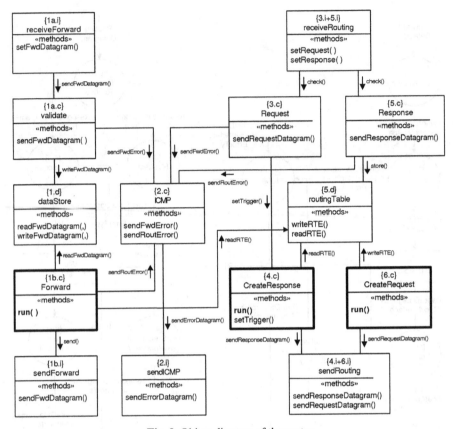

Fig. 9. Object diagram of the router

```
21              addAssoc(src,dst,"send"+string.split(f.name,'+')[0]))))
```

The definition of the function addAssoc() is given below. Its functionality is to add an association with a given name corresponding to a source and a destination element in the source model. To do this, the function queries the target model to select corresponding elements and adds the new association to the target model.

```
1   def addAssoc(source,destination,theName):
2       umlModel.ownedElement.select(lambda src:
3           src.oclIsKindOf(Class) and
4           src.name==source.name and
5           umlModel.ownedElement.select(lambda dest:
6               dest.oclIsKindOf(Class) and
7               dest.name==destination.name and
8               classDiag.addAssociation(src, dest, name=theName+"()")))
9       return 1
```

5 Conclusions

There are many reasons to encourage the use of models and the concept of *everything is a model* in system development. Models are described at the right level of abstraction and precision. Source code is too concrete, natural language is too ambiguous. New languages can easily be explored because of the common structure inherent in all models and metamodels, as given by a common meta-metamodel. This implies that it is simpler to construct a tool to extract semantic information about a design from a model of any language.

In this chapter we have presented a model-driven development method for protocol processing devices and shown how some of the steps in this process can be automated using transformation scripts. Some of the scripts presented are general enough so that they can be reused for similar, or with the necessary adaptation to different types of, applications.

This specific development method is not a general approach valid for any kind of embedded system. It is only intended to work in a particular class of systems that focus on how data is distributed in the system but not how it is stored (e.g. protocol processing applications). However, we think that that is exactly where model-driven methodologies are more valuable. The more specific our application domain, the more difficult it is to find trained developers who are familiar with the application domain and, therefore, the higher profit can be obtained from using a well-defined process and advanced tools to guide and help the developers. In any case, we believe that most of the ideas of the approach can be adapted and used in other application domains and for other implementation platforms.

We also showed that the idea behind MDA can be extended beyond the margins of software development, and can also be applied to hardware specifications. Still, because of the gap between software and hardware specifications, the PIM and PSM respectively, we proposed the use of additional information (i.e. domain information) to bridge the gap between the two. Using domain information during the platform configuration process provided basic support for reuse, and in particular proved to be helpful in platforms built around a library of components. In our opinion the idea brings benefits especially for the development of new products belonging to the same product families.

Furthermore, we have shown what we consider is the best benefit we can achieve from the MDA: we were able to script and automate our development process in the context of a case study of an IPv6 router using our TACO protocol processing architecture. Tools for model transformation are still in their infancy. However, the need is clearly evident, and related work in this field is ongoing. The Generative Model Transformer (GMT) [145] is an open source initiative that wants to fulfill the promise of MDA, and encourage exploration and research related to MDA. GMT sounds very promising, as a joint tool effort could be the missing link between everyday modeling and the software development community.

6 Acknowledgements

Dragos Truscan gratefully acknowledges financial support from the HPY and TES research foundations.

An Integrated Model-Driven Development Environment for Composing and Validating Distributed Real-Time and Embedded Systems*

Gabriele Trombetti[1], Aniruddha Gokhale[1], Douglas C. Schmidt[1], Jesse Greenwald[2], John Hatcliff[2], Georg Jung[2] and Gurdip Singh[2]

[1] Vanderbilt University, Nashville, TN 37235, USA
{gtrombetti,gokhale,schmidt}@dre.vanderbilt.edu
[2] Kansas State University, Manhattan, KS 66506, USA
{jesse,hatcliff,jung,singh}@cis.ksu.edu

Summary. Model-driven development (MDD) tools and processes are increasingly used to develop component middleware and applications for distributed real-time and embedded (DRE) systems, which have stringent requirements for timeliness, correctness, scalability, and maintainability. MDD techniques help developers of DRE systems express application functionality and quality of service (QoS) requirements at a higher level of abstraction than is possible using third-generation programming languages, such as Visual Basic, Java, C++, or C#. The state-of-the-art in MDD for large-scale DRE systems is still maturing, however, and no single MDD environment provides the capabilities needed for effective development of large-scale DRE systems.

This chapter presents three contributions to the study of integrated MDD development and model checking for large-scale DRE systems. First, we describe how our CoSMIC and Cadena MDD toolsuites have been combined to provide an integrated environment that enhances the development and validation of DRE systems. Second, we discuss how we addressed key research issues associated with implementing MDD algorithms for maintaining semantics-preserving transfer of model data between the CoSMIC and Cadena MDD tools. Third, we discuss how we overcame technical difficulties encountered when applying the integrated COSMIC and Cadena for a representative DRE system. Our results show that interoperation between different MDD tools is achievable with the proper choice of communication format, semantics, and the development of a reliable graph diff-merge algorithm. This interoperation helps identify the workflow and capabilities needed for next-generation DRE development environments.

* This work was sponsored in part by NSF ITR #CCR-0325274, NSF ITR #CCR-0312859, DARPA/AFRL #F33615-03-C-4112, and Lockheed Martin.

1 Introduction

Emerging Trends.

Developers of mission-critical distributed real-time and embedded (DRE) systems face a number of challenges, including (1) *alleviating complexity* – both inherent and accidental, (2) *reducing total ownership costs* – both initial and recurring costs, and (3) *ensuring correct end-to-end system behavior* – both functional and quality of service (QoS) requirements. Promising technologies that address various aspects of these challenges are *QoS-enabled component middleware* and *model-driven development* (MDD) with *model checking* capabilities, as we discuss below.

QoS-enabled component middleware. A key enabler in recent successes [366, 391] with DRE systems has been *middleware* [375], which is software that provides reusable services that coordinate how application components are composed and interoperate. QoS-enabled component middleware technologies enhance conventional middleware by offering (1) explicit support for configuring of policies and mechanisms for systemic aspects, such as real-time QoS and security, and (2) a programming model that decouples these systemic aspects from application functionality. These capabilities help address complexity, cost, and correctness by making the QoS-enabled component middleware responsible for (pre)allocating CPU resources, reserving network bandwidth/connections, and monitoring/enforcing the proper use of system resources at run-time to meet DRE system QoS requirements.

Our work on QoS-enabled component middleware has focused on the *Component-Integrated ACE ORB* (CIAO) [454], which is open-source (www.dre.vanderbilt.edu/CIAO) middleware that enhances *The ACE ORB* (TAO) [378] to provide Real-time CORBA [314] enhancements to the CORBA Component Model (CCM) [311]. CIAO's CCM components are interconnected via the following types of standard *ports*:

- *Facets*, which define an interface that accepts point-to-point method invocations from other components and *receptacles*, which indicate a dependency on point-to-point method interfaces provided by other components. A receptacle is connected to a facet to provide *synchronous remote method invocation* communication between a pair of components.
- *Event sources and sinks*, which indicate a willingness to exchange typed messages with one or more components. Event sources can be connected to event sinks for *asynchronous point-to-multipoint message-passing* communication between components.

CIAO abstracts component QoS requirements into metadata that can be specified in a CCM *component assembly* after a component has been implemented [453]. Decoupling the specification of QoS requirements from component implementations greatly simplifies the configuration and evaluation of DRE systems with multiple QoS requirements [452].

Model-driven development (MDD). MDD software processes and tools are a promising approach for addressing the challenges of developing, evolving and validating large-scale DRE system maintenance and modification [309, 246, 163]. The MDD paradigm systematically applies *domain-specific modeling languages* (DSMLs) to direct the understanding, design, construction, deployment, and operation of computing systems, ranging from small-scale real-time and embedded systems to large-scale business applications distributed across an enterprise. MDD tools address complexity, cost, and correctness by helping to automate (1) *analysis* and *verification* of characteristics of system behavior, such as predictability, safety, and security, and (2) *synthesis* of code that is customized for DRE system properties, such as isolation levels of a transaction, recovery strategies to handle various run-time failures, and authentication and authorization strategies modeled at higher levels of abstraction.

Our work on MDD technologies has focused on CoSMIC [153] and Cadena [198]:

- CoSMIC (www.dre.vanderbilt.edu/cosmic) is an open source MDD toolsuite that address key lifecycle development challenges of DRE middleware and applications, such as modeling of DRE system deployment and configuration capabilities [25] and their QoS requirements [260]. The CoSMIC MDD tools enable developers of DRE systems to specify, develop, compose, and integrate application and middleware software.
- Cadena (cadena.projects.cis.ksu.edu) is an MDD toolsuite that supports various aspects of component-based DRE systems, including definition of component interfaces, deployment and configuration capabilities, and configuration of underlying middleware services. In contrast to CoSMIC (which focuses on providing various forms of support for QoS management and configuration of particular component middleware frameworks, such as CIAO [454]), Cadena focuses on providing various forms of visualization and model-level analysis of system configurations, including architectural slicing, simulation, behaviors [84] and integration with multiple CCM implementations including CIAO (C++) and OpenCCM (Java).

Gaps in MDD Technologies for DRE Systems

The QoS-enabled component middleware and MDD toolsuites described above have largely evolved independently in separate R&D communities. Due to the complexity and mission-criticality of large-scale DRE systems, however, there is a need to combine (1) lightweight specification and analysis capabilities that capture functional and QoS specifications for component-based DRE systems with (2) capabilities for QoS management and middleware configuration to achieve an integrated collection of tools that can verify DRE system behavior early in the development lifecycle and enhance reliability. Such an integrated approach can help increase productivity and reduce the risk of mistakes caused by DRE system developers, who would otherwise need to port models from MDD tools manually into representations used by other tools every time a model changes.

This chapter is organized into the following three thrusts that describe our experience developing and evaluating an integrated MDD and analysis environment for QoS-enabled component middleware and DRE systems:

- Section 2 describes how CoSMIC has been combined with Cadena to provide an integrated MDD environment that accelerates the development and validation of DRE systems by addressing key production stages and providing powerful analysis capabilities for tracking errors early in the development lifecycle. This integrated environment foreshadows the types of capabilities needed in future DRE development environments to improve the creation and validation of DRE systems.
- Section 3 discusses R&D issues associated with implementing algorithms for integrating MDD tools for DRE systems, including coping with export–import cycles, storing and transferring supersets and subsets of captured information, merging and preserving information, and addressing future extensibility of the integration.
- Section 4 presents a case study of a robot assembly[3] DRE system that illustrates the technical difficulties encountered when integrating CoSMIC and Cadena tools, highlighting how the choice of an effective communication protocol, data interchange format, and a framework for semantic translators helped enable smoother tool integration.

This paper shows how our integrated CoSMIC and Cadena MDD technologies enable developers to specify DRE system requirements at higher levels of abstraction than those provided by low-level mechanisms, such as conventional third-generation programming languages, operating systems, and middleware platforms. Our case study shows how these higher-level specifications express constraints that are transformed into running lower-level code that preserves and enforces the semantics of the specifications. These "correct by construction" MDD techniques are in contrast to the "construct by correction" techniques commonly used today by post-construction tools, such as compilers, source-level debuggers, and XML descriptor validators.

2 An Overview of the CoSMIC and Cadena MDD Environments

This section presents an overview of the CoSMIC and Cadena MDD toolsuites, highlighting the capabilities of each tool in the DRE system case study presented in Section 4.

2.1 Overview of CoSMIC

The *Component Synthesis using Model Integrated Computing* (CoSMIC) [153] toolsuite is an integrated collection of MDD tools that address the key lifecycle challenges of middleware and applications in DRE systems. Figure 1 illustrates CoSMIC's MDD tools that address deployment and configuration lifecycle challenges of

---

[3] "*Assembly*" is used here as in "*assembly line*," which is a different use of the term than the concept of a "*CCM component assembly*" mentioned above.

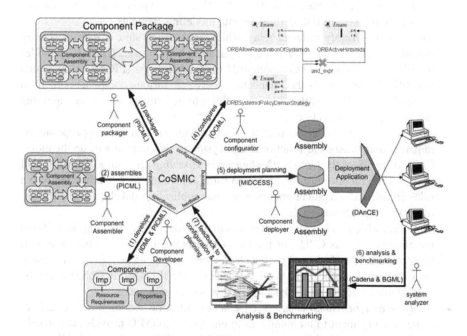

Fig. 1. The CoSMIC MDD toolsuite

DRE systems. CoSMIC supports modeling of DRE system deployment and configuration capabilities, their QoS requirements, and QoS adaptation policies used for DRE system QoS management. Its MDD tools are implemented via *domain-specific modeling languages* (DSMLs) developed using the Generic Modeling Environment (GME) [269], which is a configurable toolkit for creating domain-specific modeling and program synthesis environments. CoSMIC uses GME to define the modeling paradigms[4] for each stage of its tool chain. CoSMIC ensures that the rules of construction – and the models constructed according to these rules – can evolve together over time. Each CoSMIC tool synthesizes XML-based metadata that is used by the CIAO QoS-enabled component middleware [454] described in Section 1. In particular, CoSMIC supports CIAO's implementation of the OMG's Deployment and Configuration (D&C) specification [316] and provides the following capabilities shown in Figure 1:

- *Specification and implementation*, which enables application functionality specification, partitioning, and implementation as components. CoSMIC provides the *Interface Definition Modeling Language* (IDML), which is a DSML that can be

---

[4] A *modeling paradigm* defines the syntax and semantics of a DSML [246].

used to specify component definitions. IDML also provides an importer that can transform preexisting IDL definitions into modeling elements.

- *Component assembly and packaging*, which can bundle a suite of software binary modules and metadata representing application components. CoSMIC provides the *Platform Independent Component Modeling Language* (PICML) [25], which is a DSML that models the connections between various components to form assemblies. PICML enables these assemblies to be composed into packages that can be shipped to target nodes.
- *Configuration*, which allows packages to be customized with the appropriate parameters that satisfy the functional and systemic requirements of applications. CoSMIC provides the *Options Configuration Modeling Language* (OCML) [260] to model the middleware configuration rules, which are then synthesized into a rules engine and graphical environment that application developers use to configure the middleware.
- *Planning*, which makes appropriate deployment decisions including identifying the entities, such as CPUs, of the target environment where the packages will be deployed. The *Model Integrated Deployment and Configuration Environment for Composable Software Systems* (MIDCESS) [153] DSML in CoSMIC can be used to model deployment plans for DRE system components.
- *Analysis and benchmarking*, which enables run-time reconfiguration and resource management to maintain end-to-end QoS. CoSMIC provides the *Benchmark Generation Modeling Language* (BGML) [260], which models DRE systems' QoS requirements and synthesizes empirical benchmarking testsuites. Additional analysis capability is achieved via integration with external tools, as described in Sect. 3.
- *Deployment*, which triggers the installed binaries and brings the application to a ready state. CoSMIC is integrated with a run-time framework called *DAnCE* (Deployment And Configuration Engine), which implements the OMG's D&C specification and can be used to model the deployment of DRE system packages according to precisely specified plans.

The CoSMIC toolsuite also provides the capability to interwork with other MDA and analysis tools, such as Cadena [198] (Sect. 2.2), and aspect model weavers, such as C-SAW [159]. The integration of CoSMIC with Cadena is the focus of Sect. 3.

The core DSML provided by CoSMIC is PICML, which figures prominently in the integration of CoSMIC and Cadena described in Sect. 3. PICML allows developers to model packages of components into assemblies that can then be configured and deployed appropriately. Configuration and deployment concerns cross-cut assemblies and systems. These cross-cutting concerns are captured by the different aspects of PICML. During the configuration and deployment process, multiple concerns captured in the format of metadata in the component development process are woven together by PICML, as shown in Fig. 2.

PICML allows the specification of the component-based deployment and configuration concerns outlined above by allowing users to model them as elements in a GME paradigm. Additional constraints are defined via GME's *Object Constraint*

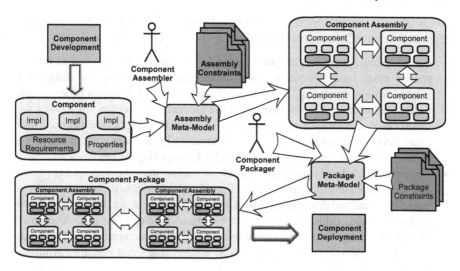

Fig. 2. The PICML Architecture

Language (OCL) [319] facilities to ensure that the models built using PICML are semantically valid. PICML's constraints check that the *static semantics* (i.e., the semantics that are required to be present at design-time) are not violated. For example, at design-time, PICML can enforce the CCM constraint that only ports with the same interface or event type can be connected together.

The generative capabilities of PICML enable the separation of cross-cutting deployment and configuration concerns, which are represented in the form of XML metadata and whose semantics can be validated automatically. The DAnCE run-time framework provided by CIAO is then responsible for weaving these concerns into component middleware and applications. The model interpreters in PICML target the configuration and deployment of DRE components for CIAO. We chose CIAO as our initial focus since it is QoS-enabled component middleware designed to meet the requirements of DRE systems. As other component middleware platforms (such as J2EE and .NET) mature and become suitable for DRE systems, we will (1) enhance CoSMIC so it supports Platform Independent Models (PIMs) and then (2) include the necessary patterns and policies to map these PIMs to Platform Specific Models (PSMs) for various component middleware platforms.

2.2 Overview of Cadena

The Cadena MDD toolsuite was built to provide a variety of forms of support for developing component-based distributed systems, including component interface specification via CCM IDL, construction of component assemblies using multiple system views, and generation of configuration and deployment XML data. A primary focus of work on Cadena has been to investigate a number of different structural and behavioral analysis techniques for component-based systems. The following is a summary of the capabilities Cadena provides to develop these types of systems:

- A collection of lightweight specification forms that can be attached to IDL to specify mode variable domains, intra-component dependencies, and component state-transition semantics. These forms have a natural refinement order so that useful feedback can be obtained with little annotation effort, and increasing the precision of annotation yields more precise analysis. Cadena specifications also allow developers to specify the same information in different ways, achieving a form of *checkable redundancy* that is useful for exposing design flaws.
- Dependency analysis capabilities that allow tracing inter/intra-component event and data dependencies, as well as algorithms for synthesizing dependency-based real-time and distribution aspect information. In essence, these dependency analyses provide different forms of architectural "slicing" that help developers identify dependencies among components for system understanding and for guiding component integration tasks, such as establishing event handling priorities and locking policies.
- A novel model-checking infrastructure (based on the Bogor model-checking framework [102]) dedicated to event-based inter-component communication via real-time middleware enables system design models (derived from component IDL, component assembly descriptions, and annotations) to be model-checked for global system properties. This enables developers to perform simple simulations of their systems to reason about, e.g., high-level mode transitions, and to check system designs against crucial system requirements phrased in the form of invariants, event/state ordering constraints, and component interaction protocols phrased as regular expressions or temporal logic formulas.
- A component assembly framework supporting a variety of visualization and programming tools for developing component connections, such as hiding or changing the color of component and connections that satisfy user-defined queries of component and connection attributes.
- A component deployment facility that auto-generates XML deployment and configuration information.

Cadena is implemented as a set of plug-ins to IBM's Eclipse IDE, which facilities an uninterrupted workflow in which component interface and architectural design can be performed in the same tool as the component implementation (e.g., using the sophisticated Java development environment of Eclipse). Implementing Cadena as an Eclipse plug-in also simplifies the incorporation of analysis tools, such as the Bogor model checking engine.

In the integration with CoSMIC, we focus on using Cadena's system configuration dependency analysis facilities. Even with small systems of ~20–30 components, relationships between components and component dependencies are often hard to determine from visual inspections of textual or graphical component assembly views. Component-based DRE system's can often have well over 1000 components [391, 366], and engineers at Boeing and Lockheed Martin with whom we collaborate have identified the development of automated support for component dependency analysis and visualization as a high priority.

Given a component library and component assembly description (along with the optional *Cadena property specification* file described below), Cadena's dependency module builds a *port dependence graph* PDG = (N,E) where each node $n \in N$ is a component/port pair $(c.p)$. Edges (i.e., dependencies) between PDG nodes arise from two sources: *inter-component dependencies* corresponding to port connections specified in component assembly descriptions and *intra-component dependencies* captured by CPS declarations in component property specifications. Cadena provides the following analysis capabilities for dependency graphs:

- **Forward and backward slices**, which detects the components that are affected by (forward) or affect (backward) a particular component or port. Note that slices can be computed at two levels of granularity: (1) a *component-level forward slice* finds all components that are affected by a given component vs. (2) a *port-level forward slice* finds all components that are affected by a port.
- **Mode-based slicing and chopping**, which leverages specifications of dependencies that capture the fact that some dependencies are only active when a component is in a particular mode. This enables more precise views of system dependencies that reflect only those dependencies that are active when the system is in a particular state. In either case, slices are constructed by considering the reachability of components in the port dependency graph described above.
- **Chopping**, which highlights all the ports and components that lie on a path between two given components/ports. Intuitively, given two components C_1 and C_2, a chop based on C_1 and C_2 finds all paths between C_1 and C_2 by intersecting the forward slice from C_1 and the backward slice from C_2.
- **Mode-based slicing and chopping**, which leverages specifications of dependencies that capture the fact that some dependencies are only active when a component is in a particular mode. This enables more precise views of system dependencies that reflect only those dependencies that are active when the system is in a particular state.
- **Cycle detection**, which detects cycles along a series of event connections in the dependency graph. In certain computational models, event cycles may indicate design flaws.

Figure 3 shows a portion of Cadena's interface for issuing dependency-related queries over the graphical structure of a system configuration. The displayed pull-down menu allows developers to select from among the dependency analysis capabilities described above. The results of an analysis are displayed in the tool by changing the color of relevant components, ports, and connections. For example, the results of a forward slice are displayed by rendering in gray all the components, ports, and connections affected by the given component.

Cadena decouples various aspects of modeling by requiring that these cross-cutting concerns be captured in the following types of files located in a common project space:

338   Gabriele Trombetti et al.

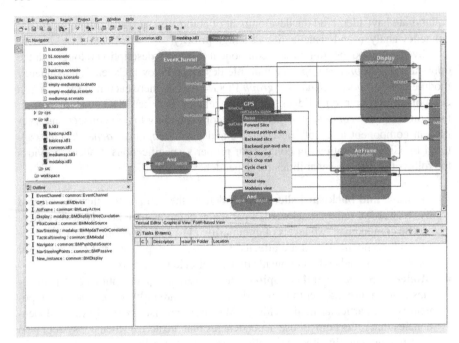

Fig. 3. Cadena Dependency Analysis Interface

- **IDL3 file** `*.idl`, which contains OMG's standard interface description language metadata describing components and their interfaces.
- **Scenario file** (`*.scenario`), which describes an assembly of interconnected CCM components, including the value of their configuration properties. Cadena provides a graphical visualizer, a text editor, and a form view editor to manipulate `*.scenario` files. The equivalent of a scenario file in CoSMIC's PICML is the CCM component *assembly* view, which enables graphical editing of properties.
- **Profile file** (`*.profile`), which acts as a scenario format definition and validation system by defining the type of the properties that can be associated with different components and/or connections. Cadena supports three types for properties: STRING, INT, and BOOLEAN. There is no equivalent for the `.profile` file on PICML, which is another motivation for integrating CoSMIC and Cadena.
- **CPS (Cadena Property Specification) file** (`*.cps`), which contains lightweight semantic annotations to capture abstract semantics that can be leveraged by Cadena's analysis facilities. For example, in DRE systems, a component's behavior is often organized into a collection of *modes* (e.g., a component can be in an active or inactive mode, or in a normal or fault-recovery mode, etc.). Modes can be used to represent the abstract state of a component. A component's mode state is often implemented as a variable with an enumerated type that includes each of the mode states, and a modal component typically varies its behavior by branching to different implementations based on the cur-

rent state of its mode variable. The `*.cps` file provides a means to capture the modes within a component and the internal interconnections within each component that depend on the mode. Information in this file includes conditional behavior, such as a set of inputs of a component having an effect on a set of outputs only when that component is in a particular mode/state. Cadena `*.cps` files can also include simple state transition systems – finite state automata that describe the abstract control flow of actions on a component's interface (e.g., method calls and event publishing) as well as transitions on mode state variables. This information can be used to generate finite state models suitable for simulation or state-space exploration (model checking) of system designs. There is no equivalent for the `*.cps` file in PICML or in CCM.

3 Approaches to Integrating MDD Tools for DRE Systems

Due to the magnitude and complexity of the DRE problem space, no single MDD toolsuite yet provides solutions to all challenges of large-scale DRE system development. For example, CoSMIC did not initially provide tools for analyzing and validating the functional correctness and QoS properties of DRE systems. Likewise, Cadena did not initially provide capabilities for modeling elements and procedures meaningful for important stages of the development of DRE systems, such as installation, packaging, and deployment. What we therefore required was an *integrated* MDD toolsuite that developers of DRE systems could use to compose, configure, and deploy their applications end-to-end to help (1) identify bugs early in the lifecycle, (2) reduce total development costs, (3) decrease time to market, and (4) increase the reliability of DRE systems.

Integrating CoSMIC and Cadena required that (1) software components and associated modeling artifacts could be manipulated via any of their MDD tools, (2) changes to the components and modeling artifacts made by one tool could be reflected in other tools, where applicable, (3) any tool capturing unique information (i.e., not captured by any other tool) required special support to preserve this information correctly, and (4) all the pieces of information captured by each integrated MDD tool could be treated as parts of a single *global project*. Achieving this level of integration was hard since different MDD tools captured different sets of properties. For example, certain CoSMIC tools captured certain parts of a project, whereas other parts are captured by certain Cadena tools.[5]

The remainder of this section describes key challenges that arose when integrating CoSMIC and Cadena and discusses our solutions to resolve these challenges. These challenges are discussed in order of increasing complexity, where a subsequent challenge could be resolved only when the previous challenge was addressed. Section 4 then presents a case study of a robot assembly application that illustrates our experiences applying the integrated CoSMIC and Cadena toolsuites to a representative DRE system.

---

[5] The subset of the project captured by one tool is referred as the tool's *model document*.

Challenge 1: Identifying an Inter-tool Communication Model

Context. Different MDD tools provide different capabilities, e.g., browsable models and visual modeling of deploy requirements vs. rate-monotonic schedulability analysis and model checking. Large-scale DRE systems, however, may require the use of multiple MDD tools. What is needed is a communication model for interoperability among various MDD tools. An important goal of our work was therefore to transfer model documents back and forth between CoSMIC and Cadena, while minimizing user intervention.

Problems. Since Cosmic and Cadena were developed independently for several years they had little/nothing in common with respect to the type of model documents they used. Moreover, under many aspects these tools do not even capture the same type of information, e.g., the `*.scenario` and `*.IDL3` model documents of Cadena appear to have equivalent representation in CoSMIC, but there are subtle differences between the model documents. Likewise, the `*.profile`, `*.cor`, and `*.cps` model documents have no equivalent in CoSMIC. Similarly, 80% of the information in the CoSMIC model documents have no direct equivalent in Cadena.

Many standard interoperability solutions available for tool interoperability cater to a specific concern. For example, the *Analysis Interchange Format* (AIF) [245] provides interoperability by promoting seamless exchange of only analysis data among tools. Similarly, the *Hybrid Systems Interchange Format* (HSIF) [328] provides model exchanges for those systems that are modeled as hybrid systems, but does not support exchanging analysis information. In many cases, therefore, an interchange format might not support a feature of a tool. Hence, a decision to use such an interchange format would preclude the use of that feature, thereby decreasing the value of the tool. It is also undesirable to create point-to-point solutions since they do not scale as the number of tools with different capability increases. It is therefore necessary to develop a framework that allows seamless interoperability between desired features among tools without creating point-to-point solutions.

Solution approach → An open tool integration framework. Our approach for integrating CoSMIC and Cadena is based on the *Open Tool Integration Framework* (OTIF) [217] developed by the Institute for Software Integrated Systems (ISIS) at Vanderbilt University. OTIF consists of a backplane, an integration repository, application-specific tool adapters, and semantic translators. The backplane provides a communication and subscription/notification mechanism for other tools. The backplane also acts as a common integration repository for the data stored in a canonical syntactical format, but which may have different semantics. OTIF's tool integration repository stores data in a format understood by at least one of the communicating tools. Custom semantic translators and tool adapters can then be plugged into the OTIF backplane and used to (1) automatically convert data in a format understood by one tool into data for another tool and (2) communicate between the tools.

A novel aspect of OTIF is its ability to integrate MDD tools that were not initially intended to interoperate, which is why we selected it for our CoSMIC↔Cadena integration. Figure 4 illustrates the interworking of CoSMIC and Cadena via the OTIF backplane. The OTIF backplane supports standard CORBA [315] communication capabilities using TAO [378], thereby allowing distributed interoperability, as well as

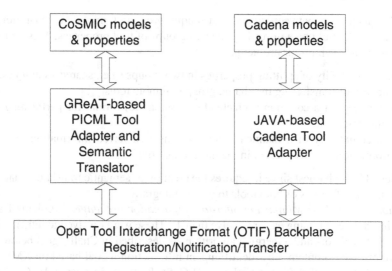

Fig. 4. CoSMIC↔Cadena Interoperability via OTIF

platform-independent interoperability. Custom tool-specific adapters must be written by developers who wish to export desired tool-specific data to the backplane. Other tools that want to interoperate with this tool must provide an adapter that converts data on the backplane to the format it desires. We have developed appropriate tool adapters for CoSMIC and Cadena, along with semantic translators that help these two toolsuites interoperate via the OTIF backplane.

Challenge 2: Devising Effective Communication Protocols and Data Interchange Formats

Context. An important concern for tool interoperability is ensuring that the tools understand each other's data formats and their semantics. What is needed is a mechanism that allows exporting and importing tool-specific data using a tool integration framework, such as OTIF.

Problems. There is often minimal overlap between tools, other than some common aspects pertaining to DRE systems. For example, the common information in CoSMIC and Cadena is restricted to the fact that both tools are tailored to support DRE systems built using the CORBA Component Model (CCM) [311]. These commonalities are localized in certain artifacts, such as the IDL descriptions and assembly information of CCM components.

The same problem seen from another perspective is that when tools are integrated, they capture and contain in their model document two types of properties: (1) *shared* properties, i.e., properties being captured also by other tools being integrated, and (2) *unique* properties, i.e., properties not captured by any of the other tools being integrated. Shared properties must often be transferred to other tools to synchronize the state amongst the tools. In contrast, unique properties cannot reasonably be transferred to another tool since they would not be understood.

The distinction between shared and unique properties implies a separation of concerns that should be enforced by the two groups of tool properties. This, in turn, implies the following four problems:

(1) The complexity of splitting properties in two groups (i.e., shared vs unique).
(2) The task of transferring the shared group to remote tools.
(3) The choice of a common syntactical (not semantic) format for performing the communication.
(4) The complexity of semantically merging the transferred information into the information already present in the destination tool.

Problem 4 is the hardest since it requires the creation of semantic translators that can understand the formats of both tools to enable integration.

Solution approach → *Minimizing inter-tool information exchange.* Problems 1 and 4 are interrelated (1 being easier to solve than 4). These were resolved together using semantic translators and a merging algorithm, as described in Challenge 3 below.

We resolved problem 3 by identifying an information model based on XML for the data that is needed for the Cadena and CoSMIC tools. For example, CoSMIC generates information captured by the `*.scenario` model document in the form of XML descriptors and then creates a plug-in to import this XML format into Cadena. The reverse direction for this format incorporates the changes suggested by the Cadena analysis tools into the CoSMIC models.

Problem 2 is more complex than problem 3, so we resolved it using OTIF, which allowed us to work at a significantly higher level of abstraction. For example, OTIF relieved us from many low-level details, such as the complexity of handling a communication among multiple tools. Each tool can be started and shut down at any time, can run in multiple instances, and might need to search for other tools and (re)establish connections to them at any time.

To function properly, OTIF requires support for document creation, persistence, and navigation to make data interchange seamless. OTIF thus supports a *Universal Data Model* (UDM) [94] interface to access and manipulate data on the OTIF backplane. UDM provides a development process and set of tools that generate C++ interfaces from data structures described using UML class diagrams. These interfaces and the underlying C++ libraries enable convenient programmatic access and automatically configured persistence services for data structures described via UML diagrams. We leverage these UDM capabilities for the data exchange between CoSMIC and Cadena.

The modeling paradigms, such as CoSMIC's PICML, built using GME were explicitly developed to expose a UDM interface. The Eclipse framework used by Cadena, however, does not support UDM natively, so we created a UML class diagram that described the Cadena models.

Challenge 3: Achieving Lossless Semantic Transfers of Data

Context. For any successful tool interoperability comprising data interchange, it is important that the exchanged data be transferred without loss of essential semantic information.

Problems. Lossless semantic transfers of tool-specific data are hard since different tools address different aspects of DRE systems and therefore deal with different types of data, with their own semantics, and representation. It is therefore possible (and common) for mismatches to arise between data supported by individual tools and how they are managed by the tool. For example, we outline the differences between CoSMIC and Cadena formats below:

- Cadena `*.scenario` files support properties on connections (such as event sources/sinks and invoke connections), whereas CoSMIC's PICML does not.
- Both PICML and Cadena support CCM connections types, such as *emit, publish*, and *invoke*, but PICML provides specialized connector types for each of these in its CCM component assembly metamodel, whereas Cadena infers the connector types from the port types.
- PICML supports QoS requirements on connections that are passed to the deployment run-time for validity checks and potential optimizations at deployment stage, whereas Cadena does not support this capability.
- PICML provides a specialized connector for a publisher/subscriber connection involving multiple publishers and multiple receivers, whereas Cadena uses multiple connections for this case.
- Cadena supports the `STRING, INT`, and `BOOLEAN` attribute types, whereas PICML supports `Boolean, Byte, ShortInteger, LongInteger, Real-Number, String, GenericObject, GenericValueObject, Generic-Value, TypeEncoding`, and `TypeKind`.

Given these constraints, it is straightforward to create simple lossy export and import algorithms that would lose information not captured by one toolsuite vs. the other. This design, however, would force users to reenter information twice for each toolsuite, thereby increasing effort and the chance of inconsistencies in information maintained across the tools. What was desired, instead, is a *write-once* approach, whereby once information was entered using either CoSMIC or Cadena tools, the data transfer algorithm would preserve the data and its semantics for all but a few exceptionally rare circumstances.

One approach to handle these issues is to merge the different data handled by individual tools to form a superset that is maintained by the OTIF backplane. Transferring the complete set of information between the tools is not maintainable, however, since whenever a feature should be added in *any one* of the tools being integrated, the set of information being transferred across *all* tools would change. At that point, *all* the semantic translators that convert documents from/to *any* two tools would need to be updated to support the enlarged information set.

Solution approach → A graph-based diff-merge algorithm. Our solution uses information captured by individual MDD tools, focusing on the features that can map between the tools, and applying graph transformation algorithms to attain the desired interoperability. The information we transferred was contained in the CCM component assembly view of CoSMIC/PICML and in the `*.scenario` and `*.profile` files from Cadena, as well as the information conveyed in IDL3 files.

In the transformation algorithm, the information from PICML is matched against the corresponding information in Cadena. Differences are detected and then, depending on the direction of communication (PICML→Cadena or Cadena→PICML), such differences are imported into the destination tool, replacing earlier information that was outdated. This approach resembles a diff-merge algorithm (web.umr. edu/~gnudoc/single/emacs1934/ediff.html), thought it is performed on data from MDD tools that were stored as a graph of interconnected information rather than sequential text. We therefore call our approach a *graph* diff-merge algorithm.

The graph diff-merge algorithm for exporting PICML data to Cadena follows the steps described below (the appendix on p. 361 of this book explains the CCM terminology used in these steps).

(1) Every CCM component assembly generates a separate *.scenario file. The full path name of the assembly from the *RootFolder* is encapsulated in a property called *PICML_pathname*, which is stored by Cadena and eventually returned to PICML unchanged. This property is needed to match the same source CCM component assembly on the PICML side when reimporting.
(2) CCM component assembly-level properties are transferred to Cadena as scenario-level properties if the type is supported by Cadena, otherwise they are retained on the PICML side.
(3) All the *PublishConnectors* are checked and the newly created ones are flagged with a unique *ConnectorID*, which is in a *DeployRequirement* having a magic name that is disregarded by the DAnCE D&C run-time system provided by CIAO.
(4) All *PublishConnectors* are checked for the presence of a *Requirement* with another magic name called *CadenaProperties*. If found, all the properties encapsulated inside such requirement are output as properties on the *EventSource-to-Sink* corresponding connection in Cadena, which compensates for the lack of properties on connectors on the PICML side.
(5) All *Components* that have an output *Emit* or an *Invocation* connection are checked for a property with a magic name: *CadenaEIProperties* (where EI stands for "Emit–Invoke"). This property contains a string that is the dump of an XML file containing multiple properties for each *Receptacle-to-Facet* or *Event Source-to-Sink Emit* connection output from that component. The embedded file is parsed and the contained information is extracted and sent to Cadena, which accounts for the lack of properties on emit and invoke connections on the PICML side.
(6) All component instances are browsed and their name and type are transferred to Cadena. The attached properties are transferred to Cadena only if they are a type supported by Cadena, otherwise they are retained on the PICML side. For all components, each connection to a remote port or to a *PublishConnector* is passed to Cadena.

At this point, the XML file containing the information about the scenario (and implicitly about the profile) is sent to the OTIF backplane. On the Cadena side it is fetched, de-encapsulated from XML, and dumped to disk, possibly overwriting a preexisting version.

During Cadena export to PICML, the transfer across the OTIF backplane acts in the reverse way. The key points of the graph diff-merge algorithm on the PICML side are as follows:

(1) Using the *PICML_pathname* information, the same CCM component assembly of the export is matched so that the modifications can be performed in the correct place.

(2) Based on the names of the component instance, the components are matched.

(3) Based on the *ConnectorIDs*, the *PublishConnectors* are matched. On the PICML side, the components and the *PublishConnectors* that have no match on the Cadena side are considered deleted by the Cadena user and thus get destroyed on the PICML side. The properties and requirement that only refer to those are also destroyed.

(4) The *Components* and *PublishConnectors* on the Cadena side that are unmatched on the PICML side are considered newly created and thus created on the PICML side.

(5) All the emit and invoke connections at the PICML side are deleted, and are recreated new from the information on the Cadena side.

(6) All the properties on PICML components and at the component assembly level are browsed. For those where the type could have been passed to the Cadena side, a match to the properties on the Cadena side is attempted. If the match fails, those PICML properties are considered to be deleted by the Cadena user, so they are destroyed on the PICML side.

(7) For all properties on *Components* on the Cadena side, a match is attempted on the PICML side. If the match succeeds, the value is updated on the PICML side, otherwise this is considered a new property created by the Cadena user so a new property gets created on the PICML side.

(8) Steps 6 and 7 are repeated again for properties on *PublishConnectors*, with the difference that the match is attempted inside the *Requirement* called *CadenaProperties*, if it exists. The newly created properties are also created there (if a requirement with such a name does not exist, it is created and attached to the *PublishConnector*).

(9) Steps 6 and 7 are also repeated again for the properties on *EmitConnector* and *PublishConnector*, but this time the match is attempted on the XML content of the magic property *CadenaEIProperties* on the component that has the outgoing emit or invoke connection, which is created if needed.

To perform these steps for the two directions of communication, we used the GReAT (Graph Rewriting And Transformation) [243] tool. GReAT is a GME-based MDD tool that can be used to visually define graph transformation among networks of objects that are accessible with UDM. GReAT shortened our development time significantly since it is much more readable and maintainable than using a third-generation programming language, such as C++ or Java. Both GME project files and

XML files whose schema can be defined with a UML diagram can be accessed via UDM.

A GReAT transformation can be run interpretatively during development and debugging. It can also be used to generate C++ header and implementation files that can be compiled for a release version of the transformation. The current version of the CoSMIC↔Cadena import/export transformation contains more than 2000 elements (graph pattern nodes) and 13500 lines of C++ code. Figure 4 illustrates the architecture of this transformation process, where a bidirectional *GReAT-based tool adapter and semantic translator* converts PICML assemblies to/from XML files conforming to the adopted interchange schema, which was chosen to conform to the semantics of Cadena *.scenario and *.profile files. The schema, known to the OTIF backplane, is used to read and validate the XML file upon arrival on the backplane. At every upload of a new interchange XML file onto the backplane, the tool adapters are notified of the availability of such new CCM component assembly and are prompted for the download. On the Cadena side, a simpler *Java-based Cadena tool adapter* converts the XML to *.scenario and *.profile files and vice versa. Our graph diff-merge algorithm is activated during the backplane-to-PICML import and is implemented inside the *GReAT-based PICML tool adapter and semantic translator*.

4 Demonstrating Integrated CoSMIC↔Cadena Capabilities via a Robot Assembly Case Study

This section describes a case study of a robot assembly application we developed using CoSMIC and Cadena in conjunction with colleagues at Lockheed Martin. This application is representative of DRE systems in the process control domain, i.e., it defines an *assembly line* with robots creating various types of *goods*, which in our case study are wrist watches assembled by robots. We describe the robot assembly application below to illustrate the benefits of integrating and applying the CoSMIC and Cadena MDD toolsuites, as described in Sect. 2 and 3. In particular, this case study illustrates how developers of the robot assembly application required multiple MDD tools, each providing different capabilities, such as configuration, deployment, schedulability analysis, and model checking. The source code and integrated MDD tools for this example are available in the CIAO release from www.dre.vanderbilt.edu/CIAO.

4.1 Structure and Functionality of the Robot Assembly Application

Figure 5 illustrates the five core components in the robot assembly application: ManagementWorkInstruction, WatchSettingManager, HumanMachineInterface, PalletConveyorManager, and RobotManager, all of which are implemented as CCM components using CIAO. These individual CCM components can be interconnected to form *CCM component assemblies* and ultimately deployed using DAnCE to create complete applications.

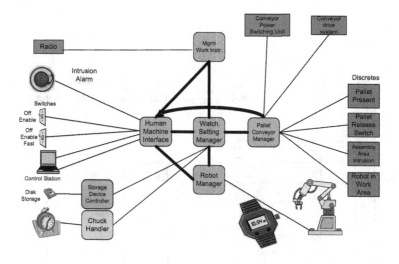

Fig. 5. Robot assembly model

Figure 6 depicts a sequence diagram for the robot assembly production process. The ManagementWorkInstruction and HumanMachineInterface components interact with humans, whereas the PalletConveyorManager and RobotManager components interact with the pallet moving and assembling tools' hardware devices, respectively. The normal operation of the robot assembly application involves the following steps:

(1) The ManagementWorkInstruction asks for a watch to be produced by sending an event to the WatchSettingManager.
(2) The WatchSettingManager emits an event to the HumanMachineInterface asking to validate the order. The HumanMachineInterface accepts the order by invoking an operation on a CCM facet belonging to the WatchSettingManager.
(3) The WatchSettingManager uses a different event to notify the ManagementWorkInstruction that the order was accepted and then displays the work on the HumanMachineInterface.
(4) The WatchSettingManager emits an event to the PalletConveyorManager to move the pallet into position. The PalletConveyorManager then responds with another event acknowledging the status of good positioning on the pallet. This event includes an enumerated type indicating status, such as acceptance, rejection, completion, failure, and/or cancellation.
(5) The WatchSettingManager again emits an event to the HumanMachineInterface asking for confirmation to perform a production step. The HumanMachineInterface accepts by invoking an operation on a facet.

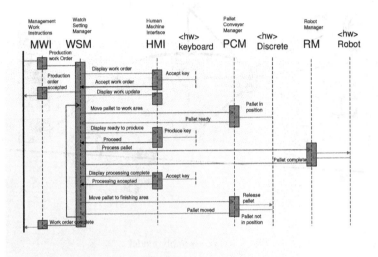

Fig. 6. Robot assembly production sequence

(6) The WatchSettingManager emits an event to the RobotManager asking it to process the pallet. The RobotManager performs the job and then responds via an event acknowledging the success (or failure) of the assembling operation.

(7) The WatchSettingManager displays the completed work to HumanMachineInterface via an event. The HumanMachineInterface validates the work via a facet operation call (same as in step 1).

(8) The WatchSettingManager sends an event asking the PalletConveyorManager to move the pallet out of the working area and into a finishing area. The PalletConveyorManager notifies the status of the operation back to the WatchSettingManager with the acknowledgement event already discussed. Steps 2–7 can be repeated if there are additional pallets to process.

(9) The WatchSettingManager sends an event to the ManagementWorkInstruction notifying it that the requested job has been completed.

4.2 Key Capabilities Provided by CoSMIC and Cadena Integration for the Robot Assembly Application

Section 4.1 described the structure and functionality of the robot assembly application. We now illustrate the key challenges encountered when integrating the CoSMIC and Cadena MDD toolsuites and applying them to the robot assembly case study.

Capability 1: Choosing Appropriate Communication Mechanisms.

Developers of large-scale component-based DRE systems must determine which communication mechanisms their components should use to interact. A key design decision is whether to use CCM *facets and receptacles*, which can perform point-to-point synchronous operation invocations between components, or *event sources and sinks*, which can exchange typed messages asynchronously with one or more components. Applying an MDD tool like PICML (Sect. 2.1) can help developers reason more effectively about which communication mechanism to select. Below, we demonstrate how our MDD tools help developers make better design choices.

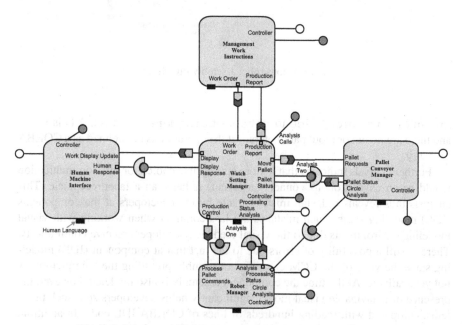

Fig. 7. Robot assembly CCM component assembly Visio drawing

Figure 7 shows a Visio drawing of the robot assembly component interaction. We used this informal drawing to guide our subsequent formal modeling and analysis of the robot assembly application. In particular, we created a model of the CCM component assembly in PICML and then used Cadena to analze, validate, and refine this model. After validation by Cadena, we used the CoSMIC toolsuite to deploy, configure, and run the robot assembly application. Figure 8 (without the connection indicated by the arrow) represents the PICML model that captures the application represented by the Visio drawing in Fig. 7.

Unlike the informal Visio drawing, the PICML model is semantically navigable, down to the data types and events exchanged by every operation and event communication. By inspecting the PICML model, we can quickly spot design fallacies and/or vulnerabilities, e.g., the return value of the facet invocation for the response of

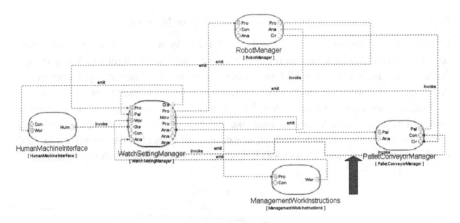

Fig. 8. Erroneous robot assembly PICML model

`HumanMachineInterface` to `WatchSettingManager` (Sect. 4.1) is void and there are no out or inout parameters, yet the operation is not defined as a CORBA oneway.

Further analysis indicates that a more appropriate choice for this communication would be an asynchronous connection (event) rather than a facet/receptacle. This analysis thus reveals a design mistake made by the developers at the components (IDL) modeling stage. Such mistakes are less common when working with visual modeling environments due to the visual feedback developers receive continuously. There is still a possibility of errors due to the fact that at component (IDL) modeling stage the view of the CCM component assembly providing the "big picture" is not yet available. At the time the component assembly is also modeled, however, the presence of a navigable visual model significantly helps developers spot such problems, compared with reading hundreds of lines of CORBA IDL code. In addition, refinement cycles for correcting such errors in the IDL and then adjusting the component assembly accordingly are much faster to perform with a visual modeler than when dealing with low-level source code.

Capability 2: Detecting Type Mismatches at Design-time vs. Run-time

As mentioned in Sect. 1, a key goal of MDD is achieving "correct by construction" programs. In particular, MDD tools should allow only correct choices and/or detect maximum number of errors at design-time rather than run-time. Constraining a correct choice or performing an early detection of mistakes significantly reduces the time needed for fixes.

To evaluate how effectively our integrated CoSMIC and Cadena tools described in Sect. 3 work in the context of our robot assembly application, we deliberately tried to introduce a mistake in our component assembly by connecting an additional port to a destination port of the wrong type. This mistake is detected by PICML's constraint checker because the two ends are not of the same type, and thus disallowed by the PICML paradigm. It would not be desirable, however, to have trivial human mistakes detected by only one tool (e.g., PICML), as this would defer the detection significantly when users work for long period of time on other tool(s) (e.g., Cadena) before going back to PICML.

Cadena (described in Sect. 2.2) also immediately detects a set of potential human mistakes, including connections with mismatched endpoints and mismatched type for properties on components. These checks are performed both at modeling time and model-import time and can be verified, e.g., by importing into Cadena an erroneous model produced by a tool that has weaker validation support. In our case, PICML is (currently) the only other tool, so testing this feature required manually disabling PICML's constraint checker, manual creation of an invalid connection, and then exporting the result to Cadena.

For this example, we chose to connect the `analysis` receptacle of the `Watch-SettingManager` to the `controller` facet of `PalletConveyorManager`, as shown in Fig. 8 with a block arrow. Figure 9 shows how Cadena detected the wrong connection, and printed an error message. Early (possibly immediate) detection of user mistakes, even when limited to simple ones, is important since it reduces the work that must be undone to roll back to a valid project state when a mistake is detected.

Capability 3: Analysis of Component Assemblies.

Another important suite of capabilities that we have developed is Cadena's collection of assembly graph analyses and architectural slicing facilities. These range from simple detection of cyclic call-chains and event feedbacks to more sophisticated forms of graph reachability and dependency analysis that also include information about certain aspects of component state.

We now consider the use of the cycle detection mechanism for the robot model example. Since all robot assembly components only interact with the `Watch-SettingManager`, any possible cycle must pass through that component. Right clicking on the `WatchSettingManager` component in the graphical scenario view of Cadena and selecting the "cycle check" feature highlights two components of the assembly – the `HumanMachineInterface` and the `WatchSetting-Manager` – which form a cycle, as shown in Fig. 10. The cycle detection stops after the first detection, which is why only two components are highlighted (darker shade) in the figure. If we disconnect those two components and repeat the cycle check, however, other components will be highlighted. The `WatchSettingManager` affects and is affected by every other component, so eventually every component is in the downstream path of every other component in the component assembly.

Since we have at least one cycle we cannot be certain that deadlocks do not occur. Deadlocks for such a model are thus "implementation defined," which means that they might or might not be avoided with a more sophisticated implementation, e.g., one that handles assumptions that cannot be (or are not) modeled. The system therefore cannot be validated from a modeling perspective. Examining the production sequence diagram in Fig. 6 above, however, clearly shows that no deadlock can

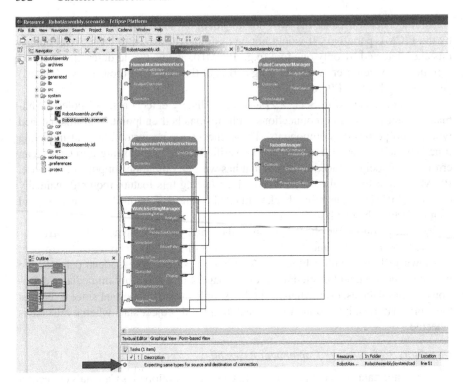

Fig. 9. Error detected by robot assembly Cadena model

occur, at least during the normal production use case. This information clashes with the analysis from Cadena, due to the fact that we have not yet specified modal information in our components, i.e., component operational modes specifying interactions between input and output ports of the same component (intra-component interactions). Specifying modal information allows a more precise detection of cycles and potential deadlocks.

For the semantics shown in Fig. 6 production sequence diagram, the most components can remain stateless. At least two components require state, however, the `WatchSettingManager` and the `HumanMachineInterface`. For the `WatchSettingManager`, the sequence diagram in Fig. 6 implicitly defines the following seven states: (1) *WaitingWorkOrder*, (2) *WaitingAcceptWorkOrder*, (3) *WaitingPalletReady*, (4) *WaitingProceed*, (5) *WaitingPalletComplete*, (6) *WaitingPalletMoved*, and (7) *WaitingProcessingAccepted*. In each state, no more than one input port affects an output port, and not all the output ports are affected (in facts, no more than three are affected for each mode). The other input and output ports behave as if they were disconnected.

For the `HumanMachineInterface`, we need to specify that a *DisplayWorkUpdate* cannot trigger an *AcceptWorkOrder*. Otherwise, a feedback cycle with

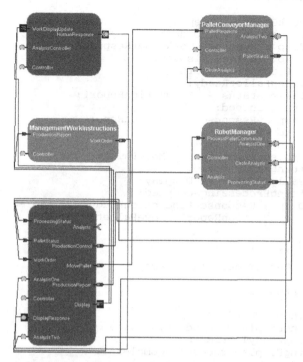

Fig. 10. Robot assembly modeless cycle detection in Cadena

the WatchSettingManager will arise. At least two states are needed, though it is better to specify all four semantically detectable states: (1) *WaitingNewWorkOrder*, (2) *WaitingDisplayWorkUpdate*, (3) *WaitingReadyToProduce*, and (4) *WaitingDisplayProcessingComplete*.

The behaviors of the WatchSettingManager and the HumanMachine-Interface components outlined above can be captured in the Cadena property specification (*.cps) file shown below:

```
module RobotAssembly {
  component WatchSettingManager {
    mode status of {
        WaitingWorkOrder,
        WaitingAcceptWorkOrder,
        WaitingPalletReady,
        WaitingProceed,
        WaitingPalletComplete,
        WaitingPalletMoved,
        WaitingProcessingAccepted
    }
    init status.WaitingWorkOrder;

    dependencydefault: none;
    dependencies {
      case status of {
        WaitingWorkOrder:
```

```
         WorkOrder -> Display;
       WaitingAcceptWorkOrder:
         DisplayResponse.WorkOrderResponse ->
           MovePallet, Display,
           ProductionReport;
       WaitingPalletReady:
         PalletStatus -> ProductionReport;
       WaitingProceed:
         DisplayResponse.ProductionReport ->
           MovePallet;
       WaitingPalletComplete:
         ProcessingStatus -> MovePallet;
       WaitingPalletMoved:
         PalletStatus -> Display;
       WaitingProcessingAccepted:
         DisplayResponse.ProductionReadyResponse ->
           ProductionReport, MovePallet;
     }
   }
 }
 component HumanMachineInterface
 {
   mode status of
   {
     WaitingNewWorkOrder,
     WaitingDisplayWorkUpdate,
     WaitingReadyToProduce,
     WaitingDisplayProcessingComplete
   }
   init status.WaitingNewWorkOrder;
   dependencydefault: none;
   dependencies {
     case status of {
       WaitingNewWorkOrder:
         WorkDisplayUpdate ->
           HumanResponse.WorkOrderResponse;
       WaitingDisplayWorkUpdate:
         WorkDisplayUpdate -> ;
       WaitingReadyToProduce:
         WorkDisplayUpdate ->
           HumanResponse.ProductionReadyResponse;
       WaitingDisplayProcessingComplete:
         WorkDisplayUpdate ->
           HumanResponse.PalletInspectionResponse;
     }
   }
 }
}
```

The Cadena *.cps file shown above sets our modal specifications for the robot assembly project. The remainder of this section refers to the modal view of the scenario illustrated in Fig. 11. The two components for which we have defined the states must be set to a globally consistent state, i.e., we cannot set the WatchSettingManager in the *WaitingPalletComplete* state while the HumanMachineInterface is in the *WaitingNewWorkOrder* state. We therefore set the WatchSettingManager in the WaitingAcceptWorkOrder state and the

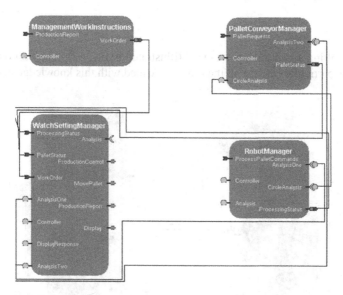

Fig. 11. Robot assembly: modal view in Cadena

HumanMachineInterface in the WaitingDisplayWorkUpdate state. As a result, only the connections that belong to the current mode will be shown (see Fig. 11). Since the cycle analysis will detect any cycles in any of the modes, the current model can be analyzed to detect deadlocks.

For contrast, we also show a variation of the robot assembly CCM component assembly that is in fact not deadlock-proof and hence cannot be validated. This variation consists of adding the connection from the WatchSettingManger/-Analysis receptacle to the RobotManager/Analysis facet.[6] We do not have any semantic or behavioral specifications for these analysis ports. We must therefore assume that (1) operation calls on the facets can affect any analysis receptacle on the same component and (2) this behavior can happen in any mode of the three components. To reflect this scenario we add the following lines for the Watch-SettingManager into the *.cps file shown below:

```
...
dependencies {
  AnalysisOne.CallingBackTwo
            -> Analysis.CicrleCallOne,
               Analysis.CallingBackOne;
  AnalysisTwo.CircleCallThree
            -> Analysis.CicrleCallOne,
               Analysis.CallingBackOne;
  case status of
```

---

[6] Figure 7 shows that the following two CCM ports were already connected: (1) Robot-Manager/CircleAnalysis receptacle to PalletConveyorManager/Circle-Analysis facet and (2) PalletConveyorManager/AnalysisTwo receptacle to WatchSettingManager/AnalysisTwo facet.

```
    . . .
}
```

The resulting scenario shows a cycle (illustrated in Fig. 12) in at least one mode (and in this particular case, in all the modes). Armed with this knowledge, therefore,

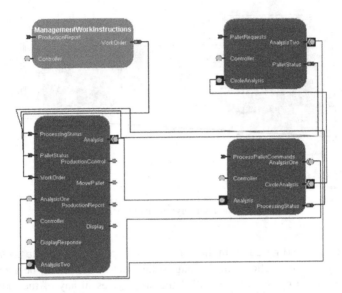

Fig. 12. Robot assembly: Cadena model after circle analysis

any deadlock avoidance must be at the implementation level, i.e., this model cannot be validated against deadlocks without further knowledge of the semantics at the modal level.

4.3 Summary of the Robot Assembly Case Study

This section used a robot assembly application case study we developed with our colleagues at Lockheed Martin to showcase our integration of CoSMIC and Cadena. The case study shows how semantic validation of models can help detect problems earlier in the software lifecycle, e.g., immediately after the planning of the interfaces, but before implementing the business logic. In our experience, early detection of defects yielded fewer code revisions, lower development costs, and shorter time to market. This "correct by construction" paradigm and the ongoing checking for human mistakes made by CoSMIC and Cadena helped ensure proper execution in mission-critical contexts, where run-time error detection and debugging alone was insufficient.

In particular, the CoSMIC PICML MDD tool helped developers formally define CCM component assemblies, while allowing better visualization and easier navigation that can be useful to improve design, spot errors more easily, and in general work at a higher level of abstraction and be more productive. The Cadena environment, likewise, provided powerful analysis and validation features, which were synergistic with those of PICML. In Cadena, a relatively straightforward declarative language was used to define high-level behavioral specifications for components. These specifications were then used for analysis and validation purposes, such as component-dependencies traversal and ensuring the robot assembly application was free of deadlocks.

5 Related Work

MDD technologies are used in a variety of contexts and domains. For example, the OMG's Model-Driven Architecture (MDA) [135] and Microsoft's Software Factories [163] focus mainly on enterprise business applications. Other MDD technologies, such as model-integrated computing (MIC) [415], focus on embedded systems. More recently, MDD technologies are aligning [307] to add QoS capabilities necessary to support DRE systems in domains ranging from aerospace [7] to telecommunications [300] and industrial process control [356]. This section describes and compares our research on MDD technologies with related work.

Our work on MDD technologies extends earlier work on MIC [246, 196, 277, 160] that focused on modeling and synthesizing embedded software. Examples of MIC technology used today include GME [269] and Ptolemy [53] (used primarily in the real-time and embedded domain) and MDA [309] based on UML [310] and XML [3] (which have been used primarily in the business domain). Previous efforts using MIC technologies for QoS adaptation have been applied to embedded systems comprising digital signal processors or signal detection systems [296, 5], which have a small number of fairly static QoS requirements. In contrast, our research on integrating CoSMIC and Cadena focuses on enhancing and applying MIC technologies at a much broader level, i.e., modeling and controlling much larger-scale DRE systems with multi-dimensional simultaneous QoS requirements.

Other related MDD tools are the Virginia Embedded System Toolkit (VEST) [403] and Automatic Integration of Reusable Embedded Systems (AIRES) [257]. VEST is an embedded system composition tool based on GME [269] that (1) enables the composition of reliable and configurable systems from COTS component libraries and (2) checks whether certain real-time, memory, power, and cost constraints of real-time and embedded applications are satisfied. AIRES provides the means to map design-time models of component composition with real-time requirements to run-time models weaving timing and scheduling attributes within the run-time models. Although VEST and AIRES provide modeling and analysis tools for real-time scheduling and resource usage, they have not been applied to QoS-enabled component middleware, which is characterized by complex interactions between the components, their containers, and the provisioned services, and across distributed components via real-time event communication or request/response. Moreover, our research on the integration of CoSMIC and Cadena involves whole-system global analysis of large-scale DRE system for end-to-end timing constraints, as well as configuration and deployment.

Another project aimed at tool integration is the Open Tool Integration Framework (OTIF) [217], which was developed by the Institute for Software Integrated Systems (ISIS) at Vanderbilt University. As opposed to our approach – where most features of Cadena and CoSMIC were developed separately and with no initial idea of subsequent integration – OTIF explicitly provides a framework for integrating tools developed as part of the DARPA MoBIES project [328]. The MoBIES workflows are fairly complex and allow interoperations in multiple directions among the tools. These flows are not lossless in most cases, however, so they were able to obtain seamless roundtrip interoperability in only one case, i.e., between the *ESML* and *OEP_Configuration* formats, inside the ESML workflow.

OTIF provides a communication framework with facilities for storing various versions of the same set of data written in different formats, subscription/notify mechanism, and automatic triggering of application-specific translators when certain data format's are submitted to the backplane (data repository). OTIF requires, however, that the actual (application-specific) semantic translators and the (application-specific) tool adapters for actually performing the communication and the translation be provided by the user. Our work with CoSMIC and Cadena helps improve upon earlier uses of OTIF by selecting interchange formats and transformation semantics that can accomplish more effective roundtrip interoperability and lossless communication between the two MDD development environments.

6 Concluding Remarks

Model-driven development (MDD) of software engineering processes is emerging as an effective paradigm for addressing key challenges of distributed real-time and embedded (DRE) systems. MDD is a software development paradigm that systematically applies domain-specific modeling languages to engineer computing systems. It is therefore a key step toward converting the *art of programming* into an *engineering process* that will industrialize the software industry [163].

This chapter showed how we have integrated *CoSMIC*, which is an MDD toolsuite consisting of modeling, analysis, and synthesis tools that address key lifecycle challenges of component-based DRE systems with *Cadena*, which is an MDD toolsuite for modeling and model checking component-based DRE systems. We demonstrated how CoSMIC can leverage Cadena/Bogor's model-checking and verification capabilities to raise the reliability of component-based DRE systems significantly, while also reducing development time and effort. We also showed how the capabilities provided by CoSMIC and Cadena are complementary and can help developers of component-based DRE system middleware and applications view and analyze models from different perspectives.

The novelty of our approach focuses on exchanging a minimal set of data between interacting tools, namely the common subset of properties captured by the tools. Modifications on a project made by CoSMIC tools can thus be transferred to

Cadena tools and merged into the model document of the destination tools and vice versa. Modifications performed on properties captured uniquely by CoSMIC tools need not be transferred to Cadena tools and vice versa. Depending on the tools being integrated, the merging of modifications into a tool's model document can be performed automatically by semantic translators (which keep state in this case) or tool adapters (which can access the internal state of the tool). In either case, our general approach can be applied to simplify the integration of various MDD tools, e.g., to provide model checking, schedulability, and stability analysis.

Section 3 describes a graph diff-merge algorithm that transfers modifications into a destination tool's model document and semantic translators that convert between the formats understood by various CoSMIC and Cadena MDD tools. Graph transformation is used to define algorithms for semantic translation and merging directly at the metamodel level, i.e., at a higher level of abstraction than provided by third-generation programming languages. This approach (1) reduces the time needed to develop semantic translators, compared with manually writing a backtracking engine to match entire graphs, (2) reduces sporadic and hard-to-track errors that stem from manually manipulating pointers, allocating resources, and handling exceptions, and (3) increases the readability and maintainability of the algorithms, compared with conventional handwritten code in third-generation languages.

The lessons learned by applying our integrated CoSMIC and Cadena toolsuite to the robot assembly case study described in Sect. 4 illustrated that:

- Not every MDD tool offers the same capabilities, but a collection of these tools is needed to develop DRE systems, which is why interoperability between the tools is necessary. For example, CoSMIC and Cadena have different modeling capabilities and validation functionalities that we combined to provide a broader range of capabilities for developers of our robot assembly application.
- Although partial, user-assisted interoperability is easier to implement, it does not prevent human mistakes when exporting model documents from one tool and importing them into another. It is therefore important to automate the communication process as much as possible to ensure consistency. For example, our use of the Open Tool Integration Framework (OTIF) [217] helped minimize the number of steps needed for users to transfer the robot assembly project between CoSMIC and Cadena MDD tools. We also carefully crafted the graph diff-merge algorithm to avoid manual replication of information.
- Bidirectional communication among MDD tools is an effective way to enable users to edit models locally on whichever tool is in use, while maintaining the ability to transfer changes to other tools automatically, thus enhancing consistency. For example, when developing the communication between CoSMIC and Cadena, we allowed developers to use the tools in any semantically valid order, and did not constrain the actions that could be performed while working with compatible tools.
- When achieving tool integration, key issues to consider are the communication model, data interchange format, and algorithms for lossless data transforms. Our CoSMIC↔Cadena integration effort focused on these three points and applied

tools that could help reduce our development time. For example, we used OTIF to provide communication features, document storage on the backplane, and automatic notification of availability of new documents to connected tools. We used XML/UDM to interchange the syntactic and semantic formats of CoSMIC and Cadena model documents. We used GReAT for our graph diff-merge algorithms to reduce development time and detect/merge variations of graph-based data formats. These tools allowed us to complete our robot assembly development and validation tasks correctly in a relatively short time.

- Complex transformation algorithms become more manageable when working at the meta-level. In particular, we found that several hundred well-structured graphical transformation rules were faster to write and easier to read and maintain than thousands of lines of equivalent C++ code. We leveraged the GReAT tool to visually define these graph rules and transformations.

- To define transformations at the meta-level requires access to the metamodels (represented as graph structures) of both the source and destination semantic formats. If any of there metamodels are not available, an alternative is to use an XML format defined with a UML diagram (i.e., the *metamodel*) acting as a proxy for the source or destination format. For example, the metamodel of the Cadena internal document format was not available, so we used GME to define an XML representation of it in UML. We could then use GReAT to define transformations between the CoSMIC metamodel and the newly defined XML format, the latter acting as a proxy for the Cadena format.

- The message flow in our robot assembly case study is largely asynchronous and most communication is performed via events, though some callbacks are performed via invocations on facet operations. It is hard to recognize this message flow from the production sequence diagram in Fig. 6. However, MDD tools, such as PICML in CoSMIC and the Cadena's Scenario graphical view, can show which communications are performed through event emissions and which are operation invocation. MDD tools also enable more efficient browsing through components and interfaces to indicate visually which data types are exchanged.

- Behavioral specifications of components can be used to perform dependency checks and stability analysis in a component-based distributed application. Underspecifying the behavior of such components might prevent a complete validation, as happened with the connection of the circle analysis port in our robot assembly application.

- When solving new problems, the time needed to learn new MDD tools appropriate for the solution must be considered. For example, we used GME interpreters, GReAT, UDM, and OTIF for our robot assembly application. Acquiring expertise with these tools occupied roughly a third of the total development time. It is therefore essential to factor the time and effort needed to learn multiple MDD tools to avoid underestimating overall development costs.

Appendix: CCM as Captured in CoSMIC and Cadena

This appendix explains key CCM concepts and terminology, and then shows how they are supported by CoSMIC and Cadena when diverging from each other or from the CCM specifications.

CCM components model units of software and contain *ports* for communicating with other components. Ports are divided into (1) asynchronous event-based ports (*EventSources* and *EventSinks*) and (2) synchronous operation-based ports (*Facets* and *Receptacles*), which can be connected together with *Invoke* connections (for operation-based ports) and *Emit* or *Publish* connections (for event-based ports).

Publish connections originating from an *EventSource* need to pass through a *PublishConnector* element in PICML before reaching any *EventSink* port, whereas Cadena has no concept of *PublishConnector*. *Emit* connections can only connect one *EventSource* to one *EventSink*, while *Publish* connections can be many-to-many. The explicit distinction between *Publish* and *Emit* connections, however, only exists in PICML, whereas in Cadena both are mapped to a generic *EventSource-to-Sink* connection.

Properties are name/type/value triplets that can belong to *Components* or to *Requirements* in PICML, whereas in Cadena they can belong to *Components* and to *Connections* between ports. *Requirements* (a.k.a. *Deploy Requirements*, PICML only) are contained in *Components* and *PublishConnectors* and serve to hold constraints (defined as a set of *Properties*) specifying where a *Component* or *Publish-Connector* can be deployed.

A PICML *Assembly* holds *Components*, connections between their ports, *PublishConnectors*, *Requirements* associated to *Components* or *PublishConnectors*, and *Properties* associated to *Components*. The correspondent of an *Assembly* in Cadena is the *Scenario*, which contains *Components*, *Connections* between their ports, and *Properties* associated to these *Components* and *Connections*. In PICML and Cadena there can be multiple *Assemblies/Scenarios* distinguished by a different path from a so-called *RootFolder*.

Acknowledgements

We would like to acknowledge our collaborators Sylvester Fernandez, Dave Bailey, Chris Andrews, Bob Parkhill, and Theckla Louchios from Lockheed Martin, Eagan and Dallas, for their help with the CoSMIC↔Cadena integration.

A Model-Driven Technique for Development of Embedded Systems Based on the DEVS Formalism

Gabriel A. Wainer, Ezequiel Glinsky, and Peter MacSween

Department of Systems and Computer Engineering, Carleton University,
4456 Mackenzie Building, 1125 Colonel By Drive, Ottawa, ON, K1S 5B6, Canada
gwainer@sce.carleton.ca

Summary. The development of embedded systems with real-time constraints has received the thorough study of the software engineering community in the last 20 years. Despite these efforts, most existing methods are still hard to scale up for large systems, or they require expensive testing efforts. We propose a model-driven method to develop this kind of application based on DEVS, a formal technique originally created for modeling and simulation of discrete-event systems. This approach combines the advantages of a simulation-based approach with the rigor of a formal methodology. We will explain how to use this framework to incrementally develop embedded applications, and to seamlessly integrate simulation models with hardware components. The use of this methodology shortens the development cycle and reduces its cost, improving quality and reliability of the final product. Our approach does not impose any order in the deployment of the actual hardware components, providing flexibility to the overall process. The use of DEVS improves reliability (in terms of logical correctness and timing), enables model reuse, and permits reducing development and testing times for the overall process.

1 Introduction

Embedded real-time software construction has usually posed interesting challenges due to the complexity of the tasks executed. Most methods are either hard to scale up for large systems, or require a difficult testing effort with no guarantee for bug-free software products. Formal methods have showed promising results; nevertheless, they are difficult to apply when the complexity of the system under development scales up. Instead, systems engineers have often relied on the use of modeling and simulation (M&S) techniques in order to make system development tasks manageable. Construction of system models and their analysis through simulation reduces both end costs and risks, while enhancing system capabilities and improving the quality of the final products. M&S techniques let users experiment with "virtual" systems, allowing them to explore changes, and test dynamic conditions in a risk-free environment. This is a useful approach, moreover, considering that testing under actual operating conditions may be impractical and in some cases impossible.

M&S methodologies and tools have provided means for cost-effective validity analysis for real-time embedded systems [381, 268]. M&S-based testing is a popular technique, which is widely used for the early stages of a project; however, when the development tasks switch towards the target environment, the early models and simulation artifacts are often abandoned. We propose a model-driven framework to develop embedded systems based on the DEVS (Discrete Event systems Specification) formalism [465]. DEVS provides a formal foundation to M&S that proved to be successful in different complex systems. This approach combines the advantages of a simulation-based approach with the rigor of a formal methodology. Another advantage of using DEVS is that different existing techniques (bond graphs, cellular automata, partial differential equations, queuing models, etc.) have been successfully transformed into DEVS models. DEVS theory has evolved since the early 1970s, providing a generic framework to model discrete-event systems. Many existing techniques that have been widely used for the development of embedded and real-time systems, have also been mapped into DEVS models. Many state-based approaches, such as Verilog [255], VHDL [286], Petri nets [228] and timed Petri nets, timed automata [148], state charts [45] and finite state machines [466] have their DEVS equivalents. This permits sharing information at the level of the model, and different submodels can be specified using different techniques, while keeping independence at the level of the execution engine. In this way, we count with a mathematical framework that can be used to describe different modeling techniques and prove properties about general aspects of the system, while having a general method for sharing model information using different approaches, and being able to apply the right technique to each part of the application development process.

CD++ [449] is M&S software that implements DEVS theory with extensions to support real-time model execution [150]. CD++ was used as the base for our development, building on previous research focused on real-time applications with hardware-in-the-loop [273]. We will discuss how to use this framework to incrementally develop embedded applications, and to seamlessly integrate simulation models with hardware components. Initially, we develop models entirely in CD++, and we replace them with hardware surrogates at later stages of the process. Our approach does not impose any order in the deployment of the actual hardware components, providing flexibility to the overall process. The use of DEVS improves reliability (in terms of logical correctness and timing), enables model reuse, and permits reducing development and testing times for the overall process. Consequently, the development cycle is shortened, its cost reduced, and quality and reliability of the final product is improved.

2 Background

The DEVS formalism [465] is M&S framework based on dynamic systems theory. DEVS is an increasingly accepted framework for understanding and supporting the activities of modeling and simulation. It is a sound formal framework based on generic dynamic systems, including well-defined coupling of components, hierarchical, modular construction, discrete-event approximation of continuous system, and support for repository reuse. A real system modeled with DEVS is described as a composite of submodels, each of them being behavioral (**atomic**) or structural (**coupled**). A DEVS atomic model is informally described in Fig. 1.

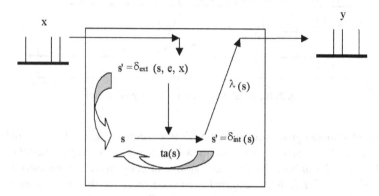

Fig. 1. Informal description of an atomic model

A DEVS atomic model is formally described as:

$$M = \langle\, X, S, Y, \delta_{int}, \delta_{ext}, \lambda, ta \,\rangle$$

Each atomic model is seen as having an interface consisting of *input* (X) and *output* (Y) *ports*. Every *state* (S) in the model is associated with a *time advance* (*ta*) function, which determines the duration of the state. The model will be in the state s during *ta* time units. The time advance is a function in the domain of the real positive numbers (including zero and infinity). Once this time is consumed, an internal transition is triggered. This involves two actions: first, the model execution results are spread through the model's output ports by activating the *output function* (λ). Then, the *internal transition function* (δ_{int}) is fired, producing a state change. Input external events are collected in the input ports, which have room for only one input, and are cleared immediately after being processed. The input ports will only receive input events for the current event time, and the external transition function (δ_{ext}) specifies how to react to those inputs.

A DEVS coupled model is composed of several atomic or coupled submodels, as seen in Fig. 2.

Coupled models are defined as a set of basic components (atomic or coupled), which are interconnected through the model's interfaces. The model's coupling defines how to convert the outputs of a model into inputs for the others, and to inputs/outputs to the exterior of the model. A DEVS coupled model is formally defined by:

$$CM = \langle\, X, Y, D, \{M_d \mid d \in D\}, EIC, EOC, IC, select \,\rangle$$

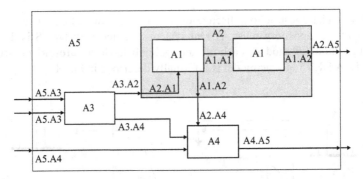

Fig. 2. Informal description of a coupled model

A coupled model groups several DEVS's into a compound model that can be regarded, due to the *closure property*, as a new DEVS model. A coupled model is composed by a set (D) of basic models (i.e., atomic or coupled) interconnected through their interfaces (X, Y). When external events are received, the coupled model has to redirect the inputs to one or more components. Similarly, when a component produces an output, it may have to map it as an input to another component, or as an output of the coupled model itself. Mapping between ports is defined by the *EIC*, *EOC*, and *IC* sets, which define how to convert the outputs of a model into inputs for others. *EIC* defines how external inputs are routed to the subcomponents; *EOC* defines how outputs of internal subcomponents are routed outside the coupled model; and *IC* takes care of the internal couplings. *select* is the tiebreaker function, which defines an order over the components.

3 The CD++ Toolkit

CD++ [449] is a modeling tool that was defined using the specifications presented in the previous section, and the basic execution techniques introduced in [465]. The toolkit includes facilities to build DEVS models. DEVS atomic models can be programmed and incorporated into a class hierarchy programmed in C++. Coupled models can be defined using a built-in specification language. CD++ is built as a class hierarchy of models related to processing entities. DEVS atomic models can be programmed and incorporated into the *Model* basic class hierarchy using C++. A new atomic model is created as a new class that inherits from the *Atomic* base class. *Atomic* is an abstract class that declares a model's API and defines some service functions the user can use to write the model.

Defining models in C++ provides the users with flexibility to define the model's behavior. Nevertheless, a non-experienced user can have difficulties in defining models using this approach. Graphical specification also improves the interaction with stakeholders and users during system specification, while allowing the modeler to think about the problem in a more abstract way. Therefore, we have used an extended graphical notation to allow defining atomic model's behavior [450, 60].

Each model is defined by a unique identifier, and states are represented by vertices (bubbles) in a directed graph. Each bubble includes an identifier and a state lifetime.

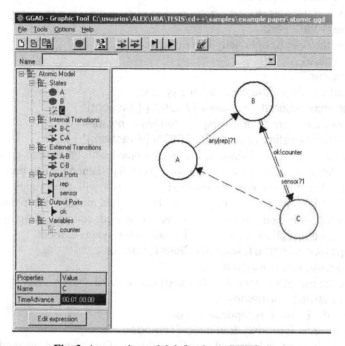

Fig. 3. An atomic model defined as a DEVS graph

Figure 3 shows a simple atomic model defined in CD++ using this notation. The model includes three states: A, B and C. Dashed lines represent internal transitions, while full lines define external transitions. In this case, if the model is in state A and it receives an external event through the *rep* input port (shown in the left panel), the *any* function is evaluated. If the result of this evaluation is 1, the model changes to state B. While in B, the model waits, its lifetime to be consumed. It then executes the output function, which will send the value of the intermediate state variable *counter* through the output port *ok*. After that, the internal transition function executes, and the model changes to state C.

Each of the elements in the graphical notation is converted into an analytical representation. This notation can be used both to check validity of the model and to run these models in CD++ [450].

[modelname] defines the atomic or coupled model name, which will be used subsequently. Model states are declared as: state: state1 state2 ... .

States are associated to a time advance value. This attribute is initialized with the name of the object and the list of valid attributes for that object, as follows: state1 : time-expression.

One of the states must be declared as the initial state of the model: initial: state-name. Then, I/O ports are declared as follows:

in : inport1 inport2 ...

out : outport1 outport2 ...

Temporary variables are declared by:

var : var1 var2 var3 ...

In addition, they can be optionally initialized as:

var1 : value1

var2 : value2

The internal transitions use the following syntax:

int : source destination [outport!value]* ({ (action;)* })?

External transitions are defined using the following notation:

ext : source destination EXPRESSION ({ (action;)* })?

Once an atomic model is defined, it can be combined with others into a multicomponent model using a specification language specially defined for this purpose. The user must define the coupling information, and CD++ will generate an analytical specification that can be used for execution. The coupled model at the higher level is always named [top]. Four properties must be configured: components, output ports, input ports, and links between models. The following syntax is used:

Components: name1[@atomicClass1] name2 ...

Out: portname1 portname2 ...

enumerate the model's output ports (optional clause), and

In: portname1 portname2 ...

enumerates the input ports (optional clause).

Link: source[@model] destination[@model]

describes the internal and external coupling scheme. If the name of the model is not included, the default will be the coupled model currently being defined.

Figure 4 shows a sample coupled model describing an Ethernet switch presented in [451].

The top model here is composed of three coupled models (*server1*, *server2*, and *client*) and one atomic component (*eth*, an instance of *EthernetSwitch*). *client* is composed of two atomic components (*clientNet* and *hsclient*) and one coupled component (*WSclient*). The input and output ports define the model's interface, and the links between components define the model's coupling. The input ports in the top model (e.g., *eth_enable*, *eth_disable*, *hss1_start*) are used to activate and deactivate the Ethernet switch, server nodes, and client. The output ports (e.g., *status*, *packets*) are used to inform the progress of the system.

Models developed in CD++ are independent of the engine in charge of driving their execution. At present, CD++ is able to execute models in single processor, parallel, or real-time mode. The execution engine uses the model's specifications, and it builds one object to control each component in the model hierarchy. These objects communicate using message passing, and they are called **processors**. There are different types of processors according to the activity they carry out: **simulators** are specialized in atomic models (executing its associated functions), **coordinators**

```
components:  server1    server2 client    eth@EthernetSwitch
in: eth_enable  eth_disable
in: hss1_start  hss1_stop  hss2_start  hss2_stop
...
out: packets    status
link: server_out@serv1  in1@eth
link: out1@eth    server_in@serv1
...
[eth]
delay:  00:00:01:000
node_1: 1    node_2: 2    node_3: 3

[client]
components: WSclient    clientNet@Network
components: hsclient@HSClient
in:  hs_start    hs_stop   client_in
out:  client_out
link: hs_start    start@hsclient
...
```

Fig. 4. Definition of the Ethernet DEVS coupled model in CD++

manage coupled models, and the **root coordinator** controls global execution aspects (time, start/stop, interfacing with the environment, etc.).

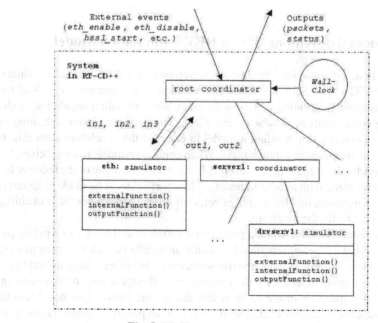

Fig. 5. RT-CD++ execution scheme

RT-CD++ [150] uses the real-time clock to trigger the processing of discrete events in the system. Thus, the same models used for simulation can be later used for execution in real time. Figure 5 outlines the processor's hierarchy generated by RT-CD++ to execute the model. The root coordinator created at the top level manages the interaction with the experimental frame that tests the model receiving inputs (via *eth_enable*, *eth_disable*, *hss1_start*, etc.), and returns outputs (via *status* and *packets*). The root coordinator exchanges messages with its children. Coordinators are created to handle the coupled models *server1*, *server2*, *client*, etc. Simulators are created to handle the components *eth* (which inherits from the atomic *EthernetSwitch*), *clientNet* (from atomic *Network*), *hsclient* (from atomic *HSClient*), *drvserv1* (from atomic *Driver*), etc.

Model execution is triggered by the real-time clock using the time of the external events. When the root coordinator receives a new event, it forwards the message to the corresponding processor. Timing constraints (deadlines) can be associated to each external event. When the processing of an event is completed, the root coordinator checks if the deadline has been met. In this way, we can obtain performance metrics (number of missed deadlines, worst-case response time).

We thoroughly tested the execution performance of RT-CD++ [151], using DEVStone, a synthetic benchmark we created to study the performance of DEVS-based simulators [152]. We conducted performance analysis using DEVStone to study the overhead of the real-time engine in CD++. These studies showed that models with more than 50 components execute with an overhead below 2%. For larger models (over 200 components), the overhead incurred by the tool is below 3%, which is reasonable considering the complexity of the tools.

4 Incremental development of a DEVS Simulation Model

In this section, we show how to develop incrementally a model based on simple components. The application executes in a simulated environment (i.e., all of the components remain executing in a virtual world). We have built a simulation model integrating components of a radar system [282]. The first stage in the definition of this example consisted of building a model to examine the synchronization effects between radar receivers and transmitters. When using a scanning radar receiver, the interception of radar signals can be severely limited if the scan rate of the receiver becomes synchronized with a radar transmitter. Every effort must be made to generate a receiver scan pattern that limits this effect, as it seriously degrades the probability of intercept (POI) for the receiver.

Synchronization occurs when a particular transmitter sends out radar pulses periodically, with the receiver scheduled to scan periodically in such a manner that the receiver is never "listening" when the transmitter is transmitting. This can lead to the transmitter *not* being detected by the receiver, even though it may be transmitting. The sequential operation of the receiver that defines the tuned frequency, listening time, azimuth, and beam width are specified by a "scan pattern". Receivers can communicate with each other, with each receiver notifying the other receivers about radar transmitters that have been detected. Each receiver is connected to a simple communications bus, and it maintains a tracking table containing all the information about the currently known transmitters. In order to analyze the behavior or this system, we built a DEVS model, whose structure is the one presented in Fig. 6.

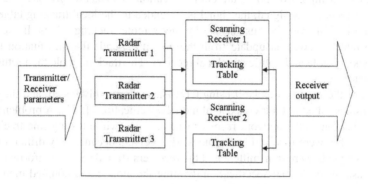

Fig. 6. Structure of the radar Tx/Rx model

The first step was to identify and define each one of the model components. Once they were identified, a DEVS atomic model was built for each subcomponent. Below, we exemplify the definition of one of these models by showing the tracking table atomic model. The tracking table model is responsible for maintaining the list of transmitters that are "known" to the local receiver.

Tracking Table = $\langle$ S, X, Y, δ_{int}, δ_{ext}, ta, λ $\rangle$

S = { Receive_Update_From_Bus, Wait, New_Signal_Detected, Send_Update_To_Bus, Notify_New_Freq }
X = { signal_props, bus_receive_freq, bus_receive_id }
Y = { bus_send_freq, bus_send_id, new_freq }
δ_{int} = { δ_{int}(Receive_Update_From_Bus) = Notify_New_Freq,
δ_{int}(Notify_New_Freq) = Wait,
δ_{int}(New_Signal_Detected) = Send_Update_To_Bus,
δ_{int}(Send_Update_To_Bus) = Wait }
δ_{ext}= { δ_{ext}(Wait, signal_props) = New_Signal_Detected,
δ_{ext}(Wait,bus_receive_freq) = Receive_Update_From_Bus }
ta = { ta(Receive_Update_From_Bus) = UPDATE_TIME,
ta(New_Signal_Detected) = PROCESS_TIME,
ta(Send_Update_To_Bus) = BUS_TIME,
ta(Notify_New_Freq) = NOTIFY_TIME }
λ(S) = { λ(New_Signal_Detected) = (bus_send_freq,bus_send_id),
λ(Receive_Update_From_Bus) = new_freq }

This model evolves through different states (S): receive an update from the bus, wait, detection of a new signal, transmission of an update to the bus, or notification of a new frequency. The model changes from one state to the other by executing the transition functions. As seen in the external transition (δ_{ext}), from a *wait* state, the tracking table receives information from either the local receiver (*signal props*, one of the external input events) or the communication bus (*receive freq*). If the local receiver detects a new signal, the signal is appended to the local tracking table, and an update is sent over the bus for use by any remote tracking tables. If the local tracking table receives an update from the bus, it appends the information to the local tracking table and notifies the local receiver. The tracking table then returns to a wait state.

Each of the models was built using CD++ and thoroughly tested, and they performed as described in their conceptual model specifications [282]. A problem with the specification of the network receiver was revealed while testing (the tracing of the signals that were received by the network receivers became very difficult when numerous signals were transmitted, and the receivers started to share information).

The use of the formal specification defining the atomic and coupled model behavior was very useful in debugging the models when they were implemented. The iterative procedure of updating the formal specification, then updating the implementation, was quite efficient. Following these iterations resulted in the models matching the specifications. Once this stage was completed, a coupled model was built, integrating all of the systems' components. The description of this model can be found in Fig. 7.

```
[top]
components: tr1@Transmitter tr2@Transmitter
            tr3@Transmitter netrx1 netrx2
out: notify1 notify2 notify3
Link: pulse_out@tr1 ext_signal@netrx1
Link: pulse_out@tr1 ext_signal@netrx2
...
[netrx1]
components: tt1@Tracking_Table rx1@Scanning_Receiver
in: ext_signal brf brid
out: notify bs_id bs_freq
Link: ext_signal ext_signal@rx1
Link: brf bus_receive_freq@tt1
Link: brid bus_receive_id@tt1
...
Link: bus_send_freq@tt1 bs_freq
...
```

Fig. 7. Coupled model definition: radar Tx/Rx

The various atomic models contained in the previously defined coupled model were tested using different scenarios. Table 1 shows the result of the testing scenario for the network with a transmitter. In this case, the transmitter sends out pulses at 24 kHz, with a pulse width of 5 ms, and a pulse interval of 40 ms. Bus message at $t=20$ ms. Receiver listening between 22 and 25 kHz. As we can see in the table, the receiver gets a signal from the transmitter every 40 ms, and a bus message at $t=20$ms. The bus message is ignored because it is not within the listening range of the receiver (19 kHz, and the receiver is listening from 22 to 25 kHz). Note that the model does not queue received pulses or bus messages. For each pulse received by the local transmitter, a bus message is generated after a delay of 15 ms. The bus message stays active for 40 ms.

Table 1. Testing scenario: network with transmitter

Events	Outputs
00:00:20 brf 19000	00:00:001 notify 1
00:00:20 brid 3	00:00:016 bs_id 1
	00:00:016 bs_freq 24000
	00:00:026 bs_id 0
	00:00:026 bs_freq 0
	00:00:041 notify 0
	00:00:081 notify 1
	00:00:096 bs_id 1
	00:00:096 bs_freq 24000
	00:00:106 bs_id 0
	00:00:106 bs_freq 0
	00:00:121 notify 0

During this phase, we were able to detect a problem with the specification of the network receiver: the signal information received by the bus was sent to the scanning receiver, which treated it like an external signal (thus causing a second bus transmission). The specification was corrected so that signal information is not re-sent over the bus.

Another component of the application describes the behavior of a simple vehicle, which seeks a target. As shown in Fig. 8, the seeker acts to steer the vehicle towards a specified position in global space. This behavior adjusts the vehicle so that its velocity is radially aligned towards the target.

Using the hierarchy of motion behaviors defined in [363], the "Action Selection" of the seek behavior is specified by dictating the destination location.

The model components specify the desired velocity of the vehicle. The model rules detail the discrete motion that was implemented to simulate the effect of a desired velocity on the vehicle. Multiple combinations of actual and desired velocity could result in the same destination for the vehicle. The model was completely implemented in CD++ following the previous rule specifications, and it was first tested using a single vehicle, with different initial velocities and different desired velocities.

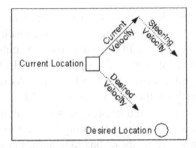

Fig. 8. Informal behavior of the Seek model.

After all the rules were implemented, all possible velocities were tested in all possible desired velocities. Following that, collisions were tested using multiple vehicles.

Figure 9 displays the two state variables employed in the definition of the model. The left-hand plane (mostly white) displays the current location and velocity of the three vehicles. The right-hand plane describes the "desired velocity vector field" of the vehicles. The "desired location" for all three vehicles is the center of the plane, and the "desired velocity vectors" steer them to that point. As we can see, the three vehicles enter from the top-right corner of the plane, and they stop when they cannot move any closer to the "desired location".

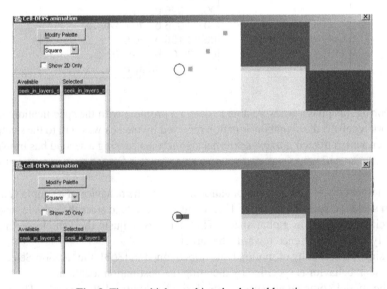

Fig. 9. Three vehicles seeking the desired location

The final stage of development consisted of showing how to provide interoperation of these models by allowing interaction between the components. This interaction is done at the level of the model, independently of the execution engine chosen (i.e., simulated, real time, or parallel), as the models only communicate at the level of their interfaces. Let us consider, for instance, the existence of a new model, *Radar*. The radar model is prepared to scan a cell space according to a given frequency. Figure 10 shows how to integrate this new model with the two other models defined earlier in this section. These three models were built independently, but they can be easily integrated thanks to the definition of DEVS interfaces.

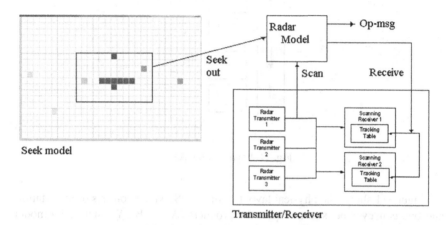

Fig. 10. Multimodel integration

The T/R model is used to start radar scanning activities. Upon activation, the radar will scan the field defined by the seeker model defined earlier, and will generate two outputs: a reception signal for the T/R, and a number of operator messages according to the values received in the field. The seeker model advances independently of the execution of the radar, because these models are built as discrete-event specifications, and each subcomponent progresses according its own internal time base. Our *top* model is now integrated by the three original components. The model produces outputs that can be used by the radar model. We have defined a *zone* in which the cells will generate outputs (by using the *out-rule* definition). Finally, the model, defined earlier in Fig. 6, includes two new input/output ports in order to provide interaction with the radar model. This model is not defined in the file, because it has been defined as a DEVS atomic model, and we just need to define the coupling between this model and the remaining components.

5 Hybrid Applications: An Automated Factory Model

We will now show how to incrementally build an application with components in hardware and simulated modules. The model here represents an automated manufacturing system (AMS) for a factory floor. The AMS is composed of dedicated stations that perform tasks on products being assembled, and conveyor belts transporting the products to/from the workstations. The production cycle is organized by a scheduler, which will define the actions to be carried out according to the type of piece being assembled. The scheduler determines which station (e.g., painting, baking, storage) should receive and work on the product.

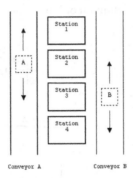

Fig. 11. Layout of the AMS

Figure 11 shows the physical layout of the AMS, which consists of four stations and two conveyor belts to transport the products (A and B). We started by modeling and simulating the entire system in CD++ based on the layout presented in this figure. The system, shown in Fig. 12, is composed of two coupled (conveyors) and three atomic components (a controller, a scheduler, and a display). Each conveyor is formed by two atomic models (an engine and a sensor controller).

The control unit receives events from the environment, and forwards them to the remaining components of the system, using the previously defined coupling scheme. The display controller handles the digital display (showing information about the pieces in each conveyor belt), based on the signals received from the controller unit. The controller receives input signals from the sensors and the scheduler, and determines where to dispatch each piece activating the engines of the conveyor belts. The scheduler stores information about which stations have to work on a specific product.

Most of the logic of the controller unit is located in the external transition function, which handles the incoming events. Events received via ports *station_ij* represent that the product in conveyor belt j has to be sent to station i. Events received at *sensor_ij* indicate that the product in conveyor j has reached station i; thus, we can schedule the next internal transition function to activate/deactivate the engine of the corresponding conveyor (via *direction_j* and *activate_j*). We can also signal the display controller when the conveyor belt starts moving or a product reaches a new station (via *direction_display_j* and *station_display_j*). Users can define the activation time for the engine, customizing its timing behavior.

Different experimental frames were applied to this model, allowing the analysis of different scenarios. We started by analyzing the behavior of each submodel independently (using the specifications for their physical counterparts) and then we conducted integration tests. Initially, we ran several experiments using the simula-

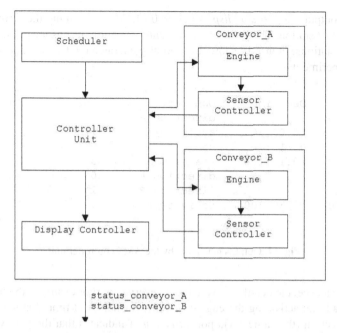

Fig. 12. Scheme of the AMS (entirely in CD++)

tion engine. This allowed us to identify some logical errors, which were fixed at this stage. Later, we repeated the tests under the real-time execution engine. This allowed us to detect problems with the model's timing constraints in runtime. Once fixed, these models were ready to become the actual software components of the application, running in real time. Figure 13 shows a sample event file for one of these experiments in the real-time environment.

```
Time        Deadline     In-port     Out-Port     Value
00:09:100   00:09:300    sta_3A      activate_A    1
00:12:500   00:12:700    sensor_2A   sta_disp_A    1
00:17:500   00:17:700    sensor_3A   sta_disp_A    1
00:35:100   00:35:300    sta_4B      activate_B    1
...
```

Fig. 13. Experimental frame for the AMS controller unit

Initially, a piece is placed in station 1 of each conveyor belt and there are no pending events. The first event represents an activity scheduled for product A in station 3. The event occurs at time 00:09:100, and the simulator receives it via input port *sta_3A*. As a result, we expect to turn on the conveyor belt in less than 200 ms to transport the product. The second event in the list represents the activation of *sensor_2A* (i.e., the product in belt A has reached the second station). In this case, we expect an output via port *sta_disp_A* before 00:12:700, informing the arrival of the product at that station. The value of 1 represents activation of sensors and scheduling of tasks in stations. Figure 14 shows the outputs generated by the real-time simulator for this experiment.

Time	Deadline	Out-port	Value
00:09:110		direction_A	1
00:09:110	00:09:300	activate_A	1
00:12:510	00:12:700	sta_disp_A	2
00:17:510	00:17:700	sta_disp_A	3
00:17:510		direction_A	0
00:35:110		direction_B	1
00:35:110	00:35:300	activate_B	1
...			

Fig. 14. Outputs generated by the AMS controller unit.

As we can see, the deadlines were met in every case. For example, the first event met its deadline, activating the engine of conveyor belt A at time 00:09:110 in the correct direction (the value 1 via port *direction_A* indicates that the belt will move forward). The third output is the result of activating the sensor at the second station in belt A, and the following one represents the product reaching the third station at time 00:17:510. The fifth line shows that the conveyor belt has stopped after product A has reached station 3. The last two lines show the initial activity that generates scheduling a job in station 4 for product B.

We used different experimental frames to thoroughly test this model, and once satisfied with its behavior, we progressively started to replace simulated components with their hardware counterparts. The first step was to replace the scheduler model, and to execute it on the microcontroller. The microcontroller generates the events to the simulated model, indicating that a product has to be sent to a given station. The remaining components are not changed. Figure 15 shows the CD++ coupled model specification for this version of the system.

Here, *conveyor_A* and *conveyor_B* are coupled components, whereas *cu* and *dis* are atomic. The top model input ports are used to receive events from the scheduler now running in the external board. Replacing a CD++ component with its counterpart running in the external devices is straightforward, since the model interfaces are not changed (an option in the executable engine will establish that a particular model is running in an external device). Likewise, testing this model only requires reusing the previously defined experimental frames. As the scheduler model was built using the hardware specifications for the actual system, and the interfaces of the submodels do not change, the transition is transparent. Figure 16 shows the output of a sample execution of this model. The results obtained are the same as before, regardless of the use of a hardware surrogate.

In this case, events generated by the scheduler running on the board are sent to CD++. These events trigger the same activities in the model as in the simulated

```
components:   conveyor_A   conveyor_B scheduler
              cu@CU dis@Display
in   : sta_1A   sta_2A   sta_3A   sta_4A
in   : sta_1B   sta_2B   sta_3B   sta_4B
out  : status_conv_A
out  : status_conv_B
link : sta_1A   sta_1A@cu
link : sta_2A   sta_2A@cu
...

[conveyor_B]
components:   sb@SensorController   eng@Engine
...
```

Fig. 15. CD++ model: scheduler in hardware

```
Time              Out-port              Value
00:08:170         status_conv_A         2
00:19:540         status_conv_A         3
00:30:130         status_conv_B         2
00:35:140         status_conv_B         3
...
```

Fig. 16. Outputs for example shown in Fig. 15

environment. In Fig. 16, *status_conv_A* and *status_conv_B* show that the products in both belts are transported to the corresponding stations.

After conducting extensive tests, we also moved the display controller to the microcontroller. The value displayed on the digital display (which is updated by the model running in CD++) represents the current station for each product. The display controller and the scheduler were combined in a single application following the previous model specifications. By simply activating the execution engine specifying that the display controller is running in a hardware surrogate, we are able to execute the new application without any modifications. Every time the models activate the output ports *status_conv_A* and *status_conv_B*, the display controller on the board is activated, showing on the LCD the current location of each product as shown in Fig. 17.

```
Time              Out-port              Value
00:27:410         status_conv_A         2
00:33:180         status_conv_A         3
00:34:390         status_conv_B         2
01:10:690         status_conv_A         2
01:15:170         status_conv_A         1
...
```

Fig. 17. Outputs for previous example

The first two lines of Fig. 17 show the product in conveyor A moving from the first to the third station. The third line shows the product in conveyor B moving to station 2 at time 00:34:390. After station 3 finished its work on product A, the product reaches station 1 at time 01:15:170. When the external display controller receives new data, it displays the value (i.e., the current position of the product in that belt) on the LCD, and then waits for more data.

The final step was to implement the complete AMS on the microcontroller. Figure 18 shows the scheme for this experimental frame, in which only the engines of the conveyor belt are still simulated in CD++.

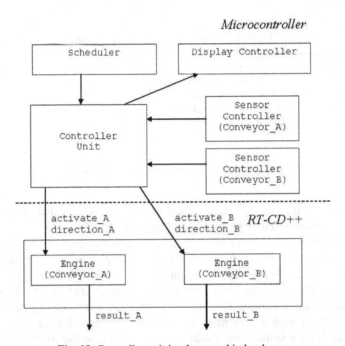

Fig. 18. Controller unit implemented in hardware

The model does not require any modification, and the model executing in the microcontroller feeds the input ports *activate* and *direction* in Fig. 15.

Figure 19 shows the events generated by the model running in the microcontroller, which represents setting the direction, activation, and deactivation of the conveyor belt engines A and B.

Figure 20 shows the activation and deactivation of the belts when the requests are received, which is the result of the activity in the microcontroller. The values issued by the port, *result_A* and *result_B*, represent that the belt is activated to move forward (1), reverse (2), or, be deactivated (0).

```
Time                Port                 Value
00:06:120           direction_A          1
00:06:130           activate_A           1
00:15:930           activate_A           0
00:56:800           direction_B          2
00:56:810           activate_B           1
01:01:130           activate_B           0
...
```

Fig. 19. Event log generated by the engines model

```
Time                Out-port                  Value
00:06:130           result_A                  1
00:15:930           result_A                  0
00:56:810           result_B                  2
01:01:130           result_B                  0
01:22:720           result_B                  2
...
```

Fig. 20. Outputs for the model in Fig. 18

6 Development Improvements

The time required to develop models in RT-CD++ is a major concern, given that time-to-market is generally a crucial factor. Component reuse is an essential aim of our approach. In the development of the AMS, we reused a controller unit that was implemented for an elevator control system in a previous prototype application. We also reused a prototype of a painting station, which mimics the procedure needed to paint pieces placed on its working area (following a predefined sequence).

We conducted experiments in the classroom, asking students with different experience in the area to build the AMS system using different approaches. Table 2 summarizes the results of this study.

Table 2. Comparing development times for the AMS application

	Beginners			*Experts*		
	Manual	**CD++**	**Combined**	**Manual**	**CD++**	**Combined**
Prototype	40 m/h	24 m/h	64 m/h	32 m/h	12 m/h	44 m/h
Test	28 m/h	10 m/h	38 m/h	22 m/h	4 m/h	26 m/h
# of bugs	17	2		9	2	
Average time to fix	20 min	7 min		18 min	5 min	

The study was conducted with two groups of students: beginners and experts. Different teams were given the same application to develop, both manually and using CD++. The first line shows the average time (in man/hours) taken by the teams to complete the prototype. As we can see, building the application using CD++ always improved when compared to building the same application manually (using a C++ compiler). This is due to the clear separation of concerns of the DEVS models: the students only needed to build the models and not pay attention to any issues related to executing those models. In the worst case (beginners), building the application using CD++ was 40% faster. The main reason for this is related to the second, third, and fourth lines. It is much easier to detect and fix errors using a DEVS-based approach. Likewise, the number of errors found was considerably smaller (mainly due to the reason that it is easy to decompose models up to the right level of abstraction, which eases finding and fixing errors).

In the third column, we added the time taken to develop the application using both approaches combined (which result in higher- quality software). That is, we use a simulation tool (like CD++) to learn about the system, and then use the knowledge gained by the simulation and experience to build the application manually. If we compare this approach against the use of a tool like CD++ and the application of the DEVS methodology, we obtain higher gains (27% of the original time, in the case of an expert user of CD++). In our case, we are able to move from the simulated world into the real-time application without changing one line of code: the application developed in CD++ and run under the simulation runtime can be later used to run the actual application just by activating the real-time execution engine.

Note that, in this study, we did not take into consideration maintenance costs, which, in any long-term project, take a large percentage of the resources spent in the development cycle. Reducing the testing time would greatly improve maintenance, and modifying models is much simpler than focusing on the application from scratch. Simultaneously, it is easy to locate the sources for modification (anything related to reaction to external events should be placed in the external transition function; internal state changes in the internal transitions; and outputs in the output function).

7 Conclusion

M&S techniques offer significant support for the design and testing of complex embedded real-time applications. We showed the use of DEVS as the basis for model-driven development of these systems. The use of different experimental frameworks permitted us to analyze the model execution in a simulated environment, checking the model's behavior and timing constraints within a risk-free environment. The integration of hardware components into the system was straightforward. Testing and maintenance phases are highly improved due to the use of a formal approach like DEVS for modeling the system's behavior. The experiments were carried out using CD++, a DEVS tool that has been built following DEVS formal definitions.

DEVS provides a sound methodology for developing discrete-event applications, which can be easily applied to improve the development of real-time embedded applications. These advantages include secure, reliable testing, model reuse, and the possibility of building models with different resolution at different levels of abstraction. Model execution is automatically verifiable, as the execution processors are built following the formal specifications of DEVS. Hence, the developer only needs to focus on the model under development. The transition from simulated models to the actual hardware counterparts can be incremental, incorporating deployed models into the framework when they are ready.

Relying on experimental frameworks facilitates testing in a cost-effective manner, allowing users to build and reuse test frames for each submodel of the system. Since the DEVS formalism is closed under coupling, models can be decomposed in simpler versions, always obtaining equivalent behavior. Finally, the semantics of models are not tied to particular interpretations, thus existing models can be reused. Likewise, models functions can be reused just by associating them with new models as needed. For instance, we are now building an extension to the examples presented here that will handle 10 conveyors and 20 stations. Extending the model presented here requires modifying only the external transition function in the controller unit, and defining a new coupled model including the new stations, while keeping the remaining methods unchanged.

8 Acknowledgements

This work has been partially supported by NSERC (National Science and Engineering Research Council of Canada), IRIS (Institute for Research on Intelligenet Systems, PRECARN, Canada), and the Intel IXA University program.

Model-Driven Service Engineering

Rolv Bræk[1] and Geir Melby[2]

[1] NTNU Department of Telematics, Trondheim, Norway
[2] Ericsson Norarc, Asker, Norway rdv.braeck@item.ntnu.no

Summary. Abstraction and platform are two of the most central concepts in MDA. To succeed with MDA means to build a clear, operational understanding of the two concepts. Two key questions are how to express the PIM and especially its behavior, and how to deal with implementation and platform dependent properties. In this chapter we offer some answers based on earlier work on model-driven development and current work on model-driven service engineering. A central aim of the latter work is to enable rapid, modular and incremental development and deployment of collaborative services. A model-driven solution supported by a layered execution framework is presented.

1 The MDA Idea

"The MDA defines an approach to IT system specification that separates the specification of system functionality from the specification of the implementation of that functionality on a specific technology platform" [171].

As illustrated in Fig. 1, the central idea in MDA is that functionality and other properties can be expressed in models that are implementation and platform independent and then be turned into efficient implementations by means of transformations. In this way the emphasis of systems development is shifted away from detailed implementations towards more abstract models that can survive changes in implementations and platforms.

The idea to describe and analyze the functionality of a system separately from the way it is implemented has been around since the very beginning of software engineering and is central to most systems and software engineering approaches. The degree of success has, however, varied tremendously, which suggests that just adopting this idea alone is not sufficient. It appears that the language and method used to define functionality are crucial.

The idea to automatically transform the functionality specification/description into executable code has been around for almost as long a time, but has been slower to materialize in practical results. Again it appears that the language and method used to define functionality are crucial. In order to enable automatic translation, it is necessary that functionality is described using a formalism with sufficient completeness,

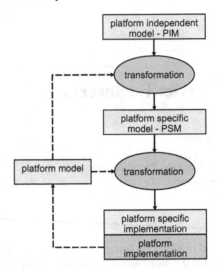

Fig. 1. MDA in a nutshell

rigor and precision. Although such formalisms have been around for more than 20 years, the general software engineering community has been quite hesitant to pick them up, preferring to stick with less formal, more illustrative approaches believed to be more practical.

The greatest promise of MDA is that this attitude is changing. The speed with which industry and research now embrace MDA is astounding considering the many hurdles that must be overcome before MDA can be turned into a mature technology. Although the basic ideas are simple, there are lots of open issues concerning how they may be implemented effectively and efficiently.

The platform concept is central in MDA because the main criterion used to classify models is their degree of platform independence. This raises two important questions:

(1) Is platform independence a sufficient abstraction criterion?
(2) Is the concept of a platform sufficiently precise?

As illustrated in Fig. 1, the platform concept is important not only as a target for implementations and as an abstraction criterion, but also as input to precisely define transformations. As pointed out on p. 119 of this book, MDA does not provide a precise platform definition, maybe deliberately, which leaves it up to implementers to define their understanding.

MDA is defined as a very open-ended and generic pattern. To make it practicable it is necessary to turn the pattern into a well-defined, rigorous approach supported by tools. This means to define the model architecture more precisely, including abstraction criteria, and to be more specific about platform properties and transformations. The purpose of this chapter is to outline and discuss ways of doing this in the service engineering domain. In order to put things into perspective, we first present an early model-driven approach and some lessons learned concerning how to express functionality and deal with platform issues. We then show how similar principles may be applied to support model-driven service engineering today and in the future.

2 Model-Driven Development *anno* 1993

Methods and tools for model-driven development (MDD) have been successfully applied on industrial development projects at least since the early 1980s and possibly earlier. In order to provide background and to clarify some important issues related to MDD we shall have a closer look at one such method defined in 1993 [50] and illustrated in Fig. 2. This was before the time of UML. Functionality was modeled using SDL [224], which is a language for communicating state machines comparable to the state machines now defined in UML 2.0. The experience gained will therefore be applicable also in a UML setting.

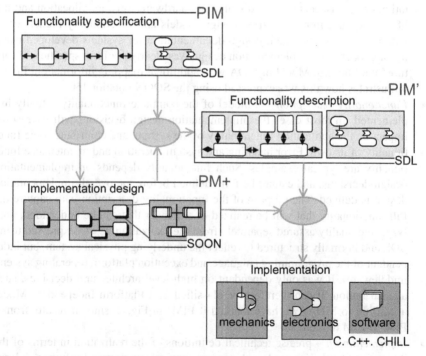

Fig. 2. Model-driven development *anno* 1993

The main models, presented in the recommended order of development, were the following:

- *Functionality specification* – a model of pure application functionality aiming to describe logical behavior and information as clearly as possible. It is expressed using a conceptual abstraction based on concurrent state machines that communicate asynchronously. It allows behavior to be fully defined in terms that enable users and developers to communicate precisely, to establish a common understanding, and to ensure that the functionality is correct according to requirements. It provides a view where the system may be seen as a whole, independently of realization platforms and technology. The behavior may be executed and analyzed to ensure that it is according to needs and without errors. In this way the quality of the application functionality can be ensured independently of how it is realized. In MDA terminology this was clearly a Platform Independent Model, a PIM.

- *Implementation design* – an architectural description of the realization (the physical system) in terms of hardware and software components and a definition of how the functionality is mapped into it. This is a high-level description of the realization using aggregation to hide irrelevant detail. The purpose is not to define behavior on a more detailed level since the behavior is precisely defined in the functionality models. It serves as an orthogonal view that focuses on implementation design aspects such as distribution, hardware/software allocation and use of middleware. Implementation design models and functionality models combine to constitute the main design documentation for systems developed using this approach. The implementation design was clearly platform specific and captured the Platform Model in MDA with additional mapping information. Figure 3 illustrates how this was expressed using the SOON notation [50].
- *Functionality description* – a model of the complete functionality actually implemented. In most cases the implementation design decisions will have some impact on the application functionality of the system, and contribute some functionality of its own. Error handling and system operation and maintenance functionality are typical examples. Such functionality depends on implementation design decisions, and cannot be fully defined before the overall implementation design is defined. The purpose of the functionality description is to capture the full functionality that will be realized in a manner that can be understood, analyzed and quality assured separately from the realization. It was expressed using SDL and normally structured to reflect the underlying physical system, but independent of the programming language and execution platform (operating system, middleware). It was only dependent on high-level architectural decisions, such as distribution. It can therefore be classified as a Platform Independent Model according to MDA. We have marked it PIM' in Fig. 2, since it results from a PIM-to-PIM refinement.
- *Implementation* – precise technical definitions of the realization in terms of the different technologies used, such as mechanics, electronics and software. A large number of realizations will normally be possible for a given functionality, and the choice will depend on what properties are desired from the realization itself (often called non-functional properties). If properly separated, a given functionality model will hold for several alternative realizations. Several translators exist that generate complete, product quality, application code from SDL. The code

can normally be optimized and adapted to different computing platforms and hardware environments using various techniques as explained in [370].

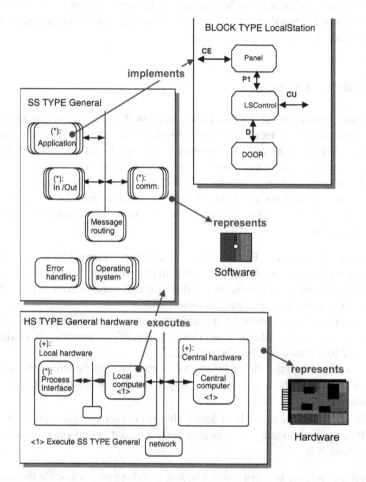

Fig. 3. Implementation Design using SOON: a PM+ (a platform model with mapping)

This and related approaches have been successfully applied to develop many industrial products, mostly within the telecom domain, but also automotive, aeronautical, instrumentation and other embedded applications, e.g. [17]. These applications are characterized by complex reactive behavior running on distributed hardware and software platforms with severe performance and real-time constraints, quite a challenging test for the MDA idea.

Although there is no PSM to be found in Fig. 2, the approach lies well within the MDA pattern because MDA allows for several PIM-to-PIM refinements and does not prescribe that a PSM must be made [174]. There was never a need for a PSM because the PIM' and the PM+ (PM with mapping information) together provided the information needed. Note that the PM+ here complements the functionality design and provides a high-level documentation of the platform (actually the complete implementation architecture) without repeating information from the functionality design. It should be possible to derive a PSM by adding functionality details to this model, but there was never a need for that.[3]

3 Abstraction Criteria

MDA defines abstraction in the usual way found in the software engineering literature: to hide irrelevant detail in order to focus on the relevant. This definition is adopted by ODP [224] as well. The problem with this definition is that it gives no clues as to what is relevant and what is irrelevant and how the irrelevant should be hidden. MDA gives just one clue: that the PIM should be platform independent and therefore hide details of the platform. Clearly, platform independence is a desirable property, but it is not sufficient. At least three other properties must also be satisfied in order to reach the goals of MDD:

- *Human comprehension.* Functionality should be represented in a way that enables human beings to fully understand it, to reason about it and to communicate precisely. To this end the concepts of the language must be well defined, match the problem domain and be easy to understand.
- *Analytical power.* It should be possible to reason about behaviors in order to compare systems, to validate interfaces and to verify properties. This requires a semantic foundation suitable for analysis.
- *Realism.* The language should build on concepts that can be effectively and efficiently realized in the real world. This requirement is essential for two important reasons:
  - (1) That it should be possible to derive efficient implementations automatically.
  - (2) That the functionality models may serve as valid documentation of the real system.

Platform independence is not in conflict with any of these properties. On the contrary, it is our experience that platform independence often is satisfied by consequence.

The first two properties, human comprehension and analytical possibilities, will normally benefit from a *conceptual abstraction*. By this we mean to use a language based on concepts that are closer to the problem domain than the implementation domain. Conceptual abstraction means more than just hiding details. It means thinking differently about a problem, because the problem is formulated using other concepts. Mathematical models used for performance analysis and strength calculations

---

[3] A PSM is normally taken to contain the same information as a PIM with additional platform specific detail. Sometimes a marked PIM is used as intermediate. The value of repeating PIM information in PSM may be questioned. Instead one may emphasize documenting the mapping and the additional information separately (here in the implementation design).

are well-known examples of conceptual abstraction. While this has obvious advantages, there is a danger that the chosen concepts cannot be effectively implemented, and therefore the realism may be lost. It is therefore important to select conceptual abstractions that are implementable in efficient ways.

The extended finite state machine is a conceptual abstraction that satisfies the three criteria (for suitable application domains) and has proven to be useful time and time again. Therefore it has been adopted in one form or another, by the major modeling languages dealing with stateful reactive behavior, notably UML and SDL.

One important property of state machines is that they lend themselves to layered implementations where the application runs on top of a state machines support layer. In this way two benefits can be gained:

- The conceptual distance from application functionality to application implementation is shortened.
- The underlying platform may be hidden from the application implementation by the state machine support layer, and in this way improve the platform independence and portability of applications.

This allows the MDA to be specialized as illustrated in Fig. 4.

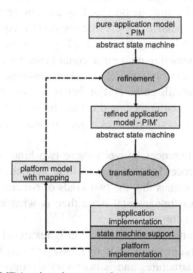

Fig. 4. MDA using abstract and concrete state machines

4 Towards Model-Driven Service Engineering

As the underlying technology gradually matures, service development or service engineering is receiving more attention and starting to become a discipline in its own right. This has been a clear trend within telecom for years. Driven by the belief that future revenues will have to come from new services, a tremendous effort has been invested in new platforms, methods and tools to enable rapid development and incremental deployment of convergent services, i.e. integrated communication, multimedia and information services delivered transparently over a range of access and transport networks. Similarly, concepts like the Service-Oriented Architecture (SOA) and Service-Oriented Computing (SOC) building on web services are being developed for the business domain. A general challenge for service engineering, be it business or ICT applications, is to enable service modules to be rapidly developed, and to be deployed and composed dynamically without undesirable service interactions. This is a formidable problem and a very challenging, yet attractive, application area for MDA.

4.1 The Nature of Services

In the information processing domain, a service is considered as a computation or information processing operation that is accessed through an interface using a request–response type of interaction. There may be many users accessing the service more or less simultaneously, but initiatives come from one side only (normally from the users). This kind of service may be provided by a client–server structure where the server side is made up of passive objects that respond to requests without taking independent initiatives. In telecom and embedded systems, services normally involve several active objects interacting on a more equal basis where initiatives may come from several sides and possibly conflict. A telecommunication conference service is a typical example. It entails collaboration between concurrently behaving, active objects taking part in the conference, and cannot be properly understood simply as an interface. This kind of service requires a peer-to-peer structure of interconnected active objects [49].

The fundamental differences between these two kinds of services and object structures have consequences for service modelling, service composition and service platforms. Convergence means that the two kinds of structure need to be combined and integrated. The most fundamental issue then is what kind of communication mechanism to use in the core.

Synchronous communication by invocation is restricted to client–server structures while asynchronous communication by messaging may be used for both client–server and peer-to-peer structures and is necessary to support general peer-to-peer structures efficiently. It may then be argued that asynchronous communication by messaging should be supported at the core of a mixed engineering approach. Recent trends in business applications point in the same direction. Business-to-business interactions need to be carried out on a loosely coupled peer-to-peer basis using asynchronous communication [173]. Consequently, in order to cover a wide range of convergent services, an approach to service engineering must support peer-to-peer services and asynchronous communication.

We consider a service in general to be *an identified (partial) functionality, provided by a system, component, or facility, to achieve a goal for its environment.* More specifically a service is seen as *a collaboration seeking to achieve some goal(s).*

This definition fits well with the UML 2.0 collaboration concept. A service may conveniently be defined as a collaboration between roles with behavior defined by means of UML behavior diagrams such as activity diagrams, sequence diagrams and state machines. Collaboration roles may be flexibly bound to actor objects as long as the actor class is compatible with the role. In this way a given class may be assigned to play several roles, and a role may be played by several different classes. The *n:m* relationship between actors and roles follows from the nature of services. Separating roles from actors provides an opportunity for flexibility and modularity in service modeling, but also poses a challenge in service composition. Similar opportunities and challenges exists within so-called aspect-oriented computing (p. 237).

4.2 Role and Actor Modeling – RAM

RAM is an experimental, model-driven approach to incremental service engineering. It is being developed and applied to develop experimental services in a joint effort between NTNU, Telenor and Ericsson [303].

An experimental service execution framework called ActorFrame [367], [287] has been developed that directly supports some of the key concepts in RAM. In this way the approach uses a conceptual abstraction based on roles and actors that are supported at the implementation level by ActorFrame, which includes a support layer for UML 2.0 state machines.

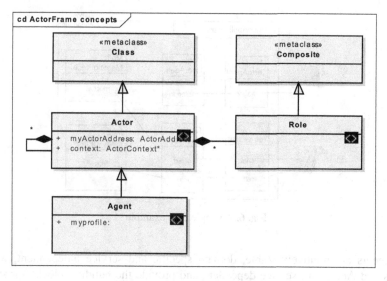

Fig. 5. The main RAM concepts

Briefly explained, the main concepts and features are as follows, see Fig. 5:

- Services and applications are performed by Agents representing and acting on behalf of application domain entities (such as users). Agents are special Actors that reflect the environment being served by an application system. RAM is therefore an Agent-oriented approach according to [49].
- Services are seen as collaborations between Roles played by Actors (that may be Agents) on a peer-to-peer basis. In Fig. 6 there are six Agents playing the Roles of three active services: a logon service, a chat service and a call service.
- Actors may perform several Roles concurrently and contain inner Actors.
- Services require that dynamic links are created between Actors playing service roles. An Actor's ability to play Roles depends on its current state, what other Roles it is playing and the policies of its enclosing Agent.
- Predefined patterns and types provide generic service functionality and support mechanisms, e.g. a role request pattern for dynamic session initiation, management functionality and dynamic deployment functionality.
- Service development is model driven and incremental with Role types, Actor types and Agent types as module types.
- Executable application systems are framework based and dynamically composed from instances of Role types, Actor types and Agent types. Figure 6 shows a simple application system corresponding to a PIM.
- New Role, Actor and Agent types may be dynamically deployed into a framework and validated.
- New types may be defined by extending Agents, Actors and Roles.

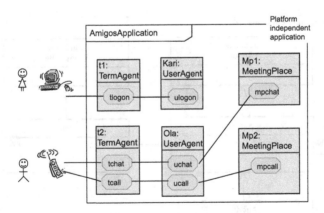

Fig. 6. A simple PIM example

Agents are relatively stable, domain specific and service independent, while Roles and Actors are service dependent and provide the building blocks for static and dynamic service composition. They are all active classes in the UML 2.0 sense with behavior defined by state machines supporting composite states and behavior inheritance.

4.3 Service Modeling

A detailed presentation of the service modeling approach is beyond the scope of this chapter. We shall only outline the approach sufficiently for the MDA aspects to be appreciated, see Fig. 7.

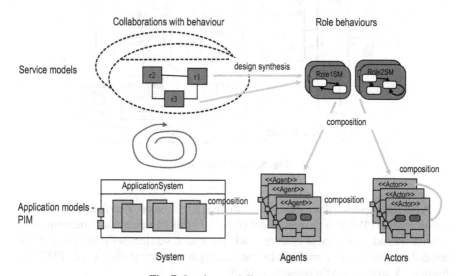

Fig. 7. Service modeling overview

Service modeling begins with collaboration diagrams identifying the roles involved and their associations. The diagrams may well contain collaboration uses (previously called collaboration occurrences) representing inner sub-collaborations. Associated with the collaboration are definitions of the service behavior expressed using sequence diagrams, activity diagrams and other suitable notations.

The next step is to define complete service role behaviors using state machines. The behavior of these state machines may be analyzed for internal consistency and their visible interface behaviors, called a-roles, on all external interfaces may be derived according to rules laid out in [127]. These a-roles are intended for later validation of dynamic links when the roles are invoked. They may also be used to support service discovery and selection.

Actor types are then defined by composition of role behaviors and inner actors. Each Actor type is defined by a UML 2.0 class diagram with inner parts and external associations. This diagram constrains the inner structure of roles and actors that instances may have and also the environment where instances may be validly instantiated. Agents are modeled in the same way as Actors. The only difference is that Agent instances may have externally visible identities, credentials and policies associated with them.

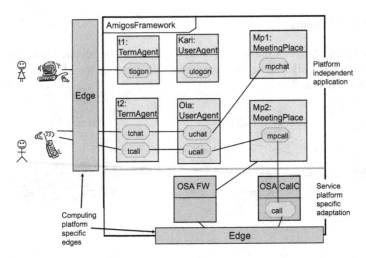

Fig. 8. A PIM' example

As in the approach described earlier, there is a refinement step from a pure application model (PIM) to a refined model (PIM'). In this particular case the refinement is needed to adapt to service enablers such as location services, map servers and Parlay call control services provided by the underlying service platform. The PIM' is a framework with two main parts, see Fig. 8:

- An application part consisting of Agents and Actors playing Roles. This part constitutes the pure application functionality PIM.
- An adaptation part also consisting of Agents and Actors playing Roles, serving as an adaptation layer towards the underlying service platform. This is service platform dependent, but implementation independent.

Figure 8 also shows Edge adaptors that provide means for applications to communicate transparently over a variety of protocols with terminals and other external entities. They serve as bridges between the internal communication mechanisms and the external. A variety of edges are provided including web access, web services access, JMS, and Java RMI.

4.4 Implementation and Platform Issues

A virtual machine layer called ActorFrame provides support for the RAM concepts. It builds on a layer below that provides support for UML 2.0 state machines including parts, ports and associations as well as behavior inheritance. This layer is currently provided in three variants, Fig. 9:

- ActorFrame, which runs directly over a Java VM and may be deployed on most Java platforms including small devices and mobile terminals.
- EJB ActorFrame, which runs on J2EE platforms and is intended for application servers.
- MIDLet ActorFrame, which runs on Java MIDLet2.0-enabled mobile phones.

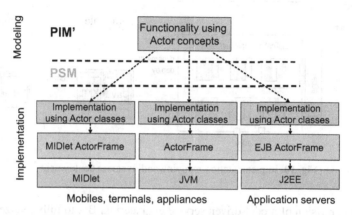

Fig. 9. Implementation layering and platform adaptation

The application code is nearly identical for the three platforms, which make's porting from one platform to another quite simple. The ActorFrame layer uses actor descriptors implemented as XML files to dynamically create actor instances according to the content and context constraints specified by the actor descriptors, see Fig. 10. New actor types may be dynamically deployed, and existing actor types may be reconfigured on-the-fly by editing the actor descriptors. A UML 2.0 to Java translator has been developed that generates the application code and the actor descriptors for both platforms. This allows flexibility to deploy actors and roles of distributed peer-to-peer services on terminals and application servers as best seem's fit.

The framework has been used to develop experimental services using the PATS laboratory infrastructure to access live network resources over a variety of interfaces including Parlay, Parlay-X and location servers.

Some challenges now being addressed in RAM are:

- Flexible, incremental translators.
- Incremental validation tools.
- Service naming, discovery and selection.
- Personalization and context awareness.

4.5 RAM and MDA

The overall approach is summarized in Fig. 11. Due to the conceptual abstractions provided by state machines there has been no need for a PSM. With the code generator now in place in the RAMSES toolset [259] we are one important step closer to

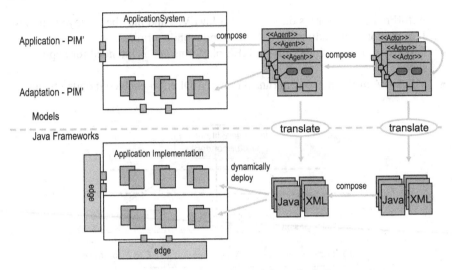

Fig. 10. Implementation mapping and dynamic deployment

realizing our vision of model-driven service engineering. But to fully realize the vision, more needs to be done to support the incremental and compositional approach on the modeling level. To that end we are currently working on compositional methods and tools to ensure that actors are internally consistent and that interfaces are compatible when composed. We aim to find means to ensure consistency and compatibility on the modeling level that can be utilized at runtime. The runtime aspect is important because services may be deployed, discovered and used dynamically at runtime in combinations that have never been planned. Work is under way in this direction based on the principles of [127] and [46].

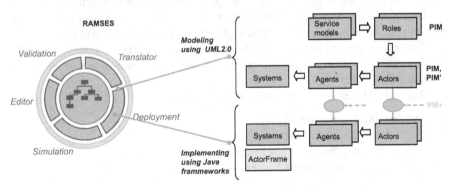

Fig. 11. RAM overview, with the RAMSES toolset

5 Concluding Remarks

MDA is a great initiative. It is ambitious, but clearly feasible as demonstrated through industrial application of early MDD approaches such as the one presented in Sect. 2. The potential benefits are easy to see if the *model-driven approach* is compared with the *elaboration approach* that has been dominating mainstream software engineering so far.

- In the *elaboration approach* functionality is normally described with insufficient precision and completeness to be fully understood and analyzed on its own terms or to be automatically implemented. This can often be attributed to the use of languages with incomplete behavioral semantics. Missing functionality details have to be added by elaboration during implementation design and realizations to compensate for this. As a result, the realization (the source code) ends up as the only complete view of the system and is often the only one that is maintained. This gradually reduces the value of the other views, and makes the documentation very realization dependent. When the technology and platforms change, as occurs rapidly these days, more than necessary must be redone, because it is hard to factor out and reuse functionality that is not changed. Mainstream software engineering has followed the elaboration approach, and this has also been the case for most UML use, including the Rational Unified Process (RUP), before MDA.
- In the *model-driven approach* it is essential that functionality is modeled more completely and with sufficient precision and realism that behavior may be fully understood, analyzed and realized on the basis of the functionality models. The implementation dependent information should be kept as orthogonal as possible to the functionality, and realization of functionality may be carried out by (manual or automatic) transformation of the functionality description. One important goal is that the functionality models can remain valid for the realization and serve as documentation. Another goal is that functionality models can survive technology and platform changes, and thereby give better return of investment, which is desirable, since functionality tends to have a longer life than realizations.

Figure 12 serves as a suggestive illustration of the two approaches. The first thing to note is how the effort pyramids are inverted. In MDD relatively more effort is spent on functionality models and implementation design than on implementations. This means that more effort is invested where the potential return's on investment in terms of quality and lifecycle cost are higher. Since functionality is expressed using formal languages, the quality of functionality can be assured separately from the quality of realization. Provided that the realization of functionality is automatically generated, the testing may concentrate on non-functional properties like performance and response times. An important point illustrated in the figure 12, is that the functionality description need not be changed if the execution platform or programming language is changed. When using the MDD approach, it is sufficient to change the implementation design and realization. The functionality description can be reused and thereby provide a better return on investment than possible when using the elaboration approach. In the MDD approach the viewpoints/aspects are well separated, while in the elaboration approach the separation is often not so clear.

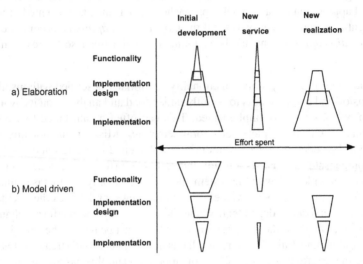

Fig. 12. Effort pyramids for the elaboration approach and the MDD approach

Among the many problems needing to be solved on the way towards MDA the following are perhaps the most challenging:

- Flexible and powerful translators (p. 19 of this book).
- Platform adaptation and optimization.
- Incremental and dynamic service composition.

Two factors seem especially crucial:

- How the PIM is expressed and especially how its behavior is expressed.
- How the implementation and platform dependent information is added, e.g. expressing the PM+ (implementation design) and making tools obey it.

In this chapter we have presented some possibilities enabled by using state machines. State machines are clearly not the solution to all application problems, but their application area is expanding as gradually more applications become distributed and collaborative with stateful peer-to-peer behavior. Web service orchestration is one new area where state machines can fit in.

6 Acknowledgements

Many people from industry and academia alike have contributed to the two model-driven approaches presented here. Øystein Haugen, Ulrik Johansen, Richard Sanders,

Jacqueline Floch, Birger Møller-Pedersen, and Knut Eilif Husa have all played key roles. Knut and Eilif Husa at Ericsson NORARC have significantly contributed to the ActorFrame service execution framework while the RAMSES toolset has been developed by Frank Kraemer, Alf K. Støyle, Dragana Korda and Rune Alsnes at NTNU. We would especially like to thank Humberto M. Castejon, Judith E.J. Rossebø, Sune Jacobsson, Richard Sanders, Fritjof B. Engelhartsen, Frank Krämer and the editors for valuable comments and inputs to this chapter.

Practical Insights into Model-Driven Architecture: Lessons from the Design and Use of an MDA Toolkit

Alan W. Brown, Jim Conallen, and Dave Tropeano

IBM Software Group,
4205 S. Miami Blvd, Durham, NC 27703, USA
{awbrown, jconallen, davetropeano}@us.ibm.com

Summary. There has been much discussion about the role and importance of model-driven development (MDD) and Model-Driven Architecture (MDA) as a way to improve the productivity and quality of enterprise application development. However, few documented experiences with the use of MDA styles of development are available. This paper provides a set of practical lessons derived from the design and use of an MDA toolkit at IBM. We describe the MDA Toolkit and its use, and highlight the key lessons in the use of an MDA approach from these experiences. We conclude with some observations on the MDA approach in general, and a brief discussion of follow, on work we are undertaking as a result of our experiences.

1 Introduction

Software development is an iterative process of understanding, discovery, and design. An increasing understanding is obtained through the application of techniques that help us discover more about the problem domain that provides the basis for the design of solutions that address the concerns of a defined set of stakeholders in the context of a set of solution delivery constraints. Throughout this process many different kinds of information must be captured, analyzed, refined, and communicated. Models, supported by modeling techniques and tools, help to enable this process.

The Unified Modeling Language (UML) is the standard modeling notation for software-intensive systems [225]. Originally conceived over a decade ago as an integration of the most successful modeling ideas of the time, UML is widely used by organizations, and supported by more than a dozen different product offerings. Its evolution is managed through a standards process governed by the Object Management Group (OMG). One of the reasons for the success of UML is its flexibility. It supports the creation of a set of models representing both the problem domain and solution domain, can capture and relate multiple perspectives highlighting different viewpoints on these domains, enables modeling of the system at different levels of abstraction, and encourages the partitioning of models into manageable pieces as required for shared and iterative development approaches. In addition, relationships between model elements can be maintained across modeling perspectives and levels of abstraction, and specialized semantics can be placed on model elements through built-in UML extension mechanisms (i.e., stereotypes and tagged values bundled into UML profiles).

As a consequence, UML is often the basis for system and software design approaches that encourage model-centric styles of development. Users of UML for modeling are supported by well-established methods that offer a set of best practices for creating, evolving, and refining models described in UML. One of the most well known is the IBM Rational Unified Process (RUP). The RUP describes a development process that helps organizations successfully apply a model-driven development (MDD) approach [262, 261]. It introduces important practical techniques to the creation, evolution, and maintenance of models, focusing on how teams of practitioners working on a large-scale development effort can reduce technical and developmental risk in a project, produce models of high fidelity, and ensure that the different models are appropriately synchronized.

Organizations have been successfully using UML in the context of RUP-based best practices for some time. Surveys indicate that almost 40% of developers use some modeling approaches based on UML, and the market-leading tool supporting UML, IBM Rational Rose, has cumulatively sold in excess of 250000 licenses [71].

As investment in these models has increased, some organizations have begun automating many of the model transformation aspects of an MDD approach. In effect, they have been using the UML/RUP/Rose combination as a platform on which to build their own model-driven approaches – writing RoseScript to manipulate models in IBM Rational Rose, or building external utilities for manipulation of the models that IBM Rational Rose externalizes in the eXtensible Markup Language (XML) Model Interchange format, XMI. In some cases customers have significant investment in these layers as a way of capturing their organization's best practices for modeling and model transformation.

A particular approach to MDD has been standardized by the OMG. The Model-Driven Architecture (MDA) approach that they have defined focuses on the creation of models using UML, and the transformation of those models between different levels of abstraction. This has led to products that support the creation, management, and sharing of such transformation. Commercial products such as Codagen [66] and arcStyler [265], and open source efforts such as AndroMDA [18] and OpenMDX [2], augment the capabilities of modeling tools such as IBM Rational Rose to support MDA and ease the creation, management and application of these transformations.

In this paper we examine MDD approaches from the perspective of the design and use of a toolkit for MDA at IBM. We describe the rationale for the introduction of this toolkit, explore its key capabilities, and highlight many of the important lessons in the application and use of a model-driven style of development based on use of this MDA toolkit in a number of customer situations. We then comment on the adaptation of traditional software lifecycle practices in regard to MDA approaches and make a number of general observations on the successful application of model-driven approaches in practice. Throughout the paper we assume a general familiarity with the Object Management Group's MDA approach, and a background in modeling using UML. Many introductions to these topics are available elsewhere.

2 The MDA Toolkit for IBM Rational XDE Java

2.1 Motivation

With the introduction of IBM Rational's next generation modeling environment in 2002, IBM Rational XDE, it was important to offer appropriate support for model-driven styles of development with that product. Since its introduction, the principal mechanism for producing custom automation in IBM Rational XDE has been the executable patterns mechanism. This mechanism allows developers to create and design executable patterns as visual models. A pattern developer uses IBM Rational XDE to create diagrams and model elements within a "pattern" element. The pattern, itself a stereotyped UML model element, could then be executed in other parts of the model or in other models. The mechanism essentially makes the specified part of the target model look like the pattern.

This type of transformation engine is inherently declarative. That is, within a diagram a structure of model elements is constructed. Elements and properties of those elements are parameterized. This is inherently a declarative style of transformation mapping. Conditional and procedural elements in the pattern are expressed with code in special "callouts". The callouts are simply callback functions that are executed during special steps in the execution of the pattern.

Our initial attempts at using the patterns mechanism to implement large-scale MDA style transformations, where entire models are processed in a batch-like operation, were disappointing. While complete and fully functional, we found in practice that the performance suffered, especially as more algorithmic complexity was added to the transformations. This highlighted our emerging opinion that although they are relatively easy to define and understand, declarative-style transformation mechanisms such as the executable patterns mechanism in IBM Rational XDE were not suited to the large-scale MDA style of transformations we were trying to build.

Our conclusions are that the patterns mechanism is best suited to small-scale transformations on discrete, individually selected model elements. Patterns are also most efficient when the transformation mapping is mostly declarative. The more algorithmically complex the transformation mapping is, the less suited a visual, executable patterns mechanism is. We recognized that what was needed was a more scalable approach to implementing MDA-style transformations, an approach that could handle the increased algorithmic complexity, and that would scale to support transformations involving large models.

It was these driving factors that led to the creation of the "MDA Toolkit for IBM Rational XDE Java". This toolkit's main goal is to make it practical to develop large-scale MDA-style transformations that use and manipulate UML models created with IBM Rational XDE.

2.2 Key Aspects of the MDA Toolkit

The MDA Toolkit for IBM Rational XDE Java provides a framework for a transformation author to develop and deploy MDA-style transformations involving UML models.[1] Toolkit-created transformations are inherently procedural since they are, for the most part, Java code. Unlike the visual, executable patterns mechanism, most of the work creating an MDA Toolkit transformation is in the development of code that directly manipulates the models and other artifacts that participate in the transformation. This approach to transformation development is simple and efficient for handling arbitrarily algorithmically complex transformation mappings.

The toolkit provides a special application programming interface (API), layered on top of the base model access API that provides many commonly used features in MDA transformations. Most UML model APIs provide only the most basic model access functionality (get, create, and update model elements and properties). It has been our experience that when developing MDA transformations involving manipulation of UML models, additional higher-level functionality is key to making the transformations robust, scalable, and maintainable. The MDA Toolkit provides an API for model access (an MDA API) that includes high-level functionality such as:

- *Intelligent and deep copying of model elements.* Copying model elements (especially when the elements can be containers or when they have relationships to other elements outside of the container) requires many discrete decisions to be made. Optional parameters to a copy method determine how relationships and sub-elements are copied. Relationships can be copied relative to the elements on their ends, or one end can be copied and the other remain fixed (i.e., a relationship to shared framework object). The toolkit's intelligent copy methods offer a callback mechanism to help resolve names.
- *Language specific behavior.* Approaches to comparing elements such as names, or operation signatures, can vary with the target language. For example, in different target programming language an operation that searches for or creates named model elements requires a target-language specific approach toward handling upper- and lowercase characters. Similarly, when comparing operations for languages like C++ or Java the operation name alone is insufficient, and operations are compared with each other by their signatures which only recognize the list of argument types, not names or return values. The ability to have the API for model access by default understand and behave with these rules makes working with the model significantly easier.

A principal design goal of the MDA API was to develop an inherent behavior in the API that supports the idea of iterative and repeated transformation invocation. We have found that most uses of an MDA transformation occur in a process where the transformation is re-executed multiple times in an iterative development process. Therefore, it is critical that any artifacts modified by the transformation preserve all information that is not directly linked to the originating elements of the transformation. For example, a transformation that converts an abstract UML class to a Java class, where the source file already exists and contains a number of helper attributes and methods, should not remove any existing code during repeated transformations.

---

[1] Further details on the MDA Toolkit for IBM Rational XDE, including access to the download, are available at http://www.ibm.com/rational/mda/toolkit.html.

2.3 The Role of UML Profiles

The MDA toolkit includes tools for creating and refreshing UML profiles. We have found that custom UML profiles are used in most transformations that involve UML models. Profiles play two different roles in a typical MDA transformation. They can be a "semantic profile" in which they are used to enable the model to accurately and appropriately capture and express specific information. This is the classical use of a UML profile: to define a set of semantics with which to interpret a model. However, they can also be used as a "marking" mechanism. Marking a model, in OMG MDA terminology, means tagging a model with extra information that is used by tools, and that is not appropriate to be captured in the semantics of the model. This is information that is not within the domain of the level of abstraction of the model content itself, but information that is necessary for an automated transformation to complete its tasks.

The toolkit includes an authoring and runtime component. The authoring component enables UML profile creation and includes a project creation wizard (with sample code). The authoring component is only required in those workstations used to create new custom MDA transformations. The runtime includes the MDA API which provides the high-level MDA functionality on top of the basic model access API, and is a shared component that is required on every machine that invokes MDA transformations.

2.4 Packaging and Delivering MDA Toolkit Transformations

Transformations created with the toolkit are packaged as Eclipse plugins making the developed transformations easy to deploy to development teams. The toolkit insulates the transformation developer from most of the details of creating Eclipse plugins, so they can focus on developing the transformation itself.

The toolkit manages most of the details of the Eclipse plugin project, including the user interface and cached preferences, thus freeing the transformation developer to focus on implementing the actual transformation logic. Once a transformation and any required custom UML profiles are created and ready for deployment, they are packaged as an Eclipse feature and made available on an internal intranet or website. Each developer installs the desired transformations and dependent plugins. Once these are installed, the developer has a new menu item and set of default preferences that when invoked prompts the developer for the required parameters before invoking the transformation itself.

All the detailed transformation logic in the mapping is encoded in and executed with the downloaded transformation. This alone is not sufficient to ensure that any given transformation is going to be used correctly. Therefore, most well-constructed transformations will include new sections to be added to the Eclipse online help. These sections should document when, why, and how a transformation should be invoked. Of course, in every environment where automation is being introduced the process should be updated and communicated accordingly.

The MDA Toolkit for IBM Rational XDE Java was made available late in 2003, and has been used in a variety of customer situations. Our experiences in the design and application of that toolkit have reinforced much of our earlier work, and highlighted a number of critical lessons for anyone interested in the practical application of MDA.

3 Lessons in the Design and Application of MDA Solutions

Over the past few years there have been a number of organizations using MDD, including use of model transformations. In fact, the authors of this paper have been directly and indirectly involved in developing models for large-scale systems, building model transformations, designing MDA tools, and using MDA tools on a number of customer engagements. As a result, a set of best practices for developing MDA-style solutions can begin to be distilled based on these experiences.

While each customer situation has its own particular concerns, we have found that there is a consistent set of steps that is followed in creating MDA solutions. Briefly, the steps followed when developing MDA style automation are:

(1) Examine the models currently used in the development process, and the semantic connections between elements across abstraction boundaries.
(2) Identify candidate transformations for automation.
(3) Specify (document) the transformation requirements.
(4) Create the necessary UML profiles.
(5) Develop the transformation code.
(6) Draft usage documents, package, and deploy.

These steps form the basis for a variety of MDA projects, and, when coupled with typical iterative design and risk-reducing development practices, offer a robust MDA approach. Most importantly, from our experiences applying these steps, a set of heuristics can be distilled that offer a set of lessons for those practicing MDA. We now examine those lessons in detail.

3.1 Semantic Model Connections

Lesson 1. *Develop transformations only when the semantic connections between the model elements are well understood.*

Before any attempt to introduce automation in the development process, you must acquire a full and thorough understanding of all the models used and managed in the process. Too often, development efforts begin with the creation of useless models, just because the untailored development process or method states that they are needed. Unless the models being developed during a software project provide clear and useful information to the effort, they should not be created or maintained. Similarly many projects are often missing some key models and abstractions that connect various parts of the system. Whenever it is apparent that a significant amount of human interpretation and creativity is employed in any particular part of a project, there might be a need for a formal model to capture the thought processes and design decisions made during those activities.

The semantic connection's between elements in models across abstraction boundaries are of particular interest in the context of MDA. Most of the practical activity around MDA today involves the automation of transformations, particularly transformations of information from models at higher level's of abstractions and model's at lower abstractions. Typically, connections like this "fan out"; that is, a single model element at a high level of abstraction (i.e., use case) is connected to multiple model elements (i.e., boundaries, entities, and controllers) in lower-level models.

The traceability of these connections is important for a number of reasons, the most important of which is to support automated transformations. But it also has important significance in iterative development environments where any given transformation is likely to be invoked many times.

It has been our experience that a transformation is rarely just a simple matter of moving information from one input model to one output model. More typically there is one primary input source, with a few extra general purpose parameters, and a set of output models. For example, in a typical J2EE system, an analysis model contains information that is transformed into a database design, Java interface and object design, a set of Java Server Pages (JSPs), and a number of configuration or deployment descriptors. All of these more detailed models must be synchronized to execute properly. Therefore it is often most convenient to develop a single transformation that manages the transfer of information from the primary high-level source model to the set of low-level models, rather than developing separate transformations for each combination of input and output models. It is this ability to coordinate the semantic content across various low-level models that makes MDA an attractive technology.

Furthermore, an important property of a transformation in this scenario is the ability for it to be executed and only update those elements of downstream models that are directly dependent on the upstream ones. Any additional information captured in the detailed models that was not generated by the transformation in the first place should remain intact. Additionally, model elements created by the transformation should not be duplicated in the downstream models during each invocation, only updated (or created if not present in the model). The MDA Toolkit API is structured so that transformations inherently follow these design principles.

3.2 Identify Candidate Transformations

Lesson 2. *Not all semantic connections make for good MDA transformations.*

When tight semantic connections are identified between elements in models they should be examined to see if the rules governing their relationships are suitable for automation. A suitable transformation can only be implemented when these rules are clear and unambiguous. They may be large and complicated, or they can be trivial and simple – in either case it may be appropriate to investigate authoring a transformation to implement them; however, if the rules that define these connections, and subsequently the rules for constructing new elements in the other models, require developer experience or judgment, then automation can be easily ruled out.

Another reason to rule out automation is the inability to programmatically access the necessary elements of the models themselves. For example, most transformation steps that involve the reading of natural language documents, regardless of the level of formality in them, are typically not suited to MDA-style automation. As an illustration, we usually find that transforming a use case specification document into an analysis model is generally not practical. However, transforming a UML sequence diagram, or activity that accompanies a use case, might be suitable for automation (given the rigor under which is was constructed).

3.3 Document Transformation Requirements

Lesson 3. *Writing MDA transforms should be treated as a software development project itself.*

The most useful transformations automate tasks that are either too tedious or complex to rely on a developer to consistently and reliably implement. MDA automation ensures consistency and in most cases significant time savings. It is not surprising that most successful transformations are in fact non-trivial examples of software. When considering the use of MDA automation, and the creation of non-trivial transformations, it should be treated as a separate software development in itself.

A transformation, especially one created with the MDA Toolkit, is an example of custom software. The requirements should be clearly understood (Lesson 1) and examined both semantically and technically. The bulk of the requirements specification is in the mapping document. The mapping document describes in detail the semantic connections between the modeling elements in the various models participating in the transformation. Other pertinent requirements may include performance, security, scalability, etc.

Most of the transformations that we have been involved with were implemented with a number of classes, and as a result underwent an analysis and a design phase. Other practical issues such as testing, deployment, and training also have their parallels in the classic software development process. While most typical MDA transformations do not require a large team to implement, they should at least be treated as an independent software development effort to ensure completeness and quality.

When specifying the requirements for a transformation implemented with the MDA Toolkit there are three distinct behaviors that should be considered:

- Validation of input parameters (and their content) for required and consistent information.
- Execution of the core transformation logic/mapping.
- Verification of the semantic connections between the model elements that participated in the transformation.

The execution of the transformation's logic and the modification of the downstream models represent the most important work of the entire transformation. However, the validation of input and verification of successful completion are also important in an iterative development environment.

Lesson 4. *Validate the integrity of all parameters and artifacts participating in a transformation before executing it.*

Since almost anything can be invoked and executed in an MDA Toolkit-created transformation, there is no inherent transactional process monitoring. That is, there are no facilities to guarantee that a transformation begun and then aborted before completion will result in the reset of all input parameters to their previous state. This is because the MDA Toolkit does not limit or restrict the types of artifacts that can participate in a transformation. It is perfectly possible for the invocation of a transformation to invoke external web services, or modify artifacts in a permanent way. It is generally up to the transformation developer to ensure the integrity of the artifacts that are manipulated in a transformation. As a result it may be necessary to ensure that the input set of artifacts is in a known state (i.e., all required parameters are specified, expected profiles applied to models, and expected content in models are verified artifacts) before the transformation takes place. This is also useful when the transformation takes a long period of time to execute (it may not be unusual for a transformation to execute over a period of hours if it is particularly complex and works on large resources). If the parameters (or any of the participating artifacts) can be determined to be invalid early on it can save user time, and preserve artifact integrity.

Lesson 5. *A verification specification is required to maintain the transform's integrity in light of downstream changes.*

When the transformation becomes part of an iterative development process it is likely that even after a transformation is executed, the artifacts, both input and output, will be manually updated. This follows the general MDD philosophy that changes are first introduced to the system in the models with the most appropriate level of abstraction, regardless of abstraction level. For example, a Customer entity described in a high-level analysis model might not contain information about persistence strategy information (optimistic, pessimistic, etc.). So changes to this strategy need not be introduced into the analysis model, but rather in the design model where they would have most impact. Consequently, the addition of a new key attribute to the Customer class would probably require a change directly to the high-level analysis model. When appropriate, and after a possible evaluation, this change would be reflected as appropriate to lower-level models, possibly as the result of an automated MDA transformation.

Because iterative development processes encourage the evolution of models throughout the development process, an important feature of a good automated transformation is the ability to analyze the current state of artifacts and compare them to what would be expected if the transformation was to execute with them. This step is encouraged in MDA Toolkit transformations with a separate and distinct verification step. The verification step is typically run separately, after the downstream artifacts have undergone not only the transformation, but subsequent modification. In a typical scenario a developer would use a transformation to update or create a set of models or code with new information in the abstract model. Then, those downstream models and artifacts might undergo further refinement that is not related to any semantic information managed by the transformation process. During this refinement, it is possible (although undesirable) for changes to be made that break the expected semantic connections between the models. Explicitly executing the verification of a transformation will produce a report to the developer of any breaks in the semantic mapping established by the original transformation. These may then be addressed appropriately by the developer, resulting in a change to either the upstream models, or downstream models, or both.

Lesson 6. *In most MDA situations, the model-to-model mappings are complex and require careful design and implementation.*

The core logic in a transformation usually expresses the algorithm in which one set of model elements is transformed into another set. In a simple declarative-style mapping, the connections are relatively simple and straightforward, and there is little ambiguity. In most large-scale MDA-style transformations that we have seen the mappings are not always so simple. Often an element in the upstream model will map to one configuration of elements under a complex set of conditions that often involve other upstream model elements, connections, and stereotypes and tag values of various UML profiles.

Take as a simple example a persistent entity called Address that defines a number of attributes, one of which is tagged as a primary key type (in the marking profile). Mapping an abstract class such as this into a Java object and database design is relatively straightforward (Fig. 1). A Java object is created, with the attributes mirrored, and the data types corrected. Getters and setters are created as well. In the database design a table and columns are created with the names adjusted to the organization's standards. The primary key (identified by a tag in the marking profile) is set. The data types are converted with some help from the marking profile. The marking profile can also be used to determine the Null and other typical database properties.

This simple example illustrates mapping a single class in the abstract model to a single class in the object model and a single table in the data model. Attributes in the abstract model map one-for-one to attributes in the object model, and columns in the data model. Operations in the object model all trace back to exactly one attribute in the abstract model.

In another example, however, the mapping is not so straightforward. Take as a second example a set of classes participating in a hierarchy in the analysis model (Fig. 2). The classes RestrictedProduct and CommericalProduct are specializations of Product. The Product class also identifies two attributes (code and supplier) as the object identifier or primary key; however, this is often identified with a tag value or stereotype which may not appear rendered in a diagram. Using the organization's

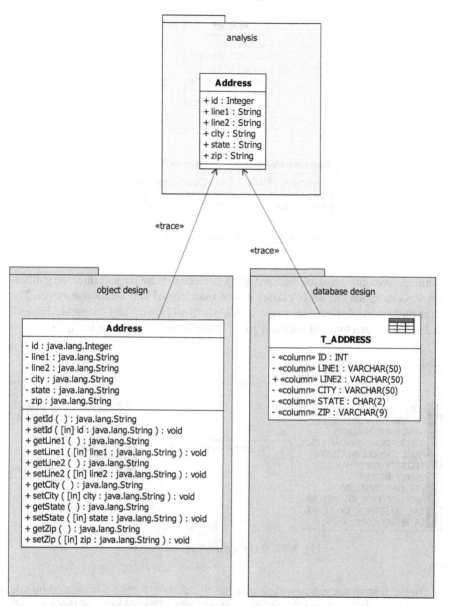

Fig. 1. Mapping a simple entity to object and data design models

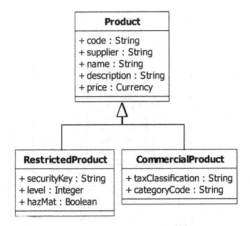

Fig. 2. Specialization in the analysis model

naming conventions and attribute mapping strategies, there are still three very different ways in which this set of classes can be transformed into a database model. The three basic strategies we refer to as "Roll Up", "Roll Down", and "Separate Tables", and are supported by IBM Rational XDE's Data Modeler as shown in Fig. 3.

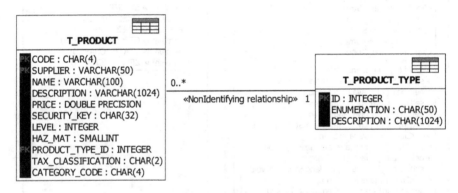

Fig. 3. "Roll Up" generalization strategy

In the first strategy, a new type of table T_PRODUCT_TYPE is created by taking the base class and appending the _TYPE suffix. The columns of this table are predefined by the mapping and always the same. This "type" table is used to simply provide an extensible means to easily add new types. All the attributes of all the sub-classes are rolled up into the one main table.

In the "Roll Down" strategy, illustrated in Fig. 4, all concrete classes are assigned their own unique table, where columns in the base class are duplicated across all the tables.

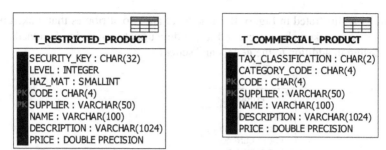

Fig. 4. "Roll Down" generalization strategy

Finally, in the "Separate Tables" strategy, illustrated in Fig. 5, all classes are mirrored with a table, and identifying relationships are created between the base class and its sub-classes so that base class attributes captured in the base class table can be accessed by corresponding rows of data in the child tables. In all three strategies the tables use the composite key implied by the main base class.

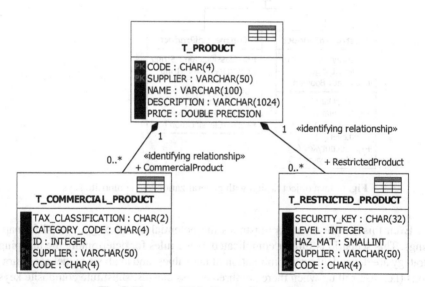

Fig. 5. "Separate Tables" generalization strategy

From this example it is clear that the mapping strategy is no longer simple, and that it is possible for some elements in the abstract model to map simultaneously to different elements in the database design. Also, in the "Roll Up" case all three analysis classes map to a pair of tables, with only one of them sharing a common name.

The resultant object model might also have requirements for only a single attribute as an object key (as in J2EE). The resultant transformation into the Java object model is illustrated in Fig. 6. Because there are two attributes that make up the object key, a new key class is created and a directional association is added to the object design in addition to the getters and setters.

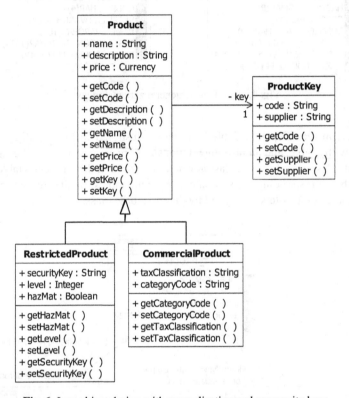

Fig. 6. Java object design with generalization and composite keys

Even this simple scenario illustrates the potential complexity in real-life mappings. This scenario is further complicated as the rules for determining the mapping strategy are dependent on a combination of tag values, and analysis model configurations (i.e., use roll up when there are three or less classes, substitute composite keys with a single auto-generated integer key unless an override tag value is set False, etc.). In the micro view, each of these issues is not insurmountable, and each case separately examined makes perfect sense, and often corresponds to what designers and developers have been doing manually for many years. However, when collected into a single transformation, one that needs to coordinate the structure and content of multiple downstream models, the intertangling of logic often makes it difficult to express simply in a declarative style. In these situations, the transformation is best expressed and implemented algorithmically, which is the default usage style of the MDA Toolkit.

Lesson 7. *Transformations can be expressed declaratively or imperatively. In general the imperative approach is more adaptable when describing complex transformations.*

While the MDA Toolkit naturally emphasizes an imperative style of thinking about implementation, it also allows XDE patterns to invoke, or support, declarative routines. The MDA Toolkit lets transformation developers create reference models with predefined sets of model elements that can be selectively copied to a target model and altered during the copy process.

Figure 7 highlights a fragment of a reference model that contains a number of classes and relationships. Some of the classes have attributes and operations. The operations have complete code templates associated with them that are used to generate complete method bodies in the code. The model element names are invalid Java identifiers as this set of classes is not expected to be used to generate code directly. Rather, this set of classes will be copied into a code model, and during the copy the element names will be updated with the actual names of classes that appear in the transformation's input model.

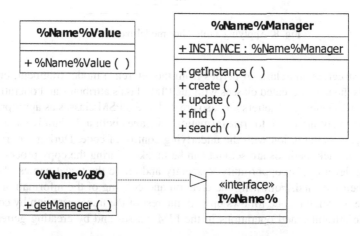

Fig. 7. A pattern of model elements in a reference model

The overall process of the transformation is to process an input model (a Platform Independent Model – PIM) and to look for classes tagged as «managed class». This marking in a PIM indicates that the class should be transformed into a set of classes in the target Platform Specific Model – PSM. So for each «managed class» in the PIM the set of classes in Fig. 7 is copied into the appropriate location of the PSM, and during the copy the names are modified with information from the originating PIM class.

Figure 8 shows the results of transforming one class in the PIM stereotyped «managed class» into the PSM. The result is the creation of four new classes, whose names are based on the originating PIM class. The transformation not only copies

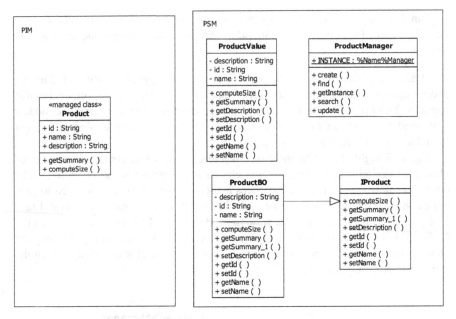

Fig. 8. Applying a reference model-based pattern

over the structure and class properties from the reference model fragment, but also augments the newly created classes with the PIM class's attributes and operations as appropriate. Getters and setters are also created in the PSM classes as appropriate.

This type of approach to transformation leverages both a declarative and visual style of pattern definition with the underlying control of code. During the transformation, callback methods are set and can be invoked during the copy process. This gives the developer an opportunity to specify and refine the target names of all elements being copied. Following the creation and copying of the information in the reference model, the code follows up with the rest of the transformation by copying all public attributes and operations in the PIM classes and by creating getters and setters.

3.4 Create UML Profiles

Lesson 8. *UML profiles can be used to manage model markups as part of the MDA transformation.*

UML profiles are used in two distinct and separate ways. First, the traditional role of UML profiles is to provide a mechanism to extend the semantics of UML for a particular domain or method. It enables UML to effectively model something concrete. IBM Rational's Business Modeling Profile and Data Modeling Profile are examples of UML profiles that enable IBM Rational XDE to effectively model business processes and logical/physical database designs, respectively. These types of profile usage can be thought of as semantic profiles, necessary for the model itself to capture and express the detail for the particular level of abstraction and domain.

Profiles are also a useful mechanism for managing model markings, a necessary element of the MDA transformation process. Marking is a step or technique in MDA in which additional information, not within the semantic scope of the model itself, can be added to a model solely for use by automation later. Marking up a model is usually a step done just before a transformation is ready to be invoked. Of course, a model can be marked as it is developed. However, typically the role and skills of the developer creating the model may not be appropriate to understand the significance and purpose of the various markings themselves.

For example, suppose a simple abstract entity model (part of the traditional analysis model) was developed in UML by a set of analysts. This model defines a number of persistent entities in the proposed system, including their attributes and relationships to each other. This information gets transformed into a logical (or physical) database design. A problem occurs when the analysis model is used to create a new database model. The information captured in the analysis model is insufficient to complete a working data model. For instance, a String attribute of an entity could be implemented as a CHAR, VARCHAR, or TEXT type of column. Additionally, the length information of the column is not information that is normally captured in an analysis model.

Transformations going from models at high levels of abstraction to models at lower levels of abstraction, and hence more detail, often suffer this problem of insufficient or incomplete information. Even in the case of mapping a UML association to a Java field, it is unclear how associations with multiplicities of 'many' are implemented. The semantics of sets, lists, and maps are beyond the semantic scope of most UML analysis models, but something critical within the scope of the implementing Java class.

UML profiles come to the rescue here by providing a mechanism through which models and model elements can be augmented with information, albeit beyond the model's official semantic scope, to be used by transformations. A marking profile, distinct and separate from any applied semantic profiles, can be applied to a model that defines stereotypes and tag values that contain information used only during the transformation. A data modeling profile would contain tags that describe a column's length or precision. A Java profile would contain information on how an association was implemented in Java.

The MDA Toolkit functionality for creating UML profiles is in fact an example of an MDA transformation itself. Profiles are created by first building a UML model and stereotyping classes and attributes in the model that in the end are used to generate the actual profile file. This stereotyping of the profile model's elements is "marking" the model with the necessary information for the transformation to build the actual profile file which is registered with IBM Rational XDE, and subsequently capable of being applied to any UML model opened by IBM Rational XDE.

3.5 Develop the Transformation

Lesson 9. *All transformations should be created such that they can participate in a iterative process, and hence can be repeatedly applied without loss of unrelated information.*

A critical design goal of any transformation is the ability for it to participate in an iterative development process. While one-time-only transformations may be easier to develop, it has been our experience that these types of transformations see very little usage as compared to the effort required to create them. Instead, transformations that can be continually applied to evolving development lifecycle artifacts tend to be far more valuable and worth the effort in developing.

Developing transformations with the MDA Toolkit that participate in an iterative development process requires some attention to all elements in the design and implementation. The MDA API that provides the primary method for model access and manipulation is designed to promote this type of transformation development. For example, when creating an attribute on a class the createAttribute() method of the MdaClass object by default will first check to see if an attribute of that name already exists, and if it does will simply return that instance of the attribute without creating a new duplicate attribute. Interestingly enough this is not the default behavior of most UML access APIs because the UML specification itself does not require unique attribute names. Therefore, in theory a UML API should permit this. However, most of our transformations target a real-life implementation language like Java or C++, and so in practice this type of behavior in a model API is not desired.

The MDA Toolkit API does have an implementation bias. When it compares class names and attribute names it looks for uniqueness in its container, and uses case-sensitive comparisons. When comparing operations, it performs a case-sensitive name match along with a comparison of input argument data types, and ignores return types. As a result, the MDA Toolkit API makes it significantly easier for a transformation developer who is targeting a Java or C++ implementations to develop iterative-friendly transformations.

The overall process of developing a MDA Toolkit transformation is little more than an exercise in developing Java code, and in particular developing an Eclipse Java plugin. Fortunately the toolkit wizard provides most of the Eclipse required code, and lets the transformation developer focus on implementing the transformation logic.

Lesson 10. *Good transformations implement discrete validation, transformation, and verification procedures.*

When the toolkit wizard creates a project, it provides stubs or sample code for three key methods:

```
public boolean validate() throws Exception {
  boolean valid = true;
  return valid;
}
```

```
public void transform() throws Exception {
}

public boolean verify() throws Exception {
  boolean verified = true;
  return verified;
}
```

The most important of these is the transform() method which is invoked when the developer using the transformation wants to invoke the transformation. It is in this method that the primary logic of the transformation is encoded. Any parameter values specified by the developer invoking the transformation are obtained with simple method calls and are typically translated into something more meaningful like MDA API references. The logic of the transformation is most often delegated to helper methods and other custom classes that perform the real work of the transformation. During the transformation it is often useful to write status messages to the visible log, so the developer can monitor the progress.

In the sample implementation below, analysis model and design model filenames are specified as parameters. Parameter values are accessed by calling a superclass method. These are then converted to MdaModel element references. In this example the analysis model is scanned for all classes that are stereotyped "PersistentObject" (in a custom profile), and that are not subclasses of another class, since entire hierarchies are processed in a single function. Most of the work is coordinated by the processPersitenceObject() helper method, which in turn uses several delegate classes to perform the bulk of the transformation work.

```
public void transform() throws Exception {
  writeln("Starting transformation");
  String analysisModelFilename =
      getStringParameter(TransformationParameters
      .P_FILE_PIM_MODEL);
  String designModelFilename =
      getStringParameter(TransformationParameters
      .P_FILE_PSM_MODEL);

  designModel = openModel("designModel",
      designModelFilename);
  analysisModel = openModel("analysisModel",
      analysisModelFilename);

  MdaClass[] allClasses = analysisModel.getMdaClasses(
      MdaOption.RECURSE);
  for(int i=0;i<allClasses.length;i++) {
    MdaClass cls = allClasses[i];
    MdaGeneralization[] generalizations =
```

```
          cls.getMdaGeneralizations();
      if( generalizations.length == 0
          && cls.isStereotyped("MyCustomProfile",
          "PersistentObject") ) {
        processPersistentObject(cls);
      }
  }

  writeln("Completed Transformation");
}
```

The validate() method is called before the transform() method, and if it returns a false value will abort any attempt to run the transform() method. In the following sample implementation the analysis model is checked to ensure that it exists and that it has the custom profile applied to it. The design model is checked for its existence and that it is an IBM Rational XDE code model, capable of roundtrip engineering Java code.

```
public boolean validate() throws Exception {
  boolean valid = true;
  writeln("Starting validation");

  String designModelFilename =
      getStringParameter(TransformationParameters
      .P_FILE_PSM_MODEL);
  MdaModel designModel = openModel("designModel",
      designModelFilename);
  if( designModel == null ) {
    valid = false;
      writeln("The design model is a required parameter"
          + " and must exist.")
  } else {
    if( !designModel.canRTE() ) {
      valid = false;
      writeln("The design model must be"
          + " an XDE Code Model");
    }
  }

  String analysisModelFilename =
      getStringParameter(TransformationParameters
      .P_FILE_PIM_MODEL);
  MdaModel analysisModel = openModel("analysisModel",
      analysisModelFilename);
  if( analysisModel == null ) {
    valid = false;
```

```
  writeln("The analysis model is a required parameter"
      + " and must exist." );
  } else {
    if( !analysisModel.hasProfile("MyCustomProfile")) {
      valid = false;
      writeln("The profile MyCustomProfile "
          + "must be applied to the Analysis model");
    }
  }

  writeln("Validation completed.");
  return valid;
}
```

Depending on the desired level of verification, the verification() method can be as complex as the transform method itself, and typically will use helper methods and classes similar to the actual transform code. In the following example the same code is used to identify elements in the analysis model that should have been transformed.

```
public boolean verify() throws Exception {
  boolean verified = true;
  writeln("Starting verification");
  String analysisModelFilename =
      getStringParameter(TransformationParameters
      .P_FILE_PIM_MODEL);
  String designModelFilename =
      getStringParameter(TransformationParameters
      .P_FILE_PSM_MODEL);

  MdaModel designModel = openModel("designModel",
      designModelFilename);
  MdaModel analysisModel = openModel("analysisModel",
      analysisModelFilename);

  MdaClass[] allClasses = analysisModel.getMdaClasses(
      MdaOption.RECURSE);
  for(int i=0;i<allClasses.length;i++) {
    MdaClass cls = allClasses[i];
    MdaGeneralization[] generalizations =
        cls.getMdaGeneralizations();
    if( generalizations.length == 0
        && cls.isStereotyped("MyCustomProfile",
        "PersistentObject") ) {
      verifyPersistentObject(cls);
    }
  }
```

```
writeln("Verification completed.");
return verified;
}
```

The development and testing of an MDA transformation proceeds like any Eclipse plugin project. A transformation can be debugging using the Eclipse runtime workbench, which essentially starts up a new instance of the Eclipse and IBM Rational XDE shells in debug mode, enabling step-by-step tracing of transformation code.

3.6 Deploy the Transformation

Lesson 11. *Use of the Eclipse plugin architecture greatly simplifies the task of installing and upgrading MDA transformations.*

When a transformation has been developed the task of deploying it and educating a large development team comes next. Fortunately, the Eclipse Update Manager mechanism provides a convenient mechanism for installing plug-ins into an Eclipse shell. Using the built-in Eclipse Plugin Development Environment (PDE) functions, the transformation can be packaged and placed on an internal HTTP site from where developers can easily download and install MDA Toolkit transformations, and other dependent plug-ins.

Once installed into a developer's workstation the menu item corresponding to the transformation can be activated in any perspective. The menu item prompts the developer for the parameters of the transformation. The developer can optionally run all three functions (validate, transform, or verify) together, or run them individually. The results will appear in the updated models and artifacts and in the log window.

Lesson 12. *Each MDA transformation must be well documented, providing samples, guidance, and support information.*

Providing the transformation functionality to a developer is not sufficient. It is important that whenever significant new functionality such as an MDA transformation is provided to a development team, they should be educated in its usage. Since most valuable transformations perform relatively complex work, it follows that in many cases the decision when to use it and exactly what to supply as parameters might be equally complex.

Updating the development process and providing online documentation to accompany the transformation should be considered essential to success. In the Eclipse environment, documentation is easily inserted into the rest of the online help, and is typically part of the transformation plugin itself or a dependent plugin that is installed with the transformation.

4 Commentary

4.1 The MDA Process

Building solutions using MDA approaches requires changes to the development process. While our experience has been that many of the current best practices for enterprise software development are still applicable, there are some important changes to those practices as a result of taking a more model-driven perspective to the development process. To explore this topic we look at a well-known development process, the Rational Unified Process, and consider the way that process is interpreted and executed on an MDA project.

RUP Overview

The Rational Unified Process®, or RUP®, is the de facto standard software engineering process in use today [262]. It provides a disciplined approach to assigning tasks and responsibilities within a development organization and has been applied to projects of varying size and complexity, with small teams and large, and on efforts lasting weeks to large-scale programs lasting years. The goal of RUP is to ensure the production of high-quality software that predictably meets the needs of its end users on schedule and within budget.

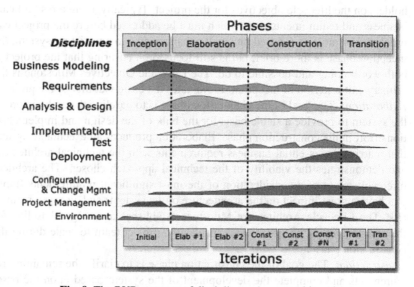

Fig. 9. The RUP concepts of disciplines, phases, and iterations

Figure 9 illustrates the overall architecture of the RUP in two dimensions. The horizontal axis represents time and shows the lifecycle aspects of the process. Both the management perspective of lifecycle phases is shown (across the top) and the software engineering and project management perspective of iterations is displayed (along the bottom).

The vertical axis represents disciplines that logically group activities by nature. This shows the static aspect of the process – how it is described in terms of process components, disciplines, activities, workflows, artifacts, and roles.

The concept within RUP is that at any point in time there is activity taking place in a variety of disciplines. What distinguishes one lifecycle phase from another is not the total absence of a discipline, but the relative amount of contribution that discipline is making in the overall work streams. The mix of activities varies over time as the emphasis and priorities of the project change. For example, in early iterations you spend more time on requirements; in later iterations you spend more time on implementation.

RUP Phases and Iterations

From a management perspective, the software lifecycle of RUP consists of four sequential phases, each concluded by a major milestone. An assessment is performed to determine whether the objectives of the phase have been met. A satisfactory assessment allows the project to move to the next phase. Briefly, the phases of a RUP lifecycle are:

- *Inception:*. The goal of the inception phase is to reach agreement among all stakeholders on the lifecycle objectives for the project. Typically, there are significant business and requirements risks which must be addressed before the project can proceed. For projects focused on small enhancements to an existing system, the inception phase is more brief, but is still focused on ensuring that the project is both worth doing and possible to do. The Lifecycle Objectives Milestone is the primary exit criterion of inception. It evaluates the basic viability of the project.
- *Elaboration:*. The goal of the elaboration phase is to baseline the architecture of the system to provide a stable basis for the bulk of the design and implementation effort in the construction phase. Elaboration produces an executable system that marries the essential business requirements with the technical architecture and demonstrates the viability of the technical approach chosen. The architecture evolves out of a consideration of the most significant requirements (those that have a great impact on the architecture of the system) and an assessment of risk. The Lifecycle Architecture Milestone establishes a managed baseline for the architecture of the system and enables the project team to scale during the construction phase.
- *Construction:*. The goal of the construction phase is to clarify the remaining requirements and complete the development of the system based upon the baselined architecture. The construction phase is in some sense a manufacturing process, where emphasis is placed on managing resources and controlling operations to optimize costs, schedules, and quality. In this sense the management mindset undergoes a transition from the development of intellectual property during inception and elaboration, to the development of deployable products during

construction and transition. The Initial Operational Capability milestone determines whether the product is ready to be deployed into a user acceptance environment.

- *Transition:*. The focus of the transition phase is to ensure that software is available for its end users. The transition phase can span several iterations, and includes testing the product in preparation for release, and making minor adjustments based on user feedback. At this point in the lifecycle, user feedback should focus mainly on fine tuning the product, configuring, installing, and usability issues; all the major structural issues should have been worked out much earlier in the project lifecycle. The Product Release Milestone is where you decide if the objectives of the project were met, and if you should start another development cycle.

From a software engineering and project management perspective, things happen day to day based on iterations. Phases consist of iterations – distinct sequences of activities with a baselined plan and valuation criteria resulting in a release of artifacts (internal or external). Every phase of the lifecycle consists of a series of iterations and the character of the iterations differs depending on where you in the lifecycle.

RUP and MDA

Currently, RUP provides no specific guidance on how to integrate an MDA approach into the overall process. This is not surprising as RUP reflects current industry best practice and typically does not codify approaches until they are well established within the field. MDA is a new and emerging approach, and significant best practice with MDA as applied to RUP projects is only now becoming available. Our experiences, however, indicate a number of important ways in which we can enhance RUP with best practices for MDA projects. In particular, the backbone of RUP, an architecture-centric iterative development process, is highly appropriate to MDA projects. As a result, the core approaches defined in RUP offer an excellent basis on which to succeed with MDA.

However, there are some areas where additional guidance on MDA is appropriate. Here, we indicate a number of the important aspects to consider in applying RUP to an MDA project:

- Elaboration is the main phase impacted by an MDA project. It is important to look at elaboration activities and briefly describe MDA modifications.
- The "Architect" role is the main role in elaboration that requires addition consideration. A specialization of architect, "MDA Architect" is appropriate to many MDA projects. This is the essential role in which specific MDA activities and artifacts are defined, transformations created, and so on. Hence, the primary MDA artifacts from this role are mapping documents, transformations, and UML profiles.
- MDA is as much about model-driven automation as it is about model-driven architecture. This provides some guidance as to how to view MDA and RUP. Typically, MDA automates activities within RUP. Rather than change RUP activities,

MDA augments them with additional tasks aimed at supporting automation of a number of the primary RUP activities.

- The application of MDA will involve many RUP roles, but these roles will typically not have additional activities. Rather, the specific activities will have details added on how those activities are automated using the specific tools and MDA approaches chosen. In the RUP we call these additional details RUP Tool mentors. For example, a team working on object-relational data mapping may be using a modeling tool with a set of MDA transformations. But their workflow related to "define design classes" will largely remain the same at a high level.
- Perhaps more pervasively, the primary changes to RUP consist of a more subtle change of perspective on the development process. MDA encourages architects and developers to work at higher levels of abstraction than typically expected in non-MDA projects. This is most apparent during construction where the code automation aspects of MDA significantly change the emphasis of the implementation tasks. Developers are able to continue to work with more abstract analysis and design models as inputs to MDA transformations. They find that they work less and less with actual implementation models and source code, and more with designing the appropriate business-focused workflow of the solution. A smaller subset of developers will be implementing the model-to-code transformations themselves.
- MDA transformations are frequently built around pre-built solution frameworks (also called "Reference Architectures" or "Application Frameworks"). The MDA transformations augment these frameworks with domain-specific business logic. This approach of coupling MDA and solution frameworks makes a great deal of sense since the entire MDA approach is centered on automating a set of repeatable approaches and assets. However, it further changes the development process toward greater emphasis on reuse, management assets, and incremental delivery of solutions.

4.2 Using MDA to Customize a Solution Framework

Today's enterprise software systems are rarely (if ever) developed from scratch line by line in an IDE. Rather, they are created by extending an existing solution framework with domain specific business logic, by connecting to (and manipulating) information from different sources, and by designing rich user display and interaction services. Hence, the development approach that is followed is not the classical "waterfall" scenario where requirements gathering is followed by analysis and design, leading to the implementation of the system. Rather, it is one of continual extension and refinement of an existing partial solution toward a desired goal through a set of iterations that add value to the solution.

These partial solutions that form the heart of a new system may come from one of several sources:

(1) An existing set of applications. The primary approach may be to take an existing solution and extend it in useful ways, as dictated by the business need. Hence,

much of the design work involves understanding how those existing applications are architected, and where meaningful extensions can be added without undue compromise on the qualities of the existing applications. In most cases the process is complicated by the fact that the original applications were not designed with the goal of reuse in mind.

(2) A proprietary application framework used by the organization. Having built many kinds of similar solutions in a particular domain, some organizations have extracted core application capabilities as reusable proprietary services to be employed in future solutions. These services help to improve productivity of a family of systems that share common characteristics, and increase the predictability of future system development. An example is Accenture's General Reusable Netcentric Delivery Solution (GRNDS) Framework.[2]

(3) An acquired application framework, whether open source or commercial in origin. Recognizing the consistent architectural patterns that are used in designing certain kinds of applications has resulted in a number of technologies being created to help organizations to create solutions conforming to those patterns. The resulting application frameworks are available both commercially and in the open source community, and are delivered as standalone frameworks or bundled with tools that help create, manage, and extend those frameworks. Examples include the Struts and JSF frameworks for creating certain kinds of n-tiered J2EE solutions.

(4) A set of extensions and customizations to packaged applications. Many organizations acquire comprehensive solutions for key business processes from packaged application vendors. However, organizations typically need to customize those solutions to meet their needs. As a result, the packaged application vendors have structured their solutions to support different kinds of extension and customization, offer well-defined APIs to access internals of the packaged application, or augment the packaged applications with detailed design documents, extension examples, and package specific tools.

Consequently, the primary task faced by many IT projects is to create a clear understanding of their domain, to express that understanding in a platform independent domain model supporting various kinds of analysis to ensure its correctness and consistency, and to map that domain model to a platform specific implementation realized by extending the solution framework. Model-to-model transformations help in refining the domain, while model-to-code transformation's map the domain model to the specific solution framework.

In model-to-code transformations the solution framework plays a key role as it constrains and guides the kinds of transformations that are meaningful. For example, if using a Struts-based application framework, the application being created has a well-understood structure, including well-known extension points where business logic will be realized. A set of transformations can be created based on that knowledge. Indeed, wizard-driven tooling can be created to automate creation of those

---

[2] See http://www.accenture.com/xd/xd.asp?it=enweb&xd=services
%5Ctechnical%5Ccapabilities%5Cgrnds.xml

transformations for domain models containing appropriate kinds of information. This is the way, for example, in which tools such as the IBM Rational Application Developer use domain-focused visual design tooling to automate code generation for Struts or Java Server Faces (JSF)-based application frameworks. More generally, by using a solution framework as the basis for a system, the task of writing model-to-code transformations is significantly eased, and we gain greater efficiency, predictability, repeatability, and manageability of the resulting solutions.

In summary, we reiterate that software is rarely created from scratch, and that model transformations (to another model or to code) help leverage existing solution frameworks. As this approach of building on existing software increases, the MDA role and value increases and helps automate how we extend and customize those frameworks. In fact, this "custom automation" is viewed by some as the only viable option for creating systems of increasing complexity, and in response to the constraints placed on us by the components and technologies we deploy.

5 Summary and Future Directions

Model-driven approaches to software and system development have been in use for some time. More recently, the focus of attention has been on how to increase automation of model-driven technologies based on the OMG's MDA approach. MDA approaches enable organizations to construct custom automations for model-to-model and model-to-code transformations. Using these transformations technical experts can share their expertise across a large development team. In particular, MDA offers a number of advantages over other approaches:

- Productivity of development is increased by helping to insulate a majority of developers from technical details that they do not need to consider to carry out their task of designing enterprise solutions to meet a business need. Consequently, more time is spent focusing on the task at hand: implementing the business capabilities of the system.
- Quality is improved by encouraging reuse of known patterns of behavior, building on existing architectural designs, and leveraging expertise more effectively. The use of automation also promotes consistency and improves the quality of the system design and implementation, particularly as the solution evolves through maintenance and upgrade.
- Predictability of the development process and the delivered solution is enhanced through a repeatable set of practices well matched to today's need for iterative delivery of solution capabilities. The use of automation speeds up development, particularly where many of the tasks of the developer are repeated and cumbersome.

In this chapter we have explored many of the practical aspects of realizing an MDA approach based on our use of modeling approaches in general, and the design and use of a specific MDA Toolkit for IBM Rational XDE for Java. These experiences reveal that while traditional design and implementation practices are relevant to MDA projects, there are a number of additional requirements that must be addressed to ensure that the approach is optimally applied. We have described many of these requirements, and illustrated them with practical examples. Our key findings have been distilled into 12 lessons for the practical application of MDA. These lessons, however, are not specific to a single set of technologies. They have also been applied within other IBM Rational tools. The latest set of solutions from IBM Rational support MDA development projects by providing capabilities that have been created based on experiences with existing technologies and practices, including those reported here. As a result, IBM Rational tools provide a rich set of functionality for all types of automation, including predefined out-of-the-box transformations and tools for customizing transformations.[3] The latest example of this support for MDA is seen in *IBM Rational Software Architect*. This is an extensive workbench of design and construction services supporting various aspects of analysis, design, and implementation of enterprise systems, including sophisticated model authoring and management capabilities to support visual modeling in UML. Specific to MDA projects, the IBM Rational Software Architect product contains an extensive custom pattern authoring environment, and supports authoring of model-to-model and model-to-code transformations in several ways (depending on preferred style and design goals):

- Generic plugins (using the Eclipse plugin development environment).
- Pluglets (small, easily installable automation assistants useful for quick one-time automation tasks).
- Transformations (a rules-based framework for structuring large and complex transformations).

Supporting these technologies is a set of best practices that assist organizations to adopt model-driven approaches. Integrated with the IBM Rational Software Architect product is context-specific process guidance for development using techniques based on the RUP. Furthermore, this guidance can be augmented with project specific additional practices and reusable assets available from online sources (such as developerWorks)[4].

6 Acknowledgements

The work reported in this chapter has been carried out by a number of people, and it is our pleasure to acknowledge their contribution. The ideas discussed here reflect the thinking of a broad team at IBM including Grady Booch, Gary Cernosek, Jim Conallen, Pete Eeles, Sridhar Iyengar, Simon Johnston, Grant Larsen, Martin Nally, Jim Rumbaugh, and Bran Selic. We also thank Mike Perrow for his helpful reviews of the chapter.

---

[3] For more details, see http://www.ibm.com/rational/mda.

[4] For more details see http://www.ibm.com/developerworks/rational.

References

1. *The Murphi Model Checker.* http://verify.stanford.edu/dill/murphi.html.
2. openmdx. www.openmdx.org.
3. Extensible Markup Language (XML) 1.0 (Second Edition). www.w3c.org/XML, October 2000.
4. AspectC++. http://www.aspectc.org/, January 2005.
5. Sherif Abdelwahed, Sandeep Neema, Joseph Loyall, and Richard Shapiro. Multi-level online hybrid control design for QoS management. In *Proceedings of the 24th IEEE International Real-time Systems Symposium (RTSS 2003)*, Cancun, Mexico, December 2003.
6. M. Abi-Antoun, J. Ho, and J. Kwan. *Inter-Library Loan Management System: Revised Life-Cycle Architecture.* Center for Software Engineering, University of Southern California, Los Angeles, CA, USA, 1999.
7. Lockheed Martin Aeronautics. Lockheed Martin (MDA Success Story). www.omg.org/mda/mda_files/LockheedMartin.pdf, January 2003.
8. Aditya Agrawal, Gábor Karsai, and Ákos Lédeczi. An end-to-end domain-driven software development framework. In *18th Annual ACM SIGPLAN Conference on Object-Oriented Programming, Systems, Languages, and Applications (OOPSLA) - Domain-driven Track*, pages 8–15, Anaheim, California, USA, October 2003.
9. K. Ahmed. *Developing Enterprise Java Applications with J2EE and UML.* Addison-Wesley, 2001.
10. A.V. Aho, R. Sethi, and J.D. Ullman. *Compilers: Principles, Techniques, and Tools.* Addison-Wesley, Reading, MA, 1988.
11. D. Akehurst and S. Kent. A relational approach to defining transformations in a metamodel. In *Proc. UML 2002 - The Unified Modeling Language. Model Engineering, Languages, Concepts, and Tools. 5th International Conference, Dresden, Germany*, volume 2460 of *LNCS*. Springer, Berlin Heidelberg New York, 2002.
12. M. Alanen, J. Lilius, I. Pores, and D. Truscan. Model driven engineering: A position paper. In *Proceedings of the 1st International Workshop on Model-based Methodologies for Pervasive and Embedded Software*, Hamilton (Ontario), Canada,, 2004.
13. Marcus Alanen and Ivan Porres. Difference and union of models. In *Proceedings of the UML 2003 Conference, San Francisco, CA*, volume 2863 of *LNCS*, pages 2–17. Springer, Berlin Heidelberg New York, October 2003.

434   References

14. R.A. Altmann, A.N. Hawke, and C.D. Marlin. An integrated programming environment based on multiple concurrent views. *Australian Computer Journal*, 20:65–72, 1988.

15. Deepak Alur, John Crupi, and Dan Malks. *J2EE Patterns*. Prentice Hall, Englemovel cliffs, NJ,.

16. S. Alvarado. An evaluation of object oriented architecture models for satellite ground systems. In *Proceedings of the 2nd Ground Systems Architecture Workshop (GSAW), El Segundo, CA*. 1998.

17. Matjaz Dolenc Ana Robnik and Milenko Alcin. Industrial experience using SDL in IskraTEL. In Rolv Bræk and Amardeo Sarma, editors, *Proceedings of Seventh SDL Forum*, Amsterdam, 1995. Elsevier Science.

18. AndroMDA: MDA Framework. http://www.andromda.org/, December 2004.

19. P. Andre, A. Romanczuk, and J.-C. Royer. Check the consistency of uml class diagrams using larch prover. In T. Clark, editor, *Proc. of 3rd Rigorous Object-Oriented Methods Workshop*. BCS, Swindor, UK, 2000.

20. Dave Astels. Refactoring with uml. In *Proceedings of 3rd International Conference on eXtreme Programming and Flexible Processes in Software Engineering (XP2002)*, pages 67–70, Alghero, Sardinia, Italy, 2002.

21. E. Astesiano and G. Reggio. An attempt at analysing the consistency problems in the uml from a classical algebraic viewpoint. In *Recent Trends in Algebraic Development Techniques, Selected Papers of the 16th International Workshop WADT'02*, volume 2755 of *LNCS*, pages 56–81. Springer, Berlin Heidelberg New York, 2003.

22. Colin Atkinson and Thomas Kühne. Aspect-oriented development with stratified frameworks. *IEEE Software*, 20(1):81–89, 2003.

23. A. Avizienis, J. Laprie, and B. Randell. Fundamental concepts of dependability. Technical report, University of Newcastle, 2001.

24. R. Back, D. Björklund, J. Lilius, L. Milovanov, and I. Porres. A workbench to experiment with new model driven engineering applications. In *UML 2003*, volume 2863 of *LNCS*. Springer, Berlin Heidelberg New York, 2003.

25. Krishnakumar Balasubramanian, Jaiganesh Balasubramanian, Jeff Parsons, Aniruddha Gokhale, and Douglas C. Schmidt. A platform-independent component modeling language for distributed real-time and embedded systems. In *Proceedings of the 11th IEEE Real-Time and Embedded Technology and Applications Symposium*, San Francisco, CA, USA,, March 2005.

26. Paolo Baldan and Barbara König. Approximating the behaviour of graph transformation systems. In Andrea Corradini, Hartmut Ehrig, Hans-Jörg Kreowski, and Grzegorz Rozenberg, editors, *Proceedings ICGT 2002: First International Conference on Graph Transformation*, volume 2505 of *LNCS*, pages 14–29, Barcelona, Spain, 2002. Springer, Berlin Heidelberg New York.

27. R. Balzer, T.E. Cheatham, and C. Green. Software technology in the 1990's: Using a new paradigm. *IEEE Computer*, pages 39–45, November 1983.

28. F. Barbier, B. Henderson-Sellers, A. Le Parc, and J.-M. Bruel. Formalization of the whole-part relationship in the unified modeling language. *IEEE Transaction on Software Engineering*, 29(5):459–470, 2003.

29. Luciano Baresi and Reiko Heckel. Tutorial introduction to graph transformation: A software engineering perspective. In *International Conference on Graph Transformation, ICGT, LNCS*, volume 2505 of *Lecture Notes in Computer Science*, pages 402–439. Springer, Berlin Heidelberg New York, 2002.

30. Len Bass, Paul Clements, and Rick Kazman. *Software Architecture in Practice*. Addison Wesley, 2nd edition, 2003.

31. D. Batory, J. N. Sarvela, and A. Rauschmayer. Scaling step-wise refinement. *IEEE Transactions on Software Engineering*, 30(6):355–371, 2004.

32. F.L. Bauer, M. Broy, R. Gnatz, W. Hesse, B. Krieg-Brückner, H. Partsch, P. Pepper, and H. Wössner. Towards a wide spectrum language to support program specification and program development. *ACM SIGPLAN Notices*, 13(12):15–24, 1978.

33. Ira D. Baxter, Christopher Pidgeon, and Michael Mehlich. Dms: Program transformations for practical scalable software evolution. In *26th International Conference on Software Engineering*, pages 625–634, Edinburgh, Scotland, 2004.

34. K. Beck. *Extreme Programming Explained*. Addison-Wesley, Reading, MA, 1999.

35. M. Belaunde. Assessment of the model driven technologies - foundations and key technologies. MODA-TEL Consortium. http://www.modatel.org/~Modatel/pub/deliverables/D2.1-final.pdf, December 2002.

36. Gerd Beneken, Tilman Seifert, Niko Baehr, Inge Hanschke, and Olaf Rauch. Referenzarchitekturen und MDA. In Peter Dadam and Manfred Reichert, editors, *GI Jahrestagung (2)*, volume 51 of *LNI*, pages 101–105. GI, Bonn, 2004.

37. Saddek Bensalem, Vijay Ganesh, Yassine Lakhnech, César Munoz, Sam Owre, Harald Rueß, John Rushby, Vlad Rusu, Hassen Saïdi, N. Shankar, Eli Singerman, and Ashish Tiwari. An overview of SAL. In C. Michael Holloway, editor, *LFM 2000: Fifth NASA Langley Formal Methods Workshop*, pages 187–196, 2000.

38. Gerard Berry and Georges Gonthier. The Esterel synchronous programming language: Design, semantics, implementation. *Science of Computer Programming*, 19(2):87–152, 1992.

39. Jean Bézivin, Nicolas Farcet, Jean-Marc Jézéquel, Benoît Langlois, and Damien Pollet. Reflective model driven engineering. In *Proceedings of UML 2003 Conference*, volume 2863 of *LNCS*, pages 175–189, San Francisco, CA, 2003. Springer, Berlin Heidelberg, New York.

40. B. Blanchet, P. Cousot, R. Cousot, J. Feret, L. Mauborgne, A. Min'e, D. Monniaux, and X. Rival. Design and implementation of a special-purpose static program analyzer for safety-critical real-time embedded software. In *The essence of computation: complexity, analysis, transformation*, pages 85–108. Springer, Berlin, Heidelberg, New York, 2002.

41. Marko Boger, Thorsten Sturm, and Per Fragemann. Refactoring browser for uml. In *Objects, Components, Architectures, Services, and Applications for a NetworkedWorld: International Conference NetObjectDays, NODe 2002*, volume 2591/2003 of *LNCS*, pages 366–377, Erfurt, Germany, 2002. Springer, Berlin Heidelberg New York.

42. G. Booch, J. Rumbaugh, and I. Jacobson. *The Unified Modeling Language User Guide*. Addison-Wesley, Reading, MA, 1999.

43. E. Börger, A. Cavarra, and E. Riccobene. Modeling the dynamics of UML State Machines. In Y. Gurevich, P. Kutter, M. Odersky, and L. Thiele, editors, *Abstract State Machines. Theory and Applications*, volume 1912 of *LNCS*, pages 223–241. Springer, Berlin Heidelberg New York, 2000.

44. Egon Börger and Robert F. Stärk. *Abstract State Machines. A method for High-Level System Design and Analysis*. Springer, Berlin Heidelberg New York, 2003.

45. S. Borland and H. Vangheluwe. Transforming statecharts to DEVS. In *Proceedings of the SCS Summer Computer Simulation Conference*, 2003.

46. Rolv Braek and Richard Sanders. Modeling peer-to-peer service goals in uml. In *2nd IEEE International Conference on Software Engineering and Formal Methods(SEFM), Beijing, China*. IEEE Computer Society Press, Silver Spring, MD, 2004.

47. F.M.T. Brazier, B.M. Dunin-Keplicz, N.R. Jennings, and J. Treur. Desire: Modelling multi-agent systems in a compositional formal framework. *International Journal of Cooperative Information Systems*, (1):67–94, 1997.

48. R. Breu, R. Grosu, F. Huber, B. Rumpe, and W. Schwerin. Systems, views and models of UML. In M. Schader and A. Korthaus, editors, *The Unified Modeling Language, Technical Aspects and Applications*, pages 93–109. Physica Verlag, Heidelberg, 1998.
49. Rolv Bræk and Jacqueline Floch. ICT convergence: Modeling issues. In Daniel Amyot and Allan Williams, editors, *System Analysis and Modeling: 4th International SDL and MSC Workshop, SAM 2004, Ottawa, Canada, June 1-4, 2004, Revised Selected Papers*, volume 3319 of *LNCS*, pages 237–256. Springer, Berlin Heidelberg New York, 2005.
50. Rolv Bræk and Øystein Haugen. *Engineering Real Time Systems. An object-oriented methodology using SDL*. Prentice Hall, Englewood Cliffs, NJ, 1993.
51. A.W. Brown. Model driven architecture: Principles and practice. *Software and Systems Modeling*, 3(4):314–327, December 2004.
52. M. Broy and M. Wirsing. Algebraic state machines. In T. Rus, editor, *8th International Conference on Algebraic Methodology and Software Technology (AMAST 2000)*, volume 1816 of *LNCS*. Springer, Berlin Heidelberg New York, 2000.
53. J. T. Buck, S. Ha, E. A. Lee, and D. G. Messerschmitt. Ptolemy: A framework for simulating and prototyping heterogeneous systems. *International Journal of Computer Simulation, Special Issue on Simulation Software Development Component Development Strategies*, 4, April 1994.
54. R. Budde, K. Kautz, K. Kuhlenkamp, and H. Züllighoven. *Prototyping. An Approach to Evolutionary System Development*. Springer, Berlin Heidelberg New York, 1992.
55. G. Caplat and J.L. Sourrouille. Model mapping in MDA. In J. Bezivin and R. France, editors, *Proceedings of UML 2002 Workshop in Software Model Engineering*, Dresden, Germany, 2002.
56. G. Caplat and J.L. Sourrouille. Considerations about model mapping. In J. Bezivin and M. Gogolla, editors, *Proceedings of UML 2003 Workshop in Software Model Engineering*, San Francisco, CA, USA, 2003.
57. Castor. Castor library. http://castor.exolab.org, June 2003.
58. S. Chaki, E. Clarke, A. Groce, S. Jha, and H. Veith. Modular verification of software components in C. *IEEE Transactions on Software Engineering*, 30(6):388–402, June 2004.
59. Sudarshan S. Chawathe, Anand Rajaraman, Hector Garcia-Molina, and Jennifer Widom. Change detection in hierarchically structured information. In *Proceedings of the ACM SIGMOD International Conference on Management of Data*, pages 493–504, Montreal, Canada, June 1996.
60. G. Christen, A. Dobniewski, and G. Wainer. Modeling state-based DEVS models in CD++. In *Proceedings of MGA, Advanced Simulation Technologies Conference 2004 (ASTC'04)*, 2004.
61. A. Christoph and M. M. Müller. GREAT: UML transformation tool for porting middleware applications. In P. Stevens, J. Whittle, and G. Booch, editors, *UML 2003 - The Unified Modeling Language. Model Languages and Applications. 6th International Conference, San Francisco, CA, USA, Proceedings*, volume 2863 of *LNCS*, pages 18–30. Springer, Berlin Heidelberg New York, 2003.
62. S. Clarke, W. Harrison, H. Ossher, and P. Tarr. Subject-oriented design: Towards improved alignment of requirements, design, and code. In *Proceedings OOPSLA 1999*, Denver, Colorado, USA, November 1999.
63. *CLI.Standard ECMA-335, Common Language Infrastructure (CLI)*, 2nd edition, 2002. ISO/IEC 23271, http://www.ecma-international.org/publications/standards/Ecma-335.htm.
64. Concern Manipulation Environment (CME) WWW site. http://www.research.ibm.com/cme/, 2004.

65. J.M. Cobleigh, L.A. Clarke, and L.J. Osterweil. Flavers: A finite state verification technique for software systems. *IBM Systems Journal*, 41(1):140–165, 2002.

66. Codagen Technologies Corporation. Codagen Architect. http://www.codagen.com/products/architect/, January 2005.

67. Compuware Corporation. OptimalJ. http://www.compuware.com/products/optimalj/, January 2005.

68. Steve Cook. Domain-specific modelling and model driven architecture. *MDA Journal, Business Process Trends*, pages 2–10, January 2004.

69. Steve Cook and Stuart Kent. The tool factory. OOPSLA 2003 Workshop on Generative Techniques in the context of Model Driven Architecture, 2003.

70. Steve Cook, Anneke Kleppe, Richard Mitchell, Bernhard Rumpe, Jos Warmer, and Alan Wills. Defining UML family members using prefaces. In Christine Mingins, editor, *Proceedings of TOOLS Pacific 1999*. IEEE Computer Society, 1999.

71. Evans Data Corp. North American Development Survey: Volume 1. Response to question on "Use of UML in Application Design", 2003.

72. Safeware Engineering Corporation. *SpecTRM User Manual*, 2003.

73. Vitech Corporation. http://www.vtcorp.com/, December 2003.

74. Andrea Corradini, Ugo Montanari, Francesca Rossi, Hartmut Ehrig, Reiko Heckel, and Michael Löwe. Algebraic approaches to graph transformation I: Basic concepts and double pushout approach. In G. Rozenberg, editor, *Handbook of Graph Grammars and Computing by Graph transformation, Volume 1: Foundations*. World Scientific, 1997.

75. Alexandre L. Correa and Cláudia Maria Lima Werner. Applying refactoring techniques to UML/OCL models. In *Proceedings of UML 2004 Conference*, volume 3273 of *LNCS*, pages 173–187, Lisbon, Portugal, 2004. Springer, Berlin Heidelberg New York.

76. Katja Cremer, André Marburger, and Bernhard Westfechtel. Graph-based tools for reengineering. *Journal of Software Maintenance and Evolution: Research and Practice*, 14:25–292, 2002.

77. I. Crnkovic, J.A. Stafford, H.W. Schmidt, and K. Wallnau, editors. *Proceedings of 7th International Symposium on Component-Based Software Engineering (CBSE)*, Edinburgh, Scotland, May 2004. Springer, Berlin Heidelberg New York.

78. György Csertán, Gábor Huszerl, István Majzik, Zsigmond Pap, András Pataricza, and Dániel Varró. VIATRA: Visual automated transformations for formal verification and validation of UML models. In Julian Richardson, Wolfgang Emmerich, and Dave Wile, editors, *Proceedings ASE 2002: 17th IEEE International Conference on Automated Software Engineering*, pages 267–270, Edinburgh, Scotland, 2002. IEEE Press, Piscataway, NJ.

79. K. Czarnecki and U.W. Eisenecker. *Generative Programming: Methods, Tools and Applications*. Addison-Wesley, Reading, MA, 2000.

80. K. Czarnecki and S. Helsen. Classification of model transformation approaches. In J. Bettin, G. van Emde Boas, and A. Agrawal, editors, *2nd OOPSLA Workshop on Generative Techniques in the Context of MDA*, Anaheim, CA, USA, 2003.

81. Juan de Lara and Hans Vangheluwe. AToM3: A tool for multi-formalism and metamodelling. In Ralf-Detlef Kutsche and Herbert Weber, editors, *Proceedings 5th International Conference, FASE 2002: Fundamental Approaches to Software Engineering, Grenoble, France*, volume 2306 of *LNCS*, pages 174–188. Springer, Berlin Heidelberg New York, 2002.

82. S. Demeyer, T. D. Meijler, O. Nierstrasz, and P. Steyaert. Design guidelines for tailorable frameworks. *Communications of the ACM*, 40(10):60–64, 1997.

83. Serge Demeyer, Sander Tichelaar, and Patrick Steyaert. FAMIX 2.0 – the FAMOOS information exchange model. http://www.iam.unibe.ch/~famoos/FAMIX/, September 1999.

84. William Deng, Matthew Dwyer, John Hatcliff, Georg Jung, and Robby. Model-checking middleware-based event-driven real-time embedded software. In *Proceedings of the 1st International Symposium on Formal Methods for Component and Objects*, volume 2582 of *LNCS*, pages 154–181, 2002.

85. E. W. Dijkstra. *A Discipline of Programming*. Prentice Hall, Englewood Cliffs, NJ, 1976.

86. J.S. Dong. State, event, time and diagram in system modelling. In *Proceedings of ICSE'01*, pages 733–734, Toronto, Canada., 2001. IEEE Press, Piscataway, NJ.

87. Heiko Dorr. *Efficient Graph Rewriting and Its Implementation*. Springer, Berlin Heidelberg New York, 1995.

88. F. L. Dotti, L. Foss, L. Ribeiro, and O. M. Santos. Verification of object-based distributed systems. In *Proceedings 6th International Conference on Formal Methods for Open Object-based Distributed Systems*, volume 2884, pages 261–275. Springer, Berlin Heidelberg New York, 2003.

89. B.P. Douglass. *Doing hard time: developing real-time systems with UML, objects, frameworks, and patterns*. Addison-Wesley Longman, Harlow, UK, 1999.

90. B.P. Douglass. *Real-Time Design Patterns: Robust Scalable Architecture for Real-Time Systems*. Addison-Wesley Longman, Harlow, UK, 2002.

91. Frank Drewes, Berthold Hoffmann, and Detlef Plump. Hierarchical graph transformation. *Journal of Computer and System Sciences*, 64(2):249–283, 2002.

92. S. Drossopoulou, F. Damiani, M. Dezani-Ciancaglini, and P. Giannini. More dynamic object reclassification: Fickleii. *ACM TOPLAS*, 24(2):153–191, 2002.

93. DSTC. Breeze: Workflow with ease. http://www.dstc.edu.au/Research/Projects/Pegamento/Breeze/breeze.html.

94. E. Magyari, A. Bakay, A. Lang, T. Paka, A. Vizhanyo, A. Agrawal, G. Karsai. UDM: An infrastructure for implementing domain-specific modeling languages. In *The 3rd OOPSLA Workshop on Domain-Specific Modeling, OOPSLA 2003*, Anaheim, CA, USA, October 2003.

95. Gregory T. Eakman. Classification of model transformation approaches. In *UML Workshop: Model Driven Architecture in the Specification, Implementation and Validation of Object-oriented Embedded Systems*, Anaheim, California, October 2003.

96. J. Ebert, K. Kontogiannis, and J. Mylopoulos. Interoperability of reengineering tools, January 2001. Seminar Number 01041, Report Number 296.

97. Eclipse Project. AspectJ. http://www.eclipse.org/aspectj/, January 2005.

98. Eclipse Project. Eclipse. http://www.eclipse.org/eclipse/, January 2005.

99. Eclipse Project. Eclipse Modeling Framework (EMF). http://www.eclipse.org/emf/, January 2005.

100. Eclipse Project. ECore. http://download.eclipse.org/tools/emf/javadoc/, package org.eclipse.emf.ecore, January 2005.

101. J. Clark (editor). XML transformations (XSLT) version 1.1, W3C working draft. http://www.w3.org/TR/xslt11, December 2000.

102. Edwin Robby, Matthew Dwyer and John Hatcliff. Bogor: An extensible and highly-modular model checking framework. In *In the Proceedings of the Fourth Joint Meeting of the European Software Engineering Conference and ACM SIGSOFT Symposium on the Foundations of Software Engineering (ESEC/FSE 2003)*, Helsinki, Finland.

103. A. Egyed. Automated abstraction of class diagrams. *ACM Transaction's on Software Engineering and Methodology*, 11:449–491, 2002.

104. A. Egyed. A scenario-driven approach to trace dependency analysis. *IEEE Transactions on Software Engineering*, 29:116–132, 2003.
105. A. Egyed and P. Kruchten. Rose/architect: A tool to visualize architecture. In *Proceedings of the 32nd Hawaii International Conference on System Sciences (HICSS), Maui, HI, USA.* 1999.
106. A. Egyed and N. Medvidovic. A formal approach to heterogeneous software modeling. In *Proceedings of 3rd Foundational Aspects of Software Engineering (FASE), Berlin, Germany*, pages 178–192. 2000.
107. A. Egyed and D. Wile. Statechart simulator for modeling architectural dynamics. In *Proceedings of the 2nd Working International Conference on Software Architecture (WICSA), Amsterdam, The Netherlands*, pages 87–96. 2001.
108. Hartmut Ehrig, Reiko Heckel, Martin Korff, Michael Löwe, Leila Ribeiro, Annika Wagner, and Andrea Corradini. Algebraic approaches to graph transformation II: Single pushout approach and comparison with double pushout approach. In G. Rozenberg, editor, *The Handbook of Graph Grammars and Computing by Graph Transformation, Volume 1: Foundations*. World Scientific, Singapore, 1997.
109. J. Ellsberger, D. Hogrefe, and A. Sarma. *SDL. Formal Object-oriented Language for Communicating Systems*. Prentice Hall, Englewood Cliffs, NJ, 1997.
110. J. Elmqvist. Analysis of intent specification and system upgrade traceability. Master's thesis, Linköpings University, December 2003.
111. Matthew Emerson and Janos Sztipanovits. Implementing a MOF-based metamodeling environment using graph transformations. In *Proceedings of OOPSLA Workshop on Domain-Specific Modeling*, pages 83–92, Vancouver, BC, Canada, October 2004.
112. Gregor Engels, Reiko Heckel, and Jochen M. Küster. The consistency workbench: A tool for consistency management in UML-based development. In Perdita Stevens, Jon Whittle, and Grady Booch, editors, *Proceedings UML 2003 - The Unified Modeling Language. Model Languages and Applications. 6th International Conference, San Francisco, CA, USA*, volume 2863 of *LNCS*, pages 356–359. Springer, Berlin Heidelberg New York, 2003.
113. A. Eriksson. Model-based development of an airbag software. Master's thesis, Linköpings University, March 2004.
114. A. Kleppe et al. *MDA Explained: The Model Driven Architecture Practice and Promise*. Addison-Wesley, Reading, MA, 2004.
115. S.J. Mellor et al. *MDA Distilled: Principles of Model-Driven Architecture*. Addison-Wesley, Reading, MA, 2004.
116. Rational Software et.al. *UML Summary*. OMG document ad/97-08-03, 1997.
117. A. Evans, R. France, K. Lano, and B. Rumpe. The UML as a formal modeling notation. *Computer Standards & Interfaces*, 19(7):325–334, 1998.
118. M.E. Fagan. Advances in software inspections. *IEEE Transactions on Software Engineering*, 12:744–751, 1986.
119. H. Fahmy and R.C. Holt. Using graph rewriting to specify software architectural transformations. In *Proceedings of the 15th IEEE International Conference on Automated Software Engineering (ASE)*, pages 187–196. 2000.
120. J.M. Favre. Towards a basic theory to model driven engineering. In M. Gogolla, P. Sammut, and J. Whittle, editors, *Proceedings of UML 2004 Workshop in Software Model Engineering*, Lisbon, Portugal, 2004.
121. M. Fayad, D. Schmidt, and R. Johnson, editors. *Building Application Frameworks: Object-Oriented Foundations of Framework Design*. Wiley, New York, 1999.
122. J. M. Fernandes. Functional and object-oriented modeling of embedded software. Technical Report 512, Turku Centre for Computer Science (TUCS), Turku, Finland, 2003.

123. J. M. Fernandes, R. J. Machado, and H. D. Santos. Modelling industrial embedded systems with UML. In *Proceedings of CODES 2000*, San Diego, CA, USA, 2000.

124. R. E. Filman, T. Elrad, S. Clarke, and M. Akşit. *Aspect-Oriented Software Development*. Addison-Wesley, Reading, MA, 2004.

125. A. Finkelstein, J. Kramer, B. Nuseibeh, L. Finkelstein, and M. Goedicke. Viewpoints: A framework for integrating multiple perspectives in system development. *International Journal of Software Engineering and Knowledge Engineering*, 2(1):31–58, 1992.

126. Thorsten Fischer, Jörg Niere, Lars Torunski, and Albert Zündorf. Story diagrams: A new graph rewrite language based on the Unified Modeling Language and Java. In *Proceedings of the 6th International Workshop on Theory and Application of Graph Transformation (TAGT)*, volume 1764 of *LNCS*, pages 296–309. Springer, Berlin Heidelberg New York, November 1998.

127. Jacqueline Floch. *Towards plug-and-play services: Design and validation using roles*. PhD thesis, The Norwegian University of Science and Technology – NTNU, 2003.

128. Institute for Software Integrated Systems. *The Generic Modeling Environment: GME 4 Users Manual*. Vanderbilt University, 2004.

129. Formal Techniques in Software Engineering. Model driven, Template based, Model Transformer (MoTMoT). http://sourceforge.net/projects/motmot/, 2004.

130. Martin Fowler. Model Driven Architecture. http://www.martinfowler.com/bliki/ModelDrivenArchitecture.html, February 2004.

131. Martin Fowler, Kent Beck, John Brant, William Opdyke, and Don Roberts. *Refactoring: Improving the Design of Existing Code*. Addison-Wesley, Reading, MA, 1999.

132. D. Fox, W. Burgard, and S. Thrun. The dynamic window approach to collision avoidance. *IEEE Robotics & Automation Magazine*, 4(1):25–40, March 1997.

133. R. France, A. Evans, K. Lano, and B. Rumpe. The UML as a formal modeling notation. *of Computer Standards & Interfaces*, 19:325–334, 1998.

134. Robert France, Sudipto Ghosh, Eunjee Song, and Dae-Kyoo Kim. A metamodeling approach to pattern-based model refactoring. *IEEE Software*, pages 52–58, September 2003.

135. David Frankel. *Model Driven Architecture: Applying MDA to Enterprise Computing*. Wiley, New York, 2003.

136. David S. Frankel. The MDA marketing message and the MDA reality. *MDA Journal, a Business Process Trends Column*, March 2004.

137. French National Institute for Research in Computer Science and Control (INRIA). Model Transformation Language (MTL). http://modelware.inria.fr/, January 2005.

138. I. Jacobsen G. Booch and J. Rumbaugh. *The Unified Modeling Language User's Guide*. Addison Wesley, Reading, MA, 1998.

139. Paolo Bottoni Gabriele Taentzer and Francesco Parisi Presicce. Specifying integrated refactoring with distributed graph transformations. In *Proceedings of AGTIVE 2003*, pages 227–242, 2003.

140. E. Gamma, R. Helm, R. Johnson, and J. Vlissides. *Design Patterns – Elements of Reusable Object-Oriented Software*. Addison-Wesley, 1995.

141. Erich Gamma and Kent Beck. *Contributing to Eclipse: Principles, Patterns, and Plug-ins*. Addison-Wesley, Reading, MA, 2003.

142. D. Garlan. Views for tools in integrated environments. In Reidar Conradi, Tor Didriksen, and Dag H. Wanvik, editors, *Advanced Programming Environments, Proceedings of an International Workshop, Trondheim, Norway, June 16-18, 1986*, volume 244 of *LNCS*, pages 314–343. Springer, Berlin Heidelberg New York, 1986.

143. Leif Geiger and Albert Zündorf. Graph based debugging with Fujaba. In *Proceedings Workshop on Graph Based Tools, International Conference on Graph Transformations*, 2002.
144. Leif Geiger and Albert Zündorf. Statechart modeling with Fujaba. In *Graph Based Tools (GraBaTs); workshop at ICGT 2004*, Rome, 2004.
145. Generative Model Transformer. http://www.eclipse.org/gmt/.
146. Gentleware corporation. http://www.gentleware.com, 2003.
147. Anna Gerber, Michael J. Lawley, Kerry Raymond, Jim Steel, and Andrew Wood. Transformation: The missing link of MDA. In *Proceedings of the 1st International Conference on Graph Transformation, ICGT'02*, volume 2505 of *LNCS*, pages 90–105. Springer, Berlin Heidelberg New York, 2002.
148. N. Giambiasi, J.L. Paillet, and F. Chane. From timed automata to DEVS models. In *Proceedings of the SCS Winter Simulation Conference*, 2003.
149. M. Glandrup and M. Aksit. Design for composition: Extending patterns with a crosscut specification. www.win.tue.nl/ipa/archive/falldays2003/UT-ipapresentation.ppt, 2003.
150. E. Glinsky and G. Wainer. Definition of real-time simulation in the CD++ toolkit. In *Proceedings of the SCS Summer Computer Simulation Conference*, 2002.
151. E. Glinsky and G. Wainer. Performance analysis of real-time DEVS models. In *Proceedings of the SCS Winter Simulation Conference*, 2002.
152. E. Glinsky and G. Wainer. A benchmarking technique for studying performance of DEVS modeling and simulation environments. Technical Report SCE-05-01, Dept. of Systems and Computer Engineering. Carleton University, 2005.
153. Aniruddha Gokhale, Krishnakumar Balasubramanian, Jaiganesh Balasubramanian, Arvind S. Krishna, George T. Edwards, Gan Deng, Emre Turkay, Jeffrey Parsons, and Douglas C. Schmidt. Model driven middleware: A new paradigm for deploying and provisioning distributed real-time and embedded applications. *The Journal of Science of Computer Programming: Special Issue on Model Driven Architecture*, 2004.
154. Adele Goldberg and David Robson. *Smalltalk-80: The Language and its Implementation*. Addison-Wesley, Reading, MA, 1983.
155. Pieter Van Gorp, Hans Stenten, Tom Mens, and Serge Demeyer. Towards automating source-consistent UML refactorings. In *Proceedings of UML 2003 Conference*, volume 2863 of *LNCS*, pages 144–158, San Francisco, CA, 2003. Springer, Berlin Heidelberg New York.
156. O.C.Z. Gotel and A.C.W. Finkelstein. An analysis of the requirements traceability problem. In *Proceedings of the First International Conference on Requirements Engineering*, pages 94–101. 1994.
157. L. Grady, J. Howard, and P. Anderson, editors. *Safety-Critical Requirements Specfication and Analysis using SpecTRM*. US Software Safety Working Group, February 2002.
158. A. Grahn. Code generation from high-level models of reactive and security-intrinsic systems. Master's thesis, Linköpings University, April 2004. LiTH-IDA-EX–04/030–SE.
159. Jeff Gray, Ted Bapty, Sandeep Neema, Douglas C. Schmidt, Aniruddha Gokhale, and Balachandran Natarajan. An approach for supporting aspect-oriented domain modeling. In *Generative Programming and Component Engineering (GPCE 2003)*, volume 2830 of *LNCS*, pages 151–168, Erfurt, Germany, September 2003. Springer, Berlin Heidelberg New York.
160. Jeff Gray, Ted Bapty, Sandeep Neema, and James Tuck. Handling crosscutting constraints in domain-specific modeling. *Communications of the ACM*, pages 87–93, October 2001.

161. Jeffrey G. Gray. *Aspect-Oriented Domain-Specific Modeling: A Generative Approach Using a Meta-weaver Framework.* Phd, Vanderbilt University, 2002.

162. Jack Greenfield and Keith Short. Software factories: Assembling applications with patterns, models, frameworks and tools. OOPSLA 2003 Workshop on Generative Techniques in the context of Model Driven Architecture, October 2003.

163. Jack Greenfield, Keith Short, Steve Cook, and Stuart Kent. *Software Factories: Assembling Applications with Patterns, Models, Frameworks, and Tools.* John Wiley & Sons, New York, 2004.

164. Object Management Group. Model-level testing and debugging rfp. OMG Document Number : realtime/03-01-12, 2001.

165. Object Management Group. MOF 2.0 Query / Views / Transformations RFP. OMG document ad/02-04-10. Available at http://www.omg.org/.

166. Object Management Group. OMG Meta-Object Facility (MOF). OMG Document formal/01-11-02. Available at http://www.omg.org/.

167. Object Management Group. OMG XML Metadata Interchange (XMI) Specification. OMG Document formal/00-11-02.

168. Object Management Group. Software Process Engineering Metamodel Specification (SPEM). OMG Document formal/02-11-14. Available at http://www.omg.org/.

169. Object Management Group. Object Constraint Language Specification, version 1.1. Available at http://www.omg.org/., September 1997.

170. Object Management Group. Interchange metamodel in xml. OMG document: formal/01-02-15, 2001.

171. Object Management Group. Model driven architecture (mda). Technical Report ormsc/2001-07-01, OMG, July 2001.

172. Object Management Group. UML profile for enterprise distributed computing (EDOC). OMG document: ptc/02-02-05, 2002.

173. Object Management Group. Uml profile for enterprise distributed object computing specification. Technical Report OMG Adopted Specification ptc/02-02-05, OMG, February 2002.

174. Object Management Group. Mda guide version 1.0.1. Technical Report omg/2003-06-01, OMG, July 2003.

175. Object Management Group. Unified Modeling Language: Diagram Interchange version 2.0, September 2003. OMG document ptc/03-09-01. Available at http://www.omg.org.

176. Object Management Group. First OMG Model-Integrated Computing (MIC) Workshop. http://www.omg.org/news/meetings/mic2004/., October 2004.

177. Progres Group. PROGRES: Programmed graph rewriting system. http://www-i3.informatik.rwth-aachen.de/research/projects/progres/, 2004.

178. L. Grunske, B. Kaiser, and R. H. Ruessner. *Embedded system development with components*, chapter Specification and evaluation of safety properties in a component-based software engineering process. 2005. To Appear.

179. Lare Grunske. Automated software architecture evolution with hypergraph transformation. In *7th International IASTED on Conference Software Engineering and Application (SEA 03)*, IASTED Proceedings, pages 613–621, Marina del Ray, CA, USA, November 3-5 2003.

180. N. Guelfi. Flexible consistency in software development using contracts and refinements. 2nd International Workshop on Living With Inconsistency, part of ICSE 2001, Toronto, Canada, May 2001.

181. Annegret Habel. *Hyperedge replacement: grammars and languages*, volume 643 of *Lecture Notes in Computer Science*. Springer, Berlin Heidelberg New York, New York, NY, USA, 1992.

182. Annegret Habel, Reiko Heckel, and Gabriele Taentzer. Graph grammars with negative application conditions. *Fundamenta Informaticae*, 26(3/4):287–313, 1996.

183. M. Hakala, J. Hautamäki, K. Koskimies, J. Paakki, A. Viljamaa, and J. Viljamaa. Generating application development environments for Java frameworks. In *Proc. GCSE 2001*, pages 163–176, Erfurt, Germany, September 2001. Springer, Berlin Heidelberg New York, LNCS 2186.

184. N. Halbwachs, P. Caspi, P. Raymond, and D. Pilaud. The synchronous data-flow programming language LUSTRE. *Proceedings of the IEEE*, 79(9):1305–1320, September 1991.

185. D. Hamlet, D. Mason, and D. Woit. Theory of software reliability based on components. In *ICSE '01: Proceedings of the 23rd International Conference on Software Engineering*, pages 361–370. IEEE Computer Society, 2001.

186. J. Hammarberg and S. Nadjm-Tehrani. Development of safety-critical reconfigurable hardware with esterel. In *8th International Workshop on Formal Methods for Industrial Critical Systems (FMICS)*. Elsevier, June 2003.

187. J. Hammarberg and S. Nadjm-Tehrani. Formal verification of fault tolerance in safety-critical configurable modules. *International Journal of Software Tools for Technology Transfer (STTT)*, December 2004. Springer, Berlin Heidelberg New York.

188. I. Hammouda, O. Guldogan, K. Koskimies, and T. Systä. Tool-supported customization of UML class diagrams for learning complex system models. In *Proc. IWPC 2004*, pages 24–33, Bari, Italy, 2004.

189. I. Hammouda and M. Harsu. Documenting maintenance tasks using maintenance patterns. In *Proc. CSMR 2004*, pages 37–47, Tampere, Finland, 2004.

190. I. Hammouda, J. Hautamäki, M. Pussinen, and K. Koskimies. Managing variability using heterogeneous feature variation patterns. In *Proc. FASE 2005*, pages 145–159, Edinburgh, Scotland, April 2005.

191. I. Hammouda, M. Katara, and K. Koskimies. A tool environment for aspectual patterns in UML. In *Proc. WoDiSEE 2004*, pages 58–65, Edinburgh, Scotland, May 2004.

192. I. Hammouda and K. Koskimies. A pattern-based J2EE application development. *Nordic Journal of Computing (NJC)*, 9(3):248–260, Fall 2002.

193. I. Hammouda, J. Koskinen, M. Pussinen, M. Katara, and T. Mikkonen. Adaptable concern-based framework specialization in UML. In *Proc. ASE 2004*, pages 78–87, Linz, Austria, September 2004.

194. Stefan Hanenberg, Arno Schmidmeier, and Rainer Unland. AspectJ Idioms for Aspect-Oriented Software Construction. In *Proceedings of the 8th European Conference on Pattern Languages of Programs, EuroPLoP*, Irsee, Germany, June 2003.

195. D. Harel and B. Rumpe. Modeling languages: Syntax, semantics and all that stuff – Part i: The basic stuff. Technical Report MCS00-16, Weizmann Institute of Science, Rehovot (Israel), 2000.

196. David Harel and Eran Gery. Executable Object Modeling with Statecharts. In *Proceedings of the 18th International Conference on Software Engineering*, pages 246–257. IEEE Computer Society Press, 1996.

197. Mary Jean Harrold. Testing: A road map. In *Proceedings of the Future of Software Engineering*, pages 61–82, Limerick, Ireland, May 2000.

198. John Hatcliff, Xinghua Deng, Matthew B. Dwyer, Georg Jung, and Venkatesh Prasad Ranganath. Cadena: An integrated development, analysis, and verification environment

for component-based systems. In *Proceedings of the 25th International Conference on Software Engineering*, pages 160–173, Portland, Oregon, May 2003. IEEE Computer Society.

199. Les Hatton. Reexamining the fault density-component size connection. *IEEE Softw.*, 14(2):89–97, 1997.

200. J.H. Hausmann, R. Heckel, and S. Sauer. Extended model relations with graphical consistency conditions. In L. Kuzniarz, G. Reggio, and J.L. Sourrouille, editors, *Proceedings UML 2002 Workshop on Consistency Problems in UML-based Software Development*, Dresden (Germany), 2002.

201. J. Hautamäki. *Pattern-Based Tool Support for Frameworks: Towards Architecture-Oriented Software Development Environment*. Publication 521, Tampere University of Technology, 2005.

202. K. Havelund and W. Visser. Program model checking as a new trend. *International Journal of Software Tools for Technology Transfer (STTT)*, 4(1):8–20, 2002.

203. Susumu Hayashi, Pan YiBing, Masami Sato, Kenji Mori, Sul Sejeon, and Shuusuke Haruna. Test driven development of UML models with smart modeling system. In *Proceedings of the UML 2004 Conference*, volume 3237 of *LNCS*, pages 295–409, Lisbon, Portugal, 2004. Springer, Berlin Heidelberg New York.

204. R. Heckel, H. Ehrig, U. Wolter, and A. Corradini. Integrating the specification techniques of graph transformation and temporal logic. In *Proceedings of Mathematical Foundations of Computer Science (MFCS'97), Slovakia*, volume 1295 of *LNCS*, pages 219–228. Springer, Berlin Heidelberg New York, 1997.

205. Reiko Heckel. Compositional verification of reactive systems specified by graph transformation. In *Proceedings of FASE: Fundamental Approaches to Software Engineering*, volume 1382 of *LNCS*, pages 138–153. Springer, Berlin Heidelberg New York, 1998.

206. M.P.E. Heimdahl and N.G. Leveson. Completeness and consistency in hierarchical state-based requirements. *Software Engineering*, 22(6):363–377, 1996.

207. Dan Hirsh, Paola Inverardi, and Ugo Montanari. Modeling software architecures and styles with graph grammars and constraint solving. *Proceedings of First Working IFIP Conference on Software Architecture (WICSA1)*, pages 127–144, 2000.

208. I.M. Holland. Specifying reusable components using contracts. In *Proceedings of ECOOP 1992*, pages 287–308, Utrecht, The Netherlands, 1992. Springer, Berlin Heidelberg New York. volume 615 of LNCS.

209. Richard C. Holt, Ahmed E. Hassan, Bruno Laguë, Sébastien Lapierre, and Charles Leduc. E/R schema for the datrix C/C++/java exchange format. In *Proceedings of the Seventh Working Conference on Reverse Engineering*, page 284. IEEE Computer Society, 2000.

210. E. Holz. Strategien zur Unterstützung der Modellkombination im Softwareentwicklungsprozess (Strategies for supporting combination of models in the software development process). In Metzger A and G. Zimmermann, editors, *Modellierung Reaktiver Systeme: Ein Fallbeispiel (Modeling Reactive Systems: A Case-Study)*, SFB 501 Report 08/03. University of Kaiserslautern, 2003.

211. G. Holzmann. The model checker SPIN. *IEEE Transactions on Software Engineering*, 23(5):279–295, 1997.

212. F. Huber, B. Schätz, A. Schmidt, and K. Spies. AutoFocus: A tool for distributed systems specification. In B. Jonsson and J. Parrow, editors, *Formal Techniques in Real-Time and Fault-Tolerant Systems, 4th International Symposium, FTRTFT'96*, volume 1135 of *LNCS*, pages 467–470, Uppsala, Sweden, 1996. Springer, Berlin Heidelberg New York.

213. E.T. Hvannberg. Combining UML and Z in a software process. In J.L. Rash, editor, *Formal Approaches to Agent-Based Systems*, volume 1871 of *LNCS*, pages 47–52. Springer, Berlin Heidelberg New York, 2001.

214. IAR. http://www.iar.com/, March 2004.

215. IBM. Rational Rose XDE Developer. http://www-306.ibm.com/software/awdtools/developer/rosexde/, 2004.

216. ILogix. http://www.ilogix.com/, March 2004.

217. Institute for Software Integrated Systems.   Open Tool Integration Framework. www.isis.vanderbilt.edu/Projects/WOTIF/.

218. Interactive Objects Software GmbH.   ArcStyler.   http://www.io-software.com/products/arcstyler_overview.jsp, January 2005.

219. International Organization for Standardization. *ISO 9126. Information technology – Software product evaluation – Quality characteristics and guidelines for their use*, December 1991.

220. P. Inverardi, H. Muccini, and P. Pelliccione. Automated check of architectural models consistency using spin. In *Proceedings of 16th IEEE International Confonference on Automated Software Engineering*, pages 346–349, San Diego, CA, USA, 2001.

221. R. Iosif and R. Sisto. dSPIN: A dynamic extension of SPIN. In *Proceedings of the 6th SPIN Workshop*, volume 1680 of *LNCS*, pages 261–276. Springer, Berlin Heidelberg New York, 1999.

222. J. Isaksson, J. Lilius, and D. Truscan. A MOF-based metamodel for SA/RT. In *Proceedings of the Rapid Integration of Software Engineering Techniques (RISE'04) Workshop*, pages 97–106, November 2004.

223. ISIS.   Model-Integrated Computing.   http://www.isis.vanderbilt.edu/Research/mic.html.

224. ITU-T. *Basic Reference Model of Open Distributed Processing - Part 1: Overview*. ITU-T, 1997. ITU-T Recommendation X.901, ISO/IEC IS 10746-1.

225. G. Booch J. Rumbaugh and I. Jacobsen. *The Unified Modeling Language Reference Manual, Second Edition*. Addison-Wesley, Reading, MA, 2004.

226. J2EE Enterprise JavaBeans technology. http://java.sun.com/products/ejb/, 2004.

227. D. Jackson and M. Rinard. Software analysis: A roadmap. In *Proceedings of the 20th International Conference on Software Engineering (ICSE)*, pages 133–145. 2000.

228. C. Jacques and G. Wainer. Using the CD++ DEVS toolkit to develop petri nets. In *Proceedings of the SCS Summer Computer Simulation Conference*, 2002.

229. P. Jalote. *An Integrated Approach to Software Engineering*. Springer, Berlin Heidelberg New York, New York, second edition, 1997.

230. P.C. Janca. Pragmatic application of information agents. BIS Strategic Decisions, Norwell, MA, USA, 1995.

231. Java Community Process. Java Metadata Interface (JMI) Specification, v1.0, June 2002.   Java Specification Request, JSR#040. http://java.sun.com/products/jmi/.

232. JSR-000026, UML/EJB Mapping Specification. http://jcp.org/aboutJava/communityprocess/review/jsr026/, 2001.

233. N.R. Jennings. On agent-based software engineering. *Artificial Intelligence*, 117:277–296, 2000.

234. N.R. Jennings and M. Wooldridge. *Agent Technology: Foundations, Applications And Markets*. Springer, Berlin Heidelberg New York, 1998.

235. L. Jin and H. Zhu. Automatic generation of formal specification from requirements definition. In *Proceedings of ICFEM'97*, pages 243–251, Hiroshima, Japan, 1997.

236. C. Jones. Patterns of large software systems: Failure and success. *Computer*, 28(3):86–87, 1995.

237. J. Jürjens. A UML statecharts semantics with message-passing. In *Symposium of Applied Computing 2002*, pages 1009–1013, Madrid, March 11–14 2002. ACM.

238. J. Jürjens. Formal Semantics for Interacting UML subsystems. In *FMOODS 2002*, pages 29–44. IFIP, Kluwer, 2002.

239. J. Jürjens. UMLsec: Extending UML for secure systems development. In J.-M. Jézéquel, H. Hussmann, and S. Cook, editors, *UML 2002 – The Unified Modeling Language*, volume 2460 of *LNCS*, pages 412–425, Dresden, Sept. 30 – Oct. 4 2002. Springer, Berlin Heidelberg New York.

240. J. Jürjens. *Secure Systems Development with UML*. Springer, Berlin Heidelberg New York, 2004.

241. J. Jürjens and Pasha Shabalin. A foundation for tool-supported critical systems development with UML. In *11th Annual IEEE International Conference on the Engineering of Computer Based Systems (ECBS 2004)*, Brno, Czech Republic, May 2004.

242. Audris Kalnins, Janis Barzdins, and Edgars Celms. Model transformation language MOLA. In *Proceedings of MDAFA 2004 (Model-Driven Architecture: Foundations and Applications 2004)*, pages 14–28, 2004.

243. Gabor Karsai, Aditya Agrawal, Feng Shi, and Jonathan Sprinkle. On the use of graph transformation in the formal specification of model interpreters. In *Journal of Universal Computer Science 9*, pages 1296–1321, 2003.

244. Gábor Karsai, Miklos Maroti, Ákos Lédeczi, Jeff Gray, and Janos Sztipanovits. Type hierarchies and composition in modeling and meta-modeling languages. *IEEE Transactions on Control System Technology, special issue on Computer Automated Multi-Paradigm Modeling Modeling*, pages 263–278, March 2004.

245. Gabor Karsai, Sandeep Neema, Arpad Bakay, Akos Ledeczi, Feng Shi, and Aniruddha Gokhale. A model-based front-end to ACE/TAO: The embedded system modeling language. In *Proceedings of the Second Annual TAO Workshop*, Arlington, VA, USA, July 2002.

246. Gabor Karsai, Janos Sztipanovits, Akos Ledeczi, and Ted Bapty. Model-integrated development of embedded software. *Proceedings of the IEEE*, 91(1):145–164, January 2003.

247. M. Katara and S. Katz. Architectural views of aspects. In *Proceedings of AOSD 2003*, Boston, MA, USA, March 2003.

248. I. Khriss, M. Elkoutbi, and R. Keller. Automating the synthesis of UML statechart diagrams from multiple collaboration diagrams. In *Proceedings of the Conference on the Unified Modeling Language*, pages 132–147. 1998.

249. Samir Khuller and Balaji Raghavachari. Graph and network algorithms. *ACM Computing Surveys*, pages 43–45, March 1999.

250. G. Kiczales. Oriented programming (AOP). http://www.theserverside.com/talks/videos/GregorKiczalesText/interview.tss, July 2003.

251. Gregor Kiczales, Erik Hilsdale, Jim Hugunin, Mik Kersten, Jeffrey Palm, and William Griswold. Getting started with AspectJ. *Communications of the ACM*, pages 59–65, October 2001.

252. Gregor Kiczales, Erik Hilsdale, Jim Hugunin, Mik Kersten, Jeffrey Palm, and William G. Griswold. An overview of AspectJ. In *Proceedings of the 15th European Conference on Object-Oriented Programming, ECOOP*, volume 2072 of *LNCS*, pages 327–353, Budapest, Hungary, 2001. Springer, Berlin Heidelberg New York.

253. Gregor Kiczales, John Lamping, Anurag Mendhekar, Chris Maeda, Cristina Videira Lopes, Jean-Marc Loingtier, and John Irwin. Aspect-oriented programming. In *Proceedings of the 11th European Conference on Object-Oriented Programming, ECOOP*, volume 1241 of *LNCS*, pages 220–242, Jyväskylä, Finland, 1997. Springer, Berlin Heidelberg New York.

254. Michael Kifer, Georg Lausen, and James Wu. Logical foundations of object-oriented and frame-based languages. *Journal of the ACM*, 42(4):741–843, 1995.

255. J.-K. Kim, Y.G. Kim, and T.G. Kim. DHMIF: DEVS-based hardware model interchange format. In *Proceedings of the European Simulation Symposium*, 2001.

256. A. Kleppe and J. Warmer. Do MDA transformations preserve meaning? an investigation into preserving semantics. In A. Evans, P. Sammut, and J.S. Willans, editors, *Proceedings of First International Workshop on Metamodelling for MDA*, York, UK, 2003.

257. Sharath Kodase, Shige Wang, Zonghua Gu, and Kang G. Shin. Improving scalability of task allocation and scheduling in large distributed real-time systems using shared buffers. In *Proceedings of the 9th Real-time/Embedded Technology and Applications Symposium (RTAS)*, Washington, DC, USA, May 2003.

258. K. Koskimies, T. Systä, J. Tuomi, and T. Männistö. Automated support for modelling oo software. *IEEE Software*, 87-94, 1998.

259. Frank Alexander Kraemer. Telecom service engineering with Eclipse. [Poster]. Eclipse Technology Exchange, ECOOP, 2004.

260. Arvind S. Krishna, Emre Turkay, Aniruddha Gokhale, and Douglas C. Schmidt. Model-driven techniques for evaluating the QoS of middleware configurations for DRE systems. In *Proceedings of the 11th IEEE Real-Time and Embedded Technology and Applications Symposium*, San Francisco, CA, USA, March 2005.

261. P. Kroll and P. Kruchten. *The Rational Unified Process Made Easy: A Practitioner's Guide to the RUP*. Addison-Wesley, Reading, MA, 2004.

262. P. Kruchten. *The Rational Unified Process: An Introduction*. Addison-Wesley, 1998.

263. V. Kulkarni and S. Reddy. Separation of concerns in model-driven development. *IEEE Software*, 20(5):64–69, October 2003.

264. Jochen M. Küster, Shane Sendall, and Michael Wahler. Comparing two model transformation approaches. In *Proceedings of Workshop on OCL and Model Driven Engineering*, October 2004. Satelite event of the Seventh International Conference on UML.

265. L. Kuzniarz, G. Reggio, J.L. Sourrouille, and Z. Huzar. Consistency problems in UML-based software development, Workshop Materials at UML'2002. Research report. Blekinge Institute of Technology., 2002.

266. J. H. Lala and R. E. Harper. Architectural principles for safety-critical real-time applications. *Proceedings of the IEEE*, 82(1):25–40, January 1994.

267. H. Ledang and J. Souquières. Integrating UML and B specification techniques. In *Proceedings of Informatik2001*, pages 641–648, Vienna University, Autria, 2001.

268. A. Ledeczi, J. Davis, S. Neema, and A. Agrawal. Modeling methodology for integrated simulation of embedded systems. *Proceedings of 7th IEEE International Conference on Engineering of Computer Based Systems*, 13(1):82–103, 2003.

269. Ákos Lédeczi, Arpad Bakay, Miklos Maroti, Peter Volgyesi, Greg Nordstrom, Jonathan Sprinkle, and Gábor Karsai. Composing domain-specific design environments. *IEEE Computer*, pages 44–51, November 2001.

270. Timothy C. Lethbridge, Sander Tichelaar, and Erhard Ploedereder. The Dagstuhl Middle Metamodel: A schema for reverse engineering. In *Proceedings of the International Workshop on Meta-Models and Schemas for Reverse Engineering (ateM 2003)*, volume 94 of *ENTCS*, pages 7–18. Elsevier, Amsterdam, 2004.

271. N. Leveson. Intent specifications: an approach to building human-centered specifications. *IEEE Transactions on Software Engineering*, 26(1):15–35, January 2000.

272. N.G. Leveson and K.A. Weiss. Making embedded software reuse practical and safe. In *SIGSOFT '04/FSE-12: Proceedings of the 12th ACM SIGSOFT Twelfth International Symposium on Foundations of Software Engineering*, pages 171–178. ACM Press, New York, 2004.

273. L. Li, T. Pearce, and G. Wainer. Interfacing real-time DEVS models with a DSP platform. In *Proceedings of the Industrial Simulation Symposium*, 2003.

274. K. Lieberherr, D. Lorenz, and M. Mezini. Programming with aspectual components. Technical report, NU-CCS-99-01, College of Computer Science, Northeastern University, Boston, MA, March 1999.

275. K.J. Lieberherr, W.L. Hursch, and C. Xiao. Object-extending class transformations. *Journal of Formal Aspects of Computing*, 6:391–416, 1994.

276. J. Lilius and I. Porres. Formalising UML state machines for model checking. In R. France and B. Rumpe, editors, *UML' 99*, volume 1723 of *LNCS*, pages 430–445. Springer, Berlin Heidelberg New York, 1999.

277. Man Lin. Synthesis of control software in a layered architecture from hybrid automata. In *Hybrid Systems: Computation and Control: Second International Workshop, HSCC'99, Berg en Dal, The Netherlands, March 1999. Proceedings*, volume 1569 of *LNCS*, pages 152–164. Springer, Berlin Heidelberg New York, 1999.

278. Martin Lippert. An AspectJ-enabled Eclipse core runtime platform. In *Proceedings of the Poster Session at the ACM SIGPLAN Conference on Object-Oriented Programming, Systems, Languages, and Applications, OOPSLA*, pages 322–323, Anaheim, CA, USA, October 2003. OOPSLA 2003 Companion, ACM Press, New York.

279. Martin Lippert. AspectJ-Enabled Eclipse Runtime. http://www.martinlippert.com/eclipse-aspectj-runtime/, January 2005.

280. Log4J: Apache Logging Services. http://logging.apache.org/log4j/, December 2004.

281. J. Ludewig. Models in software engineering – An introduction. *Software and Systems Modeling*, 1(2):5–14, 2003.

282. P. MacSween and G. Wainer. On the construction of complex models using reusable components. In *Proceedings of SISO Spring Interop-erability Workshop*, 2004.

283. P. Maes. Agents that reduce work and information overload. *Communications of the ACM*, 37(7):31–40, 1994.

284. James Martin and Carma McClure. *Software Maintenance*. Prentice-Hall, Englewood Cliffs, NJ, 1983.

285. W.E. McUmber and B.H.C. Cheng. A general framework for formalizing uml with formal languages. In *Proceedings of the 23rd International Conference on Software Engineering (ICSE)*, pages 433–442. 2001.

286. S. Mehta and G. Wainer. Modeling hybrid hardware description languages in DEVS. Technical Report SCE-05-02, Dept. of Systems and Computer Engineering. Carleton University, 2005.

287. Geir Melby and Rolv Bræk. Delivery of convergent telecom services on j2ee platforms. In *International Conference on Intelligence in Service Delivery Networks, ICIN, Bordaux, France*, October 2004.

288. S. Mellor, A. Clark, and T. Futagami. Model-driven development. *IEEE Software*, 20(5):14–18, September–October 2003.

289. Stephen J. Mellor and Marc J. Balcer. *Executable UML: A Foundation for Model Driven Architecture*. Addison-Wesley, Reading, MA, 2002.

290. Tom Mens, Serge Demeyer, and Dirk Janssens. Formalising behaviour preserving program transformations. In *Graph Transformation*.

291. Tom Mens and Tom Tourwé. A survey of software refactoring. *IEEE Transactions on Software Engineering*, pages 126–139, February 2004.

292. Microsoft, Inc. COM (Component Object Model), DCOM (Distributed COM), COM+. http://www.microsoft.com/com/, January 2005.

293. Microsoft, Inc. .NET. http://www.microsoft.com/net/, January 2005.

294. J. Miller and J. Mukerji. Model driven architecture (MDA) guide. version 1.0.1. Technical Report omg/2003-06-01, Object Management Group (OMG), 2003.

295. A. Moukas. Amalthaea: Information discovery and filtering using a multi-agent evolving ecosystem. *Journal of Applied AI*, 11(5):437–457, 1997.

296. Sandeep Neema, Ted Bapty, Jeff Gray, and Aniruddha Gokhale. Generators for synthesis of QoS adaptation in distributed real-time embedded systems. In *First ACM SIGPLAN/SIGSOFT Conference on Generative Programming and Component Engineering (GPCE '02)*, volume 2487 of *LNCS*, pages 236–251, Pittsburgh, PA, USA, 2002. Springer, Berlin Heidelberg New York.

297. C. Nentwich, W. Emmerich, and A. Finkelstein. Static consistency check for distributed specifications. In *Proceesings of 16th International Conference on Automated Software Engineering*, pages 115–124, Coronado Island, CA, USA, 2001.

298. C. Nentwich, W. Emmerich, and A. Finkelstein. Flexible consistency check. *ACM Transactions on Software Engineering and Methodology*, 12(1):28–63, 2003.

299. Netbeans project. Open source. http://mdr.netbeans.org/, 2003.

300. Looking Glass Networks. Optical Fiber Metropolitan Network. www.omg.org/mda/mda_files/LookingGlassN.pdf, January 2003.

301. Pat Niemeyer. Beanshell. http://www.beanshell.org/, 2004.

302. Novosoft NSUML project. http://nsuml.sourceforge.net/, 2003.

303. Telenor NTNU and Ericsson. The arts research project. http://www.pats.no, January 2005.

304. B. Nuseibeh, J. Kramer, and A. Finkelstein. A framework for expressing the relationships between multiple views in requirements specifications. *Transactions on Software Engineering*, 20(10):760–773, October 1994.

305. Scott Oaks and Henry Wong. *Jini in a Nutshell*. O'Reilly, Sebastopol, CA, 2000.

306. Object Management Group. MDA specifications.

307. Object Management Group. Model Integrated Computing PSIG. http://mic.omg.org.

308. Object Management Group. XML Metadata Interchange (XMI) Specification, v1.1, November 2000.

309. Object Management Group. *Model Driven Architecture (MDA)*, OMG Document ormsc/2001-07-01 edition, July 2001.

310. Object Management Group. *Unified Modeling Language (UML) v1.4*, OMG Document formal/2001-09-67 edition, September 2001.

311. Object Management Group. *CORBA Components*, OMG Document formal/2002-06-65 edition, June 2002.

312. Object Management Group. Mof 1.4 specification. http://www.omg.org/technology/documents/formal/mof.htm, April 2002.

313. Object Management Group. OMG XML Metadata Interchange (XMI) Specification. http://www.omg.org/cgi-bin/doc?formal/2002-01-01, January 2002.

314. Object Management Group. *Real-Time CORBA Specification*, 1.1 edition, August 2002.

315. Object Management Group. *The Common Object Request Broker: Architecture and Specification*, 3.0.2 edition, December 2002.

316. Object Management Group. *Deployment and Configuration Adopted Submission*, OMG Document ptc/03-07-08 edition, July 2003.

317. Object Management Group. *MDA Guide Version 1.0.1*, 2003. Version 1.0.1, OMG document omg/03-06-01.

318. Object Management Group. OMG Unified Modeling Language Specification v1.5: Revisions and recommendations, March 2003. Version 1.5. OMG Document formal/03-03-01.

319. Object Management Group. *Unified Modeling Language: OCL version 2.0 Final Adopted Specification*, OMG Document ptc/03-10-14 edition, October 2003.

320. Object Management Group. XML Metadata Interchange (XMI) Specification, v2.0, May 2003.

321. Object Management Group. Common Object Request Broker Architecture: Core Specification, v3.0.3, March 2004.

322. Object Management Group. http://www.omg.org/, January 2005.

323. Object Management Group. Committed Companies and Their Products. http://www.omg.org/mda/committed-products.htm, January 2005.

324. Object Management Group. Model Driven Architecture. http://www.omg.org/mda/, January 2005.

325. Object Technology International, Inc. Eclipse Platform Technical Overview, July 2001.

326. J. Odell, H.V.D. Parunak, and M. Fleischer. The role of roles. *Journal of Object Technology*, 2(1):39–51, 2002.

327. J. Odell and G. Ramackers. *Martin/Odell Approach: A Formalization for OO*, pages 12.1–12.9. CRC Press, Boca Raton, FL, 1999.

328. DARPA Information Exploitation Office. Model-Based Integration of Embedded Software (MoBIES). www.darpa.mil/ixo/mobies.asp.

329. Dirk Ohst, Michael Welle, and Udo Kelter. Differences between versions of uml diagrams. In *European Software Engineering Conference/Foundations of Software Engineering*, pages 227–236, Helsinki, Finland, September 2003.

330. A. Olsen, O. Faergemand, and B. Moeller-Pedersen. *Systems Engineering Using SDL-92*. Elsevier Science, Amsterdam, 1994.

331. Object Management Group. Introduction to UML. http://www.omg.org/gettingstarted/what_is_uml.htm, April 2003.

332. Object Management Group. UML 2.0 Diagram Interchange Specification version 2.0. http://www.omg.org/docs/ptc/03-09-01.pdf, 2003.

333. Object Management Group. UML Specification. http://www.omg.org/uml, April 2003.

334. Catalog of OMG Modeling and Metadata Specifications. http://www.omg.org/technology/documents/modeling_spec_catalog.htm, December 2004.

335. William F. Opdyke. *Refactoring: A program restructuring aid in designing object-oriented application frameworks*. Ph. d. thesis, University of Illinois at Urbana–Champaign, 1992.

336. Open SystemC Initiative. *SystemC*. http://www.systemc.org.

337. OptimalJ – Platform Independence. http://idevnews.com/IntegrationNews.asp?ID=76, June 2004.

338. A. Orso, L. Baresi, and M. Pezze. Introducing formal specification methods in industrial practice. In *Proc. of ICSE'97*, pages 56–66, Boston, USA, 1997.

339. G. Övergaard. A formal approach to relationships in the unified modeling language. In *Proceedings of the Workshop on Precise Semantics for Software Modeling Techniques (PSMTŠ98)*, pages 91–108. 1998.

340. Ovum. Intelligent agents: The new revolution in software. Ovum Report. London: Ovum Publications, 1994.

341. R.F. Paige, J.S. Ostroff, and P.J. Brooke. Check the consistency of collaboration and class diagrams using pvs. In *Proc. of 4th Workshop on Rigorous Object-Oriented Methods*, London, 2002. British Computer Society.

342. Z.S. Pap, I. Majzikl, A. Pataricza, and A. Szegi. Completeness and consistency analysis of uml statechart specifications. In *Proceedings of IEEE Design and Diagnostics of Electronic Circuits and Systems Workshop*, pages 83–90, 2001.

343. D.L. Parnas. On the criteria to be used in decomposing systems into modules. *Communications of the ACM*, 15(12):1053–1058, December 1972.

344. CWM Partners. Common Warehouse Metamodel specification. OMG documents: ad/01-02-{01,02,03}, 2001.

345. H.A. Partsch. *Specification and Transformation of Programs. A Formal Approach to Software Development*. Springer, Berlin Heidelberg New York, 1990.

346. J. Peckham and F. Maryanski. Semantic data models. *ACM Computing Surveys*, 20(3):154–189, 1988.

347. M. Peltier, J. Bézevin, and G. Guillaume. MTRANS: A general framework, based on XSLT for model transformations. In *WTUML'01, Proceedings of the Workshop on Transformations in UML, Genova, Italy*, 2001.

348. J. Peltonen and P. Selonen. An approach and a platform for building UML processing tools. In *Proc. WoDiSEE 2004*, pages 51–57, Edinburgh, Scotland, May 2004.

349. James Lyle Peterson. Petri nets. *ACM Computing Surveys*, pages 223–252, September 1977.

350. Thomas M. Pigoski. *Practical Software Maintenance*. John Wiley & Sons, New York, January 2000.

351. Ivan Porres. Model refactorings as rule-based update transformations. In *Proceedings of UML 2003 Conference*, volume 2863 of *LNCS*, pages 159–174, San Francisco, CA, USA, 2003. Springer, Berlin Heidelberg New York.

352. Terrence W. Pratt. Pair grammars, graph languages and string-to-graph translations. *Journal of Computer and System Sciences*, 5:560–595, 1971.

353. S. Queins. *PROBAnD – eine Requirements-Engineering-Methode zur systematischen, domänenspezifischen Entwicklung reaktiver Systeme (A requirements engineering method for the systematic, domain-specific development of reactive systems)*. PhD thesis, University of Kaiserslautern, Kaiserslautern (Germany), 2002.

354. QVT-Partners. Revised submission for mof 2.0 query / views / transformations rfp. http://qvtp.org/downloads/1.1/qvtpartners1.1.pdf, 2003.

355. F.D. Racz and K. Koskimies. Tool-supported compression of uml class diagrams. In *Proceedings of the 2nd International Conference on the Unified Modeling Language (UML)*, pages 172–187. 1999.

356. Austrian Railways. Success Story OBB. www.omg.org/mda/mda_files/SuccessStory_OeBB.pdf/, January 2003.

357. A. Rashid, A. Moreira, and J. Araujo. Modularisation and composition of aspectual requirements. In *Proceedings of AOSD 2003*, pages 11–20, Boston, MA, USA, 2003.

358. G. Reggio, E. Astesiano, C. Choppy, and H. Hußmann. Analysing UML active classes and associated state machines – A lightweight formal approach. In T. Maibaum, editor, *Fundamental Approaches to Software Engineering (FASE2000)*, volume 1783 of *LNCS*, pages 127–146. Springer, Berlin Heidelberg New York, 2000.

359. W. Reisig. *A Primer in Petri Net Design*. Springer, Berlin Heidelberg New York, Berlin Heidelberg, 1992.

360. Arend Rensink. The GROOVE simulator: A tool for state space generation. In *Applications of Graph Transformations with Industrial Relevance (AGTIVE)*.

361. Arend Rensink. Canonical graph shapes. In D. A. Schmidt, editor, *Programming Languages and Systems — European Symposium on Programming (ESOP)*, volume 2986 of *LNCS*, pages 401–415. Springer, Berlin Heidelberg New York, 2004.

362. Arend Rensink, Ákos Schmidt, and Dániel Varró. Model checking graph transformations: A comparison of two approaches. In *Proceedings of ICGT 2004: Second International Conference on Graph Transformation*, volume 3256 of *LNCS*, pages 226–241, Rome, Italy, 2004. Springer, Berlin Heidelberg New York.

363. C.W. Reynolds. Steering behaviors for autonomous characters. http://www.red.com/cwr/steer/gdc99, December 2000.

364. J. Robbins, D. Hilbert, and D. Redmiles. Software architecture critics in argo. In *The 1998 International Conference on Intelligent User Interfaces*, San Francisco, CA, USA, January.

365. Donald Bradley Roberts. *Practical Analysis for Refactoring*. Phd, University of Illinois at Urbana-Champaign, 1999.

366. Wendy Roll. Towards model-based and CCM-based applications for real-time systems. In *Proceedings of the International Symposium on Object-Oriented Real-time Distributed Computing (ISORC)*.

367. Knut-Eilif Husa Rolv Bræk and Geir Melby. Serviceframe whitepaper. Technical report, Ericsson NORARC, 2001.

368. Rational Rose WWW site. http://www.rational.com/products/rose/index.jsp, 2004.

369. M. Rosen. Which MDA tools are right for you? In *Proceedings of MDA Implementers' Workshop Succeeding with Model Driven Systems*, Orlando, FL, USA, May 2003.

370. Richard Sanders. Implementing from sdl. *Telektronikk*.

371. P. Sargent. Back to school for a brand new abc. *Guardian*, March(12):28, March 1992.

372. Stephen Schach. *Object-Oriented and Classical Software Engineering*. McGraw-Hill, 6th edition edition, 2004.

373. Stephen R. Schach. Testing: Principles and practice. *ACM Computing Surveys*, pages 277–279, March 1996.

374. T. Schäfer, A. Knapp, and S. Merz. Model checking UML state machines and collaborations. In S.D. Stoller and W. Visser, editors, *Workshop on Software Model Checking*, volume 55 of *ENTCS*. Elsevier, Amsterdam, 2001.

375. Richard E. Schantz and Douglas C. Schmidt. Middleware for distributed systems: Evolving the common structure for network-centric applications. In John Marciniak and George Telecki, editors, *Encyclopedia of Software Engineering*. Wiley, New York, 2002.

376. Hans Schippers, Pieter Van Gorp, and Dirk Janssens. Leveraging UML profiles to generate plugins from visual model transformations. In *Proceedings Int'l Workshop Software Evolution through Transformations (SETra)*, Electronic Notes in Theoretical Computer Science, 2004.

377. Ákos Schmidt and Dániel Varró. CheckVML: A tool for model checking visual modeling languages. In Perdita Stevens, Jon Whittle, and Grady Booch, editors, *Proceedings UML 2003: 6th International Conference on the Unified Modeling Language*, volume 2863 of *LNCS*, pages 92–95, San Francisco, CA, USA, October 20-24 2003. Springer, Berlin Heidelberg New York.

378. Douglas C. Schmidt, David L. Levine, and Sumedh Mungee. The design and performance of real-time object request brokers. *Computer Communications*, 21(4):294–324, April 1998.

379. H. Schmidt. Trustworthy components-compositionality and prediction. *Journal of System Software*, 65(3):215–225, 2003.

380. S. Schönberger, R.K. Keller, and I. Khriss. Algorithmic support for model transformation in object-oriented software development. *Concurrency and Computation: Practice and Experience*, 13:351–383, 2001.

381. S. Schulz, T.C. Ewing, and J.W. Rozenblit. Discrete event system specification (DEVS) and statemate statecharts equivalence for embedded systems modeling. In *Proceedings of 7th IEEE International Conference on Engineering of Computer Based Systems*, 2000.

382. Andy Schürr. Specification of graph translators with triple graph grammars. In *Proceedings of 20th Workshop on Graph-Theoretic Concepts in Computer Science*, pages 151–163, 1994.

383. Andy Schürr, Andreas J. Winter, and Albert Zündorf. Graph grammar engineering with PROGRES. In *Proceedings of 5th European Software Engineering Conference ESEC*, volume LNCS 989, pages 219–234. Springer, Berlin Heidelberg New York, 1995.

384. E. Seidewitz. What models mean. *IEEE Software*, 21(5):26–32, 2003.

385. Tilman Seifert, Gerd Beneken, and Niko Baehr. Engineering long-lived applications using MDA. In *International Conference on Software Engineering and Applications*, Cambridge, MA, USA, November 2004.

386. B. Selic. The pragmatics of model-driven development. *IEEE Software*, 20(5):19–25, September–October 2003.

387. S. Sendall, G. Perrouin, N. Guelfi, and O. Biberstein. Supporting model-to-model transformations: The VMT approach.

388. Shane Sendall and Wojtek Kozaczynski. Model transformation: The heart and soul of model-driven software development. *IEEE Software*, 20 (5):42–45, 2003.

389. L. Shan and H. Zhu. Camle: A caste-centric agent-oriented modelling language and environment. In *Proceedings of SELMAS'04 at ICSE'94*, pages 66–73, Edinburgh, Scotland, 2004.

390. L. Shan and H. Zhu. Consistency check in modelling multi-agent systems. In *Proceedings of COMPSAC'04*, pages 114–119, Hong Kong, 2004.

391. David C. Sharp and Wendy C. Roll. Model-based integration of reusable component-based avionics system. In *Proceedings of the Workshop on Model-Driven Embedded Systems in RTAS 2003*, May 2003.

392. M. Sheeran and G. Stålmarck. A tutorial on Stålmarck's proof procedure for propositional logic. In G. Gopalakrishnan and P. Windley, editors, *Proceedings of 2nd International Conference on Formal Methods in Computer-Aided Design, FMCAD'98*, volume 1522 of *LNCS*, pages 82–99. Springer, Berlin Heidelberg New York, Palo Alto, CA, USA, 1998.

393. M. Siikarla, K. Koskimies, and T. Systä. Open MDA using transformational patterns. In *Proceedings of MDAFA 2004*, pages 92–106, Linköping, Sweden, June 2004.

394. Raul Silaghi, Frédéric Fondement, and Alfred Strohmeier. Towards an MDA-oriented UML profile for distribution. In *Proceedings of the 8th IEEE International Enterprise Distributed Object Computing Conference, EDOC*, Monterey, CA, USA.

395. Raul Silaghi and Alfred Strohmeier. Integrating CBSE, SoC, MDA, and AOP in a software development method. In *Proceedings of the 7th IEEE International Enterprise Distributed Object Computing Conference, EDOC*, Brisbane, Queensland, Australia.

396. M.P. Singh. A semantics for speech acts. *Annals of Mathematics and Artificial Intelligence*, 8(II):47–71, 1993.

397. M.P. Singh. Agent communication languages: Rethinking the principles. *IEEE Computer*, 31(12):40–47, December 1998.

398. G. Snelting and F. Tip. Reengineering class hierarchies using concept analysis. In *Proceedings of the ACM SIGSOFT Symposium on the Foundations of Software Engineering*, pages 99–110. 1998.
399. C. Snook and M. Butler. Using a graphical design tool for formal specification. In G. Kadoda, editor, *The 13th Workshop of the Psychology of Programming Interest Group*, pages 311–321, Bournemouth, UK, 2001.
400. IBM Rational Software. Rational XDE. http://www.rational.com/products/xde/index.jsp, 2004.
401. Software Engineering Laboratory at the Swiss Federal Institute of Technology in Lausanne. The Parallax Project. http://parallax-lgl.epfl.ch/, January 2005.
402. Z. Somogyi, F. Henderson, and T. Conway. Mercury: An efficient purely declarative logic programming language. In *Proceedings of the Australian Computer Science Conference*.
403. John A. Stankovic, Ruiqing Zhu, Ramasubramaniam Poornalingam, Chenyang Lu, Zhendong Yu, Marty Humphrey, and Brian Ellis. VEST: An aspect-based composition tool for real-time systems. In *Proceedings of the IEEE Real-time Applications Symposium*, Washington, DC, USA, May 2003.
404. P. Stevens. Small-scale XMI programming: A revolution in UML tool use? *Automated Software Engineering*, 10(1):7–21, January 2003.
405. Giancarlo Succi and Michele Marchesi. *Extreme Programming Examined*. Addison-Wesley, Reading, MA, 2001.
406. Sun Microsystems, Inc. Java Remote Method Invocation Specification, Revision 1.7, Java 2 SDK, v1.3.0. http://java.sun.com/j2se/1.3/docs/guide/rmi/, December 1999.
407. Sun Microsystems, Inc. Java 2 Platform, Enterprise Edition Specification, v1.4, November 2003.
408. Sun Microsystems, Inc. Jini Network Technology. http://www.sun.com/jini/, January 2005.
409. Sun Microsystems, Inc. NetBeans Metadata Repository (MDR). http://mdr.netbeans.org/, January 2005.
410. Sun Microsystems. EJB 2.1 Specification Final Release 2.1. http://java.sun.com/products/ejb/docs.html, 11 2003.
411. Gerson Sunyé, Damien Pollet, Yves Le Traon, and Jean-Marc Jézéquel. Refactoring uml models. In *Proceedings of UML 2001 Conference*, volume 2185 of *LNCS*, pages 138–148, Toronto, Canada, 2001. Springer, Berlin Heidelberg New York.
412. M. Svahnberg and J. Bosch. Issues concerning variability in software product lines. In Frank van der Linden, editor, *Software Architectures for Product Families, International Workshop IW-SAPF-3*, volume 1951 of *LNCS*, pages 146–157. Springer, Berlin Heidelberg New York, 2000.
413. E.B. Swanson and E. Dans. System life expectancy and the maintenance effort: Exploring their equilibration. *MIS Quarterly*, 24(2):277–297, 2000.
414. Janos Sztipanovits. Generative programming for embedded systems. In *Keynote Address: Generative Programming and Component Engineering (GPCE)*, volume 2487 of *LNCS*, pages 32–49, Pittsburgh, PA, USA, 2002. Springer, Berlin Heidelberg New York.
415. Janos Sztipanovits and Gabor Karsai. Model-Integrated Computing. *IEEE Computer*, 30(4):110–112, April 1997.
416. C. Szyperski. *Component Software: Beyond Object-Oriented Programming*. Addison-Wesley, Reading, MA, second edition, 2002.
417. CCITT Recommendation T.81. Information technology - digital compression and coding of continuous-tone still images, September 1992.

418. Gabi Taentzer. AGG: The attributed graph grammar system. `http://tfs.cs.tu-berlin.de/agg/`, 2003.

419. P. Tarr, H. Osher, W. Harrison, and S.M.Jr. Sutton. N degrees of separation: Multi-dimensional separation of concerns. In *Proceedings of the 21st International Conference on Software Engineering (ICSE 21), Los Angeles, CA*, pages 107–119. 1999.

420. Esterel Technologies. `http://www.esterel-technologies.com/`, October 2003.

421. Telelogic. `http://www.telelogic.com`, December 2003.

422. A. Tesanovic, S. Nadjm-Tehrani, and J. Hansson. *In Embedded System Development with Components*, chapter Modular verification of reconfigurable components. Springer, Berlin Heidelberg New York, 2005.

423. A. Tesanovic, D. Nyström, J. Hansson, and C. Norström. Aspects and components in real-time system development: Towards reconfigurable and reusable software. *Journal of Embedded Computing*, 1(1), October 2004.

424. Dave Thomas. MDA: Revenge of the modelers or UML utopia? *IEEE Software*, 21(3):15–17, May 2004.

425. Sander Tichelaar, Stéphane Ducasse, Serge Demeyer, and Oscar Nierstrasz. A meta-model for language-independent refactoring. In *Proceedings of International Symposium on Principles of Software Evolution (ISPSE 2000)*, pages 157–169, Kanazawa, Japan, 2000. IEEE Computer Society Press, Silver Spring, MD.

426. D. Truscan. A model-driven approach to TTA-based processor configuration. In *Forum on specification and Design Languages (FDL'04)*, 2004.

427. D. Truscan. A UML profile for the TACO protocol processing framework. In *Proceedings of the 22nd Norchip Conference*, pages 225–228, November 2004.

428. D. Truscan, J. M. Fernandes, and J. Lilius. Tool support for DFD to UML model-based transformations. Technical Report 519, Turku Centre for Computer Science (TUCS), Turku, Finland, 2003.

429. D. Truscan, J.M. Fernandes, and J. Lilius. Tool support for DFD-UML model-based transformations. In *11th International Conference and Workshop on the Engineering of Computer Based Systems (ECBS'04)*, May 2004.

430. A. Tsiolakis and H. Ehrig. Consistency analysis of uml class and sequence diagrams using attributed graph grammars. In *Proceedings of GRATRA 2000*.

431. UML Revision Task Force. OMG UML Specification v. 1.4. OMG Document ad/01-09-67. `http://www.omg.org/uml`, 2001.

432. Pieter Van Gorp, Dirk Janssens, and Tracy Gardner. Write once, deploy N: A performance oriented mda case study. In *Proceedings of the 8th IEEE International Enterprise Distributed Object Computing Conference*, September 2004.

433. Pieter Van Gorp, Niels Van Eetvelde, and Dirk Janssens. Implementing refactorings as graph rewrite rules on a platform independent meta model. In *Proceedings of Fujaba Days 2003*, 2003.

434. R. van Ommering, F. van der Linden, J. Kramer, and J. Magee. The koala component model for consumer electronics software. *Computer*, 33(3):78–85, March 2000.

435. D. Varró and A. Pataricza. Generic and meta-transformations for model transformation engineering. In *Proceedings of the UML 2004 Conference*, volume 3237 of *LNCS*, pages 290–304, Lisbon, Portugal, October 2004. Springer, Berlin Heidelberg New York.

436. D. Varró, G. Varró, and A. Pataricza. Designing the automatic transformation of visual languages. *Science of Computer Programming*, pages 205–227, 2002.

437. Dániel Varró. Towards symbolic analysis of visual modelling languages. In Paolo Bottoni and Mark Minas, editors, *Proceedings of GT-VMT 2002: International Workshop*

on *Graph Transformation and Visual Modelling Techniques*, volume 72 (3) of *ENTCS*, pages 57–70, Barcelona, Spain, October 2002. Elsevier, Amsterdam.

438. Dániel Varró. Automated formal verification of visual modeling languages by model checking. *Journal of Software and Systems Modeling*, 3(2):85–113, May 2004.

439. Dániel Varró and András Pataricza. Automated formal verification of model transformations. In Jan Jürjens, Bernhard Rumpe, Robert France, and Eduardo B. Fernandez, editors, *CSDUML 2003: Critical Systems Development in UML; Proceedings of the UML'03 Workshop*, pages 63–78, 2003.

440. Gergely Varró, Katalin Friedl, and Dániel Varró. Graph transformations in relational databases. In *Proceedings GraBaTs 2004: International Workshop on Graph Based Tools*, ENTCS. Elsevier, Amsterdam, 2004. To appear.

441. Gergely Varró and Dániel Varró. Graph transformation with incremental updates. In *Proceedings of GT-VMT 2004, International Workshop on Graph Transformation and Visual Modelling Techniques*, ENTCS. Elsevier, Amsterdam, March 2004. To appear.

442. Velocity. http://jakarta.apache.org/velocity/, December 2004.

443. S. Virtanen, J. Lilius, T. Nurmi, and T. Westerlund. TACO: Rapid design space exploration for protocol processors. In *The Ninth IEEE/DATC Electronic Design Processes Workshop Notes*, Monterey, CA, USA, April 2002.

444. S. Virtanen, T. Lundström, and J. Lilius. A processor design tool for the TACO framework. In *Proceedings of 2002 IEEE Norchip Conference*, November 2002.

445. S. Virtanen, D. Truscan, and J. Lilius. TACO IPv6 Router - A case study in protocol processor design. Technical Report 528, Turku Centre for Computer Science, April 2003.

446. Eelco Visser. A survey of rewriting strategies in program transformation systems. In B. Gramlich and S. Lucas, editors, *Proceedings of Workshop on Reduction Strategies in Rewriting and Programming*, volume 57 of *ENTSC*. Elsevier, May 2001.

447. W. Visser, K. Havelund, G. Brat, and S. Park. Model checking programs. In *ASE'00: Proceedings of the Fifteenth IEEE International Conference on Automated Software Engineering*, page 3, 2000.

448. Attila Vizhanyo, Aditya Agrawal, and Feng Shi. Towards generation of high-performance transformations. In *Generative Programming and Component Engineering: Third International Conference, GPCE 2004, Vancouver, Canada, October 24-28, 2004. Proceedings*, volume 3286 of *LNCS*, pages 298–316. Springer, Berlin Heidelberg New York, 2004.

449. G. Wainer. CD++: A toolkit to develop DEVS models. *Software - Practice and Experience*, 32:1261–1302, 2002.

450. G. Wainer, G. Christen, and A. Dobniewski. Defining DEVS models with the CD++ toolkit. In *Proceedings of the European Simulation Symposium*, 2001.

451. G. Wainer, E. Glinsky, and Peter MacSween. A model-driven technique for development of embedded systems based on the devs formalism. Technical Report SCE-05-03, Dept. of Systems and Computer Engineering. Carleton University, 2005.

452. Nanbor Wang, Chris Gill, Douglas C. Schmidt, and Venkita Subramonian. Configuring real-time aspects in component middleware. In *Proceedings of the International Symposium on Distributed Objects and Applications (DOA'04)*, Agia Napa, Cyprus, October 2004.

453. Nanbor Wang and Christopher Gill. Improving real-time system configuration via a QoS-aware CORBA component model. In *Hawaii International Conference on System Sciences, Software Technology Track, Distributed Object and Component-based Software Systems Minitrack, HICSS 2003*.

454. Nanbor Wang, Douglas C. Schmidt, Aniruddha Gokhale, Craig Rodrigues, Balachan-dran Natarajan, Joseph P. Loyall, Richard E. Schantz, and Christopher D. Gill. QoS-enabled middleware. In Qusay Mahmoud, editor, *Middleware for Communications*. Wiley, New York, 2003.

455. Yuan Wang, David J. DeWitt, and Jin-Yi Cai. X -diff: An effective change detection algorithm for xml documents. In *Proceedings of the 19th International Conference on Data Engineering*, pages 519–530, Bangalore, India, March 2003.

456. Jos Warmer and Anneke Kleppe. *The Object Constraint Language: Precise Modeling with UML*. Addison-Wesley, Reading, MA, 1998.

457. Jos Warmer and Anneke Kleppe. *The Object Constraint Language: Getting Your Models Ready for MDA, Second Edition*. Addison-Wesley, Reading, MA, 2003.

458. R. Wieringa. A survey of structured and object-oriented software specification methods and techniques. *ACM Computing Surveys*, 30(4):459–527, 1998.

459. E.D. Willink. UMLX: A graphical transformation language for MDA. In A. Rensink, editor, *Model Driven Architecture: Foundations and Applications Workshop Proceedings*, pages 15–22, June 2003. http://trese.cs.utwente.nl/mdafa2003/proceedings.pdf.

460. World Wide Web Consortium. The extensible stylesheet language transformations specification. http://www.w3.org/TR/1999/REC-xslt-19991116, 1999.

461. World Wide Web Consortium. Web Services. http://www.w3.org/2002/ws/, January 2005.

462. Weidong Xia and Gwanhoo Lee. Grasping the complexity of is development projects. *Communications of the ACM*, 47(5):68–74, 2004.

463. J. Xu, L. Jin, and H. Zhu. Tool support of orderly transition from informal to formal descriptions in requirements engineering. In N. Terashima and E. Altman, editors, *Proceedings of IFIP'96: Advanced IT Tools*, pages 199–206. Chapman and Hall, London, 1996.

464. L. Yilmaz. Verification and validation: Automated object-flow testing of dynamic process interaction models. In *Proceedings of the 33rd Conference on Winter Simulation*, pages 586–594, Arlington, VA, USA, 2001.

465. Bernard P. Zeigler, Tag Gon Kim, and Herbert Praehofer. *Theory of Modeling and Simulation*. Academic Press, 2000.

466. T. Zheng and G. Wainer. Implementing finite state machines using the CD++ toolkit. In *Proceedings of the SCS Summer Computer Simulation Conference*, 2003.

467. H. Zhu. The role of caste in formal specification of mas. In S.T. Yuan and M. Yokoo, editors, *Intelligent Agents: Specification, Modeling and Application*, volume 2132 of *LNCS*, pages 1–15. Springer, Berlin Heidelberg New York, 2001.

468. H. Zhu. Slabs: A formal specification language for agent-based systems. *Journal of Software Engineering and Knowledge Engineering*, 11(5):529–558, 2001.

469. H. Zhu. Formal specification of evolutionary software agents. In C. George and H. Miao, editors, *Formal Methods and Software Engineering*, volume 2495 of *LNCS*, pages 249–261. Springer, Berlin Heidelberg New York, 2002.

470. H. Zhu. A formal specification language for agent-oriented software engineering. In *Proc. of AAMAS'2003*, pages 1174–1175, Melbourne, Australia, 2003.

471. H. Zhu and D. Lightfoot. Caste: A step beyond object orientation. In L. Boszormenyi and P. Schojer, editors, *Modular Programming Languages, Proceedings of JMLC'2003*, volume 2789 of *LNCS*, pages 59–62. Springer, Berlin Heidelberg New York, 2003.

472. H. Zhu, B. Zhou, X. Mao, L. Shan, and D. Duce. Agent-oriented formal specification of web services. In *GCC Workshops 2004*, pages 633–641, 2004.

473. Hong Zhu, Patrick Hall, and John May. Software unit test coverage and adequacy. *ACM Computing Surveys*, pages 367–427, December 1997.

474. Albert Zündorf. Graph pattern matching in PROGRES. In *Proceedings of 5th International Workshop on Graph-Grammars and their Application to Computer Science*, volume 1073 of *LNCS*. Springer, Berlin Heidelberg New York, 1996.
475. Albert Zündorf. The Fujaba Toolsuite. http://www.fujaba.de/, 1999.
476. Albert Zündorf. Rigorous object oriented software development. Habilitation thesis, University of Paderborn, 2001.

Index